The Humanities in the Western Tradition

Volume I

The Humanities in the Western Tradition

IDEAS AND AESTHETICS

Marvin Perry
Baruch College, City University of New York

J. Wayne Baker
The University of Akron

Pamela Pfeiffer Hollinger
The University of Akron

George Bock
Editorial Associate

HOUGHTON MIFFLIN COMPANY
Boston   New York

Cover: Theatrical scene from the House of the Tragic Poet, Pompeii. *Source: Museo Archeologico Nazionale, Naples, Italy/Canali PhotoBank Milan/Superstock.*

Senior Sponsoring Editor: Nancy Blaine
Development Editor: Julie Dunn
Senior Project Editor: Bob Greiner
Editorial Assistant: Wendy Thayer
Senior Production/Design Coordinator: Jodi O'Rourke
Manufacturing Manager: Florence Cadran
Senior Marketing Manager: Sandra McGuire

Printed in the U.S.A.

Library of Congress Catalog Number: 2002105244

ISBN: 0-395-84811-3

04 05 06 07 08 09   11

Preface   xiii

PART I
The Birth of the West: The Greco-Roman Judeo-Christian Heritage   2

CHAPTER 1   The Ancient Near East: The First Civilizations   5

CHAPTER 2   The Hebrews: A New View of God and the Individual   31

CHAPTER 3   Hellenic Civilization I: From Myth to Reason   53

CHAPTER 4   Hellenic Civilization II: The Arts and Literature   77

CHAPTER 5   The Hellenistic Age: Cultural Diffusion   107

CHAPTER 6   Roman Civilization: The Expansion of Hellenism   125

CHAPTER 7   Early Christianity: A World Religion   159

PART II
The Middle Ages: The Christian Centuries   180

CHAPTER 8   The Medieval East: Byzantium and Islam   183

CHAPTER 9   The Early Medieval West: Fusion of Classical, Christian, and
             Germanic Traditions   209

CHAPTER 10   The High Middle Ages I: The Flowering of Medieval Thought   231

CHAPTER 11   The High Middle Ages II: The Flowering of Medieval Literature,
             Art, and Music   255

CHAPTER 12   The Late Middle Ages: Crisis, Continuity, and Change   293

Glossary   325
Bibliography   332
Credits   336
Index   338

Preface   xiii

PART I
The Birth of the West: The Greco-Roman
Judeo-Christian Heritage   **2**

CHAPTER 1

**The Ancient Near East: The First
Civilizations**   **5**

Prehistory   **5**

The Paleolithic Age   5
Paleolithic Art and Music   6
The Neolithic Age   7

The Rise to Civilization   **8**

Mesopotamian Civilization   **9**

Religion: The Basis of Mesopotamian Civilization   9
World Cultures: The Origins of Hinduism in India   11
Law, Mathematics, and Medicine   12
Mesopotamian Literature   12
Mesopotamian Art and Music   15

Egyptian Civilization   **17**

From Old Kingdom to New Kingdom   17
The Pharaoh   18
Religion: The Basis of Egyptian Civilization   18
Amarna Religion: Toward Monotheism   19
Science and Mathematics   20
Egyptian Literature   20
Egyptian Art and Music   21

Persia: Unifier of the Near East   **25**

Persian Religion: Zoroastrianism   25
Persian Art   26

• The Religious Orientation of the Ancient
Near East   27
A Mythmaking Worldview   27
Near Eastern Achievements   28
Key Terms   28
Notes   29

CHAPTER 2

**The Hebrews: A New View of God
and the Individual**   **31**

Early Hebrew History   **31**

**God: One, Sovereign, Transcendent,
Good**   **34**

The Individual and Moral Autonomy   **36**

The Covenant and the Law   **37**

The Hebrew Idea of History   **38**

The Prophets   **39**

Social Justice   39
Messiah and Apocalypse   40
Universalism and Individualism   40

The Bible as Literature   **41**

The Epics: Stories and Historical Cycles   41
Lyric Poetry   44
The Wisdom Writings   45
The Hebrew Scriptures and Western Authors
and Language   48

Art and Music   **49**

• The Legacy of the Ancient Jews   50
Key Terms   51
Notes   51

CHAPTER 3

Hellenic Civilization I: From Myth to Reason 53

Early Aegean Civilizations 53

Evolution of City-States 54

Break with Theocratic Politics 54
Sparta: A Garrison State 55
Athens: The Rise of Democracy 56

The Decline of the City-States 57

Early Greek Literature 58

Homer 58
Hesiod 60

Greek Religion 62

The Olympian Religion 62
The Mystery Religions 63

Philosophy in the Hellenic Age 64

The Cosmologists: Rational Inquiry into Nature 65
The Sophists: A Rational Investigation of
 Human Culture 67
Socrates: Shaping the Rational Individual 68
Plato: The Rational Society 69
Aristotle: Synthesis of Greek Thought 72
• The Enduring Impact of Greek Philosophy 74
Key Terms 75
Notes 75

CHAPTER 4

Hellenic Civilization II: The Arts and Literature 77

Lyric Poetry 77

Sappho 78
Pindar 78

Music 79

Drama 80

Aeschylus 82
Sophocles 82

Euripides 85
Aristophanes and Greek Comedy 86
World Cultures: Confucianism 87

The Greek View of History 88
Herodotus 88
Thucydides 89

Hellenic Art 89
Vase Painting 90
Sculpture 92
Architecture 97
• The Greek Achievement: Reason,
 Freedom, Humanism 103
Key Terms 104
Notes 104

CHAPTER 5

The Hellenistic Age: Cultural Diffusion 107

Alexander the Great 108

Hellenistic Society 108

Cosmopolitanism 108
The Jews in the Hellenistic Age 110

Hellenistic Culture 110

Literature and History 110
Science 112
World Cultures: The Art of Governing
According to Han Fei Tzu 113
Philosophy 114

Hellenistic Art 116
• The Hellenistic Legacy 123
Key Terms 123
Notes 123

CHAPTER 6

Roman Civilization: The Expansion of Hellenism 125

Evolution of the Roman Republic 125

Roman Expansion to 146 B.C. 127
The Collapse of the Republic 127

The Foundations of the Roman Empire   128

Augustus   128
The Pax Romana   129

The Decline of Rome   131

Third-Century Crisis   131
Diocletian and Constantine: The Regimented State   131
Tribal Migrations and Invasions   132

Republican Culture: Philosophy and Literature   132

Lucretius   132
Cicero   132
Sallust   133
Plautus   133
Terence   133
Catullus   133

Roman Culture During the Pax Romana   134

Literature and History   134
Philosophy   137
Science   138
World Cultures: Later Hinduism—
The Bhagavad-Gita   139

Law   140

Cultural Stagnation and Transformation   140

The Spread of Mystery Religions   141
The Spiritualization of Philosophy   142

Roman Art   142

Architecture   143
Portrait Sculpture   148
Imperial Narrative Relief Sculpture   150
Painting   152
• The Roman Legacy   156
Key Terms   156
Notes   156

CHAPTER   7

Early Christianity: A World Religion   159

The Origins of Christianity   159

Judaism in the First Century B.C.   160

Jesus: Moral Transformation of the Individual   160
The Apostle Paul: From a Jewish Sect to a
World Religion   162

The Spread and Triumph of Christianity   163

The Appeal of Christianity   163
Christianity and Rome   164

Development of Christian Organization and Attitudes   165

The Primacy of the Bishop of Rome   165
The Rise of Monasticism   165
Christianity and Society   165
Christianity and the Jews   166

Early Christian Theology and Literature   167

The Scriptural Tradition and Doctrinal Disputes   167
Christianity and Greek Philosophy   168
Augustine: The Christian Worldview   169

Early Christian Art   171

Symbolism in Early Christian Art   172
Architecture   175
• Christianity and Classical Humanism:
Alternative Worldviews   178
Key Terms   179
Notes   179

PART II
The Middle Ages: The Christian
Centuries   **180**

CHAPTER   8

The Medieval East: Byzantium and Islam   183

A Survey of Byzantine History   183

Byzantine Learning   184

Byzantine Music   185

Byzantine Art and Architecture   186

The Origins and Expansion of Islam   193

The Decline of the Arab Empire   195

Islamic Theology   195

Inner Divisions: Sunnites, Shi'ites,
and Sufis   196

Muslim Society   197

The Status of Women   197
Relations with the "Peoples of the Book"   197

Islamic Learning   198

Islamic Literature   199

The Theme of Love   199
The *Rubaiyat* of Omar Khayyam   200
Jalal al-Din Rumi   200
Thousand and One Arabian Nights   201

Islamic Art and Architecture   202

• The Legacies of Byzantium and Islam   206
Key Terms   *207*
Notes   *207*

CHAPTER 9

The Early Medieval West:
Fusion of Classical, Christian,
and Germanic Traditions   209

The Rise of Latin Christendom   209

The Church: Shaper of Medieval Civilization   209
The Era of Charlemagne   211
Feudal Society   212
Agrarian Society   214
Early Medieval Thought: The Waning of
Classical Culture   215
Transmitters   215
The Carolingian Renaissance   216
World Cultures: *The Pillow-Book:* The Journal
of Sei Shonagon   217

Early Medieval Literature   218

Welsh Mythology   218
Irish Lyric Poetry and Epic Tales   218
The Old English Epic: *Beowulf*   219
Christian Themes   220

Early Medieval Art   221

• The Birth of Europe   228

Key Terms   *229*
Notes   *229*

CHAPTER 10

The High Middle Ages I: The
Flowering of Medieval Thought   231

Economic Expansion: Agricultural
Improvements, Revival of Trade,
and Growth of Towns   231

The Rise of States   233

England   234
France   234
Germany   235

Medieval Religion: Devotion, Power,
Heresy   235

The Sacraments   235
The Gregorian Reform   235
The Crusades   237
Dissenters and Reformers   238
Innocent III: The Apex of Papal Power   240
Christians and Jews   241

Revival of Learning   242
World Cultures: Lu Yu: Chinese Bard   243

Philosophy–Theology   245

Anselm   245
Abelard   245
The Recovery of Aristotle   246
Thomas Aquinas: Synthesis of Christian Belief
and Reason   247
Strict Aristotelianism: The Challenge to Orthodoxy   248
Joachim of Fiore: A Challenge to the Traditional
View of History   249

Science   250

The Recovery of Roman Law   251

• The Medieval Worldview   252

The Universe: Higher and Lower Worlds   252
The Individual: Sinful but Redeemable   252
Key Terms   *253*
Notes   *253*

CHAPTER 11

The High Middle Ages II: The Flowering of Medieval Literature, Art, and Music 255

Medieval Literature 255

Religious Hymns and Drama 255
Goliardic Poetry 256
Epics 257
The Poetry of Chivalric Love 260
World Cultures: *Popol Vuh:* Mayan Creation Myth 261
Dante Alighieri: *The Divine Comedy* 262

Medieval Art 264

Architecture 264
Sculpture 276

Pictorial Art 280

Medieval Music 284

• Christianity and the Arts 289
Key Terms 290
Notes 290

CHAPTER 12

The Late Middle Ages: Crisis, Continuity, and Change 293

The Fourteenth Century: An Age of Adversity 293

The Decline of the Papacy 295

Conflict with France 295
The Great Schism and the Conciliar Movement 295

Late Medieval Thought 296

Critics of Papal Power 296
Fourteenth-Century Heresies 296
Breakup of The thomistic Synthesis 297

Late Medieval Literature: Continuity with Traditional Themes 297

The Letters of Catherine of Siena 298
The Vision of Piers Plowman 298
Sir Gawain and the Green Knight 299
Roman de la Rose 300
World Cultures: Ibn Battuta: World Traveler 301
Everyman 302

Late Medieval Literature: New Directions 303

Francesco Petrarch 304
Giovanni Boccaccio 305
Geoffrey Chaucer 307
Christine de Pizan 309

Late Medieval Art 310

Sculpture 310
Painting 311

The *Ars Nova* (New Art) in Music 318

• The Middle Ages and the Modern World: Continuity and Discontinuity 320
Key Terms 323
Notes 323

Glossary 325
Bibliography 332
Credits 336
Index 338

The *Humanities in the Western Tradition: Ideas and Aesthetics* surveys Western thought, literature, and the arts from antiquity to the present. The text has two principal aims: (1) It explores those profound questions about the human experience elicited by a study of the ideas and aesthetics that have characterized Western thought, literature, art, and music—those cultural concerns that are called the Humanities. (2) It strives for synthesis, that is, it seeks to say something significant about the stages of Western history and the nature and meaning of the Western tradition. The text is written with the conviction that without a knowledge of Western history in general, and Western Humanities in particular, those who share in the Western tradition cannot fully know themselves. Without knowledge of our historic artistic, musical, and literary achievements, elicited from a study of the Humanities, our aesthetic tastes and moral awareness will be much the poorer. Without an understanding of the historical evolution of reason, freedom, and respect for human dignity, the dominant ideals of the Western tradition, commitment to these ideals will diminish. The authors hope to convey to students that the Western tradition is a living, vital tradition and that the study of thought, literature, and the arts—subjects that comprise the Humanities—will enrich their lives.

How this text came to be written sheds light on the authors' intent and objectives. Before his retirement, J. Wayne Baker was Course Director for the Humanities in the History Department, The University of Akron. A historian specializing in the Renaissance and Reformation, Baker, over the years of teaching the Humanities course, had also acquired an interest in art history. Pamela Hollinger, whose special interests are music history and British and American literature, had for many years worked closely with Baker in the Humanities program at The University of Akron, especially by creating a multimedia format for lecture presentations that integrated the various components of the Humanities. They had been thinking about producing a Humanities text that integrated more biographical information and human interest into discussions of music and art and provided deeper analyses of the great works of literature, a proposal they submitted to Houghton Mifflin Company.

Marvin Perry, whose special concerns are intellectual history and the evolution and nature of the Western tradition, has written several widely used texts for Houghton Mifflin, including *Western Civilization: Ideas, Politics, and Society* (senior author and general editor); *Sources of the Western Tradition* (senior editor); and *An Intellectual History of Modern Europe*. Coincidentally, he had proposed a Humanities text grounded in a solid historical framework and rich in ideas drawn from the West's philosophic, scientific, and religious traditions. It was clear that the two approaches complemented each other and the project was born.

The text took six years to complete, requiring endless hours of research, dialogue, and revision. We hope that instructors will find the finished work a helpful pedagogical instrument and that it will kindle in students an enduring appreciation for and interest in the Humanities.

APPROACH AND ORGANIZATION

To realize the project's overarching concerns, the authors devised an approach for each of the disciplines treated in a Humanities course. Realizing that many students enrolled in a Humanities program may never have studied European history, the authors provide a strong historical framework that facilitates comprehension of the Western cultural tradition. In our treatment of thought and the arts we have been careful to relate literary, art, and music productions to the historical eras in which they emerged. We also try to define the essential character of an age—classical Greece, the Middle Ages, the Enlightenment—by focusing on crucial questions: How did representative thinkers view nature, society, and the purpose of life? How did they assess the value of reason, faith, and clerical authority? What was their conception of political freedom? How did developments in literature and the arts show both an inheritance from the past and new points of departure?

Another feature of the text is the significant attention given to Western philosophy and religion in the shaping of those unique patterns of thought and systems of values that constitute the Western heritage. Thus the text contains discussions of the West's principal thinkers, often quoting passages from their works; it also devotes an entire chapter to the ancient Hebrews and another to Early Christianity, and in appropriate places throughout both volumes, important religious issues are treated. Because of the growing importance of Islam in today's world, we have included an extensive treatment of medieval Islamic civilization.

The literature sections are decidedly more than a list of books with brief summaries of plots; rather, we have tried to breathe life into literary discussions by incorporating appropriate biographical information about the authors, source extracts, and analyses of the important ideas the works convey.

The art sections reveal how people in each era interpreted their culture visually. Carefully chosen images of paintings, sculptures, and architectural works provide visual evidence of the essential values and beliefs that men and women held in a particular historical era. In some cases, images illustrate how artists were ahead of their time, cutting against the grain of contemporary thinking and introducing new artistic styles and approaches. In addressing the important issues that concern art historians, the authors have tried to make the text accessible to students with little prior knowledge of art history.

The music sections place composers in their cultural milieu; also, carefully selected details from their personal lives and careers give them a human face. Knowing that many students (and instructors) have little or no background in music theory, we have kept technical discussions to a bare minimum; however, where technical accomplishments were crucial to the development of Western music, we have made every effort to achieve clarity.

To convey to students the enduring importance of particular historical developments or the achievements in thought, literature, and the arts that they had just studied, each chapter contains an endpiece that searches for larger meaning. These endpieces are not chapter summaries, but interpretive and conceptual essays that compel students to ponder crucial questions about the Humanities and the nature and meaning of Western civilization. Examples of endpieces in Volume 1 are "The Greek Achievement: Reason, Freedom, Humanism" in Chapter 4; "Christianity and Classical Humanism: Alternative Worldviews" in Chapter 7; "Christianity and the Arts" in Chapter 11; and "The Middle Ages and the Modern World: Continuity and Discontinuity" in Chapter 12.

Endpieces in Volume 2 include "The Renaissance and the Rise of Modernity" in Chapter 13; "The Enlightenment and the Modern Mentality" in Chapter 17; "Enlightenment Values and the Arts" in Chapter 18; "The Enlightenment Tradition in Disarray" in Chapter 23; "The Modern Predicament" in Chapter 25; and "The Western Tradition in a Global Age" in Chapter 26.

The Humanities in the Western Tradition: Ideas and Aesthetics contains twenty-six chapters, twelve in Volume I and fourteen in Volume II. The chapters are grouped into five parts, two in Volume I and three in Volume II: (1) The Birth of the West: The Greco-Roman and Judaeo-Christian Heritage; (2) The Middle Ages: The Christian Centuries; (3) The Early Modern West: From the Renaissance to the Enlightenment; (4) The Modern West: From Classicism to Modernism; and (5) Modernism and Beyond.

WORLD CULTURES

We now live in a global age in which Western ideals, institutions, and cultural styles have spread throughout the world. The globalization process also means that cultural elements—particularly religious beliefs, cuisines, and music—from Asian, African, and Middle Eastern lands have moved westward. That many non-Western students now attend American universities is another illustration of globalization. Although this text is concerned essentially with the Western humanities, we of course recognize the immense achievements of the other civilizations of the world. To facilitate an understanding and appreciation of all the world's civilizations, the text incorporates a special feature—"World Cultures" boxes that contain source material from the literary traditions of non-Western cultures. For example, Volume I contains excerpts from the *Rig Veda* and the *Bhagavad-Gita*, key ancient Hindu documents, and from the writings of Confucius, the Chinese sage, Han fei Tzu, the Chinese legalist philosopher, and Lu Yu, a prominent Chinese poet. Also included are selections from the journal of Sei Shonagon, an attendant to the empress of Japan in the late tenth century; a narrative by the fourteenth-century Islamic African, Ibn Battuta, about his travels; and *Popul Vuh*, the ancient sacred book of the Mayan people of Guatemala.

Volume II contains an Aztec account of the Spanish conquest of their land and Simon Bolivar's "Proclamation to the People of Venezuela" calling for liberation from Spanish rule. Two documents concern Africa: an excerpt from the memoirs of Olaudah Equiano, an educated former slave who took part in the antislavery movement in England, and a traditional African folktale. The excerpts from Japanese literature consist of a passage from a play by Chikamatsu Monzaemon, a late-seventeenth–early-eighteenth-century dramatist, who is called the "Japanese Shakespeare," and a sampling of modern Japanese lyric poetry. Emperor Ch'ien-lung's confidence in the superiority of Chinese civilization is revealed in his haughty reply to King George III's letter requesting the establishment of a British trading center at Peking (present-day Beijing). Three representative illustrations of twentieth-century Chinese poetry are also included. Excerpted too is Mohandas Gandhi's appeal for passive resistance, which had a profound influence on Martin Luther King, Jr.

SPECIAL FEATURES

The Humanities in the Western Tradition has been designed with a variety of features to help students master the material, including:

Comparative Timelines Each of the book's five parts contains a two-page comparative timeline. These timelines allow students to visualize and compare events in four categories: Politics/Society; Art/Architecture; Literature/Music; and Philosophy/Science/Religion.

Key Terms Every chapter of the book contains a list of important terms that students should know. These terms are highlighted within the narrative and listed at the end of the chapter for easy review.

Glossary A glossary containing definitions of all the key terms appears at the end of each volume.

Annotated Bibliography Organized by chapter, this bibliography appears at the end of the text. A searchable version also appears on the text's website.

TEACHING RESOURCES

We understand the challenges that instructors face when developing and teaching a Humanities course. The resources that exist are often difficult to locate, too general for the course, or too expensive to purchase. With these concerns in mind we developed the full package of ancillaries that accompany *The Humanities in the Western Tradition.*

Online Study Guide A free study guide for students appears on the text-specific website and features chapter summaries and outlines; a glossary of key terms; web activities and links; and a self-testing quiz program. The site also features special art and music sections that trace major artistic movements, identify important terms, and allow students to explore additional works on the web.

ClassPrep CD-ROM This CD-ROM includes all the resources that a professor needs to teach with *The Humanities in the Western Tradition.* An Instructor's Manual features chapter summaries, lecture suggestions, bibliographic information, and classroom discussion questions and activities. A Testbank offers more than 700 multiple-choice, fill-in-the-blank, and essay questions. PowerPoint slides of all the maps and 100 of the art images from the text have been included to enable instructors to highlight visuals in the classroom.

Music CDs Students may purchase a two-volume CD package to help supplement the music coverage in the text. Each CD features more than one hour of music and is designed to accompany specific discussions in the text (see CD icon in the margins).

Blackboard and WebCT Course material is offered in both Blackboard and WebCT formats for those institutions that use these learning environments.

Computerized Testbank A computerized version of the Testbank is available.

ACKNOWLEDGMENTS

The authors are grateful to the staff of Houghton Mifflin Company. Both Jean Woy (Editor-in-Chief) and Pat Coryell (now Editor-in-Chief for English, Education, ESL, and Student Success titles) recognized the merit of our proposals and brought the team together. Nancy Blaine, Senior Sponsoring Editor, and Julie Dunn, Development Editor, who continually impressed us with their commitment to the project, provided effective guidance. Bob Greiner, Senior Project Editor, conscientiously and skillfully supervised the manuscript through production. Karen Slaght, who edited the manuscript, provided helpful suggestions. Carole Frohlich researched and coordinated all of the art for the book; Jodi O'Rourke coordinated the production; and Janet Theurer provided us with a beautiful design in which to showcase the text.

Marvin Perry and Wayne Baker wish to thank their spouses, Phyllis Perry and Linda Kersker, for their encouragement, support, and patience. Marvin Perry is also grateful to his wife for her computer expertise, which saved him much time and frustration.

Pamela Pfeiffer Hollinger particularly appreciates the efforts of her friend and colleague, Robert DeMass, Jr., for his capable assistance in researching, selecting, and documenting the musical selections. Similarly, without the support and encouragement of her colleagues Marjorie Keil, Chris Kolaczewski-Ferris, and Joy LiCause, she is not certain if she could have kept her good humor during stressful times. To her capable student assistants, Joshua Davis and Scott Lockett, who helped to stimulate her thinking on some of the more contemporary art and music issues, "thank you." But most importantly, she is grateful for the love, patience, and understanding of her husband Greg and their daughters, Gretchen and Jenna.

Many instructors provided valuable suggestions on early drafts of the manuscript. The authors wish to thank the following people for their critical reading and insightful comments:

Phillip N. Bebb, *Ohio University*

Sherry Blum, *Austin Community College*

William J. Bogard, *Black Hills State University*

Edward T. Bonahue, *Santa Fe Community College*

Carolyn V. Copeland, *Bethune-Cookman College*

Tina M. Crocco, *Georgia Perimeter College*

Robert Eisner, *San Diego State University*

Kimberly Felos, *St. Petersburg College*

David H. Fenimore, *University of Nevada, Reno*

Matthew David Fisher, *Ball State University*

Ann M. Green, *Jackson Community College*

Jon D. Green, *Brigham Young University*

Thomas W. Hardy, *Northern Virginia Community College*

Siegfried E. Heit, *University of Central Oklahoma*

John Jay Hilfiger, *Saint Francis College*

Seth R. Katz, *Bradley University*

Kevin Kennedy, *Arapahoe Community College*

Richard D. Kortum, *East Tennessee State University*

Charlie McAllister, *Catawba College*

Bruce Naschak, *San Diego Mesa College*

Merry Ovnick, *California State University, Northridge*

Danney Ursery, *St. Edward's University*

Theresa A. Vaughan, *University of Central Oklahoma*

Richard A. Voeltz, *Cameron University*

LeeAnn E. Westman, *Ferris State University*

Sonia Yetter, *University of Northern Iowa*

Joel Zimbelman, *California State University, Chico*

M. P.

J. W. B.

P. P. H.

The Humanities in the
Western Tradition

	3500 B.C.	3000 B.C.	2500 B.C.	2000 B.C.

Politics/Society

● Rise of civilization in Sumer (c. 3200 B.C.)

● Union of Upper and Lower Egypt (c. 2900 B.C.)

● Rise of Minoan civilization (c. 2600 B.C.)

Rise of Mycenaean civilization (c. 2000 B.C.) ●

Hammurabi of Babylon builds an empire (1792–1750 B.C.) ●

Art/Architecture

← ● Altamira Cave paintings
(15,000–10,000 B.C.)

● Statues from the Abu Temple (2700–2500 B.C.)

● Pyramids at Giza constructed
(c. 2613–c. 2494 B.C.)

Literature/Music

● *Epic of Gilgamesh*
(2000 B.C.)

Philosophy/Religion/Science

● Creation of unified Hebrew monarchy under David (1000–961 B.C.)

● Hellenic Age (c. 800–323 B.C.)

● Babylonian Captivity (586–538 B.C.)

● Formation of Roman Republic (509 B.C.)

● Persian and Peloponnesian Wars (499–404 B.C.)

● Conquests of Alexander the Great (336–323 B.C.)

● Hellenistic Age (323–30 B.C.)

● Greco-Roman Age (30 B.C.–c. A.D. 500)

● Pax Romana—height of Roman Empire (27 B.C.– A.D. 180)

End of Roman Empire in the West (A.D. 476) ●

● Oriental style of Greek vase painting (725–650 B.C.)

● Classical period of Greek art (c. 480–323 B.C.)

● Construction of the Parthenon (447–432 B.C.)

● *Laocoön Group* (c. 25 B.C.)

Dedication of Trajan's Column (113) ●

● Construction of the Pantheon (c. 118–126)

The Good Shepherd (c. 300) ●

Dedication of Old Saint Peter's Church in Rome (324) ●

● Earliest Hebrew Psalms (c. 905–805 B.C.)

● Homer's *Iliad* and *Odyssey* (c. 700s B.C.)

● Sappho, greatest female poet of antiquity (c. 600 B.C.)

● Origins of musical theory, Pythagoras defines mathematical laws for sound (6th century B.C.)

● Greek dramatists Aeschylus, Sophocles, Euripides, Aristophanes (400s B.C.)

● Golden Age of Roman Literature, Cicero, Virgil, Livy, Horace, Ovid (mid-1st century B.C. to A.D. 14)

● Amenhotep IV and movement toward monotheism in Egypt (c. 1369–1353 B.C.)

● Moses and the Exodus (1200s B.C.)

● Rise of Greek philosophy: Ionians, Pythagoreans, Parmenides (500s and 400s B.C.)

● Execution of Socrates (399 B.C.)

Alexandrian mathematicians: Euclid, Archimedes (300s and 200s B.C.) ●   ● Crucifixion of Jesus (c. A.D. 29)

Rise of Hellenistic philosophies: Epicureanism, Stoicism, Skepticism, Cynicism (300s–200s B.C.) ●

Ptolemy, influential astronomer and geographer, (A.D. 127–141) ●

Church fathers: Jerome (b. A.D. 342–d. 420), Ambrose (b. A.D. 340–d. 397), Augustine (b. A.D. 354–d. 430) ●

The Ancient Near East: The First Civilizations

IVILIZATION WAS NOT INEVITABLE; it was an act of human creativity. The first civilizations emerged some five thousand years ago in the river valleys of Mesopotamia and Egypt. There, human beings established cities and states, invented writing, developed organized religion, and constructed large-scale buildings and monuments—all characteristics of civilized life. Striving to give form and meaning to their world and their place in it, they also engaged in the arts—literature, music, art, and architecture.

PREHISTORY

The Paleolithic Age

Humanity's rise to civilization was long and arduous. Some 99 percent of human history took place before the creation of civilization, in the vast ages of prehistory. The period called the *Paleolithic Age,* or Old Stone Age, began with the earliest primitive toolmaking human beings who inhabited East Africa some three million years ago. It ended about ten thousand years ago in parts of the Near East when people discovered how to farm. Our Paleolithic ancestors lived as hunters and food gatherers. Because they had not learned how to farm, they never established permanent villages. When their food supplies ran short, they abandoned their caves or tentlike structures made of branches and searched for new dwelling places.

Although human progress was very slow during the long centuries of the Paleolithic Age, developments did occur that influenced the future enormously. Paleolithic people developed spoken language and learned how to make and use tools of bone, wood, and stone. With these simple tools, they dug up roots; peeled the bark off trees; trapped, killed, and skinned animals; made clothing; and fashioned fishnets. They also discovered how to control fire, which allowed them to cook their meat and provided warmth and protection.

Along with toolmaking and the control of fire, language was a great human achievement. Language enabled individuals to acquire and share knowledge, experiences, and feelings with one another. Thus, language was the decisive factor in the development of culture and its transmission from one generation to the next.

Most likely, our Paleolithic ancestors developed mythic-religious beliefs to explain the mysteries of nature, birth, sickness, and death. They felt that living powers operated within and beyond the world they experienced, and they sought to establish friendly relations with these powers. To Paleolithic people, the elements—sun, rain, wind, thunder, and lightning—were alive. The natural

Queen Nefertiti

New Kingdom, 18th dynasty c. 1370 B.C., painted limestone, 20˝ (50.8 cm), Staatliche Museen, Berlin. This bust shows the queen as a woman of consummate beauty who wears the crown of Upper and Lower Egypt as well as other ritualistic necklaces. The sculptor carefully detailed her makeup to craft a woman who is simultaneously sensuous and determined.

(Staatliche Museen zu Berlin, Egyptian Museum/Bildarchiv Preussischer Kulturbesitz. Photo: Margarete Busing)

Figure 1.1   Main Hall of Lascaux, 15,000–10,000 B.C., Dordogne region, France
The entire scene is called "the shaft of the dead man," which refers to the mysterious stick figure image of a man, who is falling backwards and has a bird's head and an erect penis. *(Jean Vertut)*

elements were spirits; they could feel and act with a purpose. To appease them, Paleolithic people made offerings. Gradually, shamans, priestesses, and healers emerged who, through rituals, trances, and chants, seemed able to communicate with these spirits. Paleolithic people also began the practice of burying their dead, sometimes with offerings, which suggests a belief in life after death.

Paleolithic Art and Music

Through the use of radiocarbon dating, we know that the earliest extant art was created in about 30,000 B.C., when Paleolithic people sought out the dark and silent interior of caves, which they probably viewed as sanctuaries. Using only torches for light, they painted remarkably skillful and perceptive pictures of animals, and a few humans, on the cave walls. Although the pictures are related to their lives as food gatherers and hunters, scholars can only speculate about whether they are manifestations of the artists' creative imagination or are depictions of actual events in their lives. Most likely, when these prehistoric artists drew an animal with a spear in its side, they believed that this act would bring success in hunting; when they drew a herd of animals, they probably hoped that this would cause plentiful game. This belief that something done to an image of an animal or a person would produce the same effect on the being itself is called *sympathetic magic.* Hunting societies that endured into the modern world still engaged in rituals designed to protect the hunter and to ensure a kill.

These works are all anonymous, impersonal, and somewhat standardized in their renderings of animals and humans. Though all the human figures are stylized showing only the slightest suggestion of movement, the most distinctive representations are those of women with large breasts, distended abdomens, exposed genitalia, and broad thighs, evidently linking them to fertility. Horses are the animal that appears most frequently, followed by bison, mammoth, ibex (wild goat), aurochs (wild ox), and deer. Generally portrayed in profile with an alert attitude, animals appear more naturalistic than do humans.

The first cave paintings to be discovered, in 1879, were those of the Altamira Cave (c. 15,000–10,000 B.C.), located in the province of Santander in northern Spain. Throughout the centuries, artists painted over previous scenes; thus, deciphering the meaning of the cave paintings has been tantamount to putting together several jigsaw puzzles simultaneously. For several years after the discovery of the Altamira cave paintings, scientists and archaeologists were skeptical as to their authenticity, but the discovery in southern France of other cave paintings, including the Lascaux Cave, found in 1940, dispelled all doubts. Dating from about 15,000 to 10,000 B.C., the *Main Hall of Lascaux* (Figure 1.1) is relatively small, approximately 110 yards long, and is adjacent to a side gallery and chamber. The side gallery consists of over sixty animal figures, including a cow jumping, numerous deer, and an injured stag with black hooves and expansive red antlers. The most mysterious drawing, painted in black at the back of the chamber, is the stick figure image of a man with a bird's head and an erect penis. Beneath the man, who is falling backwards, is a staff topped with a bird's head and a rhinoceros with two horns. The entire scene is called "the shaft of the dead man," but no one knows its actual meaning.

The relief carvings in many of the caves attest to the existence of a type of fertility cult—most of which is concerned with the reproductive power of animals, but that, on rare occasions, treats human figures as well. Dated to between 15,000 and 10,000 B.C., La Magdelaine Cave in southern France and the Addaura Cave near Palermo, Sicily, house such figures.

Small-scale ivory sculptures of mammoth also date from approximately the same time (c. 30,000 B.C.) as the earliest cave paintings. Later sculptures include horses and bison, but the most renowned are female figurines, which scholars assume are linked to fertility. The most famous example of this type of small-scale sculpture is the *"Venus" of Willendorf* (Figure 1.2) (c. 25,000 B.C.), so-named for the area in Austria where she was found. Sculpted in limestone and presumably painted red, her navel is formed naturally from a cleft in the rock, and her head, which lacks any facial features, is laden with circuitously styled hair. The roundness of her form suggests the oval shape of a sacred stone, but the large size of her breasts and genitalia suggests she was a symbol of human fertility.

Figure 1.2 "Venus" of Willendorf, c. 25,000 B.C., stone, height 4 3/8" (11 cm), Naturhistoriches Museum, Vienna She was named for the region in which she was found. Although the roundness of her form suggests the oval shape of a sacred stone, the large size of her breasts and genitalia suggests that she served as a symbol of human fertility. *(Naturhistorisches Museum, Vienna/Art Resource, NY)*

On December 18, 1994, the Chauvet Cave in the Ardèche region in southern France was found. Dating from about 32,000 to 30,000 B.C., the cave contains the oldest and best-preserved prehistoric paintings. Although it has not yet been completely explored, more than two hundred depictions of animals have already been discovered. The most numerous images are of rhinoceroses, followed by lions, mammoth, horses, bison, bears, reindeer, aurochs, ibex, and stags. Unlike previously discovered caves, this earliest of caves also includes an image of a panther (Figure 1.3) and a horned owl. The spotted panther is dwarfed by a larger image, which is either a bear or hyena. Although there is evidence of some human body parts, including hands and female genitalia, as yet no complete human figure has been discovered.

Through the portrayal of natural events and the human form in cave paintings and sculpted figures, our prehistoric ancestors were, in their own way, struggling to give form and clarity to their own experiences.

All human cultures have demonstrated a feeling for music. The rhythmic activity of work and play, the songs of birds, and the sound of waves crashing on the shore seem to ignite musical expression in people. Therefore, it is likely that prehistoric people beat out rhythms on primitive drums, sang softly to babies, and chanted tales about the deeds of heroes. However, this cannot be demonstrated conclusively. Ethnomusicologists and students of prehistory extrapolate this conclusion from the experience of modern tribal cultures in which dance and musical expression are a vital part of communal life. Among the artifacts left behind by prehistoric people are objects that may have been their musical instruments.

The Neolithic Age

Some ten thousand years ago, the New Stone Age, or *Neolithic Age,* began in the Near East. During the Neolithic Age, human beings discovered farming, domesticated animals, established villages, polished stone tools, made pottery, and wove cloth. So important were these achievements that they are referred to as the Neolithic Revolution.

The establishment of villages changed the patterns of life. A food surplus freed some of the people to devote part of their time to sharpening their skills as basket weavers or toolmakers. The demand for raw materials and the creations of skilled artisans fostered trade, sometimes across long distances, and spurred the formation of trading settlements. Hunting bands were egalitarian; generally, no one member had more possessions— belongings presented a burden when moving from

Figure 1.3   Chauvet Cave, 25,000 B.C., Ardèche region, France   This cave contains the oldest and best-preserved prehistoric paintings. More than two hundred animals are depicted, including rhinoceroses, lions, mammoths, horses, bison, bears, reindeer, aurochs (European bison), ibex (goats), and stags. This particular painting shows one of the earliest portrayals of a panther. *(Ministere de la Culture et de la Communication, Prefecture de la Region Rhone-Alpes: Grotte Chauvet-Pont d'Arc)*

place to place—or more power than another. In farming villages, a ruling elite emerged that possessed wealth and wielded power.

Neolithic people made great strides in technology. By shaping and baking clay, they made pottery containers for cooking and for storing food and water. The invention of the potter's wheel enabled them to form bowls and plates quicker and more precisely. The discoveries of the wheel and the sail improved transportation and promoted trade, and the development of the plow and the ox yoke made tilling the soil easier for farmers. Over time, Neolithic people learned how to fashion tools and weapons from metal—first copper then bronze—which were sharper than stone implements.

THE RISE TO CIVILIZATION

What we call civilization arose some five thousand years ago, first in Mesopotamia and Egypt and then later in East Asia (in India and China). The first civilizations began in cities that were larger, more populated, and more complex in their politi-

cal, economic, and social structure than Neolithic villages. The invention of writing enabled the first civilizations to preserve, organize, and expand their knowledge and to pass it on to future generations. It also allowed government officials and priests to conduct their affairs more efficiently. Moreover, civilized societies possessed organized governments, which issued laws and defined the boundary lines of their states. The inhabitants erected buildings and monuments on a scale much larger than Neolithic communities, engaged in trade and manufacturing, and used specialized labor for different projects. Religious life became more organized and complex, and a powerful and wealthy priesthood emerged. These developments—cities, specialization of labor, writing, organized government, monumental architecture, and a complex religious structure—differentiate the first civilizations from prehistoric cultures.

Religion was the central force in these primary civilizations. It provided satisfying explanations for the workings of nature, helped ease the fear of death, and justified traditional rules of morality. Law was considered sacred, a commandment of the gods. Religion united people in the common enterprises needed for survival—for example, the construction and maintenance of irrigation works and the storage of food. Religion also promoted creative achievements in art, literature, and science. In addition, the power of rulers, who were regarded either as gods or as agents of the gods, was derived from religion.

The emergence of civilization was a great creative act and not merely the inevitable development of agricultural societies. Many communities had learned how to farm, but only a handful made the leap into civilization. How was it possible for the Sumerians and the Egyptians, the creators of the earliest civilizations, to make this breakthrough? Most scholars stress the relationship between civilizations and river valleys. Rivers deposited fertile silt on adjoining fields, provided water for crops, and served as avenues for trade. However, environmental factors alone do not adequately explain the emergence of civilization. What cannot be omitted is the human contribution—capacity for thought and cooperative activity. Before these rivers could be of any value in producing crops, swamps around them had to be drained; jungles had to be cleared; and dikes, reservoirs, and canals had to be built. The construction and maintenance of irrigation works required the cooperation of large numbers of people, a necessary condition for civilization.

In the process of constructing and maintaining irrigation networks, people learned to formulate and obey rules and developed administrative, engineering, and mathematical skills. The need to keep records stimulated the invention of writing. These creative responses to the challenges posed by nature spurred the early inhabitants of Sumer and Egypt to make the breakthrough to civilization, thereby altering the course of human destiny.

MESOPOTAMIAN CIVILIZATION

Mesopotamia is the Greek word for "land between the rivers." It was here, in the valleys of the Tigris and Euphrates Rivers, that the first civilization began. The first people to develop an urban civilization in Mesopotamia (modern-day Iraq) were the Sumerians, who colonized the marshlands of the lower Euphrates, which, along with the Tigris, flows into the Persian Gulf. Through constant toil and imagination, the Sumerians transformed the swamps into fields of barley and groves of date palms. Around 3000 B.C., their hut settlements gradually evolved into twelve independent city-states, each consisting of a city and its surrounding countryside (Map 1.1).

The history of Mesopotamia is marked by a succession of conquests. The Sumerian cities were incorporated into various kingdoms and empires. Although the Sumerian language, replaced by a Semitic tongue, became an obscure language known only to priests, and the Sumerians gradually disappeared as a distinct people, their cultural achievements endured. Akkadians, Babylonians, Elamites, and others adopted Sumerian religious, legal, literary, and art forms. The Sumerian legacy served as the basis for a Mesopotamian civilization, which maintained a distinctive style for three thousand years.

Religion: The Basis of Mesopotamian Civilization

Religion lay at the center of Mesopotamian life. Every human activity—political, military, social, legal, literary, artistic—was generally subordinated to an overriding religious purpose. Religion was the Mesopotamians' frame of reference for understanding nature, society, and themselves; it dominated and inspired all other cultural expressions and human activities. Wars between cities, for instance, were interpreted as conflicts between the gods of those cities, and victory ultimately depended on divine favor, not on human effort. Myths—narratives about the activities of the gods—explained the origins of the human species. According to the earliest Sumerian myths, the first human beings issued forth from the earth like plant life, were shaped from clay by divine craftsmen and granted a heart by the goddess Nammu, or were formed from the blood of two gods sacrificed for that purpose.

The Mesopotamians believed that people were given life so that they could execute on earth the will of the gods in heaven. No important decisions were made by kings or priests without first consulting the gods. To discover the wishes of the gods, priests sacrificed animals and then examined their livers, or the priests might find their answers in the stars or in dreams.

The cities of Mesopotamia were sacred communities dedicated to serving divine masters, and people hoped that appeasing the gods would bring security and prosperity to their cities. A particular city belonged to a god, who was the real owner of the land and the real ruler of the city; often, a vast complex of temples was built for the god and the god's family. In the temple, the god was offered shelter, food, clothing, and the homage of dutiful servants.

Supervised by priests, the temple was a vital part of the city's life. People congregated there to take part in religious ceremonies. The temple,

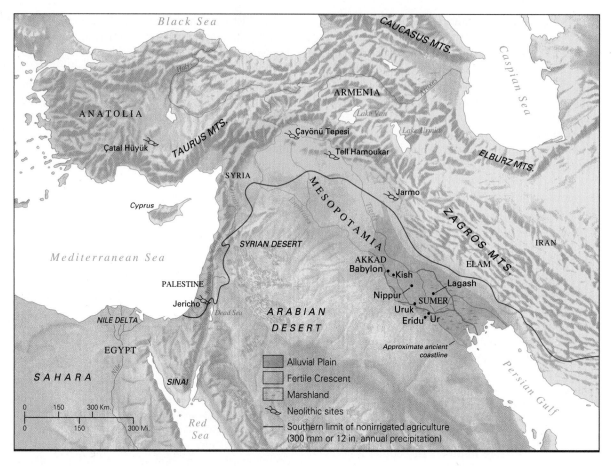

Map 1.1 Western Asia The Neolithic Revolution began after 10,000 B.C. in the Fertile Cresent, an arc-shaped region of dependable annual rainfall. In this area between the Tigris and Euphrates Rivers known as Mesopotamia, the world's first urban civilization took root about 3500–3000 B.C.

which probably owned most of the land in the city, also fulfilled important economic functions. Temple priests collected rents, operated businesses, and received contributions for festivals. Most inhabitants of the city worked for the temple priests as tenant farmers, agricultural laborers, or servants. Anxious to curry favor with the gods and goddesses who watched over the fields, peasants surrendered part of their crops to the temples. Priests coordinated the city's economic activity, which included supervising the distribution of land, overseeing the irrigation works, and storing food for emergencies.

The gods, invisible to human eyes but omnipresent, controlled the entire universe and everything in it. The moon, the sun, and the storm, the city, the irrigation works, and the fields—each was directed by a god. Mesopotamians saw gods and demons everywhere in nature. There was a god in the fire and another in the river; evil demons stirred up sandstorms, caused disease, and endangered women in childbirth. To shield themselves from hostile forces, Mesopotamians wore charms and begged their gods for help. Each Mesopotamian offered prayers and sacrifices to a personal god or goddess, who provided protection against evil spirits.

Mesopotamians believed that they were manipulated by divine beings. When misfortune befell them, people attributed it to the gods. Even success was not due to people's own efforts but to the intervention of a god who had taken a special interest in them. Compared with the gods, an individual was an insignificant and lowly creature.

Uncertainty and danger filled life in Mesopotamia. Sometimes the unpredictable river waters broke through the dikes, flooding fields, ruining crops, and damaging cities. At other times, an insufficient overflow deprived the land of water, causing crops to fail. Great windstorms left the countryside covered with a layer of sand, and heavy thunderstorms turned fields into a sea of mud that made travel impossible. Unlike Egypt, which was protected by vast deserts, Mesopotamia had no natural barriers to invasion. Feeling themselves surrounded by unfathomable and often hostile

THE ORIGINS OF HINDUISM IN INDIA

ORIGINATING IN INDIA FROM ABOUT 1500 B.C., Hinduism is one of the oldest living religions in the world. The oldest sacred writings of Hinduism are the Veda (Books of Knowledge), consisting of four collections of scripture. Although the Veda were written down sometime before 1000 B.C., they undoubtedly had existed as an oral tradition for centuries before then. The most important is the Rig-Veda, which consists of more than one thousand hymns or prayers to nature deities that are similar to the Homeric gods of the Greeks. The following hymn, addressed to Varuna, the most ancient Vedic god who personified the sky and the earth, not only describes the powers of the god but also evidences a concern with sin and the need of forgiveness.

To Varuna

1. Sing forth a hymn sublime and solemn, grateful to glorious Varuna, imperial ruler,
   Who hath struck out, like one who slays the victim, earth as a skin to spread in front of Surya [the sun god].

2. In the tree-tops the air he hath extended, but milk in kine [cows] and vigorous speed in horses,
   Set intellect in hearts, fire in the waters, Surya in heaven and Soma [the moon god] on the mountain.

3. Varuna lets the big cask, opening downward, flow through the heaven and earth and air's mid-region.
   Therewith the universe's sovereign [ruler] waters earth as the shower of rain bedews the barley.

4. When Varuna is fain for milk, he moistens the sky, the land, and earth to her foundation.
   Then straight the mountains clothe them in the raincloud: the heroes, putting forth their vigour, loose them.

5. I will declare this mighty deed of magic, of glorious Varuna, the lord immortal,
   Who, standing in the firmament, hath meted the earth out with the sun as with a measure.

6. None, verily, hath ever let or hindered this the most wise god's mighty deed of magic,
   Whereby with all their flood, the lucid rivers fill not one sea wherein they pour their waters.

7. If we have sinned against the man who loves us, have ever wronged a brother, friend, or comrade,

8. The neighbor ever with us, or a stranger, O Varuna, remove us from the trespass.
   If we, as gamesters cheat at play, have cheated, done wrong unwittingly or sinned of purpose,
   Cast all these sins away like loosened fetter, and, Varuna, let us be thine own beloved.

Source: Hindu Scriptures, *ed. Nicol Macnicol.* Everyman's Library, *no. 944*
(London: J. M. Dent; New York: E. P. Dutton, 1938), pp. 18–19.

forces, Mesopotamians lived in an atmosphere of anxiety, which permeated their civilization.

Contributing to this sense of insecurity was the belief that the gods behaved capriciously, malevolently, and vindictively. What do the gods demand of me? Is it ever possible to please them? Mesopotamians had no reassuring answers to these questions, for the gods' behavior was a mystery to mere human beings. A mood of uncertainty and anxiety, an awareness of the cosmos as unfathomable and mysterious, a feeling of dread about the fragility of human existence, and the impermanence of human achievement—these attitudes are as old as the first civilization.

Law, Mathematics, and Medicine

The king administered the laws, which came from the gods. The principal collection of laws in ancient Mesopotamia was the famous *code of Hammurabi* (c. 1792–c. 1750 B.C.), the Babylonian ruler. Unearthed by French archaeologists in 1901–1902, the code has provided invaluable insights into Mesopotamian society. In typical Mesopotamian fashion, Hammurabi claimed that his code rested on the authority of the gods; to violate it was to contravene the divine order.

The code reveals social status and mores in that area and time. Women were subservient to men, although efforts were made to protect women and children from abuse. By making death the penalty for adultery, the code probably sought to preserve family life. Punishments were generally severe— "an eye for an eye and a tooth for a tooth." The code prescribed death for housebreaking, kidnapping, aiding the escape of slaves, receiving stolen goods, and bearing false witness, but it did allow for consideration of extenuating circumstances. Class distinctions were also expressed in the code. For example, a person received more severe punishment for harming a noble than for harming a commoner. Government officials who engaged in extortion or bribery were harshly punished. The code's many provisions relating to business transactions underscore the importance of trade to Mesopotamian life.

The Mesopotamians made some impressive advances in mathematics. They devised multiplication and division tables, including even cubes and cube roots. They determined the area of right-angle triangles and rectangles, divided a circle into 360 degrees, and had some understanding of the principles that centuries later would be developed into the Pythagorean theorem and quadratic equations. However, the Babylonians, who made the chief contributions in mathematics, barely advanced to the level of devising theories; they did not formulate general principles or furnish proofs for their mathematical operations.

By carefully observing and accurately recording the positions of planets and constellations of stars, Babylonian sky watchers took the first steps toward developing the science of astronomy, and they devised a calendar based on the cycles of the moon. As in mathematics, however, they did not form theories to coordinate and illuminate their data. They believed that the position of the stars and planets revealed the will of the gods. Astronomers did not examine the heavens to find what we call cause-and-effect connections between the phenomena. Rather, they aspired to discover what the gods wanted. With this knowledge, people could organize their political, social, and moral lives in accordance with divine commands, and they could escape the terrible consequences that they believed resulted from ignoring the gods' wishes.

Consistent with their religious worldview, the Mesopotamians believed that gods and goddesses or demons caused disease. To cure a patient, priest-physicians resorted to magic; through prayers and sacrifices, they attempted to appease the gods and eject the demons from the sick body. Nevertheless, in identifying illnesses and prescribing appropriate remedies, Mesopotamians demonstrated some accurate knowledge of medicine and pharmacology.

Mesopotamian Literature

Mythological poetry treating the activities of deities was the predominant literary genre in Mesopotamia. A good example of this type of poetry is *Enuma Elish* ("When on high"), an *epic* poem that relates the creation of the world by Marduk, the chief god of Babylon. Marduk slays Tiamet, a primal mother identified with the salt sea.

> Then the lord paused to view her dead body,
> That he might divide the monster and do artful works.
> He split her like a shellfish into two parts:
> Half of her he set up and ceiled [covered] it as sky.[1]

From the other half of Tiamet's carcass, Marduk proceeded to fashion the earth. In contrast to the biblical notion of the creation of humanity in the image of God, the *Enuma Elish* "establish[es] a savage, 'man' shall be his name. . . . He shall be charged with the service of the gods that they might be at ease!"[2] Believing that they were subject to malicious gods, Mesopotamians held little hope for a happy life on earth.

Mesopotamian wisdom literature reinforced the pessimism that pervaded Mesopotamian life. Wisdom literature is moralistic and didactic; that is, it provides guidelines for proper conduct that will bring success in life. In a more sophisticated form, Mesopotamian wisdom literature also raised fundamental questions about the human condition: Does life have a meaning? Why do seemingly good people, those who are obedient to the gods and rulers, suffer? Despite the fact that the writer of the following verses had done all that he believed the gods wanted him to do, he continued to suffer. He not only laments his fate, but also wonders aloud why he must endure pain and suffering when he has endeavored to do nothing except good. This form of literature is very much present in the Hebrew Scriptures, and both his tribulation and questioning spirit foreshadow the biblical Job discussed in Chapter 2.

> I survived to the next year; the appointed time passed.
> I turned around, but it is bad, very bad;
> My *ill luck* increases and I cannot find what is right.
> I called to my god, but he did not show his face,
> I prayed to my goddess, but she did not raise her head.
> Even the diviner with his divination could not make a prediction,
> And the interpreter of dreams with his libation could not elucidate my case. . . .
> For myself, I gave attention to supplication and prayer:
> My prayer was discretion, sacrifice my rule.
> The day for worshipping the god was a joy to my heart;
> The day of the goddess's procession was profit and gain to me.
> The king's blessing—that was my joy,
> And the accompanying music became a delight for me.
> I had my land keep the god's rites,
> And brought my people to value the goddess's name,
> I made the praise for the king like a god's,
> And taught the people respect for the palace.
> I wish I knew that these things would be pleasing to one's god!
> What is good for oneself may be offense to one's god,
> What in one's own heart seems despicable may be proper to one's god.
> Who can know the will of the gods in heaven?
> Who can understand the plans of the underworld gods?
> Where have humans learned the way of a god?
> He who was alive yesterday is dead today.

He then goes on to describe the "debilitating disease" that is destroying him. He cannot eat, has lost control over his bowel movements, and is too weak to leave the house. "[Yet] My god has not come to the rescue nor taken me by the hand; My goddess has not shown pity on me nor gone by my side."[3]

Written about 2000 B.C., *The Epic of Gilgamesh,* the greatest work of Mesopotamian literature, is also an expression of the pessimism that pervaded Mesopotamian life. Utilizing legends about Gilgamesh, probably a historical figure who ruled the city of Uruk about 2600 B.C., it reveals the Mesopotamians' struggle to come to terms with reality. The story deals with a profound theme—the human protest against death. In the end, Gilgamesh learns to accept reality: There is no escape from death.

In *The Epic of Gilgamesh,* the gods are enmeshed in human activities. Because King Gilgamesh, son of a human father and the goddess Ninsun, drives his subjects too hard, they appeal to the gods for help. The gods decide that a man of Gilgamesh's immense vigor and strength requires a rival with similar attributes with whom he can contend. The creation goddess, Aruru, is instructed to create a man worthy of Gilgamesh. From clay she fashions Enkidu in the image of Anu, the god of the heavens and father of all the gods.

Enkidu is a powerful man who roams with the animals and destroys traps set by hunters, one of whom appeals to King Gilgamesh. The two of them, accompanied by a harlot, find Enkidu at a watering place frequented by animals. The harlot removes her clothes and seduces Enkidu, who spends a week with her, oblivious to everything else.

After this encounter, the bond between Enkidu and the animals is broken. He now enters civilization and is befriended by Gilgamesh, with whom he slays the terrible monster Humbaba.

Returning to Uruk after the encounter with Humbaba, Gilgamesh washes away the grime of battle and dons his royal clothes; thus arrayed, he attracts the goddess of love, Ishtar, patroness of Uruk, who proposes marriage, but because of Ishtar's previous marriages and infidelities, Gilgamesh refuses. Ishtar falls into a bitter rage and appeals to her father, the god Anu, to unleash the fearful Bull of Heaven on Gilgamesh.

However, Gilgamesh and Enkidu together slay the beast. To avenge the death of Humbaba and the Bull of Heaven, the gods decide that Enkidu shall die. Gilgamesh weeps over the loss of his dear friend:

Hear me great ones of Uruk,
I weep for Enkidu, my friend,
Bitterly moaning like a woman mourning
I weep for my brother.

O Enkidu, my brother,
You were the axe at my side,
My hand's strength, the sword in my belt,
The shield before me,
A glorious robe, my fairest ornament;
An evil Fate has robbed me.

. . .

All the people of Eridu
Weep for you Enkidu.[4]

In his despair, Gilgamesh is confronted with the reality of his own death and yearns for eternal life. In the garden of the gods, Gilgamesh speaks with Siduri, the divine winemaker, who tells him that his quest for immortality is hopeless.

"[M]y friend who was very dear to me and who endured dangers beside me, Enkidu my brother, whom I loved, the end of mortality has overtaken him. I wept for him seven days and nights till the worm fastened on him. Because of my brother I am afraid of death, because of my brother I stray through the wilderness and cannot rest. But now, young woman, maker of wine, since I have seen your face do not let me see the face of death which I dread so much."

She answered, "Gilgamesh, where are you hurrying to? You will never find that life for which you are looking. When the gods created man they allotted to him death, but life they retained in their own keeping. As for you, Gilgamesh, fill your belly with good things; day and night, night and day, dance and be merry, feast and rejoice. Let your clothes be fresh, bathe yourself in water, cherish the little child that holds your hand, and make your wife happy in your embrace; for this too is the lot of man."[5]

Gilgamesh, however, refuses to abandon his quest, so Siduri instructs him how to reach Utnapishtim, the legendary king of the city of Shurrupak, to whom the gods had granted everlasting life. Gilgamesh is ferried across the "waters of death" by a boatman and meets Utnapishtim. But he, too, cannot give Gilgamesh the immortality for which he yearns.

"Oh father Utnapishtim, you have entered the assembly of the gods, I wish to question you concerning the living and the dead, how shall I find the life for which I am searching?"

Utnapishtim said, "There is no permanence. Do we build a house to stand for ever, do we seal a contract to hold for all time? Do brothers divide an inheritance to keep for ever, does the flood-time of rivers endure? It is only the nymph of the dragon-fly who sheds her larva and sees the sun in his glory. From the days of the old there is no permanence. The sleeping and the dead, how alike they are, they are like a painted death. What is there between the master and the servant when both have fulfilled their doom? When the Anunnaki, the judges, come together, and Mammetun the mother of destinies, together they decree the fates of men. Life and death they allot but the day of death they do not disclose."[6]

When Gilgamesh asks Utnapishtim how he came to possess everlasting life, Utnapishtim responds: "I will reveal to you a mystery, I will tell you a secret of the gods." He then relates the story of a great flood, one of several Near Eastern flood tales that preceded the story of Noah in Genesis. At one time, said Utnapishtim, the world teeming with people "bellowed like a wild bull."[7] Disturbed by the clamor, the great god Enlil told a council of gods: "'The uproar of mankind is intolerable and sleep is no longer possible by reason of the babel.' So the gods agreed to exterminate mankind."[8] However, the god Ea warned Utnapishtim of the impending flood and instructed him to build a boat in which he would carry "the seed of all living creatures."[9]

The storm god let loose a tempest, which raged for six days and six nights, pouring "over the people like the tides of battle. . . . Even the gods were terrified at the flood, they fled to the highest heaven."[10] On the seventh day the storm subsided and the sea grew calm. Utnapishtim opened a hatch and wept "for on every side was the waste of water. I looked for land in vain."[11] But miles away he spied a mountain and there the boat grounded. Utnapishtim sent forth a dove, which returned because the land was still covered with water. He then loosed a raven, which found land. A hopeful Utnapishtim prepared burnt offerings for the gods, who, smelling the sweet savor, gathered over the sacrifice. When Enlil, who had ordered the flood, saw the boat, he was enraged: "Has any of these mortals escaped? Not one was to have survived the destruction."[12] Ea, Utnapishtim's protector, spoke to Enlil, wisest of gods, "Hero Enlil, how could you so senselessly bring down the flood?"[13] Instead of such indiscriminate and unjust destruction, Ea urged punishing sinners for their sins. Mindful of Ea's advice, Enlil blessed Utnapishtim and his wife and granted them immortality.

Toward the end of the epic, Utnapishtim reveals to Gilgamesh "a secret thing, . . . a mystery of the gods. . . . There is a plant that grows under the water . . . which restores his lost youth to a

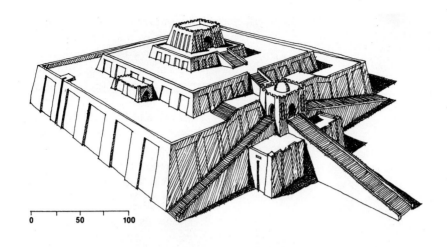

Figure 1.4   Ziggurat at Ur, reconstruction   The ziggurat was essentially a terraced pyramid with each level smaller than the one below it and with the temple itself resting on the summit. But unlike the Egyptian pyramids, which have a vertical axis as they rise like mountains high above the barren plains, the ziggurats have a serpentine axis as the spiral ascends. *(Witt et al.,* The Humanities, *Sixth Edition, Vol. 1, p. 10, Houghton Mifflin Company, ©2001.)*

man."[14] Gilgamesh then goes to the deepest water, ties stones to his feet, and plucks the plant from the bottom of the sea. He vows to return to Uruk, give the plant to the old men to eat, and finally, "I shall eat it myself and have back all my lost youth."[15] However, after traveling all day he stops for the night:

> [He] saw a well of cool water and he went down and bathed; but deep in the pool there was lying a serpent and the serpent sensed the sweetness of the flower. It rose out of the water and snatched it away, and immediately it sloughed its skin and returned to the well. Then Gilgamesh sat down and wept, the tears ran down his face, . . . "for this I wrung out my heart's blood? For myself I have gained nothing; not I, but the beast of the earth has joy of it now."[16]

Resigned to the futility of his quest for immortality, King Gilgamesh "who knew the countries of the world . . . [and] saw mysteries and knew secret things . . . was weary, worn out with labour, and returning [to Uruk] engraved on a stone the whole story."[17]

Mesopotamian Art and Music

Similar to other cultural expressions, Mesopotamian art was primarily a religious experience; artists aspired to honor the gods and to win their favor. This helps to explain why artists were anonymous and statues and reliefs were, at times, buried in a building foundation where they could be seen only by the gods. Both architecture and sculpture are evidence of the Mesopotamians' deep-seated longing to initiate contact with their gods.

The most prominent architectural structure was the *ziggurat* (Figure 1.4), a temple tower located in the heart of the city. The ziggurat was essentially a terraced pyramid with each level smaller than the one below it, with the temple itself resting on

the summit. The *cella*, the main room, was where sacrificial offerings were made to the deity for whom the temple was constructed. Here people also sought to gain knowledge of future events through omens, which they believed could be foretold by reading the entrails of the sacrificial animals or by interpreting the patterns of the sacrificial smoke. The entire complex of the ziggurat was designed to be a spiritual experience that ended with the individual's encounter with the deity. For example, worshipers were forced to proceed around numerous corners before they could ascend toward the god in the cella. Unlike the Egyptian pyramids, which have a vertical axis as they rise like mountains high above the barren plains, the ziggurats have a serpentine axis as the spiral ascends. The ziggurat was surrounded by low walls that enclosed offices and houses for the priests and shops where potters, weavers, carpenters, and tanners performed their crafts. The Tower of Babel (or Babylon) featured in the Genesis (11:1–9) story was a type of ziggurat.

A group of *Statues from the Abu Temple* (Figure 1.5) at Tell Asmar (in Iraq), which dates from about 2700 to 2500 B.C., gives further evidence of the significant place religion played in the lives of the inhabitants of Mesopotamia. At the center of a group of worshipers are two deities, known by their size and their enlarged pupils; the tallest is Abu, the god of vegetation, and the other is the Mother Goddess, Ki, also known as Ninhursag. People believed that the gods themselves were present in images of them; hence, the surrounding figures served as surrogates for actual worshipers.

Animals also played an important role in the mythic-religious outlook of the Near East. This is evident in the exquisite *Sumerian Harp* (Figure 1.6), unearthed from the tomb of Puabi, queen of Ur, from about 2600 B.C. The harp is constructed of wood, but the front panel is divided into sections and overlaid with a combination of shells,

Figure 1.5 Statues from the Abu Temple c. 2700–2500 B.C., marble with shell and black limestone inlay, tallest figure ~30" (76.2 cm), Warka, Iraq At the center of the group of worshipers are the deities Abu, the god of vegetation, and Ki, the Mother Goddess. *(Museum, Baghdad and The Oriental Institute, University of Chicago)*

bitumen, lapis lazuli, and gold. The top section features a heroic figure embracing two man-faced bulls made from shells inlaid with bitumen. The sections beneath show various animals engaged in human tasks—carrying food, drink, and musical instruments. The donkey carrying the harp is an image that survived in sculpture well into the Middle Ages. Scholars disagree over the actual meaning of the scenes. Some say the animals are part of a larger moral lesson, whereas others contend the scenes are renderings of portions of the Gilgamesh

epic or perhaps a portrayal of some sort of festive celebration in honor of the gods.

In the late 2000s B.C., a cultural outpouring occurred in the Sumerian city-state of Lagash that included public works and temples in honor of their deities. The series of powerful kings responsible for these projects included *King Gudea* (Figure 1.7), who likened himself to a shepherd of his people and had numerous pious-looking statues of himself placed in the temples. This statue, from about 2150 B.C., bears an inscription that

Figure 1.6 Soundbox of a Sumerian Harp, c. 2685–2550 B.C., wood with gold, lapis lazuli, and shell inlay, height 17" (43 cm), University Museum, University of Pennsylvania, Philadelphia This artifact demonstrates the important role that animals played in the mythic-religious outlook of the Near East. The top section features a heroic figure embracing two man-faced bulls, and the lower sections illustrate various animals engaged in human tasks—carrying food, drink, and musical instruments. *(University of Pennsylvania Museum, object B 17694)*

describes a temple dedicated to the goddess Geshtin-anna. The libation that Gudea holds is probably intended for her. The king's erect posture and the straightforward gaze of his large eyes suggest both his piety and his regal presence. Even though the sculptor has carefully detailed the muscular composition of Gudea's exposed arm and shoulder, the edges of the base are rounded to conform to the columnar configuration of the statue.

Centuries later, about 100 miles north of Lagash, King Nebuchadnezzar rebuilt Babylon. The new Babylon that arose on the bank of the Euphrates featured magnificent procession ways that led to palaces and temples. On his palace grounds, according to legend, Nebuchadnezzar created the famous Hanging Gardens—one of the "Seven Wonders of the Ancient World"—for his Median wife and erected monumental arched gates for the fortified walls of the city. Nebuchadnezzar commissioned one of these gates to honor Ishtar (Sumerian, Inanna), the mother of Marduk (Sumerian, Enlil), the sky god. The gate was sub-

sequently destroyed by the Persians, who conquered Babylon in 539 B.C. under Cyrus the Great.

Although there is no way to reconstruct how music in Mesopotamia sounded, there is abundant visual evidence that it existed and served a profoundly important ceremonial, communal, and personal function. Mesopotamian art shows musical performances and several instruments, including semielliptical harps, bow-shaped harps, trumpets, and percussion instruments. Although music served a primarily religious function in temple ceremonies and processions, it was also used at feasts and funerals and to commemorate victories on the battlefield.

EGYPTIAN CIVILIZATION

During the early period of Mesopotamian civilization, the Egyptians developed their civilization in the fertile valley of the Nile. Without this mighty river, which flows more than four thousand miles from central Africa northward to the Mediterranean, virtually all of Egypt would be a desert. When the Nile overflowed its banks, the floodwaters deposited a layer of fertile black earth that, when cultivated, provided abundant food to support the Egyptian civilization. The Egyptians learned how to control the river—a feat that required cooperative effort and ingenuity, as well as engineering and administrative skills. Natural barriers—mountains, deserts, cataracts (rapids) in the Nile, and the Mediterranean—protected Egypt from attack, allowing the inhabitants to enjoy long periods of peace and prosperity (Map 1.2). Thus, unlike Mesopotamians, Egyptians derived a sense of security from their environment.

From Old Kingdom to New Kingdom

By 2686 B.C., centralized rule had been firmly established, and great pyramids, which were tombs for the **pharaohs,** were being constructed. The pyramids required rigorous central planning to coordinate the tens of thousands of laborers drafted to build these immense monuments. During this Pyramid Age, or Old Kingdom (2686–2181 B.C.), the essential forms of Egyptian civilization crystallized. Egyptians looked to the past, convinced that the ways of their ancestors were best. For almost three thousand years, Egyptian civilization sought to retain a harmony with the order of nature instituted at creation. Believing in a changeless universe, the Egyptians did not value change or development—what we call progress—but venerated the institutions, traditions, and authority that embodied permanence.

Figure 1.7   King Gudea, 2150 B.C. Louvre Museum, Paris, France   Gudea was a powerful Sumerian king, who likened himself to a shepherd of his people and had numerous pious-looking statues of himself (such as this one) placed in countless temples. *(Réunion des Musées Nationaux/ Art Resource, NY)*

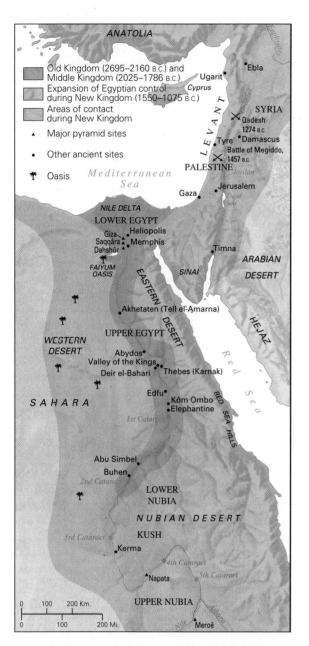

Map 1.2   Ancient Egypt and the Levant   The unique geography of the Nile Valley and its fertile soil left a stamp on ancient Egypt. Egypt enjoyed trade and cultural contact—and sometimes went to war—with nearby lands.

Rival noble families competing for the throne destroyed the Old Kingdom. During what is called the Middle Kingdom (2040–1786 B.C.), strong kings reasserted pharonic rule and reunited that state. But around 1800 B.C., the Hyksos (a mixture of Semites and Indo-Europeans) invaded Egypt. The Hyksos dominated Egypt for about a hundred years, until the Egyptians drove them out in 1570 B.C., beginning a period of empire building known as the New Kingdom (1570–1085 B.C.). During this time, aggressive pharaohs conquered territory that extended as far as the Euphrates River.

The Pharaoh

The pharaoh was viewed as both a man and a god. Divine kingship was the basic institution of Egyptian civilization. The Egyptians saw rule by a god–king as the only acceptable political arrangement: It was in harmony with the order of the universe, and it brought justice and security to the nation. The pharaoh's power extended to all sectors of society. Peasants were drafted to serve in labor corps as miners or construction workers. Foreign trade was a state monopoly, conducted according to the kingdom's needs. As the supreme overlord, the pharaoh oversaw an army of government officials, who collected taxes, supervised construction projects, checked the irrigation works, surveyed the land, kept records, conducted foreign trade, and supervised government warehouses, where grain was stored as insurance against a bad harvest. All Egyptians were subservient to the pharaoh, whose word was regarded as a divine ordinance. Most pharaohs took their responsibilities seriously and tried to govern as benevolent protectors of the people.

The pharaoh was seen as ruling in accordance with *Ma'at,* which means justice, law, right, and truth. To oppose the pharaoh was to violate the order of Ma'at and to bring disorder to society. Because the Egyptians regarded Ma'at as the right order of nature, they believed that its preservation must be the object of human activity—the guiding norm of the state and the standard by which individuals conducted their lives. Those who did Ma'at and spoke Ma'at would be justly rewarded. Could anything be more reassuring than this belief that divine truth was represented in the person of the pharaoh?

Religion: The Basis of Egyptian Civilization

Religion was omnipresent in Egyptian life and accounted for the outstanding achievements of Egyptian civilization. Religious beliefs were the basis of Egyptian art, medicine, astronomy, literature, and government. The great pyramids were tombs for the pharaohs, man–gods. Magical utterances pervaded medical practices, for disease was attributed to the gods. Astronomy evolved to determine the correct time to perform religious rites and sacrifices. The earliest examples of literature dealt entirely with religious themes. The pharaoh was a sacrosanct monarch who served as an intermediary between the gods and human beings. Justice was conceived in religious terms, something bestowed by a creator-god. The Egyptians developed an ethical code, which they believed the gods had approved. In a number of treatises compiled by high officials, now called *Books of Instruction,*

Egyptians were urged to tell the truth and to treat others fairly. In one *Book of Instruction,* which was prepared at the end of the second millennium, the author used a high ethical tone to enjoin Egyptians to express compassion for the poor, widows, and the handicapped.

The Egyptians also believed great powers in nature—sky, sun, earth, the Nile—to be gods. Thus, the universe was alive with divinities—there were about two thousand gods in the Egyptian pantheon—and human lives were tied to the movements of the sun and the moon and to the rhythm of the seasons. In the heavens the Egyptians found answers to the great problems of human existence.

A crucial feature of Egyptian religion was the afterlife. Through pyramid tombs, mummification to preserve the dead, and funerary art, the Egyptians showed their yearning for eternity and their desire to overcome death. Mortuary priests recited incantations to ensure the preservation of the dead body and the continuity of existence. Inscribed on the pyramids' interior walls were "pyramid texts," written in *hieroglyphics*—a form of picture writing in which figures, such as crocodiles, sails, eyes, and so forth, represented words or sounds that would be combined to form words. The texts contained fragments from myths, historical annals, and magical lore and provided spells to assist the king in ascending to heaven.

At first, the Egyptians believed that only the pharaoh and the royal family were immortal. In time, however, the nobility and then the commoners claimed that they, too, could share in the blessings of the "otherworld." Prayers that were hitherto reserved for the pharaoh could, for a fee, be recited by priests at the burial of commoners. To the Egyptians, the otherworld contained the same pleasures as those enjoyed on earth—friends, servants, fishing, hunting, paddling a canoe, picnicking with family members, entertainment by musicians and dancers, and good food. However, because earthly existence was not fundamentally unhappy, Egyptians did not yearn for death. The following song, inscribed in a pharaoh's tomb, reveals the Egyptians' relish for life.

> Enjoy yourself while you live,
> put on fine linen
> anoint yourself with wonderful ointments,
> multiply all your fine possessions on earth,
> follow your heart's command on earth
> be joyful and make merry.[18]

An early illustration of Egyptian belief in immortality is found in the legend of Osiris and Isis. Osiris was believed to have been the ruler of predynastic Egypt, and he later became the god of vegetation and of the underworld, the afterlife. Isis, his wife as well as his sister, was a mother goddess like Ninhursag of the Mesopotamians. At a time when Isis was not present, the god Set—Osiris' brother and great rival—killed him, cut his body into pieces, and threw them into the Nile. Isis, however, found the pieces and restored Osiris to life. This myth accounts not only for Osiris' function as god of the underworld but also for his role as guarantor of immortality—initially only for the pharaohs, then later for all Egyptians. The people also believed that the reigning pharaoh was divine because he was the manifestation of Horus—the son of Isis and Osiris—and that at his death the pharaoh became Osiris, and thus ruler of the underworld.

Amarna Religion: Toward Monotheism

During the New Kingdom, growing cultural interchange was paralleled by a movement toward monotheism during the reign of Pharaoh Amenhotep IV (c. 1369–1353 B.C.). Amenhotep sought to replace traditional polytheism—including the worship of Osiris—with the worship of Aton, a single god of all people, the supreme force in nature, who was represented as the sun disk, the provider of life. Amenhotep took the name Akhenaton ("It is well with Aton") and moved the capital from Thebes to a newly constructed holy city, called Akhetaten, near modern Tell el Amarna, which is why scholars refer to these innovations as the Amarna religion. The city contained palaces, administrative centers, and a temple complex honoring Aton, who was worshiped by Akhenaton and his family. Akhenaton and his wife, Nefertiti (see chapter opening), who played a prominent role in his court, dedicated themselves to Aton—the creator of the world, the sustainer of life, and the god of love, justice, and peace. Akhenaton also ordered his officials to chisel out the names of other gods from inscriptions on temples and monuments. With awe, Akhenaton glorified Aton:

> How manifold are thy works!
> They are hidden from man's sight.
> O sole god, like whom there is no other. Thou
>   hast made the earth according to thy desire.[19]

Akhenaton's "monotheism" had little impact on the masses of Egyptians, who retained their ancient beliefs, and it was resisted by priests, who resented his changes. After Akhenaton's death, a new pharaoh had the monuments to Aton destroyed, along with records and inscriptions bearing Akhenaton's name.

Historians are not certain why Akhenaton made such a radical break with tradition by propagating the worship of a single god. Was he trying to strike at the priests, whose wealth and prestige had increased considerably with Egypt's conquests? Did the break stem essentially from the vision of a great prophet, history's first? The most significant historical questions about Akhenaton are these two: Was his religion genuine monotheism, which pushed religious thought in a new direction? And if so, did it influence Moses, who led the Israelites out of Egypt about a century later? These questions have aroused controversy among historians. The principal limitation on the monotheistic character of Atonism is that there were really two gods in Akhenaton's religion: Aton and the pharaoh himself, who was still worshiped as a deity. Nor is there any evidence that Akhenaton influenced the monotheism of Moses.

Science and Mathematics

Similar to the Mesopotamians, the Egyptians made practical advances in the sciences. They demonstrated superb engineering skills in building pyramids and fashioned an effective system of mathematics, including geometry for measurements, which enabled them to solve relatively simple problems. The Egyptians' solar calendar, which allowed them to predict when the Nile would overflow, was more accurate than the Babylonians' lunar calendar.

In the area of medicine, Egyptian doctors were more capable than their Mesopotamian counterparts. They could identify illnesses and recognized that uncleanliness encouraged contagion. They also had some knowledge of anatomy and performed operations, such as circumcision and perhaps the draining of abscessed teeth. But their knowledge of medicine, as was that of the Mesopotamians, was handicapped by their belief that spiritual forces caused illnesses.

Egyptian Literature

Egyptian literature was distinguished by its richness and variety. In addition to religious–mythical writings, largely funerary texts, there were love poems, tales of adventure, romance, fantasy, and collections of maxims compiled by elderly sages for the benefit of young rulers.

THE BOOK OF THE DEAD   Containing litanies, hymns, and other religious texts, "The Book of the Dead," was written to guide the deceased person safely between this world and the afterlife. The texts are intimately aligned with the cult of Osiris and also contain references to a Day of Judgment. Chapter 125 describes deceased individuals,

standing before the doors of the Judgment Hall, ruled by Osiris, reciting their ordeals in the long journey from life to the Kingdom of Osiris. Once inside the main hall, every individual declares the name of Osiris and the forty-two other gods who assist him in the judgment of souls. The deceased individual then makes "a negative confession of sin"—that they did not commit any of the sins Osiris mentions.

1. "Hail, thou whose strides are long, who comest forth from Annu (Heliopolis), I have not done iniquity.*
2. . . . I have not robbed with violence.
3. . . . I have not done violence [to any man].
4. . . . I have not committed theft.
5. . . . I have not slain man or woman. . .
7. . . . I have not acted deceitfully.
8. . . . I have not purloined the things which belong unto God.
9. . . . I have not uttered falsehood.
10. . . . I have not carried away food.
11. . . . I have not uttered evil words.
12. . . . I have attacked no man. . . .
16. . . . I have never pried into matters [to make mischief].
17. . . . I have not set my mouth in motion [against any man].
18. . . . I have not given way to wrath concerning myself without a cause.
41. . . . I have not increased my wealth, except with such things as are [justly] mine own possessions.
42. . . . I have not thought scorn of the god who is in my city."[20]

LOVE, PASSION, AND MISOGYNY   As in most ancient societies, Egyptian women were concerned principally with marriage, children, and their household. In comparison to other societies, however, Egyptian women suffered fewer disabilities. They had legal rights; could enter the priesthood, a truly prestigious position; and had access to the otherworld after death.

Both men and women came under love's power, and the Egyptians wrote numerous poems that expressed both the joy and pain of love. In the following poem, a young man admires his loved one's beauty. Because the Egyptians were interested in maintaining pure bloodlines, children were often the product of incestuous relationships—father and daughter, mother and son, first cousins, and brother and sister. Therefore, the word *sister* (or *brother*), when used by a lover as an expression of endearment, may be taken either figuratively or lit-

---

* With the exception of the first confession, the acclamation to each of the gods has been omitted.

erally, depending on the circumstances; in the following poem, it is most likely used figuratively.

> The *One*, the sister without peer,
> The handsomest of all!
> She looks like the rising morning star
> At the start of a happy year.
> Shining bright, fair of skin,
> Lovely the look of her eyes,
> Sweet the speech of her lips,
> She has not a word too much.
> Upright neck, shining breast,
> Hair true lapis lazuli;
> Arms surpassing gold,
> Fingers like lotus buds.
> Heavy thighs, narrow waist,
> Her legs parade her beauty;
> With graceful step she treads the ground,
> Captures my heart by her movements.
> She causes all men's necks
> To turn about to see her;
> Joy has he whom she embraces,
> He is like the first of men!

Without his love the young man suffers.

> *Seven* days since I saw my sister,
> And sickness invaded me;
> I am heavy in all my limbs,
> My body has forsaken me.
> When the physicians come to me,
> My heart rejects their remedies;
> The magicians are quite helpless,
> My sickness is not discerned.
> To tell me "She is here" would revive me!
> Her name would make me rise;
> Her messenger's coming and going,
> That would revive my heart!
> My sister is better than all prescriptions,
> She does more for me than all medicines;
> Her coming to me is my amulet,
> The sight of her makes me well!
> When she opens her eyes my body is young,
> Her speaking makes me strong;
> Embracing her expels my malady—
> *Seven* days since she went from me!

Egyptian women also experienced love and vented their feelings:

> My heart *flutters* hastily,
> When I think of my love of you;
> It lets me not act sensibly,
> It leaps [from] its place.
> It lets me not put on a dress,
> Nor wrap my scarf around me;
> I put no paint upon my eyes,
> I'm even not anointed.
> "Don't wait, go there," says it to me,

> As often as I think of him;
> My heart, don't act so stupidly,
> Why do you play the fool?
> Sit still, the brother comes to you,
> And many eyes as well!
> Let not the people say of me:
> "A woman fallen through love!"
> Be steady when you think of him,
> My heart, do not *flutter*![21]

Sometimes Egyptian men held unflattering views of women. In his advice to his son, the priest Ankhsheshong, who lived some time between 300 B.C. and 50 B.C., expressed such misogynist views.

> Let your wife see your wealth; do not trust her with it. . . .
> Do not open your heart to your wife or to your servant.
> Open it to your mother; she is a woman of discretion. . . .
> Instructing a woman is like having a sack of sand whose side is split open.
> Her savings are stolen goods.
> What she does with her husband today she does with another man tomorrow. . . .
> Do not rejoice in your wife's beauty; her heart is set on her lover. . . .
> If a woman does not desire the property of her husband she has another man [in her] heart.[22]

Egyptian Art and Music

The archaeological evidence, particularly from Egyptian tombs, indicates that the Egyptians were greatly concerned with immortality; inscriptions and artifacts reflect their compelling desire to obtain the "good life" in the afterlife. In order to enjoy a beneficial afterlife, the deceased's physical and spiritual identity needed to be maintained. Physical identity was preserved by mummification of the body, by inscriptions written about the person in the tomb, and by provisions (food, drink, furniture, even mummified pets) stored in the tomb to be a mainstay for the departed person. Protection of the spirit (*ka*) was fostered through texts (such as variations of the Osiris myths) and inscriptions detailing spells devised to protect the dead person during his or her precarious descent into the underworld. The final step in the transition from earthly existence to life in the underworld was a ritualistic judgment by Osiris. Consequently, the Egyptians spent an inordinate amount of time in preparation for the afterlife. Even though people of moderate means could only plan for a modest afterlife, they believed it would be, at the very least, an idealized version of their earthly life.

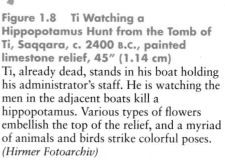

Figure 1.8 Ti Watching a Hippopotamus Hunt from the Tomb of Ti, Saqqara, c. 2400 B.C., painted limestone relief, 45" (1.14 cm)
Ti, already dead, stands in his boat holding his administrator's staff. He is watching the men in the adjacent boats kill a hippopotamus. Various types of flowers embellish the top of the relief, and a myriad of animals and birds strike colorful poses. *(Hirmer Fotoarchiv)*

Painted narrative relief panels that line the Egyptian tombs help us to understand the lives of both ordinary and extraordinary Egyptians. The episodes portrayed in these reliefs are enriched with illustrations of animals, birds, plants, and people that relate to the person's earthly existence. For example, *Ti Watching a Hippopotamus Hunt* (Figure 1.8), from the Tomb of Ti at Saqqara (c. 2400 B.C.), shows Ti nearly twice as large as the surrounding figures as he stands in his boat holding his administrator's staff. Against the vertical furrows of the background, which represent a papyrus swamp, Ti, already deceased, is merely an observer of men in adjacent boats killing a hippopotamus. Various types of flowers embellish the top of the relief, and a myriad of animals and birds strike colorful poses. Although the ripples in the water (appearing as stylized zigzags at the bottom of the relief) suggest a sense of movement, the scene also displays a sense of order seen in the parallelism of the hunters' spears and the triangular arrangement of Ti's tunic. Relief panels, such as this one, not only tell us

about the occurrences in the deceased's life, but also enable us to learn about the natural environment of the Egyptians—swamps, birds, flowers, animals—and to understand the activities associated with the hunt.

Egyptian pictorial art was characteristically stiff, formal, and lacking in realism. For example, pharaohs were depicted as austere, solid, and immobile, thus portraying the divinity of the pharaohs and the immutable cycle of life and death. During the brief reign of Akhenaton however, a naturalistic approach, known as the Amarna style, emerged in conjunction with the pharaoh's creative religious ideas. Inspired artists now sought to represent things more realistically and attempted to capture an individual's human essence. In what was a radical departure from convention, Akhenaton was, for example, portrayed in everyday situations—lifting his daughter onto his knee or leaning on a stick while walking in his garden.

As compared to Egyptians with modest incomes, a pharaoh spared no expense in prepa-

Figure 1.9   The Pyramids, Giza, c. 2500s B.C.   The pyramids were the final resting place for three of Egypt's pharaohs. Cheops' pyramid is 480 feet high, Chephren's is 470 feet in height, and Mycerinus' is 203 feet tall. *(Farrel Grehan/Photo Researchers)*

ration for his otherworldly existence. The Age of the Pyramids during the Old Kingdom lasted for slightly less than four centuries. The best-known pyramids are the three gigantic *Pyramids of Giza* (Figure 1.9), built for Khufu, Khafra, and Menkure, better known by their Greek names— Cheops, Chephren, and Mycerinus. Cheops' pyramid is the oldest and largest, at a height of 480 feet; Chephren's, 470 feet high, was the second and was erected on the same diagonal line as Cheops'; the smallest is Mycerinus' at only 203 feet. Next to the only extant valley temple at Giza, that of Chephren, is the monumental *Sphinx* (Figure 1.10). With the body of a lion

and the face of a man (most likely Chephren himself), the Sphinx watches over Giza as a testament to the divine kingship of the pharaohs. Carved from rock and originally painted, the body and head of the Sphinx are 230 feet long and 65 feet high; the paws were sculpted separately and then attached.

In contrast to women in most ancient civilizations, including Greece and Rome, Egyptian women, particularly those of the upper class, appear to have held relatively equal legal and economic status with their male counterparts. For example, the pyramids of the queens of Cheops and Mycerinus were erected parallel to the ones

Figure 1.10   The Great Sphinx, Giza, c. 2500 B.C., height 65′ (19.8 m)   With the body of a lion and the face of a man, the Sphinx watches over Giza as a testament to the divine kingship of the pharaohs. *(John Ross/Robert Harding Picture Library)*

for the pharaohs. Further evidence of female equality is found in historical inscriptions in documents, in tombs, and in sculptures where kings are often depicted with their queens. One such statue comes from Giza—*Mycerinus and His Queen* (Figure 1.11)—wherein the figures are sculpted at nearly the same height. Although the bodies are well proportioned, their blocklike portrayal exhibits a rigidity and inflexibility of form. There is no suggestion of movement, for the left foot of both figures is positioned slightly forward, and their arms are stiffly ensconced. Only the slight swelling of the queen's breasts under her clinging gown suggests her feminine character. Scholars suggest that the representation of the divinity and

grandeur of the pharaoh was far more important to the sculptor than depiction of natural human forms. This type of the positioning of the body and the rigidity of form was widely emulated during the Archaic period of Greek sculpture (see Chapter 4).

Queens were sometimes sculpted independently of the king, especially during the New Kingdom. The limestone bust of *Queen Nefertiti* (see chapter opening), wife of Akhenaton, was sculpted about 1370 B.C., some thousand years after *Mycerinus and His Queen*, and shows the queen, a woman of consummate beauty, wearing the crown of Upper and Lower Egypt as well as ritualistic necklaces. The sculptor elegantly captured her slender neck, high cheekbones, flawless nose, taut chin, and ample lips. Carefully detailing her makeup, the sculptor presents a woman who is simultaneously sensuous and determined. Although this remarkable bust was not intended for public display—the statue was actually a model for a public portrait of the queen and was found in the sculptor's studio—its naturalistic styling signaled the Amarna style of art (as a parallel to the Amarna religion) during Akhenaton's reign. This style of art was perpetuated by Akhenaton's son-in-law, Tutankhamen.

Tutankhamen (Figure 1.12), who died at the young age of eighteen, was only a minor king who ruled Egypt from about 1347 to 1338 B.C. His fame as an Egyptian pharaoh is the result of a happenstance of history—his tomb was not plundered. It was discovered in all its glory and with all its treasures intact in 1922. The solid gold sarcophagus (coffin) of "King Tut" weighs nearly 250 pounds. The cover of the coffin depicts a handsome youth with delicacy, charm, and comeliness—tendencies typical of the Amarna style. During the New Kingdom there was a reaction to the Amarna style, and Egyptian art became more ornamental. The backlash continued throughout the New Kingdom, as represented by a concerted effort to return to the rigidity of form that characterized the sculpture of the Old Kingdom. However, as the Egyptians became a conquered people, their art, like that of the Mesopotamians, began to show the influence of foreign forms.

Wall paintings in tombs and hieroglyphic accounts reveal a wide array of musical instruments: harps, lyres, lutes, flutes, percussion instruments, and trumpets. Egyptians employed music for religious ceremonies and kingly processions, as did the Mesopotamians. They were also similar to the Mesopotamians in the way they utilized music, both privately and socially—in their homes and at feasts and funerals.

Figure 1.11 Mycerinus and His Queen, Giza, 2499–2171 B.C. slate, 54 1/2" (142.3 cm), Museum of Fine Arts, Boston   Although the bodies are well proportioned, their blocklike portrayal exhibits a rigidity and inflexibility of form. Only the slight swelling of the queen's breasts under her clinging gown suggests her feminine character. *(Harvard University—Museum of Fine Arts Expedition, 11.1738)*

Figure 1.12   The Golden Coffin of Tutankhamen, 18th dynasty late Amarna period, c. 1352 B.C., gold inlaid with lapis lazuli, turquoise, and carnelian, Egyptian Museum, Cairo   Discovered with all its treasures intact in 1922, the tomb of "King Tut" contained a solid gold sarcophagus weighing nearly 250 pounds. *(Robert Harding Picture Library)*

PERSIA: UNIFIER OF THE NEAR EAST

After 1500 B.C., the Near East entered a period of empire building. In the late sixth century B.C., the Persians, the greatest of the empire builders, conquered all the land from the Nile River in Egypt to the Indus River in India. Persian kings developed an effective system of administration—based in part on an Assyrian model—that gave stability and a degree of unity to their extensive territories. The Persian empire was divided into twenty provinces (satrapies), each administered by a governor (satrap) responsible to the emperor. Besides providing impressive political and administrative

unity, the Persians fused and perpetuated the various cultural traditions of the Near East. Persian palaces, for example, boasted the terraces of Babylon, the colonnades of Egypt, the winged bulls that decorated Assyrian palace gates, and the craftsmanship of Median goldsmiths.

Persia unified the nations of the Near East into a world–state, headed by a divinely appointed king. It also synthesized the region's cultural traditions. Soon it would confront the city–states of Greece, whose political system and cultural orientation differed from those of the Near East.

Persian Religion: Zoroastrianism

Judaism and its two derivative religions, Christianity and Islam, emerged from the Near East. All were monotheistic, emphasized ethics, and believed in God as the source of justice and truth. Zoroastrianism—another monotheistic faith— also came from the Near East. It originated with the worship of Mazda—the god of light, justice, wisdom, goodness, and immortality. Zoroastrianism is a living religion; its 140,000 adherents are centered largely in Iran and India.

The most important prophet of this ancient faith is Zarathuštra (Zoroaster in Greek). Legend placed him in the late seventh and early sixth century B.C., but he may have lived earlier. In contrast to the traditional religions of the Near East, Zarathuštra rejected magic, polytheism, and blood sacrifices. Instead, his teachings stressed ethics and emphasized the individual's capacity to choose between good and evil. Zarathuštra asserted the existence of a cosmic dualism within the universe that resulted in a war within an individual's soul, whose salvation depended on choosing good over evil. Zarathuštra also referred to another cosmic deity—*Angra Mainyu* (or Ahriman)—the destructive spirit of darkness and the evil and ignorant counterpart of the good and wise Ahura Mazda. People were free to choose whom they would follow, but because of the tradition of *aša*—right order and behavior—most people would choose the good of Ahura Mazda. To serve him, one had to speak the truth and be good to others; the reward for such behavior was life eternal in paradise, the realm of light and goodness. The followers of the evil spirit could be cast into a realm of darkness and torment—a temporary form of hell—to await the end of time. Such a separation of good and evil people demanded that peoples' words and actions in their earthly life be judged. This task was assigned to Mithra, the guardian of the covenant of *aša,* who presided over the judgment of souls; and to Rašnu, the Mainyu of judgment, who held the scales of judgment.

Figure 1.13 Tomb of Xerxes (died 464 B.C.), Naqsh-i Rustam (approximately five miles north of Persepolis) The tomb is carved out of solid rock and depicts Xerxes worshiping at a fire altar in honor of the Zoroastrian All-Creator God, Ahura Mazda. *(Nat Yanna Brandt/Photo Researchers)*

Zarathuštra also developed an *eschatology*—a vision of an "end of time"* when Ahura Mazda's purpose for creating the world is fulfilled, evil is defeated, and good finally triumphs. The two major events leading up to the end of time are: the bodily resurrection of the dead, both in paradise and hell; and the final judgment—during which all of humanity is to be immersed in molten metal. Those who survive are innocent, and those who perish unwittingly aid in the abolition of evil from the universe. Hell then ceases to exist, and the earth becomes a grassy plain in which the blessed partake in a communal meal that purifies their resurrected bodies, and they dwell with Ahura Mazda forever.

Zoroastrianism came in contact with Greek culture during the Achaemenian empire—the dynasty

that ruled Iran from the time of Cyrus the Great to Alexander the Great's invasion in 330 B.C. Greek thinkers spoke of the Zoroastrians' piety, discipline, and ethical concerns. Inscriptions from this period also attest to the vitality of the faith among the Persians, as evidenced by one found on the tomb of Darius I: "Whoever shall worship Ahuramazda as long as he has strength, he will be happy, both living and dead."[23]

Persian Art

Cyrus and his successors aspired to the same sort of cultural greatness as did the Assyrian kings. The magnificent city of Persepolis (in Iran) was to be a testament to the "Persian style" of art and architecture. Darius I began the elaborate citadel; his son, Xerxes, continued its construction; and his grandson, Artaxerxes I (464–425 B.C.), completed it. The citadel, of which only portions of the audi-

---

* The end of time is the Frašo-kereti (Making Glorious).

ence hall remain, was a confluence of styles—Median, Mesopotamian, Egyptian, and Greek. The audience hall was 250 feet square, with a wooden ceiling 40 feet above the floor supported by 36 columns. The uppermost part of the columns (the capitals) are adorned with the same types of animals that the Assyrians used for their art, but the columns evidence both Egyptian and Greek (see Chapter 4) influences. Xerxes continued to use the audience hall until his death in 464 B.C., when he was buried, as were his father and his successors, in a colossal tomb. The relief narrative of the *Tomb of Xerxes* (Figure 1.13) at Naqsh-i Rustam, approximately five miles north of Persepolis, is carved out of solid rock and depicts Xerxes worshiping at a fire altar exalting Ahura Mazda. More than thirty other figures support the dais on which he stands. Below the narrative is the opening to the tomb itself, which looks much like the facade of a Greek temple—flanked by columns and apparently resting on a podium (see Chapter 4).

The Religious Orientation of the Ancient Near East

Religion dominated, suffused, and inspired all features of Near Eastern society: law, kingship, art, and science. In the first civilizations, the deepest thoughts of human beings were expressed in the form of religious myths. They were the source of the vitality and creativity of Mesopotamian and Egyptian civilizations. Priest–kings or god–kings, their power sanctioned by divine forces, furnished the necessary authority to organize large numbers of people in cooperative ventures. Religion also encouraged and justified wars—including enslavements and massacres—which were seen as conflicts between the gods.

A Mythmaking Worldview

A religious, or mythopoeic (mythmaking), view of the world gives Near Eastern civilization its distinctive form and allows us to see it as an organic whole. Mesopotamians and Egyptians inherited from their prehistoric ancestors a great variety of stories that attempted to account for the origins of the world and human life. Giving free play to the imagination, they altered and expanded these myths and spontaneously created new ones in order to answer questions that we today treat scientifically. Mythmaking was humanity's first way of thinking; it was the earliest attempt to make

nature's mysteries and life's uncertainties comprehensible. Appealing primarily to the imagination and emotions, rather than to reason, mythical thinking, as expressed in language, art, poetry, and social organization, has been a fundamental formative element of human culture.

Originating in sacred rites, ritual dances, feasts, and ceremonies, myths depicted the deeds of gods, who, in some remote past, had brought forth the world and human beings. Holding that the gods determined human destiny, Near Eastern people interpreted their experiences through myths. Myths also enabled Mesopotamians and Egyptians to make sense out of nature and to explain the world of phenomena. Through myths, the Near Eastern mind sought to give coherence to the universe and make it intelligible. These myths gave Near Eastern people a framework within which to pattern their experiences into a meaningful order, justify their rules of conduct, and try to overcome the uncertainty of existence.

The civilizations of the ancient Near East were based on a way of thinking that was fundamentally different from the modern scientific outlook. The difference between scientific and mythical thinking is profound. The scientific mind views physical nature as an *it*—inanimate, impersonal, and governed by universal law. The mythmaking mind of the Near East saw every object in nature as a *thou*—personified, alive, and with an individual will. It saw gods or demons manipulating things. The sun and stars, the rivers and mountains, the wind and lightning were either gods or the dwelling places of gods. Live agents were the forces behind natural events. An Egyptian or a Mesopotamian experienced natural phenomena—a falling rock, a thunderclap, a rampaging river—as life facing life. If a river flooded the region and destroyed crops, it was because it wanted to; the river or the gods desired to punish the people.

In other words, the ancients told myths instead of presenting an analysis or conclusions. We would explain, for instance, that certain atmospheric changes broke a drought and brought about rain. The Babylonians observed the same facts, but experienced them as the intervention of the gigantic bird Imdugud, which came to their rescue. It covered the sky with the black storm clouds of its wings and devoured the Bull of Heaven, whose hot breath had scorched the crops.[24]

The Egyptians believed that the sun rose in the morning, traveled across the sky, and set into the netherworld beyond the western horizon. Sometimes, it was maintained that the great Cow of Heaven every day gave birth to the sun, which was swallowed every evening by the sky goddess Nut.

After warding off the forces of chaos and disruption, the sun reappeared the next morning. For the Egyptians, the rising and setting of the sun were not natural occurrences—a celestial body obeying an impersonal law—but a religious drama.

The scientific mind holds that natural objects obey universal rules; hence, the location of planets, the speed of objects, and the onset of a hurricane can be predicted. The mythmaking mind of the ancient Near East was not troubled by contradictions. It did not seek logical consistency and had no awareness of repetitive laws inherent in nature. Rather, it attributed all occurrences to the actions of gods, whose behavior was often erratic and unpredictable. Witch doctors employed magic to protect people from evil supernatural forces that surrounded them. The scientific mind appeals to reason: It analyzes nature logically and systematically and searches for general principles that govern phenomena. The mythmaking mind appeals to the imagination and feelings and proclaims a truth that is emotionally satisfying, not one that has been arrived at through intellectual analysis and synthesis. Mythical explanations of nature and human experience enrich perception and feeling. Thus, they made life seem less overwhelming and death less frightening.

Of course, Near Eastern people did engage in rational forms of thought and behavior. They certainly employed reason in building irrigation works, in preparing a calendar, and in performing mathematical operations. However, because rational, or logical, thought remained subordinate to a mythic-religious orientation, they did not arrive at a *consistently* and *self-consciously* rational method of inquiring into physical nature and human culture.

Thus, Near Eastern civilization reached the first level in the development of science: observing nature, recording data, and improving technology in mining, metallurgy, and architecture. But it did not advance to the level of self-conscious philosophical and scientific thought—that is, logically deduced abstractions, hypotheses, and generalizations. Mesopotamians and Egyptians did not fashion a body of philosophical and scientific ideas that were logically structured, discussed, and debated. They had no awareness of general laws that govern particular events. These later developments were the singular achievement of Greek philosophy: It gave a "rational interpretation to natural occurrences which had previously been explained by ancient mythologies. . . . With the study of nature set free from the control of mythological fancy, the way was opened for the development of science as an intellectual system."[25]

Near Eastern Achievements

Mesopotamians and Egyptians demonstrated enormous creativity and intelligence. They built irrigation works and cities, organized governments, charted the course of heavenly bodies, performed mathematical operations, constructed large-scale monuments, engaged in international trade, established bureaucracies and schools, and considerably advanced the level of technology. Without the Sumerian invention of writing—one of the great creative acts in history—what we mean by civilization could not have emerged.

Many elements of ancient Near Eastern civilization were passed on to the West. The wheeled vehicle, the plow, and the phonetic alphabet—all inventions important to the development of civilization—derive from the Near East. In the realm of medicine, the Egyptians knew the value of certain drugs, such as castor oil; they also knew how to use splints and bandages. The innovative divisions that gave 360 degrees to a circle and 60 minutes to an hour originated in Mesopotamia. Egyptian geometry and Babylonian astronomy were utilized by the Greeks and became a part of Western knowledge. The belief that a king's power issued from a heavenly source also derived from the Near East. In Christian art, too, one finds connections to Mesopotamian art forms—for example, the Assyrians depicted winged angel-like beings.

Both the Hebrews and the Greeks borrowed Mesopotamian literary themes. For instance, some biblical stories, such as the Flood, the quarrel between Cain and Abel, and the Tower of Babel, stem from Mesopotamian antecedents. A similar link exists between the Greek and the earlier Mesopotamian mythologies.

Thus, many achievements of the Egyptians and the Mesopotamians were inherited and assimilated by both the Greeks and the Hebrews. Even more important for an understanding of the essential meaning of Western civilization are the ways in which the Greeks and the Hebrews rejected or transformed elements of the older Near Eastern traditions to create new points of departure for the human mind.

Key Terms

Paleolithic Age	ziggurat
sympathetic magic	pharaoh
Neolithic Age	Ma'at
code of Hammurabi	hieroglyphics
The Epic of Gilgamesh	eschatology

Notes

1. James B. Pritchard, ed., *Ancient Near Eastern Texts Relating to the Old Testament,* 3rd ed. with Supplement (Princeton, N.J.: Princeton University Press, 1969), p. 67.
2. Ibid., p. 68.
3. James B. Pritchard, ed., *The Ancient Near East: A New Anthology of Texts and Pictures* (Princeton, N.J.: Princeton University Press, 1975), pp. 151–154.
4. *The Epic of Gilgamesh,* intro. N. K. Sandars (New York: Penguin Books, 1972), pp. 94–95.
5. Ibid., pp. 101–102.
6. Ibid., pp. 106–107.
7. Ibid., p. 108.
8. Ibid.
9. Ibid.
10. Ibid., p. 110.
11. Ibid., p. 111.
12. Ibid., p. 112.
13. Ibid.
14. Ibid., p. 116.
15. Ibid.
16. Ibid., p. 117.
17. Ibid.
18. Quoted in Eugene Strouhal, *Life of the Ancient Egyptians* (Norman, Okla.: University of Oklahoma Press, 1992), p. 41.
19. Quoted in John A. Wilson, *The Culture of Ancient Egypt* (Chicago: University of Chicago Press, Phoenix Books, 1951), p. 227.
20. E. A. Wallis Budge, *The Book of the Dead* (London: Arkana, 1985), pp. 366–371.
21. Miriam Lichtheim, *Ancient Egyptian Literature: A Book of Readings* (Berkeley: University of California Press, 1976), Vol. II, pp. 182, 183–184, 185.
22. Ibid., Vol. III, pp. 166–180.
23. Ibid., p. 126.
24. Henri Frankfort, Mrs. H. A. Frankfort, John A. Wilson, and Thorkild Jacobsen, *Before Philosophy: The Intellectual Adventure of Ancient Man* (Baltimore: Penguin Books, 1949), p. 15.
25. Samuel Sambursky, *The Physical World of the Greeks* (New York: Collier Books, 1962), pp. 18–19.

The Hebrews: A New View of God and the Individual

ANCIENT MESOPOTAMIA AND EGYPT, the birthplace of the first civilizations, are not the spiritual ancestors of the West; for the origins of the Western tradition, we must turn to the Hebrews (Jews) and the Greeks. Both Greeks and Hebrews, of course, absorbed some elements of the civilizations of Mesopotamia and Egypt, but even more significant is how they transformed this inheritance and shaped worldviews that differed markedly from the outlooks of these first civilizations. As Egyptologist John A. Wilson writes,

> The Children of Israel built a nation and a religion on the rejection of things Egyptian. Not only did they see God as one, but they ascribed to him consistency of concern for man and consistency of justice to man. . . . Like the Greeks, the Hebrews took forms from their great neighbors; like the Greeks, they used those forms for very different purposes.[1]

In this chapter, we examine one source of the Western tradition, the Hebrews, whose conception of God broke with the outlook of the Near East and whose ethical teachings helped to fashion the Western idea of the dignity of the individual.

EARLY HEBREW HISTORY

The Hebrews originated in Mesopotamia and migrated to Canaan, a portion of which was later called Palestine (Map 2.1). The Hebrew patriarchs—Abraham, Isaac, and Jacob, so prominently depicted in the Bible—were chieftains of seminomadic clans that roamed Palestine and occasionally journeyed to Mesopotamia and Egypt. During these travels, the early Hebrews absorbed some features of Mesopotamian civilization. For example, there are parallels between biblical law and the Mesopotamian legal tradition. Several biblical stories—the Creation, the Flood, the Garden of Eden—derived from Mesopotamian sources.

Some Hebrews journeyed from Canaan to Egypt to be herdsmen and farmers, but they eventually became forced laborers for the Egyptians. Fearful of turning into permanent slaves of the pharaoh, the Hebrews yearned for an opportunity to escape. In the thirteenth century B.C., an extraordinary leader, called Moses, rose among them, was accepted by his people as a messenger of God, and led them in their exodus from Egypt. During their wanderings in the wilderness of Sinai, Moses transformed them into a nation, united and uplifted by a belief in Yahweh, the one God. During this time, Hebrew Scriptures say God also renewed his covenant with the Hebrew people.

Abraham and Isaac

Fresco, from the Ipogeo di Via Latina, Rome. God tested Abraham's faithfulness by commanding him to offer his son "as a burnt offering upon one of the mountains of which I shall tell you" (Genesis 22:2). In the upper part of the fresco, Abraham raises his hand as Isaac cowers beneath him, but at the last moment, God intervenes and prevents Abraham from sacrificing his son.

(Ipogeo de Via Latina, Rome/ Scala/Art Resource, NY)

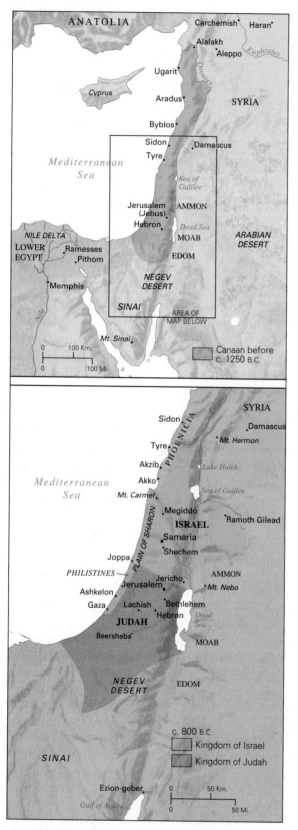

Map 2.1 Ancient Israel The Israelites settled in the Canaanite hill country west of the Jordan River and the Dead Sea after 1200 B.C. *(top map)*. Control of Israelite territory after 922 B.C. was shared between two monarchies *(bottom map)*: the kingdoms of Israel (conquered by the Assyrians in 722 B.C.) and Judah (conquered by the Chaldeans in 586 B.C.).

The wandering Hebrews returned to Canaan to rejoin other Hebrew tribes that had not migrated to Egypt. The conquest and colonization of Canaan was a gradual process, which took many generations. In Canaan, the Israelites did not form a state with a central government but were loosely organized into a tribal confederation bound by a commitment to Yahweh. Threatened by the Philistines (originally from the islands of the Aegean Sea and the coast of Asia Minor), the twelve Hebrew tribes united under the leadership of Saul, a charismatic hero, whom they acclaimed as their first king. Under Saul's successor, David, a gifted warrior and poet, the Hebrews (or Israelites) broke the back of Philistine power and subdued their neighboring peoples.

David's son, Solomon, built a royal palace in Jerusalem and beside it a magnificent temple honoring God (Figure 2.1). Under Solomon, ancient Israel was at the height of its political power and prosperity (Figure 2.2, p. 35), but opposition to Solomon's tax policies and his favored treatment of the region of Judah in the south led to the division of the kingdom after his death in 922 B.C. The tribes loyal to Solomon's son belonged to the Kingdom of Judah, whereas the other tribes organized the northern Kingdom of Israel.

In 722 B.C., Israel fell to the Assyrians, who deported many Hebrews to other parts of the Assyrian empire. These transplanted Hebrews merged with neighboring peoples and lost their identity as the people of the one God. In 586 B.C., the Chaldeans conquered Judah, destroyed Solomon's temple, devastated the land, and deported several thousand Hebrews to Babylon. The prophets Isaiah, Ezekiel, and Jeremiah declared that the destruction of Judah was a punishment that the Hebrews had brought on themselves by violating God's laws. This time was the darkest moment in the history of the Hebrews. Their state was gone, and neighboring peoples had overrun their land; their holy temple built during the reign of King Solomon, was in ruins; thousands had died in battle, been executed, or fled to Egypt and other lands; and thousands more were in exile in Babylon. This exile is known as the *Babylonian Captivity.*

Still, the Hebrews, now commonly called Jews, survived as a people—a fact that is a marvel of history. Although many of the exiles in Babylon assimilated Babylonian ways, some remained faithful to their God, Yahweh, and to the Law of Moses. Priests struggled to understand the misfortunes that had befallen their people and to prevent the erosion of faith in a foreign environment. They stressed the importance of the Sabbath and of circumcision as a means of

Figure 2.1   Solomon's Temple   In the Temple, people sang Psalms, passages from the Scriptures, and folk tunes. In 586 B.C., the Chaldeans conquered Judah, destroyed the Temple, devastated the land, and deported several thousand Hebrews to Babylon.

preserving the covenant that God made with Abraham and renewed with Moses (see following discussion). And they codified ancient traditions, records, and practices, particularly laws, and, in the process, created the Torah (see below). Thus, faith enabled the Jews to endure conquest and exile; it also fostered a longing to return to their homeland. When the Persians conquered Babylon, King Cyrus, in 538 B.C., permitted the exiles to return to Judah, now a Persian province, and to rebuild the temple. The majority of Judeans preferred to remain in prosperous and cosmopolitan Babylon. But some of them did return to Judah, and in 515 B.C., the Hebrews dedicated the second temple at Jerusalem.

The Jews regained their national independence in the second century B.C.; however, in the next century, their land fell within the Roman orbit, and after failed revolutions against Rome in succeeding centuries, the Jews became a dispersed people. Nonetheless, they never relinquished their commitment to God and his Law as recorded in the Hebrew Scriptures. Called *Tanak* (Holy Scriptures) by Jews (and the Old Testament by Christians), these Scriptures consist of thirty-nine books (see p. 34) written by several authors who lived in different centuries. Jews call the first five books—Genesis, Exodus, Leviticus, Numbers, and Deuteronomy—the *Torah* (which originally meant "teaching" or "instruction"). Often the Torah is referred to as the *Pentateuch,* a Greek word meaning "five books." The Hebrew Scriptures represent

Jewish written and oral tradition dating from about 1250 to 150 B.C. This record of more than a thousand years of ancient Jewish life includes Jewish laws, wisdom, hopes, legends, and literary expressions. In describing an ancient people's efforts to comprehend the ways of God, the Scriptures emphasize and value the human experience; their heroes are not demigods but human beings. The Scriptures depict human strength as well as weakness. Some passages exhibit cruelty and unseemly revenge against the enemies of Israel, but others express the highest ethical values. The central message of the Torah is adherence to the Law that was given to Moses and the renewal of the sacred covenant, which the entire nation entered into with God at Mount Sinai, an event that included the giving of *The Ten Commandments* (see p. 37).

Compiled by religious devotees, not research historians, the Hebrew Scriptures understandably contain factual errors, imprecisions, and discrepancies. However, they also offer passages of reliable history, and historians find these Scriptures an indispensable source for studying the ancient Near East. Students of literature explore the Scriptures for its poetry, legends, and themes, all of which are an integral part of the Western literary tradition. But it is as a work of religious inspiration that the Hebrew Bible attains its profoundest importance. As set forth there, the Hebrew idea of God and his relationship to human beings is one of the foundations of the Western tradition.

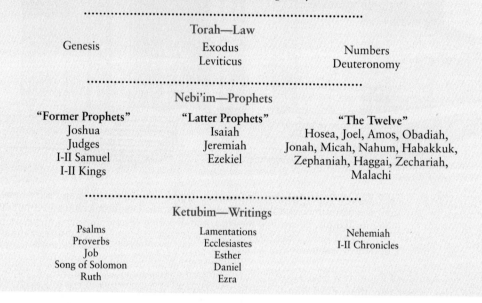

The word TaNaK (tah-náhk) is an acronym for the books that form the Hebrew canon—Torah, Nebi'im, and Ketubim ("Law, Prophets, Writings"). In ancient times, the number of books was usually given as twenty-four. Certain books are now divided into two parts, and the twelve works by the minor prophets are now counted as individual books, totaling thirty-nine.

Torah—Law

Genesis   Exodus   Numbers
Leviticus   Deuteronomy

Nebi'im—Prophets

"Former Prophets"	**"Latter Prophets"**	**"The Twelve"**
Joshua	Isaiah	Hosea, Joel, Amos, Obadiah,
Judges	Jeremiah	Jonah, Micah, Nahum, Habakkuk,
I-II Samuel	Ezekiel	Zephaniah, Haggai, Zechariah,
I-II Kings		Malachi

Ketubim—Writings

Psalms	Lamentations	Nehemiah
Proverbs	Ecclesiastes	I-II Chronicles
Job	Esther	
Song of Solomon	Daniel	
Ruth	Ezra	

GOD: ONE, SOVEREIGN, TRANSCENDENT, GOOD

The Hebrew view of God evolved through the history and experiences of the Hebrew people. In the days of the patriarchs, before the sojourn in Egypt, the Hebrews most likely were not monotheists—believers in one God. They probably devoted themselves to the god of their particular clan and expressed no hatred for the idolatrous beliefs of neighboring peoples. The chief of each clan established a special attachment to the god of his fathers, hoping that the deity would protect and assist the clan. Quite likely, the patriarchs' religion contained spiritual elements that later would aid in the transition to monotheism. But this probability cannot be documented with certainly, for much of patriarchal religion still remains a mystery.

Some historians say that Moses' religion was not pure monotheism because it did not rule out the existence of other gods. According to this view, not until the prophets, centuries later, did the Hebrews explicitly deny that other gods existed and proclaim that Yahweh stood alone. Other scholars believe that Moses proclaimed a monotheistic idea, that this idea became the central force in the life of the Hebrews at the time of the Exodus from Egypt, and that it continues to be

central today. John Bright, an American biblical scholar, suggests a judicious balance. The religion of Moses "did not deny the existence of other gods," says Bright, but it "effectively denied them status as *gods*."[2] The Hebrews could serve only Yahweh and "accorded all power and authority to Him." Consequently, Israel was

> forbidden to approach [other deities] as gods. . . . The gods were thus rendered irrelevant, driven from the field. . . . To Israel only the one God was God. . . . The other gods, allowed neither part in creation, nor function in the cosmos, nor power over events . . . were robbed of all that made them gods and rendered non-entities, in short, were "undeified." Though the full implications of monotheism were centuries in being drawn, in the functional sense Israel believed in but one God from the beginning.[3]

Monotheism became the central force in the life of the Hebrews and marked a profound break with Near Eastern religious thought. Near Eastern gods were not truly free; their power was not without limits. Unlike Yahweh, Near Eastern gods were not eternal, but were born or created; they issued from some prior realm. They were also subject to biological conditions, requiring food, drink, sleep, and sexual gratification. Sometimes, they

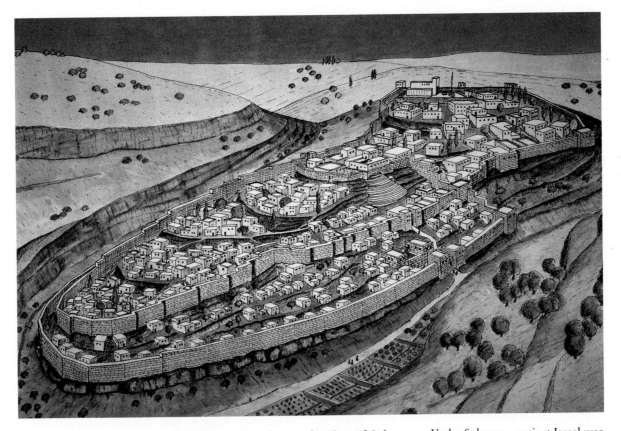

Figure 2.2   Jerusalem at the Time of Solomon   Under Solomon, ancient Israel was at the height of its political power and prosperity. As shown in this modern architectural drawing, Jerusalem was the center of Hebrew political and religious life. *(Ritmeyer Archaeological Design)*

became ill or grew old or died. When they behaved wickedly, they had to answer to fate, which demanded punishment as retribution; even the gods were subject to fate's power.

The Hebrews regarded God as *fully sovereign.* He ruled all and was subject to nothing. Yahweh's existence and power did not derive from a preexisting realm, as was the case with the gods of other peoples. The Hebrews believed that no realm of being preceded God in time or surpassed him in power. They saw God as eternal, the source of all in the universe, and having a supreme will. He created and governed the natural world and shaped the moral laws that govern human beings. He was not subservient to fate but determined what happened.

Whereas Near Eastern divinities dwelt within nature, the Hebrew God was *transcendent,* above nature and not a part of it. Yahweh was not identified with any natural force and did not dwell in a particular place in heaven or on earth. Because God was the creator and ruler of nature, there was no place for a sun god, a moon god, a god in the river, or a demon in the storm. Nature was God's creation but was not itself divine. Therefore, when the Hebrews confronted natural phenomena, they experienced God's magnificent handiwork, not

objects with wills of their own. All natural phenomena—rivers, mountains, storms, stars—were divested of any supernatural quality. The stars and planets were creations of Yahweh, not divinities or the abodes of divinities. The Hebrews neither regarded them with awe nor worshiped them.

The removal of the gods from nature—the demythicizing of nature—is a necessary prerequisite for scientific thought. But concerned with religion and morality, the Hebrews did not create theoretical science. As testimony to God's greatness, nature inspired them to sing the praises of the Lord; it invoked worship of God, not scientific curiosity. When they gazed at the heavens, they did not seek to discover mathematical relationships but admired God's handiwork. They did not view nature as a system governed by self-operating physical principles or natural law. Rather, they saw the rising sun, spring rain, summer heat, and winter cold as God intervening in an orderly manner in his creation. The Hebrews, unlike the Greeks, were not philosophical or scientific thinkers. They were concerned with God's will, not the human intellect; with the feelings of the heart, not the power of the mind; with righteous behavior, not abstract thought.

Unlike the Greeks, the Hebrews did not speculate about the origins of all things and the operations of nature; they knew that God had created everything. For the Hebrews, God's existence was based on religious conviction, not on rational inquiry; on revelation, not on reason. It was the Greeks, not the Hebrews, who originated *systematic* rational thought. But Christianity, born of Judaism, retained the Hebrew view of a transcendent God and the orderliness of his creation—concepts that could accommodate Greek science.

The Hebrews also did not speculate about God's nature. They knew only that he was good and that he made ethical demands on his people. Unlike Near Eastern gods, Yahweh was not driven by lust or motivated by evil but was "merciful and gracious, long-suffering, and abundant in goodness and truth . . . forgiving inequity and transgression and sin" (Psalm 145:8). In contrast to pagan gods, who were indifferent to human beings, Yahweh was attentive to human needs. By asserting that God was one, sovereign, transcendent, and good, the Hebrews effected a religious revolution that separated them entirely from the worldview held by the other peoples of the ancient Near East.

THE INDIVIDUAL AND MORAL AUTONOMY

This new conception of God made possible a new awareness of the individual. In confronting God, the Hebrews developed an awareness of *self*, or *I*: the individual became conscious of his or her own person, moral autonomy, and personal worth. The Hebrews believed that God, who possessed total freedom, had bestowed on people moral freedom—the capacity to choose between good and evil.

Fundamental to Hebrew belief was the insistence that God did not create people to be his slaves. The Hebrews regarded God with awe and humility, with respect and fear, but they did not believe that God wanted people to grovel before him; rather, he wanted them to fulfill their moral potential by freely making the choice to follow or not to follow God's law. Thus, in creating men and women in his own image, God made them autonomous and sovereign. In God's plan for the universe, human beings were the highest creation, subordinate only to God. Of all his creations, only they had been given the freedom to choose between righteousness and wickedness, between "life and good, and death and evil" (Deuteronomy 30:15). But having the power to choose freely, men and women must bear the responsibility for their choice.

God demanded that the Hebrews have no other gods and that they make no images "nor any manner of likeness, of any thing that is in heaven above, or that is in the earth beneath, . . . thou shalt not bow down unto them nor serve them" (Exodus 20:4–5). The Hebrews believed that the worship of idols deprived men and women of their freedom and dignity; people cannot be fully human if they surrender themselves to a lifeless idol. Hence, the Hebrews rejected images and all other forms of idolatry. A crucial element of Near Eastern religion was the use of images—art forms that depicted divinities—but the Hebrews believed that God, the Supreme Being, could not be represented by pictures or sculpture fashioned by human hands. The Hebrews rejected entirely the belief that an image possessed divine powers that could be manipulated for human advantage. Ethical considerations, not myth or magic, were central to Hebrew religious life.

By making God the center of life, Hebrews could become free moral agents; no person, no human institution, and no human tradition could claim their souls. Because God alone was the supreme value in the universe, only he was worthy of worship. Thus, to give ultimate loyalty to a king or a general violated God's stern warning against the worship of false gods. The first concern of the Hebrews was righteousness, not power, fame, or riches, which were only idols and would impoverish a person spiritually and morally.

There was, however, a condition to freedom. For the Hebrews, people were not free to create their own moral precepts or their own standards of right and wrong. Freedom meant voluntary obedience to commands that originated with God. Blind fate, malevolent demons, or arbitrary gods did not cause evil and suffering; they resulted from people's disregard of God's commandments. The dilemma is that in possessing freedom of choice, human beings are also free to disobey God, to commit a sin, which leads to suffering and death. Thus, in the Genesis story, Adam and Eve were punished for disobeying God in the Garden of Eden.

For the Hebrews, to know God was not to comprehend him intellectually, to define him, or to prove his existence; to know God was to be righteous and loving, merciful and just. When men and women loved God, the Hebrews believed, they were uplifted and improved. Gradually, they learned to overcome the worst elements of human nature and to treat people with respect and compassion. The Jews came to interpret the belief that humans were created in God's image to mean that each human being has a divine spark in him or her, giving every person a unique dignity that cannot be taken away.

Through their devotion to God, the Hebrews asserted the value and autonomy of human beings. Thus, the Hebrews conceived the idea of moral freedom—that each individual is responsible for his or her own actions. These concepts of human dignity and moral autonomy, which Christianity inherited, are at the core of the Western tradition.

THE COVENANT AND THE LAW

Central to Hebrew religious thought and decisive in Hebrew history was the *covenant,* God's special agreement with the Hebrew people: If they obeyed his commands, they would "be unto Me a kingdom of priests, and a holy nation" (Exodus 19:6). By this act, the Israelites as a nation accepted God's lordship.

The Hebrews came to see themselves as a unique nation, a "chosen people," for God had given them a special honor, a profound opportunity, and (as they could never forget) an awesome responsibility. The Hebrews did not claim that God had selected them because they were better than other peoples or because they had done anything special to deserve God's election. They believed that God had selected them to receive the Law so that their nation would set an example of righteous behavior and ultimately make God and the Law known to the other nations.

This responsibility to be the moral teachers of humanity weighed heavily on the Hebrews. They believed that God had revealed his Law—including the moral code known as the Ten Commandments (see below)—to the Hebrew people as a whole, and obedience to the Law became the overriding obligation of each Hebrew.

Israelite law incorporated many elements from Near Eastern legal codes and oral traditions. But by making people more important than property, by expressing mercy toward the oppressed, and by rejecting the idea that law should treat the poor and the rich differently, Israelite law demonstrated a greater ethical awareness and a more humane spirit than other legal codes of the Near East.

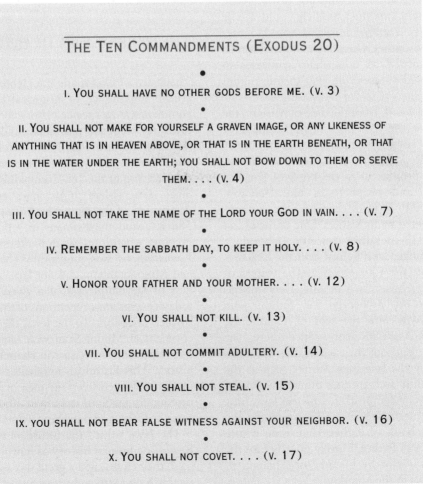

THE TEN COMMANDMENTS (EXODUS 20)

•

I. YOU SHALL HAVE NO OTHER GODS BEFORE ME. (V. 3)

•

II. YOU SHALL NOT MAKE FOR YOURSELF A GRAVEN IMAGE, OR ANY LIKENESS OF ANYTHING THAT IS IN HEAVEN ABOVE, OR THAT IS IN THE EARTH BENEATH, OR THAT IS IN THE WATER UNDER THE EARTH; YOU SHALL NOT BOW DOWN TO THEM OR SERVE THEM. . . . (V. 4)

•

III. YOU SHALL NOT TAKE THE NAME OF THE LORD YOUR GOD IN VAIN. . . . (V. 7)

•

IV. REMEMBER THE SABBATH DAY, TO KEEP IT HOLY. . . . (V. 8)

•

V. HONOR YOUR FATHER AND YOUR MOTHER. . . . (V. 12)

•

VI. YOU SHALL NOT KILL. (V. 13)

•

VII. YOU SHALL NOT COMMIT ADULTERY. (V. 14)

•

VIII. YOU SHALL NOT STEAL. (V. 15)

•

IX. YOU SHALL NOT BEAR FALSE WITNESS AGAINST YOUR NEIGHBOR. (V. 16)

•

X. YOU SHALL NOT COVET. . . . (V. 17)

Thus, there were laws to protect the poor, widows, orphans, resident aliens, hired laborers, and slaves:

> Ye shall not steal; neither shall ye deal falsely, nor lie to one another. . . Thou shalt not oppress thy neighbor nor rob him. . . . Ye shall do no unrighteousness in judgment; thou shalt not respect the person of the poor, nor favor the person of the mighty; but in righteousness shalt thou judge thy neighbor. . . . And if a stranger sojourn with thee in your land, ye shall not do him wrong. The stranger that sojourneth with you shall be unto you as the home born among you, and thou shalt love him as thyself.

(Leviticus 19:11, 13, 15, 33, 34)

Justice was the central theme of the ethics of the Hebrew Scriptures. The Israelites, liberated from slavery by a righteous and compassionate God, had a moral responsibility to overcome injustice and to care for the poor, the weak, and the oppressed.

Similar to other Near Eastern societies, the Jews placed women in a subordinate position. The husband was considered his wife's master, and she often addressed him as a servant or subject would speak to a superior. A husband could divorce his wife, but she could not divorce him. Only when there was no male heir could a wife inherit property from her husband or a daughter inherit from her father. Outside the home, women were not regarded as competent witnesses in court and played a lesser role than men in organized worship.

On the other hand, from the time of Miriam, the sister of Moses, the Jews also showed respect for women. The song of triumph after the Jews crossed the Red Sea is attributed to Miriam, depicted as a prophetess in the book of Exodus. Wise women and prophetesses like Deborah, Esther, and Judith were esteemed by the community and consulted by its leaders. One of the oldest stories in Jewish literature concerns Deborah, a prophet and judge, who helped lead the Israelites to victory over the Canaanites at the waters of Megiddo in northwestern Palestine. Deborah has been seen as the archetype for Judith, who charmed her way into the tent of Holofernes, leader of the Assyrian army. Once there, she beheaded him. Without their leader, the Assyrians were routed by the Israelites. Stories such as the one about Judith and another about the Jewish orphan Hadassah demonstrated to the Jews how God used the seemingly weak to overcome the mighty. In the book of Esther, Hadassah, whose Persian name was Esther, bravely goes before the king and foils a plot by his advisor, Haman, to destroy the Jews in the kingdom.

One of the historical books, Ruth, relates the touching story of Ruth, a Moabite, and Naomi, her Jewish mother-in-law. Naomi lived in Moab with her husband, two sons, and daughters-in-law. When Naomi's husband and sons died, she decided to return to Judah and implored Ruth to remain in Moab. Ruth, however, pled with Naomi to permit her to remain with her, "Entreat me not to leave you or to return from following you; for where you go I will go, and where you lodge I will lodge; your people shall be my people, and your God my God" (Ruth 1:16). In Judah, Naomi urged Ruth to marry Boaz. Their son Obed was the ancestor of King David, from whose line the prophets declared the Messiah would be born. Thus, the story illustrates how the lowly, even a foreign woman, could be exalted by God.

In addition, prophets compared God's love for the Hebrews with a husband's love for his wife. Jewish law regarded the woman as a person, not as property. Jewish concern for women even extended to female captives taken in war, who were not to be abused or humiliated. Finally, the law required a husband to respect and support his wife and never to strike her, and one of the Ten Commandments called for honoring both father and mother.

THE HEBREW IDEA OF HISTORY

Their idea of God made the Hebrews aware of the crucial importance of historical time. Holy days commemorating specific historical events were instituted to keep the past alive and vital. *Passover* (*Pesach*) commemorated their Exodus from Egypt, and the *Feast of Weeks* (*Chag Shavuot*) venerated the receiving of the Ten Commandments on Mount Sinai. On Tishah b'Av, Jews remembered the destruction of the temple by both the Chaldeans in 586 B.C. and the Romans in A.D. 70; during the evening, worshipers sat in darkness as the book of *Lamentations* was mournfully chanted. Egyptians and Mesopotamians did not have a similar awareness of the uniqueness of a given event; to them, today's events were repetitions of events experienced by their ancestors. To the Jews, the Exodus and the covenant at Mount Sinai were singular, nonrepetitive occurrences, decisive in shaping their national history. This historical uniqueness and importance of events derived from the idea of a universal God profoundly involved in human affairs—a God who cares, teaches, and punishes.

The Jews valued the future as well as the past. Regarding human history as a process leading to a goal, they envisioned a great day when God would establish on earth a glorious age of peace, prosperity, happiness, and human brotherhood. This utopian notion has become deeply embedded in Western thought.

The Hebrews saw history as the work of God; it was a divine drama filled with sacred meaning and moral significance. Historical events revealed the clash of human will with God's commands. Through history's specific events, God's presence was disclosed and his purpose made known. When the Hebrews suffered conquest and exile, they interpreted these events as retribution for violating God's Law and as punishments for their stubbornness, sinfulness, and rebelliousness. For the Hebrews, history also revealed God's compassion and concern. Thus, the Lord liberated Moses and the Israelites at the Red Sea and appointed prophets to plead for the poor and the oppressed. Because historical events revealed God's attitude toward human beings, these events possessed spiritual meaning and therefore were worth recording, evaluating, and remembering.

THE PROPHETS

Jewish history was marked by the emergence of spiritually inspired persons called *prophets,* who felt compelled to act as God's messengers. For the Hebrews, Moses was not only God's chosen lawgiver and the instrument by which God delivered the Israelites from Egypt; he also was the first and the greatest of the prophets. The teachings and deeds of others who followed him—Samuel, Elijah, and Elisha—were recorded in the historical books of Samuel and Kings. Samuel (eleventh century B.C.), the last of the Judges and a prototype of the later prophets, anointed Saul the first king of Israel. The dynamic prophet Elijah (c. 850 B.C.) denounced Ahab, King of Israel, for worshiping the pagan god of fertility, Baal.

The flowering of the prophetic movement—the age of classical, or literary, prophecy—began in the eighth century B.C. Among the literary prophets were Amos, a shepherd from Judea in the south; his younger contemporary, Hosea, from Israel in the north; Isaiah of Jerusalem; and Jeremiah, who witnessed the siege of Jerusalem by the Babylonians in the early sixth century B.C.

The prophets cared nothing for money or possessions, feared no one, and preached without invitation. Often emerging in times of social distress, they pleaded for a return to the covenant and the Law. They exhorted the entire nation and taught that when people forgot God and made themselves the center of all things, they would bring disaster on themselves and their community.

The prophets saw national misfortune as an opportunity for penitence and reform. They were remarkably courageous individuals, who did not quake before the powerful. In the late eighth century, an angry Isaiah warned:

> The Lord enters into judgment
>   with the elders and princes of his people:
>
> "It is you who have devoured the vineyard,
>   the spoil of the poor is in your houses.
>
> What do you mean by crushing my people,
>   by grinding the face of the poor?"
>
> (Isaiah 3:14–15)

Social Justice

In attacking oppression, cruelty, greed, and exploitation, the classical prophets added a new dimension to Israel's religious development. These prophets were responding to problems emanating from Israel's changed social structure. A tribal society generally lacks class distinctions, but this situation had been altered by the rise of Hebrew kings, the expansion of commerce, and the growth of cities. By the eighth century, there was a significant disparity between the wealthy and the poor. Small farmers in debt to moneylenders faced the loss of their land or even bondage; the poor were often dispossessed by the greedy wealthy. To the prophets, these social evils were religious sins that would bring ruin to Israel. In the name of God, they denounced the hypocrisy and pomp of the heartless rich and demanded justice.

Thus, Amos castigated the Jews for depending on ritual and sacrifices—superficial religiosity—and commanded them to return to the true worship of God, which included care of the poor and the needy. Amos accused pious Jews who kept the word of the Law and worshiped God in the prescribed manner but neglected their social obligations to their neighbor. For Amos, there was no separation between religion and social conduct.

> For I know how many are your transgressions
> and how great are your sins—
> you who afflict the righteous, who take a bribe,
> and turn aside the needy at the gate. . . .
>
> Seek good and not evil, that you may live;
> and so the Lord, the God of hosts,
> will be with you, as you have said. . . .
>
> I hate, I despise your feasts,
> And I will take no delight in your solemn
>   assemblies.
> Yea, though ye offer me burnt-offerings and your
>   meal-offerings,

I will not accept them;
Neither will I regard the peace offerings of your
    fat beasts.
Take thou away from Me the noise of thy songs;
And let Me not hear the melody of the psalteries.
But let justice well up as waters,
And righteousness as a mighty stream.

(Amos 5:12, 14, 21–24)

God is compassionate, insisted the prophets. He cares for all, especially the poor, the unfortunate, the suffering, and the defenseless. God's injunctions, declared Isaiah, were to

Put away the evil of your doings
From before mine eyes,
Cease to do evil;
Learn to do well;
Seek justice, relieve the oppressed,
Judge the fatherless, plead for the widow.

(Isaiah 1:16–17)

Prophets stressed the direct spiritual-ethical encounter between the individual and God. The inner person concerned them more than the outer forms of religious activity. Holding that the essence of the covenant was universal righteousness, the prophets criticized priests whose commitment to rites and rituals was not supported by a deeper spiritual insight or a zeal for morality in daily life. To the prophets, an ethical sin was far worse than a ritual omission. Above all, said the prophets, God demands righteousness, living justly before God. To live unjustly, to mistreat one's neighbors, to act without compassion—these actions violated God's Law and endangered the entire social order.

The prophets held out the hope that life on earth could be improved, that poverty and injustice need not be accepted as part of an unalterable natural order, and that the individual was capable of elevating himself or herself morally and could respect the dignity of others. Thus, they helped to shape a social conscience that has become a vital part of the Western tradition. For example, many observers noted that the language and vision of Martin Luther King, Jr. (see Chapter 26) echoed that of the ancient Hebrew prophets, whose teachings he knew intimately.

Messiah and Apocalypse

A recurring theme of Judaism in the postexilic era was the hope of the *Messiah* ("the anointed one"). An early rendering of this messianic hope came from an unknown writer during the exile of the sixth century B.C., who preached an unswerving trust in God, who would surely return the Jews to their homeland. Scholars attribute chapters 40–55 of the *Book of Isaiah* to this writer, called Deutero-Isaiah, or "Second Isaiah." The following passage tells of a time to come when the exiles would return to Judea. This passage and passages like it (cf. Isaiah 53) are also important to Christians, who interpret them to be prophecies concerning the coming of Jesus as Messiah.

Comfort, comfort my people,
    says your God.

Speak tenderly to Jerusalem,
    and cry to her that her
    warfare is ended,
    that her iniquity is pardoned,
    that she has received from the Lord's hand
    double for all her sins.

A voice cries:
    "In the wilderness
    prepare the way of the Lord, make
    straight in the desert a highway for our God.
    Every valley shall be lifted up,
    and every mountain and hill made low;
    the uneven ground shall become level,
    and the rough places a plain.
    And the glory of the Lord shall be revealed,
    and all flesh shall see it together,
    for the mouth of the Lord has spoken."

(Isaiah 40:1–5)

The prophetic literature after the Exile, specifically the prophecies of Obadiah, Zechariah, Malachi, and Daniel, was passionately *apocalyptic*; that is, it dealt with catastrophic upheavals and the emergence of a radically different world. Such literature included metaphors of the Messiah, denunciations of evil, and expectations of the "last day," by which was meant the cataclysmic end of the world as people knew it and the emergence of a new kingdom of peace. Daniel, the most apocalyptic book, recounts Daniel's visions of the future messianic kingdom, visions of hope for an oppressed people. The last chapter offers the assurance that the kingdom of God will be inaugurated at the end of time with great power and glory. History's goal becomes the fulfillment of God's sovereign plan for his creation. Such a utopian vision had tremendous appeal for those who were suffering and looking forward to their deliverance and restoration as God's people.

Universalism and Individualism

In Hebrew thought, universalism was closely connected to parochialism. Parochial-mindedness stressed the special nature, destiny, and needs of the chosen people, a nation set apart from others. This narrow tribal outlook was offset by *universalism*—a concern for all humanity, which found expression in those prophets who envisioned the unity of all people under God. All people were equally precious to God.

The prophets were not pacifists, particularly if a war was being waged against the enemies of Yahweh. But some prophets denounced war as obscene and looked forward to its elimination. They maintained that when people glorify force they dehumanize their opponents, brutalize themselves, and dishonor God. When violence rules, there can be no love.

The prophets' universalism was accompanied by an equally profound awareness of the individual and his or her intrinsic worth. Before the prophets, virtually all religious tradition had been produced communally and anonymously. The prophets, however, spoke as fearless individuals, who, by affixing their signatures to their thoughts, fully bore the responsibility for their religious inspiration and conviction.

The notion of individualism is particularly evident in the prophecies of Jeremiah, who, in the early sixth century B.C., predicted doom for Judah because of its collective sins in violating God's covenant. In doing so, Jeremiah explicitly placed emphasis on individual responsibility, when he envisioned the day when "everyone shall die for his own sin." At that time, God would make a new covenant with the Jews to replace the covenant that they had broken. This new covenant would not be written on stone as the Mosaic covenant had been; rather, it would be a covenant between God and each individual—God "will write it upon their hearts" (Jeremiah 31:30–34). The prophets' emphasis on the individual's responsibility for his or her own actions is a key component of Western thought.

In coming to regard God's Law as a *command to conscience, an appeal to the inner person,* the prophets heightened the awareness of the human personality. They indicated that the individual could not know God only by following edicts and by performing rituals; the individual must experience God. Precisely this *I–Thou* relationship could make the individual fully conscious of self and could deepen and enrich his or her own personality. During the Exodus, the Hebrews were a tribal people who obeyed the Law largely out of awe and group compulsion. By the prophets' time, the Jews appeared to be autonomous individuals who heeded the Law because of a deliberate, conscious inner commitment.

The ideals proclaimed by the prophets helped sustain the Jews throughout their long and often painful historical odyssey, and they remain a vital force for Jews today. Incorporated into the teachings of Jesus, these ideals, as part of Christianity, are embedded in the Western tradition.

THE BIBLE AS LITERATURE

In seeking to comprehend their relationship to God, the writers of the Hebrew Scriptures produced a treasury of themes, stories, and models of literary style and craftsmanship that have profoundly influenced Western writers over the centuries. Biblical literature falls into three chief categories: epic literature, lyric poetry, and wisdom writings. In all three categories the overarching theme is God's will and righteousness. Within the context of God's justice, tempered by his mercy, specific themes relating to the human condition are accentuated, including human wickedness, family quarrels, faithfulness (or lack thereof) to the covenant, the beguilement of man by woman, and reconciliation with family, friends, and/or God.

The Epics: Stories and Historical Cycles

The most readily recognized epic style in the West is that of the ancient Greeks, especially Homer's *Iliad* and *Odyssey*—long, serious poems that deal with great deeds of dauntless heroes. Written in a verse narrative style, the Homeric epic attempts to re-create the excitement and grandeur of the action. In contrast, the epic literature of the Hebrew Scriptures is written in prose narrative, and the narrator of the occurrences is more concerned with the unfolding of God's will than with relating heroic deeds. Emotion-filled scenes in which entire nations are destroyed, husbands are separated from their wives, people are compelled to leave their homeland to become wanderers, or loved ones die are interpreted in the light of God's intent. The epic literature of the Hebrews can be divided into two types—stories and historical cycles.

Anthropologists, historians, and theologians have discovered that people in ancient civilizations, like many people today, wondered about the creation of the universe and the origin of human life. Thus, the *Epic of Gilgamesh* and the *Enuma Elish* contained creation myths to provide meaning for the Mesopotamians, and the Greeks alternated between a creation myth associated with the Olympian deities and a creation through a natural process (see Chapter 3). Similarly, the most renowned epic story in the Hebrew Scriptures— God's creation of the physical universe—provided the Hebrews with an awesome vision of the majesty of God.

The *epic stories* of the Hebrews were often intoned in a rhythmic cadence, and they show continuity from story to story. The "Genesis Story" of creation (Genesis 1:1–31) describes a physical creation in six days. On the first day, God separated light (day) and darkness (night); on the second day, he divided the firmament (heaven) from the waters; beginning the third day, God brought forth the vegetation of the earth; on the fourth day, he provided the sun to shine during the day and the moon for the light of night; on the fifth day, God bestowed birds in the air and fish in the seas; and on the sixth day, God created animal life. Finally, "on the seventh God finished his work which he had done, and he rested on the seventh day" (Genesis 2:2).

After God's creation of the universe was complete, he resolved to create man, and subsequently woman, because "it is not good that the man should be alone" (Genesis 2:15). The first man, Adam, was created in the image of God from the dust of the earth, and God fashioned Eve from Adam's rib. "Then the man said, 'This at last is bone of my bones and flesh of my flesh; she shall be called Woman, because she was taken out of Man'" (Genesis 2:23). Because woman was derived from man, over the centuries this account has been taken to acknowledge the superiority of man over woman.

Eating of the "Tree of Knowledge" in disobedience of God led to the expulsion of Adam and Eve from the Garden of Eden. Henceforth, God decreed that men and women would suffer hardship and pain "till you return to the ground, for out of it you were taken; you are dust, and to dust you shall return" (Genesis 3:19).* The theme of human sinfulness is continued in the epic story of Cain and Abel, the sons of Adam and Eve. Cain commits the first murder in human history when he slays his brother, Abel (Genesis 4:8).

In the Hebrew Scriptures, God's justice and mercy always temper the theme of human sinfulness. For example, God expels Adam and Eve from the Garden of Eden for their disobedience, but does not kill them. Similarly, God's justice is meted out to Cain, not with death, but with the curse of the ground, which "shall no longer yield to you its strength," and he too is exiled from Eden. How God's justice is coupled with his mercy is further demonstrated when Cain, fearing for his life, complains to God:

> "My punishment is greater than I can bear. Behold, thou hast driven me this day away from the ground and from thy face I shall be hidden and I shall be a fugitive and a wanderer on the earth, and whoever finds me will slay me." Then the Lord said to him, "Not so! If any one slays Cain, vengeance shall be taken on him sevenfold." And the Lord put a mark on Cain, lest any who came upon him should kill him. Then Cain went away from the presence of the Lord, and dwelt in the land of Nod, east of Eden. (Genesis 4:13–16)

The disobedience of Adam and Eve and the first murder are followed by other acts of human wickedness. Regretting ever having made the human race, God, in the epic of "The Great Flood," decides to destroy the world:

> The Lord saw that the wickedness of man was great in the earth, and that every imagination of the thought of his heart was only evil continually. And the Lord was sorry that he had made man on the earth, and it grieved him to his heart. So the Lord said, "I will blot out man whom I have created from the face of the ground, man and beast and creeping things and birds of the air, for I am sorry that I have made them." (Genesis 6:5–7)

Nevertheless, God's justice and mercy are again apparent with Noah, who "found favor in the eyes of the Lord" and to whom God commanded, along with Noah's sons—Shem, Ham, and Japheth—to "make yourself an ark . . . and of every living thing of all flesh, you shall bring two of every sort into the ark" (Genesis 6:19). God then made a covenant with the descendants of Noah who survived the flood—"never again shall all flesh be cut off by the waters of a flood, and never again shall there be a flood to destroy the earth" (Genesis 9:17). The sign of this covenant was the rainbow, which people throughout history have interpreted as a sign of God's love and forgiveness.

The Hebrews, and later the Christians, understood Adam, Eve, Cain, and the people of Noah's time to have exhibited an overbearing pride, which led them to presume that they possessed the ability to judge right from wrong and to dispense justice independently of God's will. This theme of pride is reiterated in other biblical epic stories—the building of the Tower of Babel in a feeble attempt to reach God (Genesis 11); Jacob's rivalry with his twin brother, Esau, in which Jacob deprives Esau of his birthright through deceit and cunning (Genesis 25:19–34); and the Hebrews' apostasy by constructing an idol, "the Golden Calf"† (Exodus 32) while Moses was receiving the

---

* Adam's and Eve's disobedience of God's directive resulted in Saint Paul's doctrine of original sin.

† The Golden Calf was reminiscent of the Egyptian cult of Isis and Osiris with which a number of Jews were familiar during the period of their enslavement under the Egyptian pharaohs.

Ten Commandments on Mount Sinai. The danger of pride is also echoed in the wisdom writings (see below)—"Pride goes before destruction, and a haughty spirit before a fall. It is better to be of a lowly spirit with the poor than to divide the spoil with the proud" (Proverbs 16:18–19).

The epic cycles of the Hebrew Scriptures focus primarily on the patriarchs of the nation of Israel and their families. The best-known epic cycle, "Cycle of the Patriarchs"—including Abraham, Isaac, Jacob, and Joseph—constitutes nearly the entire Book of Genesis. The cycle begins with God's call for Abraham to leave his homeland and concludes with the death of Jacob and his son Joseph. As with the histories, the epic cycles show God's continued activity in his creation. God directs Abram (whose name will soon be changed to Abraham) to "Go from your country [Ur] and your kindred and your father's house to the land that I will show you [Canaan]" (Genesis 12:1). So that he might obey God, Abram, despite being an old man, makes the difficult decision to leave his homeland and become a wanderer. This portion of the cycle demonstrates the freedom of an individual to cooperate with God and establish a mutual relationship with him. It also portends God's divine activity in future events, as he promises to bless Abram and his descendants—"And I will make of you a great nation, and I will bless you and make your name great, so that you will be a blessing. I will bless those who bless you, and him who curses you I will curse" (Genesis 12:2–3). The Hebrews will interpret the rise and fall of all great nations in light of this proclamation.

Because Abram has passed the first of many trials of his faith, God promises to reward Abram with the land of his sojournings: "To your descendants I will give this land" (Genesis 12:7). Then at the age of ninety-nine, Abram's faith is again tested when he is charged to believe that he, along with his wife Sarai who is supposedly barren, will have children of their own. God then makes a covenant with Abram: "And I will establish my covenant between me and you and your descendants after you throughout their generations for an everlasting covenant, to be God to you and to your descendants after you" (Genesis 17:7). As a sign of the covenant, God commands Abraham to circumcise "every male among you" (Genesis 17:10).*

Abraham's fervent belief in the righteousness of God is further illustrated by the story of Sodom and Gomorrah. When God informs Abraham of his intentions to destroy these wicked cities, Abra-

ham dares to question God's justice: "Wilt thou indeed destroy the righteous with the wicked?" (Genesis 18:23). In a bantering dialogue with God, Abraham interrogates God as to whether or not he will destroy the city if fifty righteous people can be found. He then bargains with God to reduce the number by increments of ten each time he converses with God, until he finally asks God to save the cities for the sake of ten righteous people, and receives God's commitment, "For the sake of ten I will not destroy it" (Genesis 18:32). Here Abraham parallels Job—who believes in a righteous God, but demands to know why the innocent must suffer (see below). Because ten righteous could not be found, "The Lord rained on Sodom and Gomorrah brimstone and fire" but "remembered Abraham, and sent Lot [Abraham's nephew] out of the midst of the overthrow" (Genesis 19:28–29).

After Abraham's and Sarah's son Isaac is born, God again tests Abraham's faithfulness by commanding him to offer his son "as a burnt offering upon one of the mountains of which I shall tell you" (Genesis 22:2). At the last moment, God intervenes and prevents Abraham from sacrificing Isaac (see chapter opening). Because Abraham once more remains steadfast in his faith, God blesses him and promises, "by your descendants shall all the nations of this earth bless themselves, because you have obeyed my voice" (Genesis 22:18). When Abraham dies, the theme of faithfulness, forged by the covenantal bond between Abraham and God, is further developed in the portion of the epic cycle dealing with the twin sons of Isaac and Rebekah—Jacob and Esau.

When Esau thinks he is about to die from starvation, his younger brother Jacob seizes the opportunity to deprive Esau of the inheritance due the firstborn son. Preying on Esau's miserable condition, Jacob offers his brother "bread and a pottage of lentils" in exchange for his birthright (Genesis 25:34). The two brothers thus share the guilt and shame of human sinfulness—Esau, by weakly conceding to the demands of the flesh, and Jacob, by greedily procuring their father's blessing for himself.

The climax of this epic cycle centers on the theme of reconciliation between Jacob and Esau. Realizing the destructive consequences of this fraternal hatred, Jacob seeks to reunite with Esau. Once again (in the manner of Abram/Abraham and Sarai/Sarah), God symbolically changes the names of those whom he has purified and renewed. The etymology of the name Israel means "may God rule." Hereafter, Jacob is known as *Israel* and his descendants as "The Twelve Tribes of Israel." The stories of Israel's sons include the selling of his son, Joseph, into bondage; the migration of Israel and his sons to

---

* As a result of this event, Abram's name is changed to *Abraham* and Sarai's to *Sarah*.

Egypt during a period of famine; the reconciliation of Joseph and his brothers in the pharaoh's court; and the death of Joseph, which concludes the story of the patriarchs.

The themes treated within the cycle of the patriarchs—human sinfulness, sibling rivalry, feminine wiles, faithfulness to the covenant, reconciliation, and God's justice and mercy—constantly reappear in other biblical epics. But the will of God, his divine plan for creation, and the human being's obedience or disobedience to God's commands continue to overshadow all other themes.

Lyric Poetry

The best-known examples of lyric poetry come from the Book of Psalms. The Psalms consist of 150 hymns extolling God in exquisite poetic language. Some of them were written by King David, who ruled a united Israel c.1000–962 B.C. In addition to his great success as a warrior and administrator, David was renowned as a harpist and composer.

The **Book of Psalms** is composed primarily of *songs,* the most basic type of lyric poetry. The Hebrew Scriptures used songs to celebrate a special victory over an enemy (Psalm 114), deliverance from Egypt (Exodus 15:1–2, 9–11) and a thunderstorm (Psalm 29), and to render certain themes—God's justice (Isaiah 2:2–4), mercy (Psalm 40:1–5), and omnipotence (Psalm 2:1–6). Psalm 150 (CD 2.1), identified as the "Hallelujah Hymn," evokes the sound of music to celebrate God's mighty acts and to elicit feelings of joy.

Praise the Lord!

Praise God in his sanctuary;
  praise him in his mighty firmament!

Praise him for his mighty deeds;
  praise him according to his exceeding
    greatness!

Praise him with trumpet sound;
  praise him with lute and harp!

Praise him with timbrel and dance;
  praise him with strings and pipe!

Praise him with sounding cymbals;
  praise him with loud clashing cymbals!

Let everything that breathes praise the Lord!

Praise the Lord!

Psalm 46 depicts God's omniscience, omnipresence, and omnipotence and includes a "pendulum figure" in which the ideas seem to sway back and forth between the language of comfort and fear:

God is our refuge and strength,
  a very present help in trouble.

Therefore we will not fear
  though the earth should change,
  though the mountains shake in the heart
    of the sea;
  though its water roar and foam,
  though the mountains tremble with its tumult.

. . . .

The nations rage, the kingdoms totter;
  he utters his voice, the earth melts.
    The Lord of hosts is with us;
      the God of Jacob is our refuge.

Come behold the works of the Lord,
  how he has wrought desolations in the earth.

He makes wars cease to the end of the earth;
  he breaks the bow, and shatters the spear,
  he burns the chariots with fire!

"Be still, and know that I am God.
  I am exalted among the nations,
  I am exalted in the earth!"

The Lord of hosts is with us;
  the God of Jacob is our refuge.

Psalm 8 illustrates the type of poetry known as monody—a poem engendered by a unique personal experience, either addressed to God or to the poet, which is usually narrated. This Psalm rejoices in the greatness of God and marvels at the Lord's love for human beings, expressed in God's having given them dominion over the earth and its creatures.

When I look at thy heavens, the work of thy
    fingers,
  the moon and the stars which thou hast
    established;
  what is man that thou art mindful of him,
    and the son of man
  that thou dost care for him?

Yet thou hast made him little less than God, and
    dost crown him with glory and honor.

Thou hast given him dominion over the works of
    thy hands;
  thou hast put all things under his feet, . . .

O Lord, our Lord, how majestic is thy name in
    all the earth! (Psalm 8:3–6, 9)

Psalm 23, perhaps the most quoted of the Psalms, is an example of the meditation type of lyric poetry. ***Meditation poetry*** reflects on a theme, unlike songs, which celebrate a theme. In this case, the poet ponders God's love and care for Israel. The poet uses the figurative language of an extended metaphor—comparing God to a shepherd—to extol God for his guidance, spiritual nourishment, comfort, and protection from enemies.

> The Lord is my shepherd,
>
> I shall not want;
>
> He makes me lie down in green
> pastures.
>
> He leads me beside still waters;
> He restores my soul.
>
> He leads me in paths of righteousness
> for his name's sake.
>
> Even though I walk through the
> valley of the shadow of death,
> I fear no evil;
>
> for thou art with me;
> thy rod and thy staff
> they comfort me.
>
> Thou preparest a table before me
> in the presence of my enemies;
>
> thou anointest my head with oil,
> my cup overflows.
>
> Surely goodness and mercy
> shall follow me all the days of my life;
>
> and I shall dwell in the house of
> the Lord for ever.

Unlike almost all of the verse and narrative of the Hebrew Scriptures, ***The Song of Solomon*** is provocative and erotic in nature. The figurative language of *simile* (a comparison using *like* or *as*) is the primary vehicle for descriptive phraseology, as the bridegroom praises his bride.

> Behold, you are beautiful, my love,
> behold, you are beautiful!
>
> Your eyes are doves
> behind your veil.
>
> Your hair is like a flock of goats,
> moving down the slopes of Gilead.
>
> Your teeth are like a flock of shorn ewes
> that have come up from the washing.
>
> All of which bear twins,
> and not one among them is bereaved.
>
> Your lips are like a scarlet thread,
> and your mouth is lovely.
>
> Your cheeks are like halves of a pomegranate
> behind your veil.

> Your neck is like the tower of David
> built for an arsenal,
> whereon hang a thousand bucklers,
> all of them shields of warriors.
>
> Your two breasts are like two fawns,
> twins of a gazelle,
> that feed among the lilies.
>
> Until the day breathes
> and the shadows flee,
>
> I will [hasten] to the mountain of myrrh
> and the hill of frankincense.
>
> You are all fair, my love;
> there is no flaw in you.
>
> (The Song of Solomon 4:1–7)

The Wisdom Writings

The books in the Hebrew Scriptures referred to as "wisdom"—Proverbs, Job, Ecclesiastes, and Lamentations*—are intended to instruct people in their dealings with the problems of everyday life; they are concerned with practical rules of conduct and specific examples of personal morality rather than correct worship. By incorporating religion into the ordinary events of life, wisdom literature stressed the interrelationship of secular and religious life. Wisdom thus became a religious concept for the Jews: "For the Lord gives wisdom; from his mouth come knowledge and understanding" (Proverbs 2:6).

The Book of Proverbs (purported to be the sayings of King Solomon) offers practical advice about all sorts of matters, from how to deal with one's neighbors to table manners when eating with a ruler. It gives advice about the right conduct needed to attain happiness, that is, health, wealth, a good family, and a long life.

> A false balance is an abomination to the Lord,
> but a just weight is his delight.
>
> When pride comes, then comes disgrace;
> but with the humble is wisdom.
>
> The integrity of the upright guides them,
> but the crookedness of the treacherous
> destroys them.
>
> Riches do not profit in the day of wrath,
> but righteousness delivers from death.

---

* Technically speaking Psalms and The Song of Solomon also belong in the wisdom literature, but because of their poetic structure, they have been included under lyric poetry (see p. 44).

Figure 2.3 **Job's Tribulation, detail from the sarcophagus of Junius Bassus, c. A.D. 359** In this scene, two of Job's friends try to help him make sense of his suffering. The *Book of Job* recounts how Eliphaz believes that Job must be guilty of some unrighteous behavior, how Bildad asserts that God only punishes people when it is necessary, and how Zophar accuses Job of having offended God. *(Vatican City/Erich Lessing/Art Resource, NY)*

The righteousness of the blameless keeps his
  way straight,
    but the wicked falls by his own wickedness.

(Proverbs 11:1–5)

Its advice concerning the raising of children, carried to an extreme, has no doubt produced much suffering:

He who spares the rod hates his son,
  but he that loves him is diligent to
    discipline him.

. . . .

Do not withhold discipline from a child;
  if you beat him with a rod, he shall not die.

If you beat him with the rod
  you will save his life from Sheol [hell].

(Proverbs 13:24; 23:13–14)

In contrast to the ennobling sagacity of Proverbs, the wisdom offered by the author of the book of Ecclesiastes is fatalistic. The opening verse, "Vanity of vanities; all is vanity," sets the mood for the entire book—resignation to forces beyond an individual's control. The third chapter of the book advises that God's divine plan for the human race will forever remain a mystery. An individual must acknowledge that God has a plan and trust that "For everything there is a season, and a time for every matter under heaven" (Ecclesiastes 3:1).

Dealing in a philosophical manner with the problems of evil and human suffering, the Book of Job has a unique view of the relationship of the individual to God. The Torah, the prophets, and much of the wisdom literature make it clear that God punishes humans for sin, disobedience, and neglect of their responsibility for their neighbors.

The Book of Job, however, raises the question—"If God is all-loving, merciful, and just, how can he allow those who love, fear, and obey him to suffer and those who are wicked to prosper?"

In its profound and daring attempt to deal with the nature of God and human nature, the *Book of Job* is a literary masterpiece (Figure 2.3). Job is introduced as a man who "was perfect and upright, and one that feared God, and eschewed evil" (Job 1:1). Satan (in Hebrew, "adversary")* challenges God to test his loyal and obedient servant, Job. Surely, he says, Job is good because he has been so blessed by God, but he would curse God if he lost everything. God then allows Satan to strip Job of all of his possessions (including his family). Chastised and mocked by his friends, and afflicted with torturous physical pain, Job seeks to understand why he has been plagued. His three friends, Eliphaz, Bildad, and Zophar, attempt to help him comprehend his fate. They are part of a cycle of three dialogues in which Job and his friends address universal questions of human existence.

These dialogues are strikingly similar to Greek tragedy and exhibit the Greek emphasis on human reason. Eliphaz rationalizes that Job must be guilty of some unrighteous behavior and is being punished by God. Bildad depicts the lot of the wicked in history and how God punished people only when it was necessary. Finally, Zophar justifies Job's punishment by accusing Job of only pretending to be innocent; in reality, he must be guilty of wrongdoing that has offended God. The one thing Job's friends refuse to consider is that God might have made a wager with the adversary to test Job's faith.

The most significant dialogue is the one between Job and God. Beginning in Chapter 30, Job bewails his wretched condition, pleads his innocence, and demands a fair hearing before God. He expects God to explain precisely why he must undergo such misfortune, pain, and misery, because he has done no wrong. In this regard, Job mirrors the questioning spirit of every individual who has ever undergone trial, tragedy, or tribulation and wondered aloud, "Why me?"

And now my soul is poured out within me;
  days of affliction have taken hold of me.

The night racks my bones, and the pain that
  gnaws me takes no rest.

With violence it seizes my garment;
  it binds me about like the collar of my tunic.

God has cast me into the mire, and I have
  become like dust and ashes.

I cry to thee and thou dost not answer me;
  I stand, and thou dost not heed me.

Thou hast turned cruel to me; with the might
  of thy hand
    thou dost persecute me.

Thou liftest me up on the wind, thou makest me
  ride on it,
    and thou tossest me about in the roar of the
      storm.

Yea, I know that thou wilt bring me to death,
  and to the house appointed for all living.

(Job 30:16–23)

When God finally answers Job, it is through a whirlwind. First, God reminds Job that he is the creator of the physical world and all creation. He then asks why Job thinks he is capable of understanding God's all-encompassing power or the reasons for God's actions.

Who is this that darkens counsel by words
  without knowledge?

Gird up your loins like a man,
  I will question you, and you shall declare
    to me.

Where were you when I laid the foundation
  of the earth?
    Tell me, if you have understanding. . . .

Have you entered into the springs of the sea,
  or walked in the recesses of the deep?

Have the gates of death been revealed to you,
  or have you seen the gates of deep darkness?

Have you comprehended the expanse of the
  earth?
    Declare, if you know all this. . .

Shall a faultfinder contend with the Almighty?

He who argues with God, let him answer not.

Will you even put me in the wrong?
  Will you condemn me that you may
    be justified?

---

* Various interpretations of the personage of Satan emerged in Judaism. The earliest, the Book of Job, presents him as a heavenly adversary who argues the sinfulness of humans in the court of heaven.

    Later representations of Satan in Judaism include the supernatural being who lures people away from God, the angel of death, and one of the fallen angels. The New Testament, however, presents him as a vile being who is the absolute opposite of God, presiding over a kingdom that Christ would come again to destroy.

Have you an arm like god, and can you
     thunder with
   a voice like this? . . .

Upon earth there is not his like,
   a creature without fear.

He beholds everything that is high;
   he is king over all the sons of pride.

(Job 38:2–4, 16–18; 40:2, 8–9; 41:33–34)

God's response makes it clear to Job that the cause of human suffering is beyond human comprehension. God's nature, and his relationship to the individual and the universe, is too complex to be analyzed and questioned by human beings. Job is finally driven to acknowledge God's sovereignty and confesses his own subservient position.

I know that thou canst do all things,
   and that no purpose of thine can be
     thwarted. . . .

Therefore I have uttered what I did not
     understand,
   things too wonderful for me, which I did
     not know. . . .

I had heard of thee by the hearing of the ear,
   but now my eye sees thee;

therefore I despise myself, and repent in dust and
   ashes.

(Job 42:2–3, 5–6)

According to the Book of Job, the answer to the universal question: "Why do the innocent suffer?" cannot be known by humans. The answer is totally beyond human understanding; or, in the words of the Psalmist, "The fear of the Lord is the beginning of wisdom" (Psalm 111:10). Job learned that he was utterly dependent on a higher being, God. Consequently, because of Job's faith, God again blessed him in the end.

And the Lord blessed the latter days of Job more than his beginning; and he had fourteen thousand sheep, six thousand camels, a thousand yoke of oxen, and a thousand she-asses. He had also seven sons and three daughters. . . . And in all the land were no women so fair as Job's daughters; and their father gave them inheritance among their brothers. And after this Job lived a hundred and forty years, and saw his sons, and his sons' sons, four generations. And Job died, an old man, and full of days.

(Job 42:12–13, 15–17)

The Hebrew Scriptures and Western Authors and Language

The Hebrew Scriptures are an intrinsic part of the Western literary tradition. Numerous fables from the epic cycles have been incorporated in Western literature. Fabled stories within the epics are an intrinsic part of the Western religious and literary tradition—Joshua at the battle of Jericho (Joshua 5–6); Samson's strength (Judges 15:7–14) and his beguilement by Delilah (Judges 16:1–20); David, the lowly shepherd, slaying the giant Philistine, Goliath (I Samuel 17); David's lust for Bathsheba (II Samuel 11–12); David and his tragic relationship with his son, Absalom (II Samuel 15–18); Elijah and the false prophets (I Kings 18); and Jonah swallowed by "a great fish" (Book of Jonah 2), traditionally called a whale. The Hebrew Scriptures have influenced the works of important Western authors. Each division of Dante's *Divine Comedy* reflects a biblical theme—the *Inferno* demonstrates God's justice, the *Purgatorio* illustrates God's forgiveness, and the *Paradiso* considers the eternal blessedness God grants his faithful servants. John Milton's *Paradise Lost* epitomizes human sinfulness and pride after the commission of the original sin. The darker side of human nature is also evident in Nathaniel Hawthorne's *The Scarlet Letter,* whereby people appear to be righteous to those who only judge the outward actions of individuals in this world, but who actually harbor a "secret sin"—for example, the seemingly righteous Reverend Dimmesdale committing adultery with Hester Prynne. And in *Moby Dick,* Hawthorne's contemporary, Herman Melville, writes an extended metaphor for a sinister, yet Job-like character, Captain Ahab, who seeks to "pierce the mask" to discover God's true nature symbolized by "the white whale," but whose identity and will ultimately remain inscrutable. Moses' encounter with God in the burning bush in which God revealed "I Am Who I Am" (Exodus 3:14) is the foundation for William Blake's notion of God as the infinite "I Am." The novel, *East of Eden,* by John Steinbeck is a modern version of the biblical rivalry between Cain and Abel. The conniving Cathy Ames (who parallels Eve) gives birth to twin sons. The compliant son is Aron (the complement to Abel), who is favored by Adam over the insecure, tormented loner Caleb (the complement to Cain). And, a specific incident—Jacob giving a "long coat with sleeves" (the coat of many colors) to his son, Joseph—inspired Tim Rice and Andrew Lloyd Webber to compose the Broadway musical, *Joseph and the Amazing Technicolor Dreamcoat.*

Aside from the great literature inspired by biblical themes and allusions, biblical expressions have been incorporated into the everyday language of ordinary people: "From dust to dust" (Genesis 3:20) has come to refer to the insignificance of earthly life in comparison to the heavenly kingdom; "fire and brimstone" (Genesis 19:24) refers to God's wrath and judgment of the wicked; "written in stone" (Exodus 31:18) expounds a command from which one cannot waver; "escaped by the skin of my teeth" (Job 19:20) describes the extrication of oneself from utmost peril at the precise moment before a disaster occurs; "spare the rod and spoil the child" (Proverbs 23:13–14) bestows advice on parents not to be too lenient with their children; "there is nothing new under the sun" (Ecclesiastes 1:9) constitutes a fatalistic philosophy of life for people who believe "the more things change, the more they stay the same"; and "the leopard cannot change his spots" (Jeremiah 13:23) functions as a caution to those who believe that the wicked will change their ways.

ART AND MUSIC

The purpose of the commandment against making "a graven image, or any likeness of anything that is in heaven above, or that is in the earth beneath, or that is in the water" (Exodus 20:4) was to prevent the Hebrews from regarding a lifeless stone or wooden image fashioned by human beings as something divine. To a remarkable extent, the ancient Hebrews adhered to this prohibition. Although archaeologists have unearthed countless figures of the gods of other ancient Near Eastern peoples, no visual representation of the Jewish God has been discovered. Although the prohibition was at times circumvented (see Chapter 7), it did prove an effective barrier against the cultivation of the visual arts in Hebrew culture.

Because Jewish aesthetic creativity did not emphasize the visual, it found its highest expression in music, dance, prose, and poetry. According to the Scriptures, David, prior to becoming king, often played the lyre to comfort King Saul when an "evil spirit" tormented him: "And whenever the evil spirit from God was upon Saul, David took the lyre and played it with his hand; so Saul was refreshed, and was well, and the evil spirit departed from him" (I Samuel 16:23). David was also a famous singer and composer of numerous psalms, a number of which extolled the use of music as a means of praising God:

> Praise the Lord! . . .
>
> Praise him with trumpet sound;
> praise him with lute and harp!

> Praise him with timbrel and dance;
>
> praise him with strings and pipe!
>
> Praise him with sounding cymbals;
> praise him with loud clashing cymbals!

(Psalm 150:1, 3-5)

The instruments used in Temple worship bore a marked resemblance to those available in Egypt, including harps and lyres. In the Temple, people sang Psalms, passages from the Scriptures, and folk tunes.

Eventually, in both the Temple and the synagogue, the Scriptures were chanted in a style called *cantillation*—a formulaic series of melodies. Singing with instrumental accompaniment also became a central feature of religious ceremonies. The climax of Temple music was reached during the early Christian era when large choirs of trained male singers (including some boys) performed. Musical instruments—harps, lutes, taborets or tambourines (small hand drums), cymbals, trumpets, and flutes—generally had been borrowed from other peoples. Of particular importance was the *shofar* (made from a he-goat's or a ram's horn) to herald the beginning of the Jewish New Year and to mark the start of the Day of Atonement. The *shofar* is the only musical instrument to retain its prominence in Jewish worship services up to the present (Figure 2.4).

Hebrew musicians passed on their musical chants from one generation to another via an oral tradition, and hand signs (called "earmarks") came into existence to indicate the rise and fall of the human voice and to mark the beginning, any half-stops, and the end of each verse. Later, three values—tone (pitch), time (duration), and dynamics (loudness or softness of the tones)—came to be associated with this primitive type of musical notation. Eventually, with the development of a system of *accent marks,* names were given to the hand signs/earmarks. Because the identity of these figures, their classification, and their values are alike in the Jewish, ancient Greek, and medieval Byzantine traditions (see Chapter 8), some musicologists suggest that ancient Greeks and Byzantine Greeks were influenced by Jewish music. By the first century A.D, Greek music became popular with a number of educated members of the Hebrew community (much to the chagrin of the Hebrew religious leaders). Although the Greeks wrote theoretical treatises on music (see Chapter 4), it was not until the ninth century A.D that Aaron ben Asher authored a treatise describing the "accent marks" of the Hebrew *neginoth* (notes, tunes).

Figure 2.4 Shofar Made from a he-goat's or a ram's horn, the shofar is the only musical instrument to maintain a prominent place in Jewish worship services up to the present day. *(Zev Radovan, Jerusalem)*

The Legacy of the Ancient Jews

For the Jews, monotheism had initiated a process of self-discovery and self-realization unmatched by other peoples of the Near East. The great value that westerners give to the individual derives in part from the ancient Hebrews, who held that man and woman were created in God's image and possessed free will and a conscience answerable to God.

Throughout the centuries the Jewish Bible, with its view of God, human nature, divine punishment, and social justice, has played a pivotal and profound role in Jewish life. Moreover, its significance has transcended the Jewish experience; it is also a cornerstone of Western civilization.

Christianity, the core religion of Western civilization, emerged from ancient Judaism, and the links between the two, including monotheism, moral autonomy, prophetic values, and the Hebrew Scriptures as the Word of God, are numerous and strong. The historical Jesus cannot be understood without examining his Jewish background, and his followers appealed to the Hebrew Scriptures in order to demonstrate the validity of their beliefs. For these reasons, we talk of a Judeo–Christian tradition as an essential component of Western civilization.

The Hebrew vision of a future messianic age, a golden age of peace and social justice, is at the root of the Western idea of progress—that people can build a more just society, that there is a reason to be hopeful about the future. This perception of the world has greatly influenced modern reform movements.

Moreover, the Hebrew Scriptures have been a source of inspiration for Western religious thinkers, novelists, poets, artists, and composers to the present day. Historians and archaeologists find the Hebrew Scriptures a valuable source in their efforts to reconstruct Near Eastern history.

Finally, the Jewish style of cantillation based on modes (scales) was further developed in the Byzantine musical practice, where it came in contact with the Greek system of modes (see Chapter 4), and later these modes were transmitted to the West by way of the Eastern Church.

Key Terms

Babylonian Captivity	Universalism
Torah	Book of Psalms
covenant	meditation poetry
Passover	The Song of Solomon
Feast of Weeks	Book of Job
prophets	cantillation
Messiah	shofar
Apocalyptic	

Notes

1. John A. Wilson, "Egypt—The Kingdom of the Two Lands," in *At the Dawn of Civilization,* ed. E. A. Speiser, vol. I in *The World History of the Jewish People* (New Brunswick, N.J.: Rutgers University Press, 1964), pp. 267–268.
2. John Bright, *A History of Israel* (Philadelphia: Westminster Press, 1972), p. 154.
3. Ibid.

3

Hellenic Civilization I: From Myth to Reason

T HE HEBREW CONCEPTION OF ETHICAL MONOTHEISM, with its stress on human dignity, is one principal source of the Western tradition. The second major source derives from ancient Greece. Both Hebrews and Greeks absorbed the achievements of Near Eastern civilizations, but they also developed their own distinctive viewpoints and styles of thought, which set them apart from the Mesopotamians and the Egyptians. The great achievements of the Hebrews lay in the sphere of religious–ethical thought; those of the Greeks lay in the development of rational thought. As Greek society evolved, says British historian James Shiel, there

> was a growing reliance on independent reason, a devotion to logical precision, progressing from myth to logos [reason]. Rationalism permeated the whole social and cultural development. . . . Architecture . . . developed from primitive cultic considerations to sophisticated mathematical norms; sculpture escaped from temple image to a new love of naturalism and proportion; political life proceeded from tyranny to rational experiments in democracy. From practical rules of thumb, geometry moved forward in the direction of the impressive Euclidian synthesis. So too philosophy made its way from "sayings of the wise" to the Aristotelian logic, and made men rely on their own observation and reflection in facing the unexplained vastness of the cosmos.[1]

The Greeks conceived of nature as following general rules, not acting according to the whims of gods or demons. They saw human beings as having a capacity for rational thought, a need for freedom, and a worth as individuals. Although the Greeks never dispensed with the gods, they increasingly stressed the importance of human reason and human decisions. They came to assert that reason is the avenue to knowledge and that people—not the gods—are responsible for their own behavior. In this shift of attention from the gods to human beings, the Greeks broke with the mythmaking orientation of the Near East and created the rational outlook that is a distinctive feature of Western civilization.

EARLY AEGEAN CIVILIZATIONS

Until the latter part of the nineteenth century, historians placed the beginning of Greek (or Hellenic) history in the eighth century B.C. Now it is known that two other civilizations preceded Hellenic Greece: the Minoan and the Mycenaean. Although the ancient Greek poet Homer had spoken of an earlier Greek civilization in his works, historians believed that Homer's epics dealt with

Bust of Plato, 350–340 B.C., Roman marble copy of an original bronze bust.

Plato saw the world of phenomena as unstable, transitory, and imperfect, whereas his realm of Ideas was eternal and universally valid. For him, true wisdom was to be obtained through knowledge of the Ideas, not the imperfect reflections of the Ideas perceived with the senses.

(Staatliche Glypothek Munich/Dagli Orti/ The Art Archive)

Figure 3.1 Penelope at Her Loom For ten years, Penelope remained at home—loyal, faithful, and obedient to her husband, Odysseus. To ward off her suitors, she promised that she would marry one of them as soon as she completed her weaving. But each night she undid that day's weaving. Therefore, she never finished her work nor was she forced into an unwanted marriage.
(Museo Archeologico, Chiusi/Scala/Art Resource, NY)

myths and **legends** (Figure 3.1), not with an actual historical past. In 1871, however, a successful German businessman, Heinrich Schliemann, began a search for earliest Greece. In excavating several sites mentioned by Homer, Schliemann discovered tombs, pottery, ornaments, and the remains of palaces of what hitherto had been a lost Greek civilization. The ancient civilization was named after Mycenae, the most important city of the time.

In 1900, Arthur Evans, a British archaeologist, excavating on the island of Crete, southeast of the Greek mainland, unearthed a civilization even older than that of the Mycenaean Greeks. The Cretans, or Minoans, were not Greeks and did not speak a Greek language, but their influence on mainland Greece was considerable and enduring. Minoan civilization lasted about 1,350 years (2600–1250 B.C.) and reached its height during the period from 1700 to 1450 B.C.

Judging by the archaeological evidence, the Minoans were peaceful. Generally, Minoan art did not depict military scenes, and Minoan palaces, unlike the Mycenaean ones, had no defensive walls or fortifications. Thus, the Minoans were vulnerable to the warlike Mycenaean Greeks, whose invasion contributed to the decline of Minoan civilization.

Mycenaean civilization, which consisted of several small states, each with its own ruling dynasty, reached its height in the period from 1400 to 1230 B.C. Mycenaean arts and crafts owed a considerable debt to Crete. A script that permitted record keeping probably also came from Crete. Constant warfare among the Mycenaean kingdoms (and perhaps foreign invasions) led to the destruction of its palaces and the abrupt disintegration of Mycenaean civilization about 1100 B.C. But to the later Greek civilization, the Mycenaeans left a legacy of religious forms, pottery making, metallurgy, agriculture, language, a warrior culture and code of honor immortalized in the Homeric epics, and myths and legends that offered themes for Greek drama.

EVOLUTION OF CITY–STATES

Break with Theocratic Politics

From 1100 to 800 B.C., the Greek world passed through the *Dark Age,* an era of transition between a dead Mycenaean civilization and a still unborn Hellenic civilization. During this period the Greeks experienced insecurity, warfare, poverty, and isolation. After 800 B.C., however, town life revived. Gradually, Greek cities founded settlements on the islands of the Aegean, along the coast of Asia Minor and the Black Sea, and to the west in Sicily and southern Italy. These colonies, established to relieve overpopulation and land hunger, were independent, self-governing city–states, not possessions of the homeland city–states.

From 750 B.C. to the death of Alexander the Great in 323 B.C., Greek society comprised many independent city–states. The city–state based on tribal allegiances was generally the first political association during the early stages of civilization. Moreover, Greece's many mountains, bays, and islands—natural barriers to political unity—favored this type of political arrangement.

The scale of the city–state, or *polis,* was small; most city–states had fewer than 5,000 male citizens. Athens, which was a large city–state, had some 35,000 to 40,000 adult male citizens at its height in the fifth century B.C.; the rest of its population of 350,000 consisted of women, children, resident aliens, and slaves, none of whom could participate in lawmaking. The polis gave individuals a sense of belonging, for its citizens were intimately involved in the political and cultural life of the community.

In the fifth century B.C., at its maturity, the Greeks viewed their polis as the only avenue to the good life—"the only framework within which man could realize his spiritual, moral, and intellectual capacities."[2] The mature polis was a self-governing community that expressed the will of free citizens, not the desires of gods, hereditary kings, or priests. In the Near East, religion dominated political activity, and to abide by the mandates of the gods was the ruler's first responsibility. The Greek polis also had begun as a religious institution, in which the citizens sought to maintain an alliance with their deities. Gradually, however, the citizens de-emphasized the gods' role in political life and based government not on the magic powers of divine rulers, but on human intelligence as expressed through the community. The great innovation introduced by the Greeks into politics and social theory was the principle that law did not derive from gods or divine kings, but from the human community.

The emergence of rational attitudes did not, of course, spell the end of religion, particularly for the peasants, who retained their devotion to their ancient cults, gods, and shrines. Worshiping the god of the city remained a required act of patriotism, to which Greeks unfailingly adhered. Thus, the religious–mythical tradition never died in

Figure 3.2 Spartan Woman Statuette
Spartan women were expected to marry before the age of twenty and to have children. Moreover, it was assumed that while the men and boys underwent military training, the women would keep the household in order. *(National Archaeological Museum, Athens/Archaeological Receipts Fund)*

Greece but existed side by side with a growing rationalism and became weaker as time passed.

What made Greek political life different from that of earlier Near Eastern civilizations, as well as gave it enduring significance, was the Greeks' gradual realization that community problems are caused by human beings and require human solutions. The Greeks also valued free citizenship. An absolute king, a tyrant who ruled arbitrarily and by decree and who was above the law, was abhorrent to them.

The ideals of political freedom are best exemplified by Athens. But before turning to Athens, let us examine another Greek city, which followed a different political course.

Sparta: A Garrison State

Situated on the Peloponnesian peninsula, Sparta conquered its neighbors, including Messenia, in the eighth century B.C. Instead of selling the Messenians abroad, the traditional Greek way of treating a defeated foe, the Spartans kept them as state serfs, or helots. Helots were owned by the state rather than by individual Spartans. Enraged by their enforced servitude, the Messenians, also a Greek people, desperately tried to regain their freedom. After a bloody uprising was suppressed, the fear of a helot revolt became indelibly stamped on Spartan consciousness.

To maintain their dominion over the Messenians, who outnumbered them ten to one, the Spartans—with extraordinary single-mindedness, discipline, and loyalty—transformed their own society into an armed camp. Agricultural labor was performed by helots; trade and crafts were left to the *perioikoi,* conquered Greeks who were free but who had no political rights. The Spartans learned only one craft—soldiering—and were inculcated with only one conception of excellence—fighting bravely and dying in battle for their city. Military training for Spartan boys began at age seven; they exercised, drilled, competed, and endured physical hardships. Other Greeks admired the Spartans for their courage, obedience to laws, and achievement in molding themselves according to an ideal. But the Spartans were also criticized for having a limited conception of areté (excellence).

In comparison to women in other parts of Greece, Spartan women (Figure 3.2) were more autonomous, and unlike Athenian women, they could inherit property. While the men and boys underwent military training, the women were placed in charge of keeping the household in order. Spartan women were also expected to marry before the age of twenty and to have children.

Athens: The Rise of Democracy

The contrast between the city–states of Athens and Sparta is striking. Whereas Sparta was a land power and exclusively agricultural, Athens was located on the peninsula of Attica near the coast, possessed a great navy, and was the commercial leader among the Greeks. To the Spartans, freedom meant preserving the independence of their fatherland; this overriding consideration demanded order, discipline, and regimentation. The Athenians also were determined to protect their city from enemies, but unlike the Spartans, they valued political freedom and sought the full development and enrichment of the human personality. Thus, whereas authoritarian and militaristic Sparta turned culturally sterile, the relatively free and open society of Athens became the cultural leader of Hellenic civilization.

During the eighth century B.C., aristocrats (*aristocracy* is a Greek word meaning "rule of the best") usurped power from hereditary kings. Through the efforts of reformers, notably Solon (c. 640–559 B.C.) and Cleisthenes (c. 570–c. 508 B.C.), the power of the aristocracy was reduced, and the Assembly, which was open to all male citizens, became the supreme authority in the state. But before Athenian democracy reached full bloom, Athens had to fight a war of survival against the mighty Persian empire.

In 499 B.C., the Ionian Greeks of Asia Minor rebelled against their Persian overlord. Sympathetic to the Ionian cause, Athens sent twenty ships to aid the revolt. Bent on revenge, Darius I, king of Persia, sent a small detachment to Attica. In 490 B.C., on the plains of Marathon, the citizen army of Athens defeated the Persians—for the Athenians, one of the finest moments in their history. Ten years later, Xerxes, Darius' son, organized a huge invasion force—some 250,000 men and more than 500 ships—with the aim of reducing Greece to a Persian province. Setting aside their separatist instincts, most of the city–states united to defend their independence and their liberty. The inventive intelligence with which the Greeks had planned their military operations and a fierce desire to preserve their freedom enabled them to defeat the greatest military power the Mediterranean world had yet seen. The confidence and pride that came with victory propelled Athens into a golden age.

The mature Athenian state was a direct democracy, in which the citizens themselves, not elected representatives, made the laws. In the Assembly, which was open to all adult male citizens and which met some forty times a year, Athenians debated and voted on key issues of state: They declared war, signed treaties, and spent public funds. The lowliest cobbler, as well as the wealthiest aristocrat, had the opportunity to express his opinion in the Assembly, to vote, and to hold office. By the middle of the fifth century, the will of the people, as expressed in the Assembly, was supreme.

Athens has been aptly described as a government of amateurs; there were no professional civil servants, no professional soldiers and sailors, no state judges, and no elected lawmakers. Ordinary citizens performed the duties of government. Such a system rested on the assumption that the average citizen was capable of participating intelligently in the affairs of state and that he would, in a spirit of civic patriotism, carry out his responsibilities to his city. In Athens of the fifth century B.C., excellence was equated with good citizenship—a concern for the good of the community that outweighed personal aspirations.

Athenian democracy achieved its height in the middle of the fifth century B.C., under the leadership of Pericles (c. 495–429 B.C.), a gifted statesman, orator, and military commander. In the opening stage of the monumental clash with Sparta, the Peloponnesian War (431–404 B.C.), Pericles delivered an oration in honor of the Athenian war casualties. The oration, as reported by Thucydides, the great Athenian historian of the fifth century B.C., contains a glowing description of the Athenian democratic ideal:

> We are called a democracy, for the administration is in the hands of the many and not of the few. But while the law secures equal justice to all alike in their private disputes, the claim of excellence is also recognized; and when a citizen is any way distinguished, he is [selected for] public service . . . as the reward of merit. Neither is poverty a bar, but a man may benefit his country whatever may be the obscurity of his condition. . . . There is no exclusiveness in our public life, and in our private intercourse we are not suspicious of one another, nor angry with our neighbor if he does what he likes; we do not put on sour looks at him which though harmless are unpleasant. . . . a spirit of reverence pervades our public acts; we are prevented from doing wrong by respect for authority and for the laws. . . .[3]

Athenian democracy undoubtedly had its limitations and weaknesses. Modern critics point out that resident aliens were almost totally barred from citizenship and therefore from political participation. Slaves, who constituted about one-fourth of the Athenian population, enjoyed none of the freedoms that Athenians considered so precious. The Greeks regarded slavery as a necessary precondition for civilized life; for some to be free and prosperous, they believed, others had to be enslaved. Slaves were generally prisoners of war or captives of pirates. In Athens, some slaves were Greeks, but most were foreigners. Slaves usually did the same work as Athenian citizens: farming, commerce, manufacturing, and domestic chores. However, those slaves, including preadolescent children, who toiled in the mines suffered a grim fate.

Athens was an exclusive men's club; women were denied legal and political rights. Most Greeks, no doubt, agreed with Aristotle, who said: "[T]he male is by nature superior, and the female inferior; and the one rules, and the other is ruled."[4] A girl usually married at age fourteen to a man twice her age, and the marriage was arranged by a male relative. The wedding day might be the first time that the young bride saw her future husband. Although either spouse could obtain a divorce, the children remained with the father after the marriage was dissolved. Wives did not dine with their husbands and spent much of their time in the women's quarters.

Athenian women were barred from holding public office and generally could not appear in court without a male representative. They could not act in plays, and when attending the theater, they sat in the rear, away from the men. Greek women received no formal education, although some young women learned to read and write at home. Training in household skills was considered the only education a woman needed. Because it was believed that a woman could not act independently, she was required to have a guardian—normally her father or husband—who controlled her property and supervised her behavior. Convinced that financial dealings were too difficult for women and that they needed to be protected from strangers, men, not women, did the marketing. When a woman left the house, she was usually accompanied by a male. The Athenian wife was treated as a minor; in effect, she was her husband's ward.

The flaws in Athenian democracy should not cause us to undervalue its extraordinary achievement. The idea that the state represents a community of free, self-governing citizens remains a crucial principle of Western civilization. Athenian democracy embodied the principle of the legal state—a government based not on force, but on laws debated, devised, altered, and obeyed by free citizens. Both democratic politics and systematic political thought originated in Greece. There, people first asked questions about the nature and purpose of the state, rationally analyzed political institutions, speculated about human nature and justice, and discussed the merits of various forms of government. It is to Greece that we ultimately trace the idea of democracy and all that accompanies it: citizenship, constitutions, equality before the law, government by law, reasoned debate, respect for the individual, and confidence in human intelligence.

THE DECLINE OF THE CITY–STATES

Although the Greeks shared a common language and culture, they remained divided politically. A determination to preserve city–state sovereignty prevented the Greeks from forming a larger political grouping, which might have prevented the intercity warfare that ultimately cost the city–state its vitality and independence. Immediately after the Persian Wars, more than 150 city–states organized a confederation, the *Delian League* (named after its treasury on the island of Delos), to protect themselves against a renewed confrontation with Persia. Because of its wealth, its powerful fleet, and the restless energy of its citizens, Athens assumed leadership of the Delian League. Athenians consciously and rapaciously manipulated the league for their own economic advantage, seeing no contradiction between imperialism and democracy. Athenian control of the Delian League frightened the Spartans and their allies in the Peloponnesian League. Sparta and the Peloponnesian states decided on war because they saw a dynamic and imperialistic Athens as a threat to their independence (Map 3.1).

The war began in 431 B.C. and ended in 404 B.C., when a besieged Athens, with a decimated navy and a dwindling food supply, surrendered. Sparta dissolved the Delian League and left Athens with only a handful of ships. The Peloponnesian War shattered the spiritual foundations of Hellenic society. During its course, selfish individualism triumphed over civic duty, moderation gave way to extremism, and in several cities, including Athens, politics degenerated into civil war between oligarchs, who wanted to concentrate power in their own hands by depriving the lower classes of political rights, and democrats, who sought to preserve the political rights of all adult male citizens.

The Peloponnesian War was the great crisis of Hellenic history. The city–states never recovered from their self-inflicted spiritual wounds. In the fourth century, the quarrelsome city–states formed new systems of alliances and persisted in their ruinous conflicts. While the Greek cities battered one another in fratricidal warfare, a new power was rising in the north—Macedonia. To the Greeks, the Macedonians, a wild mountain people who spoke a Greek dialect and had acquired a sprinkling of Hellenic culture, differed little from other non-Greeks, whom they called barbarians. In 359 B.C., at the age of twenty-three, Philip II (382–336 B.C.) ascended

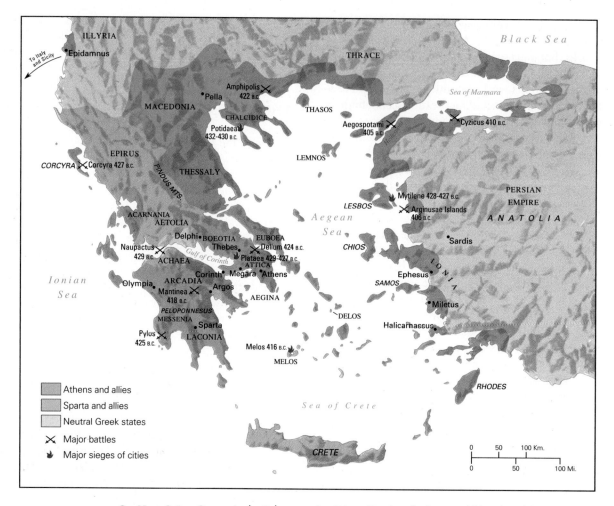

Map 3.1 Greece in the Peloponnesian War   During the long and bloody Peloponnesian War (431–404 B.C.), much of the Greek world was divided in two camps: one led by Sparta, the other by Athens.

the Macedonian throne. He converted Macedonia into a first-rate military power and began a drive to become master of the Greeks.

Incorrectly assessing Philip's strength, the Greeks were slow to organize a coalition against Macedonia. In 338 B.C., at Chaeronea, Philip's forces decisively defeated the Greeks, and all of Greece was his. The city–states still existed, but they had lost their independence. The world of the small, independent, and self-sufficient polis was drawing to a close, and Greek civilization was taking a different shape.

EARLY GREEK LITERATURE

Homer

The poet Homer lived during the eighth century B.C., just after the Dark Age. His great epics, the *Iliad* and the *Odyssey,* helped to shape the Greek spirit and Greek religion. Although scholars gener-

ally agree that Homer composed the *Iliad,* some of them hold that the *Odyssey* was probably the work of an unknown poet, who lived sometime after Homer; others say that Homer composed both epics in their earliest forms and that others altered them. Despite the controversy, we do know that Homer was the earliest molder of the Greek outlook and character. For centuries, Greek youngsters grew up reciting the Homeric epics and admiring the Homeric heroes, who strove for honor and faced suffering and death with courage. Greek thinkers quoted Homer to illustrate moral truths.

In contrast to earlier works of mythology, Homer dealt not just with a hero's actions but also with what the hero thought and felt about his behavior. Homer was a poetic genius, able to reveal a human being's deepest thoughts, feelings, and conflicts in a few brilliant lines. His characters were complex in their motives and expressed powerful human emotions—wrath, vengeance, guilt, remorse, compassion, and love—that would intrigue and inspire Western writers into the twenty-first century.

The *Iliad* and the *Odyssey* deal with events that had taken place centuries before Homer's time, during the Mycenaean period. They express a single tradition, yet are very different in spirit. The *Iliad* deals, in poetic form, with a small segment of the tenth and last year of the Trojan War. At the very beginning, Homer states his theme:

> The Wrath of Achilles is my theme, that fatal wrath which, in fulfillment of the will of Zeus, brought the Achaeans [Greeks] so much suffering and sent the gallant souls of many noblemen to Hades, leaving their bodies as carrion for the dogs and passing birds. Let us begin, goddess of song, with the angry parting that took place between Agamemnon King of Men and the great Achilles Son of Peleus.[5]

The story goes on to reveal the cause and tragic consequences of this wrath. In depriving "the swift and excellent" Achilles of his rightful war prize (the captive young woman Briseis), King Agamemnon has insulted Achilles' honor and has violated the solemn rule that warrior heroes treat each other with respect. His pride wounded, Achilles refuses to rejoin Agamemnon in battle against Troy and plans to affirm his honor by demonstrating that the Achaeans need his valor and military prowess. Not until many brave men have been slain, including his dearest friend Patroclus, does Achilles set aside his quarrel with Agamemnon and enter the battle.

Homer employs a particular event, the quarrel between an arrogant Agamemnon and a revengeful Achilles, to demonstrate a universal principle: that "wicked arrogance" and "ruinous wrath" will cause much suffering and death. Homer grasps that there is an internal logic to existence. For Homer, says British classicist H. D. F. Kitto, "actions must have their consequences; ill-judged actions must have uncomfortable results."[6] People, and even the gods, operate within a certain unalterable framework; their deeds are subject to the demands of fate, or necessity. With a poet's intuition, Homer sensed what would become a fundamental attitude of the Greek mind: There is a universal order to things. Later Greeks would formulate this insight in philosophical terms.

Although human life is governed by laws of necessity, the Homeric warrior expresses a passionate desire to assert himself, to demonstrate his worth, to gain the glory that poets would immortalize in their songs—that is, to achieve *areté*, excellence. In the *Iliad*, Hector, prince of Troy, does battle with Achilles, even though defeat and death seem certain. He fights not because he is a fool rushing madly into a fray nor because he relishes combat, but because he is a prince bound by a code of honor and conscious of his reputation and of his responsibility to his fellow Trojans. In the code of the warrior–aristocrats, cowardice brought unbearable shame, and honor meant more than life itself. When Hector knows that he is going to be slain by Achilles, he expresses this overriding concern with heroism and glory: "So now I meet my doom. Let me at least sell my life dearly and have a not inglorious end, after some feat of arms that shall come to the ears of generations still unborn."[7] The audience knew that Hector would die at the hands of Achilles; consequently their interest was not in the action of the battle poetry but rather in the pathos of death and how Hector would face his inexorable fate.

Of necessity, Hector must be killed to avenge the death of Patroclus, but Achilles, in another act of **hubris**—excessive pride or arrogance that leads to suffering—attempts to mutilate Hector's corpse by dragging it around the grave of Patroclus at dawn for twelve days. He compounds the atrocity by burning twelve Trojan prisoners on Patroclus' funeral pyre. For these excesses, he incurs the displeasure of the gods. Yet, Achilles is also capable of compassion. When a grief-stricken Priam, Hector's father, goes to Achilles and requests Hector's body, Achilles responds with tenderness. This scene shows that although Homer sees the essence of life as the pursuit of glory, he is also sensitive to life's brevity and to the suffering that pervades human existence.

> Priam had set Achilles thinking of his own father and brought him to the verge of tears. Taking the old man's hand, he gently put him from him; and overcome by their memories they both broke down. Priam, crouching at Achilles' feet, wept bitterly for man-slaying Hector, and Achilles wept for his father, and then again for Patroclus. The house was filled with the sounds of their lamentation. But presently, when he had enough of tears and recovered his composure, the excellent Achilles leapt from his chair, and in compassion for the old man's grey head and grey beard, took him by the arm and raised him. Then he spoke to him from his heart: "You are indeed a man of sorrows and suffered much. How could you dare to come by yourself to the Achaean ships into the presence of a man who has killed so many of your gallant sons? You have a heart of iron. But pray be seated now, here on this chair, and let us leave our sorrows, bitter though they are, locked up in our own hearts, for weeping is cold comfort and does little good. We men are wretched things, and the gods, who have no cares themselves, have woven sorrow into the very pattern of our lives."[8]

Heroism, the pursuit of glory, and war's exhilaration are central to the *Iliad*, but Homer is also sensitive to the suffering caused by war. Battlefields littered with dead and maimed warriors fill soldiers with tears. And the grief of widows, orphans, and parents is unremitting. Homer grasped war's tragic character: It confers honor and dignity on the victorious, but suffering, grief, enslavement, and death on the defeated. And one day, the hero, who had been lauded for his courage and prowess and had brought glory to his family and city, will also perish by the sword. This is his destiny. Homer's insights into life's tragic nature instructed the great Greek dramatists (see Chapter 4) and future Western writers.

The *Iliad* is concerned with noble and proud warriors relentlessly competing with each other for glory and with the suffering and mourning stemming from this all-consuming passion. The *Odyssey* has a different character. Odysseus, the hero of the *Odyssey*, battles fantastic monsters drawn from an older mythological tradition and scoundrels beneath his social class, not other noble warriors aspiring through military prowess to win honor. Odysseus is cunning and resourceful, but ultimately less memorable than the intense Achilles who displays in powerful ways a wide range of human qualities—pride, anger, self-doubt, grief, and compassion. There is nothing in the *Odyssey* comparable to the overwhelming passion that ignites Achilles' wrath when Agamemnon insults his honor, the pathos elicited by Hector as he resolves to fight the mighty Achilles despite the pleas of his father and wife, and the tenderness displayed by Achilles to the grieving Priam. Because Odysseus has insulted the gods, his return to Ithaca from the siege of Troy takes ten years. The tension of his journey home is, however, far less gripping than the theme of Achilles' wrath.

When Odysseus, in disguise, arrives home after the long absence, he discovers that several villains—called suitors because they pursue his wife—have taken over his house; they appropriate and abuse his property, sleep with his servants, plot to murder his son, and attempt to steal his wife, Penelope, who resists them. Remaining at home for ten years, loyal, faithful, and obedient to her husband, Penelope demonstrates the Greek view of the proper relationship of a woman to her husband. Finally, a vengeful, but patient and cunning, Odysseus waits for the right moment to kill the suitors. That these wicked people pay with their lives for their evil acts indicates that a principle of justice, no doubt installed by the gods, operates in the world. The conclusion of the *Odyssey*, the happy reunion of husband, wife, and son, contrasts with the tragic consequences of Achilles'

wrath—the death of many noble heroes and the devouring grief of their kin and comrades.

In the warrior–aristocrat world of Homer, excellence was principally interpreted as bravery and skill in battle. Homer's portrayal also bears the embryo of a larger conception of human excellence, one that combines thought with action. A man of true worth, says the wise Phoenix to the stubborn Achilles, is both "a speaker of words and a doer of deeds." In this passage, we find the earliest statement of the Greek educational ideal: the molding of human beings who, says classicist Werner Jaeger, "united nobility of action with nobility of mind," who realized "the whole of human potentialities."[9] Thus, in Homer we find the beginnings of Greek humanism—a concern with human beings and with their achievements.

Homeric humanism was expressed in another way. To Mesopotamian and Egyptian minds, the gods were primarily responsible for the good or evil that befell human beings. In Homer's work, the gods are still very much involved in human affairs, but he also makes the individual a decisive actor in the drama of life. Human actions and human personality are very important. Homer's men demonstrate a considerable independence of will. Human beings pay respect to the gods but do not live in perpetual fear of them; they choose their own way, at times even defying the gods. Homer's claim that humans and gods are part of the same family led the Greeks to believe that humans are capable of godlike actions. From the beginning, Homer's epics are not only about divine intervention in behalf of human beings, but also they are about human actions that are subject to human standards of justice. This is not to say that humans accept total responsibility for their actions. At times, they prefer to attribute human misery, misfortune, and suffering to "the will of the gods." But as British classicist C. M. Bowra notes, "the human actors . . . pursue their own aims and deal their own blows; the gods may help or obstruct them, but success or failure remains their own. The gods have the last word, but in the interval men do their utmost and win glory for it."[10]

Essentially, Homer's works are an expression of the poetic imagination and mythical thought. But his view of the eternal order of nature and his conception of the individual striving for excellence form the foundations of the Greek outlook.

Hesiod

The poet Hesiod (c. 700 B.C.), who lived on a farm in Boetia, in central Greece, wrote two major poems, *Theogony*, which deals with the formation of the universe, and *Works and Days*, which depicts the life of peasants. Similar to Homer's epics, Hesiod's poems contain ideas that contributed to the shaping of the Greek outlook and the emergence of philosophy. For example, utilizing inherited ethical maxims and driven by his own deep concern for justice, Hesiod raised questions about the origin of evil, the existence of a moral order within nature, and what constitutes the good life, which would greatly influence later Greek dramatists and philosophers.

In the earlier poem, *Theogony (Generation of the Gods),* Hesiod produced a **cosmogony**—an account of the genesis of the universe. He did this through a systematic treatment of the lineage of the gods. Whereas Homer's epics are silent about creation and the origin of life, Hesiod's poem links the creation of the natural world (Heaven, Earth, Sea, Night, and Day), and human life to the existence of immortal gods and goddesses. The poem begins with a mystical dream in which Hesiod encounters the Muses (nine daughters of Zeus), "who by their singing delight the great mind of Zeus, their father, who lives on Olympos, as they tell of what is, and what is to be, and what was before now."[11] The Muses then relate to Hesiod the origins, genealogies, and functions of the gods. The creation of the first generation of deities began with Chaos who gave rise to Gaia, Mother Earth, "to be the unshakable foundation of all the immortals who keep the crests of snowy Olympos," and to Tartaros "the foggy in the pit of the wide-wayed earth." Chaos also produced Erebus, Night, who "lay in love" with Day. Gaia's firstborn was Ouranos who became the ruler of the world and the personification of Heaven. Gaia then brought forth many other children, including "the tall Hills, those wild haunts that are beloved by the goddess Nymphs," and Pontos, the sea.[12]

The Titans, led by Kronos, were Hesiod's second generation of gods. The transference of power to the Titans, and subsequently to the Olympians, was violent. Kronos castrated his father, Ouranos, to win the kingdom and devoured his own children to maintain control of it. However, Kronos' son, Zeus, who was saved by his mother, led the Olympian deities (so named because they lived on Mount Olympos, the highest mountain) in their conquest of the Titans. Hesiod viewed Zeus' triumph over the Titans and their imprisonment in Tartaros as a great victory for order and law. Firmly established as the omnipotent ruler of creation, Zeus could secure justice for human beings.

Although Hesiod's *Theogony* is replete with mythical imagery, for several reasons scholars regard it as a precursor of Greek philosophy. First, in explaining the origins of the world through the genealogy of the gods, he produced an ordered and structured mythology that can be interpreted as nascent rational speculation. Second, the gift of law bestowed by Zeus on humanity can be viewed as an early expression of natural law—the recognition of both a physical and moral order inherent in the universe. Crucial for philosophic thought, the concept of natural law, which Hesiod had expressed in mythical–religious terms, was explicitly formulated in the rational categories of philosophy by Greek thinkers after Hesiod.

Whereas Homer's epics concentrate on heroes striving to win honor as defined by a chivalric aristocratic ideal, Hesiod's later poem, *Works and Days,* describes the daily ordeal of common folk struggling to feed their families. A man of the soil, Hesiod also maintains that honest labor promotes the good life.

> [G]et all necessary gear in your house
>   in good order,
> lest . . . the season pass you by, and your work
>   be undone.
> Do not put off until tomorrow and the day after.
> A man does not fill his barn by shirking his
>   labors
> or putting them off; it is keeping at it that gets
>   the work done.[13]

For Hesiod, the farmer who perseveres in his daily labor demonstrates *areté* (excellence); heroes are not made only on the battlefield, but also on the farm in the farmer's confrontation with the land and nature.

But it is Hesiod's concern with justice that gives the poem stature. Cheated by his brother, Perses, out of part of their father's estate, Hesiod feels compelled to instruct Perses and others about the virtues of justice. He attributes the wretched condition of social life, including "civil war and slaughter," to a breakdown of moral standards. Using the myth of the five ages of humanity, he demonstrates the progressive deterioration of human conduct. Once human beings lived in a golden age, which eventually perished; succeeding ages also perished, victims of injustice and violence. His own age, the Iron Age, he said, is marked by drudgery, pain, and wickedness. And pessimistic about human nature, Hesiod speaks of a coming sixth age when "there shall be no defense against evil."

Hesiod employs another myth to account for the origins of evil. When Prometheus deceived Zeus and also stole fire to aid men, Zeus retaliated by thinking up "dismal sorrows for mankind." He did this by making it hard for men to earn a livelihood and by creating Pandora, the first woman. Pandora was endowed with all the wiles and beauty of a goddess. But Zeus commanded

Hermes "to put in her the mind of a hussy, and a treacherous nature."[14] Before her creation, all passions, vices, spites, and sicknesses had been sealed in a jar, but Pandora took the lid from the jar and released the evils into the world. Hope, however, clung relentlessly to the inside lip of the jar. Ever since, humanity has been plagued with misfortune, pain, and suffering—but not without hope.

Although he was generally pessimistic, Hesiod still believed that human beings could improve their lot if they embraced justice, which "is proved the best thing they have." An awareness of justice is what distinguishes human beings from other creatures:

> You, Perses, should store away in your mind all
>   that I tell you,
> and listen to justice, and put away
>   all notions of violence.
> Here is the law, as Zeus established it
>   for human beings;
> as for fish, and wild animals, and the flying birds,
> they feed on each other, since there is no idea
>   of justice among them;
> but to men he gave justice, and she in the end
>   is proved the best thing
> they have. If a man sees what is right
>   and is willing to argue it,
> Zeus of the wide brows grants him prosperity.[15]

Human beings are faced with the choice between *Dikê* (straight judgment and justice), which safeguards society, and *Hubris* (excessive pride), which destroys it. Honoring justice is what distinguishes a civilized society from a state of savagery.

Throughout *Theogony* and *Works and Days*, Hesiod used the language and imagery of myth to express a curiosity about the genesis of the universe, a concern for justice, and an awareness of a universal moral order. In succeeding centuries, Greek thinkers would discuss these issues using the language and categories of philosophy.

GREEK RELIGION

During the Dark Age, Greek religion was a mixture of beliefs and cults of gods and goddesses inherited from the Mycenaen past and from an even older Indo-European past imported from Asia Minor. Like many other primitive religions, primitive Greek religion was directly linked to fertility—both of the tribe and of the earth. Local Chthonic or earth deities embodied an earth mother who was the mother of corn and fruit. Initially, she was barren and inanimate, but in the spring she was viewed as the *Kore* ("maiden"), who was to mate and become fruitful.

Over time, however, the Olympian deities, as organized by Homer and Hesiod, replaced the tribal beliefs. Although neither Homer nor Hesiod intended their poetry to have any theological significance, their treatment of the gods had important religious implications for the Greeks. In time, the mythology in their epics formed the basis of the Olympian religion accepted throughout Greece.

Greek religion lacked the holy books, dogmas, priestly class, and creeds that came to permeate Judaism and Christianity. The lack of legalisms freed the Greeks to embellish and to reorder inherited myths so that no rigid belief system guarded by priests and no fixed form of ritual developed. As classicist Edith Hamilton noted: "Greek religion was developed not by priests nor by prophets nor by saints nor by any set of men who were held to be removed from the ordinary run of life because of a superior degree of holiness; it was developed by poets and artists and philosophers, all of them people who instinctively leave thought and imagination free, and all of them in Greece, men of practical affairs."[16]

The Olympian Religion

The Olympian religion generally replaced the old Chthonic deities. The Olympian deities (see p. 63) had a broader appeal than the local cults, which were often unique to each tribe. Moreover, the Olympian creation myths defined the gods and goddesses in more human terms than the mysterious Chthonian deities. Not only did the idea of a powerful Zeus convey order to creation, but it also clarified human existence—mortal beings should submit themselves to the Olympians, who, in return, would watch over them and fulfill their needs. Olympian religion inspired great works of art, provided the thematic material for the great Greek dramatists, and served as the focus for many of the hymns composed by Greek musicians and poets.

Homer claimed that humans were capable of godlike actions; conversely, he also ascribed human attributes and behavior to the Olympian deities. The sexual escapades of Zeus are the subject of the most famous myths. These myths describe the notorious love affairs of Zeus and his fathering of many children with various female deities as well as with mortal women. The most famous cycle of myths is centered on the jealousy of Zeus' wife, Hera. One tale deals with Zeus' love for Hera's priestess, Io. Attempting to deceive Hera while he pursued Io, Zeus turned himself into a cloud. In spite of this deception, Hera's suspicions were aroused, and Zeus attempted to

The identity, significance, and symbols of the twelve Olympian deities are summarized in the chart below. Greek Olympian religion was largely appropriated by the Romans.

Greek/Roman Name	Significance	Symbols
Zeus/Jupiter	King of the Gods, God of the Sky	Thunderbolt, scepter, eagle
Hera/Juno	Goddess of Marriage	Crown, scepter, peacock
Poseidon/Neptune	God of the Sea	Trident, horse
Hades/Pluto	God of the Underworld	(no fixed symbol)
Hestia/Vesta	Goddess of the Hearth	(no fixed symbol)
Apollo/Apollo	Light, Purification, Music	Lyre, bow, shepherd's crook
Athene/Minerva	Wisdom, Patron of Athens	Owl, spear, helmet, winged victory (Nike)
Aphrodite/Venus	Goddess of Love and Beauty	(no fixed symbol)
Ares/Mars	God of War and Carnage	(no fixed symbol)
Hermes/Mercury	Messenger of the Gods, Travel, Luck, Conductor of the Dead	Caduceus (staff)
Artemis/Diana	Goddess of the Hunt, Protectress of wild animals and women	Bow
Hephaistos/Vulcan	God of the Forge, Fire	Hammer, tongs

stymie his wife by transforming Io into a white heifer. Undaunted, Hera then tortured the heifer, Io, with a gadfly, which unremittingly stung her until she was driven mad.

The Olympian deities could also be arrogant and quarrelsome, often acting like defiant children who insist on having their own way. Because many of the Olympians' squabbles were played out on earth, humans became victims of the Olympians' anger and pride. Those Greeks who looked to the Olympian deities for moral standards found them sorely deficient. In the sixth century B.C. the philosopher Xenophanes disparaged the gods for their immorality and advanced a single god—a conceptual abstraction, not a living god in human form—who came to embody perfection. After Xenophanes' attack on the Olympians, further attempts were made to promote Zeus from simply the lord of the cosmos to the position of preeminent deity and the moral arbiter of justice and law.

The Mystery Religions

Olympianism did not answer many of the spiritual and emotional needs of men and women. It lacked the mystery and ecstasy of the earlier Chthonic cults and did not satisfy a yearning for immortality, which for the most part it reserved for the gods. Many Greeks found an outlet for their religious feeling in the sacred ceremonies of *mystery religions* whose initiates engaged in secret forms of worship. The Eleusinian and the Orphic-Dionysian mysteries were the two most important cults.

The Eleusinian mystery was based on the tragic myth of Demeter, the goddess of grain and fertility. Demeter searched for her daughter, Persephone, who had been kidnapped by Hades to become his queen in the Underworld. Participants in the cult purified themselves by bathing in the sea; to show their devotion to Demeter, they sacrificed a piglet and fasted in imitation of the goddess who fasted while mourning the loss of her daughter. These rituals provided an outlet for religious feelings, and the promise of a happy life beyond the grave eased the terror of death.

Orphism was named for Orpheus, a poet whose music on the lyre could calm animalistic passions. Said to have lived in Thrace in the distant past, Orpheus was most likely a purely mythical figure. His life was tragic. His beloved wife, Eurydice, died from a snakebite, and Orpheus' attempt to rescue her from the Underworld failed. He died an agonizing death, torn to pieces by the *maenads,* "mad women," who were driven into a frenzy by the god Dionysos.

Participants in the Orphic cult believed that Orpheus had shown them the way to eternal life. It consisted of purifying the soul through sacramental rituals and ascetic practices, including fasting. Like the Pythagoreans (see p. 65), Orphics believed that the soul was contaminated by the body, and that it would live in several different bodies before attaining perfection and eternal peace.

As Orphism evolved, it found a place for Dionysos, around whom an elaborate myth had developed. Dionysos' mother was Persephone, the daughter of Demeter, and his father was Zeus. Hera, Zeus' wife, was enraged by her husband's liaison with Persephone and enlisted the help of the Titans, who tore Dionysos apart and ate his limbs. But a new Dionysos was created from his heart, which had been preserved. In ecstatic rituals, cult members memorialized Dionysos' death and celebrated his rebirth. In imitation of Dionysos' ordeal, they savagely tore apart sacrificial animals. By releasing pent-up, primitive emotions, these frenzied orgies served as a *catharsis* for the cult members.

Orphics believed that human beings possessed a dual nature—a corrupt body and a pure soul. Ascetic practices and the ritualistic consumption of wine—symbolizing both the blood of Dionysos when he was eaten by the Titans and that he was the god of wine—aided the soul in its liberation from the body.

In the early stages of Greek history, most people sought to live in accordance with the wishes of the gods. Through prayer, offerings, and ritual purification, they tried to appease the gods and consulted oracles to divine the future. Although religion pervaded daily life, the Greeks had no official body of priests who ruled religious matters and could intervene in politics. Instead, religious ceremonies were conducted by citizens chosen to serve as priests. Nor was there an official creed with established doctrines. For many Greeks, religion was more social than spiritual; that is, it was more a way of expressing attachment to the community than finding inner peace through personal communion with a higher reality. In time, traditional religion would be challenged and undermined by a growing secular and rational spirit.

PHILOSOPHY IN THE HELLENIC AGE

The Greeks broke with the mythopoeic outlook of the Near East and conceived a new way of viewing nature and human society, which is the basis of the Western scientific and philosophic tradition. After an initial period of mythical thinking, by the fifth century B.C., the Greek mind had gradually applied reason to the physical world and to all human activities. This emphasis on reason marks a turning point for human civilization.

The development of rational thought in Greece was a process, a trend, not a finished achievement. The process began when some thinkers rejected mythical explanations for natural phenomena. The nonphilosophical majority never entirely eliminated the language, attitudes, and beliefs of myth from its life and thought. For them, the world remained controlled by divine forces, which were appeased through cultic practices. Even in the mature philosophy of Plato and Aristotle, mythical modes of thought persisted. Plato's thought, especially, retained a certain religious–mystical tone. What is of immense historical importance is not the degree to which the Greeks successfully integrated the norm of reason, but that they originated this norm, defined it, and applied it to their intellectual development and social life.

The first thinkers in human history to raise thought to the level of self-conscious theory emerged in the sixth century B.C., in the Greek cities of Ionia in Asia Minor. Curious about the essential composition of nature and dissatisfied with earlier creation legends, the Ionians sought physical, rather than mythic–religious, explanations for natural occurrences. In the process, they arrived at a new concept of nature and a new method of inquiry. They maintained that nature was not manipulated by arbitrary and willful gods and that it was not governed by blind chance. The Ionians said that nature is a uniform whole; it contains a hidden structure—principles of order or general laws—that govern phenomena, and these fundamental rules are ascertainable by the human mind. They implied that the origin, composition, and structure of the world can be investigated rationally and systematically. Thus, in seeking to account for rainbows, earthquakes, and eclipses, the Ionians posited entirely naturalistic explanations that excluded the gods. This new outlook marks the beginning of scientific thought.

What conditions enabled the Greeks to make this breakthrough? Perhaps their familiarity with Near Eastern achievements in mathematics and science stimulated their ideas. But this influence should not be exaggerated, says Greek scholar John N. Theodorakopoulos, for Egyptians and Mesopotamians "had only mythological systems of belief and a knowledge of practical matters. They did not possess those pure and crystal-clear products of the intellect which we call science and philosophy. Nor did they have any terminology to describe them."[17] Perhaps the poets' conception of human behavior as subject to universal destiny was extended into the philosophers' belief that nature was governed by law. Perhaps the breakthrough was fostered by the Greeks' freedom from a priesthood and rigid religious doctrines that limit thought. Or perhaps Greek speculative thought was an offspring of the city, because if law governed human affairs, providing balance and order, should not the universe also be regulated by principles of order?

The Cosmologists: Rational Inquiry into Nature

The first Ionian philosophers are called cosmologists because they sought knowledge about the universe—how nature came to be the way it was. They held that some single, eternal, and imperishable substance, which underwent various modifications, gave rise to all phenomena in nature. Their search for the unity underlying the phenomena—the "One"—became a focus of philosophy in the ancient world; it also would have great significance for religious thought.

Ionian philosophy began with Thales (c. 624–548 B.C.) of Miletus, a city in Ionia. He was a contemporary of Solon of Athens and concerned himself with understanding the order of nature. Thales said that water was the basic element, the underlying substratum of nature, and that through some natural process—similar to the formation of ice or steam—water gave rise to everything else in the world.

Thales revolutionized thought because he omitted the gods from his account of the origins of nature and searched for a natural explanation of how all things came to be. He broke with the commonly held belief that earthquakes were caused by Poseidon, god of the sea, and offered instead a naturalistic explanation for these disturbances: that the earth floated on water and that when the water experienced turbulent waves, the earth was rocked by earthquakes. Thales was the first person to predict an eclipse of the sun. To do this, he had to dismiss traditional mythical explanations and to grasp a crucial scientific principle—that heavenly objects move in regular patterns, which can be known.

Anaximander (c. 611–547 B.C.), another sixth-century Ionian, rejected Thales' theory that water was the original substance. He rejected any specific substance and suggested that an indefinite, undifferentiated substance, which he called the Boundless, was the source of all things. He believed that from this primary mass, which contained the powers of heat and cold, there gradually emerged a nucleus, the seed of the world. According to Anaximander, the cold and wet condensed to form the earth and its cloud cover, while the hot and dry formed the rings of fire that we see as the moon, the sun, and the stars. The heat from the fire in the sky dried the earth and shrank the seas. From the warm slime on earth arose life, and from the first sea creatures there evolved land animals, including human beings. Anaximander's account of the origins of the universe and nature understandably contained fantastic elements. Nevertheless, by offering a natural explanation for the origin of nature and life and by holding that nature was lawful, it surpassed the creation myths.

Similar to his fellow Ionians, Anaximenes, who died around 525 B.C., made the transition from myth to reason. He also maintained that a primary substance, air, underlay reality and accounted for nature's orderliness. Air that was rarefied became fire, whereas wind and clouds were formed from condensed air. If the process of condensation continued, it produced water, earth, and eventually, stones. Anaximenes also rejected the old belief that a rainbow was the goddess Iris; instead, he saw it as the consequence of the sun's rays falling on dense air.

The Ionians have been called "matter philosophers" because they held that everything issued from a particular material substance. Other sixth-century B.C. thinkers tried a different approach. Pythagoras (c. 580–507 B.C.) and his followers, who lived in the Greek cities in southern Italy, did not find the nature of things in a particular substance but in mathematical relationships. The Pythagoreans discovered that the intervals in the musical scale can be expressed mathematically. Extending this principle of proportion found in sound to the universe at large, they concluded that the cosmos also contained an inherent mathematical order. Thus, the Pythagoreans shifted the emphasis from matter to form, from the world of sense perception to the logic of mathematics.

The Pythagoreans were also religious mystics who valued the soul more than the body and believed in the immortality and transmigration of souls. Consequently, they refused to eat animal flesh, fearing that it contained former human souls. The religious beliefs of the Pythagoreans as well as their stress on mathematics would greatly influence Plato.

Parmenides (c. 515–450 B.C.), a native of the Greek city of Elea in southern Italy, challenged the fundamental view of the Ionians that all things emerged from one original substance. In developing his position, Parmenides applied to philosophical argument the logic used by the Pythagoreans for mathematical thinking. In putting forth the proposition that an argument must be consistent and contain no contradictions, Parmenides became the founder of formal logic.

Despite appearances, asserted Parmenides, reality—the cosmos and all that is within it—is one, eternal, and unchanging. All change or "Becoming" is actually only the appearance of the single Reality or "Being," which Parmenides also called the "Existent" or "that which is." Therefore, Reality is not made known through the senses, which are misleading, but through the mind; not through experience, but through pure thought. Truth could be reached only through abstract thought.

Parmenides' concept of an unchanging reality apprehended by thought alone and the distinction he drew between the senses and reason influenced Plato and are the foundations of **metaphysics**—the branch of philosophy that deals with ultimate reality or Being.

Parmenides' thought also had religious implications. Although he did not refer to True Being as God, he did ascribe to it the attributes of oneness, transcendence, permanence, and perfection. Such a description of Being abounds with religious meaning. Particularly as developed by Plato, the quest for Being would greatly influence religious thought, including Christian theology, in the ancient world.

Democritus (c. 460–370 B.C.), from the Greek mainland, renewed the Ionians' concern with the world of matter and reaffirmed their confidence in knowledge derived from sense perception—and the senses indicated that change did occur in nature, in contrast to Parmenides' view. But Democritus also retained Parmenides' reverence for reason. His model of the universe consisted of two fundamental realities: empty space and an infinite number of atoms. Eternal, indivisible, and imperceptible, these atoms moved in the void. All things consisted of atoms, and combinations of atoms accounted for all change in nature. In a world of colliding atoms, everything behaved according to mechanical principles. (Of course Democritus' atomic theory did not derive from any empirical evidence of atoms, but was purely speculative.)

Concepts that are essential to scientific thought thus emerged in embryonic form with Greek philosophers: natural explanations for physical occurrences (Ionians), the mathematical order of nature (Pythagoras), logical proof (Parmenides), and the mechanical structure of the universe (Democritus). By giving to nature a rational, rather than a mythical, foundation and by holding that theories should be grounded in evidence and that one should be able to defend them logically, the early Greek philosophers pushed thought in a new direction. This new approach allowed a critical analysis of theories, whereas myths, accepted unconditionally on faith and authority, did not promote discussion and questioning. For the most part these early Greek philosophers rejected the old mythical explanations of nature. Nevertheless, when they proclaimed the unity and orderliness of nature and that an ultimate reality underlies the finite world, they were also expressing ideas crucial to religious thought.

These early philosophers made possible theoretical thinking and the systematization of knowledge—as distinct from the mere observation and collection of data. This systematization of knowledge extended into several areas. Greek mathematicians, for example, organized the Egyptians' practical experience with land measurements into the logical and coherent science of geometry; they established mathematics as an ordered system based on fundamental premises and necessary connections, and they developed logical procedures for mathematical proofs. Both Babylonians and Egyptians had performed fairly complex mathematical operations, but unlike the Greeks, they made no attempt to prove underlying mathematical principles—to demonstrate that certain conclusions must flow from certain hypotheses. In another area, Babylonian priests observed the heavens for religious reasons, believing that the stars revealed the wishes of the gods. The Greeks used the data collected by the Babylonians, but not for a religious purpose; they sought to discover the geometrical laws that underlie the motions of heavenly bodies.

A parallel development occurred in medicine. No Near Eastern medical text explicitly attacked magical beliefs and practices. In contrast, Greek doctors, because of the philosophers' work, were able to distinguish between magic and medicine. The school of the Greek physician Hippocrates (c. 460–c. 377 B.C.), located on the island of Cos, off the Asia Minor coast, was influenced by the thought of the early Greek cosmologists. Hippocratic physicians recorded in detail their observations of ill patients, classified symptoms, predicted the future course of the disease, and denounced supernatural and magical explanations and cures.

I am about to discuss the disease called "sacred." It is not, in my opinion, any more divine or sacred than any other disease, but has a natural cause, and its supposed divine origin is due to men's inexperience, and to their wonder at its peculiar character. Now . . . men continue to believe in its divine origin because they are at a loss to understand it. . . . My own view is that those who first attributed a sacred character to this malady were like the magicians, purifiers, charlatans, and quacks of our own day; men who claim great piety and superior knowledge. Being at a loss, and having no treatment which would help, they concealed and sheltered themselves behind superstition, and called this illness sacred, in order that their utter ignorance might not be manifest.[18]

In rejecting the concept of sacred diseases, the Hippocratic school inaugurated the growth of a scientific approach to medicine.

The Sophists: A Rational Investigation of Human Culture

In their effort to understand the external world, the cosmologists had created the tools of reason. These early Greek thinkers were developing a new and profound awareness of the mind's capacity for theoretical thinking. And equally important, they were establishing the mind's autonomy—its ability to inquire into any subject relying solely on its own power to think. Greek thinkers then turned away from the world of nature and attempted a rational investigation of people and society. The *Sophists* exemplified this shift in focus. They were professional teachers who wandered from city to city teaching rhetoric, grammar, poetry, gymnastics, mathematics, and music. The Sophists insisted that it was futile to speculate about the first principles of the universe, for such knowledge was beyond the grasp of the human mind. Instead, they urged individuals to improve themselves and their cities by applying reason to the tasks of citizenship and statesmanship.

The Sophists answered a practical need in Athens, which had been transformed into a wealthy and dynamic imperial state after the Persian Wars. Because the Sophists claimed that they could teach *political* areté—the skill to formulate the right laws and policies for cities and the art of eloquence and persuasion needed for success in public life—they were sought as tutors by politically ambitious young men, especially in Athens. The Western humanist tradition owes much to the Sophists, who examined political and ethical problems, cultivated the minds of their students, and invented formal secular education.

Traditionally, the Greeks had drawn a sharp distinction between Greeks, the bearers of an enlightened civilization, and uncivilized and immoderate non-Greeks, whom they called barbarians, and they held that some people were slaves by nature. Euripides expressed these sentiments: "It is natural for Hellenes to rule barbarians and not . . . for barbarians to rule Hellenes. They are a slave race, Hellenes are free."[19] Some Sophists in the fourth century B.C. arrived at a broader conception of

humanity. They asserted that slavery was based on force or chance, that people were not slaves or masters by nature, and indeed that all people, Greek and non-Greek, were fundamentally alike.

The Sophists were philosophical relativists; that is, they held that no truth is universally valid. Protagoras, a fifth-century Sophist, said that "man is the measure of all things." By this he meant that good and evil, truth and falsehood, are matters of individual judgment; there are no universal standards that fit all people at all times.

In applying reason critically to human affairs, the Sophists attacked the traditional religious and moral values of Athenian society. Some Sophists taught that speculation about the divine was useless. Others went further by asserting that religion was just a human invention to ensure obedience to traditions and laws.

The Sophists also applied reason to law, with the same effect: the undermining of traditional authority. The laws of a given city, they asserted, did not derive from the gods; nor were they based on any objective, universal, and timeless standards of justice and good, for such standards did not exist. Each community determined for itself what was good or bad, just or unjust. Beginning with this premise, some Sophists simply urged that laws be changed to meet new circumstances. More radical Sophists argued that law was merely something made by the most powerful citizens for their own benefit. This principle had dangerous implications: first, law did not need to be obeyed because it rested on no higher principle than might; and second, the strong should do what they have the power to do, and the weak must accept what they cannot resist. Both interpretations were disruptive of community life, for they stressed the selfish interests of the individual over the general welfare of the city.

Some Sophists combined this assault on law with an attack on the ancient Athenian idea of *sophrosyne*—moderation and self-discipline—because it denied human instincts. Instead of moderation, they urged that individuals maximize pleasure and trample underfoot the traditions that restricted them from fully expressing their desires. To these radical Sophists, the concept of sophrosyne was invented by the weak to enslave nobler natures.

In subjecting traditions to the critique of reason, the radical Sophists triggered an intellectual and spiritual crisis. Their doctrines encouraged loss of respect for authority, disobedience to law, neglect of civic duty, and selfish individualism. These attitudes became widespread during and after the Peloponnesian War, dangerously weakening community bonds.

Figure 3.3 Bust of Socrates Socrates wanted to subject all human beliefs and behavior to the scrutiny of reason. He believed that reason was the only proper guide to the most crucial problem of human existence: the question of good and evil. *(Hirmer Fotoarchiv)*

Socrates: Shaping the Rational Individual

In attempting to comprehend nature, the cosmologists had discovered theoretical reason. The Sophists then applied theoretical reason to society. In the process, they created a profound problem for Athens and other city–states: the need to restore the authority of law and a respect for moral values. Conservatives argued that the only way to do so was by renewing allegiance to the sacred traditions that the Sophists had undermined.

Socrates (Figure 3.3), one of the most extraordinary figures in the history of Western civilization, took a different position. Born in Athens, probably in 469 B.C., about ten years after the Persian Wars, he was executed in 399 B.C., five years after the end of the Peloponnesian War. His life spanned the glory years of Greece, when Athenian culture and democracy were at their height, as well as the tragic years of the lengthy and shattering war with Sparta.

Both the Sophists and Socrates continued the tradition of reason initiated by the cosmologists, but unlike the cosmologists, both felt that knowledge of the individual and society was more important than knowledge of nature. For both, the old mythological traditions, which had served as a foundation for religion and morality, were no longer valid. Socrates and the Sophists endeavored to improve the individual and thought that this could be accomplished through education. Despite these similarities, Socrates' teaching marks a profound break with the Sophist movement.

Socrates attacked the Sophists' relativism, holding that people should regulate their behavior in accordance with universal values. As he saw it, the Sophists taught skills but had no insights into questions that really mattered: What is the purpose of life? What are the values by which humans should live? How do people perfect their character? Here the Sophists failed, said Socrates; they taught the ambitious to succeed in politics, but persuasive oratory and clever reasoning do not instruct a person in the art of living. He felt that the Sophists had attacked the old system of beliefs but had not provided the individual with a satisfactory replacement.

Socrates' central concern was the perfection of individual human character, the achievement of moral excellence. Moral values, for Socrates, did not derive either from a transcendent God, as they did for the Hebrews, or from an inherited mythic-religious tradition. They were attained when the individual regulated his life according to objective standards arrived at through rational reflection; that is, when reason became the formative, guiding, and ruling agency of the soul. For Socrates, true education meant the shaping of character according to values discovered through the active use of reason.

Socrates wanted to subject all human beliefs and behavior to the scrutiny of reason and in this way remove ethics from the realm of authority, tradition, dogma, superstition, and myth. He believed that reason was the only proper guide to the most crucial problem of human existence: the question of good and evil. Socrates taught that rational inquiry was a priceless tool, allowing one to test opinions, weigh the merit of ideas, and alter beliefs on the basis of knowledge. To Socrates, when people engaged in critical self-examination and strove tirelessly to perfect their nature, they liberated themselves from prevailing opinions and traditions and based their conduct on convictions that they could rationally defend. Socrates believed that people with questioning minds could not be swayed by sophistic eloquence nor delude themselves into thinking that they knew something when they really did not.

DIALECTICS In urging Athenians to think rationally about the problems of human existence, Socrates offered no systematic ethical theory, no list of ethical precepts. What he did supply was a method of inquiry called *dialectics,* or logical discussion. As Socrates used it, a dialectical exchange between individuals (or with oneself), a *dialogue,* was the essential source of knowledge. It forced people out of their apathy and smugness and made them aware of their ignorance. It compelled them to examine their thoughts critically; to confront illogical, inconsistent, dogmatic, and imprecise assertions; and to express their ideas in clearly defined terms.

Dialectics affirmed that the acquisition of knowledge was a creative act. The human mind could not be coerced into knowing; it was not a passive vessel into which a teacher poured knowledge. The dialogue compelled the individual to play an active role in acquiring ideas and values by which to live. In a dialogue, individuals became thinking participants in a quest for knowledge. Through relentless cross-examination, Socrates induced his partner in discourse to explain and justify his opinions rationally, for only thus did knowledge become a part of one's being.

Dialogue implied that reason was meant to be used in relations between human beings and that they could learn from each other, help each other, teach each other, and improve each other. It implied further that the human mind could and should make rational choices. To deal rationally with oneself and with others is the distinctive mark of being human. Through the dialectical method, people could make ethical choices, impose rules on themselves, and give form to their existence.

For Socrates, the highest form of excellence was taking control of one's life and shaping it according to ethical values reached through reflection. The good life is attained by the exercise of reason and the development of intelligence—this precept is the essence of Socratic teaching. Socrates made the individual the center of the universe, reason central to the individual, and moral worth the central aim of human life. In Socrates, Greek humanism found its highest expression.

THE EXECUTION OF SOCRATES Socrates devoted much of his life to the mission of persuading his fellow Athenians to think critically about how they lived their lives. "No greater good can happen to a man than to discuss human excellence every day,"[20] he said. Always self-controlled and never raising his voice in anger, Socrates engaged any willing Athenian in conversation about his values. Through probing questions, he tried to stir people out of their complacency and make them realize how directionless and purposeless their lives were.

For many years, Socrates challenged Athenians without suffering harm, for Athens was generally distinguished by its freedom of speech and thought. In the uncertain times during and immediately after the Peloponnesian War, however, Socrates made enemies. When he was seventy, he was accused of corrupting the youth of the city and of not believing in the city's gods but in other, new divinities. Underlying these accusations was the fear that Socrates was a troublemaker, a subversive, a Sophist who threatened the state by subjecting its ancient and sacred values to the critique of thought.

Socrates denied the charges and conducted himself with great dignity at his trial, refusing to grovel and beg forgiveness. Instead, he defined his creed:

> If you think that a man of any worth at all ought to . . . think of anything but whether he is acting justly or unjustly, and as a good or a bad man would act, you are mistaken. . . . If you were therefore to say to me, "Socrates, . . . we will let you go, but on the condition that you give up this investigation of yours, and philosophy. If you are found following these pursuits again you shall die." I say, if you offered to let me go on these terms, I should reply: . . . "As long as I have breath and strength I will not give up philosophy and exhorting you and declaring the truth to every one of you whom I meet, saying, as I am accustomed, 'My good friend, you are a citizen of Athens . . . are you not ashamed of caring so much for making of money and for fame and prestige, when you neither think nor care about wisdom and truth and the improvement of your soul?'"[21]

Convicted by an Athenian court, Socrates was ordered to drink poison. Had he attempted to appease the jurors, he probably would have been given a light punishment, but he would not disobey the commands of his conscience and alter his principles, even under threat of death.

Socrates did not write down his philosophy and beliefs. We are able to construct a coherent account of his life and ideals largely through the works of his most important disciple, Plato.

Plato: The Rational Society

Plato (c. 429–347 B.C.) used his master's teachings to create a comprehensive system of philosophy, which embraced the metaphysical world, the natural world, and the social world. But Plato had a more ambitious goal than Socrates' moral reformation of the individual. He tried to arrange political life according to rational rules and held that

Socrates' quest for personal morality could not succeed unless the community was also transformed on the basis of reason. Virtually all the problems discussed by Western philosophers for the past two millennia were raised by Plato. We focus on two of his principal concerns, the theory of Ideas and that of the just state.

THEORY OF IDEAS   Socrates had taught that universal standards of right and justice exist and are arrived at through thought. Building on the insights of his teacher Socrates and of Parmenides, who said that reality is known only through the mind, Plato postulated the existence of a higher world of reality, independent of the world of things that we experience every day. This higher reality, he said, is the world of true Being, the realm of Ideas, or *Forms*—unchanging, eternal, absolute, and universal standards of beauty, goodness, justice, and truth. To live in accordance with these standards constitutes the good life; to know these forms is to grasp ultimate truth.

Truth resides in this world of Forms and not in the world of change, the world of Becoming, which is made known through the senses. For example, a person can never draw a perfect square, but the properties of a perfect square exist in the world of Forms. Also, a sculptor observes many bodies, and they all possess some flaw; in his mind's eye, he tries to penetrate the world of Ideas and to reproduce with art a perfect body. Again, the ordinary person only forms an opinion of what beauty is from observing beautiful things; the philosopher, aspiring to true knowledge, goes beyond what he sees and tries to grasp with his mind the Idea of beauty. Similarly, the ordinary individual has only a superficial understanding of justice or goodness; a true conception of justice or goodness is available only to the philosopher, whose mind can leap from worldly particulars to an ideal world beyond space and time.

It is possible for the philosopher to come to a knowledge of the Ideas in the world of Being, said Plato, because he understands the relationship between the body and the immortal soul. Plato taught that the soul (the mind or the *psyche*) originates in the higher world of Being and thus has an affinity with the eternal Ideas. However, because in this life the soul exists in the body, it is inhibited from knowing the Ideas.

Plato said that genuine philosophers are "those whose passion it is to see the truth." They will attempt to know the eternal standards of beauty, justice, and goodness that exist in the world of Forms through their minds, or psyches, not through the senses. Plato says that the ordinary person, basing opinion on everyday experience, has an imperfect understanding of beauty, goodness, and justice, whereas the philosopher, through reason, reaches beyond sense perception to the realm of Being and discovers truth.

The distinction between a higher world of truth and a lower world of imperfection, deception, and illusion is illustrated in Plato's famous Allegory of the Cave (Figure 3.4) in which he compares those persons without a knowledge of the Forms to prisoners chained to the walls in a dark cave. There is a screen in front of them and a light behind the screen that throws shadows onto the screen of artificial objects such as wooden and stone figures of men and animals. To the prisoners, the shadows of the artificial objects constitute reality. When a freed prisoner ascends from the cave to the sunlight, he sees a totally different world. Returning to the cave, he tries to tell the prisoners that the shadows are only poor imitations of reality, but they laugh at him, for their opinions have been shaped by the only world they know. The meaning of the parable is clear: The philosophers who ascend to the higher world of Forms possess true knowledge; everyone else possesses mere opinions, deceptive beliefs, and illusions. The philosophers have a duty to guide the ignorant.

Plato saw the world of phenomena as unstable, transitory, and imperfect, whereas his realm of Ideas was eternal and universally valid. For him, true wisdom was to be obtained through knowledge of the Ideas, not the imperfect reflections of the Ideas perceived with the senses. A champion of reason, Plato aspired to study human life and arrange it according to universally valid standards. In contrast to sophistic relativism, he maintained that objective and eternal standards do exist.

Although Plato advocated the life of reason and wanted to organize society according to rational rules, his writing also reveals a religious–mystical side. This facet of Plato's thought can be seen in his idea of reincarnation, or the transmigration of souls. Each human soul preexisted in the world of Ideas. When the soul is born into a human body, it forgets the Ideas because the body obstructs such knowledge. When the philosopher achieves the difficult task of knowing the Ideas, he is in essence remembering what his psyche once knew. Learning, therefore, is a process of recollecting what one already knew prior to the soul becoming incarnate in a body. At times, Plato seems like a mystic seeking to escape from this world into a higher reality, a realm that is without earth's evil and injustice. Because Platonism is a two-world philosophy, it has had an important effect on religious thought. In subsequent chapters, we examine the influence of Platonic otherworldliness on later philosopher–mystics and Christian thinkers.

Figure 3.4 Allegory of the Cave Plato distinguished between a higher world of truth and a lower world of imperfection. He compares people without knowledge of the higher world to prisoners chained to the walls in a dark cave. There is a screen in front of them and a light behind the screen that throws shadows onto the screen of artificial objects, which the prisoners interpret as reality. When a freed prisoner ascends from the cave into the sunlight (the realm of Truth), he realizes that a totally different reality exists. *(From* The Great Dialogues of Plato, *translated by W. H. D. Rouse. Used by permission of Dutton Signet, a division of Penguin Books USA Inc.)*

THE JUST STATE In adapting the rational legacy of Greek philosophy to politics, Plato constructed a comprehensive political theory. What the Greeks had achieved in practice—the movement away from mythic and theocratic politics—Plato accomplished on the level of thought: the fashioning of a rational model of the state.

Similar to Socrates, Plato attempted to resolve the problem caused by the radical Sophists: the undermining of traditional values. Socrates tried to dispel this spiritual crisis through a moral transformation of the individual, whereas Plato wanted the entire community to conform to rational principles. Plato said that if human beings are to live an ethical life, they must do it as citizens of a just and rational state. In an unjust state, people cannot achieve Socratic wisdom, for their souls will mirror the state's wickedness.

Plato had experienced the ruinous Peloponnesian War and the accompanying political turmoil. He saw Athens undergo one political crisis after another; most shocking of all, he had witnessed Socrates' trial and execution. Disillusioned by the corruption of Athenian morality and politics, Plato refused to participate in political life. He came to believe that under the Athenian constitution neither the morality of the individual Athenian nor the good of the state could be enhanced, and that Athens required moral and political reform founded on Socrates' philosophy. As Socrates had, and in contrast to the Sophists'

relativism, Plato sought permanent truth and moral certainty.

In his great dialogue, *The Republic,* Plato devised an ideal state, based on standards that would rescue his native Athens from the evils that had befallen it. *The Republic* attempted to analyze society rationally and to reshape the state so that individuals could fulfill the best within them and attain the Socratic goal of moral excellence. For Plato, the just state could not be founded on tradition (for inherited attitudes did not derive from rational standards) or on the doctrine of might being right (a principle taught by radical Sophists and practiced by Athenian statesmen). A just state, for Plato, conformed to universally valid principles and aimed at the moral improvement of its citizens, not at increasing its power and material possessions. Such a state required leaders distinguished by their wisdom and virtue, rather than by sophistic cleverness and eloquence.

Fundamental to Plato's political theory, as formulated in *The Republic,* was his criticism of Athenian democracy. An aristocrat by birth and temperament, Plato believed that it was foolish to expect the common person to think intelligently about foreign policy, economics, or other vital matters of state. Yet the common man was permitted to speak in the Assembly, to vote, and to be selected, by lot, for executive office. A second weakness of democracy was that leaders were chosen and followed for nonessential reasons, such as persuasive speech, good looks, wealth, and family background.

A third danger of democracy was that it could degenerate into anarchy, said Plato. Intoxicated by liberty, the citizens of a democracy could lose all sense of balance, self-discipline, and respect for law. A fourth weakness was that a demagogue could gain power by promising to plunder the rich to benefit the poor. Because of these inherent weaknesses of democracy, Plato insisted that Athens could not be saved by more doses of liberty. He believed that Athens would be governed properly only when the wisest people, the philosophers, attained power.

> Unless either philosophers become kings in their countries or those who are now called kings and rulers come to be sufficiently inspired with a genuine desire for wisdom; unless, that is to say, political power and philosophy meet together . . . there can be no rest from troubles . . . for states, nor yet, as I believe, for all mankind.[22]

Philosophers are the natural rulers of the state; only they are capable of a correct understanding of justice; only they have the wisdom to reform the state in the best interests of all its citizens.

Plato rejected the fundamental principle of Athenian democracy: that the average person is capable of participating sensibly in public affairs. People would not entrust the care of a sick person to just anyone, said Plato, nor would they allow a novice to guide a ship during a storm. Yet, in a democracy, amateurs were permitted to run the government and to supervise the education of the young; no wonder that Athenian society was disintegrating. Plato felt that these duties should be performed only by the best people in the city, the philosophers who would approach human problems with reason and wisdom derived from knowledge of the world of unchanging and perfect Ideas. Only those possessors of truth would be competent to rule, said Plato. Whereas Socrates believed that all people could base their actions on reason and acquire virtue, Plato maintained that only a few were capable of philosophical wisdom, and that these few were the state's natural rulers.

The organization of the state, as formulated in *The Republic,* is consistent with Plato's theory of Ideas and corresponds to his conception of the individual soul and of human nature. Plato held that the soul had three major capacities: reason (the pursuit of knowledge), spiritedness (self-assertion, courage, ambition), and desire (the "savage many-headed monster" that relishes food, sex, and possessions). In the well-governed soul, spiritedness and desire are guided by reason and knowledge—standards derived from the world of Ideas.

Plato divided people into three groups: those who demonstrated philosophical ability should be rulers; those whose natural bent revealed exceptional courage should be soldiers; and those driven by desire, the great masses, should be producers (tradespeople, artisans, or farmers). In what was a radical departure from the general attitudes of the times, Plato held that men and women should receive the same education and have equal access to all occupations and public positions, including philosopher–ruler. Generally speaking, Plato's view of women is ambivalent. Although the progressive position he took in the *Republic* is also evident in the *Symposium,* where he introduces a female philosopher whose wisdom even Socrates respects, in a later dialogue, *Timaeus,* Plato admits the natural inferiority of women.

Plato felt that the entire community must recognize the primacy of the intellect, and he sought to create a harmonious state in which each individual performed what he or she was best qualified to do and preferred to do. This would be a just state, said Plato, for it would recognize human inequalities and diversities and make the best possible use of them for the entire community.

In *The Republic,* the philosophers were selected by a rigorous system of education open to all children. Those not demonstrating sufficient intelligence or strength of character were to be weeded out to become workers or warriors, depending on their natural aptitudes. After many years of education and practical military and administrative experience, the philosophers were to be entrusted with political power. If they had been properly educated, the philosopher–rulers would not seek personal wealth or personal power; they would be concerned only with pursuing justice and serving the community. The philosophers were to be absolute rulers. Although the people would have lost their right to participate in political decisions, they would have gained a well-governed state, whose leaders, distinguished by their wisdom, integrity, and sense of responsibility, sought only the common good. Only thus, said Plato, could the individual and the community achieve well-being.

Aristotle: Synthesis of Greek Thought

Aristotle (384–322 B.C.) stands at the apex of Greek thought because he achieved a creative synthesis of the knowledge and theories of earlier thinkers. Aristotle studied at Plato's Academy for twenty years. Later, he became tutor to young Alexander the Great, the son of Philip of Macedon. After Alexander had inherited his father's throne, Aristotle returned to Athens and founded a school, the Lyceum.

The range of Aristotle's interests and intellect is extraordinary. He was the leading expert of his time in every field of knowledge, with the possible exception of mathematics. Even a partial listing of his works shows the universal character of his mind and his all-consuming passion to understand the worlds of nature and of humankind: *Logic, Physics, On the Heavens, On the Soul, On the Parts of Animals, Metaphysics, Nicomachean Ethics, Politics, Rhetoric,* and *Poetics.*

Aristotle undertook the monumental task of organizing and systematizing the thought of the Pre-Socratics, Socrates, and Plato. He shared with the natural philosophers a desire to understand the physical universe; he shared with Socrates and Plato the belief that reason was a person's highest faculty and that the polis was the primary formative institution of Greek life. Out of the myriad of Aristotle's achievements, we will discuss only three: his critique of Plato's theory of Ideas, his ethical thought, and his political thought.

CRITIQUE OF PLATO'S THEORY OF IDEAS   As Democritus did before him, Aristotle renewed confidence in sense perception; he wanted to swing the pendulum back from Plato's higher world to the material world. Aristotle possessed a scientist's curiosity to understand the facts of nature and appreciated the world of phenomena, of concrete things. He respected knowledge obtained through the senses.

Aristotle retained Plato's stress on universal principles, but he wanted these principles to derive from human experience with the material world. To the practical and empirically minded Aristotle, the Platonic notion of an independent and separate world of Forms beyond space and time seemed contrary to common sense. To comprehend reality, said Aristotle, one should not escape into another world. For him, Plato's two-world philosophy suffered from too much mystery, mysticism, and poetic fancy; moreover, Plato slighted the world of facts and objects revealed through sight, hearing, and touch, a world that Aristotle valued. Like Plato, Aristotle desired to comprehend the essence of things and held that understanding universal principles is the ultimate aim of knowledge. But unlike Plato, he did not turn away from the world of things to obtain such knowledge.

For Aristotle, the Forms were not located in a higher world outside and beyond phenomena but existed in things themselves. He said that through human experience with such things as human beings, horses, and white objects, the essence of human, horse, and whiteness can be discovered through reason; the Form of Human, the Form of Horse, and the Form of Whiteness can be determined. These universals, which apply to all men, all horses, and all white things, were for both Aris-

totle and Plato the true objects of knowledge. For Plato, these Forms existed independently of particular objects; the Forms for men or horses or whiteness or triangles or temples existed, whether or not representations of these Ideas in the form of material objects were made known to the senses. For Aristotle, however, universal Ideas could not be determined without examination of particular things. Whereas Plato's use of reason tended to stress otherworldliness, Aristotle tried to bring philosophy back to earth.

By holding that certainty in knowledge comes from reason alone and not from the senses, Plato was predisposed toward mathematics and metaphysics. By stressing the importance of knowledge acquired through the rational examination of sense experience, Aristotle favored the development of empirical sciences—physics, biology, zoology, botany, and other disciplines based on the observation and investigation of nature and the recording of data. Aristotle maintained that theory must not conflict with facts and must make them more intelligible, and that it was the task of science to arrange facts into a system of knowledge.

ETHICAL THOUGHT   Aristotle believed, as Socrates and Plato did, that a knowledge of ethics was possible and that it must be based on reason. For him, ethical thought derived from a realistic appraisal of human nature and a commonsense attitude toward life. In *Nicomachean Ethics,* he offered this appraisal, as well as a practical guide to proper conduct. The good life, for Aristotle, was the examined life; it meant making intelligent decisions when confronted with specific problems. Individuals could achieve happiness when they exercised the distinctively human trait of reasoning, when they applied their knowledge relevantly to life, and when their behavior was governed by intelligence and not by whim, tradition, or authority.

Aristotle recognized that people are not entirely rational, that the human personality reveals a passionate element that can never be eradicated or ignored. Aristotle held that surrendering completely to desire meant descending to the level of beasts, but that denying the passions and living as an ascetic was a foolish and unreasonable rejection of human nature. He maintained that by proper training, people could learn to regulate their desires. They could achieve moral well-being, or virtue, when they avoided extremes of behavior and rationally chose the way of moderation, which he defined as the mean between two extremes. For example, some people "become angry at the wrong things, more than is right, and longer, and cannot be appeased until they inflict vengeance or punishment." At the other extreme, foolish and slavish people endure every insult without defending themselves. Between these extremes is "the man who is angry at the right thing and with the right people, and, further, as he ought, when he ought, and as long as he ought. . . . [T]he good-tempered man tends to be unperturbed and not to be led by passion."[23] "Nothing in excess" is the key to Aristotle's ethics.

Aristotle believed that the contemplative life of the philosopher would yield perfect happiness. The pursuit of philosophical wisdom and beauty, he stated, offered "pleasures marvelous for their purity and their enduringness."[24] But Aristotle did not demand more from an individual than human nature would allow. He did not set impossible standards for behavior, recognizing that all persons cannot pursue the life of contemplation, for some lack sufficient leisure or intelligence. However, by applying reason to human affairs, all individuals could experience a good life.

POLITICAL THOUGHT   Aristotle's *Politics* complements his *Ethics*. To live the good life, he said, a person must do it as a member of a political community. Only the polis would provide people with an opportunity to lead a rational and moral existence, that is, to fulfill their human potential. With this assertion, Aristotle demonstrated a typically Greek attitude. At the very moment when his pupil Alexander the Great was constructing a world-state that unified Greece and Persia, Aristotle defended the traditional system of independent city–states. Indeed, his *Politics* summed up the polis-centered orientation of Hellenic civilization.

Also in typically Greek fashion, Aristotle did not want women to participate in the political life of the city. Unlike Plato, who, in *The Republic,* wished to give women an equal opportunity with men, Aristotle, in his *Politics,* put women in an inferior category and maintained that the free male should rule over women. Because Aristotle believed that women shared in the rational faculty of soul to a lesser degree than men, he also asserted that it was a woman's place to obey and to be silent.

Like Plato, Aristotle presumed that political life could be rationally understood and intelligently directed. In *Politics,* as in *Ethics,* he adopted a commonsense, practical attitude. He did not aim at utopia but wanted to find the most effective form of government for most men in typical circumstances. In typically Greek fashion, Aristotle held that enhancing the good of the community is nobler and more virtuous than doing good for oneself, however worthy the act.

Aristotle emphasized the importance of the rule of law. He placed his trust in law rather than in individuals, for they are subject to passions. Aristotle recognized that at times laws should be altered, but he recommended great caution; otherwise, people would lose respect for law and legal procedure.

> For the law has no power to command obedience except that of habit, which can only be given by time, so that a readiness to change from old to new laws enfeebles the power of the law.[25]

Tyranny and revolution, Aristotle said, can threaten the rule of law and the well-being of the citizen. To prevent revolution, the state must maintain

> the spirit of obedience to law, more especially in small matters; for transgression creeps in unperceived and at last ruins the state. [This cannot be done] unless the young are trained by habit and education in the spirit of the constitution. [To live as one pleases] is contradictory to the true interests of the state. . . . Men should not think it slavery to live according to the rule of the constitution, for it is their salvation.[26]

Aristotle held "that the best political community is formed by citizens of the middle class [those with a moderate amount of property], and that those states are likely to be well-administered in which the middle class is large and stronger if possible than the other classes [the wealthy and the poor]." Both the rich, who excel in "beauty, strength, birth, [and] wealth," and the poor, who are "very weak or very much disgraced [find it] difficult to follow rational principle. Of these two the one sort grow into violence and great criminals, the other into rogues and petty rascals." The rich are unwilling "to submit to authority . . . for when they are boys, by reason of the luxury in which they are brought up, they never learn even at school, the habit of obedience." Consequently, the wealthy "can only rule despotically." On the other hand, the poor "are too degraded to command and must be ruled like slaves."[27] Middle-class citizens are less afflicted by envy than the poor and are more likely than the rich to view their fellow citizens as equals. Aristotle saw the rule of the middle class as the best formula for balancing the well-being of the individual with that of the community.

The Enduring Impact of Greek Philosophy

Philosophy is a Greek word meaning "love of wisdom." The Greeks are regarded as the founders of Western philosophy because they were the first to self-consciously and critically examine inherited beliefs. In the process, they rejected mythical explanations for natural occurrences and attempted a rational analysis of both physical nature and human society. They established a crucial principle of Western thought: the autonomy of reason. The mind accepts no higher authority—inherited religious beliefs, for example—than the conclusions of reason.

The Greeks laid the foundations of the principal fields of philosophy still explored today—cosmology, metaphysics, ethics, political theory, and logic. Many of the great questions discussed by philosophers for more than two thousand years were first raised by the Greeks: How did all things in nature come to be? What is reality? What is the good life? Are there universal standards of truth, justice, and beauty that apply to all people at all times? What is the best form of government? Greek philosophers explored these fundamental questions with such great insight that contemporary thinkers still read and quote their writings.

There is also a close link between Greek philosophy and Christian thought. Many early Christian thinkers respected Greek learning and recognized its value for Christianity. They used the logic and terminology of Greek philosophy to demonstrate that Christian teachings, which they knew to be true on the basis of faith—the existence of God, for example—could also be shown to be logically true. This practice of demonstrating and explaining the revealed truth of Christianity in a rational and systematic way became a crucial feature of Christian thought during the Middle Ages. Consequently, Christian thinkers kept Greek philosophy alive with its rigorous demand for logical thinking. That medieval Christian thinkers produced a richly structured theology, which has remained an indelible part of the Christian tradition, was due to their employing the methods and language of Greek philosophy.

But medieval Christian thinkers, unlike the ancient Greeks, did not regard reason as autonomous. They used Greek philosophy to demonstrate the truth of Christian teachings, never to challenge or reject them. Reason, they held, must be guided by God's revelation as taught by the church. In the modern world, reason would again reassert its autonomy. This rejection of medieval views of nature and society because they seemed to conflict with reason is a crucial factor in the emergence of modern Western civilization.

Key Terms

myths	mystery religions
legends	catharsis
Dark Age	metaphysics
polis	Sophists
Delian League	dialectics
hubris	Forms
cosmogony	

Notes

1. James Shiel, ed., *Greek Thought and the Rise of Christianity* (New York: Barnes & Noble, 1968), pp. 5–6.
2. H. D. F. Kitto, *The Greeks* (Baltimore: Penguin Books, 1950), p. 78.
3. Thucydides, *The Peloponnesian War,* trans. Benjamin Jowett (Oxford: Clarendon Press, 1881), bk. 2, chap. 37.
4. Aristotle, *Politics,* in *Basic Works of Aristotle,* ed. Richard McKeon (New York: Random House, 1941), p. 1132.
5. Homer, *The Iliad,* trans. E. V. Rieu (Baltimore: Penguin Books, 1950), p. 23.
6. Kitto, *The Greeks,* p. 60.
7. Homer, *The Iliad,* p. 405.
8. Ibid., pp. 450–451.
9. Werner Jaeger, *Paideia: The Ideals of Greek Culture,* trans. Gilbert Highet (New York: Oxford University Press, 1945), 1:8.
10. C. M. Bowra, *Homer* (London: Gerald Duckworth, 1972), p. 72.
11. *Hesiod,* trans. Richmond Lattimore. (Ann Arbor: The University of Michigan Press, 1973), p. 125.
12. Ibid., pp. 130–132.
13. Ibid., p. 67.
14. Ibid., p. 25.
15. Ibid., p. 51.
16. Edith Hamilton, *The Greek Way to Western Civilization* (New York: New American Library, 1963), p. 208
17. John N. Theodorakopoulos, "The Origins of Science and Philosophy," in *History of the Hellenic World: The Archaic Period,* ed. G. A. Christopoulos and J. C. Bastias (University Park, Pa.: Pennsylvania State University Press, 1975), p. 438.
18. Quoted in George Sarton, *A History of Science,* vol. 1 (Cambridge, Mass.: Harvard University Press, 1952), pp. 355–356.
19. Euripides, *Iphigenia at Aulis in Ten Plays by Euripides,* trans. Moses Hadas and John McClean (New York: Bantam Books, 1960) p. 348 (lines 1400–1401).
20. Plato, *Apology,* trans. F. J. Church, rev. R. D. Cummings (Indianapolis: Bobbs-Merrill, 1956), sec. 28.
21. Ibid., secs. 16–17.
22. Plato, *The Republic,* trans. F. M. Cornford (New York: Oxford University Press, 1945), pp. 178–179.
23. *Nichomachean Ethics,* in *Basic Works of Aristotle,* ed. Richard McKeon (New York: Random House, 1941), p. 996.
24. Ibid., p. 1104.
25. *Politics,* in *Basic Works of Aristotle,* ed. McKeon, p. 1164.
26. Ibid., pp. 1246, 1251.
27. Ibid., pp. 1220–1221.

Hellenic Civilization II: The Arts and Literature

THE TRENDS SEEN IN GREEK PHILOSOPHY—a rational inquiry into nature and society and an awareness of human personality—were also evident in Greek art and literature. As in Greek philosophy and politics, Greek art and literature, too, applied reason to human experience and made the transition from a mythopoeic–religious worldview to a world perceived as orderly and rational. Greek writers and artists gradually transformed the supernatural religious themes with which they were at first preoccupied into secular human themes.

Greek artists, just as Greek philosophers did, proclaimed the importance and creative capacity of the individual. They exemplified the humanist spirit that characterized all aspects of Greek culture. Classical art placed people in their natural environment, made the human form the focal point of attention, and exalted the nobility, dignity, self-assurance, and beauty of the human being.

As a Greek sculptor shaped a clear visual image of the human form, so a Greek dramatist brought the inner life of human beings, their fears, and their hopes into sharp focus and tried to find the deeper meaning of human experience. Thus, both art and drama evidenced the growing self-awareness of the individual.

The natural philosophers searched for principles or laws that they thought governed the physical world. Consistent with this emerging rational–scientific outlook, dramatists believed there were inherent principles of order in the social world that, if violated, brought disaster to the individual and the community. And Greek artists and musicians tried to capture with their art the harmony, unity, and principles of movement that operate in nature.

Greek art and literature served as models for the Romans, inspired the humanists and artists of the Italian Renaissance, and continued to stir the creative energies of writers and artists into modern times.

LYRIC POETRY

During the seventh century B.C., *lyric poetry* began to supplant epic poetry. Greek lyric poetry was intended to be sung to the musical accompaniment of a lyre, a stringed instrument. In fact the word *lyric* means "accompanied by the lyre." The earliest examples of lyric poetry (in which rhythm, melody, and words were inseparably linked) have all been lost. Unlike the epic poetry of Homer, which focused on the deeds of great warriors, lyric poetry was much

Praxiteles, *Aphrodite of Knidos*, c. 350 B.C., Roman copy, marble, height 6′8″ (2 m), Vatican Museum, Rome

The statue was rendered for Aphrodite's sanctuary at Knidos in Asia Minor. It is significant because it is one of the earliest depictions of a female nude.

(Vatican Museums)

more concerned with a poet's own opinions and inner emotions.

Sappho

Sappho, who lived around 600 B.C. on the island of Lesbos, in Asia Minor, was the greatest female lyric poet in antiquity. A member of the aristocracy, Sappho was married to a man named Cercylas, and she had one daughter, Cleïs. She was famous for her lyric poetry, but only one complete poem, of 28 lines, remains; the rest of her poems exist only in fragments. Sappho actually created a metric stanza that bears the name *Sapphic*.

Sappho established a "finishing" school to teach music and singing to well-to-do girls and to prepare them for marriage. With great tenderness, she wrote poems of friendship and love: "Some say the fairest thing on earth is a troop of horsemen, others a band of foot-soldiers, others a squadron of ships. But I say the fairest thing is the beloved."[1] And of her daughter Cleïs, she wrote:

> I have a child; so fair
> As golden flowers is she,
> My Cleïs, all my care.
> I'd not give her away
> For Lydia's* wide sway
> Nor lands men long to see.[2]

Although some of her poems are about love between women and men, some verses addressed to women suggest a homoerotic interest. In one ode, Sappho implores the goddess Aphrodite to assist her in making her female lover come back to her. Aphrodite replies:

> Who now, oh Sappho, who wrongs you?
> If she flees you now, she will pursue you;
> if she won't accept what you give, she'll give it;
> if she doesn't love you, she'll love you soon now,
>   even unwilling.

To which Sappho responds:

> Come to me again, and release me from this
> want past bearing. All that my heart desires to
> happen—make it happen. And stand beside me,
>   goddess, my ally.[3]

Sappho also expressed homoerotic desire in this surviving fragment:

> Please Abanthis, your Sappho calls you:
> won't you take this Lydian lyre and play
> another song to Gongyla† while desire still
>   flutters your heart-strings
> for that girl, that beautiful girl: her dress's
> clinging makes you shake when you see it[4]

The sensual and erotic nature of these poems indicates that Sappho was bisexual. This form of sexual behavior was tolerated in ancient Greece, says classicist Lyn Hatherly Wilson, "because it was not procreative, because it did not alter a woman's virginal status, or affect her entry into marriage and male/female relations, except in ways that were considered positive."[5]

Sappho's fame radiated widely. She was honored with coins and statues; six comedies were written with the title "Sappho"; and in Athens, her poetry was so popular that her portrait was placed in the Acropolis (see pp. 99, 101). Centuries later, Roman poets alluded to Sappho's poetry, and her influence continued into the Christian era.

Pindar

The aristocratic Pindar (c. 518–438 B.C.), another Greek lyric poet, was celebrated in antiquity as the greatest of all the lyric poets. Born near Thebes, as a boy he studied poetry in Athens, and about 474 B.C., he wrote a poem in praise of "glorious Athens . . . city of the gods."[6] The democratic ideals of Athens, however, challenged Pindar's idea of patrician privilege, and by the time he died in 438 B.C., the aristocratic society that he praised in his poems was nearing its end. Pindar's odes, which were meant to be sung or chanted, celebrated the virtues of victorious athletes in the Greek Games. Athletic talents and virtues, he believed, could not be acquired, but were innate in the athlete's aristocratic blood. In one of his poems of praise for a victorious athlete, Pindar expressed the aristocratic view of excellence. Although life is essentially tragic—triumphs are short-lived, misfortunes are many, and ultimately death overtakes all—man must still demonstrate his worth by striving for excellence.

> He who wins of a sudden, some noble prize
> In the rich years of youth
> Is raised high with hope; his manhood takes
>   wings;
> He has in his heart what is better than wealth
> But brief is the season of man's delight.
> Soon it falls to the ground;
> Some dire decision uproots it.
> —Thing of a day! such is man: a shadow in a
>   dream.
> Yet when god-given splendour visits him
> A bright radiance plays over him, and how
>   sweet is life![7]

---

* Kingdom in Asia Minor, to the east of Lesbos.

† Gongyla, a female friend of Abanthis, was also Sappho's friend.

The last of the great lyric poets, Pindar represented the earlier aristocratic era with its celebration of individual *areté*. After Pindar, lyric poetry declined and was replaced by tragedy.

MUSIC

Music was an important component of Greek culture. Vase paintings from the second millennium B.C. show musicians playing stringed and wooden instruments and dancers in processions accompanied by musical instruments. In the *Iliad,* Achilles tries to relieve his grief by singing and playing a stringed instrument. Lyric poetry was intended to be sung with instrumental accompaniment before an audience. Solo and choral singing were essential features of dramatic performances, and contests, festivals, and religious ceremonies included music. Greek thinkers, including Plato and Aristotle, wrote treatises on music in which they discussed its power to sway emotions and its role in educating youth. Aristotle, for example, valued music because it brought people pleasure and promoted relaxation. Maintaining that music also affected character by igniting a variety of moods—anger, pity, fear, frenzy, calmness—he said that some melodies are better suited than others for the ethical upbringing of youth.

The Greek contribution to music is consistent with its achievement in science, philosophy, literature, and the visual arts. Although music itself is a basic human activity extending back to prehistory, finding different expressions among the Mesopotamians, Egyptians, and Hebrews, it is only with the Greeks that music was lifted to the level of self-reflection and theory.

The design of instruments in earlier civilizations, such as the stringed instruments of Mesopotamia and Egypt, suggests awareness of the relationship between the length of a string and the pitch of the sound it produced. But the Greeks were the first to discern that the length of a string and the pitch of a sound could be expressed in mathematical ratios. The shorter the string, the greater the frequency of vibrations, and the higher the pitch; the longer the string, the slower the vibrations, and the lower the pitch.

In the sixth century B.C., the mathematician and philosopher Pythagoras formulated and defined mathematical laws governing the production of sound, which mark the origins of musical theory. Pythagoras observed that there was a change in intonation as a blacksmith struck an anvil with various hammers. Extending this principle, he determined that if a person stretched two strings to the same tension and divided one of them in half, the pitch of the shorter string was an octave higher than that of the longer string. Pythagoras concluded that music contains an inherent mathematical structure: There is a numerical ratio underlying each interval of a scale. This inherent mathematical order is the basis of harmony and accounts for sounds that are pleasing to the ear. He then extended this insight to the universe at large, concluding that mathematical ratios also governed the cosmos, which he referred to as "the music of the spheres."

Pythagoras asserted that each of the seven planets generated a specific note based on its distance from the stationary center of the universe, which was thought to be the earth. To parallel the notes associated with the seven planets, Pythagoras devised seven *modes* (modern-day musical scales)—the Hypodorian, Hypophrygian, Hypolydian, Dorian, Phrygian, Lydian, and Mixolydian—which, he believed, could make people sad, sentimental, angry, calm, or even moral. Like Plato and Aristotle after him, Pythagoras believed that music had an *ethos*—an inherent moral value—and that different types of music affected human temperament in a variety of ways. Pythagoras reputedly cured a man of drunkenness by using the Hypophrygian mode, whose melodies contained a curative power. Extending the principle that music was a branch of science, physicians at Epidauros and Pergamum also drew on its purported healing power.

Today, numerous doctors refer to the healing power of music as "The Mozart Effect" and use music therapy to relieve pain, to alleviate fatigue, and to promote mental health. Industrialists also have found that music fights fatigue, thereby promoting greater productivity among workers.

Plato applied Pythagoras' teachings about the music of the spheres, calling them "celestial harmonies." In his *Laws, Republic,* and *Timaeus,* Plato used musical metaphors to describe his vision of society patterned on the cosmic principles of harmony, symmetry, and balance. By the second century A.D., music was still viewed as a branch of mathematics by Ptolemy (see p. 138), as well as Nicomachus of Gerasa, a Pythagorean, who compiled *The Manual of Harmonics*—the first inclusive commentary on the universal principles inherent within the musical scale. During the Early Middle Ages, Boethius (see p. 215) was instrumental in transmitting the Pythagorean system of modes to the medieval world. Church musicians then transformed the Greek modes to correspond to the organization of the church service.

MUSICAL TERM	DEFINITION	EXAMPLE
Pitch	Refers to the frequency of vibration which produces a high or low quality of musical sound	Within an octave—do, re, mi, fa, so, la, ti, do—the vibration increases as the note gets higher
Interval	The distance in pitch between two notes (tones)	For example—*do-mi, re-fa, mi-so*, etc.
Tetrachord	A group of four notes the lowest and highest of which are separated by the interval of a perfect fourth	Based on four strings of the lyre; Pythagoras added an eighth string so that it had an octave
Octave	The interval that includes eight notes (e.g. *do-do, re-re,* etc); the highest note gives the impression of being a simple duplication of the first note. The ratio is 2:1, because the string for the higher note vibrates twice as fast per second as the string for the lower note and is said to be an octave higher	*Somewhere Over the Rainbow* the interval between "some" and "where" is an octave
The Interval of a Fifth	The fifth note above the first note (e.g. C-G or *do-so*)	*Twinkle, Twinkle, Little Star* the interval between the first "twinkle" and the second "twinkle" is a fifth
The Interval of a Fourth	The fourth note above the first note (e.g. C-F or *do-fa*)	*Here Comes the Bride* the interval between the "here" and "comes" is a fourth

Modern Extension of Pythagoras' Ratios—		Pythagoras' Ratios Applied		Combination of a Fifth and a Fourth—Creating an Octave
		Pitch literally has to do with frequency of vibration, i.e., cycles per second expressed as Hz = hertz; the following example is in the Key of C		
Prime	1:1			
Second	9:8			
Major Third	5:4	C	256 Hz	
Fourth	4:3	D	288 Hz	
Fifth	3:2	E	320 Hz	
Major Sixth	5:3	F	341 1/4 Hz	
Major Seventh	15:8	G	384 Hz	
Octave	2:1	A*	426 2/3 Hz	

(*very close to modern tuning pitch of A 440 Hz)

DRAMA

Greek tragedy, or drama, is inextricably linked to music and dance, as well as to religion. Originating in the sixth century B.C., in the religious festivals honoring Dionysos, the god of wine and agricultural fertility, Greek drama is the high point of Greek poetry. During the Great Dionysia, the religious festival celebrated in March in Athens, participants danced and sang hymns in honor of Dionysos. The hymns were performed by a group of singers called a **chorus**, a word derived from the Greek noun meaning "dance." The emotional impact of these hymns was intensified by the music, which was played on either a lyre or a wind instrument called an aulos. These hymns expressed a variety of emotions, such as courage, solemnity, frailty, boldness, enthusiasm, and sorrow, by means of one of the seven Greek modes.

Tragedy (*tragoidia*), which literally means "goat song," is an art form that developed before the Classical age, the height of Greek civilization. The Archaic age lasted from approximately 650 B.C. to 480 B.C. and the Classical age from about 480 B.C. to the death of Alexander the Great in 323 B.C. The early choric performances were probably linked to satyr plays, which dealt with the mythical half-man, half-goat attendants of Dionysos. In the latter part of the sixth century (c. 535 B.C.), the first actor, Thespis, stepped away from the chorus and engaged it in dialogue. By separating himself from the choral group, Thespis demonstrated a new awareness of the individual.

With only one actor and a chorus, however, the possibilities for dramatic action and human conflict were limited. Then Aeschylus introduced a second actor in his dramas, and Sophocles a third. Dialogue between individuals thus became possible. The Greek actors wore masks, and by changing them, each actor could play several roles in the same performance. This flexibility allowed the dramatists to depict the clash and interplay of human wills and passions on a greater scale. By the middle of the fifth century B.C., tragedies were performed regularly at religious and civic festivals.

The audience sat on wooden bleachers in the open-air, hillside theater (*theatron*). The acoustics of these stone theaters was so superb that a clear voice projected from the orchestra could be heard, without amplification, in the last row of the theater. In the staging of these tragedies, the all-male chorus generally danced and sang in a circular area called the *orchestra* ("dancing place"), which encircled an altar. Their costumes consisted of goatskins (only later did the costumes become elaborate), larger-than-life masks, and elevated shoes. Behind the orchestra, which occupied one-third of the theater, was the *skênê*, a structure through which performers could enter and exit; when painted, it was the only backdrop for the action. There were also two mechanical devices that were used for special effects. One was the *ekkyklêma,* a platform on wheels that could be moved onto the stage through one of the doors of the *skênê*. It contained an indoor tableau representing the result of an action, such as a murder, that the audience had not previously seen. The other device was a crane, which was attached to a cable with a harness, allowing an actor portraying a god or goddess to appear on the scene from the sky. These cranes were called *mêchanê,* hence the Latin phrase ***deus ex machina***—"the god from the machine." Today, this phrase is used to refer to any improbable event or character employed in literature to resolve a confounding dilemma.

The plays that the dramatists submitted for the festival competitions comprised a *tetralogy* (set of four), which included a *trilogy* (set of three) of tragedies and a satyr play. They began with the chorus' hymn to the gods and ended with a lamentation over the fate of the hero or heroine. The plots, generally drawn from mythology, often concerned royal families. Of the many tetralogies that were performed, only a small fraction have survived.

The subject matter of the tragedies concentrated on grand themes of the human condition—the sufferings, weaknesses, and triumphs of individuals. Because of the grandeur of the dramatists' themes, the eminence of their heroes, and the loftiness of their language, Greek spectators felt intensely involved in the tragedies of the lives portrayed. What they were witnessing went beyond anything in their ordinary lives, and they experienced the full range of human emotions.

A development parallel to Socratic dialectics— dialogue between thinking individuals—occurred in Greek drama. Through the technique of dialogue, early dramatists first pitted human beings against the gods and destiny. Later, by placing characters in conflict with each other, dramatists arrived at the idea of individuals as active subjects responsible for their behavior and decisions, which were based on their own feelings and thoughts. Greek tragedy evolved as a continuous striving toward humanization and individualization.

Like the natural philosophers, Greek dramatists saw an inner logic to the social universe and called it Fate or Destiny. When people were stubborn, narrow-minded, arrogant, or immoderate, they were punished. The order in the universe required it, said Sophocles:

> The man who goes his way
> Overbearing in the word and deed,
> Who fears no justice,
> Honors no temples of the gods—
> May an evil destiny seize him.
> And punish his ill-starred pride.[8]

The freedom to make decisions, the dramatist says, gives individuals the potential for greatness, but in choosing wrongly or unintelligently, they bring disaster on themselves and others. Also similar to philosophy, Greek tragedy entailed rational reflection. Tragic heroes were not passive victims of fate. They were thinking human beings who felt a need to comprehend their position, explain the reasons for their actions, and analyze their feelings.

The essence of Greek tragedy lies in the tragic heroes' struggle against cosmic forces and insurmountable obstacles, which eventually crushes them. But what impressed the Greek spectators (and impresses today's readers of Greek drama) was not the vulnerability or weaknesses of human beings, but their courage and determination in the face of these forces.

Aeschylus

Aeschylus (525–456 B.C.), an Athenian nobleman, had fought in the battle of Marathon. It was Aeschylus who introduced the second actor to interact with the chorus. He wrote more than eighty plays, of which only seven survive, and he won the grand prize of the Great Dionysia thirteen times. His plays have common themes. As an Athenian patriot, Aeschylus urged adherence to traditional religious beliefs and moral values. He believed, as did Solon, the statesman, that the world was governed by divine justice that could not be violated with impunity; when individuals evinced *hubris* (overweening pride or arrogance), which led them to overstep the bounds of moderation, they had to be punished. Another principal theme was that through suffering came knowledge: The terrible consequences of sins against the divine order should remind all to think and act with moderation and caution.

Aeschylus' first play, *The Persians,* dealt with an actual event, the defeat of Xerxes, the Persian emperor, by the Greeks. Xerxes' intemperate ambition to become master of Asia and Greece conflicted with the divine order of the universe. For this hubris, Xerxes had to pay:

A single stroke has brought about the ruin of
    great
Prosperity, the flower of Persia fallen and
    gone.[9]

The suffering of Xerxes should make people aware of what they can and cannot do:

And heaps of corpses even in generations
    hence
Will signify in silence to the eyes of men
That mortal man should not think more than
    mortal thoughts.
For hubris blossomed forth and grew a crop
    of ruin,
And from it gathered in a harvest full of tears.
In face of this, when Xerxes, who lacks good
    sense, returns
Counsel him with reasoning and good advice,
To cease from wounding God with over-boastful
    rashness.[10]

His *Orestia* trilogy, consisting of three interconnected plays, first performed in 458 B.C. when Aeschylus was sixty-seven years old, was his last and greatest work. The only trilogy still extant, it won the grand prize in Athens. The tragedies address issues such as immortality, familial strife, human relationships with the gods and goddesses, and especially blood vengeance. This blood vengeance theme appears in *Agamemnon,* the first play of the trilogy. Agamemnon is forced by Zeus, through his prophet, Calchas, to choose between abandoning his faltering campaign or sacrificing his daughter, Iphigenia, to receive the favor of the gods. After much soul-searching he chooses public duty and sacrifices Iphigenia. When he returns home, however, his wife, Clytemnestra, murders him in revenge for Iphigenia's death. Though her apparent motive is retribution, the audience comes to realize that it is also her selfish desire to replace Agamemnon, king and husband, with her lover, Aegisthus.

The theme of blood vengeance continues in the second play of the trilogy, *The Libation Bearers.* Orestes and Electra, the children of Clytemnestra and Agamemnon, are faced with difficult options—kill their mother or allow her to live and leave their father's death unavenged. They choose to kill Clytemnestra and her lover. It is Orestes who actually commits the terrible crime of matricide. As punishment, he is driven mad by the earth goddesses, the *Furies,* who have hair of snakes and whose eyes drip blood.

The final play of the trilogy, *Eumenides,* asserts the power of human reason over uncontrollable passion, of civilization over barbarism. With the help of the Olympian deities Athena and Apollo, Orestes succeeds in setting up a court in Athens to try cases of blood vengeance, thereby lifting the issue from the level of a personal vendetta to the higher level of law. In the final courtroom drama, Orestes is absolved of his crime, which is adjudged to be an act of justifiable homicide. This decision ends the cycle of blood vengeance and demonstrates the triumph of Dikê (justice).

Whereas Aeschylean drama dealt principally with the cosmic theme of the individual in conflict with the moral universe, later dramatists, although continuing to use patterns fashioned by Aeschylus, gave greater attention to the psychology of the individual.

Sophocles

Another outstanding Athenian dramatist was Sophocles (c. 496–406 B.C.). A personal friend of the Athenian leader Pericles, Sophocles' life spanned the triumphs and disasters of the fifth century B.C. He was the most prolific of the Greek tragedians and the most successful—winning the grand prize in Athens on numerous occasions. Of the more than 100 plays that Sophocles wrote, only seven (written during his later life) have survived.

Sophocles' greatness as a playwright lay in both the excellence of his dramatic technique and the skill with which he portrayed characters. Aristotle credited Sophocles with three important innovations in the form of tragedy—enlarging the chorus from twelve to fifteen people, introducing a third actor, and using painted scenery. Disregarding the interconnectedness of the plays of Aeschylus' trilogies, Sophocles chose to write three single, unrelated plays each of which focused on a unique hero or heroine. The people that he created possessed violent passions and tender emotions; they were noble in their nature, though their actions showed human frailty. Sophocles consciously formulated a standard of human excellence: Individuals should shape their character in the way a sculptor shapes a form, according to laws of proportion. Sophocles felt that when these principles of harmony were violated by immoderate behavior, a person's character would be thrown off balance and misfortune would strike. Both the physical and social worlds obey laws, said Sophocles, and human beings cannot violate these laws with impunity.

Whereas Aeschylus concentrated on religious matters and Euripides (see discussion later in the chapter) dealt with social issues, Sophocles wrote about the perennial problem of well-intentioned human beings struggling valiantly, but unwisely and vainly, against the tide of fate. His characters, bent on some action fraught with danger, resist all appeals to caution and inescapably meet with disaster.

Sophocles' portrayal of individuals is matched by his immense adaptability of style. The language of his plays moves skillfully and easily between lofty rhetoric and simple, casual speech, enabling Sophocles to juxtapose contrasting characters without impeding the progress of the play. Finally, there is an intrinsic relationship between the beginnings and endings of Sophocles' plays. Whereas Sophocles opens each play with a prologue that sets up the action for the entire play, he prolongs the action far beyond the climax, which makes the conclusion of each play anticlimactic. This compelled the audience to reflect on the consequences of the actions of the central characters and to ponder the comparable merit of divine and human accountability in the events of life.

In keeping with this structure, Sophocles' tragedy *Antigone*—quite possibly the first play to present a woman as an estimable being adept at devising her own destiny—opens with a prologue, spoken by Antigone to her sister, that characterizes the entire range of dramatic action:

> O Ismene, Ismene my dear sister,
> We are the last survivors, you and I,
> Of the house of Oedipus—and still Zeus
> Torments us with our father's crimes. What pain
> Or suffering, what shame or dishonour
> Have we not endured together? Now they say
> That general Creon has proclaimed another law
> In Thebes. Have they told you yet?
> Have you heard the latest outrage, heard
> How they are treating those we love as
>   enemies?[11]

Antigone highlights a theme that recurs in Western thought over the centuries: the conflict between individual morality and the requirements of the state, between personal conscience and the state's laws. Creon, king of Thebes, forbids the burial of Polyneikes, Antigone's beloved brother, because he rebelled against the state. The body, decrees Creon, shall remain unburied, food for dogs and vultures, despite the fact that Antigone is his niece and betrothed to his son, Haimon. Antigone (whose name means "born to oppose") believes that a higher law compels her to bury her brother, even though this means certain death for her and for her sister Ismene, if the latter helps Antigone.

Because King Creon fears instability, even anarchy, in Thebes if he allows his niece's crime to go unpunished, he asks his son, Haimon, to repudiate Antigone and renounce his love for her. Creon's argument is based on the belief that he is acting in behalf of order and the good of the community:

> . . . For there is
> No greater evil than disobedience:
> Great cities are devoured by it, their homes
> Left empty, their armies scattered and destroyed.
> In a prosperous state, where all is well,
> Obedience is the cause. That's why
> I mean to uphold the law, and not give way,
> Defeated by a woman.[12]

In his reply, Haimon affirms two principles that have reverberated throughout Western history: There exists a moral law that is higher than the decrees of the state, and basing one's behavior on this law is a worthy act; the state is not the private possession of a ruler to do with as he wishes. "Of course, if what I say is right! It's not my age that matters—it's knowing right from wrong! . . . No city belongs to any single man. . . . I defy you only when I see you're wrong. . . . To be a slave of evil—that is worse [than being defeated by Antigone, a woman]. . . . Is it insolence to argue with a fool?"[13] Nevertheless, Creon decrees Antigone be arrested, imprisoned, and left alone to die—a decision that has dire consequences. Antigone commits suicide, and her death is followed by the suicides of Haimon and his mother. Losing his wife and son finally leads King Creon to recognize his terrible mistake.

In *Oedipus the King,* first performed about 429 B.C., Sophocles probes deeply into the human psyche. Oedipus is warned not to pursue the mystery of his birth, but he insists on searching for the truth about himself: "Nothing will move me. I will find the whole truth." For this determination, born more of innocence than a consuming arrogance, he will suffer. Events do not turn out, as Oedipus discovers, the way a person thinks and desires that they should; the individual is impotent before a relentless fate, which governs human existence. It seems beyond imagining that Oedipus, whom all envied for his intelligence, courage, and good works, would suffer such dreadful misfortune. The play considers the issue of freedom and determinism—whether individuals are masters of their fate or victims of forces beyond their control. From Aristotle, who used the play as the model for tragedy in his *Poetics,* to Sigmund Freud, who spoke of the "Oedipus complex," the impact of this tragedy has been enormous.

The action centers on the prophecy known to Oedipus' birth parents, that he would kill his father and marry his mother. Attempting to circumvent the prophecy, King Laius and Queen Iocaste give their son away to die of exposure on Mount Kithairon. The name Oedipus means "swollen foot" and refers to his parents having his heels pinned together to prevent his movement on Mount Kithairon. Oedipus was rescued by a shepherd and raised by adoptive parents, King Polybus and Queen Meropé, in Corinth. Later, as an adult, Oedipus hears the prophecy repeated and goes to the Delphic oracle, which verifies its truth. Attempting to flee his fate, Oedipus encounters an entourage that runs him off the road to Thebes. In his great anger and impetuousness (his tragic flaw), he kills several men, including King Laius. When he arrives in Thebes, he finds that the city is suffering from a great famine because the murder of King Laius (unbeknownst to him, his real father) has gone unavenged. Showing himself to be quite wise, Oedipus solves the "riddle of the Sphinx" and becomes the leader of Thebes. He then marries dead Laius' wife, Iocaste (unbeknownst to him, his real mother) and vows to find the murderer of Laius and to punish him.

The play is laden with tragic irony. Oedipus dooms himself, no less than seven times, with his pronouncements of what will happen to those who withhold knowledge of the king's murder and what will transpire once the murderer is discovered. For example, in addressing the Theban people, he decrees that if anyone knows the murderer and conceals it,

> I solemnly forbid the people of this country,
> Where power and throne are mine, ever to
>   receive that man
> Or speak to him, no matter who he is, or let him
> Join in sacrifice, lustration,* or in prayer.
> I decree that he be driven from every house,
> Being, as he is, corruption itself to us: the Delphic
> Voice of Zeus has pronounced this revelation.
> Thus I associate myself with the oracle
> And take the side of the murdered king.
> As for the criminal, I pray to God—
> Whether it be a lurking thief, or one of a
>   number—
> I pray that that man's life be consumed in evil
>   and wretchedness.
> And as for me, this curse applies no less
> If it should turn out that the culprit is my guest
>   here,
> Sharing my hearth.
>   You have heard the penalty.[14]

Turning a blind eye to all evidence that it was he who murdered Laius, Oedipus relentlessly continues the search for the killer. His actions are motivated both by his concern for the Theban people, who must suffer until Laius' murderer is found, and by his own hubris, which compels him to prevent anyone from getting the better of him, including the god Apollo, whose oracle had prophesied Oedipus' doom.

Oedipus reveals to Iocaste his dread of the prophecy that he will kill his own father and share his mother's bed. Iocaste, who realizes that no good can come from Oedipus' quest for the truth, urges him not to give a second thought to oracles, for prophets and prophecies are worthless; no craft gives knowledge of what cannot be known. Moreover, says Iocaste, sleeping with one's mother is a common male dream; ignore it and you will be untroubled.

Iocaste:
  From now on never think of those things
  again.

Oedipus:
  And yet—must I not fear my mother's bed?

Iocaste:
  Why should anyone in this world be afraid,
  Since Fate rules us and nothing can be
    foreseen?

---

* Lustration was an ancient ceremony by which a person defiled by a crime was purified.

A Man should live only for the present day.
Have no more fear of sleeping with your
  mother:
How many men, in dreams, have lain with
  their mother!
No reasonable man is troubled by such things.

Oedipus:
  That is true; only—
  If only my mother were not still alive!
  But she is alive. I can not help my dread.[15]

When the terrible truth of his past is certain to
him, Oedipus, using the brooches of Iocaste who
has hanged herself, gouges out his eyes. It was the
god Apollo, he says, that brought this "sick fate"
upon him. "But the blinding hand was my own!
How could I bear to see when all my sight was
horror everywhere?"[16] Thus tragedy also gives
Oedipus the strength to assert his moral independence.
Although struck down by fate, Oedipus
remains an impressive figure. The *catharsis* of the
tragedy (the purging of the audience's emotions
through a work of art) comes from Oedipus'
choice of his own punishment, self-inflicted blindness.
Oedipus demonstrates that he still possesses
the distinctly human qualities of choosing and acting,
that he still remains a free man responsible for
his actions. Despite his misery, Oedipus is able to
confront a brutal fate with courage and to demonstrate
nobility of character.

Euripides

Euripides (c. 485–406 B.C.) wrote more than
ninety tragedies, of which only nineteen have survived.
The rationalist spirit of Greek philosophy
permeated his tragedies. Like the Sophists, Euripides
subjected the problems of human life to critical
analysis and challenged human conventions. This
critical spirit prompted the traditionalist Aristophanes
(see next section) to attack Euripides for
introducing the art of reasoning into tragedy. The
role of the gods, women's conflicts, the horrors of
war, the power of passion, and the prevalence of
human suffering and weakness were carefully
scrutinized in Euripides' plays. Euripides blends a
poet's insight with a psychologist's probing to
reveal the tangled world of human passions and
souls in torment. Thus, in *Medea,* he presents the
deepest feelings of a Greek woman:

  It was everything to me to think well of one
    man,
  And he, my own husband, has turned out
    wholly vile.
  Of all things which are living and can form a
    judgment

We women are the most unfortunate creatures.
Firstly, with an excess of wealth it is required
For us to buy a husband and take for our
  bodies
A master; for not to take one is even worse.
And now the question is serious whether we
  take
A good or bad one; for there is no easy escape
For a woman, nor can she say no to her
  marriage.
She arrives among new modes of behaviour
  and manners,
And needs prophetic power, unless she has
  learnt at home,
How best to manage him who shares the bed
  with her.
And if we work out all this well and carefully,
And the husband lives with us and lightly
  bears his yoke,
Then life is enviable. If not, I'd rather die.
A man, when he's tired of the company in his
  home,
Goes out of the house and puts an end to his
  boredom
And turns to a friend or companion of his
  own age.
But we are forced to keep our eyes on one
  alone.
What they say of us is that we have a peaceful
  time
Living at home, while they do the fighting in
  war.
How wrong they are! I would very much
  rather stand
Three times in the front of battle than bear
  one child.[17]

Euripides recognized the power of irrational,
demonic forces that seethe within people—what
he called "the bloody Fury raised by fiends of
Hell."[18] A scorned Medea, seeking revenge against
her husband by murdering their children, says:

  I know indeed what evil I intend to do,
  But stronger than all my afterthoughts is my
    fury,
  Fury that brings upon mortals the greatest
    evils.[19]

In his plays, Euripides showed that the great
tragedy of human existence is that reason can offer
only feeble resistance against these compelling,
relentless, and consuming passions. The forces
that destroy erupt from the volcanic nature of
human beings.

Euripides' rationalism led him to conclude that
the gods and goddesses were unworthy of worship
and esteem. In *The Trojan Women* he expresses

the futility of praying to the gods. Hecuba, forced to leave Troy, knowing that she will become a slave, remarks: "Lo, the flame hath thee, and we, thy children, pass away to slavery . . . God! O God of mercy! . . . Nay: Why call I on the Gods? They know, they know, my prayers, and would not hear them long ago."[20]

A second distinctive feature of Euripidean tragedy is its humanitarianism. No other Greek thinker expressed such concern for a fellow human being, such compassion for human suffering. Though Euripides' plots still came from mythological sources, his tragedies had obvious references to contemporary events, particularly the Peloponnesian War. For example, in *The Trojan Women,* it is almost impossible to miss the parallel between the enslavement of the Trojan women by the Greeks in Homer's epic and the cruel treatment of the people of the island of Melos, invaded by the Athenians during the Peloponnesian War. Athens massacred the men of the small island, sold its women and children into slavery, and sacked the city. In this same play he depicts war as agony and not glory, and the warrior as brutish and not noble. He described the torments of women, for whom war meant the loss of homes, husbands, children, and freedom. *The Trojan Women* was performed one year after the atrocity on Melos. Here Euripides warned the Athenians:

> How are ye blind,
> Ye treaders down of cities, ye that cast
> Temples to desolation, and lay waste
> Tombs, the untrodden sanctuaries where lie
> The ancient dead; yourselves so soon to die![21]

By exposing war as barbaric, Euripides was expressing his hostility to the Athenian leaders, who persisted in continuing the disastrous Peloponnesian War. Euripides' political and social views help to account for the unpopularity of his tragedies in his own lifetime.

Aristophanes and Greek Comedy

When comedy began as an art form is open to much debate. The word *comedy* comes from the Greek word *komos,* which means "ritual revel." From the earliest of Greek times, revelers would travel to local communities often telling obscene jokes and wearing huge artificial phalluses. The *komos* would always end with a sexual union—an orgy or marriage—as a symbol of increased fertility. Dionysos, who was the god of fertility as well as revelry and intoxication, is the link between tragedy and comedy. By the time of Aristophanes, comedy was a well-established art form.

Aristophanes (c. 448–c. 380 B.C.), the greatest of the Greek comic playwrights, similar to Euripides, was a political and social commentator. Only eleven of his forty-four comedies are extant. He lampooned Athenian statesmen and intellectuals, censured government policies, and as an aristocrat, protested against the decay of traditional Athenian values. Behind Aristophanes' sharp wit lay a deadly seriousness: He recognized that the ruinous Peloponnesian War must end. In the process of serving as a social critic, Aristophanes wrote some of the most hilarious lines in world literature.

His sexually explicit play, *Lysistrata,* first produced in 411 B.C., when the Peloponnesian War still raged, attacked the folly of war. It is laden with obscenities as the Athenian women, led by Lysistrata, discuss how best to prevent their men from engaging in further warfare. They arrive at a practical conclusion—they will abstain from sexual relations with their husbands and lovers until warfare has ceased. Lysistrata reveals the plan:

> For if we women will but sit at home,
> Powdered and trimmed, clad in our daintiest
> lawn [fine linen dress],
> Employing all our charms, and all our arts
> To win men's love, and when we've won it,
> then
> Repel them firmly, till they end the war,
> We'll soon get Peace again, be sure of that.[22]

After the plan has been implemented, many women become "husband-sick" and seek to desert the temple where they have gathered. But the men also suffer:

> Oh me! these pangs and paroxysms of love,
> Riving my heart, keen as a torturer's wheel![23]

Through these unorthodox methods, the women achieve their goal—peace. Performed during the darkest days of the war, this play reminded its audiences to concentrate their efforts in the real world on securing peace.

In *The Clouds,* Aristophanes ridiculed the Sophist method of education both for turning the youth away from their parents' values and for engaging the youth in useless, hairsplitting logic. To Aristophanes, the worst of the Sophists was Socrates, who is depicted in *The Clouds* as a fuzzy-minded thinker with both feet planted firmly in the clouds. Socrates is made to look ridiculous, a man who walks on air, contemplates the sun, and teaches such absurd things as "Heaven is one vast fire extinguisher" or "How many feet of its own a flea could jump." The Sophists in the play teach only how "to succeed just enough for my need and to slip through the clutches of the law." A student

CONFUCIANISM

THE TEACHINGS OF CONFUCIUS (551–479 B.C.) helped to shape the character of the Chinese people and have influenced Chinese society and life for twenty-five hundred years. Blending his teachings with earlier Chinese beliefs and traditions, Confucius taught patience, peace, moderation, and respect for one's ancestors. He was concerned with the earthly happiness of human beings rather than with any concept of an afterlife. Although Confucius himself wrote little, he compiled a series of ancient writings that became part of the sacred scripture of Confucianism. The *Lun Yu,* or *The Analects of Confucius,* is a collection of sayings by Confucius that were written down after his death. In it, Confucius, the "Master," answers questions asked by his disciples on moral and social topics.

I,16. The Master said, (the good man) does not grieve that other people do not recognize his merits. His only anxiety is lest he should fail to recognize theirs.

II,3. The Master said, Govern the people by regulations, keep order among them by chastisements, and they will flee from you, and lose all self-respect. Govern them by moral force, keep order among them by ritual and they will keep their self-respect and come to you of their own accord.

IV,16. The Master said, A gentleman takes as much trouble to discover what is right as lesser men take to discover what will pay.

IV,17. The Master said, In the presence of a good man, think all the time how you may learn to equal him. In the presence of a bad man, turn your gaze within!

IV,18. The Master said, In serving his father and mother a man may gently remonstrate with them. But if he sees that he has failed to change their opinion, he should resume an attitude of deference and not thwart them; he may feel discouraged, but not resentful.

VII,15. The Master said, He who seeks only coarse food to eat, water to drink and a bent arm for a pillow, will without looking for it find happiness to boot. Any thought of accepting wealth and rank by means that I know to be wrong is as remote from me as the clouds that float above.

VII,25. The Master said, A Divine Sage I cannot hope ever to meet; the most I can hope for is to meet a true gentleman. The Master said, A faultless man I cannot hope ever to meet; the most I can hope for is to meet a man of fixed principles. Yet where all around I see Nothing pretending to be Something, Emptiness pretending to be Fullness, Penury pretending to be Affluence, even a man of fixed principles will be none too easy to find.

IX,4. There were four things that the Master wholly eschewed: he took nothing for granted, he was never over-positive, never obstinate, never egotistic.

XIV,5. The Master said, One who has accumulated moral power will certainly also possess eloquence; but he who has eloquence does not necessarily possess moral power. A Good Man will certainly also possess courage; but a brave man is not necessarily Good.

XIV,29. The Master said, A gentleman is ashamed to let his words outrun his deeds.

XV,35. The Master said, When it comes to Goodness one need not avoid competing with one's teacher.

Source: The Analects of Confucius, *trans. Arthur Waley (New York: The Macmillan Company, 1939; copyright 1938 by George Allen & Unwin, Ltd.)*

of these Sophists becomes a "concocter of lies . . . a supple, unprincipled, troublesome cheat."[24] To Aristophanes, Socrates was a subversive who caused Athenians to repudiate civil morality and to speculate about nonsense questions. The play contributed to the Athenians' disaffection with Socrates, and his trial and execution. Clearly, Aristophanes admired the Athens that had bested the Persians at the battle of Marathon and feared the rationalism that Euripides, the Sophists, and Socrates had injected into Athenian intellectual life.

THE GREEK VIEW OF HISTORY

The Mesopotamians and the Egyptians kept annals that purported to narrate the deeds of gods and their human agents, the priest-kings or god-kings. These chronicles, filled with religious sayings, royal records, and boastful accounts of military campaigns, are devoid of critical analysis and interpretation. The Hebrews valued history, but believing that God acted in human affairs, they did not remove historical events from the realm of religious–mythical thought. The Greeks initiated a different approach to the study of history. For the Greeks, history was not the record of God's wrath or benevolence—as it was for the Hebrews—but the actions of human beings. As the gods were eliminated from the nature philosophers' explanations for the origins of things in the natural world, mythical elements were also removed from the writing of history. Greek historians asked themselves questions about the deeds of people, based their answers on available evidence, and wrote in prose, the language of rational thought. They not only narrated events but also examined causes.

Herodotus

Often called the "father of history," Herodotus (c. 484–c. 424 B.C.) wrote a history of the Persian Wars. Herodotus valued the present and recognized that it is not timeless, but that it has been shaped by earlier happenings. To understand the conflict between Persia and Greece, the most important event during his lifetime, he first inquired into the histories of these societies. Much of his information was derived from posing questions to the inhabitants of the lands he visited. Herodotus was interested in everything and frequently interlaced his historical narrative with a marvelous assortment of stories and anecdotes.

The central theme of Herodotus' *Histories* is the contrast between Near Eastern despotism and Greek freedom and the subsequent clash of these two worldviews in the Persian Wars. Certain of their superiority, the Greeks considered the non-Hellenic world to be steeped in ignorance and darkness. But Herodotus was generally free of this arrogance. A fair-minded, sympathetic, and tolerant observer, he took joy in examining the wide range of human character and experience.

Though Herodotus found much to praise in the Persian Empire, he was struck by a lack of freedom and by what he considered barbarity. Herodotus emphasized that the mentality of the free citizen was foreign to the East, where men were trained to obey the ruler's commands absolutely. Not the rule of law but the whim of despots prevailed in the East. When a Persian official urged some Greeks to submit to Xerxes, Herodotus wrote that the Greeks said: "You understand well enough what slavery is, but freedom you have never experienced, so you do not know if it tastes sweet or bitter. If you ever did come to experience it, you would advise us to fight for it not with spears only, but with axes too."[25] Of all the Greek city–states, Herodotus admired Athens most. Freedom had enabled Athens to achieve greatness, said Herodotus, and it was this illustrious city that had rescued the Greek world from Persia.

Another theme evident in Herodotus' work was punishment for hubris. In seeking to become king of both Asia and Europe, Xerxes had acted arrogantly; although he behaved as if he were superhuman, "he too was human, and was sure to be disappointed of his great expectations."[26] As did the Greek tragedians, Herodotus drew universal moral principles from human behavior.

In several ways, Herodotus was a historian rather than a teller of tales. First, he recognized that there is value to studying and preserving the past. Second, he asked questions about the past, instead of merely repeating ancient legends; he tried to discover what had happened, analyzed the motivations behind actions, and searched for cause-and-effect connections. Third, he demonstrated at times a cautious and critical attitude toward his sources, refusing to rely on legends based on little or no objective evidence.

> The course of my story now leads me to Cyrus: who was this man who destroyed the empire of Croesus, and how did the Persians win their predominant position in Asia? I could, if I wished, give three versions of Cyrus' history, all different from what follows; but I propose to base my account on those Persian authorities who seem to tell the simple truth about him without trying to exaggerate his exploits.[27]

Fourth, rising above inherited prejudices and a narrow parochialism, he attempted to examine disinterestedly and critically the histories of both Greeks and Persians. Fifth, although the gods appeared in Herodotus' narrative, they played a far less important role than they did in Greek popular mythology. Still, by retaining a belief in the significance of dreams, omens, and oracles and by allowing divine intervention, Herodotus fell short of being a thoroughgoing rationalist. Herodotus' writings contain the embryo of rational history; Thucydides brought it to maturity.

Thucydides

Thucydides (c. 460–c. 400 B.C.) also concentrated on a great political crisis confronting the Hellenic world: the Peloponnesian War. Living in Periclean Athens, whose lifeblood was politics, Thucydides regarded the motives of statesmen and the acts of government as the essence of history. He did not merely catalogue facts, but sought those general concepts and principles that the facts illustrated. His history was the work of an intelligent mind trying to make sense of his times.

Thucydides applied to the sphere of political history a rationalist empiricism worthy of the Ionian natural philosophers. He searched for the truth underlying historical events and attempted to present it objectively. From the Sophists, Thucydides learned that the motives and reactions of human beings follow patterns. Therefore, a proper analysis of the events of the Peloponnesian War would reveal general principles that govern human behavior. He intended his history to be a source of enlightenment for future ages, a possession for all time, for the kinds of behavior that caused the conflict between Sparta and Athens would recur regularly through history.

> Of the events of the war I have not ventured to speak from any chance information, nor according to any notion of my own; I have described nothing but what I either saw myself, or learned from others of whom I made the most careful and particular inquiry. The task was a laborious one, because eyewitnesses of the same occurrences gave different accounts of them, as they remembered or were [partial to] one side or the other. And very likely the strictly historical character of my narrative may be disappointing to the ear. But if he who desires to have before his eyes a true picture of the events which have happened, and of the like events which may be expected to happen hereafter in the order of human things shall pronounce what I have written to be useful, then I shall be satisfied. My history is an everlasting possession, not a prize composition which is heard and forgotten.[28]

In Thucydides' history, there was no place for myths, for legends, for the fabulous—all hindrances to historical truth. He recognized that a work of history was a creation of the rational mind and not an expression of the poetic imagination. The historian seeks to learn and to enlighten, not to entertain.

Rejecting the notion that the gods interfere in history, Thucydides looked for the social forces and human decisions behind events. Undoubtedly, he was influenced by Hippocratic doctors, who frowned on divine explanations for disease and distinguished between the symptoms of a disease and its causes. Where Herodotus occasionally lapsed into supernatural explanations, Thucydides wrote history in which the gods were absent, and he denied their intervention in human affairs. For Thucydides, history was the work of human beings. And the driving force in history was men's will to power and domination.

In addition to being a historian, Thucydides was also an astute and innovative political thinker with a specific view of government, statesmen, and international relations. He had contempt for statesmen who waged war lightly, acting from impulse, reckless daring, and an insatiable appetite for territory. Although Thucydides admired Athens for its democratic institutions, rule of law, sense of civic duty, and cultural achievements, he recognized an inherent danger in democracy: the emergence of demagogues, who rise to power by stirring up the populace. He extended the Sophists' insight that people tend to act out of self-interest to international relations; national interest, he maintained, was the motivating force in relations between states. And he explicitly formulated the principle of balance of power as a basic formula governing international relations. What caused the Peloponnesian War, he said, was the sudden and spectacular increase of Athenian power and the Spartans' fear that this would upset the balance.

Political scientists, historians, and statesmen still turn to Thucydides for insights into the realities of power politics, the dangers of political fanaticism, the nature of imperialism, the methods of demagogues, and the effects of war on democratic politics.

HELLENIC ART

The same rational and humanistic outlook that pervaded Greek philosophy, drama, and historiography also found expression in art, which showed a progressive development toward naturalism and realism—a self-conscious striving to represent the objective world as it appeared to the human eye. Greek dramatists, philosophers, and historians searched for general rules that governed human behavior. Similarly, Greek artists sought to understand and to depict general patterns that distinguished the human form. And the heightened awareness of human personality demonstrated by Greek thinkers was paralleled by Greek artists, who focused on the human form and took great pride in their works, to which they affixed their signature. Spanning the period from about 1100 B.C. until the death of Alexander the Great in 323 B.C., Greek art passed through three stages: Formative (c. 1100–650 B.C.), Archaic (c. 650–480 B.C.), and Classical (c. 480–c. 323 B.C.).

The only extant works from the Formative period are painted vases portraying fixed, solid geometric designs. In the Archaic period, the artists' attempts at duplicating nature were rudimentary, because they still generally expressed visual realities in geometric shapes, recognizable as horses, or men, but distinctly nonrealistic. During the Classical period, artists depicted reality with greater accuracy: Painters and sculptors produced a truer copy of the human form, and vase painting showed a growing awareness of perspective—reproducing a three-dimensional scene on a two-dimensional surface. Yet, although it was increasingly realistic and naturalistic, Greek art during this period was also idealistic, aspiring to a finer, more perfect representation of what was seen, depicting the essence and form of a thing more truly than it actually appeared. In achieving an accurate representation of objects while holding that there were rules of beauty that minds could discover, the Greek artist employed an approach consistent with the new scientific outlook. The Greek temple, for example, is an organized unity obeying nature's laws of equilibrium and harmony; Classical sculpture captures the basic laws that govern life in motion. Such art, based on reason, which draws the mind's attention to the clear outlines of the outer world, also draws attention to the mind itself, making human beings the center of an intelligible world and the masters of their own persons. During the Classical era, the Greeks succeeded in establishing standards that would dominate Western art until the emergence of modern art in the late nineteenth century.

Our knowledge of the Hellenic visual arts in painting, sculpture, and architecture comes from a variety of sources—extant original works, Roman copies of Greek originals, literature of the period, and (in the last 250 years) archaeological discoveries. All wall paintings or murals that were done in the formative years from 1100–650 B.C. were long ago destroyed through either conquest or decay. The same is true of the wooden sculpture and architecture that, according to archaeological evidence, preceded the monumental works executed in stone. Nevertheless, several painted vases have survived from this early period; they act as windows to the past and give us some information about Greek social customs and religious beliefs.

Vase Painting

The oldest style of Greek vase painting, beginning after 800 B.C., is the *Geometric Style*. It is characterized by a wide variety of solid, fixed shapes—concentric circles, triangles, dots, and diamonds—that decorated the vases. When animals and human figures began to appear, they were still only an accessory intended to blend with the other geometric patterns. The majority of these

Figure 4.1 Dipylon Vase, 8th c. B.C., height 40 1/2" (102.8 cm), The Metropolitan Museum of Art, New York The *Geometric Style,* of which this vase is an example, is characterized by a wide variety of solid, fixed shapes—concentric circles, triangles, dots, and diamonds. The majority of these early vases were used as grave monuments. *(The Metropolitan Museum of Art, Rogers Fund, 1914 (14.130.14). Photograph © 1996 The Metropolitan Museum of Art)*

early vases, such as the *Dipylon Vase* (Figure 4.1), were used as grave monuments. Liquid offerings flowed through holes in the bottom of the vase and into the ground, thus honoring the person who had died. Because no reference to an afterlife can be found on the vases, their only purpose must have been to memorialize the dead.

Throughout the eighth century B.C., the Greeks emphasized epic poetry, relegating sculpture and painting to a subordinate position. Therefore, most of our knowledge of the eighth century B.C. derives from Homer's epics, not from the visual arts. However, when the Greeks embarked on the **Oriental Style** of vase painting between 725 and 650 B.C., late Formative period new motifs appeared that give us a striking view of the Greek past.

The Oriental Style exhibits powerful Egyptian and other Near Eastern influences. Egyptian influence can be seen in the designs, including spirals, rosettes, and interwoven borders, and Mesopotamian influence is apparent in the figures of the animals. Rather than emphasizing design, these vases demonstrate a narrative technique, which deals with the larger questions of human existence—the origin of the universe, life after death, and the relationship of immortal deities to finite humans. For answers to these questions, the artists drew inspiration from both the local Chthonic deities and the Olympian pantheon as described by Homer and Hesiod.

The more realistic depiction of the human figure marks the transition to the Archaic period, which is regarded as the most productive, original, and inventive phase of vase painting. Because they were no longer used as grave markers, the vases of the Archaic Period are smaller than their predecessors. The vases of this period, especially those from Athens, emphasize pictorial designs that exult the human form. Modern westerners continue to admire the vases, which were virtually unsurpassed in the ancient world.

Black-figure vase painting—silhouettes in black against a red clay background—was the predominant style in the earlier part of the Archaic period. One of the most famous black-figure designs was rendered by Exekias (fl. c. 545–530 B.C.) for a *kylix* (drinking cup) in honor of the god-man, Dionysos (Figure 4.2). The interior of the cup delineates a Homeric myth in which Dionysos was attacked by pirates. As the god of the vine, Dionysos caused grapevines to sprout over the boat, thus revealing his identity and frightening the pirates, who jumped overboard and were transformed into dolphins. Exekias depicts Dionysos reclining in his boat, horn in hand, drinking. He is on his journey home, accompanied

Figure 4.2 Exekias, *Dionysos in Boat*, kylix, c. 540 B.C., diameter 12" (30.5 cm), Staatliche Antikensammlungen, Munich The interior of the cup delineates a Homeric myth in which Dionysos was attacked by pirates. Defying the Athenian tradition of painting numerous figures enclosed by a border, Exekias portrayed Dionysos as a singular figure in an unenclosed, natural setting. *(Antikensammlungen, Munchen/Bildarchiv Preussischer Kulturbesitz)*

by seven dolphins and surrounded by seven grapevines—seven being the symbolic number for good luck. Defying the Athenian tradition of painting numerous figures enclosed by a border, Exekias portrayed Dionysos as a singular figure in an unenclosed, natural setting, and thus further advanced naturalistic vase painting.

Toward the end of the sixth century B.C., vase painters discovered they could create more lifelike figures and the impression of depth if they retained the red color for the figures and made the background black. One of the earliest, and finest, red-figure vases, *The Death of Sarpedon* (Figure 4.3), was executed by Euphronios (fl. c. 510–465 B.C.). The intent of Euphronios is clear, because he included the Greek names of each figure on the vase. The vase illustrates a scene from Homer's *Iliad* concerning the dead Trojan warrior, Sarpedon. Under the direction of Hermes, the god who guides souls to Hades, *Hypnos* (Sleep) and *Thanatos* (Death) carry Sarpedon from the battlefield so his body can be prepared for burial. Euphronios demonstrates his fascination with the human form through the muscular body of Sarpe-

Figure 4.3 Euphronios, *Death of Sarpedon,* **calyx-krater, c. 515 B.C., height 18 1/2" (45.7 cm), The Metropolitan Museum of Art, New York** Under the direction of Hermes, the god who guides souls to Hades, *Hypnos* (Sleep) and *Thanatos* (Death) carry Sarpedon, a Trojan warrior, from the battlefield so his body can be prepared for burial. *(The Metropolitan Museum of Art, Purchase, Bequest of Joseph H. Durkee, Gift of Darius Ogden Mills and Gift of C. Ruxton Love, by exchange, 1972 (1972.11-10). Photograph © 1999 The Metropolitan Museum of Art)*

don, and he conveys a sense of movement by the curl of Sarpedon's toes, his grimaced face, and the sharply defined wings of Sleep and Death.

Vase painters were as highly valued as were poets in ancient Greece. However, unlike poets, who were able to gain fame regardless of gender, female artists were not accorded the same stature as their male counterparts, who were often lauded for their unique, intimate style. Following the Persian Wars, vase painting declined and wall painting, which surpassed vase painting in accurately depicting the human form and the handling of perspective, became prominent.

We know of the prominence of wall paintings from the writings of the Roman encyclopedist and naturalist, Pliny the Elder (A.D. 23–79). In his *Natural History,* Pliny describes the attempt of Apollodorus of Athens to imitate reality by creating illusions of space. Today, the best extant examples of wall paintings, dating from approximately 470 B.C., reside in the National Archaeological Museum of Paestum, Italy.

Sculpture

Hellenic sculpture passed through two major phases—the Archaic and the Classical. During the Archaic period, sculptors created statues that are discernible as animals or humans, but their block-

like or columnar shape is not naturalistic. The most popular and recognizable statues from this period are the highly formalized, free-standing human figures—*Kouros,* the young male, and *Kore,* the maiden—which are rigid and tense, yet exude a sense of life characterized by their enigmatic smile, known as the "Archaic smile."

In some ways, the *Kouroi* (plural of Kouros) and *Korai* (plural of Kore) are reminiscent of earlier Egyptian sculptures. Although the Egyptians did not sculpt nude male figures, the pose of the broad-shouldered *Standing Youth Kouros* (Figure 4.4), from about 600 B.C., evidences Egyptian influence—stiff arms and clenched fists, forward positioning of the left leg, and an unnatural, stilted styling of the hair. Throughout the Archaic period, the *Kouroi* were produced in large numbers, always rendered in the same fashion, but their purpose remains unclear. Some bear inscriptions dedicating them to a deity, but because they were often placed on graves, scholars are uncertain whether they represent a deity, the deceased, or some other esteemed person.

Sculpted around 570 B.C., *The Calf-Bearer* (Figure 4.5), a variation on the form of the *Kouros,* shows a man carrying a sacrificial animal to be offered to Athene. Even though his pose is similar to the earlier *Kouroi,* the sculptor's representation of him not as a youth, but rather as a mature man with a beard, marks an advancement in sculptural

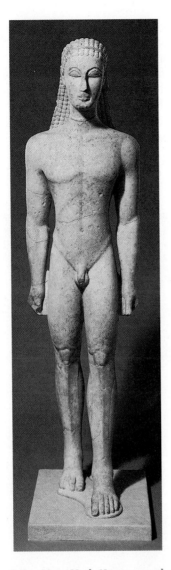

Figure 4.4 *New York Kouros,* end of 7th c. B.C., marble, height without plinth 76″ (193 cm), height of head 12″ (30.5 cm.) The Metropolitan Museum of Art, New York Although the Egyptians did not sculpt nude male figures, this kouros shows Egyptian influence— stiff arms and clenched fists, forward positioning of the left leg, and unnaturally styled hair. *(The Metropolitan Museum of Art, Fletcher Fund, 1932 (31.11.1). Photograph © 1997 The Metropolitan Museum of Art)*

Figure 4.5 *Calf-Bearer,* c. 570 B.C., marble, height 65″ (165 cm), Acropolis Museum, Athens The pose is similar to earlier kouroi, but the sculptor has chosen to represent him as a mature man with a beard, rather than as a youth. The statue is unique in its depiction of the sacrificial calf, which conforms to the shoulders of the man in a somewhat naturalistic way. *(Acropolis Museum/Archaeological Receipts Fund, Athens)*

naturalism. Also unlike his predecessors, he is clothed, with his tunic fitting like a second skin. Although his face is no longer masklike, it still bears the Archaic smile. A particularly unique aspect of this statue is the depiction of the sacrificial calf, which conforms to the shoulders of the man in a somewhat natural way, yet appears to be more vital than the man himself.

The corresponding female form, *Kore,* also was mass produced with a rigid representation similar to the *Kouros.* Because Greek women never

appeared nude in public, *Korai,* unlike the *Kouroi,* were all clothed. But because male athletes competed in the nude, some scholars suggest that the nude *Kouroi* represent athletes. In the later sixth century B.C., as the sculptors' technique advanced, the figures became more organic—that is, the various features formed a unified whole—revealing a greater appreciation of the human form. A good example of this advancement in sculpture is *The Peplos Maiden* (Figure 4.6), so named because of her garment, called a peplos, which clothes her but does not conceal her natural form. The less artificial flow of her hair and her more subdued smile augment her more lifelike representation.

With the advent of the Classical period, the further growth of sculptural realism, particularly in human figures, is apparent. Classical sculptors abandoned the Archaic geometricizing formality and aimed at a more naturalistic realism. Each object was depicted in a style as faithful to reality as possible, but it was reality idealized or made more perfect than any individual object could be. The proportions of the human form were determined by a fixed set of measurements, a reflection of the perfect, not the actual. Classical sculpture abandoned the impassivity of the Archaic smile and aimed to communicate physical dynamism and active conscious thought with the stone figure. Greek artists carefully observed nature and human beings and sought to achieve an exact knowledge of human anatomy; they tried to portray accu-

Figure 4.6 *Peplos Maiden,* c. 530 B.C., marble, height 48" (1.22 m), Acropolis Museum, Athens   Her name is derived from her garment, called a peplos. The less artificial flow of her hair and her more subdued smile indicate that sculpture was moving in the direction of more lifelike representations. *(Acropolis Museum/ Archaeological Receipts Fund, Athens)*

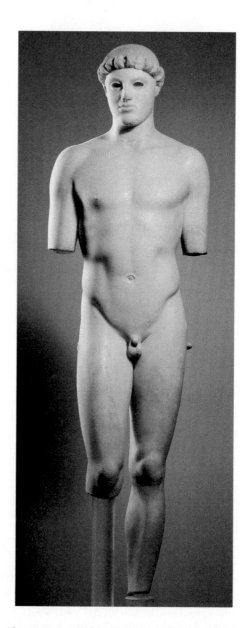

Figure 4.7 *Kritios Boy,* c. 480 B.C., marble, height 34" (86.3 cm), Acropolis Museum, Athens   Kritios succeeded in creating a sense of real movement by deflecting the boy's knee, rotating his pelvis, and angling his shoulders. *(Acropolis Museum/Archaeological Receipts Fund, Athens)*

rately the body at rest and in motion. They knew when muscles should be taut or relaxed, one hip lower than the other, the torso and neck slightly twisted—in other words, they succeeded in transforming marble or bronze into a human likeness that seemed alive. Thus, a Classical Greek statue resembled no specific individual but revealed a flawless human form, without wrinkles, warts, scars, or other imperfections.

Scholars refer to the early Classical period of

Figure 4.8 *Charioteer of Delphi,* c. 470 B.C., bronze, height 71″ (1.8 m), Archaeological Museum, Delphi   The statue was intended to commemorate Polyzalos' victory in a chariot race as part of the Delphic Games. Originally, the charioteer stood in a chariot and commanded four bronze horses, but the chariot no longer exists and only fragments of the horses remain. *(Delphi Museum/Archaeological Receipts Fund, Athens)*

Hellenic sculpture (480–450 B.C.) as the *Severe Style* in which figures are executed with simplicity and fidelity to texture and form. The *Kouros, Kritios Boy* (Figure 4.7), which dates from the early fifth century B.C., is often viewed as the line of demarcation between Archaic sculptural depictions and those classified as Classical. The statue is believed to be the work of the sculptor Kritios (fl. 470) who, along with his colleague, Nesiotes, specialized in bronze statues extolling Athenian democracy. The break with Archaic design principles is clear—Kritios has abandoned the contrived frontal pose of all previous *Kouroi,* and the boy literally stands with his weight evenly distributed. Instead of the determined, rigid symmetry of the earlier *Kouroi,* Kritios has sculpted the boy with a steady, nonsymmetrical stance, and he appears to be completely at rest. However, because of the deflection of the boy's knee, rotation of his pelvis, torque of his spine, and angle of his shoulders, Kritios also succeeded in creating a sense of real movement, thereby freeing other sculptors to create more flexible, nonmechanical figures that were more true to life.

One of the most monumental bronze statues of the Severe Style is the *Charioteer of Delphi* (Figure 4.8) (c. 470 B.C.), dedicated to the tyrant Polyzalos, who ruled the Greek city–state of Gela in Sicily. The statue was intended to commemorate Polyzalos' victory in a chariot race as part of the Delphic Games. Originally, the charioteer stood in a chariot and commanded four bronze horses, but the chariot no longer exists and only fragments of the horses remain. The resolution in the charioteer's eyes is apparent and his demeanor is calm, but the malleability of his form is innovative for the Severe Style. The configuration of his feet indicates that he bears his weight on his left foot as he turns his head to the right. Although he wears a simple garment, the sculptor manipulated its folds to display a suppleness and pliability that far surpasses anything attempted in the Archaic period. The effect of gravity on the garment and the constriction of the bindings that hold it in place demonstrate the sculptor's understanding of both an object's form and function.

The greatest contribution of the artists of the Severe Style was their concept of monumental, freestanding statues that appear to be in motion. The *Zeus* (Figure 4.9) statue epitomizes the climax of this style. The statue, which dates from around 460 B.C., was found in 1926 in the sea off the Greek coast. At one time the statue was thought to be that of Poseidon about to throw his trident. But because the immense size of the trident would have obscured the statue's face, scholars now contend that it shows Zeus about to throw a thunderbolt.

Figure 4.9 *Zeus*, c. 460 B.C., bronze, height 6'10" (2.08 m), National Archaeological Museum, Athens The statue was found off the Greek coast in 1926. Although his face is still stylized, his athletic body pulsates with life, capturing the essence of Zeus as the omnipotent ruler of the gods. *(National Archaeological Museum/Archaeological Receipts Fund, Athens)*

Although his face is still stylized (note his beard and eyebrows), his 6'10" athletic form seems to pulsate with life, capturing the essence of Zeus as the omnipotent ruler of the gods. From this time forward, the sculptor's attention to anatomical detail included the rendering of pubic hair.

The most famous statue during the golden age of Pericles prior to the Peloponnesian War was the *Doryphoros,* or Spear Bearer (Figure 4.10), which is known only through Roman copies. Polykleitos sculpted the original marble statue some time around 450–440 B.C., and he is credited with inventing a technique called ***contrapposto***—a pose suspended between resting and walking in which one side of the body is relaxed and the other side tense with the weight carried by one leg. By turning Doryphoros' hip and slightly turning his head downward, Polykleitos sculpted the figure to give the impression of being about to act or speak. He thus created a model type that was based on mathematical rules, which he explained in a treatise; this model also had a moral dimension, for harmonious proportions were tantamount to thinking about the Good. Polykleitos' *Doryphoros* became the personification of the Greeks' Classical ideal of beauty. Later, the Romans referred to Polykleitos' treatise and the statue as "The Canon," because the statue was sculpted according to the normative principles of *rhythmos* (composition and movement) and *symmetria* (harmony).

Praxiteles (fl. c. 370–330 B.C.), another important Athenian sculptor, preserved the proportions of Polykleitos, but altered his pose. His *Aphrodite of Knidos* (see chapter opening) demonstrates Praxiteles' fondness for depicting his figures slightly off balance. He thrusts her hips sideways to create an S-shaped body profile. The statue was rendered for Aphrodite's sanctuary at Knidos in Asia Minor and was completed around 350 B.C., but it is known only through Roman copies. The statue is significant because it is one of the earliest depictions of a female nude, reputedly modeled after a courtesan named Phryne, and the first to represent the goddess of love in such a fashion. Whereas Praxiteles was well known for depicting emotion in his statues, it was their luminescent, crystalline marble surfaces that made him legendary.

Such an impeccable approach to the surface of statues is the reason scholars are confident that *Hermes with the Infant Dionysos* (Figure 4.11) was the work of Praxiteles some time around 320–300 B.C.* Praxiteles found a way to polish the edges of his statues so that no rough edges

---

* Scholars dispute the existence of any extant original sculptures done by the great sculptors of the Classical period. Heretofore, scholars have conjectured that *Hermes with the Infant Dionysus* was either created by a Hellenistic sculptor or is a Roman copy. Nevertheless, most now agree that even if it is not the original work of Praxiteles, it is, at the very least, an excellent Greek copy.

remained. Also, by softening the edges of body surfaces such as the lips, eyelids, appendages, and muscles, he was able to blend one into another, thus creating even more lifelike statues than his predecessors. In this statue, Praxiteles portrays Hermes with a half smile as he dangles a bunch of grapes (no longer visible) before the desirous infant Dionysos, the god of wine and intoxication. The treatment of Hermes' form and the rendering of the mythology associated with Dionysos make this sculpture by Praxiteles a precursor of the Hellenistic and Roman pictorial sculpture (see p. 148).

Like no others before them, Classical sculptors were able to capture *symmetria* and *rhythmos*—a clarity of structure and a sense of life and motion—in their statues, thus defining Greek aesthetic principles. The architects and engineers who designed the Greek temples and the magnificent public buildings during the Periclean Age built on the same aesthetic principles. In fact, the unity of sculpture and architecture was so intense that art historians refer to it as "Sculptural Architecture" (see p. 100).

Architecture

The Greek temple, the center of Greek religious and civic life, differed structurally from the tem-

Figure 4.10   Polykleitos, *Doryphoros* (Spear Bearer), c. 450–440 B.C., Roman copy, marble, height 6'6" (2. m), Museo Archeologico Nazionale, Naples   With this statue, Polykleitos is credited with inventing *contrapposto*—a pose suspended between resting and walking in which one side of the body is relaxed and the other side tense with the weight carried by one leg. *(Archeologico Nazionale, Naples/Scala/Art Resource, NY)*

Figure 4.11   Praxiteles, *Hermes with the Infant Dionysos*, c. 330–320 B.C., marble, height 7'1" (2.16 m), Archaeological Museum, Olympia   Praxiteles portrays Hermes with a half smile as he dangles a bunch of grapes (no longer visible) before the desirous infant Dionysos, the god of wine and intoxication. *(Olympia Museum/ Archaeological Receipts Fund, Athens)*

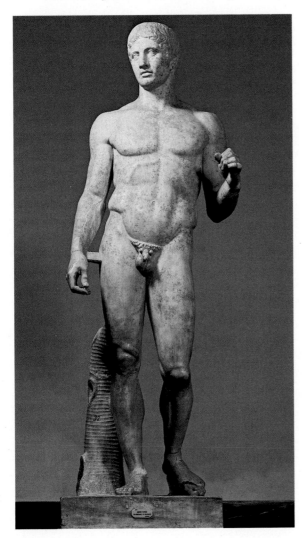

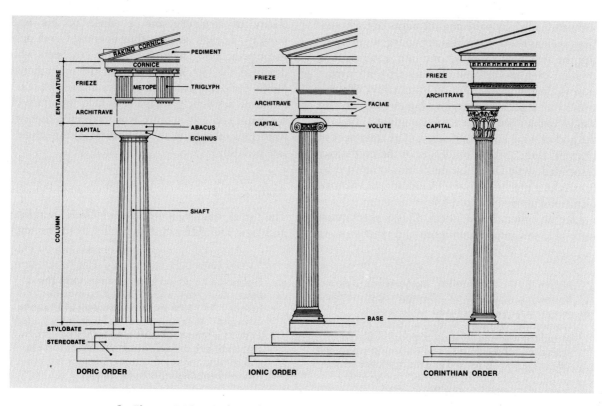

Figure 4.12 **Orders of Architectures: Doric, Ionic, Corinthian** The three main divisions of Doric architecture are the stepped platform, the columns, and the entablature, which consists of everything situated on top of the columns. Each column of the Ionic order has an elaborate contoured base, a shaft that is leaner and significantly less tapered, and a capital, called a *volute*, which simulates a large double scroll. The Corinthian capital is an embellished variation of the Ionic volute. *(Witt, et al.,* The Humanities: Cultural Roots and Continuities, *Sixth Edition, Houghton Mifflin Company, 2001)*

ples of all other peoples. Most temples, such as the ziggurat of the Mesopotamians, had such a wide variety of different expressions that it is impossible to speak of a general architectural type. In contrast, the Greeks superimposed on temples several mathematically definable "patterns," identified since Roman times as architectural orders. In architecture the Greeks developed two distinctive orders—Doric, named for a region on the Greek mainland, and Ionic, which developed on the coast of Asia Minor and the Greek islands in the Aegean. Corinthian formerly was seen as a separate order of architecture, but now is viewed as a variation of Ionic. Unlike other styles of architecture, the orders of Greek architecture are both consistent and explicitly identifiable. Ancient writers associated a degree of personality to the orders—Doric was seen as masculine and stalwart, and Ionic was viewed as feminine and exquisite (Figure 4.12).

DORIC ORDER *Doric order* refers to the standard features of the exterior, which are clearly distinguishable. The three main divisions of Doric architecture are the stepped platform, the

columns, and the entablature, which consists of everything situated on top of the columns. The two main parts of the temples, which apply to both orders of architecture, are the *cella* (area where the figure of the deity was placed) and the *pronaos* (porch). Doric architects were undoubtedly influenced by structures previously built by the Egyptians and Mycenaeans. Although scholars disagree about the specifics, most of them acknowledge that the Greeks borrowed the mathematical concepts of temple construction, and probably their stonecutting and masonry methods as well, from the Egyptians. Mycenaean influence is evident in the sculptures and the capitals of the columns.

The oldest extant Doric temple is the *Temple of Hera I* (Figure 4.13) at Paestum, located about 50 miles southeast of Naples, Italy. The temple, constructed about 550 B.C., appears to be squat and elongated, and the shafts of the columns and the capitals that cap them are thick and heavy. Inexperienced architects, who had worked previously only on wooden structures, exaggerated the tapering of the columns and the narrowing of the gaps between the capitals

Figure 4.13 Temple of _Hera I_, c. 550 B.C., Paestum, Italy Located about 50 miles southeast of Naples, this is the oldest extant Doric temple. It is squat and elongated, and the shafts of the columns and the capitals that cap them are thick and heavy. (_The Ancient Art & Architecture Collection_)

(uppermost parts) of the columns, thus overcompensating the design for the purpose of stability. Only later, during the Classical period, did the renowned design principles of harmony, symmetry, and rational order become evident in the structures of the Athenian Acropolis.

Following the Persians' destruction of the Archaic Acropolis in 480 B.C., the Athenians intended to leave it in its ravaged condition as a memorial to the savagery of the Persians. However, in 449 B.C., under the leadership of Pericles, the Athenians launched a building program on the Acropolis that was unparalleled in the history of Western culture until the High Renaissance in Italy.

The first temple erected on the Classical Acropolis, the _Parthenon_ (Figure 4.14) was constructed between 447 and 432 B.C. and dedicated to the

Figure 4.14 Iktinos, Kallikrates, Phidias, _Parthenon_, c. 447–432 B.C., Athens, Greece Dedicated to the patron goddess of the city, Athene Parthenos, the "warrior maiden," the shining marble temple seems to grow naturally out of the rocky height of the Acropolis itself, towering above the city as a symbol of Athenian power. (_John Ross/ Photo Researchers_)

Figure 4.15 Mnseicles, *Propylaea*, c. 437–432 B.C., Athens, Greece Pericles authorized the monumental gateway to the Acropolis, but Mnseicles further modified the enhancements of the Doric design to fit the asymmetric, precipitous slope of the Propylaea. Thus, he converted the rugged passage among the stones into a hallowed entryway to the Parthenon. *(Robert Frerck/Woodfin Camp & Associates)*

patron goddess of the city, Athene Parthenos, the "warrior maiden." It was the work of some of the greatest artists of the day, the architects Iktinos and Kallikrates and the sculptor Phidias. Their collaboration produced a model of perfection from which subsequent Classical sculptors and architects drew inspiration. The shining marble temple seems to grow naturally out of the rocky height of the Acropolis itself, towering above the city as a fit dwelling for the Athenian goddess and a symbol of Athenian power.

Although the Parthenon reflects *symmetria* and *rhythmos*, it exhibits some irregularity and departure from conventional temple style. The Parthenon has virtually no *pronaos,* and the *cella* is uncommonly wide and slightly shorter than most other temples. Iktinos also deviated from severe geometric standards to make the Parthenon more beautiful.

Though the stepped platform and entablature appear to the eye as a rectangular box placed on a horizontally level base, this is an illusion. The columns actually curve; thus, the center of each column is tangibly thicker than at the ends. Also, the columns lean slightly inward, and the upper-

most portion of each column is somewhat distorted to fit the curving architrave—the lowermost member of the entablature. The vertical lines also deviate from the perpendicular. These deviations were carefully designed to give an optical illusion of perfect verticality and horizontality and reduce the sense of weightiness. Thus, Greek aesthetic delight in perspectivism—the relationship of the parts to the whole—was achieved through a subtle plasticity of design.

The architectural sculpture of the Parthenon, designed by Phidias, has *rhythmos*—a patterning that conveys a liveliness and sense of motion to the building. For example, the sculpture of the Ionic frieze is uninterrupted by triglyphs—the part of a Doric frieze that separated the metopes (the square panels) from each other. It fills the space between the capitals and the roof and runs to the length of 550 feet; this area is composed of a great procession of humans and animals, probably celebrating the Panathenaic festival.

On the western end of the Classical Acropolis, Pericles subsequently authorized the monumental gateway to the Acropolis—the *Propylaea* (Figure 4.15). Begun in 437 B.C. under the direction of

Mnseicles, the body of the marble Propylaea was finished in five years, but construction was terminated during the Peloponnesian War. Using the enhancements of the Doric design in the Parthenon, Mnseicles further modified them to fit the asymmetric, precipitous slope of the Propylaea. He thereby converted the rugged passage among the stones into a hallowed entryway to the Parthenon. Only the eastern porch of the Propylaea is in viable condition. The western porch, now barely discernible, once had a northernmost wing, which served as the first known *Pinakotheke*—a gallery for paintings—where the portrait of Sappho was hung. These paintings on wood presumably were hung just beneath the windows. In a style reminiscent of the Ionic *cella* of the Parthenon, the central passageway through the Propylaea has two rows of Ionic columns, indicating a preference among Athenian architects to use Ionic elements for the interiors of Doric structures.

IONIC ORDER During the Archaic period, huge Ionic temples, which are no longer extant, were built at Ephesus and on the island of Samos. The only Ionic structures built on the Greek mainland prior to the Classical period were small treasuries built at Delphi in the eastern Peloponnesus. The most noticeable feature of the *Ionic order* is its column (see Figure 4.12 on p. 98). The "female" Ionic column differs in both essence and design from its "male" Doric predecessor. Each column has an elaborate contoured base, a shaft that is leaner and significantly less tapered, and a capital, called a *volute,* that simulates a large double scroll.

Athenian architects appear to have appropriated Ionic order architecture about 450 B.C., but only for small temples. The first Ionic temple built on the Acropolis, the *Temple of Athene Nike* (Figure 4.16), was begun in 425 B.C., approximately four years after Pericles died. Scholars

Figure 4.16 Kallikrates, *Temple of Athene Nike,* c. 427–424 B.C., Athens, Greece The purpose of this small Ionic temple was to commemorate an Athenian victory during the Peloponnesian War. The frieze above the architrave depicts the Greek victory over the Persians at Plataea in 479 B.C. *(Scala/Art Resource, NY)*

assume it was designed by Kallikrates, who worked with Iktinos on the Parthenon. Its purpose was celebratory—to commemorate an Athenian victory during the Peloponnesian War. The frieze above the architrave depicts the Greek victory over the Persians at Plataea in 479 B.C. Most scholars acknowledge that the artists who sculpted the frieze probably were trained under Phidias, but admit the work could also have been done by Kallimachos, who is credited with inventing the Corinthian capital as an embellished variation of the Ionic *volute*—the spiral-like ornamentation on Ionic columns.

The last building constructed on the northern edge of the Acropolis, opposite the Parthenon, was the *Erechtheion* (Figure 4.17), named for Erechtheus, the legendary king and founder of Athens. Begun in 421 B.C. by the architect Mnseicles, it stands at the site where Athene and Poseidon supposedly competed with one another to be the patron of Athens. This contest is portrayed in part of the west pediment sculptures of the Parthenon. Because Mnseicles had to account for the positioning of sacred artifacts—Erechtheus' tomb, Poseidon's trident mark on a rock from which a salt spring poured, and Athene's olive tree—the Erechtheion is as complicated as the

Parthenon is simple. It has four rooms, which climax in three porches, facing three divergent directions. Two porches are Ionic, but the third one, "The Porch of the Maidens," has six *korai* (called caryatids) to hold up the transformed Doric zcapitals and the Ionic entablature. When the Erechtheion was completed in 405 B.C., the pediment sculptures were not finished, conceivably because of the Peloponnesian War. Nevertheless, according to the inscriptions on the structure, cost may also have been a factor—the embellishments of the columns and capitals were more expensive than the figures of the frieze.

Such adornments were characteristic of architectural sculpture in the late fifth century B.C., and led to the development of the Corinthian capital to replace the Ionic one. The elaborate Corinthian capital resembles an upturned bell, ornamented with offshoots and leaves of the acanthus plant, which appear to grow from the crown of the column shaft. Initially, the Corinthian capital was only used for interiors, but in the fourth century B.C., it became the prototype for exterior capitals on large buildings. Eventually the Romans appropriated this style of capital and made it the model for all of their structures.

Figure 4.17   Mnseicles, *Erechtheion*, c. 421–405 B.C., Athens, Greece
This was the last building built on the Acropolis, and it stands at the site where Athene and Poseidon reputedly competed with one another to be the patron of Athens. It is named for Erechtheus, the legendary king and founder of Athens. *(Max Hunn /Photo Researchers)*

Figure 4.18   Patterned after Polykleitos the Younger, *Theater at Epidauros*, 5th century B.C., Epidauros, Greece   The concentric rows of stone seats curved to conform to the natural slope of the hillside and stepped aisles were placed at consistent intervals. This well-preserved theater had no stage, for the building behind the orchestra housed the scenery. *(William Hubbell/Woodfin Camp & Associates)*

Except for the great open-air theaters, development of Hellenic architecture stagnated between the end of the Peloponnesian War in 404 B.C. and the conquest of the Hellenistic world by the Romans. Prior to the fourth century B.C., the stone seats of the theaters curved to conform to the natural slope of the hillside. However, the *Theater at Epidauros* (Figure 4.18) demonstrates the use of a modified *tholos* plan as mastered by the architect Polykleitos the Younger—concentric rows of seats with stepped aisles placed at consistent intervals. Initially, this well-preserved theater had no stage, for the building behind the orchestra maintained the scenery. The design of the *Theater at Epidauros* further defined the architecture for public theaters in subsequent Western culture.

The achievements of Greek artists in defining aesthetic principles left a lasting legacy in Western culture. The Romans consistently copied Greek sculptural masterpieces and refined various architectural models for use in their public buildings and private homes. The artists and architects of the Italian Renaissance revived the Greeks' emphasis on the human form as well as the principles of *symmetria*, *rhythmos*, and rational order in their sculpture, painting, and architecture. In the eighteenth and nineteenth centuries, European and American sculptors, painters, and architects revived Greek aesthetic principles and forms in a style of art known as Neoclassical (see Chapter 19).

The Greek Achievement: Reason, Freedom, Humanism

Like other ancient peoples, the Greeks warred, massacred, and enslaved; they could be cruel, arrogant, contentious, and superstitious; and they often violated their ideals. But their achievement was unquestionably of profound historical significance. Western thought begins essentially with the Greeks, who first defined the individual by the capacity to reason. It was the great achievement of the Greek spirit to rise above magic, miracles, mystery, authority, and custom and to discover the means of giving rational order to nature and society. Every aspect of Greek civilization—science, philosophy, art, literature, politics, and historical writing—showed a growing reliance on human reason and a diminishing dependence on the gods.

In Mesopotamia and Egypt, people had no clear conception of their individual worth and no understanding of political liberty. They were not citizens, but subjects who marched to the command of a ruler, whose power originated with the gods. Such royal power was not imposed on an unwilling population, but was religiously accepted and obeyed.

In contrast, the Greeks created both civic politics and political freedom. They saw the state as a community of free citizens who made laws in their own interest; the citizen had no other master but himself. The Greeks held that men are capable of governing themselves, and they valued active citizenship. Denouncing arbitrary rule, they argued that power should be regulated by law and justice. For the Greeks, the state was a civilizing agent that permitted people to live the good life. Greek political thinkers arrived at a conception of the rational or legal state in which law was an expression of reason, not of whim or divine commands; of justice, not of might; of the general good of the community, not of self-interest.

The Greeks also gave to Western civilization a conception of inner, or ethical, freedom. People were free to choose between shame and honor, cowardice and duty, moderation and excess. The heroes of Greek tragedy suffered not because they were puppets manipulated by higher powers, but because they possessed the freedom of decision. The idea of ethical freedom reached its highest point with Socrates, who self-consciously shifted the focus of thought from the study of nature to the moral life. To shape oneself according to ideals known to the mind, to develop into an autonomous and self-directed person, became for the Greeks the highest form of freedom.

Underlying everything accomplished by the Greeks was a humanist attitude toward life. The Greeks expressed a belief in the worth, significance, and dignity of the individual. They called for the maximum cultivation of human talent, the full development of human personality, and the deliberate pursuit of excellence. In valuing human personality, the Greek humanists did not approve of living without restraints; they aimed at creating a higher type of person. Individuals could mold themselves according to worthy standards; they could make their lives as harmonious and flawless as a work of art. This aspiration required effort, discipline, and intelligence. Fundamental to the Greek humanist outlook was the belief that human beings could master themselves.

Despite their lauding of the human being's creative capacities, the Greeks were not naive about human nature. Rather, intensely aware of the individual's inherent capacity for evil, Greek thinkers repeatedly warned that without the restraining forces of law, civic institutions, moral norms, and character training, society would be torn apart by the savage elements within human nature.

By discovering theoretical reason, defining political freedom, and affirming the worth and potential of human personality, the Greeks broke with the past and founded the rational and humanist tradition of the West. "Had Greek civilization never existed," wrote poet W. H. Auden, "we would never have become fully conscious, which is to say that we would never have become, for better or worse, fully human."[29]

Key Terms

lyric poetry	contrapposto
chorus	Doric order
deus ex machina	cella
komos	pronoas
Geometric Style	Ionic order
Oriental Style	volute
Severe Style	

Notes

1. Cited in Werner Jaeger, *Paideia: The Ideals of Greek Culture,* trans. Gilbert Highet (New York: Oxford University Press, 1945), vol. 1, p. 135.
2. Sappho, "A Girl," in *The Oxford Book of Greek Verse in Translation,* ed. T. F. Highham and C. M. Bowra (Oxford: Clarendon Press, 1938), p. 211.
3. Sappho, *Sappho A Garland: The Poems and Fragments of Sappho,* trans. Jim Powell (New York: Farrar Straus Giroux, 1993), pp. 4–5.
4. Ibid., p. 23.
5. Lyn Hatherly Wilson, *Sappho's Sweet Bitter Songs: Configurations of Female and Male in Ancient Greek Lyric* (London and New York: Routledge, 1996), p. 70.
6. Cited in C. A. Trypanis, *Greek Poetry from Homer to Seferis* (Chicago: University of Chicago Press, 1981), p. 109.
7. Cited in H. D. F. Kitto, *The Greeks* (Baltimore: Penguin Books, 1957), pp. 174–175.
8. Sophocles, *Oedipus the King,* trans. Bernard M. W. Knox (New York: Washington Square Press, 1959), p. 61.
9. Aeschylus, *The Persians,* trans. Anthony J. Podlecki (Upper Saddle River, N.J.: Prentice-Hall, 1970), p. 49, lines 250–251.
10. Ibid., pp. 96–97, lines 818–822, 829–831.
11. Sophocles, *Antigone,* trans. Kenneth McLeish, *Sophocles: Electra, Antigone, Philoctetes* (Cambridge: Cambridge University Press, 1979), p. 61, lines 1–10.

12. Ibid., p. 82, lines 658–667.
13. Ibid., pp. 83–84, lines 719, 723, 725, 729, 735.
14. Sophocles, *Oedipus Rex,* in *The Oedipus Cycle: An English Version,* trans. Dudley Fitts and Robert Fitzgerald (San Diego: Harcourt Brace Jovanovich, 1977), p. 13.
15. Ibid., p. 49.
16. Ibid., p. 70.
17. Euripides, *Medea,* trans. Rex Warner (London: The Bodley Head, 1944), p. 18.
18. Euripides, *The Medea,* trans. Rex Warner, in Euripides, Vol. 3 of *The Complete Greek Tragedies,* ed. David Grene and Richmond Lattimore (Chicago: University of Chicago Press, 1959–1960), p. 101, line 1260.
19. Ibid., p. 96, lines 1078–1080.
20. Euripides, *The Trojan Women,* in *Five Play of Euripides: Alcestis, Medea, The Trojan Women, Iphigenia in Tauris, Electra,* trans. Gilbert Murray (New York: Oxford University Press, 1934), p. 74.
21. Ibid., p. 16, lines 95–97.
22. Aristophanes, *Lysistrata,* in *Five Comedies of Aristophanes,* trans. Benjamin Bickley Rogers (Garden City, N.Y.: Doubleday Anchor Books, 1955), p. 292.
23. Ibid., p. 320.
24. Aristophanes, *The Clouds,* in Five Comedies of Aristophanes, trans. Rogers, pp. 156–157, 169–170.
25. Herodotus, *The Histories,* trans. Aubrey de Sélincourt (Baltimore: Penguin Books, 1954), p. 458.
26. Ibid., p. 485.
27. Ibid., p. 53.
28. Thucydides, *The Peloponnesian War,* trans. Benjamin Jowett (Oxford: Clarendon Press, 1881), bk. 1, chap. 22.
29. W. H. Auden, ed., *The Portable Greek Reader* (New York: Viking, 1952), p. 38.

The Hellenistic Age: Cultural Diffusion

GREEK CIVILIZATION, OR HELLENISM, passed through three distinct stages: the Hellenic Age, the Hellenistic Age, and the Greco-Roman Age. The Hellenic Age began around 800 B.C. with the early city–states, reached its height in the fifth century B.C., and endured until the death of Alexander the Great in 323 B.C. At that time, the ancient world entered the *Hellenistic Age,* which ended in 30 B.C., when Egypt, the last major Hellenistic state, fell to Rome. The Greco-Roman Age lasted five hundred years and encompassed the period of the Roman Empire up to the collapse of the Empire's western half in the last part of the fifth century A.D.

Although the Hellenistic Age absorbed the heritage of classical (Hellenic) Greece, its style of civilization changed. During the first phase of Hellenism, the polis was the center of political life. The polis gave Greeks an identity, and only within the polis could a Greek live a good and civilized life. With the coming of the Hellenistic Age, this situation changed. Kingdoms and empires eclipsed the city–state in power and importance. Even though cities retained a large measure of autonomy in domestic affairs, they lost their freedom of action in foreign affairs. No longer were they the self-sufficient and independent communities of the Hellenic period. Unable to stand up to kingdoms, the city–state became an outmoded institution. The bonds between the individual and the city loosened. People had to deal with the feelings of isolation and insecurity produced by the decline of the polis.

As a result of Alexander the Great's conquests of the lands between Greece and India, tens of thousands of Greek soldiers, merchants, and administrators settled in eastern lands. Their encounters with different peoples and cultures of the Near East widened the Greeks' horizons and weakened their ties to their native cities. Because of these changes, the individual had to define a relationship not to the narrow, parochial society of the polis, but to the larger world. The Greeks had to examine their place in a world more complex, foreign, and threatening than the polis. They had to fashion a conception of a community that would be more comprehensive than the parochial city–state.

Hellenistic philosophers struggled with these problems of alienation and community. They sought to give people the inner strength to endure in a world where the polis no longer provided security. In this new situation, philosophers no longer assumed that the good life was tied to the affairs of the city. Freedom from emotional stress—not active citizenship and social responsibility—was the avenue to the good life. This pronounced tendency of people to withdraw into themselves and seek emotional comfort helped shape a cultural environment that contributed to the spread and triumph of Christianity in the Greco-Roman Age.

Hagesandros, Polydoros, and Athanadoros, *Laocoön Group*

c. 1st century B.C.–1st century, A.D. marble, height 7′ (2.1 m), Vatican Museum, Rome. According to the *Aeneid,* written by the Roman poet, Virgil, the priest Laocoön warned the Trojans not to bring the wooden horse—filled with Greek soldiers in its underbelly—into the city. As punishment, a deity, who sided with the Greeks, sent sea serpents to strangle Laocoön and his two sons.

(Scala/Art Resource, NY)

In the Hellenic Age, Greek philosophers had a limited conception of humanity, dividing the world into Greek and barbarian. In the Hellenistic Age, the intermingling of Greeks and peoples of the Near East caused a shift in focus from the city to the *oikoumene* (the inhabited world); parochialism gave way to cosmopolitanism and universalism as people began to think of themselves as members of a world community. Philosophers came to regard the civilized world as one city, the city of humanity. This new concept was their response to the decline of the city–state and the quest for an alternative form of community.

By uniting the diverse nationalities of the Mediterranean world under one rule, Rome gave political expression to the Hellenistic philosophers' longing for a world community. But the vast and impersonal Roman Empire could not rekindle the sense of belonging, the certainty of identity, that came with being a citizen of a small polis. In time, a resurgence of the religious spirit, particularly in the form of Christianity, helped to overcome the feelings of alienation by offering an image of community that stirred the heart.

ALEXANDER THE GREAT

After the assassination of Philip of Macedon in 336 B.C., his twenty-year-old son, Alexander, succeeded to the throne. Alexander inherited a proud and fiery temperament from his mother. From his tutor Aristotle, Alexander gained an appreciation for Greek culture, particularly the Homeric epics. Undoubtedly, the young Alexander was stirred by these stories of legendary heroes, especially of Achilles, and their striving for personal glory. Alexander acquired military skills and qualities of leadership from his father.

Philip had intended to protect his hold on Greece by driving the Persians from Asia Minor. But Alexander, whose ambition knew no bounds, aspired to conquer the entire Persian empire. Daring, brave, and intelligent, Alexander possessed the irrepressible energy of a romantic adventurer. With an army of thirty-five thousand men, Macedonians and Greeks combined, he crossed into Asia Minor in 334 B.C. and eventually advanced all the way to India. In these campaigns, Alexander proved himself to be a superb strategist and leader of men. His army won every battle and in the process carved an empire that stretched from Greece to India.

The world after Alexander differed sharply from the one that existed before he took up the sword. Alexander's conquests brought West and East closer together, marking a new epoch. Alexander himself helped to implement this transformation. He took a Persian bride, arranged for eighty of his officers and ten thousand of his soldiers to marry Near Eastern women, and planned to incorporate thirty thousand Persian youths into his army. Alexander founded Greek-style cities in Asia, where Greek settlers mixed with the native populations.

As Greeks acquired greater knowledge of the Near East, the parochial-mindedness of the polis gave way to a world outlook. As trade and travel between West and East expanded, Greek merchants and soldiers settled in Asiatic lands, and Greek culture spread to non-Greeks, the distinctions between barbarian and Greek lessened. Although Alexander never united all the peoples in a world-state, his career pushed the world in a new direction, toward a fusion of disparate peoples and the intermingling of cultural traditions.

HELLENISTIC SOCIETY

In 323 B.C., Alexander, who was not yet thirty-three years old, died after a sickness that followed a drinking party. After his premature death, his generals engaged in a long and bitter struggle to see who would succeed the conqueror. Because none of the generals or their heirs had enough power to hold together Alexander's vast empire, the wars of succession ended in a stalemate. By 275 B.C., the empire was fractured into three dynasties: the Ptolemies in Egypt, the Seleucids in Asia, and the Antigonids in Macedonia. Macedonia—Alexander's native country—continued to dominate the Greek cities, which periodically tried to break its hold. Later, the kingdom of Pergamum in western Asia Minor emerged as the fourth Hellenistic monarchy. Rome, a new power to the west, became increasingly drawn into the affairs of the quarrelsome Hellenistic kingdoms. By the middle of the second century B.C., Rome had imposed its will on them. From that time on, the political fortunes of the western and eastern Mediterranean were inextricably linked.

Cosmopolitanism

A mingling of peoples and an interchange of cultures characterized Hellenistic society. Greek traditions spread to the Near East, whereas Mesopotamian, Egyptian, Hebrew, and Persian traditions—particularly religious beliefs—moved westward. A growing cosmopolitanism replaced the parochialism of the city–state. Although the

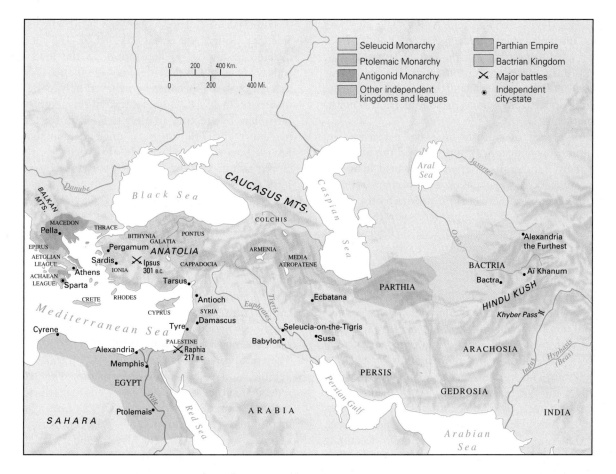

Map 5.1 The Hellenistic World After Alexander's death, his empire lost its political unity. Great new cities and kingdoms arose in the lands he had conquered.

rulers of the Hellenistic kingdoms were Macedonians and their high officials and generals were Greeks, the style of government was modeled after that of the ancient oriental kingdoms. In the Hellenic Age, the law had expressed the will of the community, but in this new age of monarchy, the kings were the law. The Macedonian rulers encouraged the oriental practice of worshiping the king as a god or as a representative of the gods. In Egypt, for example, the priests conferred on the Macedonian king the same divine powers and titles traditionally held by Egyptian pharaohs; in accordance with ancient tradition, statues of the divine king were installed in Egyptian temples.

Following Alexander's lead, the Seleucids founded cities in the east patterned after the city–states of Greece. Hellenistic kings generally did not intervene in the cities' local affairs. Thousands of Greeks settled in these cities, which were Greek in architecture and contained Greek schools, temples, theaters, where performances of classical plays were staged, and gymnasia. Gymnasia were essentially places to exercise,

train in sports, and converse, but some had libraries and halls, where public lectures and competitions of orators and poets were held. Hellenistic kings brought books, paintings, and statues to their cities from Greece. Hellenistic cities, inhabited by tens of thousands of people from many lands and dominated by a Hellenized upper class, served as centers and agents of Hellenism, which non-Greeks adopted. The cities in Egypt and Syria saw the emergence of a native elite who spoke Greek, wore Greek-style clothing, and adopted Greek customs. Koine, a form of Greek, came to be spoken throughout much of the Mediterranean world.

The greatest city of the time and the one most representative of the Hellenistic Age was Alexandria in Egypt, founded by Alexander the Great. Strategically located at one of the mouths of the Nile, Alexandria became a center of commerce and culture. The most populous city of the Mediterranean world, Alexandria at the beginning of the Christian era contained perhaps a million people: Egyptians, Persians, Macedonians,

Greeks, Jews, Syrians, and Arabs. The city was an unrivaled commercial center; goods from the Mediterranean world, east Africa, Arabia, and India circulated in its marketplaces. This cosmopolitan center also attracted poets, philosophers, physicians, astronomers, and mathematicians.

All phases of cultural life were permeated by cultural exchange. Sculpture showed the influence of many lands. Historians wrote world histories, not just local ones. Greek astronomers worked with data collected over the centuries by the Babylonians. Greeks increasingly demonstrated a fascination with oriental religious cults. Philosophers helped to break down the barriers between peoples by asserting that all inhabit a single fatherland.

The spread of Greek civilization from the Aegean to the Indus River gave the Hellenistic world a cultural common denominator, but Hellenization did not transform the East and make it one with the West. Hellenization was limited almost entirely to the cities, and in many urban centers it was often only a thin veneer. Many Egyptians in Alexandria learned Greek, and some assumed Greek names, but for most, Hellenization did not go much deeper. In the countryside, there was even less. Retaining traditional attitudes, the countryside in the East resisted Greek ways. In the villages, local and traditional law, local languages, and family customs remained unchanged; religion, the most important ingredient of the civilizations of the Near East, also kept its traditional character.

The Jews in the Hellenistic Age

Like other Near Eastern people, the Jews—both in Judea and the Diaspora (Jews who lived outside their ancient homeland)—came under the influence of Hellenism. Some Jewish scholars admired Greek learning and expressed Jewish religious ideas in Greek philosophical terms; God was identified with reason and Moses' laws with the rational order of the universe. The Hebrew Scriptures were translated into Greek for use by Greek-speaking Jews living in Alexandria and other areas outside of Judea, many of whom could not understand Hebrew or *Aramaic*—a Semitic language related to Hebrew, which became the common tongue of the Jews after the Exile in Babylon. Greek words entered the Hebrew language, and newly constructed synagogues employed Hellenistic architectural styles. Radical Hellenizers, mainly prosperous aristocrats, adopted Greek games, dress, entertainment, and eating habits. These efforts to assimilate pagan ways were resisted by simple folk and the devout who clung tenaciously to Mosaic Law.

The clash of cultures came to a head when the Seleucid king Antiochus IV (174–163 B.C.) decided to impose Hellenization on the Jews of Judea. He assumed the title *theos epiphanes* ("god made manifest") because he believed he was Zeus incarnate. In 167 B.C., he desecrated the Temple in Jerusalem by erecting an altar to Zeus in the temple court and offering pigs, unclean animals in Jewish law, as a sacrifice. He also forbade ritual circumcision, the sign of the covenant between Jews and their God.

Mattathias, a priest who slew the Syrian officer carrying the king's decree to make sacrifices to Zeus, epitomized the outrage of loyalist Jews against forced Hellenization. Mattathias' battle cry was "Let everybody who is zealous for the Law and stands by the covenant come out after me." Led by one of Mattathias' sons, Judah the Maccabeus (the "hammerer"), the Jews successfully fought the Syrians, venting their anger also against the Hellenized Jews who sided with Antiochus. They recaptured Jerusalem in 165 B.C., purified the Temple, and restored Jewish worship. The Jews rededicated the Temple and renewed themselves to the covenant. (Ever since, this act has been commemorated by Hanukkah—The Festival of Lights.) In 140 B.C., the Jews, under Judah's brother Simon, regained their independence. The Syrians finally abandoned Judea, and the descendants of Judah and Simon ruled an independent Judea until 63 B.C. when the Romans stepped in and made Judea into a Roman province.

HELLENISTIC CULTURE

Literature and History

In several ways Hellenistic literature gave expression to the new world that emerged after Alexander the Great's conquests. Unlike their Hellenic predecessors, who flourished in the vibrant world of the independent city–state, Hellenistic poets and dramatists dwelled in cities that were dominated by monarchies. As a result, their interest gravitated away from politics to everyday concerns and ordinary people. They wrote about common workers, lovers, children, pets, nature, and so on. There is a close parallel between the subject matter of literature, which focused on the particulars of the human condition, and the visual arts, which also depicted daily events and common people, including fishermen, drunken women, hunchbacks, infants, and a boy with a deer. Also like the visual arts, Hellenistic literature evidenced a sophisticated realism, giving careful attention to detail. Finally, literature reflected the broader frontiers of the age: Some of the themes selected by Greek writers showed the impact of Near Eastern cultures, and some of the writers of the period were not Greek by birth.

POETRY There was a great outpouring of literary works during the Hellenistic Age. Callimachus (c. 305–240 B.C.), an Alexandrian scholar–poet, felt that no one could duplicate the great epics of Homer or the plays of the fifth-century B.C. dramatists. He urged poets to write short, finely crafted poems, instead of composing on a grand scale.

Apollonius of Rhodes (third–second century B.C.) took issue with Callimachus and wrote the *Argonautica*. This Homeric-style epic tells the story of Jason's search for the Golden Fleece. Apollonius was a gifted poet, although the epic was not the best genre for expressing his talent. His poetic talent is shown in this description of how love for Jason takes possession of Medea:

> Time and again she darted a bright glance at Jason. All else was forgotten. Her heart, brimful of this new agony, throbbed within her and over-flowed with the sweetness of the pain. A working woman, rising before dawn to spin and needing light in her cottage room, piles brushwood on a smouldering log, and the whole heap kindled by the little brand goes up in a mighty blaze. Such was the fire of Love, stealthy but all-consuming, that swept through Medea's heart. In the turmoil of her soul, her soft cheeks turned from rose to white and white to rose.[1]

Theocritus (c. 315–250 B.C.), who lived on the island of Sicily, wrote pastorals that showed great sensitivity to natural beauty. With uncommon feeling, Theocritus responded to the sky and wind; to the hills, trees, and flowers; and to the wildlife of the countryside:

> We soon were lying joyously couched upon
>   soft deep beds
> Heaped with scented rushes and vine-leaves
>   newly stripped.
> And high above our heads there swayed and
>   quivered many a branch
> Of poplar and of elm-tree, while close behind
>   us welled
> The sacred water gushing from the cavern
>   of the Nymphs.
> Amid the shadowing foliage the brown cicalas
>   chirped
> And chattered busily without pause; and far
>   away was heard
> From the dense bramble-thicket the tree-frog's
>   fluted note.[2]

The term *New Comedy* is used to describe Athenian comedy from the death of Alexander the Great in 323 B.C. to the death of Philemon (c. 361–263 B.C.), an important New Comedy dramatist. A distinguishing feature of New Comedy was the shift away from Athenian politics to a depiction of private life, particularly of prosperous families. Dominated by a Macedonian king, the Athenians had lost much of their enthusiasm for the give-and-take of democratic politics that they had evidenced earlier. The leading dramatist of Attic New Comedy was Menander (c. 342–291 B.C.), who authored some one hundred plays. Because his plays were lost, our knowledge of Menander came largely from passages from his works quoted by numerous ancient authors and the adaptations of his comedies made by the Roman playwrights, Plautus and Terence (discussed in Chapter 6). It was not until 1957 that *Dyskolos (The Grouch)*, a complete play, and sizable fragments of several other plays were discovered.

Aristophanes, the great comic playwright of the fifth century, had mocked inept and corrupt Athenian statesmen. In an age when Athenian citizens no longer exercised political power—Macedonian soldiers were stationed in Athens—interest in high politics had waned. Grasping the changing mood of his fellow Athenians, Menander dealt with private life, not public affairs. In the daily life and personal habits of ordinary Athenians, Menander found much material to interest audiences and make them laugh. He drew his characters—the greedy, wealthy, grumpy old men, cruel fathers, jealous lovers, seduced girls, insolent servants, cunning slaves, bragging soldiers, and compassionate prostitutes—true to life and made them convincing. The plays also accurately portrayed the happenings and problems of everyday life.

At times, Menander demonstrated unusual insight into the human condition, as in this example: "Everything that dies, dies by its own corruption; all that injures is within." The apostle Paul preserved another sample of Menander's wisdom: "Bad company destroys good morals." Menander also expressed a warm concern for people, urging them to recognize the humanity of their fellows—whether Greeks, barbarians, or slaves—and to treat each other with kindness and respect. Some historians maintain that the Roman playwright Terence (c. 185–c. 159 B.C.) borrowed his famous line, "I am a man, and consider nothing human to be alien to me," from Menander.

THE HELLENISTIC ROMANCE The **Hellenistic romance** was introduced in the first century B.C. and reached its height in the second and third centuries A.D. As historical fiction, the Hellenistic romance was the precursor of the modern romance novel. It involves a praiseworthy heroine who is separated from her gallant lover, either because of natural disasters or human maliciousness; she eventually reunites with him. The best known of the later Hellenistic romances is *Daphnis and Chloë* written by Longus in the third century A.D. Daphnis and Chloë were orphans in Lesbos who were raised by shepherds; they met, fell in love, and eventually married. Unlike most romances of the period, their story has a picturesque, country setting, instead of a historical one. Although the two are not physically separated, they are, nevertheless, initially detached psychologically. Consequently, the romance focuses on the emotional development of the lovers as they move from immature infatuated children to complete sexual adulthood.

HISTORY   The leading historian of the Hellenistic Age was Polybius (c. 200–118 B.C.), whose history of the rise of Rome is one of the great works of historical literature. Reflecting the universal tendencies of the Hellenistic Age, Polybius endeavored to explain how Rome had progressed from a city–state to a world conqueror. As a disciple of Thucydides, Polybius sought rational explanations for human events. Like Thucydides, he relied on eyewitness accounts (including his own personal experiences), checked sources, and strove for objectivity.

Science

During the Hellenistic Age, Greek scientific achievement reached its height. When Alexander invaded Asia Minor, the former student of Aristotle brought along surveyors, engineers, scientists, and historians, who continued with him into Asia. The vast amount of data in botany, zoology, geography, and astronomy collected by Alexander's staff stimulated an outburst of activity. To integrate so much information, scientists had to specialize in the various disciplines. Hellenistic scientists preserved and expanded the tradition of science developed in the Hellenic Age. They attempted a rational analysis of nature; they engaged in research, organized knowledge in logical fashion, devised procedures for mathematical proof, separated medicine from magic, grasped the theory of experiment, and applied scientific principles to mechanical devices. Hellenistic science, says historian Benjamin Farrington, stood "on the threshold of the modern world. When modern science began in the sixteenth century, it took up where the Greeks left off."[3]

Although Alexandria was the principal center of scientific research, Athens still retained some of its former luster in this area. After Aristotle died in 322 B.C., he was succeeded as head of the Lyceum first by Theophrastus and then by Strato. Both wrote treatises on many subjects—logic, ethics, politics, physics, and botany. Theophrastus systematized knowledge of botany in a manner similar to Aristotle's treatment of animals. Strato is most famous for his study of physics. It is likely that Strato, in his investigation of physical problems, did not rely on logic alone but also performed a series of experiments to test his investigations.

Because of its state-supported museum, Alexandria attracted leading scholars and superseded Athens in scientific investigation. The museum (so named for the nine goddesses of art and wisdom—the Muses) contained a library of more than half a million volumes, as well as botanical gardens and an observatory. It was really a research institute—the first institution in history specifically established for the purpose of scientific research—in which some of the best minds of the day studied and worked.

MEDICINE AND ANATOMY*   Alexandrian doctors advanced medical skills. They improved surgical instruments and techniques and, by dissecting bodies, added to anatomical knowledge. Through their research, they discovered organs of the body not known until then, made the distinction between arteries and veins, divided nerves into those comprising the motor and the sensory systems, and identified the brain as the source of intelligence. Their investigations advanced knowledge of anatomy and physiology to a level that was not significantly improved until the sixteenth century A.D.

Herophilus (c. 335 B.C.–c. 280 B.C.), a physician in Alexandria and a follower of Hippocrates (see p. 66), is regarded as "the father of anatomy." Herophilus timed the human pulse with a water clock, believed that the heart distributed blood throughout the body, emphasized exercise as part of a healthy lifestyle, and engaged in dissection to increase his knowledge of human anatomy. He was provided with condemned prisoners whom he dissected alive to observe various organs of the body as they functioned. Regarding the brain to be the center of the human nervous system, Herophilus classified the nerve trunks as either sensory or motor. In addition, he wrote treatises

---

* Galen, who synthesized medical knowledge, is treated in the next chapter, on Rome.

THE ART OF GOVERNING ACCORDING TO HAN FEI TZU

HAN FEI TZU (C. 280–233 B.C.) WAS A LEADING SPOKESMAN of the Legalist or Realist school of ancient Chinese philosophy. Unlike Confucianism, Legalism made no attempt to preserve morality or religion; its only aim was to instruct the ruler in survival. Han Fei's major interest was the fine art of governing. Han Fei's hard-headed counsel on how the ruler should wield authority in order to maintain and strengthen his state has been justifiably compared with Machiavelli's advice in his treatise, *The Prince,* written more than seventeen hundred years later.

When the scholars of today discuss good government, many of them say, "Give land to the poor and destitute so that those who have no means of livelihood may be provided for." Now if men start out with equal opportunities and yet there are a few who . . . are able to keep themselves well supplied, it must be due either to hard work or to frugal living. If men start out with equal opportunities and yet there are a few who, without having suffered from some calamity, . . . still sink into poverty and destitution, it must be due either to laziness or to extravagant living. The lazy and extravagant grow poor; the diligent and frugal get rich. Now if the ruler levies money from the rich in order to give alms to the poor, he is robbing the diligent and frugal and indulging the lazy and extravagant. If he expects by such means to induce the people to work industriously and spend with caution, he will be disappointed. . . .

When a sage rules the state, he does not depend on people's doing good of themselves; he sees to it that they are not allowed to do what is bad. If he depends on people's doing good out of themselves, then within his borders he can count on ten instances of success. But if he sees to it that they are not allowed to do what is bad, then the whole state can be brought to a uniform level of order. Those who rule must employ measures that will be effective with the majority and discard those that will be effective with only a few. Therefore they devote themselves not to virtue, but to law. . . .

Nowadays, those who do not understand how to govern invariably say, "You must win the hearts of the people!" If you could assure good government merely by winning the hearts of the people, then . . . you could simply listen to what the people say. The reason you cannot rely on the wisdom of the people is that they have the minds of little children. . . .

Now the ruler presses the people to till the land and open up new pastures to increase their means of livelihood, and yet they consider him harsh; he draws up a penal code and makes the punishments more severe in order to put a stop to evil, and yet the people consider him stern. He levies taxes in cash and grain in order to fill the coffers and granaries so that there will be food for the starving and funds for the army, and yet the people consider him avaricious. He makes sure that everyone within his borders understands warfare and sees to it that there are no private exemptions from military service; he unites the strength of the state and fights fiercely in order to take its enemies captive, and yet the people consider him violent. These four types of undertaking all insure order and safety to the state, and yet the people do not have sense enough to rejoice in them.

Source: *Burton Watson, trans.,* Basic Writings of Mo Tzu, Hsün Tzu, and Han Fei Tzu *(New York and London: Columbia University Press, 1967), pp. 120–121, 125, 128–129.*

on midwifery, anatomy, and sudden death and a commentary on Hippocrates.

MATHEMATICS In geometry, Euclid, an Alexandrian mathematician who lived around 300 B.C., creatively synthesized earlier developments. He founded a school at Alexandria during the reign of Ptolemy I (323–285/283 B.C.) and wrote *Elements,* an original synthesis of the works of predecessors. Euclid's hundreds of geometrical proofs, derived from reasoning alone, are a profound witness to the power of the rational mind.

Archimedes (b. c. 287 B.C.) studied in Alexandria but spent most of his life in his native Syracuse, in Sicily. He was a mathematician, a physicist, and an ingenious inventor. His father, Phidias, was an astronomer, and Archimedes was associated with the king of Syracuse, Hieron II, and his son, Gelon. Archimedes' mechanical inventions included the water screw, which is still used for irrigation purposes in Egypt, and war engines, which for more than three years warded off the Roman ships attacking Syracuse. However, Archimedes dismissed his practical inventions, preferring to be remembered as a theoretician. In one treatise, he established the general principles of hydrostatics, a branch of physics that treats the pressure and equilibrium of liquids at rest. The so-called *"Archimedes Principle"* states that a body immersed in a fluid displaces its own weight. He also wrote treatises on curves, planes, spheres, cylinders, parabolas, centers of gravity, and floating bodies, all of which are based on mechanical considerations in problem solving. In his *Measurement of the Circle,* he calculated the relationship of the circumference of a circle to its diameter— 3.14, known by the Greek letter Pi (π). In 212 B.C., during Rome's siege of Syracuse, Archimedes was stabbed to death while drawing a mathematical figure in the sand.

ASTRONOMY AND GEOGRAPHY* Knowledge in the field of astronomy also increased. Eighteen centuries before Copernicus, Alexandrian astronomer Aristarchus (310–230 B.C.) was the first to claim that the earth rotated on its axis and revolved around the sun (the heliocentric theory) and that the stars were situated at great distances from the earth. He was accused of impiety and challenged by Hipparchus of Nicaea (c. 190–c. 127 B.C.), who successfully reasserted the geocentric, or earth–centered, theory of the universe. Therefore, Aristarchus' revolutionary ideas were not accepted, and the belief in an earth-centered universe persisted. Eratosthenes of Cyrene (c. 275–194 B.C.), an Alexandrian intellectual, estimated the earth's circumference at 24,660 miles, an error of less than 10 percent.

The astronomer–geographer Hipparchus catalogued more than 800 stars according to their magnitude and brightness and fixed their positions by latitude and longitude in relation to the path of the sun. He also calculated the lunar month and the solar year with astonishing precision.

Philosophy

Hellenistic thinkers preserved the rational tradition of Greek philosophy, but they also transformed it, for they had to adapt thought to the requirements of a cosmopolitan society. In the Hellenic Age, the starting point of philosophy was the citizen's relationship to the city; in the Hellenistic Age, the point of departure was the solitary individual's relationship to humanity, the individual's destiny in a complex world. Philosophy tried to deal with the feeling of alienation resulting from the weakening of the individual's attachment to the polis and sought a conception of community that corresponded to the social realities of a world grown larger. It aspired to make people ethically independent so that they could achieve happiness in a hostile and competitive world.

In striving for tranquillity of mind and relief from conflict, Hellenistic thinkers reflected the general anxiety that pervaded their society. They retained respect for reason and aspired to the rational life, but by stressing peace of mind and the effort to overcome anxiety, they were performing a quasi-religious function. Philosophy was trying to provide comfort for the individual suffering from feelings of loneliness and insignificance. This attempt indicated that Greek civilization was undergoing a spiritual transformation. (We examine the full meaning of this transformation in Chapters 6 and 7.) The gravitation toward religion in an effort to relieve despair gathered momentum in the centuries that followed. Thus, Hellenistic philosophies helped prepare people to accept Christianity, which promised personal salvation. Ultimately, the Christian answer to the problems of alienation and the need for community would predominate over the Greco-Roman attempt at resolution.

The Hellenistic world gave rise to four principal schools of philosophy: Epicureanism, Stoicism, Skepticism, and Cynicism.

---

* Ptolemy, who synthesized known astronomical knowledge, is treated in the next chapter, on Rome.

EPICUREANISM In the tradition of Plato and Aristotle, Epicurus (342–270 B.C.) founded a school in Athens at the end of the fourth century B.C. Epicurus broke with the attitude of the Hellenic Age in significant ways. Unlike classical Greek philosophers, Epicurus reflected the Greeks' changing relationship to the city by teaching the value of passivity and withdrawal from civic life. To him, citizenship was not a prerequisite for individual happiness. Wise persons, said Epicurus, would refrain from engaging in public affairs, for politics could deprive them of their self-sufficiency, their freedom to choose and to act. Nor would wise individuals pursue wealth, power, or fame, as these pursuits would only provoke anxiety. For the same reason, wise persons would not surrender to hate or love, desires that distress the soul. They would also try to live justly because those who behave unjustly are burdened with troubles. Nor could people find happiness if they worried about dying or pleasing the gods.

To Epicurus, the superstitious fear that the gods intervened in human life and could inflict suffering after death was the principal cause of anxiety. To remove this source of human anguish, he favored a theory of nature that had no place for the activity of gods. Therefore, he adopted the physics of *Democritus,* which taught that all things consist of atoms in motion. In a universe of colliding atoms, there could be no higher intelligence ordering things; there was no room for divine activity. Epicurus taught that the gods probably did exist but that they could not influence human affairs; consequently, individuals could order their own lives.

People could achieve happiness, said Epicurus, when their bodies were "free from pain" and their minds were "released from worry and fear." Although Epicurus wanted to increase pleasure for the individual, he rejected unbridled hedonism. Because he believed that happiness must be pursued rationally, he urged avoidance of the merely sensuous pleasures that have unpleasant aftereffects (such as overeating and excessive drinking). In general, Epicurus espoused the traditional Greek view of moderation and prudence. By opening his philosophy, called *Epicureanism,* to men and women, slave and free, Greek and barbarian, and by separating ethics from politics, Epicurus fashioned a philosophy adapted to the post-Alexandrian world of kingdoms and universal culture.

STOICISM Around the time when Epicurus founded his school, Zeno (335–263 B.C.) also opened a school in Athens. Zeno's teachings, called *Stoicism* (because his school was located in the stoa, or colonnade), became the most important philosophy in the Hellenistic world. By teaching that the world constituted a single society, Stoicism gave theoretical expression to the world-mindedness of the age. Through its concept of a world–state, the city of humanity, Stoicism offered an answer to the problem of community and alienation posed by the decline of the city–state. By stressing inner strength in dealing with life's misfortunes, it opened an avenue to individual happiness in a world fraught with uncertainty.

At the core of Stoicism was the belief that the universe contained a principle of order, variously called the Divine Fire, God—more the fundamental force of the universe than a living person—and Divine Reason (Logos). This ruling principle underlay reality and permeated all things; it accounted for the orderliness of nature. The Stoics reasoned that, being part of the universe, people too shared in the Logos that operated throughout the cosmos. The Logos was implanted in every human soul; it enabled people to act intelligently and to comprehend the principles of order that governed nature. Because reason was common to all, human beings were essentially brothers and sisters and fundamentally equal. Reason gave individuals dignity and enabled them to recognize and respect the dignity of others. To the Stoics, all people—Greek and barbarian, free and slave, rich and poor—were fellow human beings, and one law, the law of nature, applied to everyone. Thus, the Stoics, like the Hebrews, arrived at the idea of a common humanity subject to the same moral obligations.

Like Socrates, the Stoics believed that a person's distinctive quality was the ability to reason, and that happiness came from the disciplining of emotions by the rational part of the soul. Also like Socrates, the Stoics maintained that individuals should progress morally, or should perfect their character. In the Stoic view, wise persons ordered their lives according to the natural law, the law of reason, that underlay the cosmos. This harmony with the Logos would give them the inner strength to resist the torments inflicted by others, by fate, and by their own passionate natures. Self-mastery and inner peace, or happiness, would follow. Such individuals would remain undisturbed by life's misfortunes, for their souls would be their own. Even slaves were not denied this inner freedom; although their bodies were subjected to the power of their masters, their minds still remained independent and free.

Stoicism had an enduring influence on the Western mind. To some Roman political theorists, the Empire fulfilled the Stoic ideal of a world community, in which people of different nationalities held citizenship and were governed by a worldwide law that accorded with the law of reason, or natural law, operating throughout the universe. Stoic beliefs—that by nature we are all members of one family, that each person is significant, that distinctions of rank and race are of no account, and that human law should not conflict with natural law—were incorporated into Roman jurisprudence, Christian thought, and modern liberalism. There is continuity between the Stoic idea of natural law—a moral order that underlies nature—and the principle of inalienable rights—rights to which all are entitled by nature—stated in the American Declaration of Independence.

SKEPTICISM   The Epicureans tried to withdraw from the evils of this world and to attain personal happiness by reducing physical pain and mental anguish. The Stoics sought happiness by actively entering into harmony with universal reason. Both philosophies sought peace of mind, but the Stoics did not disengage themselves from political life and often exerted influence over Hellenistic rulers. *Skepticism,* another school of philosophy, attacked the Epicurean and Stoic beliefs that there is a definite avenue to happiness. Skeptics held that one could achieve spiritual comfort by recognizing that none of the beliefs by which people lived was true or could bring happiness.

Some Skeptics taught indifference to all theory and urged conformity to accepted views whether or not they were true. This attitude would avoid arguments and explanations. Gods might not exist, said the Skeptics, but to refuse to worship or to deny their existence would only cause trouble; therefore, individuals should follow the crowd. The life of the mind—metaphysical speculation inquiring into the origin of things, and clever reasoning—did not bring truth or happiness, so why should one bother with it? Suspending judgment, recognizing the inability to understand, not committing oneself to a system of belief—by these means one could achieve peace of mind. Instead of embracing doctrines, said the Greek writer Lucian, individuals should go their way "with ever a smile and never a passion."[4] This was the position of those Skeptics who were suspicious of ideas and hostile to intellectuals.

The more sophisticated Skeptics did not run away from ideas but pointed out their limitations; they did not avoid theories but refuted them. In doing so, they did not reject reason but focused on a problem of reason: whether indeed it could arrive at truth. Thus, Carneades of Cyrene (213–129 B.C.) insisted that all ideas, even mathematical principles, must be regarded as hypotheses and assumptions, not as absolutes. Just because the universe showed signs of order, Carneades argued, one could not assume that God had created it. Because there was never any certainty, only probability, morality should derive from practical experience rather than from dogma.

CYNICISM   The *Cynics* were not theoretical philosophers but supreme individualists who rebelled against established values and conventions—against every barrier of society that restrained individuals from following their own natures. Cynics regarded laws and public opinion, private property and employment, and wives and children as hindrances to the free life. Extreme individualists, the Cynics had no loyalty to family, city, or kingdom and ridiculed religion, philosophy, and literature. They renounced possessions and showed no respect for authority. When Diogenes, a fourth-century B.C. Cynic, met Alexander the Great, he is supposed to have asked only that the great conqueror get out of his light.

Cynics put their philosophy into practice. They cultivated indifference and apathy. To harden themselves against life's misfortunes, they engaged in strenuous exercise, endured cold and hunger, and lived ascetically. Not tied down by property or employment Cynics wandered shoeless from place to place, wearing dirty and ragged clothes and carrying staffs. To show their disdain for society's customs, Cynics grew long scraggly beards, used foul language, and cultivated bad manners. Diogenes supposedly said: "Look at me, . . . I am without a home, without a city, without property, without a slave; I sleep on the ground; I have neither wife nor children, no miserable governor's mansion, but only earth, and sky, and one rough cloak. Yet what do I lack? Am I not free from pain and fear, am I not free?"[5] In their attack on inherited conventions, Cynics strove for self-sufficiency and spiritual security. Theirs was the most radical philosophical quest for meaning and peace of soul during the Hellenistic Age.

HELLENISTIC ART

Hellenistic artists preserved the forms of the Classical period but also introduced new subjects and styles that reflected the peculiar character of the age, namely the subordination of cities to dynastic monarchies and the increased interaction of Greeks with Near Eastern peoples. Spurring artistic innovation was a new kind of patronage. Wealthy merchants commissioned artists to embellish their private homes, and monarchs, eager to glorify their reigns, sought the services of

Figure 5.1   *Battle of Issus, Roman mosaic*, 100 B.C., height 10'3 1/4" (3.13 m), **Museo Archeologico Nazionale, Naples**   The subject of the mosaic is believed to be Alexander's victory over the Persian king, Darius III, in 333 B.C. at the Battle of Issus. On the right side of the mosaic, we see a realistic battle scene filled with both commotion and emotion. *(Scala/Art Resource, NY)*

eminent artists to produce royal portraits, victory monuments, paintings of great battles, temples, and tombs. Continuing a practice initiated during the Hellenic age, Hellenistic cities also commissioned artists. What was new, however, was the proliferation of portrait statues honoring prominent civic leaders, orators, poets, philosophers, and playwrights. In fulfilling their commissions, painters, sculptors, and architects searched for novel forms of expression, often with the encouragement of their patrons.

Hellenistic art, like Hellenistic philosophy, was preoccupied with a heightened awareness of the universal and individual elements in human experience. It was an art of great extremes and range, easily as capable of the restraint and repose of classical Hellenic art—evidenced by such serene compositions as the *Aphrodite of Cyrene* or the *Apollo Belvedere*—as it was of lavish exaggerations and dramatic excesses—witnessed in such works as the *Nike of Samothrace* and *The Laocoön Group*. It could depict imaginative themes of cosmic sweep, such as the turbulent *Battle of Issus,* and in a burst of feeling glorify heroism, as in the numerous extant likenesses of Alexander the Great. At the same time, it also represented the world in a rigorously realistic manner, probing human personality, sometimes with heart-rending detail, as in the *Old Market Woman,* the *Dying Trumpeter,* and the *Gaul and Wife.*

The adventuresome spirit and heroic personality of Alexander the Great significantly influenced Hellenistic art. His importance is apparent in a painting by Philoxenos of Eretria, from about 300 B.C. The subject of the painting is believed to be Alexander's victory over the Persian king, Darius III, in 333 B.C. at the *Battle of Issus.* However, the scene only survives in Roman mosaic form (100 B.C.) (Figure 5.1). Many such mosaics are assumed to be copies of Greek paintings, lost after the fourth century B.C., which were discovered at Pompeii and Herculaneum in the eighteenth century. Although the left side of this mosaic is severely damaged, the right side still displays a realistic battle scene filled with commotion and emotion—light reflects from the armor, bodies, horses, and weapons. The foreshortening of the horses, from both the front and rear, and the twisted, tormented faces of the defeated soldiers enhance the sense of movement.

Long after Alexander's death, portrait sculptures of him were still prevalent. One of these (Figure 5.2) was found at Pergamum, a fourth Hellenistic kingdom that emerged in western Asia Minor in the middle of the third century B.C. Presumably it was commissioned by the wealthiest purveyors of art in Pergamum—the Attalids. The Attalid dynasty was named for Attalus I, who proclaimed himself king of the city in 240 B.C. After a

Figure 5.2 *Alexander the Great,* from Pergamum, c. 1st half of 2nd century B.C., height 16 1/8" (41 cm), Archaeological Museum, Istanbul   His ambition knew no bounds, and Alexander aspired to conquer the entire Persian empire. Daring, brave, and intelligent, he possessed the irrepressible energy of a romantic adventurer. *(Archeological Museum, Istanbul/Erich Lessing/Art Resource, NY)*

series of triumphs over the Gauls,* and an alliance with Rome, the Attalids became a profound cultural influence in the Hellenistic world. Eumenes II, son of Attalus I, authorized a burst of scholarship and art in Pergamum that lasted until his death in 159 B.C. *The Acropolis of Pergamum* (Figure 5.3), paid for with burdensome taxes exacted from his subjects, incorporated a gymnasium, a theater, a library, a marketplace, a temple for Athene, and a magnificent altar in honor of Zeus.

The *Altar to Zeus* (Figure 5.4), the most important religious shrine on the acropolis of Pergamum, was commissioned by Eumenes II about 180 B.C. to commemorate his father's victories over the Gauls. In 1873, archaeologists discovered fragments of the sculpture, and in 1930 the west front was reconstructed in Berlin. The design is basically a rectangular court with two wings surrounded by an Ionic colonnade, which ascends 100 feet from the monumental flight of stairs. The magnificent frieze on the base depicts the battle of the gods and the giants, a traditional theme for

---

* A Celtic people from north of the Alps to Iberia, Gauls had migrated south and southeast, thrusting into Italy, Greece, and Asia Minor.

Figure 5.3 *Acropolis of Pergamum,* reconstruction, Staatliche Museen zu Berlin— Preussischer Kulturbesitz   The Attalids became a profound cultural influence in the Hellenistic world. Their acropolis was paid for with burdensome taxes. It incorporated a gymnasium, a theater, a library, a marketplace, a temple for Athene, and a magnificent altar in honor of Zeus. *(Staatliche Museen zu Berlin/Bildarchiv Preussischer Kulturbesitz. Photo: Christa Begall)*

Figure 5.4   *Altar to Zeus,* c. 180 B.C., Staatliche Museen zu Berlin   Eumenes II commissioned the altar to commemorate his father's victories over the Gauls. In 1873, archaeologists discovered fragments of the sculpture, and in 1930 the west front was reconstructed in Berlin. *(Staatliche Museen zu Berlin/Bildarchiv Preussischer Kulturbesitz. Photo: Reinhard Saczewski)*

Ionic friezes, although here it represents the triumph of Attalus over the Gauls. Also unlike the customary representation of Greek triumphs—Greeks fighting Amazons, Lapiths battling Centaurs, or Greeks warring with the Persians—Attalus here is equated with Zeus in his victory against the Gauls. Such an exaltation of the ruler suggests Near Eastern influence. The frieze, over 400 feet long and seven and one-half feet tall, is rendered in such high relief that the writhing arms and legs of the figures project from the frieze and rest on the steps. The intense emotion, violence,

and drama reveal the incredible skill of the artists who worked on the project.

In stark contrast to the glory of victory portrayed on the *Altar of Zeus,* the *Dying Trumpeter* (c. 230–220 B.C.) (Figure 5.5) depicts a wounded trumpeter who has crawled off to die alone. The statue exists only as a marble Roman copy of the bronze original, but scholars, following the Roman writer–naturalist Pliny, presume Epigonos of Pergamum completed the original. The school of sculpture at Pergamum is regarded as the most dramatic of the Hellenistic schools. The sculptor shows

Figure 5.5   *The Dying Trumpeter,* marble copy of the bronze original, c. 230–220 B.C., life size, Capitoline Museum, Rome   Mortally wounded in his side, the Gaul trumpeter dauntlessly supports the full weight of his body with his right arm, as if resisting some invisible burden that is about to crush him. *(Musei Capitolini, Rome/Scala/Art Resource, NY)*

the Gauls to be worthy opponents of the Attalids and evokes great pathos for them. Mortally wounded in his side, the Gaul trumpeter dauntlessly supports the full weight of his body with his right arm as if resisting some invisible burden that is about to crush him. The realistic depiction of the trumpeter is defined by the torque necklace around his neck, the structure of his face, and his bristly hair.

An even more dramatic piece, evoking a similar pathos, is *Gaul and His Wife* (Figure 5.6). Executed sometime after 220 B.C., it portrays the murder–suicide of a man and his wife who refuse to be taken as prisoners by the approaching Attalids. As he courageously plunges the dagger into his own chest, the drooping body of his wife slips from his grasp. Such violence elicits feelings of sympathy from people who wonder what decision they personally might make if faced with the imminent capture of one's family by a foreign power. Such violence, drama, and emotion contrasts with the Classical Age of Hellenic sculpture, which idealized the human being.

Like the *Altar of Zeus,* the *Nike of Samothrace* (Figure 5.7), was reputedly rendered to commemorate a great triumph—the naval victory of Rhodes over the Seleucids in 190 B.C. Considered to be one of the most significant statues of the Hellenistic age, it originally stood in the Sanctuary of the Gods on the island of Samothrace in the northern Aegean Sea. Although scholars disagree over the person who executed it, many assume it to be the work of Phythokritos on the island of Rhodes around 200–190 B.C. The monument demonstrates an interrelatedness between the statue and the space that it occupies. The wings of the goddess, who has just landed on the prow of a ship, still seem to beat against a powerful headwind. The reality of the wind is intangible, but the wind under her wings is distinctly tangible—it appears to balance the figure as well as to shape every inch of the garment that surrounds her form. The rendering of the drapery was innovative. Whereas the drapery of the Classi-

Figure 5.6 *Gaul and His Wife,* **c. 225 B.C., marble copy of bronze original, height 6'11" (2.11 m), Museo Nazional Romano, Rome** The statue portrays the murder–suicide of a man and his wife who refuse to be taken as prisoners by the approaching Attalids. As he courageously plunges the dagger into his own chest, the drooping body of his wife slips from his grasp. *(Museo Nazionale Romano, Rome/ Scala/Art Resource, NY)*

Figure 5.7   Phythokritos of Rhodes, *Nike of Samothrace*, c. 200–190 B.C., marble, height 8′ (2.4 m), Musee du Louvre, Paris   The sculpture originally stood in the Sanctuary of the Gods on the island of Samothrace, in the northern Aegean Sea. It demonstrates an interrelatedness between the statue and the space that it occupies. For example, the wings of the goddess, who has just landed on the prow of a ship, still seem to beat against a powerful headwind. *(Louvre/Reunion des Musees Nationaux/Art Resource, NY)*

Figure 5.8   *Apollo Belvedere*, c. late fourth century B.C., marble, height 7′4″ (2.24 m), Vatican Museum, Rome   Viewed as the essence of male beauty, this statue combines the repose of Classical statuary with a realistic simulation of soft, warm flesh. *(Vatican Museums/Scala/Art Resource, NY)*

cal period of Hellenic art was idealized and static, the *Nike of Samothrace* illustrates the effect of the environment on natural space.

Perhaps the most admired statue from the Hellenistic age is the *Laocoön Group* (see chapter opening). Many consider it to be the epitome of noble tragedy. According to Pliny, this realistic scene of human suffering and torment was an original work executed during the first century B.C. by the Rhodians Hagesandros, Polydoros, and Athanadoros. But because they are now known to have been outstanding copyists of Greek statues, some scholars assert that it could be a copy of a statue done by some other sculptor as late as the first century A.D. According to the *Aeneid* written by the Roman poet Virgil (see Chapter 6), the priest Laocoön warned the Trojans not to bring the wooden horse—filled with Greek soldiers in its underbelly—into the city. The Trojans, however, did not believe Laocoön and brought the horse

inside the city walls with disastrous consequences. As punishment for his warning, a god or goddess, who sided with the Greeks, sent sea serpents to strangle Laocoön and his two sons. Precisely which god or goddess punished Laocoön and his sons is open to debate. Some claim it was Athene protecting Athens; others assert Laocoön offended Apollo; still others maintain it was Poseidon who sided with the Greeks during the Trojan War. The anguish of Laocoön's suffering is captured in stone, as he and his sons struggle against the serpents. When the statue was discovered in 1506, it also made a profound impression on Michelangelo and other artists of the Renaissance, who were inspired by its passion and drama.

Like the Classical Hellenic sculptors, Hellenistic sculptors showed an appreciation of the human form. Just as the Laocoön was seen as the epitome of tragedy, the *Apollo Belvedere* (late fourth century B.C.) (Figure 5.8) was viewed as the essence

Figure 5.9 *Aphrodite of Melos,* c. 150–100 B.C., marble, height 6′10″ (2.10 m), Louvre, Paris The serene expression and facial features of the statue best known as "Venus de Milo" are reminiscent of Classical Greek style, but her sensuality is purely Hellenistic. *(Louvre/Reunion des Musees Nationaux/Art Resource, NY)*

age. In both form and subject matter, genre sculpture was radically different from Classical Hellenic sculpture and further defined individualized realism. Hellenistic genre sculpture depicted people in everyday situations, as individuals, rather than as types. Originally from the third or second century B.C., the *Old Market Woman* survives only as a Roman copy of the original bronze statue. Her shoulders, which are stooped from the weight of her groceries, suggest the harsh physical conditions that have worn her down over the years. Scholars debate whether the number of statues of old women—rendered either as drunk, tired, or beggarly—illustrates the sculptors' realism or a disdain for the women's pathetic situations.

Patrons encouraged artists to be creative and surpass the achievements of the artists of classical

Figure 5.10 *Old Market Woman,* c. 2nd century B.C., marble, height 4′1″ (1.26 m), Metropolitan Museum of Art, New York Hellenistic genre sculpture depicted people in everyday situations, as individuals, rather than as types. Her stooped shoulders, weighed down by her groceries, also suggest the harsh physical conditions that have worn her down over the years. *(The Metropolitan Museum of Art, Rogers Fund, 1909 (09.39) © 1997 The Metropolitan Museum of Art)*

of male beauty. Hellenistic sculptors had no rivals when it came to combining the repose of Classical statuary with a realistic simulation of soft, warm flesh in their marble statues. This is clearly illustrated by the celebrated *Aphrodite of Melos* (Figure 5.9)—better known as "Venus de Milo"—which dates from some time between 150 and 100 B.C. Although the serene expression of her face and the outline of her facial features are reminiscent of Classical Greek style, the utter sensuality of her partially draped body is purely Hellenistic.

The *Old Market Woman* (Figure 5.10) is an example of the **genre sculpture** of the Hellenistic

Greece. The individualized realism of Hellenistic art and its depiction of human emotions were unsurpassed in the ancient world. Although the Romans appreciated art and copied many Hellenistic works, there were no further significant developments in sculpture until the Renaissance in Italy in the fifteenth century A.D.

THE HELLENISTIC LEGACY

The Hellenistic Age encompassed the period from the death of Alexander to the formation of the Roman Empire. During these three centuries, Greek civilization spread eastward as far as India and westward to Rome. As Greeks settled in the Near East and intermingled with Egyptians, Syrians, Persians, and others, the parochialism of the Greek polis gave way to a new cosmopolitanism, an interest in the culture of other ethnic groups, and universalism, an awareness that people were members of a world community that transcended citizenship in one's native city, which were reflected in philosophy and the arts.

Rome, conqueror of the Mediterranean world and transmitter of Hellenism, inherited the universalist tendencies of the Hellenistic Age and embodied them in its law, institutions, and art. So, too, did Christianity, which welcomed converts from every ethnic background and held that God loved all people, that Christ died for all humanity. The Stoic idea of natural law that applies to all human beings and its corollary that human beings are fundamentally equal were crucial to the formulation of the modern idea that the individual is endowed with natural rights that no government can violate. A parallel can be drawn between the Hellenistic Age, in which Greek culture spread far and wide, and our own age in which the ideas, institutions, and technology of Western civilization have been exported throughout the globe.

Key Terms

Hellenistic Age	Epicureanism
Aramaic	Stoicism
New Comedy	Skepticism
Hellenistic romance	Cynics
"Archimedes Principle"	genre sculpture
Democritus	

Notes

1. Apollonius of Rhodes, *The Voyage of Argo*, trans. E. V. Rieu (Baltimore: Penguin Books, 1959), p. 117.
2. Theocritus, *The Idylls of Theocritus*, trans. R. C. Trevelyan (London: The Casanova Society, 1925), p. 28.
3. Benjamin Farrington, *Greek Science* (Baltimore: Penguin Books, 1961), p. 301.
4. Quoted in J. H. Randall, Jr., *Hellenistic Ways of Deliverance and the Making of the Christian Synthesis* (New York: Columbia University Press, 1970), p. 74.
5. Epictetus, *The Discourses as Reported by Arrian, the Manual and Fragments*, trans. W. A. Oldfather (Cambridge, Mass.: Harvard University Press, 1966), 2:147.

MVNIF·PI·IX·P·M.
AN·XVIII

Roman Civilization: The Expansion of Hellenism

ROME'S GREAT ACHIEVEMENT WAS TO TRANSCEND the narrow political orientation of the city–state and to create a world–state, which unified the different nations of the Mediterranean world. Regarding the polis as the only means to the good life, the Greeks had not desired a larger political unit and had almost totally excluded foreigners from citizenship. Although Hellenistic philosophers had conceived the possibility of a world community, Hellenistic politics could not shape one. But Rome overcame the limitations of the city–state mentality and developed an empirewide system of law and citizenship. The Hebrews were distinguished by their prophets and the Greeks by their philosophers; Rome's genius found expression in law and government.

Historians divide Roman history into two broad periods. The period of the Republic began in 509 B.C. with the overthrow of the Etruscan monarchy; that of the Empire started in 27 B.C., when Octavian (Augustus) became in effect the first Roman emperor, ending almost five hundred years of republican self-government. By conquering the Mediterranean world and extending its law and, in some instances, citizenship to different nationalities, the Roman Republic transcended the parochialism typical of the city–state. The Republic initiated the trend toward political and legal universalism, which reached fruition in the second phase of Roman history, the Empire.

EVOLUTION OF THE ROMAN REPUBLIC

By the eighth century B.C., peasant communities existed on some of Rome's seven hills near the Tiber River in central Italy. To the north stood Etruscan cities and to the south, Greek cities. The Romans gradually absorbed the more advanced civilizations of both Etruscans and Greeks. The origin of the Etruscans remains a mystery, although some scholars believe that they came from Asia Minor and settled in northern Italy. From them, Romans acquired architectural styles and skills in road construction, sanitation, hydraulic engineering (including underground conduits), metallurgy, ceramics, and portrait sculpture. Etruscan words and names entered the Latin language, and Roman religion absorbed Etruscan gods.

Rome became a republic at the end of the sixth century B.C.—the traditional date is 509 B.C.—when the landowning aristocrats, or patricians, overthrew the Etruscan king. The early Republic was dominated by a conflict—known as the *Struggle of the Orders*—between the patricians and the commoners, or plebeians. At the beginning of the fifth century B.C., patricians owned most of the land and controlled the army and the government. The chief organ of patrician

Augustus of Prima Porta, original c. 15 B.C., marble, height 6′8″ (2 m), Vatican Museum, Rome.

The naked feet signify Augustus' divinity; the small cupid riding the dolphin alludes to Augustus' claim that the Julian line descended from Venus, and the breastplate commemorates his victory over the Parthians, the triumph that ushered in the Augustan peace.

(Scala/Art Resource, NY)

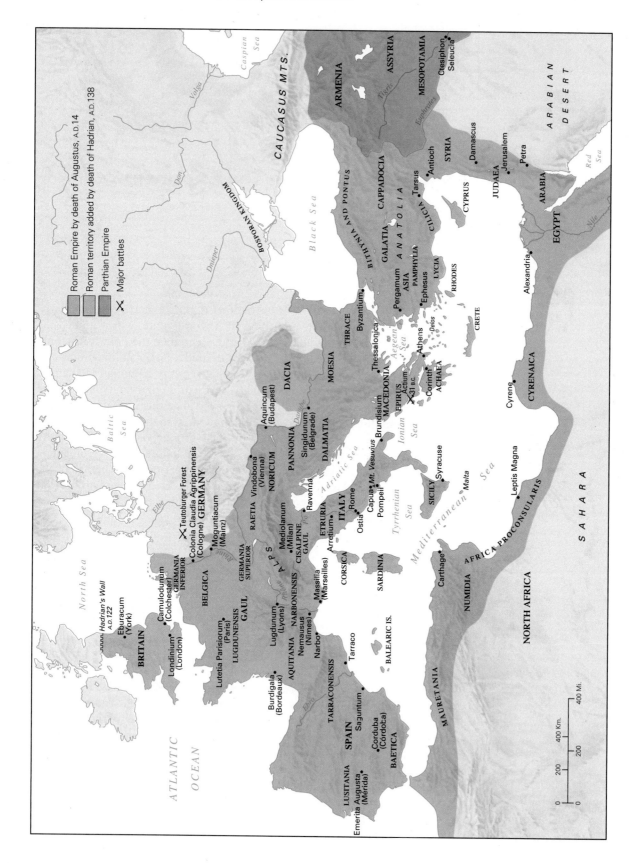

Roman Empire by death of Augustus, A.D.14

Roman territory added by death of Hadrian, A.D.138

Parthian Empire

X   Major battles

power, the Senate, controlled public finances and foreign policy. Plebeian grievances included enslavement for debt, discrimination in the courts, prevention of intermarriage with patricians, lack of political representation, and the absence of a written code of laws. Resenting their inferior status and eager for economic relief, the plebeians organized and waged a struggle for political, legal, and social equality.

The plebeians had one decisive weapon: their threat to secede from Rome, that is, not to pay taxes, work, or serve in the army. Realizing that Rome, which was constantly involved in warfare on the Italian peninsula, could not endure without plebeian help, the pragmatic patricians grudgingly made concessions. Thus, the plebeians slowly gained legal equality. By the early third century B.C., plebeians had gained the right to intermarry with patricians; access to the highest political, judicial, and religious offices in the state, including the Senate; and the elimination of slavery as payment for debt. Nevertheless, Rome was still ruled by an upper class. The oligarchy that held power now consisted of patricians and influential plebeians who had joined forces with the old nobility. Marriages between patricians and politically powerful plebeians strengthened this alliance. Deeming themselves Rome's finest citizens, the ruling oligarchy led Rome during its period of expansion and demonstrated a sense of responsibility and a talent for statesmanship.

Roman Expansion to 146 B.C.

At the time of the Struggle of the Orders, Rome was also extending its power over the Italian peninsula. In conquering Italy, Romans were united by a moral and religious devotion to their city that was strong enough to overcome social conflict, factional disputes, and personal ambition.

Shortly after asserting supremacy in Italy, Rome began a march to empire. By 146 B.C., Rome had totally destroyed Carthage, a once formidable power in the western Mediterranean, and had reduced the Hellenistic kingdoms—Macedonia, Seleucia, Egypt, and Pergamum—to client kingdoms, deprived of their freedom of action in for-

eign affairs. Rome had not yet reached the limits of its expansion, but there was no doubt that the Mediterranean world had been subjected to its will. No power could stand up to Rome.

Expansion had important consequences for Rome and the Mediterranean world. The influx into Rome of enslaved Greeks, many of them educated persons, accelerated the process of Hellenization that had begun earlier through Rome's contact with the Greek cities of southern Italy. Contact with the legal experience of other peoples, including the Greeks, led Roman jurists to incorporate into Roman law elements of the legal codes and traditions of these nations (see p. 140).

It is estimated that between 80 and 8 B.C. more than two million enslaved aliens were transported to Italy. By the middle of that century, slaves constituted about one-third of Italy's population, compared with about 10 percent before the Second Punic War. The more fortunate slaves worked as craftsmen and servants; the luckless and more numerous toiled on the growing number of plantations or died early laboring in mines. Roman masters often treated their slaves brutally. Although slave uprisings were not common, their ferocity terrified the Romans. In 73 B.C., gladiators, led by Spartacus, broke out of their barracks and were joined by tens of thousands of runaways. The slave army defeated Roman armies and devastated southern Italy before the superior might of Rome prevailed. Some six thousand of the defeated slaves were crucified.

Roman governors, lesser officials, and businessmen found the provinces a source of quick wealth; they were generally unrestrained by the Senate, which was responsible for administering the overseas territories. Exploitation, corruption, looting, and extortion soon ran rampant. The Roman nobility proved unfit to manage a world empire.

Despite numerous examples of misrule in the provinces, Roman administration had many positive features. Rome generally allowed its subjects a large measure of self-government and did not interfere with religion and local customs. Usually, the Roman taxes worked out to be no higher, and in some instances were lower, than those under previous regimes. Most important, Rome reduced the endemic warfare that had plagued these regions.

The Collapse of the Republic

During Rome's march to empire, all its classes had demonstrated a magnificent civic spirit in fighting foreign wars. With Carthage and Macedonia no longer threatening Rome, this cooperation deteriorated. Internal dissension tore Rome apart as the

Map 6.1 Roman Expansion Under the Empire The Roman Empire came to encompass all the lands surrounding the Mediterranean Sea, as well as parts of continental Europe. Deserts and seas provided solid natural boundaries, but the long vulnerable river border in central and eastern Europe would eventually prove too expensive to defend and vulnerable to invasion by Germanic and Central Asian peoples.

ferocious drive for domination formerly directed against foreign enemies turned inward, against fellow Romans. Civil war replaced foreign war. The Republic had conquered an empire only to see the spiritual qualities of its citizens decay.

The downhill slide of the Republic began with an agricultural crisis. In the long war with Hannibal in Italy, farms were devastated, and with many Roman soldier–farmers serving long periods in the army, fields lay neglected. Returning veterans lacked the money to restore their land and were forced to sell their farms to wealthy landowners at low prices.

The dispossessed peasantry found little to do in Rome, where there was not enough industry to provide them with employment and where slaves did much of the work. The once sturdy and independent Roman farmer, who had done all that his country had asked of him, was becoming part of a vast urban underclass, poor, embittered, and alienated.

Distressed by the injustice done to the peasantry and recognizing that the Roman army depended on the loyalty of small landowners, Tiberius Gracchus (163–133 B.C.), who came from one of Rome's most honored families, took up the cause of land reform. Tiberius proposed a moderate solution for the problem of the landless peasants. However, Rome's leading families viewed Tiberius as a revolutionary, who threatened their property and political authority. To preserve the status quo, with wealth and power concentrated in the hands of a few hundred families, senatorial extremists killed Tiberius and some three hundred of his followers, dumping their bodies into the Tiber.

The cause of land reform was next taken up by Gaius Gracchus (153–121 B.C.), a younger brother of Tiberius. But like his brother, Gaius aroused the anger of the senatorial class. A brief civil war raged in Rome, during which Gaius Gracchus (who may have committed suicide) and three thousand of his followers perished.

In the first century B.C., civil wars, marked by terrible massacres, raged in Rome. Rival commanders used their troops for their own political advantage and fought each other with Rome as the prize. The most able of these commanders was Julius Caesar (c. 100–44 B.C.). Caesar's victories in Gaul alarmed the Senate, which feared that Caesar would use his devoted troops and soaring reputation to seize control of the state. When the Senate ordered Caesar to relinquish his command, he decided instead to march on Rome. After he crossed the Rubicon River into Italy in 49 B.C., civil war again ravaged the Republic. The Senate's army proved no match for so talented a general; the Senate acknowledged Caesar's victory and appointed him to be dictator, a legal office, for ten years.

Caesar realized that republican institutions no longer operated effectively and that only strong and enlightened leadership could permanently end the civil warfare destroying Rome. He fought exploitation in the provinces and generously extended citizenship to more provincials. To aid the poor in Rome, he began a public works program, which provided employment and beautified the city. He also relocated more than a hundred thousand veterans and members of Rome's lower class to the provinces, where he gave them land.

On March 15, in 44 B.C., a group of nobles, who were jealous of Caesar's success and power and afraid that he would set himself up as a monarch and end republican government and aristocratic rule, assassinated Caesar. The assassination of Julius Caesar did not restore republican liberty but plunged Rome into renewed civil war, which did not end until Octavian, Caesar's adopted son, defeated his rivals and emerged as master of Rome.

The Roman Republic, which had amassed power to a degree hitherto unknown in the ancient world, was wrecked not by foreign invasion but by internal weaknesses: the degeneration of senatorial leadership, and the willingness of politicians to use violence; the formation of private armies, in which soldiers gave their loyalty to their commander rather than to Rome; the transformation of a self-reliant peasantry into an impoverished and demoralized city rabble; and the deterioration of the ancient virtues that had been the source of the state's vitality.

THE FOUNDATIONS OF THE ROMAN EMPIRE

Augustus

Like Caesar before him, Octavian recognized that only a strong monarchy could restore order to a world exhausted by civil war and anarchy. But learning from Caesar's assassination, he also knew that republican ideals were far from dead. To exercise autocratic power openly, like a Hellenistic monarch, would have aroused the hostility of the Roman ruling class, whose assistance and goodwill Octavian desired.

Octavian demonstrated his political genius by reconciling his military monarchy with republican institutions: He held absolute power without abruptly breaking with a republican past. Magistrates were still elected and assemblies still met; the Senate administered certain provinces, retained its treasury, and was invited to advise Octavian. With some truth, Octavian could claim that he ruled in partnership with the Senate. By maintaining the facade of the Republic, Octavian camouflaged his absolute power and contained senatorial opposition, which had already been weakened by the deaths of leading nobles in battle or in the purges that Octavian had instituted against his enemies.

In keeping with his policy of maintaining the appearance of traditional republican government, Octavian refused to be called king or even, like Caesar, dictator; instead, he cleverly disguised his autocratic rule by taking the inoffensive title of princeps (first citizen). The Senate also conferred on him the semireligious and revered name of Augustus. The rule of Augustus and his successors is referred to as the *principate.*

The reign of Augustus signified the end of the Roman Republic and the beginning of the Roman Empire—the termination of aristocratic politics and the emergence of one-man rule. Despite his introduction of autocratic rule, however, Augustus was by no means a self-seeking tyrant, but a creative statesman. Heir to the Roman tradition of civic duty, he regarded his power as a public trust, delegated to him by the Roman people. He was faithful to the classical ideal that the state should promote the good life by protecting civilization from barbarism and ignorance, and he sought to rescue a dying Roman world.

Augustus instituted reforms and improvements throughout the Empire. He reformed the army to guard against the reemergence of ambitious generals like those whose rivalries and private armies had wrecked the Republic. He improved the distribution of free grain to the impoverished proletariat and financed the popular gladiatorial combats out of his own funds. He earned the gratitude of the provincials by correcting tax abuses and fighting corruption and extortion, as well as by improving the quality of governors and enabling aggrieved provincials to bring charges against Roman officials. An imperial bureaucracy, which enabled talented and dedicated men to serve the state, gradually evolved.

The Pax Romana

The brilliant statesmanship of Augustus inaugurated Rome's greatest age. For the next two hundred years, the Mediterranean world enjoyed the blessings of the *Pax Romana,* the Roman peace. The ancient world had never experienced such a long period of peace, order, efficient administration, and prosperity.

The Romans called the Pax Romana the "Time of Happiness." This period was the fulfillment of Rome's mission: the creation of a world–state that provided peace, security, ordered civilization, and the rule of law. Roman legions defended the Rhine–Danube river frontiers from incursions by Germanic tribesmen, held the Parthians at bay in the east, and subdued the few uprisings that occurred. These Roman emperors did not use military force needlessly but fought for sensible political goals. Generals did not wage war recklessly; instead, they tried to limit casualties, avoid risks, and deter conflicts through a show of force.

CONSTRUCTIVE RULE   Roman rule was constructive. The Romans built roads, improved harbors, cleared forests, drained swamps, irrigated deserts, and cultivated undeveloped lands. The aqueducts they constructed brought fresh water for drinking and bathing to large numbers of people, and the effective sewage systems enhanced the quality of life. Goods were transported over roads made safe by Roman soldiers and across a Mediterranean Sea swept clear of pirates. A wide variety of goods circulated throughout the Empire. A stable currency, generally not subject to depreciation, contributed to the economic well-being of the Mediterranean world.

Scores of new cities sprang up, and old ones grew larger and wealthier. Imperial troops guarded against civil wars within the cities and prevented warfare between cities—two traditional weaknesses of city life in the ancient world. The municipalities served as centers of Greco-Roman civilization, which spread to the farthest reaches of the Mediterranean, continuing a process initiated during the Hellenistic Age. Citizenship, generously granted, was finally extended to virtually all free men by an edict of A.D. 212.

IMPROVED CONDITIONS FOR SLAVES AND WOMEN   Conditions improved for those at the bottom of society, the slaves. At the time of Augustus, slaves may have accounted for a quarter of the population of Italy. But their numbers declined as Rome engaged in fewer wars of conquest. The freeing of slaves also became more common during the Empire. Freed slaves gained citizenship, with most of the rights and privileges of other citizens; their children suffered no legal disabilities whatsoever. During the Republic, slaves had been terribly abused; they were often mutilated, thrown to wild beasts, crucified, or burned alive. Several emperors issued decrees protecting slaves from cruel masters.

The status of women had also gradually improved during the Republic. In the early days of the Republic, a woman lived under the absolute authority first of her father and then of her

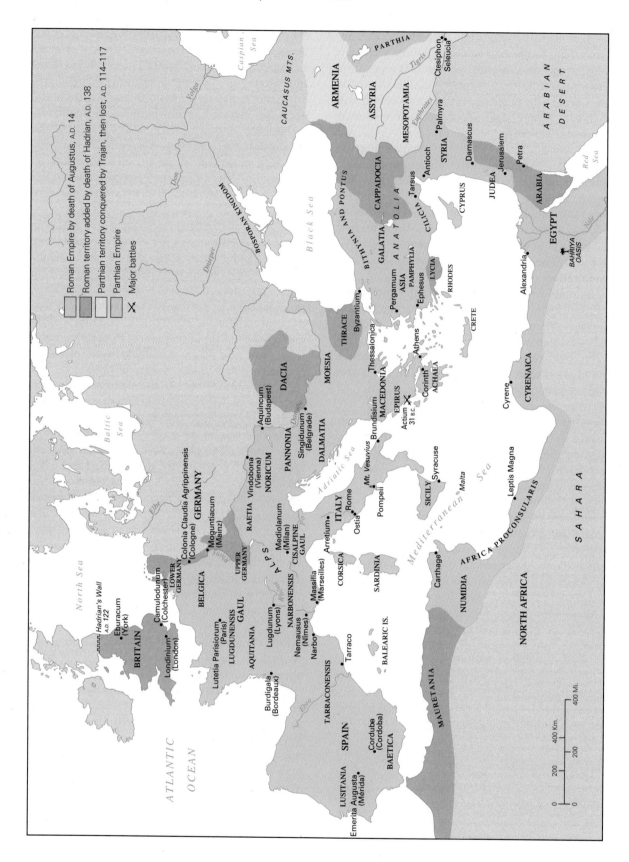

Roman Empire by death of Augustus, A.D. 14

Roman territory added by death of Hadrian, A.D. 138

Parthian territory conquered by Trajan, then lost, A.D. 114–117

Parthian Empire

X Major battles

husband. By the time of the Empire, a woman could own property and, if divorced, keep her dowry. A father no longer forced his daughter to marry against her will. Women could make business arrangements and draw up wills without the consent of their husbands. Unlike their Greek counterparts, Roman women were not secluded in their homes but could come and go as they pleased. Upper-class women of Rome also had far greater opportunities for education than those of Greece. The history of the Empire, indeed Roman history in general, is filled with talented and influential women. Cornelia, the mother of Tiberius and Gaius Gracchus, influenced Roman politics through her sons. Livia, the dynamic wife of Augustus, was often consulted on important matters of state, and during the third century there were times when women controlled the throne.

WORLD COMMUNITY   From Britain to the Arabian Desert, from the Danube River to the sands of the Sahara, some 70 million people with differing native languages, customs, and histories were united by Roman rule into a world community. Unlike officials of the Republic, when corruption and exploitation in the provinces were notorious, officials of the Empire felt a high sense of responsibility to preserve the Roman peace, institute Roman justice, and spread Roman civilization.

By constructing a world community that broke down barriers between nations, by preserving and spreading Greco-Roman civilization, and by developing a rational system of law that applied to all humanity, Rome completed the trend toward universalism and cosmopolitanism that had emerged in the Hellenistic Age.

THE DECLINE OF ROME

Third-Century Crisis

In the third century A.D., the ordered civilization of the Pax Romana ended. The degeneration of the army was a prime reason for the crisis. During the great peace, the army had remained an excellent fighting force, renowned for its discipline, organization, and loyalty. In the third century, however, there was a marked deterioration in the quality of Roman soldiers. Lacking loyalty to Rome and

Map 6.2   The Roman World in the Early Empire Many modern cities are built on the sites of Roman foundations, evidence of the immense extent of the Roman Empire at its height.

greedy for spoils, soldiers used their weapons to prey on civilians and to make and unmake emperors. Fearful of being killed by their unruly troops who wanted spoils or of being murdered by a suspicious emperor, generals were driven to seize the throne. Once in power, they had to buy the loyalty of their soldiers and guard against assassination by other generals. From A.D. 235 to 285, military mutiny and civil war raged, as legion fought legion. Many emperors were assassinated. The once stalwart army neglected its duty of defending the borders and disrupted the internal life of the Empire.

Taking advantage of the military anarchy, Germanic tribesmen crossed the Rhine–Danube frontier to loot and destroy. A reborn Persian empire, led by the Sassanid dynasty, attacked and, for a while, conquered Roman lands in the east. Some sections of the Empire, notably in Gaul, attempted to break away; these moves reflected an assertion of local patriotism over Roman universalism. The "city of mankind" was crumbling.

These eruptions had severe economic repercussions. Cities were pillaged and destroyed, farmlands were ruined, and trade was disrupted. To obtain funds and supplies for the military, emperors confiscated goods, exacted forced labor, and debased the coinage, causing inflation. These measures brought ruin to the urban middle class. The urban centers of the ancient world, creators and disseminators of high civilization, were caught in a rhythm of breakdown.

Diocletian and Constantine: The Regimented State

The emperors Diocletian (A.D. 285–305) and Constantine (A.D. 306–337) tried to contain the awesome forces of disintegration. At a time when agricultural production was steadily declining, they had to feed the city poor and an expanded army of more than 500,000, strung out over the Empire. They also had to prevent renewed outbreaks of military anarchy, drive the Germanic tribes back across the Danube frontier, and secure the eastern region against renewed aggression from Persia. Their solution was to tighten the reins of government and to squeeze more taxes and requisitions out of the citizens, sapping their civic spirit. To guard against military insurrection, Diocletian appointed a loyal general as emperor to govern the western provinces of the Empire while he ruled the eastern regions. Constantine furthered this trend of dividing the Empire into eastern and western halves by building an imperial capital, Constantinople, at the Bosporus, a strait where Asia meets Europe.

Tribal Migrations and Invasions

By imposing some order on what had been approaching chaos, Diocletian and Constantine prevented the Empire from collapsing. Rome had been given a reprieve. But in the last part of the fourth century, the problem of guarding the frontier grew more acute. The Germanic tribes and the Huns, a Mongol people from central Asia, increased their pressure on the Empire's borders; Rome itself was looted twice, in 410 by the Visigoths (West Goths) and again in 455 by the Vandals.

Economic conditions continued to deteriorate. Cities in Britain, Gaul, Germany, and Spain lay abandoned. Other metropolises saw their populations dwindle and production stagnate. The great network of Roman roads was not maintained, and trade in the west almost disappeared or passed into the hands of Greeks, Syrians, and Jews from the east.

Germanic soldiers in the pay of Rome gained control of the government and dictated the choice of emperor. In 476, Germanic officers overthrew the Roman emperor Romulus and placed one of their own, Odoacer, on the throne. This act is traditionally regarded as the end of the Roman Empire in the west.

REPUBLICAN CULTURE: PHILOSOPHY AND LITERATURE

One of the chief consequences of expansion in the Republic was increased contact with Greek culture, which exercised an increasing and fruitful influence on the Roman mind. Greek teachers, both slave and free, came to Rome and introduced Romans to Hellenic cultural achievements. As they conquered the eastern Mediterranean, Roman generals began to ship libraries and works of art from Greek cities to Rome. Roman sculpture and painting imitated Greek prototypes. In time, Romans acquired from Greece knowledge of scientific thought, philosophy, medicine, and geography. Roman writers and orators used Greek history, poetry, and oratory as models. Adopting the humanist outlook of the Greeks, the Romans came to value human intelligence and eloquent and graceful prose and poetry. Wealthy Romans retained Greek tutors, poets, and philosophers in their households and sent their sons to Athens to study. By the late Republic, educated Romans could speak and read Greek. Thus, Rome creatively assimilated the Greek achievement and transmitted it to others, thereby extending the orbit of Hellenism. To be sure, some conservative Romans were hostile to the Greek influence, which they felt threatened traditional Roman values, but the tide of Hellenism could not be stemmed.

Lucretius

Distraught by the seemingly endless strife, Lucretius (c. 96–c. 55 B.C.), the leading Roman Epicurean philosopher, yearned for philosophical tranquillity. Like Epicurus, he believed that religion prompted people to perform evil deeds and caused them to experience terrible anxiety about death and eternal punishment. In his work, *On the Nature of Things,* Lucretius expressed his appreciation of Epicurus. Like his mentor, Lucretius denounced superstition and religion for fostering psychological distress and advanced a materialistic conception of nature, one that left no room for the activity of gods—mechanical laws, not the gods, governed all physical happenings. To dispel the fear of punishment after death, Lucretius marshaled arguments to prove that the soul perishes with the body. He proposed that the simple life, devoid of political involvement and excessive passion, was the highest good and the path that would lead from emotional turmoil to peace of mind. Epicurus's hostility to traditional religion, disparagement of politics and public service, and rejection of the goals of power and glory ran counter to the accepted Roman ideal of virtue. On the other hand, his glorification of the quiet life amid a community of friends and his advice on how to deal with life's misfortunes with serenity had great appeal to first-century Romans like Lucretius, who were disgusted with civil strife.

Cicero

The Roman Republic's finest orator, as well as a leading statesman, Marcus Tullius Cicero (106–43 B.C.) was an unsurpassed Latin stylist and a student of Greek philosophy. Cicero's mother was of noble lineage and his father was a country squire, so he received an excellent education in philosophy, rhetoric, and law and was considered by many to be a child prodigy. Because Cicero held numerous political offices, including the position of consul beginning in 63 B.C., his letters, more than eight hundred of which have survived, provide modern historians with valuable insights into late republican politics. Dedicated to republicanism and public-spiritedness, Cicero sought to prevent one-man rule and in his writings exhorted fellow Romans to serve their city. His Senate speeches have been models of refined rhetoric for all students of the Latin language. His command of the Latin language was widely emulated throughout the ancient world and, after being supplanted by medieval Latin, was revived as the "pure" Latin of the Renaissance humanists.

Cicero was drawn to Stoicism, the most influential philosophy in Rome. Stoicism's stress on virtuous conduct and performance of duty coincided with Roman ideals, and its doctrine of natural law that applies to all nations harmonized with the requirements of a world empire. Cicero admired the Stoic goal of the self-sufficient sage who sought to accord his life with standards of virtue inherent in nature. Natural law commends people to do what is right and deters them from doing what is wrong, and our gift of reason enables us to abide by its commands. Thus, knowledge and virtue are closely linked. Cicero adopted the Stoic belief that the law of the state should conform with the rational and moral norms embodied in natural law, for adherence to such rationally formulated law creates a moral bond among citizens.

He also shared the Stoic view that natural law applies to all; we are all citizens of a single commonwealth and belong to a society of humanity. As he expressed it,

> there is no difference in kind between
> man and man; for Reason, which alone raises
> us above the level of the beasts and enables us
> to draw inferences, to prove and disprove, to
> discuss and solve problems, and to come to
> conclusions, is certainly common to us all, and
> though varying in what it learns, at least in the
> capacity to learn it is invariable. . . . In fact,
> there is no human being of any race who, if he
> finds a guide, cannot attain virtue.[1]

Sallust

The Roman politician and historian Gaius Sallustius Crispus, or Sallust (86–35 B.C.), a partisan of Julius Caesar, wrote in the dark days of the Republic after Caesar's assassination. Influenced by the Greek historian Thucydides, Sallust's major work, which survives only in fragments, is a history of the turbulent years from 78–67 B.C. In his antisenatorial pamphlets *Conspiracy of Catiline* and the *Jugurthine War*, Sallust contrasted the virtues of the early Republic with the moral decline that set in after the destruction of Carthage.

> To the men who had so easily endured toil and
> peril, anxiety and adversity [in building the empire
> of Rome and annihilating its enemies], the leisure
> and riches which are generally regarded as so
> desirable proved a burden and a curse. Growing
> love of money, and the lust for power which followed
> it, engendered every kind of evil. Avarice
> destroyed honour, integrity, and every other
> virtue, and instead taught men to be proud and
> cruel, to neglect religion, and to hold nothing too
> sacred to sell.[2]

Plautus

Rome's greatest playwright, Plautus (c. 254–184 B.C.), adopted features of fourth- and third-century Greek comedy. His plays had Greek characters, they took place in Greek settings, and the actors wore the Greek style of dress. His characters resembled those found in the New Comedy of Menander, the fourth-century Athenian playwright (see p. 111): a cunning slave, a lovesick youth, a foolish old man, and a braggart soldier. The plots often consisted of a struggle between two antagonists over a woman or money or both. The plays usually had the ending desired by the audience: The "good guy" won and the "bad guy" received a fitting punishment. The pains of love was a common theme:

> Not the throes of all mankind
> Equal my distracted mind.
> I strain and I toss
> On a passionate cross;
> Love's goad makes me reel,
> I whirl on Love's wheel,
> In a swoon of despair
> Hurried here, hurried there—
> Torn asunder, I am blind
> With a cloud upon my mind.[3]

Terence

Another playwright, Terence (c. 185–159 B.C.), was originally from North Africa and had been brought to Rome as a slave. His owner, a Roman senator, provided the talented youth with an education and freed him. Like Plautus, Terence was influenced by Menander. Terence's Latin style, graceful and polished, was technically superior to that of Plautus. But Terence's restrained and refined humor lacked the boisterousness of Plautus, which appealed to the Roman audience. For this reason, Terence's plays were less popular. Terence demonstrated more humaneness than Plautus, a quality that can be seen in his attitude toward child rearing:

> I give—I overlook; I do not judge it necessary
> to exert my authority in everything. . . . I
> think it better to restrain children through a
> sense of shame and liberal treatment than
> through fear. . . . This is the duty of a parent
> to accustom a son to do what is right rather of
> his own choice, than through fear of another.[4]

Catullus

Gaius Valerius Catullus (c. 84–c. 54 B.C.) is generally regarded as one of the greatest lyric poets in world literature. He was a native of northern Italy whose father, a friend of Julius Caesar, provided him with a gentleman's education. He wrote seven long poems imitating Alexandrian poetry, including *Marriage of Peleus and Thetis* and his most famous poem, *Attis*. In his early twenties, Catullus came to Rome and fell in love with Clodia; she was the wife of the governor of Cisalpine Gaul, who was away at the time. For the older Clodia, Catullus was a refreshing diversion from her many other lovers. In one of his many poems to her, Cattulus reveals his torment by Clodia's numerous affairs, as he struggles to break away from passion's grip:

> I look no more for her to be my lover as I love
> her.
> That thing could never be.
> Nor pray I for her purity—that's over.
> Only this much I pray, that I be free.
> Free from insane desire myself, and guarded in
> peace at last.
> O heaven, grant that yet the faith by which I've
> lived may be rewarded.
> Let me forget.[5]

These poems to Clodia, as well as others like them, were written in Sapphic verse (see p. 78) to express diverse types of passion. Despite Catullus's early death, he was judged by his own countrymen to be one of the greatest of all lyric poets, a view with which modern critics concur.

ROMAN CULTURE DURING THE PAX ROMANA

Literature and History

Cultural historians use the term *Golden Age* to describe Latin literature during the Ciceronian and Augustan periods. Whereas Latin prose reached its apex with Cicero in the late Republic, the reign of Augustus was distinguished by the greatest poetry ever composed in Latin. The literary activity of the *Silver Age*—the period from the death of Augustus in A.D. 14 to about A.D. 150—saw a decline in the quality of Latin prose and poetry. In comparison to the preceding period, the literature of the Silver Age was characterized by a new type of rhetoric intended more to impress than to persuade and enlighten. Hence, it often appeared affected, pompous, and superficial.

VIRGIL Publius Vergilius Maro, or Virgil (70–19 B.C.), the first important poet of the Augustan Age, was born of humble stock and educated in rhetoric and literature, as well as philosophy, particularly Epicureanism. Unlike most Romans of his day, who misused Epicureanism to justify the pursuit of physical pleasure, Virgil was drawn to the true teachings of Epicurus, which emphasized serenity and freedom from worry. He yearned to be a great poet of the caliber of Homer, and in 29 B.C. he seized the opportunity to be the "Homer of the Romans." At the request of Augustus, who wanted a literary epic to glorify the Empire and his role in founding it, Virgil wrote the *Aeneid,* a masterpiece in world literature.

The *Aeneid* is a long poem that recounts the tale of Aeneas and the founding of Rome. The first six books, which describe the wanderings of Aeneas, a survivor of Troy, show the influence of Homer's *Odyssey*; the last six, which relate the wars in Italy, show the *Iliad*'s imprint. Virgil was intensely patriotic and ascribed to Rome a divine mission to bring peace and civilized life to the world. He praised Augustus as a divinely appointed ruler who had fulfilled Rome's mission. The Greeks might be better sculptors, orators, and thinkers, said Virgil in a famous passage, but only the Romans knew how to govern an empire.

> Others will cast more tenderly in bronze their
> breathing figures, I can well believe, and bring
> more lifelike portraits out of marble;
> Argue more eloquently, use the pointer to trace
> the paths of heaven accurately and accurately
> foretell the rising stars.
> Roman, remember by your strength to rule
> earth's peoples—for your arts are to be these:
> To pacify, to impose the rule of law, to spare the
> conquered, battle down the proud.[6]

Whereas Homer's epics dealt with the deeds and misdeeds of heroic warriors, the *Aeneid* is a literary epic of national glory. The deepest ideas and feelings expressed in the *Aeneid* are Roman virtues—patriotic passion, devotion to family, duty to the state, and a deep sense of religion.

A famous passage of the *Aeneid* is Virgil's vision of the underworld that is contained in Book VI. Aeneas's encounter with his father, Anchises, enables Virgil to prophesy about the fleeting greatness of Rome under the leadership of Augustus. As Aeneas watches a procession of figures from the great Roman past, Augustus appears. Unsure who this godlike, yet dejected, man is, Aeneas questions his father:

> But here Aeneas broke in, seeing . . . a young
> man beautifully formed and tall in shining
> armor, but with clouded brow and downcast
> eyes:
> "And who is that one, Father, . . .
> How strong His presence is!
> But night like a black cloud about his head whirls
> down its awful gloom."

Anchises then relates to Aeneas the burdens a ruler must bear as he carries the weight of his people's concerns, knowing he can only correct a limited number of problems before his finite time on earth comes to an end. Anchises also weeps because he knows that the Augustan Golden Age will never again be repeated in the history of Rome:

> His father Anchises answered, and the tears
>   welled up as he began:
> "Oh, do not ask about this huge grief of your
>   people, son.
> Fate will give earth only a glimpse of him, not let
>   the boy live on.
> Lords of the sky, you thought the majesty of
>   Rome too great if it had kept these gifts. . . .
> Never will any boy of Ilian race exalt his Latin
>   forefathers with promise equal to his; never
>   will Romulus' land take pride like this in any
>   of her sons.
> Weep for his faithful heart, his old-world honor,
>   his sword arm never beaten down!"[7]

LIVY In his *History of Rome,* Livy (59 B.C.–A.D. 17) also glorified Roman character, customs, and deeds. He praised Augustus for attempting to revive traditional Roman morality, to which Livy felt a strong attachment. Although Livy was a lesser historian than Thucydides or Polybius, his work was still a major achievement, particularly in its depiction of the Roman character, which helped make Rome great.

HORACE Quintus Horatius Flaccus, or Horace (65–8 B.C.), the son of a freed slave and a friend of Virgil, was a major poet of the Augustan Age. He broadened his education in Athens by studying literature and Stoic and Epicurean philosophy, and his writings often reflect Greek ideals. Horace enjoyed the luxury of country estates, banquets, fine clothes, and courtesans, along with the simple pleasures of mountain streams and clear skies, but he was also capable of tirades against social situations that he found to be repulsive. In early poems, called *Epodes* (c. 30 B.C.), Horace made the transition from satirist to lyric poet. His *Epodes* are indictments of the aristocrats for their licentious behavior and political stupidity, which often lead to the horrors of war. In *Epodes 8* and *12* Horace exhibits a personal animosity toward old women. As he thinks of lecherous old women he has seen during the course of his life, he expresses his revulsion in these lines from *Epode 12:*

> What do you want with me, woman?
> An elephant's more your type.
> Why do you send me gifts, and why the letters?
> I'm not a muscular boy, and my nose isn't
>   stuffed.

> I have one sharp sense; I can scent a polyp or a
>   stinking goat lurking in hairy armpits more
>   keenly than hounds a sow in hiding.
> What a sweat and what a rank smell rise all
>   over her flabby flesh, when a penis is primed,
>   and she fumbles to ease her insatiable frenzy,
>   and then her makeup runs, her complexion of
>   moist chalk and crocodile dung, and then as
>   she reaches the peak of her spasm, she tears at
>   the mattress and sheets.[8]

In 23 B.C. Horace began to write his most famous lyric poems about Roman society, the *Carmina,* better known as his *Odes.* In this collection of 88 poems, he assumed many voices, including satire, and patterned the meters after Greek poets such as Sappho. Unquestionably a civilized man, Horace sought to rise above the Roman masses whose crassness, materialism, and pleasure seeking he found to be repugnant. In his *Odes,* Horace touches on many themes—the joy of good wine, the virtues of moderation and self-discipline, and the beauty of friendship. In the six lyrics that open Book III, called the "Roman Odes," and in Book IV, Horace admonishes his fellow Romans to temper desire with reason and to seek pleasure but to avoid extremes. In the following lines, he entreats his friend, Leuconoë, to enjoy life while he still can and not to worry about tomorrow or the next day, for the future is known only to the gods:

> Don't ask, Leuconoë, the forbidden question,
>   how long the gods have given to you and to
>   me; don't imagine fortunetellers know.
> Better to take what is coming, whether Jove
>   [Jupiter] allows us more winters, or this that
>   now wearies the Etruscan sea as it beats on the
>   cliffs is the last.
> Be sensible: strain the wine: in a little life, take no
>   long looks ahead.
> As we talk, time spites us and runs: reap today:
>   save no hopes for tomorrow.[9]

In the opening ode of Book II, Horace reminds Romans of the terrible civil wars that had ruined the Republic:

> Is there a field not fertile with Latin blood, that
>   will not speak with its graves of unholy
>   battles? . . .
> Is there a gorge or a river not touched by war
>   and its sorrows?
> Is there a sea that has not been discolored by
>   slaughtered Romans?
> Is there a shore that has not seen our blood?[10]

OVID Publius Ovidius Naso, or Ovid (43 B.C.–A.D. 17), was the greatest of the Latin elegists during the Golden Age. Unlike Horace, Virgil, or Livy,

Ovid did not experience the civil wars during his adult years. Consequently, he was less inclined to praise the Augustan peace. He was married three times. His first wife was chosen for him by his family, and the marriage soon dissolved; his second marriage was one of respect, rather than affection, and lasted no longer than the first; his third marriage was one of devotion, ease, and pleasure. Ovid also supposedly had a mistress, Corinna, to whom he wrote *Amores* (love letters). As a result of his marriages and affairs, Ovid's poetry reveals a preference for romance and humor and a fondness for love and sensual themes. Examples of these themes are evident in his *Heroides*—letters from famous Greek heroines in antiquity to their absent lovers—and *Metamorphoses*, in which he transformed Greek myths into enticing stories. Nevertheless, Ovid is best remembered for his advice to lovers contained in his most famous work—*Ars Amatoria* (Art of Love). Written when Ovid was 50 years old, the poem concerns itself with the art of seduction and is divided into three books. Book I deals with how to attract a woman who is the object of a man's desire:

> First of all, be quite sure that there isn't a woman who cannot be won, and make up your mind that you will win her. Only you must prepare the ground.
>
> You must play the lover for all you're worth. Tell her how you are pining for her.
>
> Never cease to sing the praises of her face, her hair, her taper fingers, and her dainty foot.
>
> Tears too are a mighty useful resource in the matter of love. They would melt a diamond. Make a point, therefore, of letting your mistress see your face all wet with tears.
>
> Women are things of many moods. You must adapt your treatment to the special case.[11]

Book II of the *Ars Amatoria* explains how a man can keep a woman, and Book III advises women about men. In A.D. 8, presumably because of the immoral influence of the *Ars Amatoria*, Ovid, at the age of 60, was banished by Augustus to Tomi (modern Costanza) on the Black Sea. Another possible reason for Ovid's banishment was his knowledge of the adulterous affair of Augustus's daughter, Julia, with her lover, Silanus. As Augustus sought to put an end to licentiousness and corruption in society, and in his own household, Ovid's (as well as Julia's) banishment was to be an example to others. Ovid spent the last ten years of his life in melancholic exile and lost most of his artistic inspiration.

MARTIAL   Marcus Valerius Martialis, or Martial (c. A.D. 38/41–c. 104), tells us much about life in the Silver Age in his well-known *Epigrams*. (An epigram is a short, witty poem that often makes a satirical point.) Born in Bilbilis, Spain, Martial lived in Rome for 34 years, but spent his last years in the Spanish countryside, where he died. Martial is famous for his practical wisdom, for example, the value he gives to writing a short book: "First, less paper is wasted; next, my copyist gets through it in a single hour, and he will not be wholly busied with my trifles,"[12] and finally, the book will not be boring. And for those who contemplate suicide, he offers this assessment:

> I like not much the man who buys
>   with blood an easy fame.
> Give me the man who glorifies,
>   but not with death, his name.[13]

In spite of the caustic tone of much of his poetry, Martial could also be sentimental when speaking about children, his friends, and his slaves. Concerning the death of the slave girl, Erotion, in A.D. 89, Martial wrote three epigrams. In one, he reveals that the memory of Erotion continued to haunt him several years later:

> In gloom that came before its time
>   Erotion's here at rest,
> Whom her sixth winter through the crime
>   of Destiny oppressed.
>
> O You, who e'er will, after me,
>   Lord of my land be made,
> Bestow its tribute annually
>   upon her tiny shade.[14]

JUVENAL   The last of the great Latin poets of the Silver Age was the satirist Decimus Junius Juvenalis, or Juvenal (A.D. c. 55–138), who, like Martial, lived most of his life in poverty. Considered to be the master of the "satire of indignation," Juvenal denounced Roman society at the time of the emperors Trajan and Hadrian. In *Satires I–VI*, Juvenal attacked evils of Roman society, such as the misconduct of emperors, the haughtiness of the wealthy, the barbaric tastes of commoners, and the failures of parents. He also described the noise, congestion, and poverty of the capital, as well as its dangers:

> . . . a piece of pot
> Falls down on my head, how often a broken
>   vessel is shot
> From the upper windows, with what force it
>   strikes and dints
>
> The cobblestones! . . .
> But these aren't your only terrors. For you can
>   never restrain
> The criminal element. Lock up your house,
>   put bolt and chain

On your shop, but when all's quiet, someone
   will rob you or he'll
Be a cutthroat perhaps and do you in quickly
   with cold steel.[15]

In addition, Juvenal expressed venomous views toward women. The most vitriolic of Juvenal's satires, *Satire VI*, is nearly 700 lines long and deals with the vices and crimes of Roman women. The satire is supposedly written to his friend, Postumus, whom Juvenal attempts to dissuade from taking a wife:

If you don't intend to love the woman who was
   your betrothed
and is now your lawfully wedded wife, why
   marry at all? . . .
If your love for your wife is pure and simple,
   and your heart is devoted to her alone,
then bow your head and prepare your neck for
   the yoke.
No woman has any regard for the man who
   loved her.
She may be passionate; still, she loves to fleece
   and torment him.
And so, the better a husband is, and the more
   attractive,
the smaller the benefit that he receives from
   having a wife.
You will give no gift without your spouse's
   permission; no item
will be sold where she says no, or bought if she is
   against it.
She will prescribe your affections. A friend who
   was known to your door
when his beard first grew, now late in life will be
   turned away.[16]

Juvenal then relates stories and descriptions of various types of misconduct and betrayal by married women, particularly those of the aristocratic class—spending money needlessly, lusting for fame and fortune, taking eunuchs and homosexuals as lovers, participating in secret orgies, procuring abortions, and killing their children and stepchildren. Likening poverty to morality and luxury to immorality, he advocates a return to the days when women knew their place and chastity reigned. *Satire VI* generally condemns female behavior within the context of marriage and describes the humiliations husbands must face—infidelity, poisonings, public harlotry, and being ignored, intimidated, and dominated. All of this, says Juvenal, is a consequence of a wife's failure to live up to the obligations of the married state—being silent, loyal, obedient, respectful of her husband, and caring for the children.

After Juvenal's death, poetry went into decline, and despite efforts to revive it in the fourth century, no poetry of comparable stature was produced.

TACITUS   Although the writers of the Silver Age of Latin literature were mostly of a lesser literary quality than their predecessors and more pessimistic and cynical in their outlook about the future of the Empire, the writing of the historian Tacitus (A.D. 55–c. 118) is an exception. Sympathetic to republican institutions, Tacitus denounced Roman emperors and the imperial system in his *Histories* and *Annals*. In *Germania*, he turned his sights on the habits of the Germanic peoples, describing them as undisciplined but heroic, with a strong love of freedom.

Philosophy

Stoicism was the principal philosophy of the Pax Romana, and its leading exponents were Seneca, Epictetus (c. A.D. 60–c. 117), and Marcus Aurelius. Perpetuating the rational tradition of Greek philosophy, Roman Stoics saw the universe as governed by reason, and they esteemed the human intellect. Like Socrates, they sought the highest good in this world, not in an afterlife, and envisioned no power above human reason. Moral values were obtained from reason alone. The individual was self-sufficient and depended entirely on rational faculties for knowing and doing good. Stoics valued self-sufficient persons who attained virtue and wisdom by exercising rational control over their lives. Roman thinkers also embraced the Stoic doctrine that all people, because of their capacity to reason, belong to a common humanity. They wanted the Roman elite to be motivated by **lex caritatis,** the law of love that spurs service to the world community.

SENECA   Lucius Annaeus Seneca (4 B.C.–A.D. 65), like other Stoics before him, sought the rational order inherent within the universe, which is evident in everything he wrote, including his *Natural Questions,* which was viewed as an authoritative work on cosmology in western Christian Europe during the Middle Ages. The melodramatic moralizing of his tragedies, nine of which are extant, protests against the evils of his day—the brutality of gladiatorial contests, the degradation of political offices to the extent that pimps and horses were appointed as consuls, and the assassinations and insurrections that characterized succession to the throne. Finally, his twelve *Moral Dialogues* illustrate how his Stoic ideals of virtue, duty, and honor were in conflict with the licentious environment in which he lived.

As tutor to the young Nero, Seneca advised the future emperor to rule mildly and with compassion in writings such as his *De Clementia (On Mercy)*—advice that Nero ignored. Seneca retired from public life in A.D. 62 to pursue philosophy and wrote 124 *Epistles,* which reveal a Stoic's quest for virtue.

Seneca's Stoic humanitarianism was expressed in his denunciation of the gladiatorial combats and in his concern for slaves.

> Were you to consider, that he whom you call your slave, is sprung from the same origin, enjoys the same climate, breathes the same air, and is subject to the same condition of life and death as yourself, you will think it possible to see him as a free-born person, as he is free to see you as a slave. . . .
>
> I will not discuss at length the treatment of slaves towards whom we behave cruelly and arrogantly. But this is the essence of what I would prescribe: treat your inferiors as you would have a superior treat you. As often as you think of the power that you have over a slave, reflect on the power that your master has over you. But you say, "I have no master." Be it so. The world goes well with you at present; it may not do so always. You may one day be a slave yourself.[17]

In A.D. 65, after Nero accused him of participating in a conspiracy against the throne, Seneca was forced to commit suicide.

MARCUS AURELIUS Emperor Marcus Aurelius (A.D. 121–180), the last of the great Stoics and the last of the group known as the "five good emperors,"* also had to deal with serious problems confronting the Empire. While commanding troops engaged in fighting plundering tribesmen in the Balkans, he wrote in Greek the *Meditations,* a classic work of Stoic thought. In Stoicism, he sought the strength to overcome the burdens of ruling an empire, the fear of death, and the injustices and misdeeds committed by his fellows.

> Hour by hour resolve firmly, like a Roman and a man, to do what comes to hand with correct and natural dignity, and with humanity, independence, and justice. Allow your mind freedom from all other considerations.
>
> This you can do, if you will approach each action as though it were your last, dismissing the wayward thought, the emotional recoil from the commands of reason, the desire to create an impression, the admiration of self, the discontent with your lot. See how little a man needs to master, for his days to flow on in quietness and

> piety: he has but to observe these few counsels, and the gods will ask nothing more.[18]

Early Roman Stoics, perpetuating the rational tradition of Greek philosophy, saw the universe as governed by reason. They esteemed the human intellect, and they valued virtue and wisdom in individuals who exercised rational control over their lives. For the early Stoics, God was an intellectual necessity, an impersonal principle that gave order to the universe. The Stoic conception of God underwent a gradual transformation, reflecting the religious yearnings of the times. For later Roman Stoics, like Marcus Aurelius, God had become a moral necessity, comforting and reassuring people. Although they maintained the traditional Stoic belief that the individual can attain virtue through unaided reason, later Roman Stoics came close to seeking God's help to live properly. The gap between Greek philosophy and Christianity was narrowing.

Science

The two most prominent scientists during the Greco-Roman Age were Ptolemy (c. A.D. 90–168), a mathematician, geographer, and astronomer who worked at Alexandria, and Galen (c. A.D. 130–c. 201), who investigated medicine and anatomy. Ptolemy's thirteen-volume work, *Mathematical Composition*—more commonly known as the *Almagest,* a Greek–Arabic term meaning "the greatest"—summed up antiquity's knowledge of astronomy and became the authoritative text during the Middle Ages. In the **Ptolemaic system,** a motionless, spherical earth stood in the center of the universe; the moon, sun, and planets moved about the earth in circles or in combinations of circles. Ptolemy also established the traditional order of the planets—Earth, Moon, Mercury, Venus, Sun, Mars, Jupiter, and Saturn. Influenced by Aristotle, he asserted that the stars were "fixed"; that is, they did not move from their appointed place in the cosmos. The Ptolemaic system was built on faulty premises, as modern astronomy eventually showed. However, it did work—that is, it did provide a model of the universe that adequately accounted for most observed phenomena. The Ptolemaic system was not challenged until the middle of the sixteenth century.

Just as Ptolemy's system dominated astronomy, so too did the theories of Galen dominate medicine down to modern times. The most important physician since Hippocrates, Galen was associated with the medical school at Pergamum and in A.D. 157 became chief physician to the gladiators there. In A.D. 161, he became a physician in the

---

*The other four "good" emperors were Nerva, Trajan, Hadrian, and Antoninus Pius.

LATER HINDUISM—*THE BHAGAVAD-GITA*

THE CENTRAL CONCEPT OF HINDUISM IS REINCARNATION (rebirth of the soul). The belief in reincarnation is closely connected with the Hindu stratification of society into four classes or castes. A person is born into the highest caste because of good behavior in a past life and into a lower caste because of misbehavior in a past life. The individual may have to pass through many reincarnations, for atonement must be made for all evil actions in a past life. The more one's actions reflect the ideals of purity, self-control, detachment, truth, nonviolence, charity, and compassion for all living creatures, the closer that person comes to approaching union with *Brahman* (the one God or the ultimate reality) and the state of *Nirvana* (the peaceful escape from the cycle of reincarnation). The practice of yoga, the path of union with Brahman, is closely related to this belief in the evolving soul. A yogi seeks to free himself from dependence on earthly objects and to withdraw from the uncertainties and evils of this world. He accomplishes this by cultivating his spiritual powers until he reaches a state of "desirelessness" and Nirvana.

The *Bhagavad-Gita,* a long devotional poem that originated sometime close to the dawn of the Christian era, advances many of these beliefs, including the doctrines of the immortality of the soul and the concept of ultimate salvation from sin. The following passage describes the perfect yoga.

If a yogi has perfect control over his mind, and struggles continually in this way to unite himself with Brahman, he will come at last to the crowning peace of Nirvana. . . .

When can a man be said to have achieved union with Brahman? When his mind is under perfect control and freed from all desires, so that he becomes absorbed in the Atman [the self or one's innermost soul], and nothing else. . . . When, through the practise of yoga, the mind ceases its restless movements, and becomes still, he realizes the Atman. It satisfies him entirely. Then he knows that infinite happiness which can be realized by the purified heart but is beyond the grasp of the senses. . . .

To achieve this certainty is to know the real meaning of the word yoga. . . . Renounce all your desires, for ever. . . .

A man who is born with tendencies toward the Divine, is fearless and pure in heart. He perseveres in that path to union with Brahman. . . . He is charitable. He can control his passions. . . . He is straightforward, truthful, and of an even temper. He harms no one. He renounces the things of this world. He has a tranquil mind and an unmalicious tongue. He is compassionate . . . . He is not greedy. He is gentle and modest. He abstains from useless activity. He has faith in the strength of his higher nature. He can forgive and endure. He is clean in thought and act. He is free from hatred and from pride. . . .

When a man is born with demonic tendencies, his birthright is hypocrisy, arrogance, conceit, anger, cruelty and ignorance. The birthright of the divine nature leads to liberation. The birthright of the demonic nature leads to greater bondage.

Source: *Swami Prabhavananda and Christopher Isherwood, trans.,* The Song of God: Bhagavad-Gita, *with an Introduction by Aldous Huxley (New York: Mentor Books, The New American Library, 1951), pp. 65–66, 114. Copyright, 1944, 1951 by The Vedanta Society of Southern California.*

service of the emperor Marcus Aurelius, and he continued in that capacity under the new emperor, his son, Commodus. Galen dissected both dead and living animals, thereby attempting a rational investigation of the body's working parts. Although his work contains many errors, he made essential contributions to the knowledge of anatomy. Having studied Plato, Aristotle, the Epicureans, and the Stoics, Galen believed that a good physician should also be a good philosopher. Asserting that Aristotle had best defined reality, Galen was critical of the monotheistic beliefs of both Jews and Christians. Due to Arab physicians who preserved his writings during the Middle Ages, Galen's influence continued in the West into early modern times.

LAW

Expressing the Roman yearning for order and justice, law was Rome's great legacy to Western civilization. Roman law passed through two essential stages: the formation of civil law (*jus civile*) and the formation of the law of nations (*jus gentium*). The basic features of civil law evolved during the two-hundred-year Struggle of the Orders, at the same time as Rome was extending its dominion over Italy. The **Twelve Tables,** drawn up in the early days of the patrician–plebeian struggle, established written rules of criminal and civil law for the Roman state that applied to all citizens. Over the centuries, the civil law was expanded through statutes passed by the assemblies and through the legal decisions of jurisdictional magistrates, the rulings of emperors, and the commentaries of professional jurists, who, aided by familiarity with Greek logic, engaged in systematic legal analysis.

During the period of the Republic's expansion outside Italy, contact with the Greeks and other peoples led to the development of the second branch of Roman law, **jus gentium,** which combined Roman civil law with principles selectively drawn from the legal tradition of Greeks and other peoples. Roman jurists identified the *jus gentium* with the natural law (*jus naturale*) of the Stoics. The jurists said that a law should accord with rational principles inherent in nature: uniform and universally valid laws that can be discerned by rational people. Serving to bind different peoples together, the law of nations harmonized with the requirements of a world empire and with Stoic ideals. As Cicero pointed out,

True law is right reason in agreement with nature; it is of universal application, unchanging and ever-

lasting. And there will not be different laws at Rome and at Athens or different laws now and in the future, but one eternal and unchangeable law will be valid for all nations and all times.[19]

The law of nations came to be applied throughout the Empire, although it never entirely supplanted local law. In the eyes of the law, a citizen—and by A.D. 212, virtually all free people had been granted citizenship—was not a Syrian or a Briton or a Spaniard, but a Roman.

After the fall of the western Roman Empire, Roman law fell into disuse in western Europe. Gradually reintroduced in the twelfth century, it came to form the basis of the common law in all Western lands except Britain and its dependencies. Some provisions of Roman law are readily recognizable in modern legal systems, as the following excerpts illustrate:

Justice is a constant, unfailing disposition to give everyone his legal due. . . . No one is compelled to defend a cause against his will. . . . No one suffers a penalty for what he thinks. . . . In the case of major offenses it makes a difference whether something is committed purposefully or accidentally. . . . In inflicting penalties, the age . . . of the guilty party must be taken into account.[20]

CULTURAL STAGNATION AND TRANSFORMATION

During the second century A.D., Greco-Roman civilization lost its creative energies, and mythic-religious movements challenged the values of classical humanism. No longer regarding reason as a satisfying guide to life, the educated elite subordinated the intellect to feelings and an unregulated imagination. No longer finding the affairs of this world to have purpose, people placed their hope in life after death. The Roman world was undergoing a religious revolution and was seeking a new vision of the divine.

The application of reason to nature and society was the great achievement of the Greek mind. Yet despite its many triumphs, Greek rationalism never entirely subdued the mythic–religious mentality, which draws its strength from human emotion. The masses of peasants and slaves remained attracted to religious forms. Ritual, mystery, magic, and ecstasy never lost their hold on the ancient world—nor, indeed, have they on our own scientific and technological society. During the Hellenistic Age, the tide of rationalism gradually receded, and the nonrational, an ever-present undercurrent, showed renewed vigor. This resurgence of the mythical mentality could be seen in the popularity of the occult, magic, alchemy, and astrology. Burdened by danger, emotional stress, and fearing fate as fixed in the stars, people turned for deliverance to magicians, astrologers, and exorcists.

They also became devotees of the many Near Eastern religious cults that promised personal salvation. More and more people felt that individuals could not achieve the good life through their own efforts; they needed outside help. Philosophers eventually sought escape from this world through union with a divine presence greater than human power. Increasingly, the masses, and then even the educated elite, came to believe that the good life could not be found on earth but only in a world beyond the grave. Seeing themselves as isolated souls wandering aimlessly in a social desert, people sought refuge in religion. Reason had been found wanting; the time for faith and salvation was at hand.

The Roman Empire had imposed peace and stability, but it could not alleviate the feelings of loneliness, anxiety, impotence, alienation, and boredom, which had been gaining ground in the Mediterranean world since the fourth century B.C. A spiritual malaise had descended on the Greco-Roman world. Among the upper classes, the philosophical and scientific spirit withered; rational and secular values were in retreat. Deprived of the excitement of politics and bored by idleness and pleasure, the best minds, says historian M. I. Rostovtzeff,

> lost faith in the power of reason. . . . Creative genius dwindled; science repeated its previous results. The textbook took the place of research; no new artistic discoveries were made, but echoes of the past were heard . . . [writers] amuse[d] the mind but [were] incapable of elevating and inspiring it.[21]

The Spread of Mystery Religions

The proliferation of Eastern mystery religions was a clear expression of this transformation of classical values. During the Hellenistic era, slaves, merchants, and soldiers brought many religious cults westward from Persia, Babylon, Syria, Egypt, and Asia Minor. The various mystery cults possessed many common features. Converts underwent initiation rites and were bound by oath to secrecy. The initiates, in a state of rapture, attempted to unite with the deity after first purifying themselves through baptism (sometimes with the blood of a bull), fasting, having their heads shaved, or drinking from a sacred vessel. Communion was achieved by donning the god's robe, eating a sacred meal, or visiting the god's sanctuary. This sacramental drama propelled initiates through an intense mystical experience of exaltation and rebirth. Cultists were certain that their particular savior–god would protect them from misfortune and ensure their soul's immortality.

Of special significance was the *cult of Mithras,* which had certain parallels with early Christianity and was its principal competitor. The devotion to Mithras began in the Near East over 2000 years before the Pax Romana. Fusing with Babylonian religious doctrines, it later spread westward from Persia into the Roman Empire. The god Mithras, whose birth date was celebrated on December 25, had as his mission the rescue of humanity from evil. Once Mithras' earthly mission was finished, his followers believed he ascended to heaven in order to watch over and guard his devotees from above.

Those who had faith in Mithras referred to him as "the light of the world" and viewed him as a symbol of justice, wisdom, and fidelity. Because they believed that the human soul descended to earth, their goal was union with the divine through an ascent of the soul through the seven levels of heaven. Symbolically climbing this celestial ladder, the initiate was reborn a new man. Mithraic rituals included a form of baptism and a service in which the participants ate bread and drank wine, which signified the god's body and blood.

Mithras was said to demand high standards of morality to fight the forces of evil. His devotees believed that there would be a final day of judgment in which Mithras would resurrect his faithful followers after death and grant them eternal life in a heaven of bliss. His adherents thus affirmed the ultimate victory of the forces of light over the forces of darkness, who would be condemned to a fiery hell.

Because Mithraism stressed respect for the masculine virtues of bravery and camaraderie and espoused celibacy, it became a militantly male religion, which barred women and was particularly popular with the Roman army. In the late third century A.D., Mithras was worshiped as *sol invictus* (invincible sun), and emperor Diocletian conferred the title of "The Protector of the Empire" upon Mithras. During the first four centuries, the Roman army was most responsible for spreading Mithraism throughout the Empire, including the more remote regions of Britain, Spain, North Africa, and Germany, where numerous Mithraic temples can still be found.

The popularity of magic and mystery demonstrates that many people in Roman society either did not comprehend or had lost faith in the rational and secular values of classical humanism. Religion proved more comforting to the spirit. People felt that the gods could provide what reason, natural law, and civic affairs could not: a sure way of overcoming life's misfortunes and discouragements, a guarantee of immortality, a sense of belonging to a community of brethren who cared, an exciting outlet for bottled-up emotions, and a sedative for anxiety at a time when dissatisfaction with the human condition showed itself in all phases of society and life.

The Spiritualization of Philosophy

The religious orientation also found expression in philosophy, which demonstrated attitudes markedly at odds with classical humanism. These attitudes, commonly associated with religion, included indifference to the world, withdrawal, and pessimism about the earthly state. From trying to understand nature and individuals' relationships to one another, the philosophers more and more aspired to a communion with a higher reality. As did the mystery religions, philosophy reached for something beyond this world in order to comfort the individual. In *Neo-Platonism,* which replaced Stoicism as the dominant school of philosophy in the Late Roman Empire, religious yearnings were transformed into a religious system that transcended reason.

Plotinus (c. A.D. 205–c. 270), the most influential spokesman of Neo-Platonism, went far beyond Marcus Aurelius's natural religion; in aspiring to the ecstatic union of the soul with God, he subordinated philosophy to mysticism. Plato's philosophy, we have seen, contained both a major and a minor key. The major key stressed a rational interpretation of the human community and called for reforming the polis on the basis of knowledge, whereas the minor key urged the soul to rise to a higher world of reality. Although Plotinus retained Platonic rationalism (he viewed the individual as a reasoning being and used rational argument to explain his religious orientation), he was intrigued by Plato's otherworldliness.

What Plotinus desired was union with the One, or the Good, sometimes called God—the source of all existence. Plotinus felt that the intellect could neither describe nor understand the One, which transcended all knowing, and that joining with the One required a mystical leap, a purification of the soul so that it could return to its true eternal home. For Plotinus, philosophy became a religious experience, a contemplation of the eternal. His successors held that through acts of magic the soul can unite with the One. Compared with this union with the divine One, of what value was knowledge

of the sensible world or a concern for human affairs? For Plotinus, this world was a sea of tears and troubles from which the individual yearned to escape. Reality was not in this world but beyond it, and the principal goal of life was not comprehension of the natural world nor fulfillment of human potential nor betterment of the human community, but knowledge of the One. Thus, his philosophy broke with the essential meaning of classical humanism.

Neo-Platonism, concludes historian of philosophy W. T. Stace, "is founded upon . . . the despair of reason." It seeks to reach the Absolute not through reason but through "spiritual intoxication." This marks a radical transformation of philosophical thinking.

> For philosophy is founded upon reason. It is the effort to comprehend, to understand, to grasp the reality of things intellectually. Therefore it cannot admit anything higher than reason. To exalt intuition, ecstasy, or rapture, above thought—this is the death of philosophy. . . . In Neo-Platonism, therefore, ancient philosophy commits suicide. This is the end. The place of philosophy is taken henceforth by religion.[22]

By the time of the Late Roman Empire, mystery religions intoxicated the masses, and mystical philosophy beguiled the educated elite. Classical civilization was being transformed. Philosophy had become subordinate to religious belief; secular values seemed inferior to religious experience. The earthly city had raised its eyes toward heaven. The culture of the Roman world was moving in a direction in which the quest for the divine was to predominate over all human enterprises.

ROMAN ART

The Romans copied art forms profusely from other peoples, especially the Etruscans and the Greeks. However, the Romans borrowed creatively, transforming and enhancing their inheritance. The Romans were most creative in transforming the Greek architectural inheritance, which was best suited to express their overriding concern with Rome's imperial mission. Roman sculpture also gave expression to the imperial ideal. Statues of emperors conveyed nobility and authority; reliefs commemorating victories glorified Roman might and grandeur. In both portraiture and narrative relief sculpture, Romans showed a commitment to accuracy and detail that rivaled Hellenistic realism. Sculptors realistically carved every distinctive detail of a subject's face.

Architecture

The skills developed by the Romans in their extensive engineering projects were also incorporated into the construction of temples, public baths, entertainment complexes, and private villas. The roads, bridges, and aqueducts of the Romans were the finest in the ancient world, and many of them still survive. Roman engineers carefully selected routes with an eye for circumventing natural barriers and minimizing drainage problems. By the third century A.D., there were more than 53,000 miles of paved roads connecting the far reaches of the empire, which spanned the equivalent of the forty modern countries in the region. Using concrete, originally invented in the Near East approximately a thousand years before the Romans, these engineers supervised the construction of great embanked roads, stone bridges across rivers, ports along the Mediterranean and other major waterways, as well as aqueducts to carry water to Roman cities. The Romans' concrete was a mixture of mortar made from lime and volcanic sand, which was strengthened with the addition of small stones. Unlike modern concrete, Roman concrete could not be poured, so it was initially used only to fill in the spaces between courses of brick in horizontal walls. Nevertheless, concrete eventually emerged as a durable, pliable, and inexpensive building material to facilitate the construction of arches, vaults, and domes.

Although the Egyptians and the Greeks were familiar with the arch, they used it mainly in subterranean structures. In Mesopotamia, the arch was often used for the gates of cities. Knowledge of arches and vaults, which they acquired from the Etruscans, enabled Roman engineers and architects to design structures that spanned wide distances and supported heavy loads. The **arch and vault** (Figure 6.1) was a crucial advancement over the "post-and-lintel" design of the Greeks. Post-and-lintel construction is the generic term used to describe the manner in which Greek architects used vertical members (e.g., columns) to support horizontal members (e.g., a wall or roof).

The Etruscans' arch consisted of wedge-shaped stones (*voussoirs*), which were fitted one next to another to displace the load of the structure inwardly on to the *keystone*—the piece at the summit of the arch that held the other stones in place. The vertical load, which the arch supported, also generated an outward thrust that Roman engineers accounted for with massive walls or supporting piers—heavy columns, usually square, used to support the arches. They learned to create a barrel vault by simply extending, or deepening, the arch. By intersecting two barrel vaults at right

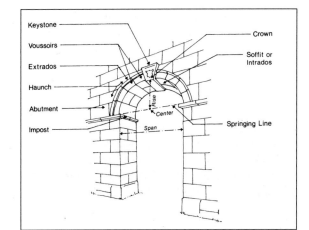

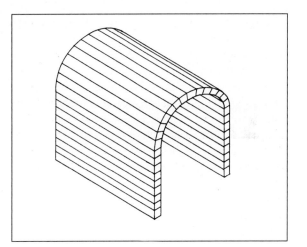

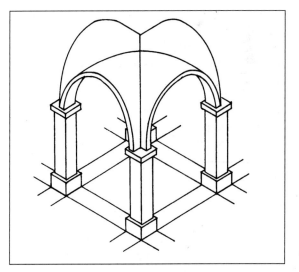

Figure 6.1 Arch, barrel vault, and groin vault
The voussoirs were fitted one next to another to displace the load of the structure inwardly onto the keystone. The vertical load, which the arch supported, was accounted for with massive walls or supporting piers. Roman engineers created a barrel vault by simply extending, or deepening, the arch, and by intersecting two barrel vaults at right angles, they fashioned a groin (cross) vault. *(Witt, et al.,* The Humanities: Cultural Roots and Continuities, *Sixth Edition, Houghton Mifflin Company, 2001)*

Figure 6.2 *Pont du Gard,* 1st century Nîmes, France   Spanning the gorge of the Gardon River near Nîmes, the aqueduct, when functional, transported 4.4 million gallons of water a day to the city of Nîmes from a spring 30 miles away. *(George Haling/Photo Researchers)*

angles they fashioned a groin (cross) vault, and by further broadening the principles of the vault, they were then able to construct domes. These advancements displaced the weight of the ceiling area to the outer edges, making possible expansive interiors. By customizing arches, vaults, and domes, the Romans built a variety of monumental public structures, including temples, amphitheaters, public baths, and private villas.

PUBLIC ARCHITECTURE   Some of the best-preserved public monuments from the age of Augustus are found at Nîmes, in southern France, which was established as a Roman outpost in the first century B.C. The monumental aqueduct, *Pont du Gard* (Figure 6.2), built by Augustus's son-in-law, Marcus Agrippa, in the late first century B.C., spans the gorge of the Gardon River near Nîmes. The aqueduct bridge consists of three stories of arches standing 160 feet high and includes protruding stones designed to support scaffolding during construction and to facilitate repair work. When functional, the aqueduct transported 4.4 million gallons of water a day to the city of Nîmes from a spring thirty miles away. Another structure at Nîmes, also built during the reign of Augustus in 16 B.C., was the temple

Maison Carrée (Figure 6.3). It marked a significant development in monumental architecture—the use of the Corinthian column (see p. 98)—which became the standard for Roman public architecture. Almost the entire structure has survived, except for the platform that surrounded the podium. The deep-seated portico has three exposed alcoves on each side, and a Corinthian arcade surrounds the walls of the narrow cella (or central room).

The *Pantheon* (Figure 6.4), Rome's most magnificent temple, built during the reign of Hadrian in the early second century A.D. to honor the seven planetary gods, came to symbolize the power and majesty of the Roman world–state. The exterior is an ungainly merger of the circular base of the cella with a porch of granite Corinthian columns, which was used as an atrium. The extremely thick concrete exterior walls, faced with brick, bear the outward thrust of the massive dome. In contrast, the vast interior, which exudes a sense of warmth and light, culminates in the overarching dome— the largest dome ever built in world history. The interior (Figure 6.5) demonstrates the architects' sense of proportion and harmony—the diameter of the dome and of the interior of the cella beneath

Figure 6.3 *Maison Carrée, 16 B.C., Nîmes, France* The temple marked a significant development in monumental architecture—the use of the Corinthian column—which became the standard for Roman public architecture. *(Giraudon/Art Resource, NY)*

it is nearly 143 feet, a distance equal to the distance from the floor to the dome's opening or *oculus* (eye). The load-bearing outer walls and the eight internal vertical supports sustain the dome, the thickness of which varies from almost 20 feet at the base to about six feet at the oculus. The niches in the walls once housed statues of Roman deities. The original coffered ceiling of the dome was painted blue with golden accents to simulate "the Dome of Heaven."

Despite its many achievements, Roman civilization presents a paradox. On the one hand, Roman culture and law evidence high standards of civilization. On the other, the Romans institutional-ized barbaric practices such as battles to the death between armed gladiators and the tormenting and slaughtering of wild beasts. The major forms of entertainment in both the Republic and the Empire were chariot races, wild-animal shows, and gladiatorial combat. Chariot races were gala events, in which the most skillful riders and the finest and best-trained stallions raced in an atmosphere of rabid excitement. The charioteers, many of them slaves hoping that victory would bring them freedom, became popular heroes.

The two main venues of Roman entertainment were the Circus Maximus and the *Colosseum* (Figure 6.6). Completed in A.D. 80, the Colosseum

Figure 6.4 *The Pantheon (exterior), early 2nd century A.D., Rome* Built by Hadrian to honor the seven planetary gods, the Pantheon came to symbolize the power and majesty of the Roman world–state. *(Ronald Sheridan/Ancient Art & Architecture Collection Ltd.)*

Figure 6.5 *The Pantheon* (interior), early 2nd century A.D., Rome   This structure demonstrates the architects' sense of proportion and harmony—the diameter of the dome and of the interior of the cella beneath it is nearly 143 feet, a distance equal to the distance from the floor to the dome's opening. *(Marcello Bertinetti /Photo Researchers)*

was an amphitheater that accommodated between 50,000 and 70,000 spectators. Each story of the exterior employed an architectural order borrowed from the Greeks. At the foot of the complex was the Doric order, followed by the Ionic and Corinthian; the fourth story, a wall that incorporated Corinthian pilasters, was added later. A canvas covering was stretched between poles, which were anchored to the upper story in order to shield spectators from the elements. To facilitate the flow of people in and out of the Colosseum, the interior was constructed with both barrel and groin vaults, which created unimpeded passageways. Beneath the wooden floor of the interior were service areas that housed the animals and equipment used in the various types of brutal spectacles that the Romans craved.

In the Colosseum, spectators saw wild beasts pitted against each other or against men armed with spears, and highly trained *gladiators* fought each other, sometimes until death. The gladiators, mainly slaves and condemned criminals, learned their craft at schools run by professional trainers. Some gladiators entered the arena armed with a sword, others with a trident and a net. The spectators were transformed into a frenzied mob that lusted for blood. If they were displeased with a losing gladiator's performance, they would call for

his immediate execution. Over the centuries, these spectacles grew more bizarre and brutal. For example, the greatest games of the Emperor Trajan (A.D. 98–117) lasted for 123 consecutive days in which 11,000 animals and 5,000 humans were killed. Hundreds of tigers were set against elephants and bulls; wild bulls tore apart men dressed in animal skins; women battled in the arena; dwarfs fought each other.

Because the business day for the Romans generally concluded at approximately three o'clock in the afternoon, those Romans who did not participate in the games and circuses frequented the *thermae* (public baths), which served as the location of numerous business and social functions from the early first century A.D. onward. Because few Romans outside of the aristocratic class could afford elaborate baths at home, they attended public ones where they met friends, received a massage, ate and drank, and participated in sports, including handball, field hockey, dodge ball, and soccer. By the middle of the fourth century there were 952 public baths in operation in the city of Rome.

One of the most impressive baths ever built was constructed during the reign of Caracalla (A.D. 188–217). Covering twenty-six acres, the *Baths of*

Caracalla contained a specially constructed aqueduct that carried water to it, a central hall more than 700 feet long, and adjoining halls to accommodate the various types of baths. The Romans could choose from a variety of baths—the *natatio* (pool), *frigidarium* (cold bath), *tepidarium* (tepid bath), *caldarium* (hot bath), and the *laconicum* (steam bath). The halls were adjacent to service rooms for heating both the air and the water and rooms designed for exercise. The great hall of the *frigidarium* was over 200 feet long and contained a vaulted ceiling. The groin vaults of the decorated, painted, and coffered ceiling were supported by piers, which were hidden by the massive marble-covered columns. Light permeated the interior through the windows, which were grouped beneath the arches of the groin vaults.

Beside the marketplace, or forum, located in the town center, the Romans constructed a basilica, a large public hall used for civic and administrative proceedings. A basilica was designed around its nave (the Latin word for ship), which is a long, rectangular hall with aisles on either side of it. The nave terminated in either a semicircular area (apse) or a tribune, a raised platform from which speeches were presented or legal cases were heard. Lateral windows above the colonnades of the side aisles lighted the interior. The ceilings could be either flat or vaulted and were ornamented with stuccoed or painted coffers.

DOMESTIC ARCHITECTURE The Roman emperors not only commissioned extraordinary public structures and monuments for the greater glory of the empire, but they also built magnificent private villas where they could retire to relax and indulge in their favorite amusements and passions. For example, Tiberius spent the last ten years of his life on the isle of Capri, where he had built at least twelve opulent villas, which included banquet halls, sculpted grottoes, and swimming pools. Hadrian built a villa at Tivoli that contained reproductions of scenes that he admired from his eastern campaigns. But perhaps the most renowned structure was the *Domus Aurea* (Golden House) of the Emperor Nero, which he authorized to be built in the center of Rome shortly after the great fire of A.D. 64.

When Mount Vesuvius erupted in A.D. 79, the towns of Pompeii and Herculaneum were covered

Figure 6.6 *Colosseum*, completed A.D. 80 , Rome This free-standing amphitheater accommodated between 50,000 and 70,000 spectators, who witnessed wild beasts fighting against each other or against men armed with spears and highly trained gladiators battling one another, sometimes until death. *(Scala/Art Resource, NY)*

Figure 6.7 *Insula at Ostia,* Italy   The exterior was constructed primarily of brick and concrete, which remained unadorned, and the interior was covered with plaster. Light and air were furnished by large windows, which, in the more expensive insulae, opened to an internal courtyard. *(Alinari/Art Resource, NY)*

with lava and volcanic ash and were thus preserved for posterity in almost pristine condition. Excavations of these towns have permitted modern people to view the private lives of both the patrician and plebeian classes. The aristocrats' *domus* (house) had an *atrium* (spacious hall), which was linked to the reception hall (*tablinum*) and the living quarters. The atrium, with its open roof, was the place where family portraits were hung; it was connected to the reception hall, where the ancestral archives were kept. The domus was generally surrounded by a colonnaded garden called a peristyle, but was shielded from the street by walls that had no windows. The more lavish homes also incorporated a portico, which extended into another garden that was ornamented with fountains, statuary, and mosaics. However, the most important room was the dining room (*triclinium*), where the master of the house and his friends indulged in sumptuous banquets.

The ordinary citizens of the cities resided in tenements (*cenacula*), which they rented in city blocks of tenements (*insulae*). By arranging the living quarters of the plebeians in such a manner, the Romans were the first town planners in the West. The first insulae appeared in the late Republic when enterprising real estate brokers combined a number of domus, built additional stories, and added balconies, which jutted into the narrow, winding streets. By the middle of the fourth century A.D., there were approximately 46,602 insu-

lae and 1,797 domus in the fourteen districts of Rome. The insulae, which often housed as many as 200 to 300 people, were shabbily constructed and had no water, no sanitary facilities, no source of heat, and only a brazier on which to cook food. Essentially these structures were slums, which tended to accentuate the cultural gap between the aristocracy and the masses. The reconstruction of the *Insula at Ostia,* a port on the Tiber, (Figure 6.7) shows that the street level was lined with shops (*tabernae*) topped by a mezzanine with small windows. The balcony encircled the entire first floor, and the remaining stories provided additional housing. Light and air were furnished by large windows, which, in the more expensive insulae, opened to an internal courtyard. The exterior of these structures was constructed primarily of brick and concrete, which remained unadorned, and the interiors were covered with plaster, in contrast to the mosaics and paintings that lined the walls of the domus of the aristocrats.

Portrait Sculpture

The Romans used portrait sculpture to glorify their emperors, honor their friends, and venerate their ancestors. The practice of the Republican period was to produce precise wax casts of the heads of those who died, which relatives held during the funeral service. This type of modeling was used for the *Roman Patrician with Portrait Heads*

(Figure 6.8). The visages of the two heads the patrician is holding bear a striking familial resemblance, but the original head was lost and replaced by the present one in approximately 40 B.C. According to the Roman custom, all of the men are clean-shaven.

The sculpting of realistic portrait busts emerged and reached its apogee during the reign of Augustus. Imitating Hellenistic models, Roman sculptors realistically carved every detail of a subject's face: unruly hair, prominent nose, lines and wrinkles, a jaw that showed weakness or strength. Statues of emperors conveyed nobility, authority, and often divinity—a reflection of the impact of the eastern provinces of the Empire, where the ruler was traditionally worshiped as divine. This Near Eastern influence is evident in *Augustus as Pontifex Maximus* (Figure 6.9; 1st century A.D. copy of the

Figure 6.8 *Roman Patrician with Busts of His Ancestors*, late 1st century B.C., marble, life size, Museo Capitolino, Rome Portrait busts emerged and reached their apogee during the reign of Augustus. Roman sculptors, according to custom, sculpted the men cleanly shaven and realistically carved each detail of their faces. *(Galleria Nazionale d'Arte Antica, Rome/Alinari/Art Resource, NY)*

Figure 6.9 *Augustus as Pontifex Maximus*, 1st century A.D., marble, height 6'9 1/2" (2.07 cm), Museo Nazionale Romano, Rome This statue shows the emperor as the Roman high priest preparing to offer a sacrifice; his dignified and reverent demeanor exudes a sense of wisdom. *(Galleria Borghese, Rome/Alinari/Art Resource, NY)*

Figure 6.10 *Equestrian Statue of Marcus Aurelius*, A.D. 161–180, bronze, 9'10" (3 m), **Piazza del Campidoglio, Rome** The emperor's demeanor reveals his pensive nature and stoic resignation to his duties. He has no armor or weapon, and he is raising his hand in a typically Roman oratorical flourish, rather than wielding a sword. *(Scala/Art Resource, NY)*

and the breastplate commemorates his victory over the Parthians, the triumph that ushered in the Augustan peace.

Emperors were commonly portrayed as great conquerors astride their horses, but the bronze *Equestrian Statue of Marcus Aurelius* (Figure 6.10; A.D. 161–180) is the only statue of its kind to survive intact. The sculptor rendered him with a beard, instead of the customary clean-shaven Roman model, to reflect the emperor's affinity for Greek philosophy. The emperor's demeanor reveals his pensive nature and stoic resignation to his duties—he has no armor or weapons, and his hand is raised with a typical Roman oratorical flourish rather than wielding a sword. The modeling of the horse's sinews, bones, tendons, and veins evidences the sculptor's concern with form and anatomy. Beneath the right foreleg of the horse, there was once, according to medieval accounts, a fettered foreign chieftain to emphasize the triumphant nature of the emperor. This statue was one of a very few to be displayed publicly during the Middle Ages because people believed it was a representation of Constantine—the first Christian emperor. The statue was widely emulated in the Renaissance and continues to be imitated even in the present day.

Imperial Narrative Relief Sculpture

The relief sculpture carved into triumphal arches, victory columns, and sacred altars combined the emperors' interest in public architecture with their desire to commemorate significant events of Roman history that glorified both the empire and the imperial throne. The *Ara Pacis Augustae* (Altar of Augustan Peace, Figure 6.11) authorized by the Roman Senate in 13 B.C., is an exceptional example of this type of monument. Completed in 9 B.C., the altar is reminiscent of the *Altar of Zeus* at Pergamum (see p. 118), although it is less theatrical and monumental.

A marble blocklike structure surrounding the altar contains intricately carved symbolic and fabled scenes, which are divided by embellished pilasters. The reliefs incorporate both mythological and historical subject matter, including Romulus and Remus, the ancestors of Aeneas; Aeneas sacrificing; a sacrificial procession that includes some of Augustus' grandchildren; and Tellus, representing the fertility of the earth, and two nymphs who accompany her, symbolizing air and water as representative of Rome's peace and prosperity under Augustus. These relief sculptures utilize *linear perspective,* for the participants in the foreground are larger and project from the stone whereas those closest to the background appear to be fused with

20 B.C. original), which shows the emperor as the Roman high priest (*pontifex maximus*) preparing to offer a sacrifice. The dignified and reverent demeanor of the emperor exudes a sense of wisdom. The heroically idealized expression and deportment of the *Augustus Prima Porta* (see chapter opening) stands in contrast to the *Pontifex Maximus* by hearkening back to the Doryphoros of Polykleitos (see chap. 4). The sculpting of Augustus' face draws attention to his eyes in a manner evocative of statues of Alexander the Great. The *Prima Porta* is also laden with symbolism: the naked feet signify Augustus' divinity; the small cupid riding the dolphin alludes to Augustus' claim that the Julian line descended from Venus;

the stone. This creates a sense of depth and real space, making the *Ara Pacis* more realistic than the flattened perspectives of the Hellenic friezes.

Evidence of this same type of perspective can be found among the sculpted white marble panels that face the *Arch of Titus* (Figure 6.12), especially in the two that flank the interior of the piers. The single concrete arch, which rises between square piers and stands at the crest of the Sacred Way, was dedicated in A.D. 81 by the Emperor Domitian to immortalize his brother Titus' successful capture of Jerusalem in A.D. 70. *Titus' Triumph* and the *Spoils from the Temple of Jerusalem*—Roman troops carrying off trumpets, the menorah, and the golden table from the temple—are both innovative and dramatic. The relief panels are executed in higher relief than those of the Ara Pacis to enhance the drama of the event as well as the play of light and shadow. The depiction of the emperor in his chariot is quite traditional, yet the other animated scenes mark a shift away from the decorum of Augustan relief sculpture.

Because most Roman triumphal monuments were arches, *Trajan's Column* (Figure 6.13) is unique. Both the architectural model for the victory column and the identity of the artists who designed and carved the monument are unknown. Some scholars assert the influence of the Egyptian obelisks, and others believe the relief carving is similar to Assyrian reliefs and Mesopotamian victory columns. Some scholars conjecture that the sculptor of the Roman Forum, Apollodoros of Damascus, was responsible for the column. The column, which commemorates the emperor's two successful campaigns against the Dacians (early inhabitants of western Romania) in A.D. 101–102 and 105–106, was dedicated in A.D. 113. Rising to the height of 125 feet, it is a continuous spiral relief carving that would measure 656 feet in length if it were uncoiled. After Trajan died in A.D. 117, his ashes were placed in a golden urn and buried within the sculpted podium of the column. The gilded bronze statue of Trajan that capped the column was destroyed in the Middle Ages, but was replaced in the sixteenth century with a statue of the Apostle Peter. The sculptural technique employed to narrate the two campaigns is essentially journalistic sculpture, that is, the reliefs are a

Figure 6.11   *Ara Pacis Augustae,* **completed 9 B.C., marble, 36' x 33' (11 x 10. 7 m), Museum of the Ara Pacis, Rome**   The reliefs of this blocklike structure incorporate both mythological and historical subject matter, including Romulus and Remus, the ancestors of Aeneas, Aeneas sacrificing, and a sacrificial procession that includes some of Augustus' grandchildren. *(Museum of the Ara Pacis, Rome/Alinari/Art Resource, NY)*

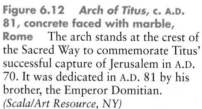

Figure 6.12 *Arch of Titus*, c. A.D. 81, concrete faced with marble, Rome   The arch stands at the crest of the Sacred Way to commemorate Titus' successful capture of Jerusalem in A.D. 70. It was dedicated in A.D. 81 by his brother, the Emperor Domitian. *(Scala/Art Resource, NY)*

narration of events, a sort of documentary. The sculptor's inventive technique is evidenced in three significant ways: (1) the figures are carved in low relief so that deep shadows, which could visually distort the bands, do not appear; (2) the most significant participants in the campaign are sculpted larger than the surrounding elements (e.g., horses, weapons, landscape, city walls); and (3) the panoramic view of the campaign occurs on an alpine terrain, which is adjusted for the optical distortion of the human eye as the spiral ascends, thus making each band appear to be of an equal width.

The last and most elaborate triumphal arch to be erected in Rome was constructed near the Colosseum to commemorate Constantine's victory on October 28, 312, over his rival, Maxentius. This victory was the one in which Constantine, according to Eusebius, saw an angel carrying a cross who said, "In this sign thou shalt conquer." *The Arch of Constantine* (Figure 6.14) has triple lateral openings, making it like the earlier *Arch of Septimus Severus* and unlike the *Arch of Titus*, the arches that stand at opposite ends of the Roman Forum. Much of the sculpture on the arch was plundered from

earlier imperial monuments honoring Trajan, Hadrian, and Marcus Aurelius. Not only were the portraits of these earlier emperors recast to portray Constantine as the restorer of the glory of Rome, but the inscriptions above the frieze depicting his battle with Maxentius laud Constantine as "the Liberator of the City" and "the State's avenger upon the tyrant and his faction." Other friezes, especially those above the lateral openings, were sculpted in the new Constantinian style—the figures are done in low relief and are flattened against the framework of the arch. Because there is neither foreshortening nor a sense of movement, the Hellenic veneration of the human form has vanished. The focus is now on the spiritual rather than on the worldly life—a trend in relief sculpture that would dominate the art of the Middle Ages.

Painting

Roman painters, like Roman sculptors, utilized themes from Roman history, particularly imperial expansion. They adopted Hellenistic art styles and used them to produce realistic representations of landscapes and individuals. They sought to replicate individual traits and to reveal the essence of a person's character. The degree to which they pushed the depiction of the individual fringes on photographic fidelity and rivals Hellenistic antecedents. In crafting the perspectives of their wall paintings, Roman artists were able to create an identifiable space that was homogenous with the surrounding structure. Landscapes were rendered with an eye for the details of bushes, trees, clouds, birds, animals, and the topography of the land.

Some of the wall murals and mosaics painted in the homes of Roman patricians still survive, such as those from the late first century B.C. in the *Villa of Livia* (Figure 6.15), located at Prima Porta, on the outskirts of Rome. Because many of the interiors of these homes were windowless, the Romans created courtyards, gardens, and open architectural settings by painting such scenes on the stucco walls. The illusion of walls fashioned of stone or marble was made possible by creating textured panels—mixing marble dust with stucco, adding pigments, and smoothing the stucco into a marblelike swirl. Later, architectural perspectives were created by painting imaginary Corinthian columns, which supported the illusionary architraves of a porch. The vision was furthered by fashioning a garden full of sunlight, which terminated in a garden gate surrounded by a colonnade. In the case of Livia's villa, the artist envisioned a garden devoid of human beings in which birds sing, wildflowers bloom, and flowering shrubs and fruit trees abound. The artist's skill in depicting the secluded grandeur of the

Figure 6.13 *Trajan's Column,* dedicated A.D. 113, marble, height 125′ (38.1 m), Rome The column commemorates Trajan's two successful campaigns against the Dacians. Rising to the height of 125 feet, it is a continuous spiral relief carving that would measure 656 feet in length if it were uncoiled. *(Scala/Art Resource, NY)*

Figure 6.14 *Arch of Constantine,* c. A.D. 312–315, Rome   The triple arch commemorates Constantine's victory over his rival Maxentius, and the inscriptions above the frieze laud Constantine as "the Liberator of the City" and "the State's avenger upon the tyrant and his faction." *(Alinari/Art Resource, NY)*

Figure 6.15 *Villa of Livia, Garden Room,* late 1st century, Prima Porta, Museo Nazionale Romano, Rome   Because many of the interiors of these homes were windowless, the Romans created courtyards, gardens, and open architectural settings by painting murals or fashioning mosaics on the stucco walls. *(Museo Nazionale Romano delle Terme, Rome/Scala/Art Resource, NY)*

Figure 6.16 *Scenes of a Dionysiac Mystery Cult,* c. 50 B.C., wall painting, Villa of the Mysteries, Pompeii These fanciful paintings illustrate scenes in which humans and gods carry on conversations and participate in rites of purification, in an illusory theater, painted on the walls of the room. *(Scala/Art Resource, NY)*

garden makes these murals among the world's finest landscape paintings.

Roman artists, however, did not feel bound by the demand of any design principles that they represent the play of light and shadow precisely or create optical perspectives exactly. Sometimes they produced scenes that have no consistent perspective, neither from above, nor below, nor straight on; consequently, these paintings seem to distort reality. This fanciful type of painting facilitated scenes drawn from mythology. This is evident in *Scenes of a Dionysiac Mystery Cult* (c. 50 B.C. Figure 6.16) unearthed at the Villa of the Mysteries in Pompeii. The artist painted an illusory theater on the walls of the room in which both humans and gods carry on conversations and participate in the rites of purification. The "stage" for these life-size figures consists of a green ledge against a red backdrop, which is divided into panels by strips of black that facilitate the movement of the eye from frame to frame as the drama unfolds. The demeanor of the participants is both dignified and intense, but the positioning of the bodies demonstrates the influence of classical Greece.

Like portrait sculpture, portrait painting began in the Republican period, but unlike sculpture, it is difficult to trace its development because only a few Roman portraits have survived. However, a group of portraits from the Faiyum district in Lower Egypt did survive because of the technique the artist used—the paint was dispersed in hot wax, thus making the pigment endure longer than pigments suspended in water or egg yolk. *Portrait of a Boy* (Figure 6.17), executed some time in the second century A.D., is an example of this type of painting. The realistic rendering of the boy's facial features is reminiscent of the modeling used in the *Roman Patrician with Busts of his Ancestors.* He has neatly combed hair and a prominent nose, but his wide-set eyes, which evoke a sense of honesty, trust, and love, overshadow his countenance.

The *mosaic* was the last notably evocative technique for Roman pictorial design. Adapting the method of the Hellenistic Greeks, the Romans made the tiles even smaller to affect the appearance of painting. Although initially little color was used in the tiles of the mosaics in public structures, once the Romans discovered that they could fuse color into

Figure 6.17 *Portrait of a Boy,* **2nd century A.D., 15 1/8" x 7 1/4" (39 x 18.3 cm), The Metropolitan Museum of Art, New York** Portrait painting began in the period of the Republic, using a technique in which paint was dispersed in hot wax. Here we see how the boy's facial features evoke a sense of honesty, trust, and love. *(The Metropolitan Museum of Art, Gift of Edward S. Harkness, 1918 (18.9.2). Photograph © 1997 The Metropolitan Museum of Art)*

glass tiles they began to cover the interior walls of their villas with mosaics. For example, by using various shades of blue, yellow, and red, an artist could capture the essence of light appropriate to the sea and Neptune as the god who presides over it.

Roman mosaic art became the rich inheritance of both Early Christian artists and the Byzantine craftsmen of the Eastern Roman Empire, who fashioned the most impressive mosaics ever created and who used them profusely until the Byzantine Empire collapsed in 1453.

The Roman Legacy

Rome left the West a rich heritage, which has endured for centuries. The idea of a world empire united by a common law and effective government never died. In the centuries following the collapse of Rome, people continued to be attracted to the idea of a unified and peaceful world–state. By preserving and adding to the philosophy, literature, science, and art of ancient Greece, Rome strengthened the foundations of the Western cultural tradition. Latin, the language of Rome, lived on long after Rome perished. The Western church fathers wrote in Latin, and during the Middle Ages, Latin was the language of learning, literature, music and law. From Latin came Italian, French, Spanish, Portuguese, and Romanian. Roman law, the quintessential expression of Roman genius, influenced church law and formed the basis of the legal codes of most European states. Finally, Christianity, the core religion of the West, was born within the Roman Empire and was greatly influenced by Roman culture and organization.

Key Terms

Struggle of the Orders	*jus gentium*
principate	cult of Mithras
Pax Romana	Neo-Platonism
Golden Age	arch and vault
Silver Age	gladiators
lex caritatis	linear perspective
Ptolemaic system	mosaic
Twelve Tables	

Notes

1. Cicero, *De Re Publica,* trans. C. W. Keyes (Cambridge, Mass.: Harvard University Press, Loeb Classical Library, 1928), p. 211.

2. Sallust, *The Conspiracy of Catiline,* trans. S. A. Handford. (Baltimore: Penguin Books, 1963), p. 127.

3. Quoted in J. Wright Duff, *A Literary History of Rome* (New York: Barnes & Noble, 1960), pp. 136–137.

4. Terence, *The Brothers,* trans. H. T. Riley (London: Henry G. Bohn, 1853), pp. 202–203.

5. Catullus, quoted in E. A. Havelock, *The Lyric Genius of Catullus* (New York: Russell & Russell, 1929), p. 63.

6. Robert Fitzgerald, *The Aeneid—Vergil* (New York: Vintage Books, 1984), p. 190.

7. Ibid., pp. 190–191.

8. Joseph P. Clancy, *The Odes, and Epodes of Horace* (Chicago: The University of Chicago Press, 1960), p. 219.

9. Ibid., p. 37.

10. Ibid., p. 74.

11. *The Art of Love and Other Love Books of Ovid* (New York: Grosset & Dunlap, The Universal Library, 1959), pp. 117–118, 130–132, 135.

12. A. G. Carrington, *Aspects of Martial's Epigrams* (Eton, Windsor, England: The Shakespeare Head Press, 1960), p. 24.

13. Ibid., p. 27.

14. Ibid., pp. 39–40.

15. *The Satire of Juvenal,* trans. Hubert Creekmore (New York: Mentor Books, 1963), pp. 58–61, lines 242–248, 269–272, 302–305.

16. Juvenal, *The Satires,* trans. Niall Rudd (Oxford: Clarendon Press, 1991), pp. 43–45, lines 200–216.

17. Adapted from Seneca, *The Epistles,* trans. Thomas Morell (London: W. Woodfall, 1786), I, Epistle 47.

18. Marcus Aurelius, *Meditations,* trans. Maxwell Stanforth (Baltimore: Penguin Classics, 1964), bk. 2.

19. Cicero, *De Re Publica,* trans. C. W. Keyes (Cambridge, Mass.: Harvard University Press, 1928), p. 211.

20. Excerpted in Naphtali Lewis and Meyer Reinhold, eds., *Roman Civilization, Sourcebook II: The Empire* (New York: Harper & Row, 1966), pp. 535, 539, 540, 547, 548.

21. Michael Rostovtzeff, *Rome* (New York: Oxford University Press, 1960), p. 322.

22. W. T. Stace, *A Critical History of Greek Philosophy* (London: Macmillan, 1924), p. 377.

Early Christianity: A World Religion

AS CONFIDENCE IN HUMAN REASON AND HOPE for happiness in this world waned in the last centuries of the Roman Empire, a new outlook began to take hold. As evident in philosophy and in the popularity of Near Eastern religions, this viewpoint stressed escape from an oppressive world and communion with a higher reality. Christianity evolved and expanded within this setting of declining classicism and heightening otherworldliness. As one response to a declining Hellenism, Christianity offered a spiritually disillusioned Greco-Roman world a reason for living: the hope of personal immortality. The triumph of Christianity marked a break with classical antiquity and the beginning of a new stage in the evolution of the West, for there was a fundamental difference between the classical and the Christian concepts of God, the individual, and the purpose of life.

THE ORIGINS OF CHRISTIANITY

A Palestinian Jew named Jesus was executed by the Roman authorities during the reign of Tiberius (A.D. 14–37), who had succeeded Augustus. At the time, few people paid much attention to what proved to be one of the most pivotal events in world history. In the quest for the historical Jesus, scholars have stressed the importance of both his Jewishness and the religious ferment that prevailed in Palestine in the first century B.C. Jesus' ethical teachings are rooted in the moral outlook of the Old Testament prophets. Jesus, who prayed as a Jew, taught as a Jew to fellow Jews, and valued Jewish law and prophetic teachings, could only conceive of himself as a Jew. Hans Küng, the prominent German student of religion, elaborates on this point:

> Jesus was a Jew, a member of a small, poor, politically powerless nation living at the periphery of the Roman Empire. He was active among Jews and for Jews. His mother Mary, his father Joseph, his family, his followers were Jews. His name was Jewish (Hebrew *Yeshu'a*). . . . His Bible, his worship, his prayers were Jewish. In the situation at that time he could not have thought of any proclamation among the gentiles. His message was for the Jewish people, but for this people in its entirety without any exception. From this basic fact it follows irrevocably that without Judaism there would be no Christianity. The Bible of the early Christians was the "Old Testament." The New Testament Scriptures became part of the Bible only by being appended to the Old. The gospel of Jesus Christ everywhere quite consciously presupposes the Torah and the Prophets.[1]

Interior Santa Costanza, c. 350, Rome

The interior is illuminated by clerestory windows and encased with mosaics.

(Canali Photobank)

159

Judaism in the First Century B.C.

In the first century B.C., four principal social-religious parties, or sects, existed among the Palestinian Jews: Sadducees, Pharisees, Essenes, and Zealots. Composed of the upper stratum of Jewish society—influential landed gentry and hereditary priests, who controlled the temple in Jerusalem—the religiously conservative *Sadducees* insisted on a strict interpretation of Mosaic Law and the perpetuation of temple ceremonies. The Sadducees claimed to be the descendants of Sadok, the high priest of Solomon, and believed they were maintaining the ancient Hebrew teachings concerning Torah, which they interpreted literally. Rejecting ideas of the resurrection of the dead and an afterlife, they held that God meted out rewards and punishments on earth.

Challenging the Sadducees were the *Pharisees,* who adopted a more liberal attitude toward Mosaic Law (Torah). The Pharisees allowed discussion on varying interpretations of the Law and granted authority to oral tradition—an "oral Torah," which was communicated from one generation to another—as well as to written Scripture. Unlike the Sadducees, the Pharisees believed in life after death. The concept of personal immortality is barely mentioned in the Hebrew Scriptures. A later addition to Hebrew religious thought, probably acquired from Persia, the idea had gained wide acceptance by the first century A.D. The Pharisees had the support of most of the Jewish people. All later forms of Judaism developed from the Pharisees.

The third religious party, the *Essenes,* established a semimonastic community near the Dead Sea. Like the Sadducees, they saw themselves as the true descendants of Sadok, but they rejected the Temple priests as corrupt. Only those priests affiliated with their sect were seen as pure. In 1947, leather scrolls in hermetically sealed cylinders were found near the community of Qumran, about fourteen miles from Jerusalem, close to the Dead Sea. Dated from between c. 200 B.C. and A.D. 66–70, the *Wady Qumran Manuscripts,* commonly called "The Dead Sea Scrolls," contain the oldest extant Hebrew manuscripts and also documents that are unique to the sect of the Essenes, founded by a man they refer to as the "Teacher of Righteousness." *The Manual of Discipline,* one of the scrolls, counsels the Essenes to be true to the "counsel of the law . . . until there shall come a prophet and the Messiahs of Aaron [Moses' brother] and Israel."[2] The Messiah of Aaron would be a priestly ruler; the Messiah of Israel would come from the line of David; and the

Prophet, a priestly Messiah (perhaps a reference to their own "Teacher of Righteousness"), would return from heaven. The Essenes believed in the physical resurrection of the body, like the Pharisees, but gave this doctrine a more compelling meaning by tying it to the immediate coming of God's kingdom. Certain that the Messiah was about to come, the Essenes believed they were the final generation of God's people. In the scroll, *The War of the Sons of Light with the Sons of Darkness,* a forty-year plan of attack is outlined in which the "sons of light" conquer the world for God.

By adding to our knowledge of Palestinian Judaism in the first century, the scrolls shed light on the period in which Christianity arose and the Christian New Testament was written. Because of the similarity between the beliefs of the Essenes and many of the teachings of Jesus, particularly in the "Sermon on the Mount" (Matthew 5–7), and the imminent coming of the Kingdom of God, some modern scholars have suggested that Jesus may have been a member of the Essenes' community.

The fourth sect, the *Zealots,* demanded that the Jews neither pay taxes to Rome nor acknowledge the authority of the Roman emperor. The Zealots were devoted patriots and engaged in acts of resistance to Rome, which culminated in the great revolt of A.D. 66–70, which was crushed by superior Roman might.

Jesus (c. 4 B.C.–c. A.D. 29) performed his ministry within this context of Jewish religious–national expectations and longings. The hopes of Jesus' early followers stemmed from a lower-class dissatisfaction with the aristocratic Sadducees; the Pharisee emphasis on prophetic ideals and the afterlife; the Essene preoccupation with the end-of-days and the belief in the nearness of God and the need for repentance; and a conquered people's yearning for the Messiah, who would liberate their land from Roman rule and establish God's reign of peace, unity, and prosperity.

Jesus: Moral Transformation of the Individual

Jesus himself wrote nothing, and nothing was written about him during his lifetime. In the generations following his death, both Roman and Jewish historians paid him scant attention. Consequently, virtually everything we know about Jesus comes from the New Testament, which was written decades after Jesus' death by devotees seeking to convey a religious truth and to propagate a faith. Modern historians have rigorously and critically analyzed the New Testament; their analyses have provided some insights into Jesus and his beliefs, though much about him remains obscure.

Around the age of thirty, no doubt influenced by John the Baptist, Jesus began to preach the coming of the reign of God and the need for people to repent—to undergo moral transformation so that they could enter God's kingdom. For Jesus, the coming of the kingdom was imminent; the process leading to its establishment on earth had already begun. A new order would soon emerge, in which God would govern his people righteously and mercifully. Hence, the present moment was critical—a time for spiritual preparedness and penitence—because an individual's thoughts, goals, and actions would determine whether he or she would gain entrance into the kingdom. People had to change their lives radically. They had to eliminate base, lustful, hostile, and selfish feelings; stop pursuing wealth and power; purify their hearts; and show their love for God and their fellow human beings.

Although Jesus did not intend to draw away his fellow Jews from their ancestral religion, he was distressed by the Judaism of his day. The rabbis taught the Golden Rule, as well as God's love and mercy for his children, but it seemed to Jesus that these ethical considerations were being undermined by an exaggerated rabbinical concern with ritual, restrictions, and the fine points of the Law. Jesus believed that the center of Judaism had shifted from prophetic values to obeying the rules and prohibitions regulating the smallest details of daily life. (To Jewish leaders, of course, these detailed regulations governing eating, washing, Sabbath observance, family relations, and so forth were God's commands, intended to sanctify all human activities.) To Jesus, such a rigid view of the Law distorted the meaning of prophetic teachings. Rules dealt only with an individual's visible behavior; they did not penetrate to the person's inner being and lead to a moral transformation based on love, compassion, and selflessness. The inner person concerned Jesus, and it was an inner change that he sought. With the fervor of a prophet, he urged a moral transformation of human character through a direct encounter between the individual and God.

Jewish scribes and priests, guardians of the faith, regarded Jesus as a troublemaker who threatened ancient traditions and undermined respect for the Sabbath. Stated succinctly, Jewish leaders believed that Jesus was setting the authority of his person over Mosaic Law—an unpardonable blasphemy in their eyes. To the Romans who ruled Palestine, Jesus was a political agitator who could ignite Jewish messianic expectations into a revolt against Rome. After Jewish leaders turned Jesus over to the Roman authorities, the Roman procurator, Pontius Pilate, sentenced him to death by crucifixion, a customary punishment for someone guilty of high treason. Jesus' execution was consistent with Roman policy in Judea, for the Romans routinely arrested and executed Jews suspected of inciting unrest against Roman rule.

Believing that Jesus was an inspired prophet or even the long-awaited Messiah, some Jews had become his followers; the chief of these were the Twelve Disciples. But at the time of Jesus' death, Christianity was still just a small Hebrew sect, with dim prospects for survival. What established the Christian movement and gave it strength was the belief of Jesus' followers that he was raised from the dead on the third day after his burial. The doctrine of the resurrection made possible the belief in Jesus as divine, a savior–god who had come to earth to show people the way to heaven. For early Christians, Jesus' death and resurrection took on greater importance than his life.

It is the nature of the prophet to propose a new religious–moral vision or to reinterpret an older conception in a profoundly novel way. That is what the charismatic Jesus did, but there is no evidence that he intended to establish a new church. His followers accomplished this. In the years immediately following the crucifixion, the religion of Jesus was confined almost exclusively to Jews, who could more appropriately be called Jewish–Christians. Soon after the crucifixion, they gathered together and formed the first Christian church. The word **Christian** derives from a name given Jesus: *Christ* (the Lord's Anointed, the Messiah). These Jewish–Christians believed that they were the true Israel, the real people of God, who had recognized the Messiah when he came. Though they were faithful in obeying the Jewish Law, they also held their own special services, and they preached to their fellow Jews that Jesus was the true Messiah. Furthermore, those Jews who accepted Jesus as Messiah and repented of their sins would be baptized in his name and would share in the immortality promised in Jesus' resurrection.

Before Christianity could realize the universal implications of Jesus' teachings and become a world religion, distinct from a Jewish sect, it had to extricate itself from Jewish ritual, politics, and culture. This achievement was the work of a Hellenized Jew, named Saul—known to the world as Paul.

The Apostle Paul: From a Jewish Sect to a World Religion

The Apostle Paul (A.D. c. 5–c. 67) came from the Greek city of Tarsus, in southeastern Asia Minor. He belonged to the Diaspora, or the "Dispersion"—the millions of Jews living outside Palestine. The non-Jews, or *Gentiles* (from Latin *gens,* or "nation"), who came into contact with Jews of the Diaspora were often favorably impressed by Hebrew monotheism, ethics, and family life. Some Gentiles embraced Hebrew monotheism but refused to adhere to provisions of the Law requiring circumcision and dietary regulations. Among these Gentiles and the non-Palestinian Jews who were greatly influenced by the Greco-Roman milieu, Jesus' Apostles would find receptive listeners.

At first, Saul persecuted the followers of Jesus, but then he underwent a spiritual transformation and became a convert to Jesus. Serving as a zealous missionary of Jewish Christianity in the Diaspora, the Apostle Paul preached to his fellow Jews in synagogues. Maintaining that the Christian message applied to non-Jews as well, Paul urged spreading it to the Gentiles. In the process of his missionary activity—and he traveled extensively through the Roman Empire—Paul formulated ideas that represented a fundamental break with Judaism and became the heart of this new religion. He taught that the crucified Messiah had suffered and died for humanity's sins; that through Jesus, God had revealed himself to all people, both Jews and Gentiles; and that this revelation supplanted God's earlier revelation to the Jewish people. Alone, one was helpless, possessed by sin, and unable to overcome one's wicked nature. Jesus was the only hope, said Paul. Through the ritual of baptism—purification by water—individuals could enter into a personal union with Christ.

CHRIST: A SAVIOR–GOD

To the first members of the Christian movement, Jesus was both a prophet, who proclaimed the power and purpose of God, and the Messiah, whose coming heralded a new age. To Paul, Jesus was a resurrected redeemer who offered salvation to all peoples. This was possible because Jesus was not only the Christ, the Messiah, but he also was the Son of God, who existed prior to his coming in human form. Although Paul was not very precise about the divinity of Jesus and his prior existence, he did frequently refer to him as the Son of God and as the divine wisdom, through whom all things were created, in whom God's purpose is revealed. Paul's emphasis on the resurrection of Jesus and his assertions of the special divine status and preexistence of Jesus ensured that Christianity would not remain a Jewish sect but could become a religion for all people.

The idea of a slain savior–god was well known in the mystery religions of the eastern Mediterranean. Like these religions, Christianity initiated converts into the mysteries of the faith, featured a sacramental meal, and in time developed a priesthood. But the similarities between Christianity and the mystery cults should not be overstressed, because the differences are more profound.

Unlike the cultic gods, Jesus had actually lived in history. Hence, people could identify with him, which enormously increased the appeal of this new religion. Moreover, the deities of the mystery religions were killed against their will by evil powers. In Jesus, it was said, God had become human and suffered pain and death out of compassion for human beings, to show a floundering humanity the way that would lead from sin to eternal life. This suffering Savior evoked from a distressed humanity deep feelings of love and loyalty. Adherents of the mystery cults were not required to undergo a profound moral transformation. Christian converts, however, felt a compelling obligation to make their behavior, in the words of Paul, "worthy of the God who calls you" (Thessalonians 2:12)* and obey Jesus' command: "Be perfect as your heavenly Father is perfect" (Matthew 5:48). Finally, Christians, with their Jewish heritage, would tolerate no other divinity but God. Pagans, on the other hand, often belonged to more than one cult, or at least recognized the divinity of gods in other cults.

THE BREAK WITH JUDAISM

In attempting to reach the Gentiles, Paul had to disentangle Christianity from a Jewish sociocultural context. Thus, he held that neither Gentile nor Jewish followers of Jesus were bound by the hundreds of rituals and rules that constitute Mosaic Law. As a consequence of Jesus' coming, Paul insisted, Mosaic regulations were obsolete and hindered missionary activity among the Gentiles. For Paul, not the Law of Moses, but love of and faith in Christ were the avenue to God and salvation. To Paul, the new Christian community was the true fulfillment of Judaism. The Jews regarded their faith as a national religion, bound inseparably with the his-

---

* The biblical quotations in this chapter are from the Holy Bible, Revised Standard Version (New York: Thomas Nelson & Sons, 1972).

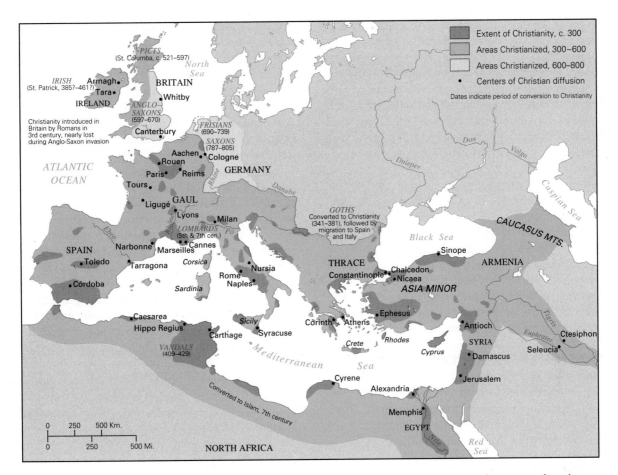

Map 7.1   The Spread of Christianity   Originating in Judea, the southern part of modern Israel and Jordan, Christianity spread throughout the Roman world. Roman sea lanes and Roman roads facilitated the expansion.

tory of their people. Paul held that Jesus fulfilled not only the messianic aspirations of the Jews, but also the spiritual needs and expectations of all peoples. For Paul, the new Christian community was not a nation, but an *oikoumene,* a world community. To this extent, Christianity shared in the universalism of the Hellenistic Age.

In preaching the doctrine of the risen Savior and insisting that Mosaic Law had been superseded, Paul (whatever his intentions) was breaking with his Jewish roots and transforming a Jewish sect into a new religion. Separating Christianity from Judaism enormously increased its appeal for the non-Jews, who were attracted to Hebrew ethical monotheism but repelled by circumcision, dietary rules, and other strict requirements of Mosaic Law. Paul built on the personalism and universalism implicit in the teachings of Jesus (and the Hebrew prophets) to create a religion intended not for a people with its own particular history, culture, and land, but for all humanity.

THE SPREAD AND TRIUMPH OF CHRISTIANITY

By establishing Christianity's independence from Judaism, Paul made the new religion fit for export to the Greco-Roman world. But its growth was slow. Originating in the first century, Christianity took firm root in the second, grew extensively in the third, and became the official religion of the Roman Empire at the end of the fourth century.

The Appeal of Christianity

The triumph of Christianity was linked to a corresponding decline in the vitality of Hellenism and a shift in cultural emphasis: a movement from reason to emotion and revelation. Offering comforting solutions to the existential problems of life and death, religion demonstrated a greater capacity than reason to stir human hearts. Hellenism had invented the tools of rational thought, but the

power of mythical thought was never entirely subdued. By the Late Roman Empire, science and philosophy could not compete with mysticism and
myth. Mystery cults, such as Mithraism and the
cult of Cybele (see p. 141), which promised personal salvation, were spreading and gaining followers. Neo-Platonists yearned for a mystical
union with the One. Astrology and magic, which
offered supernatural explanations for the operations of nature, were also popular. This recoil from
rational and worldly values helped prepare the
way for Christianity. In a culturally stagnating and
spiritually troubled Greco-Roman world, Christianity gave a new meaning to life and a new hope
to disillusioned men and women.

The Christian message of a divine Savior and a
concerned Father, as well as of brotherly love,
inspired men and women who were dissatisfied
with the world of the here and now—who felt no
attachment to city or empire, derived no inspiration from philosophy, and suffered from a profound sense of loneliness. Christianity offered the
individual what the city and the Roman
world–state could not: an intensely personal relationship with God, an intimate connection with a
higher world, and membership in a community of
the faithful who cared for one another.

Stressing the intellect and self-reliance, Greco-
Roman thought did not provide for the emotional
needs of the ordinary person. Christianity
addressed itself to this defect in the Greco-Roman
outlook. The poor, slaves, women, and the
oppressed were attracted to the personality, life,
death, and resurrection of Jesus, his love for all,
and his concern for suffering humanity. They
found spiritual sustenance in a religion that
offered a hand of love and taught that a person
need not be wellborn, rich, educated, or talented
to be worthy. To people burdened with misfortune
and terrified by death, Christianity held the
promise of eternal life, a kingdom of heaven,
where they would be comforted by God the
Father. Thus, Christianity gave the common person what the aristocratic values of Greco-Roman
civilization generally did not: hope, a sense of dignity, and inner strength.

Christianity succeeded not only through the
appeal of its message, but also through the power
of its institution, the Christian church, which grew
into a strong organization uniting the faithful. For
city dwellers, lonely, alienated, and disillusioned
with public affairs—stranded mortals groping for
a sense of community—the church that called its
members "brother" and "sister" filled an elemental
need of human beings to belong. The church welcomed women converts, who were often the first to

join and brought their menfolk after them. Among
the reasons that the church drew women was its
command to husbands to treat their wives kindly,
remain faithful, and provide for the children. The
church won new converts and retained the loyalty
of its members by furnishing social services for the
poor and infirm; welcoming slaves, criminals, sinners, and other outcasts; and offering a hand of
brotherhood and comfort during difficult times.

The ability of an evolving Christianity to assimilate elements from Greek philosophy and even
from the mystery religions also contributed in no
small measure to its growth. By utilizing Greek
philosophy, Christianity was able to present itself
in terms intelligible to those versed in Greek learning and thus attract educated people. Converts to
Christianity trained in philosophy proved to be
able defenders of their newly adopted faith.
Because some Christian doctrines (the risen Savior–God, the Virgin and child, life after death,
communion with the divine), practices (purification through baptism), and holy days (December
25 was the birth date of the god Mithras) either
paralleled or were adopted from the mystery religions, it became relatively easy to win converts
from these rivals.

Christianity and Rome

Generally tolerant of religions, the Roman government at first did not significantly interfere with the
Christian movement. Indeed, Christianity benefited in many ways from its association with the
Roman Empire. Christian missionaries traveled
throughout the Empire, over roads and across seas
made safe by Roman arms. The common Greek
dialect, *Koine*, which was spoken in most parts of
the Empire, facilitated the missionaries' task. Had
the Mediterranean world been fractured into separate and competing states, the spread of Christianity might well have faced an insurmountable
obstacle. The universalism of the Roman Empire,
which made citizenship available to peoples of
many nationalities, prepared the way for the universalism of Christianity, which welcomed membership from all nations.

As the number of Christians increased, Roman
officials began to fear the Christians as subver-
sives, preaching allegiance to God and not to
Rome. To many Romans, Christians were enemies
of the social order: strange people who would not
accept the state gods, would not engage in Roman
festivals, scorned gladiator contests, stayed away
from public baths, glorified nonviolence, refused
to honor deceased emperors as gods, and worshiped a crucified criminal as Lord. Romans ulti-

mately found in Christians a universal scapegoat for the ills burdening the Empire, such as famines, plagues, and military reverses. In an effort to stamp out Christianity, emperors several times resorted to persecution. Christians were imprisoned, beaten, starved, burned alive, torn apart by wild beasts in the arena for the amusement of the Romans, and crucified. However, the persecutions were too sporadic to severely threaten the new religion. Actually, they strengthened the determination of most of the faithful and won new converts, who were awed by the extraordinary courage of the martyrs willingly dying for their faith.

Unable to crush Christianity by persecution, Roman emperors decided to gain the support of the growing number of Christians within the Empire. In A.D. 313, Constantine, who was genuinely attracted to Christianity, issued the Edict of Milan, granting toleration to Christians. By A.D. 392, Theodosius I had made Christianity the state religion of the Empire and declared the worship of pagan gods illegal.

DEVELOPMENT OF CHRISTIAN ORGANIZATION AND ATTITUDES

Early in its history, the church developed along hierarchical lines. Those members of the Christian community who had the authority to preside over the celebration of the Mass—breaking bread and offering wine as Christ had done at the Last Supper—were called either priests or bishops. Gradually, the designation *bishop* was reserved for the one clergyman in the community with the authority to resolve disputes over doctrines and practices. Regarded as the successors to Jesus' twelve disciples, bishops supervised religious activities within their regions. In creating a diocese that was supervised by a bishop and had its center in a leading city, the church adapted Roman administrative techniques.

The Primacy of the Bishop of Rome

The bishop of Rome, later to be called the pope, claimed primacy over the other bishops. In developing the case for their supremacy over the church organization, bishops of Rome increasingly referred to the famous New Testament passage in which Jesus says to his disciple Simon (also called Peter): "'And I tell you, you are Peter, and on this rock I will build my church'" (Matthew 16:18). Because Peter in Greek means "rock" (petra), it was argued that Christ had chosen Peter to succeed him as ruler of the universal church. Because it was commonly accepted that Saint Peter had established a church in Rome and was martyred there, it was argued further that the Roman bishop inherited the power that Christ had passed on to Peter.

The Rise of Monasticism

Some devout Christians committed to living a perfect Christian life were distressed by the wickedness of the world about them, including the moral laxity of those clergy who chased after wealth and pomp. Seeking to escape from the agonies and corruptions of this world, some ardent Christians withdrew to deserts and mountains in search of spiritual renewal. In their zeal for holiness, they sometimes practiced extreme forms of asceticism: self-flogging, wearing spiked corsets, eating only herbs, or living for years on a column high above the ground. Gradually, colonies of these hermits sprang up, particularly in Egypt; in time, the leaders of these monastic communities drew up written rules that required monks to refrain from bodily abuses and to engage in manual labor.

The monastic ideal spread from east to west. The principal figure in the shaping of monasticism in the west was Benedict (c. 480–c. 543), who founded a monastery at Monte Cassino, Italy, in 529. The Rule of Benedict called for the monks to live in poverty and to study, labor, and obey the abbot, the head of the monastery. Monks were required to pray often, work hard, talk little, and surrender private property. In imposing discipline and regulations, Benedict eliminated the excessive and eccentric individualism of the early monks; he socialized and institutionalized the spiritual impulse that led monks to withdraw from the world. Benedict demonstrated the same genius for administration as the Romans had shown in organizing and governing their Empire. His rule became the standard for monasteries in western Europe.

Christianity and Society

Although salvation was their ultimate aim, Christians still had to dwell within the world and deal with its imperfections. In the process, Christian thinkers challenged some of the mores of Greco-Roman society and formulated attitudes that would endure for centuries. Influenced by passages in the New Testament that condemned acts of revenge and the shedding of blood, some early Christians refused military service. After Roman emperors professed Christianity, Christians began to serve the government more often. With the barbarians menacing the borders, these Christian officials could not advocate nonviolence. Christian theorists began to argue that under certain circumstances—to punish injustice or to restore peace—war was just. But even such wars must not entail unnecessary violence.

Christians waged no war against slavery, which was widely practiced and universally accepted in the ancient world. Paul commanded slaves to obey their masters, and many Christians were themselves slave owners. However, Christians taught that slaves, too, were children of God, sought their conversion, and urged owners not to treat them harshly. In the modern world, the Christian teaching that all persons are spiritually equal before God would impel some Christians to fight for the abolition of slavery.

The early Christian view of women was rooted in the patriarchal tradition of Jewish society. Paul echoed this tradition when he subjected the wife to her husband's authority. "Wives, be subject to your husbands, as to the Lord. For the husband is the head of the wife as Christ is the head of the church" (Ephesians 5:22–23). But Paul also held that all are baptized in Christ: "There is neither Jew nor Greek, there is neither slave nor free, there is neither male nor female; for you are all one in Christ Jesus" (Galatians 3:28). Consequently, both sexes were subject to divine law; both men and women possessed moral autonomy. The early church held to strict standards on sexual matters. It condemned adultery and esteemed virginity pledged for spiritual reasons.

The Christian understanding of a woman's subservient position was underscored in the thought of Augustine, the greatest Christian theologian in the ancient world. He believed that marriage itself was holy: it was instituted by God for companionship and the procreation of children. However, after the fall of the human race, with the original sin of Adam and Eve, sexual lust and sin became the driving force of procreation. Therefore, for Augustine, sexual pleasure or lust is always evil, whether in or out of marriage. Sexual relations in marriage for the purpose of procreation are guiltless, but, Augustine maintained, it is through the pleasure of sexual intercourse, "the lust of the flesh," that the stigma of original sin (Adam's and Eve's) is passed from parents to children. From his belief that sexual pleasure is evil emerged a distinctively negative view of women, for he held further that it is the woman who seduces the man into sin. A good Christian husband loves the woman as a creature of God, but hates "the corruptible and mortal conjugal connection and sexual intercourse"; he loves "in her what is characteristic of a human being" and hates "what belongs to her as a wife."[3] Perpetuated by the church, Augustine's largely negative view of women and their inferior status to men predominated in Western society for centuries to come.

Christianity and the Jews

The central theme of the New Testament gospels is love of both God and fellow human beings. But the gospels also devote considerable attention to the fallen angel, Satan, and the evil demons that inhabit his kingdom. Increasingly, Christians identified opponents—Jews, pagans, and heretics—with Satan and viewed conflicts in a moral context—a struggle between God's faithful and Satan's servants. Over the centuries, the view that they were participants in a cosmic struggle between good and evil led Christians to demonize adversaries, a practice that exacerbated hatred and justified mistreatment, even massacre. Christian attitudes and behavior toward Jews poignantly illustrate this point.

Numerous links connect early Christianity and Judaism. Jesus himself and his earliest followers, including the Twelve Apostles, were Jews who were faithful to Jewish law. Jesus' message was first spread in synagogues throughout the Roman Empire. Early Christianity's affirmation of the preciousness of the human being, created in God's image, its belief that God rules history, its awareness of human sinfulness, its call for repentance, and its appeal to God for forgiveness are rooted in Judaism. The Christian reference to God as a "merciful Father" derives from Jewish prayer. Also rooted in Judaism are the moral norms proclaimed by Jesus in the Sermon on the Mount and on other occasions. For example, "Thou shalt love thy neighbor as thyself" was the motto of the Jewish sage Hillel, a contemporary of Jesus who founded a school. Christianity inherited the great value that the Torah gives to charity. Jesus' use of parables to convey his teachings, the concept of the Messiah, respect for the Sabbath, the practice of giving alms to the poor, and congregational worship likewise stem from Judaism. And, of course, Christians viewed the Hebrew Scriptures as God's Word.

Over the years, however, Christians forgot or devalued this relationship to Judaism, and some thinkers began to show hostility toward Judaism and Jews, which had tragic consequences in later centuries. Several factors fueled this anti-Judaism: resentment against Jews for their refusal to accept Jesus; the polemics of the Jewish establishment against the followers of Jesus; the role in Jesus' death ascribed to Jews by the New Testament; resentment against those Christians who Judaized, that is, continued to observe Jewish festivals and the Jewish Sabbath, to regard the synagogue as holy, and to practice circumcision; and anger that Judaism remained a vital religion, for this undermined the conviction that Christianity was the fulfillment of Judaism and the one true faith.

What made Christian anti-Judaism particularly ominous was the effort of some theologians to demonize the Jewish people. The myth emerged that Jews, murderers of the incarnate God who embodied all that was good, were a cursed people, children of the Devil, whose suffering was intended by God. Thus, Origen (c. 185–c. 251) maintained that "the blood of Jesus [falls] not only upon those who lived then but also upon all generations of the Jewish people following afterward until the end of the world."[4] In the late fourth century, John Chrysostom (c. 344/354–407) described Jews as "inveterate murderers, destroyers, men possessed by the Devil. . . . [T]hey murder their offspring and immolate them to the devil." The synagogue, he said, was "the domicile of the devil as is also the soul of the Jews." Their rites are "criminal and impure," their religion is "a disease." For the "odious assassination of Christ," there is "no expiation possible, . . . no pardon." Jews will live "under the yoke of servitude without end."[5] Because the Devil was very real to early and medieval Christians, the Jew became identified with evil. Christians developed a mind-set, concludes the Reverend Robert A. Everett, that was "unable to see anything positive in Judaism. . . . Judaism and the Jewish people came to have no real value for Christians except as a negative contrast to Christianity."[6] Because of this "teaching of contempt" and the "diabolization of the Jew," the Christian ethic of love did not extend to Jews.

> . . . [O]nce it is established that God has cursed the Jews, how can one argue that Christians should love them? If Jews have been fated by God to have . . . a long history of suffering, who are Christians to alter their history by doing anything to relieve Jewish suffering? The theology of victimization thus precludes Christian love as a basis of relating to Jews.[7]

The diabolization of the Jew, which bore no relationship to the actual behavior of Jews or to their highly ethical religion, and the "theology of victimization," which held that the Jews were collectively and eternally cursed for denying Christ, became powerful myths. Over the centuries, these myths poisoned Christians' hearts and minds against Jews, spurring innumerable humiliations, persecutions, and massacres. Alongside this hatred of Jews and antipathy to their suffering, there also evolved the belief that Jews, faithless and perfidious though they were, should be permitted to survive, for one day they would see the light and convert to the true faith.

EARLY CHRISTIAN THEOLOGY AND LITERATURE

The Scriptural Tradition and Doctrinal Disputes

Christ's sayings and actions were preserved by word of mouth. Sometime around A.D. 66–70, Mark formulated the Christian message from this oral tradition and perhaps from some material that had been put in writing earlier. Mark presents Jesus as the Messiah, whom God acknowledged as his Son at his baptism (Mark 1:11) by John the Baptist. Between A.D. 80 and 90, Matthew and Luke, relying heavily on Mark's account, wrote somewhat longer Gospels. The Gospels of Mark, Matthew, and Luke are called *synoptic* because their approach to Jesus is very similar. Matthew and Luke do, however, introduce other material about Jesus. In particular, they hold that Jesus, born of a virgin was the divine son from the beginning of his earthly life.

The remaining Gospel, written by John around A.D. 110, varies significantly from the *Synoptic Gospels*. The Gospel of John uses the Stoic concept of *logos* (see p. 115) to present Jesus as a divine being. In the beginning of his gospel, John identifies Jesus with the eternal word, or *logos*; the Word became the incarnate Son of God:

> In the beginning was the Word, and the Word was with God, and the Word was God. He was in the beginning with God; all things were made through him, and without him was not anything made that was made. . . . And the Word became flesh and dwelt among us, full of grace and truth; we have beheld his glory, glory as the only Son from the Father. . . . For the law was given through Moses; grace and truth came through Jesus Christ.
> (John 1:1–3, 14, 17)

Unlike the Synoptic Gospels, which are largely concerned with moral precepts and ethical issues in their narrations of the life of Jesus, John focuses more on Jesus' message of the hope of salvation and eternal life.

The Synoptic Gospels; the Gospel of John; The Acts of the Apostles; the twenty-one Epistles, including those written by Paul; and Revelation constitute the twenty-seven books of the Christian New Testament. Christians also accepted the Hebrew Scriptures as God's Word and came to refer to them as the Old Testament. The New Testament was not written by historians with the critical spirit of a Thucydides or a Polybius, but by men moved by the fervor of faith. Under these circumstances, it is understandable that it contains discrepancies, some nonhistorical legends, and polemics.

Western culture has been inextricably tied to the New Testament (and the Hebrew Scriptures). Until the twentieth century, virtually all educated people were intimately acquainted with the Bible. New Testament images (the Annunciation, Christ on the cross, the resurrection, heaven); themes (a sinful human nature, repentance, the golden rule, confronting life's misfortunes, the power of faith); and characters (Mary, John the Baptist, Peter, Judas) pervaded literature, art, and music. The Christian vision, with its capacity to arouse an individual's deepest feelings, inspired many literary masterpieces—Dante's *Divine Comedy,* John Bunyan's *Pilgrim's Progress,* and John Milton's *Paradise Lost*; artistic triumphs—the Cathedral of Chartres, Masaccio's *The Tribute Money,* and Leonardo da Vinci's *Last Supper*; and great sacred music—Giovanni Pierluigi da Palestrina's *Lamentations,* Johann Sebastian Bach's *St. Matthew's Passion,* and G. F. Handel's *Messiah.*

The early Christians had a Bible and a clergy to teach it. But believers could interpret the Holy Writ differently, and controversies over doctrine threatened the loose unity of the early church. The most important controversy concerned the relationship of Jesus to God the Father. Arius (A.D. 250–336), a Greek priest in Alexandria, led one faction; he denied the complete divinity of Christ. Arius argued that Jesus did not preexist and was not eternal, but was made, created. To Arius, Christ was more than human but less than God; the Father and the Son did not possess the same nature, or essence. Arius said that there was no permanent union between God and Christ; the Father alone is eternal and truly God. The other faction, led by Athanasius (A.D. 295–373), argued that Jesus was of the very nature and substance of God the Father and that he had preexisted.

The emperor Constantine called the **Council of Nicaea** (A.D. 325), the first assembly, or ecumenical council, of bishops from all parts of the Roman world, to settle the controversy. The council condemned Arius and ruled that God and Christ were of the same substance, coequal and coeternal. The positions adopted at Nicaea became the basis of the Nicene Creed, which still remains the official doctrine of the church. Although Arianism, the

name given the heresy of Arius, won converts for a time, it eventually lost supporters.

Another controversy arose over the relationship between Christ's divine and human natures. Some theologians viewed Christ as a great ethical soul and tended to emphasize his human nature at the expense of his divine nature. Other theologians argued that Christ's human nature had been absorbed by his divine nature—in effect, that Christ possessed a single divine nature. The Council of Chalcedon in A.D. 451 formulated the orthodox position that Christ is truly God and truly human and that two distinct natures, one divine and the other human, are joined and preserved in his person. The other views were declared heretical but continued to persist in the eastern part of the Empire.

Christianity and Greek Philosophy

Christianity synthesized both the Hebrew and the Greco-Roman traditions. Having emerged from Judaism, it assimilated Hebrew monotheism and prophetic morality and retained the Hebrew Scriptures as the Word of God. As the new religion evolved, it also assimilated elements of Greek philosophy. The ability to combine a historic Judaic monotheism, which had many admirers in the Gentile world, with Greek rational philosophy was a crucial reason for Christianity's triumph in the Roman Empire. But there was a struggle between conservatives, who wanted no dealings with pagan philosophy, and those believers who recognized the value of Greek thought to Christianity.

To conservative church fathers—early Christian writers whose works are accepted as authoritative by the church—classical philosophy was all in error because it did not derive from divine revelation. As the final statement of God's truth, Christianity superseded both pagan philosophy and pagan religions. These conservatives feared that studying classical authors would contaminate Christian morality (Did not Plato propose a community of wives, and did not the dramatists treat violent passions?) and promote heresy (Was not classical literature replete with references to pagan gods?). For these church fathers, there could be no compromise between Greek philosophy and Christian revelation.

Tertullian (c. 150–225), the first of the Latin (Western) church fathers, is the best example of this attitude. Though he was thoroughly familiar with Greek philosophy, he believed that no attempt should be made to bring Christian beliefs into adjustment with Greek philosophy. The

Gospel of Jesus required no reinforcement from pagan ideas. The doctrines of the church, he insisted, should be accepted simply by faith, even when the church's teachings seemed to be contrary to reason. "What indeed has Jerusalem to do with Athens, the Church with [Plato's] Academy, the Christian with the heretic? . . . When we come to believe, we have no desire to believe anything else; for we begin by believing that there is nothing else which we have to believe."[8]

Some early church fathers, including several that had a Greek education, defended the value of studying classical literature. They maintained that Greek philosophy contained a dim glimmer of God's truth, a pre-Christian insight into divine wisdom. Christ had corrected and fulfilled an insight reached by the philosophical mind. Knowledge of Greek philosophy, they also contended, helped Christians explain their beliefs logically and argue intelligently with pagan critics of Christian teachings. Thus, Clement of Alexandria (c. 150–220) brought reason to the support of faith in his attempt to make Christianity more intellectually respectable in his world.

> Rather philosophy is a clear image of truth, a divine gift to the Greeks. Before the advent of the Lord, philosophy helped the Greeks to attain righteousness, and it is now conducive to piety; it supplies a preparatory teaching for those who will later embrace the faith. God is the cause of all good things: some given primarily in the form of the Old and the New Testament; others are the consequence of philosophy. Perchance too philosophy was given to the Greeks primarily till the Lord should call the Greeks to serve him. Thus philosophy acted as a schoolmaster to the Greek, preparing them for Christ, as the laws of the Jews prepared them for Christ.[9]

Utilizing the language and categories of Greek philosophy, these Christian intellectuals transformed Christianity from a simple ethical creed into a theoretical system, a theology. This effort to express Christian beliefs in terms of Greek rationalism is referred to as the Hellenization of Christianity. Greek philosophy enabled Christians to explain rationally God's existence and revelation. Using philosophical concepts, church fathers attempted to show that the Trinity, although a mystery, did not violate the law of contradiction: that God the Father, God the Son, and God the Holy Spirit did not conflict with monotheism. They attributed the order and regularity of nature and the natural law (moral principles that apply to all people)—two cardinal principles of Stoic thought—to God, the designer of the universe.

Christ was depicted as the divine Logos (reason) in human form. The Stoic teaching that all people are fundamentally equal because they share in universal reason could be formulated in Christian terms: that all are united in Christ. Christians could interpret the church to be the true fulfillment of the Stoic ideas of a polity embracing the entire world. Stoic ethics, which stressed moderation, self-control, and brotherhood, could be assimilated by Christian revelation. Particularly in Platonism, which drew a distinction between a world perceived by the senses and a higher order—a transcendent world that should be the central concern of human existence—Christian thinkers found a congenial vehicle for expressing Christian beliefs. The perfect and universal Forms, or Ideas, which Plato maintained were the true goal of knowledge and the source of ethical standards, were held by Christians to exist in God's mind.

That Greek philosophy exerted an influence on church doctrine is of immense importance; it meant that rational thought, the priceless achievement of the Greek mind, was not lost. However, the Hellenization of Christianity did not mean the triumph of classicism over Christianity, but rather the reverse: Christianity triumphed over Hellenism. Greek philosophy had to sacrifice its essential autonomy to the requirements of Christian revelation; that is, reason had to fit into a Christian framework. Although Christianity made use of Greek philosophy, Christian truth ultimately rested on faith, not reason.

Augustine: The Christian Worldview

During the early history of Christianity, many learned men, "fathers of the church," explained and defended church teachings. Most of the leading early fathers wrote in Greek, but in the middle of the fourth century, three great Latin writers—Jerome, Ambrose, and Augustine—profoundly influenced the course of Christianity in the West.

Jerome (A.D. c. 340–420) wrote about the lives of the saints and promoted the spread of monasticism. But his greatest achievement was the translation of the Old and New Testaments from Hebrew and Greek into Latin. Jerome's text, the common, or Vulgate, version of the Bible, became the official edition of the Bible for the Western church.

Ambrose (A.D. 340–397), bishop of Milan, Italy, instructed the clergy to deal humanely with the poor, the old, the sick, and the orphaned. He urged clerics not to pursue wealth, but to practice humility and avoid favoring the rich over the poor.

Ambrose sought to defend the autonomy of the church against the power of the state. His dictum that "the Emperor is within the church, not above it" became a cardinal principle of the medieval church.

The most important Christian theoretician in the Late Roman Empire was Augustine (A.D. 354–430), bishop of Hippo, in North Africa, and author of *The City of God*. Augustine became the principal architect of the Christian outlook that succeeded a dying classicism.

Augustine was born in the North African province of Numidia. His father was a pagan, his mother, Monica, a Christian. He attended school at Carthage, where he studied the Latin classics. Struggling to find meaning in a world that abounded with evil, Augustine turned to Manichaeism, an eastern religious philosophy that had roots in the cosmic dualism of Zoroastrianism. Its central doctrine was the struggle of the universal forces of light and good against those of darkness and evil. But Augustine still felt spiritually restless. In 383, he moved to Rome and then to Milan to be a teacher of rhetoric. In Milan he came under the influence of Neoplatonic writings. Then, in 386, inspired by the sermons of Ambrose, Bishop of Milan, he was converted to Christianity and devoted his life to following Christ's teachings. After his conversion Augustine returned to North Africa, where he was ordained to the priesthood in 391. Four years later he was appointed bishop of Hippo. In his autobiography, the *Confessions,* Augustine described his spiritual quest and appealed to devotees of Manichaeism and to adherents of pagan philosophy to embrace Christianity.

After the Visigoths sacked the city of Rome in 410, when Augustine was in his fifties, Neoplatonists argued that this disaster had occurred because the Romans had abandoned the old gods for Christianity. Throughout the Empire, people panicked. Even Christians expressed anxiety. Why were the righteous also suffering? Where was the kingdom of God on earth that had been prophesied? This was the setting for Augustine's *The City of God*, which he began to write in 412. *The City of God* is, therefore, both a defense of Christianity and a deliberate confrontation with Neo-Platonic doctrines. It is also a statement of Augustine's Christian philosophy of history, by which he reassured Christians that history was the unfolding of God's will. What really mattered in history, said Augustine, was not the coming to be or the passing away of cities and empires, but the individual's entrance into heaven or hell. For Augustine, history is teleological: It has a purpose. God directs the course of human events according to a predetermined plan. Prior to the incarnation of Christ, God was directing history toward this event; after

Christ, all history is moving toward the Last Judgment, when Jesus shall come again to attest to an individual's faithfulness to God's commandments and teachings.

Augustine maintained that all of history is a great conflict between two cities—the Heavenly City and the Earthly City. The Earthly City is composed of those sinners who will be condemned by God in the end. The City of God is composed of the elect, whom God chose for salvation, the small number endowed with God's grace. These people live on earth as visitors only, for they await deliverance to the Kingdom of Christ. Most inhabitants of the earthly city are destined for eternal punishment in hell. A perpetual conflict exists between the two cities and between their inhabitants: One city stands for sin and corruption; the other stands for God's truth and perfection. The City of God is represented on earth by the Christian church. In this life, then, the two cities are entangled with each other. Therefore, the church could not neglect the state but must guide it to protect human beings from their own sinful natures. The state must employ repression and punishment to restrain people, who were inherently sinful, from destroying each other and the few good men and women that God had elected to save from hell. But the earthly city would never know tranquillity, said Augustine, for it would always be inhabited predominantly by wretched sinners. People should be under no illusion that it could be transformed into the City of God, for everywhere in human society we see

> love for all those things that prove so vain and . . . breed so many heartaches, troubles, griefs, and fears; such insane joys in discord, strife, and war; such wrath and plots of enemies . . . such fraud and theft and robbery; such perfidy . . . homicide and murder, cruelty and savagery, lawlessness and lust; all the shameless passions of the impure— fornication and adultery . . . and countless other uncleanness too nasty to be mentioned; the sins against religion—sacrilege and heresy . . . the iniquities against our neighbors—calumnies and cheating, lies and false witness, violence to persons and property . . . and the innumerable other miseries and maladies that fill the world, yet escape attention.[10]

Augustinian Christianity is a living philosophy because it still has something vital to say about the human condition. To those who believe that people have the intelligence and goodwill to transform their earthly city into a rational and just community that promotes human betterment, Augustine offers a reminder of human sinfulness, weakness, and failure. Nor will new and ingenious political and social arrangements alter a defective human nature. He cautions the optimist that progress is not certain, that people, weak and ever prone to wickedness, are their own worst enemies, that success is illusory, and that misery is the essential human reality.

Augustine repudiated the distinguishing feature of classical humanism: the autonomy of reason. For him, ultimate wisdom could not be achieved through rational thought alone; reason had to be guided by faith. Without faith, there could be no true knowledge, no understanding. Philosophy had no validity if it did not first accept as absolutely true the existence of God and the authority of his revelation. Thus, Augustine upheld the primacy of faith. But he did not necessarily regard reason as an enemy of faith, and he did not call for an end to rational speculation. The part of the classical view that he denied was that reason alone could attain wisdom. The wisdom that Augustine sought was Christian wisdom, God's revelation to humanity. The starting point for this wisdom, he said, was belief in God and the Scriptures. To Augustine, secular knowledge for its own sake was of little value; the true significance of knowledge lay in its role as a tool for comprehending God's will. "Let us utilize truths useful to the faith that pagan philosophers have chanced upon," he said. Augustine adapted the classical intellectual tradition to the requirements of Christian revelation. With Augustine, the human-centered outlook of classical humanism, which for centuries had been undergoing transformation, gave way to a God-centered worldview. The fulfillment of God's will, not the full development of human capacities, became the chief concern of life.

Augustinian philosophy had a profound influence on medieval thought, particularly the distinction he drew between a higher world of perfection and lower world of corruption, his conception of human nature as essentially corrupt and sinful, his belief that reason alone could not serve as a proper guide to life, and his view that history moves toward a foreordained end.

During the Middle Ages, the church, rejecting Augustine's doctrine that only a limited number of people are predestined for heaven, emphasized that Christ had made possible the salvation of all who would embrace the precepts and injunctions of the church. The Protestant Reformers of the sixteenth century, however, accepted Augustine's position. Martin Luther taught that salvation from sin results entirely from God's grace, which is completely undeserved and absolutely free; and the belief that some men and women had been predestined to eternal life and others to eternal punishment in hell became a core doctrine of Calvinism.

EARLY CHRISTIAN ART

For thousands of years before the advent of Christianity, human beings had combined a creative impulse—a need to express themselves through visual images—with a religious impulse—a need to confront and explain the often frightening mysteries of life and death. Both in prehistoric cultures and in the early civilizations there was an inseparable link between art and religion. Christian artists also used the medium of visual arts to express spiritual feelings and to convey the teachings of their faith.

From the Jews, early Christians inherited the prohibition against making graven images. Consequently, the ancient Hebrews did not distinguish themselves in the visual arts. However, the prohibition, already bent by Hellenized Jews of the Diaspora who painted biblical scenes on synagogue walls, was not strictly observed by Christians, particularly those without Jewish roots. Showing the same flexibility that enabled Christian thinkers to absorb elements from Judaism, pagan religions, Greek philosophy, and Roman administration, while still retaining the core beliefs of their faith, early Christian artists decorated the walls of catacombs (underground burial places), sarcophagi (stone coffins), and churches with images and styles borrowed from contemporary art forms. In the process, however, they gave a Christian slant to their productions, focusing always on God's power and benevolence, the coming of Christ, and the promise of salvation. Early Christian artists reoriented art away from the rational and secular and toward the spiritual, a trend that lasted until the Renaissance.

For Christians, art was a means of expressing and strengthening devotion, rather than producing an accomplished imitation of nature. They did not aspire to create something beautiful for its own sake. This is one reason for the limited artistic merit of early Christian art. Another is that the pagan art of the Late Roman Empire, which served as a model for Christians, had already deteriorated, a pattern that is seen also in philosophy, literature, and science. According to art historian Ernst Kitzinger, "neither pagan nor Christian works of art of that period lived up to the highest standards of classical art. The Greco-Roman style had completely degenerated by the time it was taken over by Christians. . . . The artists imitated the traditional forms without entering into their

Figure 7.1 *Catacomb of Saints Peter and Marcellinus, "The Good Shepherd," early 4th century, Rome* The four semicircles, illustrating the story of Jonah and the "great fish," come together to form a cross. The center medallion symbolizes Christ as the Good Shepherd surrounded by the sheep who are entrusted to his care. *(Canali Photobank)*

spirit, and the beauty of the best classical art had disappeared altogether."[11]

Symbolism in Early Christian Art

Early Christian artists worked with specifically Christian subjects such as the magi commemorating Jesus' birth, Jesus as a miracle worker, the sacraments of baptism and the Eucharist, Christ resurrecting Lazarus, and Jesus' crucifixion and resurrection. A characteristic feature of Christian art was the use of images as symbols or image-signs, that is, a material object represented an abstract idea. Early Christian artists found passages in the Gospels, especially the Gospel of John in which Jesus spoke of himself in symbolic terms—"I am the bread of life," "I am the Light of the World," "I am the Good Shepherd," "I am the resurrection and the Life," and "I am the true vine" (John 6:35; 8:12; 10:11; 11:25; 15:1). These and other symbols were then incorporated into Christian frescoes (wall or ceiling paintings in which pigment is applied to wet plaster), sarcophagi, and mosaics.

Christian artists often used a fish to symbolize Christ and the missionary activity of his disciples. Christ had called his apostles "fishers of men" (Matthew 4:19; Mark 1:17) who, in his name, baptized people in the "waters of life." During the first and second centuries, many Christians adopted the symbol of the fish. When Christians encountered people they did not know to be Christians—especially during times of persecution or when traveling to unfamiliar cities—they would use a stick to scratch the first half of the fish symbol into the sand. If the strangers were actually Christians, they would scratch the other half of the fish. Later, they often embedded the Greek word *ichthys* (fish) within the symbol, which was an acronym formed by using the first letter of the Greek words *Iesous Christos Theou Yios Soter* (Jesus Christ God's Son Savior) to describe the character of Jesus (see example on p. 173).

Another sign of hope for the persecuted Christian minority was an anchor or a ship, wherein an orant—a figure standing with arms outstretched sideways—probably represented departed souls. Renderings of the sacraments of baptism and the

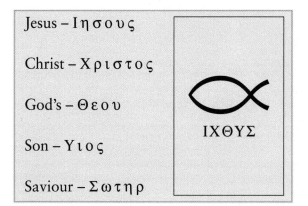

Jesus – Ι η σ ο υ ς

Christ – Χ ρ ι σ τ ο ς

God's – Θ ε ο υ

Son – Υ ι ο ς

Saviour – Σ ω τ η ρ

ΙΧΘΥΣ

Eucharist alluded to the key Christian themes of sin and redemption. An excellent illustration of Christian symbolism is the fresco, done in the early fourth century, found in the *Catacomb of Saints Peter and Marcellinus* (Figure 7.1). A small dome, modeled after the Roman Pantheon, suggests The Dome of Heaven. The four semicircles, which illustrate the biblical story of Jonah and the "great fish," join together to form a cross—the universal Christian symbol of the resurrection and heaven. The medallion in the center repeats the image of Christ as the Good Shepherd surrounded by the sheep—a symbol for the human soul— entrusted to his care.

In order not to arouse the suspicions of the Roman authorities, early Christian artists often used familiar Roman scenes to disguise a religious message. For example, the sculptured figures on the *Sarcophagus of Baebia Hertofila* (Figure 7.2), from the late third century, symbolize the Christian Eucharist. The central figure is Jesus distributing the bread and the wine of the Last Supper to his disciples. However, to the nondiscriminating observer, the scene looks like a Roman funeral feast, with mourners enjoying the feast.

The oldest images, from about 230, were drawn from Old Testament themes and figures—Adam and Eve standing beside the tree of knowledge as the serpent tempts Eve to eat of its fruit, Noah and the Ark, the Sacrifice of Abraham, Moses striking the rock, Samuel anointing David, David battling Goliath, Jonah being cast up by the sea monster, and Daniel in the Lions' Den. These scenes, frequently depicted on catacomb walls, were interpreted allegorically to give them a Christian meaning. For example, Moses raising his staff to draw water from a rock for the exiles wandering in the Sinai Desert was interpreted to mean that God would also assist persecuted Christians. An even more imaginative interpretation pointed to Christ, who told the faithful that "he who believes in me will never thirst" (John 6:35). Similarly, Abraham's willingness to sacrifice his son Isaac to show his love for God pointed to God's willingness to sacrifice his only Son because of his love for humanity. From Psalm 23, in which God is

Figure 7.2 *Sarcophagus of Baebia Hertofila,* late 3rd century, Museo delle Terme, Rome Symbolizing the Christian Eucharist, Jesus distributes the bread and the wine of the Last Supper to his disciples. *(Scala/Art Resource, NY)*

Figure 7.3 *Sarcophagus of Junius Bassus, c. 359, marble, 3'10 1/2 " x 8' (1.2 x 2.4 m), Museo Petriano, St. Peter's, Rome* The Roman prefect Junius Bassus was baptized as a Christian shortly before his death. His sarcophagus contains four scenes drawn from the Hebrew Scriptures and six from the New Testament. *(St. Peter's Basilica, Vatican State/Alinari/Art Resource, NY)*

described as a watchful shepherd, came the image of Christ as the Good Shepherd who brings strays back to the flock. The lavishly carved exterior (Figure 7.3) of the *Sarcophagus of Junius Bassus* (Junius Bassus was a Roman prefect who was baptized as a Christian shortly before his death around 359 B.C.) contains ten panels—four scenes from the Hebrew Scriptures and six from the New Testament, which are read from left to right, top to bottom. The panels are grouped systematically to illustrate the theme of salvation. Adam and Eve (panel G) represent the original sin, which could be overcome through Christ. The artist included the other Old Testament images, Isaac, Job, and Daniel (panels A, F, and I), to portend Christ's sacrifice on the cross. God's intervention to prevent Abraham from sacrificing his son, to deliver Job from his misery, and to free Daniel from the lions' den foreshadowed the saving grace brought through Christ's suffering. Christ's mission and the crucifixion are suggested by the scenes from the New Testament—Jesus' entry into Jerusalem

(panel H), his hearing before Pilate (panel D), Pilate washing his hands (panel E), and Christ enthroned (panel C) between the martyred apostles, Peter and Paul (panels B and J).

Christians also utilized images from pagan sources, which they placed within a Christian framework. Borrowing from the mystery religions, they pictured Christ ascending to heaven bathed in a halo of light. Adapting the tale of Orpheus from Greco-Roman mythology, Christ was depicted as taming wild beasts with song and lyre. Sometimes Christ was pictured on a stool reading a book—"the true philosopher." Classical mythology also had its Good Shepherd, who symbolized piety, which Christian artists transformed into an image of Christ.

Sculpture was of secondary importance in early Christian art, but *The Good Shepherd* (Figure 7.4), dating from about 300, is a notable exception. Standing nearly three and one-half feet tall, it differs markedly from other early Christian sculpture, which was executed on a smaller scale to avoid the appearance of idolatry. The pose bears a striking resemblance to the Archaic Greek statue, *The Calf-Bearer*, and the idealized features of the shepherd are reminiscent of the sculptures of Praxiteles (see Chapter 4). After Christianity was granted toleration by Emperor Constantine (Figure 7.5), Roman and Christian elements overlapped: Roman emperors were made to appear saintlike, the Virgin Mary was situated on a throne, and Christ, also on a throne, was depicted as a heavenly emperor. Even the resurrection was portrayed using imperial iconography—the cross is raised in triumph and awarded like a trophy. Moreover, after Constantine's edict, early Christian artists felt a new freedom to express their faith more overtly. This led to the use of the more obvious Christian symbols for the Holy Spirit and the resurrection—for example, a dove descending and women at Christ's empty tomb, respectively.

Figure 7.5 *The Emperor Constantine,* **c. 314, marble, height 8′ (2.5 m), Palazzo di Conservatori, Rome**   Following the Edict of Milan in 313, Constantine commissioned a number of churches that were patterned after the Roman basilica. He also decreed that basilica style be the form for Christian churches throughout the Empire. *(Scala/Art Resource, NY)*

Figure 7.4 *The Good Shepherd,* **2nd century, marble, height 39″ (99 cm), Vatican Museum**   Standing nearly three and one-half feet tall, this statue differs markedly from other early Christian sculptures, which were executed on a much smaller scale to avoid any appearance of idolatry. *(Vatican Museums/Scala/Art Resource, NY)*

Architecture

Following the Edict of Milan in 313, Constantine became the great patron of church construction. He commissioned a number of churches, which were patterned after the Roman basilica (assembly hall). As the emperor, Constantine dictated *basilica-form* architecture (the long rectangular church with a horizontal focus) as the style for Christian churches throughout the Empire. There are six main parts of a basilica-form church (Figure 7.6).

A. Nave—the main part where the people gather for worship
B. Transept—the cross arm, placed at right angles to the nave, which separates it from the apse
C. Apse—the area at the front where the altar is placed
D. Side aisles—passageways running parallel with and along either side of the nave, separated from the nave by an arcade or colonnade
E. Atrium—an open courtyard, often colonnaded
F. Narthex—vestibule, the transverse entrance hall

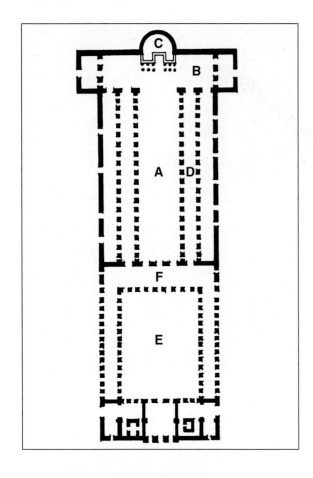

Although none of the churches built under Constantine have survived, it is possible to reconstruct models of some churches in Rome—Saint John Lateran, Saint Agnes Outside the Walls, and Old Saint Peter's—from documents that predate their transformations by later popes. The first Christian basilica, consecrated by Pope Sylvester I in 324, probably was Saint John Lateran. *Old Saint Peter's in Rome* (Figure 7.7) was the most important early basilica form church, not only because of its architecture, but also because the vault of the apse covered the area where Saint Peter is reputed to have been buried. Dedicated about 330, it was still incomplete when Constantine died in 337. Scholars call it "Old" Saint Peter's because it was razed by Pope Julius II in the early sixteenth century and replaced by the present Saint Peter's Basilica.

Old Saint Peter's church set the tone for much of Western church architecture for centuries to come.

Figure 7.6 **Floor plan of *Old Saint Peter's in Rome*, early 4th century, Rome** A—nave, B—transept, C—apse, D—side aisles, E—atrium, and F—narthex. *(Witt, et al., The Humanities: Cultural Roots and Continuities, Sixth Edition, Houghton Mifflin Company, 2001)*

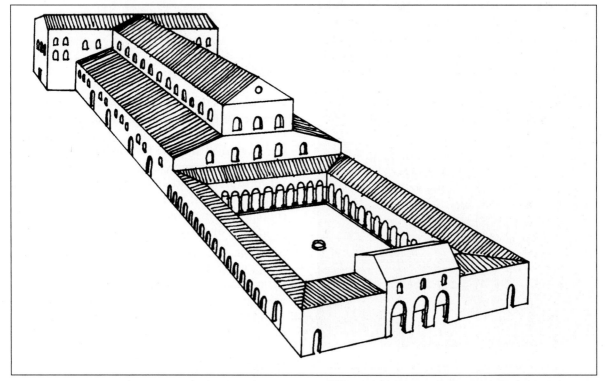

Figure 7.7 **Cutaway schematic of *Old Saint Peter's in Rome*, early 4th century, Rome** The vault of the apse reputedly covers the place where Saint Peter is buried. It is called "Old" Saint Peter's because it was razed in the early sixteenth century by Pope Julius II, who wanted a finer church. *(Witt, et al., The Humanities: Cultural Roots and Continuities, Sixth Edition, Houghton Mifflin Company, 2001)*

Figure 7.8 *Christ Gives the Law to Saints Peter and Paul*
5th century, Santa Costanza, Rome. This mosaic portrays a haloed, beardless Christ
bestowing the law in the manner of an emperor delivering an edict. *(Scala/Art Resource, NY)*

Although many early churches had a triumphal arch
to frame the altar and the apse, Old Saint Peter's
made use of a transept to suggest the Latin cross,
which became a standard feature of later basilica-
form churches. The nave of Old Saint Peter's had a
timbered roof, and the roofs covering the double
side aisles were lower than the nave, to provide
space for windows in the clerestory—the area above
the side aisle roofs. Even though some later churches
had a vaulted nave and no transept, the basic elements of basilica-form church architecture endured
throughout the Middle Ages and beyond.

Centralized form, the other popular style of
early Christian architecture, was influenced by
both Greek and Roman models—the round Greek
temple called a *tholos* and Roman structures, such
as public baths, the Pantheon (see p. 144), and
mausoleums. Centralized-form churches, which
became especially important in the fifth century in
Ravenna, Italy, and in the Byzantine Empire, were
either round or polygonal structures with a vertical focus, which was finished with a dome.
Because the number eight was the Christian symbol of the resurrection, the most common geometric design was the octagon, which was used for
both baptisteries and funeral chapels. The most

outstanding surviving example using the centralized form is the mausoleum for Constantia, Constantine's daughter, originally attached to the
Roman church of Saint Agnes Outside the Walls.
The interior of the domed mausoleum, converted
into the church *Santa Costanza* in 1256, is illuminated by clerestory windows and encased with
mosaics (see chapter opening). *Mosaics* are
designs composed of individual tiles called
tesserae, which are made from a variety of materials, including marble, colored glass, and gold. First
used as an art form by the Sumerians in the third
millennium B.C., mosaics were also employed by
the Hellenistic Greeks (see p. 117, *The Battle of
Issus*) and the Romans. With their flat, less-than-
realistic representations, mosaics enabled the early
Christian artisans to create religious art without
violating the second commandment. The apse
mosaic, *Christ Gives the Law to Saints Peter and
Paul* (Figure 7.8), portrays a haloed, beardless
Christ bestowing the law in a manner suggesting
an emperor delivering an edict.

In *Putti Harvesting Grapes* (Figure 7.9) the
putti, or children, seem to be engaged in a simple
agricultural act, but to the discerning Christian,
the scene conveyed a religious meaning, for vines

Figure 7.9 *Putti Harvesting Grapes,* c. 350, Santa Costanza, Rome   The children, called putti, are busy harvesting grapes. But to the discerning Christian, the scene contains image-signs: vines represent Jesus as the Christ and the grapes symbolize the Eucharist. *(S. Costanza, Rome/Scala/Art Resource, NY)*

and grapes were image-signs for the Lord and the Eucharist. Mosaics eventually supplanted the fresco paintings of the catacombs and became the preeminent artistic expression of Byzantine culture until the middle of the fifteenth century.

Christianity and Classical Humanism: Alternative Worldviews

Christianity and classical humanism are the two principal components of the Western tradition. The value that modern Western civilization places on the individual derives ultimately from classical humanism and the Judeo-Christian tradition. Classical humanists believed that human worth came from the capacity of individuals to reason and to shape their character and life according to rational standards. Christianity also places great stress on the individual. In the Christian view, God cares for each person; he wants people to behave righteously and to enter heaven; Christ died for all because he loves humanity. Christianity espouses active love and genuine concern for fellow human beings. Without God, people are as Augustine described them: "foul, crooked, sordid, . . . vicious." With God, the human personality can undergo a moral transformation and become loving, good, and free.

But Christianity and classical humanism also represent two essentially different worldviews. The triumph of the Christian outlook signified a break with the essential meaning of classical humanism; it pointed to the end of the world of

antiquity and the beginning of an age of faith, the Middle Ages. With the victory of Christianity, the ultimate goal of life shifted. Life's purpose was no longer to achieve excellence in this world through the full and creative development of human capacities, but to attain salvation in a heavenly city. A person's worldly accomplishments amounted to very little if he or she did not accept God and his revelation. The Christian ideal of the isolated and contemplative monk, who rejected the world in order to serve God, was alien to the spirit of classical humanism, which valued active citizenship. Equally foreign to the Greco-Roman mind was another idea introduced by Christianity: the need to escape from a sinful human nature, a consequence of Adam and Eve's defiance of God.

In the classical view, history had no ultimate end and no ultimate meaning; periods of happiness and misery repeated themselves endlessly. In the Christian view, history is filled with spiritual meaning. It is the profound drama of individuals struggling to overcome their original sin in order to gain eternal happiness in heaven. History began with Adam and Eve's fall and would end when Christ returns to earth, evil is eradicated, and God's will prevails.

Classicism held that there was no authority higher than reason, that individuals had within themselves the ability to understand the world and life; Christianity teaches that, without God as the starting point, knowledge is formless, purposeless, and prone to error. Classicism held that ethical standards were laws of nature, which reason could discover. Through reason, individuals could discern the normative values by which they should regulate their lives. Reason would enable them to govern desires and will; it would show where their behavior was wrong and teach them how to correct it. Because individuals sought what was best for themselves, they would obey the voice of reason. Christianity, on the other hand, maintains that ethical standards emanate from the personal will of God. Without submission to God's commands, people are prone to wickedness; the human will, essentially sinful, cannot be transformed by the promptings of reason. Only when individuals turn to God for forgiveness and guidance can they find the inner strength to overcome their sinful nature. People cannot perfect themselves through scientific knowledge; it is spiritual insight and belief in God that they require and that must serve as the first principle of their lives. For classicism, the ultimate good was sought through independent thought and action; for Christianity, the ultimate good comes through knowing, obeying, and loving God.

Christian thinkers respected Greek philosophy, however, and did not seek to eradicate the intellectual heritage of Greece. Rather, they sought to fit it into a Christian framework. By preserving the Greek philosophical tradition, Christian thinkers performed a task of immense historical significance.

Christianity inherited the Hebrew view of the overriding importance of God for humanity: God, who is both Lawgiver and Judge, makes life intelligible and purposeful. For the Christian, God is a living being, loving and compassionate, in whose company one seeks to spend eternity; one knows God essentially through faith and feeling. Although the Greek philosophers had a conception of God, it was not comparable to the God of Hebrews and Christians. For the Greeks, God was a logical abstraction, a principle of order, the prime mover, the first cause, the mind of the universe, pure thought, the supreme good, the highest truth; God was a concept, impersonal, unfeeling, and uninvolved with human concerns. The Greeks approached God through the intellect, not the heart; they neither loved nor worshiped God. In addition, because religion was at the periphery, not the center, of classical humanism, the idea of God did not carry the same significance for the Greeks as it did for Christianity.

In the classical world, the political community was the avenue to justice, happiness, and self-realization. In Christianity, the good life was not identified with worldly achievement but with life eternal, and the ideal commonwealth could only be one that was founded and ruled by Christ. It was entrance into God's kingdom that each person must make the central aim of life. For the next thousand years, this distinction between heaven and earth, this otherworldly, theocentric outlook, would define the Western mentality.

In the Late Roman Empire, when classical values were in decay, Christianity was a dynamic and creative movement. Possessing both institutional and spiritual strength, Christianity survived the fall of Rome. Because it retained elements of Greco-Roman civilization and taught a high morality, Christianity served as a civilizing agent in the centuries that followed Rome's collapse. Indeed, Christianity was the essential shaper of the European civilization that emerged in the Middle Ages.

Key Terms

Sadducees	bishop
Pharisees	Synoptic Gospels
Essenes	Council of Nicaea
Zealots	*ichthys*
Christian	basilica form
Gentiles	centralized form
oikoumene	mosaics

Notes

1. Hans Küng, "Christianity and Judaism," in *Jesus' Jewishness*, ed. James H. Charlesworth (New York: Crossroad, 1991), p. 259.
2. Millar Burrows, *The Dead Sea Scrolls* (New York: The Viking Press, 1956), p. 383.
3. William Findlay, trans., *The Sermon on the Mount*, I, XV, 41 in *The Works of Aurelius Augustine, Bishop of Hippo*, ed. Marcus Dods (Edinburgh: T & T Clark, 1873), 8: 32–33.
4. "Commentaria in Evangelium secundum Mathaeum," in *Patrologiae Cursus Completus*, Series Graeca Prior, ed. J. P. Migne, trans. for this text by Joseph Castora (Paris, 1862), 13: 1775–1776.
5. Quoted in Edward H. Flannery, *The Anguish of the Jews* (London: Macmillan, 1965), p. 48.
6. Randolph Braham, ed., *The Origins of the Holocaust: Christian Anti-Semitism* (Boulder, Colo.: Social Science Monographs and Institute for Holocaust Studies of the City University of New York, 1986), p. 36.
7. Ibid., p. 37.
8. Tertullian, "Prescriptions Against Heretics," *Early Latin Theology*, ed. and trans. S. L. Greenslade, Vol. 5, *Library of Christian Classics* (Philadelphia: Westminster Press and London: SCM Press, 1960), p. 183.
9. *The Writings of Clement of Alexandria* (Edinburgh: T. & T. Clark, 1867–1872), pp. 303–305, 307–310, 318.
10. St. Augustine, *The City of God*, abridged, ed. Vernon J. Bourke, trans. Gerald G. Walsh, Demitrius B. Zema, and Grace Monahan (Garden City, N.Y.: Doubleday Image Books, 1958), p. 519
11. Ernst Kitzinger, *Early Medieval Art in the British Museum* (London: Charles Skilton Ltd., 1969), p. 6.

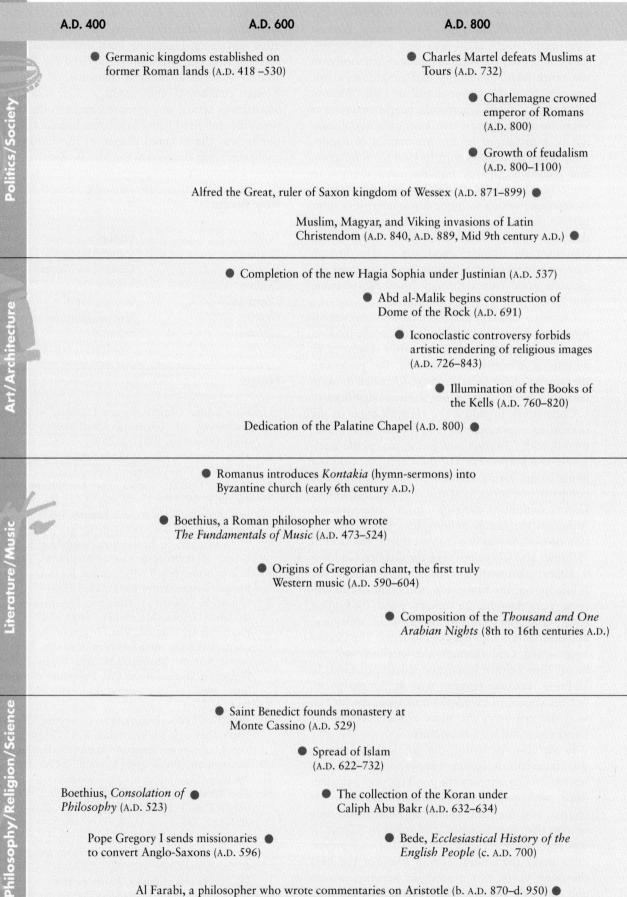

A.D. 400   A.D. 600   A.D. 800

Politics/Society

● Germanic kingdoms established on former Roman lands (A.D. 418–530)

● Charles Martel defeats Muslims at Tours (A.D. 732)

● Charlemagne crowned emperor of Romans (A.D. 800)

● Growth of feudalism (A.D. 800–1100)

Alfred the Great, ruler of Saxon kingdom of Wessex (A.D. 871–899) ●

Muslim, Magyar, and Viking invasions of Latin Christendom (A.D. 840, A.D. 889, Mid 9th century A.D.) ●

Art/Architecture

● Completion of the new Hagia Sophia under Justinian (A.D. 537)

● Abd al-Malik begins construction of Dome of the Rock (A.D. 691)

● Iconoclastic controversy forbids artistic rendering of religious images (A.D. 726–843)

● Illumination of the Books of the Kells (A.D. 760–820)

Dedication of the Palatine Chapel (A.D. 800) ●

Literature/Music

● Romanus introduces *Kontakia* (hymn-sermons) into Byzantine church (early 6th century A.D.)

● Boethius, a Roman philosopher who wrote *The Fundamentals of Music* (A.D. 473–524)

● Origins of Gregorian chant, the first truly Western music (A.D. 590–604)

● Composition of the *Thousand and One Arabian Nights* (8th to 16th centuries A.D.)

Philosophy/Religion/Science

● Saint Benedict founds monastery at Monte Cassino (A.D. 529)

● Spread of Islam (A.D. 622–732)

Boethius, *Consolation of Philosophy* (A.D. 523) ●

● The collection of the Koran under Caliph Abu Bakr (A.D. 632–634)

Pope Gregory I sends missionaries ● to convert Anglo-Saxons (A.D. 596)

● Bede, *Ecclesiastical History of the English People* (c. A.D. 700)

Al Farabi, a philosopher who wrote commentaries on Aristotle (b. A.D. 870–d. 950) ●

● German king Otto I becomes first Holy Roman Emperor (A.D. 962)

● Hundred Years' War (A.D. 1337–1453)

● Norman conquest of England (A.D. 1066)

● Black Death (A.D. 1347–1351)

● Start of First Crusade (A.D. 1096)

● Development of common law in England (A.D. 1135–1154)

● Philip Augustus expands central authority in France (A.D. 1180–1223)

● Magna Carta (A.D. 1215)

● Destruction of Baghdad by Mongols (A.D. 1258)

● Romanesque period of architecture (A.D. 1050–1200)

● *The Very Rich Hours of the Duke of Berry* illuminated manuscript (A.D. 1413)

● The Bayeux Tapestry, commissioned by William the Conqueror (c. A.D. 1073–1083)

● Gothic period of architecture begins (c. A.D. 1150)

● Notre-Dame de Chartres is rebuilt in the High Gothic style (A.D. 1194–1224)

● Height of stained glass typified in rose windows at Chartres (A.D. 1200–1250)

● Giotto designs thirty-nine frescoes for the Arena Chapel (A.D. 1305–1306)

● *Rubiayat* of Omar Khayyam (A.D. 1044–1123)

● Guillaume de Lorris writes the French allegory *The Romance of the Rose* (c. A.D. 1237)

● First written account of Irish fictional hero Cuchulainn (A.D. 1100)

● Boccaccio writes the *Decameron* (A.D. 1358)

● Chaucer's *Canterbury Tales* (c. A.D. 1386)

● *The Song of Roland,* epic poem on life of Charlemagne's nephew (c. A.D. 1130–1170)

● The Pearl Poet writes *Sir Gawain and the Green Knight* (c. A.D. 1375)

Origin of the literary genre "romance" in France (A.D. 1130–1150) ●

● First complete German text of the *Nibelungenlied* (c. A.D. 1195–1205)

● Dante Alighieri writes *The Divine Comedy* (A.D. 1292)

Poetry of Marie de France (A.D. 1160–1214) ●

● Petrach's sonnets (A.D. 1304–1374)

Philippe de Vitry's *Ars nova* characterizes musical style of fourteenth century (A.D. 1320) ●

● Christine de Pizan writes *The Book of the City of Ladies* (A.D. 1405)

● Ibn-Sina (Avicenna), doctor, scientist, and philosopher (b. A.D. 980–d. 1037)

● Ibn-Rushd (Averroes) attempts to reconcile scripture and philosophy (A.D. 1179–1180)

● Pontificate of Innocent III: height of papal power (A.D. 1198–1216)

● Thomas Aquinas, *Summa Theologica* (A.D. 1267–1273)

● Abelard, a French philosopher and theologian who supported the application of reason to faith (b. A.D. 1079–d. 1142)

● William of Ockham, an English scholastic philosopher who held that reason cannot prove truth of Christian dogmas (b. A.D. 1280–d. 13049)

● Great Schism of papacy (A.D. 1378–1417)

● Split between the Byzantine and Roman churches (A.D. 1054)

● Roger Bacon, an English scientist and philosopher who maintained that science leads to mastery of nature (b. A.D. 1220–d. 1292)

Moses ben Maimon, leading ● Jewish thinker of Middle Ages (b. A.D. 1135–d. 1204)

● Albertus Magnus, a scientist, philosopher, and theologian who urged application of reason to study of nature (b. A.D. 1206–d. 1280)

181

The Medieval East: Byzantium and Islam

T HE TRIUMPH OF CHRISTIANITY and the establishment of Germanic kingdoms on once-Roman lands constituted a new phase in Western history:
the end of the ancient world and the beginning of the Middle Ages, a period
that spanned a thousand years. In the ancient world, the locus of Greco-
Roman civilization had been the Mediterranean Sea; the heartland of Western
medieval civilization gradually shifted to the north, to regions of Europe that
Greco-Roman civilization had barely penetrated. Latin Christendom (western
and central Europe) was only one of three new civilizations based on religion
that emerged after the decline of the Roman Empire; Byzantium and Islam
were the other two. Both of these Eastern civilizations influenced the emerging
Europe in important ways.

A SURVEY OF BYZANTINE HISTORY

Although the Roman Empire in the West fell to the Germanic tribes, the eastern provinces of the Empire survived. They did so because they were richer,
more urbanized, and more populous and because the main thrust of the Germanic and Hunnish invaders had been directed at the West. In the eastern
regions, Byzantine civilization took shape. Its religion was Christianity, its culture Greek, and its machinery of administration Roman. The capital, Constantinople, was built on the site of the ancient Greek city of Byzantium, on a
peninsula in the Straits of Bosporus—the dividing line between Asia and
Europe. Constantinople was a fortress city perfectly situated to resist attacks
from both land and sea.

During the Early Middle Ages, Byzantine civilization was far more economically and culturally advanced than the Latin West. At a time when few
westerners (Latin Christians) could read or write, Byzantine scholars studied
the literature, philosophy, science, and law of ancient Greece and Rome.
Whereas trade and urban life had greatly declined in the West, Constantinople was a magnificent Byzantine city of schools, libraries, open squares, and
bustling markets.

Over the centuries, many differences developed between the Byzantine
church and the Roman church. The pope resisted domination by the Byzantine
emperor, and the Byzantines would not accept the pope as head of all Christians. The two churches quarreled over ceremonies, holy days, and most
importantly, the display of images, or icons. The Western church, although
cognizant of the biblical injunctions against the worship of images, nevertheless believed that images were tools for instruction and were valuable aids

**Great Mosque
of Córdoba
(horseshoe-shaped
arches, 786, Spain)**

The mosque is best
known for its double set
of horseshoe-shaped
arches, one above the
other, both of which are
mounted on the capitals
of the granite and marble
columns, which were
plundered from Roman
and early Christian
structures.

*(Christopher
Rennie/Robert Harding
Picture Library)*

during worship. Some Christians in the Eastern church, however, took biblical injunctions concerning the use of images more literally, which resulted in two iconoclastic controversies—from 726 to 787 and from 813 to 842—when extremists deliberately destroyed images throughout the Byzantine Empire. These differences led ultimately to a final break in 1054. The Christian church split into the Roman Catholic in the West and the Eastern (Greek) Orthodox in the East, a division that still persists.

Political and cultural differences widened the rift between Latin Christendom and Byzantium. In the Byzantine Empire, Greek was the language of religion and intellectual life; in the West, Latin predominated. Latin Christians refused to recognize that the Byzantine emperors were, as they claimed, successors to the Roman emperors. Byzantine emperors were absolute rulers who held that God had chosen them to rule and to institute divine will on earth. As successors to the Roman emperors, they claimed to rule all the lands that had once been part of the Roman Empire.

The greatest of the Byzantine emperors was Justinian, who reigned from 527 to 565. He chose as his wife the daughter of a circus performer who had led a life of prostitution in her youth. Until she died in about 548, the strong-willed and astute Empress Theodora was Justinian's closest adviser and often a figure of great authority and power. For example, during the famous Nika Riot in 532, when a mob devastated Constantinople and besieged the imperial palace itself, Theodora persuaded Justinian not to flee as he planned, but instead to resist.

Subsequently, Justinian sought to regain the lands in the western Mediterranean that had been conquered by Germanic invaders. During his reign, the Byzantine Empire reached its height and included Greece, Asia Minor, Italy, southern Spain, and parts of the Near East, North Africa, and the Balkans.

Over the centuries, the Byzantines faced attacks from the Germanic Lombards and Visigoths, Persians, Muslim Arabs, Seljuk Turks, and Latin Christians. During the Fourth Crusade (see p. 237), Latin Christians headed for Constantinople, instead of Palestine, to reinforce the Christians battling Muslims. In April 1204, the Crusaders plundered the city. The devastation was so complete that the city was never able to recover its former glory. Many of its treasures did, however, survive—shiploads of gold, silver, jewels, works of art, and relics were shipped to Venice, including the four great bronze horses above the main door of Saint Mark's Basilica.

The deathblow to the empire was dealt by the Ottoman Turks. Originally from central Asia, they had accepted Islam and had begun to build an empire. They drove the Byzantines from Asia Minor and conquered much of the Balkans. By the beginning of the fifteenth century, the Byzantine Empire consisted of only two small territories in Greece and the city of Constantinople. In 1453, the Ottoman Turks broke through Constantinople's great walls and looted the city. After more than ten centuries, the Byzantine Empire had come to an end.

BYZANTINE LEARNING

Byzantium was heir to the rich cultural tradition of the Greco-Roman world. During the Early Middle Ages, when higher learning had virtually ceased in the Latin West, in Constantinople and other cities of the Byzantine Empire, the works of ancient Greek thinkers were still studied and appreciated. To be sure, philosophy had lost its autonomy: It was no longer seen as an independent search for truth but as a preparation for theology—as a way of structuring, clarifying, and explaining Christian doctrines. Byzantine theologians took relevant ideas from Plato, Aristotle, the Stoics, and the Neo-Platonists in order to prove that God exists, that the world was his creation, and that Christ was divine. Although philosophy was subordinate to theology, ancient Greek philosophers continued to be read and, during periods of revival, earnestly studied. This legacy would be passed on to emerging Islamic civilization and eventually to western Europe.

The most lasting achievement of Byzantine civilization was in the field of law. Justinian appointed a commission of scholars to collect and codify Rome's ancient laws and the commentaries of learned jurists. The result was the monumental ***Corpus Juris Civilis,*** which became the official body of law of the Byzantine Empire. The Corpus is divided into four parts—*Code, Novels, Institutes,* and *Digest.* The Code contains decisions of emperors prior to Justinian; the Novels, which present the Emperor as the only foundation of law, comprise legislation promulgated by Justinian himself. The Institutes is a short textbook for novice law students. Covering a wide range of issues, the Digest details the decisions of Roman jurists on questions of law. After the Digest was finished, Justinian commanded that the originals be destroyed, thereby ensuring that only his version of the law would remain in use by succeeding generations. In the twelfth century, Roman law was gradually reintroduced into western Europe. Today the basis of law in many European lands can be traced back to this period.

In their writing of history, the Byzantines were influenced by the methodology and style of their Greek ancestors, Herodotus and Thucydides, who had recognized the value of history and initiated a rational approach to its study. Three prominent Byzantine historians were Procopius of Caesarea, Michael Psellus, and Anna Comnena.

The histories written by Procopius of Caesarea (c. 490–c. 562) are important sources of knowledge about the reign of Justinian. In 562, Procopius published *The Wars,* which describes the campaigns of the famous general Belisarius, to whom Procopius served as adviser in Persia, North Africa, and Italy. *The Buildings,* published in 561, details the accomplishments of Justinian in the construction of important public buildings, such as the Hagia Sophia (see p. 191). The *Secret History,* written about 550 but not published until after Procopius' death, is best known for its vociferous defamation of Justinian and Theodora.

How Theodora, most depraved of all courtesans, won his [Justinian's] love . . . and in what manner she was born and bred, and, wedded to this man, tore up the Roman Empire by the very roots, I shall now relate. . . . [A]s soon as she arrived at the age of youth, . . . she became a courtesan, and such as the ancient Greeks used to call a common one, at that: for she was not a flute or harp player, nor was she even trained to dance, but only gave her youth to anyone she met, in utter abandonment. . . . There was no shame in the girl, and no one ever saw her dismayed: no role was too scandalous for her to accept without a blush. . . . On the field of pleasure she was never defeated. . . . Often, even in the theater, in the sight of all the people, she removed her costume and stood nude in their midst, except for a girdle about the groin: not that she was abashed at revealing that, too, to the audience, but because there was a law against appearing altogether naked on the stage, without at least this much of a fig-leaf.[1]

After Procopius, there were few historians of any note until Michael Psellus (1018–c. 1078), who was also a philosopher, a statesman, and the finest classical scholar of his day. He was imperial secretary to Emperor Michael V (1041–1042) and secretary of state to his successor, Constantine IX (1042–1054). When Constantine revived the University of Constantinople in 1045, he appointed Psellus to head the philosophy faculty. During his tenure, Psellus reformed the curriculum to accentuate the classics of ancient Greece. He also reversed

the increasing dominance of Aristotelian philosophy and reestablished Neo-Platonism (which he believed was compatible with Christian revelation) as the leading philosophy in Byzantium. In the *Chronographia,* his best-known work, he wrote:

Philosophy, when I first studied it, was moribund . . . and I alone revived it, untutored by any masters worthy of mention. . . . There is a new philosophy, based on the mystery of our Christian religion, which transcends the ancient systems. . . . It was this philosophy rather than the profane which became the object of my special study.[2]

The *Chronographia* is a history of Byzantium from 976 to 1078, the year of Psellus' death. In the chapter on Constantine IX (1042–1055), he explains his motivation and his methodology in writing the history:

My history must be written in a methodical way: first the reference to my source, then the sifting of evidence, and finally the account of subsequent events. . . . I can assure you that my evidence will avoid all falsehood; whatever is not said, will remain hidden, but none of the things I am going to say will be of doubtful veracity.[3]

Anna Comnena (1083–c. 1148), the daughter of Emperor Alexius I Comnenus (1081–1118), wrote the *Alexiad,* a history of her father's life and reign. After she conspired unsuccessfully to depose her brother John, who had recently ascended to the throne, Anna's property was confiscated, she was banned from the imperial court, and she was compelled to enter a convent, where she wrote the *Alexiad.* In her *Preface* to the *Alexiad,* Anna acknowledged her indebtedness to classical learning:

I, Anna, the daughter of . . . Alexius and Irene . . . was not ignorant of letters, for I carried my study of Greek to the highest pitch, and was also not unpractised in rhetoric; I perused the works of Aristotle and the dialogues of Plato carefully, and enriched my mind by the "quaternion" of learning.[4]

Anna knew and admired the work of Michael Psellus; she did not, however, meet his strict standards of accuracy and objectivity. Nonetheless, the *Alexiad* is a valuable source for the history of her father's reign, including the First Crusade (see p. 237).

BYZANTINE MUSIC

Byzantium served as an intermediary between antiquity and the medieval West as a transmitter not only of Greco-Roman learning, literature, and art, but also of the ancient world's rich musical traditions. Byzantium not only appropriated for Christianity the antiphonal and cantillation style of chanting the Scriptures practiced by Jews in the temple and synagogues, but also the Greek system of modes, which later evolved into the Christian liturgical plainchants that characterized so much of medieval music (see Chapter 11). Byzantium also passed on their understanding of Greek musical theory, which provided the Latin church with the beginnings of its tonal system and method of musical notation. Latin Christian musicians eventually transformed the Greek tonal system into the eight church modes, which later, during the High Middle Ages, became the substructure for the major and minor scales used in modern music.

As the Byzantine church grew in importance and power under Justinian, hymn writing flourished. Initially, hymn writers followed models drawn from the churches of Jerusalem, Antioch, and Alexandria, but eventually a uniquely Byzantine style of hymnody emerged, called *Kontakia* ("hymn-sermons"). The *Kontakion* is best known through the work of Romanus (fl. first half of the sixth century), a clergyman who introduced the form into the Byzantine liturgy. In the age of Justinian, Romanus was viewed as "the truly Christian poet."

A Kontakion contains as few as eighteen and sometimes more than thirty stanzas, all of which are structured identically. A single stanza, called a Troparion, is between three and thirteen lines long. An independent Troparion opens a Kontakion and is linked to the refrain, another Troparion. A soloist sings each stanza, and the choir sings the refrain.

Romanus' *Hymn of Pentecost* relates the miracle of the Holy Spirit descending on the disciples and their "speaking in other tongues" (Acts 2). Romanus maintains that the words of Christ's disciples are superior to the writings of ancient Greek philosophers and poets:

> Why do the Greeks boast
> and puff themselves up?
> Why do they dream of Aratos
> the thrice cursed?
> Why do they err after Plato?
> Why do they love Demosthenes
> the feeble?
> Why do they not see that Homer
> is a vain dream?
> Why do they prate of Pythagoras
> who rightly has been silenced?
> And why do they not hasten
> and honour those to whom the All-holy Spirit
> appeared?

> Let us praise, brethren,
> the voices of the disciples,
> because they captured
> all men by divine power,
> and not by fine words.[5]

The following hymn, honoring the Virgin Mary, is an example of a Theotokion:

> Mystically we hymn thee,
>   Mary, Mother of God!
> For thou has been made the throne
>   of the Great King.
> Most holy tabernacle!
>   More spacious than the heavens!
> Chariot of the Cherubim,
>   and more exalted than the Seraphim!
> Bridal chamber of glory!
> For from thee came forth
>   Incarnate the God of all.
> Supplicate Him
>   for the salvation of our souls.[6]

Of particular importance in venerating Mary was the *Staurotheotokion*—a Troparion that commemorates Mary's vigil at the foot of the cross as her son was crucified. In this regard, it is very much like the *Stabat Mater* of the Western church (see Chapter 11).

> Standing by the cross
> of thy Son and the Son of God,
> and beholding
> His long-suffering,
> with tears,
> pure Mother,
> thou saidst, Woe is me!
> Why sufferest Thou thus unjustly,
> my dearest Son,
> Word of God, to save man?[7]

BYZANTINE ART AND ARCHITECTURE

In the visual arts, just as in music, Byzantium served as a transmitter of the artistic legacy of the ancient world to the medieval West. During the reign of Justinian, who was a zealous patron of the arts, Constantinople became the artistic capital of the empire. A concern of Byzantine art—one that showed continuity with the Roman past—was the glorification of the empire and its ruler. But, from the beginning, Byzantine art subordinated art to religion; it was primarily concerned with reinforcing the theology of the Orthodox Church and expressing the solemnity of its message. Eschewing innovation, artists chose subjects—themes taken from the Bible and the lives of the saints—and

Figure 8.1 *The Good Shepherd,* 425–450, mosaic, Mausoleum of Galla Placidia, Ravenna, Italy   Within a naturalistic setting, Christ, portrayed as a beardless young shepherd, is holding a large cross and is surrounded by the sheep entrusted to his care. *(Mausoleum of Galla Placidia, Ravenna/Scala/Art Resource, NY)*

portrayed expressions in ways that conveyed to the faithful the beliefs of the Orthodox Church.

The *iconoclastic controversy,* which centered on the depiction of Christ in human form, commenced in 726 with an imperial edict against making images and curtailed artistic production for more than a century. Although it was never totally enforced throughout the empire, the ban compelled many artists to eliminate the human form from their religious productions. However, because the ban did not apply to nonreligious art, it may have stimulated a renewed interest in the secular motifs of classical art. After the defeat of the iconoclasts in 843, even religious art adapted certain classical elements—the figures became more naturalistic and were positioned in a more realistic space. But it was in the West, not in Byzantium, where a trend toward realism and naturalism had the most profound and enduring effect. In contrast to Byzantium, the ancient prohibition against religious images did not hold sway over Latin Christendom, where church officials regarded visual representation of Christian figures as a useful vehicle for conveying church teachings to the illiterate masses. Over the centuries, the use of imagery proved a powerful impetus to a more naturalistic and realistic depiction of the world and the human form. This unique trend in the art of the West eventually resulted in the emancipation of art from religion and the emergence of modern art forms during the era of the Renaissance.

Ravenna, in northern Italy, which became the capital of the western part of the empire in 402,

was a crucial early site for Byzantine art. The most important surviving churches of Ravenna are associated with three significant people of the period, the empress, Galla Placidia (c. 390–450), who ruled the West from 425 to 450; the Ostrogothic (East Gothic) king, Theodoric (455–526), who ruled Italy from 493 to 526; and Maximian, who was bishop of Ravenna from 546 to 556.

From 425 to 433, a Mausoleum was built under the direction of Empress Galla Placidia; it was attached to the narthex of the Church of the Holy Cross, which no longer exists in its original form. Fashioned in the shape of a Latin cross and capped by a square tower, the Mausoleum of Galla Placidia is renowned for the mosaics above the marble-faced walls of its interior, which date from about 440. The barrel vaults are ornamented with decorative medallions on a deep blue background; the dome appears as a star-studded sky with a cross in the center. The symbols for the four evangelists are in the pendentives, which are a distinctively Byzantine contribution to the construction of domes. This architectural feature makes the transition from a square floor plan to a circular or polygonal dome. The term refers to spherical triangles formed by the intersection of the dome with its two pairs of opposite arches. The remaining wall surfaces of the mausoleum are covered with scenes depicting Christ, his apostles, and the saints. *The Good Shepherd* (Figure 8.1) appears in a naturalistic setting in the lunette, the area enframed by the arch above the entrance of the

Figure 8.2 *Saint Apollinare Nuovo* (interior), c. 500 and after, Ravenna, Italy   The twenty-six Theodoric mosaics, thirteen on each side, detail scenes of Christ's miracles and passion. The Gospel scenes of the middle tier alternate with sixteen tall standing figures above them. The Justinian mosaics on the north wall depict twenty-six female saints, as they join with the three magi to offer their gifts to the Virgin Mary and Jesus. The Justinian mosaics on the south wall portray twenty-six male saints being led into the presence of Christ. *(Scala/Art Resource, NY)*

mausoleum. Christ, portrayed as a beardless young shepherd holding a large cross, is surrounded by the sheep entrusted to his care. After Galla Placidia died, her body was embalmed, dressed in royal garments, and placed in a seated position within the tomb.

Soon after the death of Galla Placidia, a period of disorder ensued, which ended in 476 when the German mercenary Odoacer captured Ravenna. He ruled Italy until his death in 493, when he was succeeded by the Ostrogothic ruler Theodoric, an Arian Christian (see p. 168). Early in his reign, Theodoric built his own basilica-style palace church, which was consecrated to Arian Christianity. However, when the relics of Saint Apollinaris (who, according to tradition, was made bishop of Ravenna by Saint Peter himself) were brought there from Classe (the port of Ravenna) in the ninth century, the church was reconsecrated to Roman Catholicism. Henceforward, it has been known as Saint Apollinare Nuovo ("the new"). Saint Apollinare Nuovo has a nave and two side aisles, which are divided by twenty-four columns of Greek marble, twelve on each side. The mosaics that decorate the interior (Figure 8.2) come from two separate periods—the uppermost scenes were completed during Theodoric's reign, whereas the section below the windows was fashioned during the reign of Justinian.

The twenty-six Theodoric mosaics, thirteen on each side, detail scenes of Christ's miracles and passion, but do not include his crucifixion. The sixteen tall standing figures on each side of the middle tier, which alternate with the Gospel scenes above them, were originally thought to be Old Testament prophets and the apostles of the New Testament; today, however, scholars are uncertain as to their meaning. The Justinian mosaics on the lowest tier of the north and south walls are procession mosaics. Scholars acknowledge that the Justinian mosaics have been altered to fit various religious intentions, but the focus of the processions—Christ and the Virgin and her Son—were retained from the earlier scheme.

The palm tree–studded scene on the north wall depicts twenty-six beautifully dressed female saints, carrying their martyrs' crowns, as they depart from Classe. They join with the three magi, and all of them offer their gifts to the Virgin and her Son. The scene on the south wall shows twenty-six male saints, carrying their martyrs' crowns and dressed in simple garments like those of the apostles, being led into the presence of Christ.

Theodoric died in 526, and Ravenna was "liberated" from the Arian Goths by Justinian's orthodox army in 540. In 546, Bishop Maximian came to Ravenna to ensure that the two churches—San Vitale and Saint Apollinare in Classe—begun by the Gothic banker Julianus would be consecrated as orthodox churches.

San Vitale, located a short distance from the mausoleum of Galla Placidia, was begun around 530 and consecrated by Bishop Maximian in 547. In contrast to the customary basilican plan of Western Christianity, San Vitale has a centralized plan (see Chapter 6), which was typical of the Eastern Orthodox Church. Therefore, unlike any other church in Ravenna, it has a floor plan (Figure 8.3) in the shape of an octagon, which is capped by a dome. Eight marble piers sustain eight arches, which lead from the ambulatory (the walkway around the nave) into the interior space of the lower level and the gallery above the ambulatory, which was set aside for women.

Utilizing a magnificent range of color, the mosaics that line the walls of the interior illustrate both biblical and historical themes. The Byzantine-styled panels in the apse (Figure 8.4) are a symbolic representation of Christ in his Second Coming. Flanked by two angels, he holds the scroll of the seven seals (Revelation 5:1). On his

Figure 8.4   *San Vitale*, mosaic, Ravenna, Italy The entire mosaic symbolizes the Second Coming of Christ. Christ, flanked by two angels, holds the scroll of the seven seals described in the Book of Revelation. To his left is Saint Vitalis, to whom Christ hands a martyr's crown, and on his far right is Bishop Ecclesius, who offers Christ a model of San Vitale. *(Scala/Art Resource, NY)*

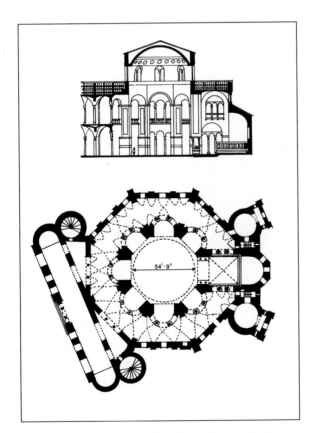

Figure 8.3   *San Vitale* (floor plan), c. 500 and after, Ravenna, Italy The centralized plan is in the shape of an octagon, capped by a dome. Eight marble piers sustain eight arches leading from the ambulatory. *(Witt et al.,* The Humanities: Cultural Roots and Continuities, *Sixth Edition, Houghton Mifflin Company, 2001)*

far left is Saint Vitalis,* to whom Christ hands a jeweled martyr's crown, and on his far right is Bishop Ecclesius (who began the construction of San Vitale), who offers a model of the church to Christ. On the side walls of the apse at the level of the windows are the more naturalistic processional mosaics of Justinian and Theodora, figures fashioned in the traditional style of Ravenna. To the left of the altar (Figure 8.5), Justinian is accompanied by courtiers, soldiers, and priests,

---

* Some time in the second century, the Roman judge Paulinus ordered Saint Vitalis to be tortured and then buried alive for having encouraged Saint Ursicinus not to disavow his faith at the prospect of death. The church of Saint Vitale is reputedly built on the site of his martyrdom.

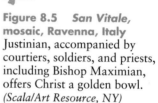

Figure 8.5 *San Vitale, mosaic, Ravenna, Italy* Justinian, accompanied by courtiers, soldiers, and priests, including Bishop Maximian, offers Christ a golden bowl. *(Scala/Art Resource, NY)*

Figure 8.6 *San Vitale, mosaic, Ravenna, Italy* Theodora, with her attendants, offers Christ a golden chalice full of wine. *(Scala/Art Resource, NY)*

including Bishop Maximian; to the right (Figure 8.6) is the empress Theodora with her attendants. Both figures are robed in the imperial purple and gaze serenely ahead as they make their offerings to Christ—Justinian a golden bowl and Theodora a golden chalice.

Saint Apollinare in Classe (Figure 8.7), just south of Ravenna, was begun in 532 and consecrated in 549 by Maximian. Like Saint Apollinare Nuovo, the interior is split into a nave and two aisles, which are divided by twenty-four columns of Greek marble. It has a timbered ceiling and a stone floor. The focal point, however, is the apse, which is filled with figures from the account of The Transfiguration of Christ when he took Peter, James, and John to a high mountain—

> and he was transfigured before them, and his garments became glistening, intensely white. . . . And there appeared to them Elijah with Moses; and they were talking to Jesus. . . . And a cloud overshadowed them, and a voice came out of the cloud, "This is my beloved Son; listen to him." (Mark 9: 2–10)

This is symbolically portrayed in the half dome where the hand of God emerges from stylized clouds between the figures of Moses and Elijah and above a jeweled cross. Peter is represented by the single lamb and James and John by the two lambs on the right. The twelve sheep above the half dome represent the twelve apostles. The face of *Christ Pantocrator* (i.e., Christ the All-Sovereign) appears at the top of the entire scene between the four beasts, which symbolize the four evangelists. This image of Christ Pantocrator was traditionally used to fill the dome of Byzantine churches. In one hand the stern-faced Christ holds the Law and gestures as if pronouncing a commandment with the other. Because Christians believed that God the Father was invisible, they were able to render his awesome power and majesty through a depiction of his incarnate son. This representation was designed to unite the everlasting nature of the All-Sovereign with the historical nature of the human Jesus. Theologian Jaroslav Pelikan acknowledges that the icon of

Christ Pantocrator "succeeded in conceptualizing the one who was the embodiment not only of the True in his teaching and the Good in his life, but of the Beautiful in his form as 'the fairest of the sons of men'" (Psalm 45:2).[8] The twelve sheep on either side of Saint Apollinaris, at the bottom of the half dome, represent the Christians entrusted to his care.

The most awesome architectural achievement of Justinian's reign was the construction of the new *Hagia Sophia* ("Holy Wisdom"; see Figure 8.8). During the Nika Riot of 532, half of Constantinople was devastated; several churches were burned to the ground, including the basilica of Hagia Sophia, constructed in 360. Justinian, intending that the new Hagia Sophia would be unlike any other church in the empire, employed two mathematicians who had studied ancient treatises on vaulting and curved surfaces. Procopius, in *The Buildings,* refers to Anthemius of Tralles as "the

Figure 8.7 *Saint Apollinare in Classe* (interior), Italy   In the half dome of the apse, the hand of God emerges from the clouds between Moses and Elijah. Peter is represented by the single lamb and James and John by the two lambs on the right. The twelve sheep above the half dome represent the twelve apostles. The face of Christ Pantocrator appears at the top of the entire scene between the four beasts, symbolizing the four evangelists. *(Scala/Art Resource, NY)*

most learned man in the skilled craft which is known as the art of building," and to his partner, Isidorus of Miletus, as "another master-builder . . . a man who was intelligent and worthy to assist the Emperor Justinian." The resulting structure, Procopius rejoices,

> proudly reveals its mass and the harmony of its proportions, having neither any excess nor deficiency, since it is both more pretentious than the buildings to which we are accustomed, and considerably more noble than those which are merely huge, and it abounds exceedingly in sunlight and in the reflection of the sun's rays from the marble. Indeed one might say that its interior is not illuminated from without by the sun, but that the radiance comes into being within it, such an abundance of light bathes this shrine.[9]

The design of Hagia Sophia is unique, blending the longitudinal axis of a basilica with features of a centralized plan. The nave of the church (Figure 8.9) was constructed using four great piers upon which were built four great arches forming a basically square unit. The triangular stonework

between the arches, the pendentives, were topped with a circular structure with windows on which the dome was placed. The windows in the base of the dome and those that pierce the walls at each level flood the interior with an ethereal light. Half domes were placed at each end of the nave, which gives the interior an elliptical shape. The effectiveness of the interrelated elements is summarized by Procopius:

> All these details, fitted together with incredible skill in mid-air and floating off from each other and resting only on the parts next to them, produce a single and most extraordinary harmony in the work, and yet do not permit the spectator to linger much over the study of any one of them, but each detail attracts the eye and draws it on irresistibly to itself.[10]

Soon after the church was completed in 537, the original dome began to push its pendentives out of line, and it finally collapsed in 558 as the result of an earthquake. The present dome, designed by Isidorus of Miletus, was consecrated in 562; it is 112 feet in diameter and, at 184 feet, is 23 feet higher than the original dome.

Figure 8.8 *Hagia Sophia* (exterior), c. 532–537, Istanbul, Turkey Justinian intended for the Hagia Sophia to be unlike any other church in the empire, and he engaged two mathematicians, who had studied ancient treatises on vaulting and curved surfaces, to work on a design for it. Upon completion, it was regarded as the most awesome architectural achievement of Justinian's reign. *(David Lomax/Robert Harding Picture Library)*

Figure 8.9 *Hagia Sophia* **(interior), c. 532–537, Istanbul, Turkey** The design blends the longitudinal axis of a basilica with features of a centralized plan. The nave was constructed using four great piers on which were built four great arches forming a basically square unit. Half domes were placed at each end of the nave to give the interior an elliptical shape. At each level, the windows flood the interior with an ethereal light. *(Werner Forman/Art Resource, NY)*

Justinian's Hagia Sophia was a landmark of Byzantine imperial glory. The Ottoman Turks, however, transformed Hagia Sophia into a mosque after their conquest of Constantinople in 1453. They added the four minarets and built massive buttresses to support the thrust of the vaults and the dome. In 1934, Hagia Sophia was turned into a museum by Kemal Atatürk (1881–1938), the first president of the republic of Turkey.

Islamic artisans produced works of art, especially mosaics, for Islamic structures that showed a Byzantine influence. Byzantine art forms were also acquired by some Slavic peoples, particularly the Russians. As in Byzantium, the art of medieval Russia was almost exclusively religious. Byzantine Greeks built the cathedral Saint Sophia at Kiev, the most prominent monument in the medieval Russian state, and the mosaics and frescoes that adorn the cathedral's interior were crafted by Greek painters.

THE ORIGINS AND EXPANSION OF ISLAM

The second Eastern civilization to arise after Rome's fall was based on the vital new religion of *Islam,* which emerged in the seventh century among the Arabs of Arabia. Its founder was Muhammad (c. 570–632), a prosperous merchant in Mecca, a trading city near the Red Sea. As an adult, Muhammad often meditated in a cave near Mecca, and when he was about forty, he believed that he was visited in his sleep by the angel Gabriel, who ordered him to "recite in the name of the Lord!" Transformed by this experience, Muhammad came to believe that he had been chosen to serve as a prophet, that he had been sent to reveal the identity of the one true God— "Allah [God], the Compassionate, the Merciful." Initially, Muhammad was distraught by the message he received, because it appeared to promise the immi-

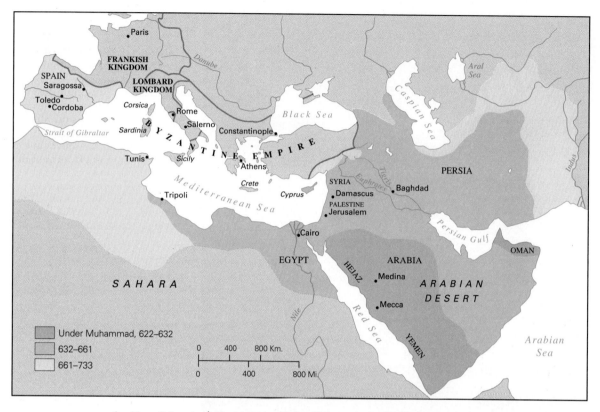

Map 8.1   Arab Conquests to 733   This map vividly illustrates the spectacular gains by the Arabs in the time of Muhammad under the first caliphs and under the Umayyads. Later, slow, steady gains in Africa, central Asia, and India expanded the empire even farther.

nent judgment of God: "This is indeed an admonition. Let him that will, take the right path to his Lord. Yet you cannot will, except by the will of Allah. Allah is wise and all-knowing. He is merciful to whom He will; but for the wrongdoers He has prepared a grievous punishment" (Sura 76:29–31).[11]

In Muhammad's time, most desert Arabs worshiped tribal gods, but in the towns and trading centers, many Arabs were familiar with Judaism and Christianity, and some had even accepted the idea of one God. Rejecting the many deities of the tribal religions, Muhammad offered the Arabs a new monotheistic faith, Islam, which means "surrender to Allah."

Muhammad's religion began to win followers, but the ruling elite of Mecca would not accept this new faith. To escape persecution, Muhammad and his small band of followers left Mecca in 622 for Medina, a town about two hundred miles away. Their flight, known as the *Hegira,* or "emigration," is one of the most important events in Muslim history and is commemorated by yearly pilgrimages. The date of the Hegira became year one of the Muslim calendar.

In Medina, Muhammad gained converts and won respect as a judge, rendering decisions on

such matters as family relations, property inheritance, and criminal behavior. Preaching a holy war against unbelievers, Muhammad urged followers to raid the trading caravans from Mecca and to subdue unfriendly Bedouin tribes (Arabs of the desert). He tried to convert the Jews of Medina, but they would not accept him as a prophet and mocked his unfamiliarity with the Hebrew Scriptures and the learned writings of the rabbis. To a large extent, political considerations determined Muhammad's policy toward Jews, who had conspired with his Meccan enemies against him. He expelled several thousand from Medina, seized Jewish property, beheaded some six hundred Jewish men, and enslaved women and children. Later, he permitted the Arabian Jews the free exercise of their religion and guaranteed the security of their property. In 630, Mecca surrendered to a Muslim army without a fight. Soon Bedouin tribes all over Arabia embraced Islam and recognized the authority of the Prophet Muhammad.

In a little more than two decades, Muhammad had united the often-feuding Arabian tribes into a powerful force dedicated to God and the spreading of the Islamic faith. After Muhammad's death in 632, his friend and father-in-law, Abu Bakr, became his successor, or caliph. Regarded as the defender of the faith, whose power derived from God, the caliph governed in accordance with Muslim law.

Islam gave the many Arab tribes the unity, discipline, and organization to succeed in their wars of conquest. Under the first four caliphs, who ruled from 632 to 661, the Arabs overran the Persian empire with breathtaking speed, seized some of Byzantium's provinces, and invaded Europe. Muslim warriors often engaged in *jihad*,* or "holy war," to spread Islam to nonbelievers. Moreover, they believed that those who died in the *jihad* were assured a place in paradise. A desire to escape from the barren Arabian Desert and to exploit the rich Byzantine and Persian lands was another compelling reason for expansion. In the east, Islam's territory eventually extended into India and to the borders of China; in the west, it encompassed North Africa and most of Spain. But the Muslims' northward push lost momentum and was halted in 717 by the Byzantines at Constantinople and in 732 by the Franks at the battle of Tours, in central France.

Under the Umayyad dynasty, the Islamic Arab empire expanded from Spain to India, and a distinctively Islamic culture emerged with Arabic as the official language. In 750, al-Abbas, a descendent of Muhammad, overthrew the Umayyads and moved the capital from Damascus, Syria, to Baghdad, Iraq. In the eighth and ninth centuries, under the Abbasid caliphs, Muslim civilization entered its golden age. Islamic civilization creatively integrated Arabic, Byzantine, Persian, and Indian cultural traditions.

THE DECLINE OF THE ARAB EMPIRE

By the eleventh century the Arabs began to lose their dominance in the Islamic world. The Seljuk Turks, who had taken Asia Minor from the Byzantines, also conquered the Arabic lands of Syria, Palestine, and much of Persia. Although the Abbasid caliphs remained the religious and cultural leaders of Islam, political power was exercised by Seljuk sultans. In the eleventh and twelfth centuries, the Muslims lost Sicily and most of Spain to Christian knights, and European Crusaders carved out kingdoms in the Near East.

In the thirteenth century came a new wave of invaders—the Mongols from central Asia. Led by

---

* The meaning of *jihad* is "to strive for moral and religious perfection." Because Muslims view their religion as universal, *jihad* is employed to spread Islam or to defend it against its enemies. For this reason, *jihad* is often translated "holy war."

Chingis Khan, Mongolian archers, mounted on fast-moving ponies, poured across Asia into Muslim lands. By 1227, when Chingis Khan died, the eastern part of the Muslim world had fallen to the Mongols. Their brutal advance westward was finally stopped in 1260 in Palestine by Egyptian forces.

In the late fourteenth century, however, the Mongols, who had by this time converted to Islam, again menaced the Near East. Tamerlane, another bloody conqueror, cowed opposition with huge pyramids built from the skulls of thousands of slaughtered victims. After Tamerlane's death in 1404, his empire disintegrated, and its collapse left the way open for the Ottoman Turks, still another people from central Asia who had adopted Islam. Under Mehmed II, the Ottoman Turks were able to consolidate their territories, and in 1453, they captured Constantinople, renamed the city Istanbul, and made it their capital.

The Ottoman Empire reached its height in the sixteenth century with the conquest of Egypt, North Africa, Syria, and the Arabian coast. The Turkish conquest of much of Hungary in the 1520s and the siege of Vienna (1529) spread panic in Europe. The Ottomans developed an effective system of administration, but could not restore the cultural brilliance, the thriving trade, or the prosperity that the Muslim world had known under the Abbasid caliphs of Baghdad.

ISLAMIC THEOLOGY

The **Quran** (or Koran), which in Arabic means "recitation," contains standards of morality and is the source of the rules that govern Islamic daily life. The Quran is the book that Muslims believe contains the words of God as revealed to Muhammad; it is also the first example of Arabic prose. Muslims see their religion as the completion and perfection of Judaism and Christianity. They regard the ancient Hebrew prophets as sent from God and value their messages about compassion and the oneness of humanity. Muslims also regard Jesus as a great prophet but do not consider him divine. Not only do Muslims see Muhammad as the last and greatest of the prophets, but they also believe that his revelations were the final stage of God's plan for humanity. They do not, however, believe that Muhammad was divine; he was entirely human. Muslims worship only Allah, the creator and ruler of heaven and earth, a single, all-powerful God who is merciful, compassionate, and just. According to the Quran, unbelievers and the wicked shall be punished on the Day of

Judgment: "On that day the heaven will shake and reel, and the mountains crumble away and cease to be. On that day woeful shall be the plight of the unbelievers . . . On that day they shall be sternly shoved into the fire of Hell . . . Burn in its flames" (Sura 52: 1–6).[12] Faithful Muslims who have lived virtuously are promised paradise, which they believe to be a garden where they will experience bodily pleasures and spiritual delights.

> But in fair gardens the righteous shall dwell in bliss, rejoicing in what their Lord will give them. He will say: "Eat and drink in joy. This is the reward of your labours." They shall recline on couches ranged in rows. To dark-eyed houris [beautiful virgins] We shall wed them. . . . Fruits We shall give them, and such meats as they desire. They will pass. . . a cup inspiring no idle talk, no sinful urge; and there shall wait on them young boys of their own as fair as virgin pearls.[13]
> (Sura 52:17–26)

An essential feature of Islam is the obligation of the faithful to obey the *Five Pillars* of the faith. The first pillar is called "The Witness"—a Muslim must accept and repeat the statement of faith: "There is no God but Allah, and Muhammad is his Prophet." The four other pillars—Prayer, Alms, Fasting, and Pilgrimage—are acts of worship. The five daily prayers—at dawn, at midday, in the afternoon, at dusk, and at night—are considered to be the duty of all faithful Muslims. Prior to their prayers, Muslims perform ritualistic acts, such as washing, before they turn to face the holy city of Mecca and pray. Because part of Muhammad's mission was to correct injustices committed against the poor, widows, and orphans, Muslims of means give thanks to God for their material well-being by being generous to the poor. Fasting, inspired by Muhammad's fasts when he was being instructed by God, is another way of offering thanks. Although physically exacting, it is seen as spiritually gratifying. Fasting is especially significant during the holy month of Ramadan, when believers abstain from food, drink, and sexual relations from just before sunrise until just after sunset. Finally, Muslims who are both physically and economically able are expected to make at least one pilgrimage to the holy city of Mecca, where as one of his last acts, Muhammad made a pilgrimage to reassert the meaning for the shrine of the Kaaba.* Pilgrimages to the Kaaba in Mecca begin in the tenth month of the Islamic year (the one following Ramadan) and last until the twelfth month.

After the death of Muhammad, Muslims sought authoritative guidance on religious, social, and moral questions that the Quran did not specifically address. The most important source for such guidance was *Hadith*—a collection of sayings, stories, and actions of the Prophet on a wide range of topics. The early Hadith were transmitted by his trusted companions and constitute the literary record of his sunna, or customary practice. Aisha, Muhammad's youngest wife, was the source of several thousand Hadith, but within two centuries about 600,000 Hadith existed. The Quran coupled with the Hadith provided directions for a complete way of life for Muslims.

INNER DIVISIONS: SUNNITES, SHI'ITES, AND SUFIS

Muslims perceived themselves as members of a single community of the faithful, but the emergence of sects ruptured the unity of Islam. The principal division—one that still incites bitter animosity—was between the Sunnites and the Shi'ites. The *Sunnites,* who were in the majority, followed traditional teachings and established practices as defined by the consensus of the Muslim community. The *Shi'ites* maintained that not the existing caliphs, but the descendants of Muhammad, starting with Ali, were the rightful rulers of the Islamic community. The massacre in 680 of Ali's younger son, Husayn, along with some of his followers and relatives, produced a passionate devotion to the house of Ali, which is still expressed in processions, poetry, and self-mortification. To Shi'ites, the anniversary of Husayn's death is the most important Shi'ite religious holiday. Because martyrdom for the faith is central to Shi'a, it continues to have great appeal.

Shi'ites view Ali and his descendants as Imams, holy men, innocent of all sin, the most excellent of beings, selected by God to inherit Muhammad's spiritual and political powers; the Imams linked the new generation with Muhammad's original inspiration. Without the Imams' guidance, the true meaning of Islam cannot be grasped. The leading branch of Shi'a, known as the Twelvers, holds that counting from Ali there have been twelve Imams. The twelfth Imam is still alive but remains in hiding; one day he will

---

* According to the Muslims' sacred history, Arabs are the descendants of Ishmael, whose parents were Hagar and Abraham. When Hagar and Ishmael were banished (see Chapter 2), Abraham accompanied them to Mecca where he and Ishmael constructed the true House of God, called the *Kaaba,* on the site of Adam's temple. However, by Muhammad's time, the site had become a center of pagan idol worship, and he sought to reestablish worship in the manner of Abraham.

return as a messianic leader, the Mahdi, and, guided by God, will set the world right. This form of Shi'a has been the official religion of Iran since the sixteenth century.

While the Sunnites and Shi'ites debated orthodoxy and who were the true successors of Muhammad, a mystical movement called *Sufism* began within Islam. The name for the Sufis is believed to derive from the Arabic word *suf*—the undyed, woolen robe these mystics wore—as a sign of their asceticism. The Sufis were opposed to the rational speculation of Muslim philosophers, and preferred poverty to worldly wealth. Both the rational discourse about truth and the rituals and ceremonies associated with the accepted worship of God left them spiritually unfulfilled. Instead, they sought to achieve union with God through direct, fervid experience.

One of the most renowned figures of early Sufism was Al-Husayn ibn Mansur al-Hallaj. Al-Hallaj preached in Baghdad, admonishing people for their moral laxity and calling for political reform. His mystical doctrine aroused the suspicion of the religious leaders, who wanted to preserve the status quo of Muslim society and who questioned his orthodoxy. In 922, al-Hallaj was arrested, imprisoned, and finally executed in a vicious manner. Sacrificing his life for his beliefs, he was beaten, whipped, nailed to a scaffold, and decapitated, and his body was burned. Al-Hallaj's death was subsequently viewed by Sufis as a model of death through love.

In succeeding centuries, Sufism grew into a mass movement emphasizing love of God, his creation, and the prophet Muhammad. The disastrous invasion of the Mongols in the thirteenth century marked the high point of Sufism; with the destruction of their material world, many Muslims sought spiritual solace in Sufism.

MUSLIM SOCIETY

The Islamic state was a theocracy in which government and religion were inseparable; there could be no distinction between secular and spiritual authority. Muslims viewed God as the source of all law and political authority and the caliph as his earthly deputy. Divine law regulated all aspects of human relations. The ruler who did not enforce Quranic law failed in his duties. Thus, Islam was more than a religion; it was also a system of government, society, law, and thought that bound its adherents into an all-encompassing community. The idea of a society governed by the Quran and the Hadith has remained in the Muslim mind for centuries.

The Status of Women

With Muhammad's affirmation of the spiritual equality of women and their right to inheritance, the status of women in Arabia improved. This revelation from the Quran was revolutionary and diametrically opposed to the prevailing Arabic view of women as inferiors and as objects of inheritance.

> Men, have fear of your Lord, who created you from a single soul. From that soul He created its mate, and through them He bestrewed the earth with countless men and women. . . . Men as well as women shall be rewarded for their labours (Sura 4:1, 32).[14]

Nonetheless, women's inheritance rights were not equal to those of men, for the Quran also states, "A male shall inherit twice as much as a female" (Sura 4:11).[15] Furthermore, the issue of the status of women was also complicated by the Hadith, so that at Muhammad's death the place and rights of women within Muslim society were yet to be fully defined.

According to the Hadith, when Muhammad heard that the Persians had named a woman to rule them he said, "Those who entrust their affairs to a woman will never know prosperity." Muhammad's comment was recalled when a Muslim army led by Aisha, Muhammad's favorite wife, was defeated in 656, and it was interpreted to mean that those who permitted themselves to be led by a woman would face certain defeat. As the Hadith continued to develop, two competing motives were at work—the first to remain true to the Prophet and the other to recapture the patriarchy of the Arabic past.

In time, a patriarchy that emphasized female inferiority was reestablished. Even though they were permitted to own property, women were socially segregated from men and veiled in public, following the Quranic admonition that women protect their modesty and not arouse men's carnal desires. Islam also retained polygamy from its Arabic past and the right of men to have concubines. Husbands had the right to divorce at will, but women were not permitted to divorce. Women did not have the religious duty of attending prayer on Fridays as did the men, nor were they promised the same sensual pleasures as the men were in Paradise.

Relations with the "Peoples of the Book"

Christians and Jews who lived in Islamic lands had fewer rights than Muslims—they could not bear arms, were assessed a special tax, and at times were barred from testifying in court against a Muslim. Nevertheless, Muslims viewed both Jews and Christians as "people of the book." They were, therefore, protected communities, and despite instances of loss of property and/or life, both groups generally went about their business and practiced their religions free of persecution. Certainly Jews were physically safer in Muslim than Christian lands, and unlike medieval Christians, Muslims did not demonize Jews as a hateful and cursed people deserving of divine punishment.

ISLAMIC LEARNING

During the Early Middle Ages, when learning was at a low point in western Europe, the Muslims forged a high civilization. Muslim thinkers translated and preserved ancient philosophical, mathematical, and medical texts, including works of Hippocrates, Galen, and Aristotle. From India, the Muslims acquired the concept of the zero and "Arabic" numerals, passing these ideas on to the West, along with their understanding of place value in units of tens, hundreds, and thousands. Muslim mathematicians also did original work in algebra (*al-jabr*), geometry, and trigonometry. Muslim astronomers corrected the observations made by ancient astronomers, particularly Ptolemy.

Building on the medical knowledge of the Greeks, Muslim physicians became the best-trained and most skillful doctors of the time. Muslims were the first to license physicians and pharmacists. Surgeons performed amputations, removed cancerous tissue, devised new medicines, and used anesthetics in performing operations. The best Muslim hospitals had separate wards for fevers, surgical cases, eye diseases, and dysentery, and physicians excelled in clinical observation. Muslim doctors who recommended humane treatment for the mentally ill were well ahead of their time. The Persian al-Razi, or Rhazes, who headed the hospital in Baghdad in the ninth century, wrote a medical encyclopedia in which he discussed measles, kidney stones, poisons, skin diseases, and ways of maintaining one's health, including proper nutrition. The works of Rhazes, translated into Latin, were widely consulted in Latin Christendom.

In physics, the Muslim Arabs' most significant contribution was in the field of optics. Rejecting Euclid's and Ptolemy's explanation that the eye emits visual rays, they recognized that vision is a consequence of rays of light. Moreover, they studied the refraction and reflection of light and made

the first documented studies of the *camera obscura*. Using a lens in a box to project an image onto a wall or screen, artists were able to trace the projected object—thus reproducing it with "photographic" realism. This technique was appropriated by artists such as Leonardo da Vinci and Jan Vermeer (see Chapters 13 and 16) and the scientist Johannes Kepler (see Chapter 17).

Both Platonic and Aristotelian studies experienced a remarkable renaissance during the ninth century under the Abbasid caliphate, when Muslim philosophers began to translate the works of the Greek philosophers and to use Greek ideas to validate the truth of the Quran. Their quest was to live in a rational manner—in harmony with the principle of reason that ruled the universe. They concluded that God himself was the principle of reason. However, as a result of their philosophical speculations, they were separated from the mainstream of Muslim thinkers who believed that God had revealed all essential truth. Nonetheless, Muslim philosophers were able to disseminate Greek ideas among the more educated Muslims and make a contribution to the development of philosophy in the West.

Al-Farabi (c. 870–950), who believed that philosophy and Islamic theology were in agreement, felt justified in using philosophical argumentation to buttress the proof of God's existence. He connected the Neo-Platonic idea of the One (see p. 142) to Aristotle's concept of the First Cause and linked both notions with God. He concluded that God's essential attribute is his existence, which has neither beginning nor ending; that his being is necessary; and that the nonexistence of something eternal is impossible. Al-Farabi's argument for the existence of God is an ontological proof and is similar to Anselm's proof (see Chapter 10). An ontological proof is an a priori argument, which is based entirely on logic, not on empirical evidence; it attempts to show that God's actual existence can be logically deduced from the concept.

Ibn-Sina, known to the West as Avicenna (980–1037), was one of the most eminent Muslim thinkers; he was a poet, doctor, scientist, and philosopher who wrote on every field of knowledge, including medicine. In fact, his *al-Qanun* (Canon of Medicine) was the most famous treatment of medicine until the eighteenth century. In it, he demonstrated that diseases could be spread by water, concluded that tuberculosis was contagious, and discussed the nature of 760 different drugs. As a philosopher, Avicenna equated God with Aristotle's First Cause, but he did not follow Aristotle in employing arguments drawn from the physical world to prove God's existence. Instead, in the fashion of al-Farabi, Avicenna argued the necessity of God's existence—God is a *necessarily* existent being, not a *possibly* existent being, for the nonexistence of a *necessarily* existent being is impossible.

Another giant of Muslim learning was the Spanish scholar Ibn-Rushd, whom westerners call Averroës (1126–1198). Initially a Neo-Platonist like al-Farabi and Avicenna, he later sought to restore the true thought of Aristotle and wrote commentaries on most of Aristotle's works. When legalistic Muslim theologians attacked him for his use of philosophy, Averroës insisted that the Quran did not oppose the study of philosophy and held that the ancient Greeks—even though they were not Muslims—had discovered truth. Using Aristotelian methodology, he argued that only the philosopher could understand the inner meaning of the Quran. Although Averroës' thought had little influence with the Muslim faithful, he did revive the study of Aristotle in the Islamic West. His commentaries on Aristotle were studied in Western universities, where they sparked an important controversy (see Chapter 10).

Ibn Khaldûn (1332–1406) wrote on philosophy, theology, and mathematics, but it is as an historian and philosopher of history that he has achieved lasting fame. He descended from Spanish Arabs who, during the reconquest of Spain by the Christians, migrated to North Africa in 1248. Born and educated in Tunisia, he traveled widely in North Africa and the Near East—often because of political turmoil—eventually settling in Cairo, where he served the sultan of Egypt as chief justice.

While living in Algeria between 1375 and 1379, Ibn Khaldûn wrote *Muqaddimah* (Prolegomena)—one of the earliest secular philosophies of history—which was the introduction to his immense *Universal History*. His world history includes information about the ancient Egyptians, Greeks, Romans, Hebrews, Arabs, and Persians, as well as histories of contemporary rulers in Europe and within Islam. The final volume, his autobiography, set the standard for an analytical account of one's life. The immense work delineates the social, economic, environmental, psychological, and human factors that affect the growth and decay of civilizations. He advocates a just monarchy in which the ruler is both kind and beneficent, but neither too clever nor shrewd.

> The concomitants of good rulership are being kind to one's [subjects] and defending them. The true meaning of royal authority is realized when the ruler defends his subjects. To be kind and beneficent toward them is part of being mild to them and showing an interest in how they are living. These things are important for the ruler in gaining the love of his subjects. . . . The Lawgiver, [Muhammad] . . . made it a condition . . . that the ruler should not be too shrewd and clever. . . For such [qualities] are accompanied by tyrannical and bad rulership and by a tendency to make the people do things that it is not in their nature to do. . . . The conclusion is that it is a drawback in a political leader to be [too] clever and shrewd. Cleverness and shrewdness imply that a person thinks too much, just as stupidity implies that he is too rigid.[16]

In addition, he attributes the ruin of civil society and the destruction of dynasties, such as the Persian empire (see Chapter 1), to injustice:

> Whoever takes someone's property, or uses him for forced labor, or presses an unjustified claim against him, or imposes upon him a duty not required by the religious law, does an injustice to that particular person. People who collect unjustified taxes commit an injustice. Those who infringe upon property (rights) commit an injustice. Those who take away property commit an injustice. Those who deny people their rights commit an injustice. Those who, in general, take property by force, commit an injustice. It is the dynasty that suffers from all these acts, in as much as civilization, which is the substance of the dynasty, is ruined where people have lost all incentive.[17]

ISLAMIC LITERATURE

Prior to Islam, Arabic literature included epic, lyric, and proverbial poetry, all of which was graphically descriptive and metrically intricate. Epics treated such themes as nomadic life, tribal rivalries, familial honor, and justice. Lyric poems were generally odes that could be subtly understated or blatantly erotic in covering topics from the harshness of the desert to love of wine and women and praise for camels.

The Theme of Love

Islamic poets appropriated the Bedouin *qasida* (ode)—which often praised the poet or the tribe and mocked their adversaries, but which could also describe nature and address ethical themes—and transformed it into a song of love. The theme of love interested several Muslim writers, among them Ibn Hazm (994–1064), who is regarded as "the greatest scholar and the most original thinker in Spanish Islam." His most significant contribution to scholarship was a study of comparative religion. But he also composed love poetry and wrote a delightful analysis of romantic love.

Love has certain signs which the intelligent man quickly detects and the shrewd man readily recognizes. Of these the first is the brooding gaze: the eye is the wide gateway of the soul, the scrutinizer of its secrets, conveying its most private thoughts and giving expression to its deepest-hid feelings. You will see the lover gazing at the beloved unblinkingly; his eyes follow the loved one's every movement, withdrawing as he withdraws, inclining as he inclines, just as the chameleon's stare shifts with the shifting of the sun.

The lover will direct his conversation to the beloved even when he purports, however earnestly, to address another: the affection is apparent to anyone with eyes to see. When the loved one speaks, the lover listens with rapt attention to his every word, he marvels at everything the beloved says, however extraordinary and absurd his observations may be. . . .

I have tested all manner of pleasures, and known every variety of joy; and I have found that neither intimacy with princes, nor wealth acquired, nor finding after lacking, nor returning after long absence, nor security after fear, and repose in a safe refuge—none of these things so powerfully affects the soul as union with the beloved, especially if it comes after long denial and continual banishment. For then the flame of passion waxes exceeding hot, and the furnace of yearning blazes up, and the fire of eager hope rages ever more fiercely.[18]

The *Rubaiyat* of Omar Khayyam

As local rulers began to break away from the Abbasid caliphate in the tenth century, Islamic literature became increasingly influenced by Persia, with an emphasis placed on elegance, gentility, lavishness, effusiveness, and grace. Nowhere is this more evident than in the *Rubaiyat* of the Persian poet Omar Khayyam (1044–1123). *Rubaiyat* literally means "quatrains," referring to a poem of four lines that usually rhymes. Khayyam was an accomplished astronomer, doctor, philosopher, and poet, and was renowned during his lifetime for his work as a mathematician. He not only advanced a geometrical approach to solving algebraic equations, developed a binomial theorem, and furthered Euclid's work on ratios, but he also devised a more accurate solar calendar, which established the length of a year at 365.24219858156 days. This figure is astonishingly close to the modern figure of 365.242190 days in a year. Khayyam's calendar was accurate

to within one day every 3,770 years. In the West, he became best known as a poet through the nineteenth-century classic Victorian translation by Edward FitzGerald of what came to be called the "Rubaiyat of Omar Khayyam." The *Rubaiyat* is still one of the most popular poems in the English language, especially the frequently quoted eleventh quatrain:

Here with a Loaf of Bread beneath the Bough,
A Flask of Wine, a Book of Verse—and Thou
Beside me singing in the Wilderness—
And Wilderness is Paradise enow [enough].[19]

In the other seventy-four quatrains of this work, such as those that follow, Khayyam reveals a philosophical attitude toward life, which is characterized by skepticism without despair and disillusionment without despondency.

Ah, my Beloved, fill the Cup that clears
TO-DAY of past Regrets and future Fears—
To-morrow?—Why, To-morrow I may be
Myself with Yesterday's Sev'n Thousand Years.
[Quatrain 20]

Ah, make the most of what we yet may spend,
Before we too into the Dust descend;
Dust into Dust, and under Dust, to lie,
Sans [without] Wine, sans Song, sans Singer,
    and—sans End!
[Quatrain 23]

Oh, come with old Khayyam, and leave the Wise
To talk; one thing is certain, that Life flies;
One thing is certain, the Rest is Lies;
The Flower that once has blown for ever dies.
[Quatrain 26][20]

Jalal al-Din Rumi

One of the most important writers of Sufism, Jalal al-Din Rumi (1207–1273), was born in Balkh (present-day Afghanistan). For political reasons, Rumi's family was forced to leave Balkh and eventually settled at Konya in Asia Minor, where his father, Baha al-Din, was a Sufi professor. Upon the death of his father, Rumi succeeded him in his post and subsequently became famous for his mystical insights, religious acumen, and the founding of the Mevlevi order of dervishes. His two most famous literary works are *Mathnawi,* a lengthy poem that deals with ethical, metaphysical, and religious concerns, and *Diwan,* a collection of lyric poetry. In the following poem from the *Diwan,* Rumi likens the ascent of the soul toward God to a lover contemplating his beloved:

This is Love: to Fly heavenward,
To rend, every instant, a hundred veils.

The first moment, to renounce life;
The last step, to fare without feet.
To regard this world as invisible,
Not to see what appears to one's self.
'O heart,' I said, 'may it bless thee
To have entered the circle of lovers,
To look beyond the range of the eye,
To penetrate the windings of the bosom!
Whence did this breath come to thee, O my soul,
Whence this throbbing, O my heart?
O bird, speak the language of birds:
I can understand thy hidden meaning.'
The soul answered: 'I was in the (divine) factory
While the house of water and clay was a-baking.
I was flying away from the (material) workshop
While the workshop was being created.
When I could resist no more, they dragged me
To mould me into shape like a ball.'[21]

The Thousand and One Arabian Nights

The collection of tales titled *The Thousand and One Arabian Nights* is one of the most famous works of popular fiction in world literature. Since the colorful court of the fifth Abbasid caliph, Harun ar-Rashid, who ruled from Baghdad between 786 and 809, is mentioned in several of the stories, scholars assume that it was the historical backdrop for many of the tales.

The enchanting stories of *The Thousand and One Arabian Nights* were composed between the eighth and sixteenth centuries, but drew on earlier oral traditions. The tales blended familiar anecdotes with Persian and Indian fairy tales, Arabic legends and romances, as well as Egyptian tales of love; the stories, replete with adventure, heroism, amorous encounters, magic, and the sights and flavor of the East, excite the imagination. The various authors were able to skirt the Islamic prohibition on fictional writing—which was seen as equivalent to lying—by making use of the literary device called *hyperbole*. Hyperbole is the literary technique of exaggeration resulting in caricatures of real people or parodies of actual events that, because they were not actually lying, enabled Arabic authors to sidestep the ban on fictional writing. To give the entire work definition, each individual tale exists within a larger framework story. The framework story takes place "in the islands of India and China," where Shahryar, in the prime of manhood and a better horseman than his younger brother, Shah Zaman, accedes to the empire of their father, while his younger brother becomes "King of Samarkand in Barbarian land."[22] On the night before he is to depart for his brother's court, Shah Zaman discovers his wife and a male cook "asleep on his carpet bed embrac-

ing."[23] With a single blow, he cuts the two into four pieces and departs for the court of King Shahryar. Once Shah Zaman arrives, King Shahryar finds him to be miserably ill and depressed about his wife's unfaithfulness.

While at his brother's court, Shah Zaman also witnesses his brother's wife committing adultery and other illicit acts with a slave named Saeed. "Now when Shah Zaman saw this conduct of his sister-in-law, he said to himself: 'By Allah, my calamity is lighter than this! My brother is a greater King among the Kings than I am, yet this infamy goeth on in his very palace, and his wife is in love with that filthiest of filthy slaves.' "[24] When Shah Zaman tells King Shahryar of his wife's betrayal, Shahyar confirms her illicit activities with his own eyes and vows revenge. He commands that his wife be put to death as well as all of her attendants and their companions. He then swears an oath—to marry a maiden every night, to violate her virginity, and to slay her the next morning. For the next three years, King Shahryar's Chief Wazir—better known as *vizier*, a term used for an Islamic minister of state—furnished him with a maiden each evening. Eventually, there were virtually no virgins left in the realm, except for the two daughters of his Chief Wazir, the elder of whom was Scheherazade—an intelligent and capable woman.

> [She] had perused the books, annals, and legends of preceding kings, and the stories, examples, and instances of bygone men and things. Indeed it was said that she had collected a thousand books of histories relating to antique races and departed rulers. She had perused the works of the poets and knew them by heart; she had studied philosophy and the sciences, arts, and accomplishments. And she was pleasant and polite, wise and witty, well read and well bred.[25]

Trusting in her own intelligence and wit, Scheherazade asks her father to give her in marriage to King Shahryar, because she believes she can offer herself as a ransom for other women like herself, successfully deceive the king, and gain her deliverance. Her father objects, but Scheherazade remains intransigent and prepares for her night with the Shahryar by concocting a plan with her sister, Dunyazade.

> When I have gone into the King I will send for thee, and when thou comest to me and seest that he hath had his carnal will of me, do thou say to me: "O my sister, an thou be not sleepy, relate to me some new story, delectable and delightsome, the better to speed our waking hours." And I will tell thee a tale which shall be our deliverance, if so

Allah please, and which shall turn the King from his bloodthirsty custom.[26]

Once Scheherazade is ravished by Shahryar, she follows through with their plan, signaling for Dunyazade, who then begs Shahryar to allow Scheherazade to tell her a story. The trick is never to finish the tale, thereby prolonging her life. King Shahryar grants his permission and "was pleased with the prospect of hearing her story. So Scheherazade rejoiced, and thus, on the first night of the Thousand Nights and a Night, she began her recitations."[27]

For three years, approximately a thousand and one nights, Scheherazade begins stories for King Shahryar that she never finishes. Finally, on behalf of the three sons they have had together, Scheherazade asks Shahryar to release her from "the doom of death," which he does by saying:

> I pardoned thee before the coming of these children, for that I found thee chaste, pure, ingenuous, and pious! Allah bless thee and thy father and thy mother and thy root and thy branch! I take the Almighty to witness against me that I exempt thee from aught that can harm thee.[28]

Scheherazade and Shahryar then marry, as do Dunyazade and Shah Zaman, and the families of the two sisters and two brothers live together in great splendor. King Shahryar summons his "chroniclers and copyists" and tells them to write down all of the stories his wife had told him: "So they wrote this and named it The Stories of the Thousand Nights and a Night. The book came to thirty volumes, and these the King laid up in his treasury."[29] After the death of the two kings the realm was ruined until—

> a wise ruler . . . found in the treasury these marvelous stories and wondrous histories . . . [and he] read therein of description and discourse and rare traits and anecdotes and moral instances and reminiscences, and bade the folk copy them and dispread them over all lands and climes, wherefore their report was bruited [well known] abroad and the people named them The Marvels and Wonders of the Thousand Nights and a Night.[30]

In the nineteenth century, Sir Richard Burton (1821–1890), the man who discovered Lake Tanganyika in southeast Africa, was the first European granted a license to penetrate the mysterious regions of Mecca and Medina. His translation of *The Thousand and One Arabian Nights* into English has become the standard version of the work in the West, in spite of its somewhat arcane and flowery language. Since that time, stories and movies derived from the tales—"The Seven Voyages of Sinbad the Sailor," "Aladdin: Or, His Wonderful Lamp," "Ali Baba and the Forty Thieves" (including its famous injunction: "Open, Sesame")—have become standard fare for westerners, who continue to be fascinated by these Islamic tales.

ISLAMIC ART AND ARCHITECTURE

Like the art of Byzantium and Latin Christendom, Islamic visual art was essentially religious, designed to evoke contemplation of the divine. Also like Byzantium, Islamic art was confronted with the problem of representing living forms. In the second century of Islam, Muslim theologians began to prohibit the portrayal of living creatures in the belief that artists who did so were engaged in idolatry, for they were presumptuously delegating to themselves God's power of creating life. Although at times the prohibition was circumvented, Muslim art became largely ornamental—stylized decorations, often intricate patterns of swirling plants and geometric shapes. These frequently exquisite patterns adorned tapestries, rugs, and the floors and walls of public buildings and mosques.

Because the Arabs had no architectural tradition on which to build, they drew on the expertise of the peoples, particularly Persians and Christian Byzantines, whom they had conquered. The Umayyad dynasty ushered in a new era of architectural and cultural opulence, building elegant palaces, government residences, and mosques.

The first important Islamic shrine to be built was the celebrated Dome of the Rock (Figure 8.10), begun in 691 in Jerusalem by the caliph Abd al-Malik on the spot where faithful Muslims believe that Muhammad began his Night-Journey as he ascended to heaven. The story of Muhammad's ascension did not become popular until the sixteenth century, and there is no evidence to indicate that Muslims knew of the tale when the Dome of the Rock was constructed. "Glory be to Him [God] who made His servants go by night from the Sacred Temple [of Mecca] to the farther Temple [of Jerusalem] whose surroundings We have blessed, that We might show him some of Our signs" (Sura 17:1).[31] The structure, which was intended to rival the splendor of the Christian Church of the Holy Sepulcher, was built over the rock on which Jews believed Abraham was about to sacrifice Isaac when the angel of the Lord intervened (Genesis 22: 9–12; see Chapter 2). Thus, Jerusalem became a holy city for Muslims, as well as for Jews and Christians.

Figure 8.10 *Dome of the Rock* (exterior), c. 680s–692, Jerusalem   This structure was the first important Islamic shrine. It was constructed on the spot where faithful Muslims believe that Muhammad began his Night-Journey as he ascended to heaven. *(R. Harding/Robert Harding Picture Library)*

Both the octagonal shape of the centralized plan (similar to the plan of Saint Vitale in Ravenna) and the lavishly ornamented interior of the *Dome of the Rock* (Figure 8.11) demonstrate the influence of Byzantine architecture. The shrine is capped by a gilded dome, which shines in the sun like a crown above Jerusalem. The interior has a double ambulatory that permits the Muslim faithful to walk around "The Rock." The ambulatory is the passageway around the central space of the interior that corresponds to the side aisles of basilica-style church architecture. Delicately pointed arches are utilized in the ambulatories as well as in the exterior windows and the courtyard. Because the pointed arch could be adapted to almost any proportion, architects in the West began to employ it (instead of the round arch) in the late eleventh century. The windows are encased with a fine lattice of stone that was designed to diminish the harsh rays of the sun. The marble interior is decorated with glass mosaics using various plant motifs because the depiction of figures, either human or animal, was forbidden in Islam. The ban on figural representations stemmed from the same fear of idolatry shown by the ancient Hebrews. The ban drew support from Muhammad's reputed chastisement of his wife Aisha for making a pillow with a picture on it, saying that angels would not enter a house that had a picture in it and that on the Last Day, those who made pictures would be punished.

Islamic religious architecture made use of ***calligraphy*** to carry the sacred message of the Quran. For Muslims, calligraphy was the art of writing the divine book and was valued above all other art forms. Instead of imitating the naturalistic styles of Greco-Roman culture, Muslim calligraphers developed a mathematically based architectural ornamentation that was decidedly abstract in form. Beyond architecture, calligraphy was also utilized as decoration for ceramics, metalwork, and textiles, such as pillows and carpets.

The calligraphic inscriptions within the Dome of the Rock are particularly rich. Various inscriptions hail God as the Eternal One (Sura 112), praise Muhammad as the Prophet of God (Sura 33:34), make reference to Sura 17 (the one that contains the Night-Journey), and declare the absolute power of God (Suras 57 and 64). The longest inscription defines the position of Jesus and the prophets who preceded him, makes references to the "Peoples of the Book," and tells of the uniqueness and importance of Muhammad's mission (see preceding discussion).

Early Muslims used existing buildings—pagan temples, Christian churches, and private homes—for worship; beginning in the early eighth century, Muslim architects began to construct ***mosques.*** The basic plan—a square structure, broad arches, and a courtyard—was influenced by Muhammad's own house. Each mosque has a *Qibla* wall (the

Figure 8.11 *Dome of the Rock* (interior), c. 680s–692, **Jerusalem** The marble interior is decorated with glass mosaics using various plant motifs, because the depiction of figures, either human or animal, was forbidden in Islam. *(Georg Gerster /Photo Researchers)*

one that faces Mecca), the interior of which contains a carved niche known as the *mihrab*, which is the central focus of the mosque. The courtyard in front of the mosque has a fountain for purposes of ritualistic cleansing before prayer. Originally, a *muezzin* ascended to the rooftop of the mosque to call the faithful to prayer five times each day; later, towers called minarets were constructed outside the mosque for that purpose. The main mosque of each city is the "Friday" mosque, where the religious leader preaches a sermon on Friday from the *minbar*, which stands in front of the Qibla wall.

One of the earliest mosques still extant is the Great Mosque of Damascus, built between 706

and 715 under the Umayyad caliph, al-Walid. The site of the Great Mosque was originally the location of a Roman temple dedicated to Jupiter, which was later transformed into a Christian church. The Great Mosque set the architectural standard for subsequent mosques built during the Umayyad caliphate. In 750, the Abbasid family conquered the Umayyads and moved their capital from Damascus to Baghdad.

During the golden age of Islam under the Abbasid caliphate, many mosques were constructed, including the monumental mosque at Samarra, northwest of Baghdad on the Tigris River, which served as the Abbasid capital from 836 until 883. The *Great Mosque of Samarra* was built under the caliph al-Mutawakkil between 848 and 852 and was designed to accommodate most of the inhabitants of Samarra. Originally, the rectangle of the exterior that surrounded the mosque measured 784 by 512 feet; the mosque was constructed of fired brick walls, 464 mud-brick piers, and a wooden roof; the interior was decorated with mosaics. Virtually nothing remains of the mosque itself except its fabulous spiral-shaped minaret (Figure 8.12), which resembles a Mesopotamian ziggurat (see Chapter 1).

When the Abbasids attempted to massacre 800 family members of the Umayyad dynasty at a dinner of peace, a few of them escaped, fled to Spain, and established Córdoba as their capital. The *Great Mosque of Córdoba* (see chapter opening), begun in 786, contains all of the usual features of a mosque, but it is best known for its double set of horseshoe-shaped arches, one above the other, both of which are mounted on the capitals of the granite and marble columns, which were plundered from Roman and early Christian buildings. There are nineteen aisles with 850 columns supporting the double-tiered arches. These soaring arches originally supported a wooden roof, but during the sixteenth century, vaulting replaced it.

When the Great Mosque of Córdoba was built in the eighth century, all of Spain except for the northwest corner was under Muslim rule. Although there was resistance to the Muslims from the beginning, the active Christian reconquest of Spain began in the eleventh century. By 1212, only the southern third of Spain was under Muslim control. By 1300, only Granada, along the Mediterranean coast, remained in Muslim hands.

The *Alhambra,* a fortress overlooking the city of Granada, was begun in the thirteenth century, but it was Muhammad III (1302–1308) who made it into a palace–city that accommodated as many as 40,000 people. By the end of the fourteenth century, there were several royal palaces within the complex. The *Palace of the Lions* (Figure 8.13), the most fascinating of the structures that remain, receives its name from the fountain in the middle of its courtyard, which is supported by twelve white marble lions. The inscription on the courtyard wall refers to the water of the fountain in the center of the courtyard as being like the believer's

Figure 8.12 *Mosque of al-Mutawakkil, minaret, 848–853, Samarra, Iraq* During the golden age of Islam under the Abbasid caliphate, many mosques were constructed, including the monumental mosque at Samarra, which served as the Abbasid capital from 836 until 883. Today, however, only its fabulous spiral-shaped minaret remains intact. *(Copyright reserved to the Creswell Archive, Department of Eastern Art, Ashmolean Museum, Oxford)*

Figure 8.13 *Alhambra—The Palace of the Lions, 1354–1391, Granada, Spain* The name of the palace derives from the fountain, supported by twelve white marble lions, in the middle of its courtyard. The inscription on the courtyard wall refers to the water of the fountain as being like the believer's soul resting in the remembrance of God. *(George Holton/Photo Researchers)*

soul resting in the remembrance of God. The slender columns of the walls support arches of varying shapes that lead into rooms surrounding the courtyard. The decorative geometric patterns of tile and stucco create an ethereal effect that was intended to suggest the idea of paradise to the believer. The vaulted, painted, and carved interior evokes a sense of tranquillity and inward reflection. The Palace of the Lions was the personal residence of Muhammad V (1354–1391), who completed the Alhambra complex. The Alhambra was the last work of Muslim art in Spain, for the Christians conquered Granada in 1492, and between 1509 and 1614 they expelled the Muslims from Spain.

The Legacies of Byzantium and Islam

During its thousand years, Byzantium made a significant impact on world history. A considerable portion of Europe might have converted to the new faith of Islam, if the Arabs had been able to break through Byzantine defenses and advance into east-

ern Europe. Other far-reaching developments in the Byzantine East were the codification of the laws of ancient Rome under Justinian, the preservation of the philosophy, science, mathematics, and literature of ancient Greece, the execution of mosaics, which adorned churches, and the refinement of domes through the use of the pendentive.

Contacts with Byzantine civilization stimulated learning in both the Islamic world to the east and Latin Christendom to the west. Speros Vryonis, a student of Byzantine civilization, states: "The Byzantines carried the torch of civilization unextinguished at a time when the barbarous Germanic and Slav tribes had reduced much of Europe to near chaos; and they maintained this high degree of civilization until Western Europe gradually emerged and began to take form."[32] Byzantium exerted an important religious, cultural, and linguistic influence on Latin Romanians, eastern Slavs (Russians and Ukrainians), and southern Slavs (Serbs and Bulgars). From Byzantium, the Slavs acquired legal principles, art forms, and an alphabet (the Cyrillic, based on the Greek) for writing their languages. (On the other hand, the western Slavs—Poles, Czechs, and Slovaks—came under the influence of Latin Christianity and the culture of Catholic Europe.)

At a time when Latin Christendom had lost a great deal of the Greco-Roman thought and culture, Muslims scholars preserved much of it. By translating Greek works into Arabic and commenting on them, Muslim thinkers performed the great historical task of preserving the philosophical and scientific heritage of ancient Greece. Along with this heritage, the original contributions of Muslim scholars and scientists were also passed on to Christian Europe; as the historian, W. Montgomery Watt, concludes:

> When one becomes aware of the full extent of Arab experimenting, Arab thinking and Arab writing, one sees that without the Arabs European science and philosophy would not have developed when they did. The Arabs were no mere transmitters of Greek thought, but genuine bearers, who both kept alive the disciplines they had been taught and extended their range. When about 1100 Europeans became seriously interested in . . . science and philosophy, . . . [they] had to learn all they could from the Arabs before they themselves could make further advances.[33]

Key Terms

Corpus Juris Civilis	Quran
Kontakion	Five Pillars
iconoclastic controversy	Sunnites
Christ Pantocrator	Shi'ites
Islam	Sufism
Hegira	calligraphy
jihad	mosques

Notes

1. *Secret History of Procopius,* trans. Richard Atwater (New York: Covici Friede, 1927), pp. 98–103.
2. *Fourteen Byzantine Rulers: The Chronographia of Michael Psellus,* trans. E. R. A. Sewter (Baltimore: Penguin Books, 1966), pp. 173, 176.
3. Ibid., pp. 165–166, 179.
4. *The Alexiad of the Princess Anna Comnena Being the History of the Reign of Her Father, Alexuis I, Emperor of the Romans, 1081–1118* A.D., trans. Elizabeth A. S. Dawes (London: Kegan Paul, Trench, Trubner & Co. Ltd., 1928), p. 1.
5. Quoted in Egon Wellesz, *A History of Byzantine Music and Hymnography* (Oxford: Clarendon Press, 1961), p. 189.
6. Ibid., p. 243.
7. Ibid.
8. Jaroslav Pelikan, *Jesus Through the Centuries: His Place in the History of Culture* (New Haven and London: Yale University Press, 1985), p. 93.
9. Procopius, *Buildings,* trans. H. B. Dewing, in *Procopius in Seven Volumes.* The Loeb Classical Library (Cambridge: Harvard University Press, 1935), 7:17.
10. Ibid., 7:21.
11. *The Koran,* trans. N. J. Dawood, Penguin Classics (Harmondsworth, Middlesex, England and New York: Penguin Books, 1974), p. 19.
12. Ibid., p. 117.
13. Ibid.
14. Ibid., pp. 366, 370.
15. Ibid., p. 367.
16. Ibn Khaldûn, *The Muqaddamah: An Introduction to History,* trans. Franz Rosenthal. Bollingen Series 43 (New York: Pantheon Books, 1958), Vol. 1, pp, 383–385.
17. Ibid., Vol. 2, pp. 106–107.
18. Ibn Hazm, *The Dove's Necklace,* trans. A. J. Arberry, in *Anthology of Islamic Literature from the Rise of Islam to Modern Times,* ed. James Kritzeck (New York: Meridian, Penguin Books, 1975), pp. 129–130, 136.
19. Edward FitzGerald, *Rubaiyat of Omar Khayyam,* [Online] Available http://tehran.stanford.edu/ Literature/Poetry/Omar_Khayyam.html. (May 25, 1998), p. 2.
20. Ibid., pp. 3, 4, 7, 13.
21. R. A. Nicholson, trans. "Rumi: Love Poems," in *Anthology of Islamic Literature from the Rise of Islam to Modern Times,* ed. James Kritzeck (New York: Meridian, Penguin Books, 1975), p. 241.
22. Sir Richard Burton, *The Arabian Nights' Entertainments (Alf Laylah Wa Laylah) Story of King Shahryar and His Brother,* 1850, [Online] Available http://persia.org. (May 27, 1998), p. 2.
23. Ibid., p. 5.
24. Ibid., pp. 9–10.
25. Ibid., p. 20.
26. Ibid., p. 33.
27. Ibid., p. 34.
28. Ibid., pp. 35–36.
29. Ibid., p. 47.
30. Ibid., pp. 47–48.
31. *The Koran,* p. 233.
32. Speros Vryonis, Jr., *Byzantium and Europe* (New York: Harcourt, Brace & World, 1967), p. 193.
33. W. Montgomery Watt, *The Influence of Islam on Medieval Europe* (Edinburgh: University Press, 1972), p. 43.

generatio

The Early Medieval West: Fusion of Classical, Christian, and Germanic Traditions

T HE CENTURIES OF CULTURAL GREATNESS of both Islamic and Byzantine civilizations enriched the Western world. However, neither Islam nor Byzantium made the breakthroughs in science, technology, philosophy, economics, and political thought that gave rise to the modern West. That process was the singular achievement of Europe. During the Early Middle Ages (500–1050), Latin Christendom was culturally far behind the two Eastern civilizations, but by the twelfth century it had caught up. In succeeding centuries, it produced the movements that ushered in the modern age: the Renaissance, the Reformation, the Scientific Revolution, the Age of Enlightenment, the French Revolution, and the Industrial Revolution.

THE RISE OF LATIN CHRISTENDOM

From the sixth to the eighth century, Europeans struggled to overcome the disorders created by the breakup of the Roman Empire and the deterioration of Greco-Roman civilization. In the process, a new civilization, with its own distinctive style, took root. It grew out of the intermingling of Greco-Roman civilization, the Christian outlook, and Germanic traditions. But centuries would pass before it would come to fruition.

In the fifth century, Germanic invaders founded kingdoms in North Africa, Italy, Spain, Gaul, and Britain—lands formerly belonging to Rome. The Roman world was probably too far gone to be rescued, but even if it had not been, the Germanic tribes were culturally unprepared to play the role of rescuer. By the end of the seventh century, the old Roman lands in the west showed a marked decline in central government, town life, commerce, and learning. The distinguishing feature of classical civilization, its vital urban institutions, had deteriorated in the Late Roman Empire. Under the kingdoms created by Germanic chieftains, the shift from an urban to a rural economy accelerated. Although towns did not vanish altogether, they continued to lose control over the surrounding countryside and to decline in wealth and importance.

The Church: Shaper of Medieval Civilization

Christianity was the integrating principle, and the church was the dominant institution of the Middle Ages. During the Late Roman Empire, as the Roman state and its institutions decayed, the church gained power and importance. Its organization grew stronger, and its membership increased. Unlike the Roman

Book of Kells, c. 760–820, 13" x 9 1/2" (33 x 24.1 cm), Trinity College Library, Dublin.

The manuscript was illuminated between 760 and 820 in southeastern Ireland, at Iona. This page, one of the most famous, contains the first three Greek letters of Christ's name: Chi (X), Rho (P), and Iota (I).

(Trinity College Library, Dublin)

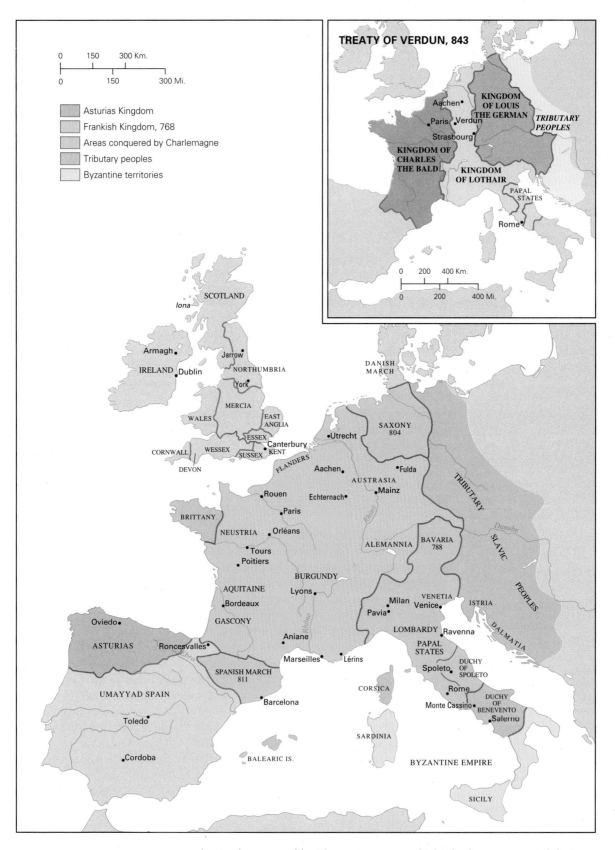

TREATY OF VERDUN, 843

KINGDOM OF LOUIS THE GERMAN

TRIBUTARY PEOPLES

Aachen

Paris • Verdun

Strasbourg

KINGDOM OF CHARLES THE BALD

KINGDOM OF LOTHAIR

PAPAL STATES

Rome

0   200   400 Km.

0   200   400 Mi.

Legend:
- Asturias Kingdom
- Frankish Kingdom, 768
- Areas conquered by Charlemagne
- Tributary peoples
- Byzantine territories

0   150   300 Km.

0   150   300 Mi.

SCOTLAND

Iona

Armagh

IRELAND   Dublin

Jarrow

NORTHUMBRIA

York

WALES   MERCIA

EAST ANGLIA

ESSEX

CORNWALL   WESSEX   Canterbury   KENT   SUSSEX

DEVON

DANISH MARCH

•Utrecht

SAXONY 804

FLANDERS

Aachen   •Fulda

AUSTRASIA

Rouen   Echternach•   •Mainz

Paris

BRITTANY

NEUSTRIA   •Orléans

Tours   Poitiers

ALEMANNIA   BAVARIA 788

BURGUNDY

AQUITAINE   Lyons

Bordeaux

GASCONY

Oviedo

ASTURIAS   Roncesvalles

Aniane

Marseilles   •Lérins

SPANISH MARCH 811

UMAYYAD SPAIN   Barcelona

Toledo

Cordoba

BALEARIC IS.

CORSICA

SARDINIA

TRIBUTARY

SLAVIC

PEOPLES

Milan   VENETIA

Pavia   Venice   ISTRIA

LOMBARDY   Ravenna   DALMATIA

PAPAL STATES

Spoleto   DUCHY OF SPOLETO

Rome

Monte Cassino   DUCHY OF BENEVENTO

Salerno

BYZANTINE EMPIRE

SICILY

Rhine

Danube

Rhône

Ebro

Map 9.1   The Carolingian World   The territory over which Charlemagne exerted direct or indirect control was vast. The lands beyond the Rhine and Danube, almost all of which were never part of the Roman Empire, became under the Carolingians a permanent part of Western civilization. The Treaty of Verdun (see insert), signed by Charlegmagne's grandsons in 843, was the first and most important of many divisions of the Carolingian Empire that eventually led to the emergence of France and Germany.

state, the church was a healthy and vital organism. The elite of the Roman Empire had severed its commitment to the values of classical civilization, whereas the church leaders were intensely devoted to their faith.

THE CHURCH AS UNIFIER When the Roman Empire collapsed, the church retained the Roman administrative system and preserved elements of Greco-Roman civilization. A unifying and civilizing agent, the church provided people with an intelligible and purposeful conception of life and death. In a dying world, the church was the only institution capable of reconstructing civilized life. Thus, the Christian outlook, rather than the traditions of the Germanic tribes, formed the foundation of medieval civilization. During the course of the Middle Ages, people came to see themselves as participants in a great drama of salvation. There was only one truth: God's revelation to humanity. There was only one avenue to heaven, and it passed through the church. Membership in a universal church replaced citizenship in a universal empire. Across Europe, from Italy to Ireland, a new society centered on Christianity was taking shape.

MONKS AND THE PAPACY Monks helped construct the foundations of medieval civilization. During the seventh century, intellectual life on the Continent continued its steady decline. In the monasteries of Ireland and England, however, a tradition of learning persisted. Early in the fifth century, Saint Patrick began the conversion of the Irish to Christianity. In Ireland, Latin became firmly entrenched as the language of both the church and scholars at a time when it was in danger of disappearing in many parts of the Continent. Irish monks preserved and cultivated Latin and even kept some knowledge of Greek alive; during their missionary activities they revived the use of Latin on the Continent. Irish scholars engaged in biblical analysis, and, in addition to copying manuscripts, they decorated them, with an exquisite eye for detail (see chapter opening). In England, the Anglo-Saxons, both women and men, who converted to Christianity mainly in the seventh century, also established monasteries that kept learning alive. Double monasteries existed, in which monks and nuns obeyed a common rule and one superior, sometimes an abbess. The Venerable Bede (673–735) wrote commentaries on Scripture and translated the Gospel of John into Anglo-Saxon. Bede is best known for his *Ecclesiastical History of the English People*, one of the finest medieval historical works. Because it was the first history of any sort to be written in England, Bede is justifiably referred to as "the Father of English History."

In the sixth and seventh centuries, Irish monks and nuns built monasteries on the Continent and converted people in the surrounding areas. Many converted Anglo-Saxons embraced Benedictine monasticism and, continuing the efforts of Irish monks, became the chief agents in Christianizing people in Northern Europe. Thus, monks and nuns made possible a unitary European civilization based on a Christian foundation. By copying and preserving ancient texts, they also kept alive elements of ancient civilization. During the Early Middle Ages, when cities were in decay, monasteries were the main cultural centers; they would remain so until the rebirth of towns in the High Middle Ages. To the medieval mind, the monks' and nuns' selfless devotion to God, adoption of apostolic poverty, and dedication to prayer and contemplation represented the highest expression of the Christian way of life; it was the finest and most certain path to salvation.

The Early Middle Ages were a formative period for the papacy, as well as for society in general. A decisive figure in the strengthening of the papacy was Gregory I, known as the Great (590–604). One of the ablest of medieval popes, Gregory used Roman methods of administration to organize effectively papal property in Italy, Sicily, Sardinia, Gaul, and other regions. He strengthened his authority over bishops and monks and dispatched missionaries to England to win over the Anglo-Saxons. He also wrote commentaries on the books of the Bible and authored many works dealing with Christian themes: the duties of bishops, the lives of saints and monks, miracles, and purgatory. Because of his many writings, Gregory is regarded as a father of the Latin Church.

The Era of Charlemagne

From their homeland in the Rhine River valley, the Frankish tribes had expanded into Roman territory during the fourth and fifth centuries. Clovis, the first Merovingian ruler (so named after Merovech, a semilegendary ancestor of Clovis), united the various Frankish tribes. Most of our knowledge about Frankish history comes from the *History of the Franks*, written about a century after Clovis by Gregory, Bishop of Tours (538–594). Gregory's account covers the conversion of the Franks to Christianity, including the conversion of Clovis himself in 496; the conquest of Gaul under Clovis; and a detailed account of the Frankish kings up to Gregory's own time. By the seventh century, the various Merovingian rulers had become ineffective and lost much of their power to great landowners. In 687, Pepin II (687–714) became the first of the Carolingian rulers (named for Charlemagne—Charles the

Great—the greatest of the Carolingian rulers). Under Charlemagne, who ruled from 768 to 814, Frankish power reached its height, and his empire covered much of western and central Europe.

On Christmas Day in Rome in the year 800, Pope Leo III crowned Charlemagne emperor of the Romans. The title signified that the tradition of a world empire still survived, despite the demise of the western Roman Empire three hundred years earlier. But because the pope crowned Charlemagne, the emperor now had a spiritual responsibility to spread and defend the faith. Thus, Roman universalism was fused with Christian universalism.

The Carolingian empire, of course, was only a dim shadow of the Roman Empire. The Franks had no Roman law or Roman legions; there were no cities that were centers of economic and cultural activity; and officials were not trained civil servants with a world outlook, but uneducated war chieftains with a tribal viewpoint. Yet Charlemagne's empire did embody the concept of a universal Christian empire—an ideal that would endure throughout the Middle Ages.

The crowning of a Germanic ruler as emperor of the Romans by the head of the church represented the merging of Germanic, Christian, and Roman traditions, which is the essential characteristic of medieval civilization. This blending of traditions was also evident on a cultural plane, for Charlemagne, a Germanic warrior-king, showed respect for classical learning and Christianity, both non-Germanic traditions (see discussion later in the chapter).

During the era of Charlemagne, a distinct European civilization took root. It blended the Roman heritage of a world empire, the intellectual achievement of the Greco-Roman mind, Christian otherworldliness, and the customs of the Germanic peoples. This nascent western European civilization differed from Byzantine and Islamic civilizations, and Europeans were growing conscious of the difference. But the new medieval civilization was still centuries away from its high point, which would be reached in the twelfth and thirteenth centuries.

After Charlemagne's death in 814, his heirs could not preserve the empire, whose strength rested more on the personal qualities of Charlemagne than on any firm economic or political foundation. Moreover, the empire was simply too large and consisted of too many diverse peoples to be governed effectively. As central authority waned, large landowners increasingly exercised authority in their own regions. Simultaneous invasions of southern Europe, by Muslims, from bases in North Africa, and Vikings, from Scandinavia, and Magyars, originally from western Asia, furthered this movement toward localism and decentralization. Villages were devastated, ports were destroyed, and the population was decimated. Trade came to a standstill, coins no longer circulated, and farms turned into wastelands. Already gravely weakened, the European economy collapsed. The political authority of kings disappeared, and cultural life and learning withered.

These terrible attacks heightened political insecurity and accelerated anew the process of decentralization that had begun with the decline of Rome. During these chaotic times, counts came to regard as their own the land that they administered and defended for their king. Similarly, the inhabitants of a district looked on the count or local lord as their ruler, for his men and fortresses protected them. In their regions, nobles exercised public power formerly held by kings. Europe had entered an age of *feudalism,* in which the essential unit of government was not a kingdom, but a county or the land belonging to a castle, and political power was the private possession of local lords.

Feudal Society

Arising during a period of collapsing central authority, invasion, scanty public revenues, and declining commerce and town life, feudalism* attempted to provide some order and security. Feudalism was not a planned system derived logically from general principles, but rather an improvised response to the challenge posed by ineffectual central authority. Feudal practices were not uniform; they differed from locality to locality, and in some regions barely took root. Although it was only a stopgap means of governing, feudalism did bring some order, justice, and law during an era of breakdown, localism, and transition. It remained the predominant political arrangement until kings reasserted their authority in the High and Late Middle Ages.

VASSALAGE Feudal relationships enabled lords to increase their military strength. The need for military support was the principal reason for the practice of *vassalage,* in which a knight, in a solemn ceremony, pledged loyalty to a lord. This feature of feudalism derived from an ancient Germanic ceremony, during which warriors swore personal allegiance to the head of the war band. Among other things, the vassal gave military service to his lord and received in return a fief, which was usually land. Peasants inhabited this fief, and

---

* Because the term *feudalism* was not coined until the seventeenth century, some medieval historians prefer the term *fief-holding.*

Map 9.2 The Great Invasions of the Ninth Century   Raids by Vikings, Magyars, and Muslims weakened the European economy and the political power of monarchs, contributing to the rise of feudalism.

the crops that they raised provided the vassal with his means of support.

FEUDAL WARRIORS Feudal lords viewed manual labor and commerce as degrading for men of their rank. They considered only one vocation worthy: that of warrior. Through combat, the lord demonstrated his valor, earned his reputation, measured his individual worth, derived excitement, added to his wealth, and defended his rights. Warfare gave meaning to his life. During the twelfth century, to relieve the boredom of peacetime, nobles staged gala tournaments, in which

knights, fighting singly or in teams, engaged each other in battle to prove their skill and courage and to win honor. The feudal glorification of combat became deeply ingrained in Western society and endured into the twentieth century. Over the centuries, a code of behavior, called *chivalry,* evolved for the feudal nobility. A true knight was expected to fight bravely, demonstrate loyalty to his lord, and treat other knights with respect and courtesy.

NOBLEWOMEN Girls from aristocratic families were generally married at age sixteen or younger to a man often twice as old. The wife of a lord was at the mercy of her husband; if she angered him, she might expect a beating. A French law code of the thirteenth century stated: "In a number of cases men may be excused for the injuries they inflict on their wives, nor should the law intervene. Provided he neither kills nor maims her, it is legal for a man to beat his wife when she wrongs him."[1] Even church law condoned wife beating.

As the lady of the castle, the lord's wife performed important duties. She assigned tasks to the servants, made medicines, preserved food, taught young girls how to sew, spin, and weave—she was responsible for providing the lord and his companions with most of the clothes they required—and, despite her subordinate position, took charge of the castle when her husband was away. If the lord was taken prisoner in war, she raised the ransom to pay for his release. Sometimes she put on armor and went to war. For amusement, noblewomen enjoyed chess and other board games, played musical instruments, or embroidered tapestries to cover castle walls. A lady might also join her husband on the hunt, a favorite recreation of the medieval nobility.

Feudal society was very much a man's world. In theory, women were deemed to be physically, morally, and intellectually inferior to men; and in practice, they were subjected to male authority. Fathers arranged the marriages of their daughters. Although the church taught that both men and women were precious to God and spiritual equals, church tradition also regarded women as agents of the devil—evil temptresses who, like the biblical Eve, lured men into sin.

Mary, the mother of Jesus, was seen as the antithesis to Eve; elevated to a position of the highest honor, Mary offered Christians an alternative image of women to that of the sinful Eve. The highest expression of devotion to the Virgin Mary was reached in the twelfth and thirteenth centuries with the growing notion that Mary was preserved from original sin and remained free of sin throughout her life.*[2] Moreover, medieval Christians believed that Mary, by devoting her entire life to her Son in his work of redemption, cooperated with him in his ministry. Therefore, as the Mother of God, she was able to intercede with her Son in behalf of individual Christians. The numerous artistic depictions of Mary as the Mother of God and the Queen of Heaven, as well as the multitude

of churches named after the Virgin, are evidence of the popular piety the cult of Mary generated throughout the Middle Ages.

Aristocratic girls who did not marry often entered a convent. (Peasant daughters, because they were needed on the farm—they probably worked as hard and as well as men—rarely became nuns. Moreover, their parents could not afford the dowry, payable in land, cash, or goods, required by the convent for admission.) The nunneries provided an outlet for the talents of unmarried noblewomen. Abbesses demonstrated organizational skills in supervising the convent's affairs. Some nuns acquired an education and, like their male counterparts, copied manuscripts and thus preserved knowledge and ideas of the past.

A few nuns distinguished themselves as writers. For example, Hroswitha (c. 935–c. 1001) of Gandersheim, in Saxony was the first Saxon poet, the first known Christian dramatist, and the first female historian in Germany history. Writing in Latin, she composed eight narrative poems drawn from legends, two epic historical works, one of which celebrated the foundation of her own convent, and six plays; in her works, she attempted to present a positive image of women.

Hildegard of Bingen (1098–1179), a German abbess, wrote works on the lives of the saints, on medicine, on natural history, and on music (see Chapter 11), but she is best known for her mystical visions, which began when she was five years old. At the age of eight, she moved into the monastery of Disibodenberg, and at fifteen, she made her profession as a nun. Twenty-three years later, she was elected abbess of the convent at Disibodenberg. Soon thereafter, a blinding vision compelled Hildegard to write *Scivias*, a contraction of *Know the Ways of the Lord (Sci vias Domini)*. In the preface, she describes the impact of the vision: "And so it kindled my whole heart and breast like a flame, not burning but warming . . . and suddenly I understood the meaning of the expositions of the books, that is to say of the psalter, the evangelists, and other catholic books of the Old and New Testaments."[3] At her death, a medieval writer reported a mysterious light in the form of a cross appeared above Hildegard's bed, and those in attendance believed it was a sign from God welcoming her into heaven.

Agrarian Society

Feudalism was built on an economic foundation known as *manorialism*. Although pockets of free peasantry remained, a village community (manor), consisting of serfs bound to the land, became the essential agricultural arrangement for much of the

---

* In 1854, this notion became the Roman Catholic dogma of the Immaculate Conception when Pope Pius IX promulgated the bull, *God Ineffible*, which states: "The doctrine which holds that the Most Blessed Virgin Mary was preserved from all stain of original sin in the first instant of her conception . . . must . . . firmly and constantly be believed by all the faithful."

Middle Ages. The manorial village was the means of organizing an agricultural society with limited markets and money. Neither lords nor priests performed economically productive work. Their ways of life were made possible by the toil of serfs. A lord controlled at least one manorial village; great lords might possess hundreds. A small manor had a dozen families; a large one had as many as fifty or sixty. The manorial village was never completely self-sufficient because salt, millstones, and metalware were generally obtained from outside sources. It did, however, constitute a balanced economic setting. Peasants grew grain and raised cattle, sheep, goats, and hogs; blacksmiths, carpenters, and stonemasons did the building and repairing; the village priest cared for the souls of the inhabitants; and the lord defended the manor and administered the customary law. The serf and his family lived in a dismal, one-room cottage, which they shared with chickens and pigs. In the center burned a small fire, the smoke escaping through a hole in the roof. In cold weather when the fire was strong, the room was filled with smoke. When it rained, water came through the thatched roof and turned the earth floor into mud. The odor from animal excrement was ever present.

When another lord attacked a manor, the peasants found protection inside the walls of their lord's house. By the twelfth century, in many places this building had become a well-fortified stone castle. Peasants generally lived, worked, and died on the lord's estate and were buried in the village churchyard. Few had any contact with the world beyond the village of their birth.

In return for protection and the right to cultivate fields and to pass these holdings on to their children, the serfs owed obligations to their lord, and their personal freedom was restricted in a variety of ways. Bound to the land, they could not leave the manor without the lord's consent. Before a serf could marry, he had to obtain the lord's permission and pay a fee. The lord could select a wife for his serf and force him to marry her. In addition to working their allotted land, the serfs had to tend the fields reserved for the lord. Other services exacted by the lord included digging ditches, gathering firewood, building fences, repairing roads and bridges, and sewing clothes. Probably somewhat more than half of a serf's workweek was devoted to fulfilling these labor obligations. Serfs also paid a variety of dues to the lord, including payments for using the lord's mill, bake-oven, and winepress.

Serfs did derive some benefits from manorial relationships. They received protection during a chaotic era, and they possessed customary rights, which the lord often respected, to cottages and farmlands. If a lord demanded more services or dues than was customary, or if he interfered with their right to cottages or strips of farmland, the peasants might demonstrate their discontent by refusing to labor for the lord. Until the fourteenth century, however, open rebellion was rare because lords possessed considerable military and legal power. The manorial system promoted attitudes of dependency and servility among the serfs; their hopes for a better life were directed toward heaven.

EARLY MEDIEVAL THOUGHT: THE WANING OF CLASSICAL CULTURE

Greco-Roman humanism, in retreat since the Late Roman Empire, continued its decline in the centuries immediately following Rome's demise. The old Roman upper classes abandoned their heritage and absorbed the ways of their Germanic conquerors, the Roman schools closed, and Roman law faded into disuse. Aside from clerics, few people could read and write Latin, and even learned clerics were rare. Europeans' knowledge of the Greek language was almost totally lost, and the Latin rhetorical style deteriorated. Many literary works of classical antiquity were either lost or unread. European culture was much poorer than the high civilizations of Byzantium, Islam, and ancient Rome.

Transmitters

During this period of cultural poverty, the few persons who were learned generally did not engage in original thought but salvaged and transmitted remnants of classical civilization. Given the context of the times, this was a considerable achievement. These individuals retained respect for the inheritance of Greece and Rome while remaining devoted to Christianity. In a rudimentary way, they were struggling to create a Christian culture that combined the intellectual tradition of Greece and Rome with the religious teachings of the Christian church.

An important figure in the intellectual life of this transitional period was Boethius (480–c. 525), a descendant of a noble family. Boethius had received a classical education at the Platonic Academy at Athens before Emperor Justinian closed it in 529. He was the last Latin-speaking scholar of the Roman world to have mastered the Greek language and to have intimate knowledge of Greek philosophy. Later, Boethius served the Ostrogoth

Theodoric I, who ruled Italy. Recognizing that Greco-Roman civilization was dying, Boethius tried to rescue the intellectual heritage of antiquity and translated into Latin some of Aristotle's treatises on logic. He also wrote commentaries on Aristotle, Cicero, and Porphyry (a Neoplatonist philosopher), as well as treatises on theology and textbooks on arithmetic, astronomy, and music. A sudden turn of fortune deprived him of power, prestige, and possessions and confronted him with imminent death when Theodoric ordered him executed in 524 or 525 for allegedly participating in a plot against the throne.

While in prison awaiting execution, Boethius wrote *The Consolation of Philosophy*, which is regarded as one of the masterpieces of world literature. In it, Boethius pondered life's meaning: "Think you that there is any certainty in the affairs of mankind when you know that often one swift hour can utterly destroy a man?"[4] Alone in his dungeon, he turned for guidance and consolation not to Christ, but to the philosophical training of his youth. He derived comfort from Lady Philosophy, who reassured him, in the tradition of Socrates and the Stoics, that "if then you are master of yourself, you will be in possession of that which you will never wish to lose, and which Fortune will never be able to take from you."[5] No tyrant can "ever disturb the peculiar restfulness which is the property of a mind that hangs together upon the firm basis of its reason."[6] In the life and thought of Boethius, the classical tradition lived on. He was a bridge between a classical civilization too weakened to be revived and a Christian civilization still in embryo.

Until the twelfth century, virtually all that Latin Christendom knew of Aristotle came from Boethius's translations and commentaries. Similarly, his work in mathematics, which contains fragments from Euclid, was the principal source for the study of that discipline in the Early Middle Ages. He also bequeathed to future generations basic philosophical definitions and terms. In his theological writings, he strove to demonstrate that reason did not conflict with orthodoxy—an early attempt to attain a rational comprehension of belief, or as he expressed it, to join faith to reason. Boethius's effort to examine Christian doctrines rationally, a principal feature of medieval philosophy, would grow to maturity in the twelfth and thirteenth centuries. Writing in the sixth century, Boethius was a forerunner of this movement.

Cassiodorus (c. 490–575), a contemporary of Boethius, was born in southern Italy of a good family; he served three Ostrogoth kings. Although Cassiodorus wrote the twelve-volume *History of the Goths* and some theological treatises, his prime legacies were the establishment of a monastic library containing Greek and Latin manuscripts and his advocacy of higher education to improve the quality of the clergy. In his educational writings, he justified the importance of studying secular literature as an aid to understanding sacred writings. Even though his works were not original, they did rescue some ideas of the ancients from oblivion; these ideas would bear fruit again in later centuries. Cassiodorus's plans for founding a university in Rome modeled after the one in Alexandria did not materialize; in fact, six hundred years would elapse before universities would arise in Latin Christendom. After leaving political office, Cassiodorus retired to a monastery, where he initiated the monastic practice of copying ancient texts. Without this tradition, many key Christian and Greco-Roman works would undoubtedly have perished.

In Spain, Isidore of Seville (c. 576–636) compiled an encyclopedia, *Etymologiae*, covering a diversity of topics from arithmetic and God to furniture. Isidore derived his information from many secular and religious sources. Quite understandably, his work contained many errors, particularly in its references to nature. For centuries, though, the *Etymologiae* served as a standard reference work and was found in every monastic library of note.

The translations and compilations made by Boethius, Cassiodorus, and Isidore, the books collected and copied by monks and nuns, and schools established in monasteries (particularly those in Ireland, England, and Italy) kept intellectual life from dying out completely in the Early Middle Ages. These three men were also responsible for giving expression to the importance of music for medieval people (see Chapter 11).

The Carolingian Renaissance

Charlemagne felt that it was his religious duty to raise the educational level of the clergy so that they understood and could properly teach the faith. To do so required overcoming the illiteracy or semi-literacy of clergymen and preparing sacred Scriptures that were uniform, complete, and free of errors. Charlemagne also fostered education to train administrators who would be capable of overseeing his empires and royal estates; such men had to be literate.

To achieve his purpose, Charlemagne gathered some of the finest scholars in Europe. In 781, Charlemagne invited Alcuin of York, England (735–804), to Aachen and placed him in charge of the Palace School, which was attended by Charlemagne and his sons and daughters, high lords, and youths training to serve the emperor. Throughout

THE PILLOW-BOOK: THE JOURNAL OF SEI SHONAGON

SEI SHONAGON WAS BORN IN ABOUT 967 into a family that had been committed to learning and literature for centuries. She was an attendant to the Empress of Japan from 991, when the Empress was fifteen years old, until 1000, when the Empress died in childbirth. Little is known about the life of Shonagon except for her years at court when she wrote *The Pillow-Book,* a journal that consists of reminiscences about court life and lists of things that she found disagreeable, disappointing, or amusing. *The Pillow-Book* is viewed as a classic of Japanese literature as well as a rich source of information on eleventh-century Japan. This first excerpt is taken from Sei's list of "Annoying Things":

> One is staying with a provincial Governor or some small official of that kind, and a servant comes from some grand house. He speaks and behaves with the utmost rudeness and an air as much as to say "I know I am being rude; but people like you can't punish me for it, so what do I care?" I find that very annoying. . . .
>
> A lady is out of humour about some trifle, and leaving her lover's side goes and establishes herself on another couch. He creeps over to her and tries to bring her back, but she is still cross, and he, feeling that this time she has really gone too far, says: "As you please," and returns to the big bed, where he ensconces himself comfortably and goes to sleep. It is a very cold night and the lady, having only an unlined wrap to cover herself with, soon begins to suffer. She thinks of getting up; but everyone else in the house is asleep and she does not know what to do or where to go. . . . Then she begins to hear strange noises both in the women's quarters and outside. She becomes frightened and softly creeps towards her lover, plucks at the bedclothes, and raises them. But he vexingly pretends to be fast asleep; or merely says: "I advise you to go on sulking a little longer."

Among "Pretty Things," Shonagon includes,

> The face of a child that has its teeth dug into a melon.
> A baby sparrow hopping towards one when one calls "*chu chu*" to it; or being fed by its parents with worms or what not, when one has captured it and tied a thread to its foot.
> A child of three or so, that scurrying along suddenly catches sight of some small object lying on the ground, and clasping the thing in its pretty little fingers, brings it to show to some grown-up person.

Under "Children," Shonagon observes,

> Sometimes when in the course of conversation I have expressed an opinion about someone and perhaps spoken rather severely, a small child has overheard me and repeated the whole thing to the person in question. This may get one into a terrible fix.

Source: Sei Shonagon, The Pillow-Book of Sei Shonagon, *trans. Arthur Waley (London: George Allen & Unwin Ltd, 1957 [First published in 1928]), pp. 89–90, 123–125.*

France, Alcuin expanded schools and libraries, promoted the copying of ancient manuscripts, and imposed basic literary standards on the clergy. One of Alcuin's most significant accomplishments was the creation of the **Carolingian minuscule script,** which standardized the written hand in the empire. Later, it became the model for early type-faces during the Renaissance and for the modern printed Latin type.

Perhaps Alcuin's most famous student was Einhard (770–840), who came to the Palace School in 791. Einhard soon became a close adviser and friend of Charlemagne. About fifteen years after the death of Charlemagne, Einhard wrote his *Life of Charles the Great,* a short and accurate account of the emperor's rule, his family, and his achievements. Einhard patterned his biography after the *Life of Augustus,* written by the Roman biographer Suetonius (c. A.D. 69–122).

The focus of the **Carolingian Renaissance** was predominantly Christian—an effort to train clergymen and improve their understanding of the Bible and the writings of the church fathers. This process raised the level of literacy and improved the Latin style. Most important, monastic copyists continued to preserve ancient texts, which otherwise might never have survived; the oldest surviving manuscripts of many ancient works are Carolingian copies. Carolingian scholars thus helped to fertilize the later cultural flowering known as the Twelfth-Century Awakening—the high point of medieval civilization.

Compared with the Greco-Roman past, with the cultural explosion of the twelfth and thirteenth centuries, or with the great Italian Renaissance of the fifteenth century, the Carolingian Renaissance seems slight indeed. Although it did rediscover and revive ancient works, it did not recapture the spirit of Greece and Rome. Carolingian scholars did not engage in independent philosophical speculation or search for new knowledge, nor did they achieve that synthesis of faith and reason that would be constructed by the great theologians of the twelfth and thirteenth centuries. The Carolingian Renaissance did, however, reverse the process of cultural decay, which had characterized much of the Early Middle Ages. Learning would never again fall to the low level it had reached during the centuries following the decline of Rome.

EARLY MEDIEVAL LITERATURE

Much of early medieval literature was written in the vernacular and recorded native Irish, Welsh, and Germanic traditions. At times, early medieval writers, particularly clergy, expressed Christian concerns, but classical Latin models continued to influence the poetry of the age.

Welsh Mythology

The source of Celtic British vernacular literature was the oral tradition of the Irish and the Welsh. The *Mabinogion,* the oldest Welsh literature, summarizes the mythology of the Welsh people in narrative form. It was not well known until 1849, when Lady Charlotte Guest translated it into English. It is she who gave it the title, **Mabinogion—** from the Welsh word *mab,* which means "boy" or "son." Guest then concluded that the Welsh noun mabinogi means "a story for children." The *Mabinogion* is a collection of pre-Christian stories based on remembered myths and histories about Celtic Britain. The four branches of the story line, set primarily in Wales and the "other" world, were based on Welsh fairy tales and nursery rhymes and were intended to entertain young chieftains. The various tales were associated with the four portions of the manuscript—*Pyll, Branwen, Manawyden,* and *Math*—each of which ends with the phrase, "So ends this branch of the Mabinogi." In the West, the *Mabinogion* is best known as the source of the themes and adventures associated with King Arthur (see Chapter 11).

Irish Lyric Poetry and Epic Tales

Irish lyric poetry was dependent on the rhythm, meter, and accents of Latin models. One common theme was love of nature as is evident in the poem *Spring,* which employs descriptive language designed to affect one's senses.

> Green cold icy spring,
> cold is produced in the wind,
> ducks of pools of water have cried out,
> fiercely complaining is the cranes' harsh cry.
>
> Green, cool, quiet, quivering—
> cold in the wind wakening;
> wailing ducks on distant ponds,
> doleful cranes are chorusing.
>
> They hear the wolves on the wilderness;
> on rising early in the morning,
> the birds awake from the islands;
> many wild beasts flee before them
> from wood, from green grass.
>
> Calls are heard on highland moors.
> Hurry, daybreak, dawning hour:
> darting fowl from far-off isles
> fleeing wild beasts, wanderers
> from wood, waste, and green. Green.[7]

In contrast to lyric poetry, which often built on classical models, Old Irish epics bear virtually no resemblance to the epic literature of Homer's *Iliad* and *Odyssey* or to Virgil's *Aeneid*. Unlike the great Greek and Roman epics, Irish epics were written in prose rather than in poetic form. The subject matter of Irish epic literature (except for a reference to a legend that the Irish were descendants of the Trojans) is also purely devoid of classical influence. The Irish epics are about Irish settlements, the kings of antiquity, heroes, otherworldly beings—fairies and leprechauns—the beauty of nature, and love.

The authors of the two principal epic cycles—the Ulster cycle and the Leinster cycle—were unconcerned with a consistent, logical approach to the plot of the narrative, did not develop the personalities of their characters, and were given to exaggeration and diversion. The cycles are, nevertheless, rich with sensuous descriptions, local color, and delightful plays on words.

The **Ulster cycle** (so named for the people of northeastern Ireland, the Ulaid) dates from the first century B.C. and reflects a tradition that is older than any other epic cycle in western Europe. However, the story of the fictional hero, Cuchulainn, was not written down until 1100 A.D. Although Cuchulainn has seven eyes, seven fingers on each hand, and seven toes on each foot, he is endowed with a sharp mind, keen wit, and athletic skill. As a youth he romances women with his physical prowess and knack for solving riddles. When Cuchulainn decides to marry, his soon-to-be father-in-law stipulates that Cuchulainn must first gain an education in arms. Through a series of otherworldy adventures, Cuchulainn surmounts all obstacles and becomes a hero. However, on his way back to his ladylove in Ireland, he falls in love with a maiden whom he has saved from imminent disaster. Cuchulainn and his new fiancée (apparently oblivious to the fact that he is engaged to another woman) proceed to Ireland, where he encounters his first fiancée in the form of a bird, which he accidentally kills while on a hunt. Once his love problems are resolved, Cuchulainn is involved in other adventures, including a war precipitated by a lovers' quarrel. One particularly amusing incident of this war involves a young girl positioned in a tower so as to warn her fellow citizens of the advance of Cuchulainn and his men. However, she becomes so enamored by the grandeur and glory of the horses, weapons, and war machinery that she neglects to announce the assault.

Whereas the Ulster cycle is about a fictional hero, the **Leinster cycle** depicts the adventures of Finn (Irish for "fair" or "white")—an actual Irish warlord who lived during the third century A.D. Although some of the texts can be dated as early as the eighth century, the stories of Finn did not become popular until the early thirteenth century. All the numerous versions of the cycle detail Finn's love life, his battles with natural and supernatural beings, and each ultimately concludes with his betrayal in battle and his death at the hands of Viking invaders. In much the same way that the Ulster cycle served to popularize the legend of King Arthur, the Leinster cycle is the Celtic source for one of the most tragic romances in the West—the story of Tristan and Iseult, which evolved into the equally tragic love story of Lancelot and Guinevere.

The Old English Epic: *Beowulf*

Other medieval epics—*The Legend of King Arthur, Beowulf, The Song of Roland,* and *The Nibelungenlied*—found their origins as early as the sixth century in the oral tradition of tribal folk legends, songs, and actual historical events, which preceded the written accounts by 300 to 500 years. Although these four medieval epics were not inspired by the epic literature of classical antiquity, they did serve a similar purpose; they focused on an idealized hero whose escapades became the foundation for a grand and glorious past and contributed to the formation of a nascent national identity. Each story centers on a kingly protagonist who demands absolute loyalty from his retainers, especially in time of battle; in the end, however, he is betrayed by one or more of his trusted vassals, who violate the code of honor. In this chapter we treat *Beowulf,* the only one of the four epics to be put into writing during the Early Middle Ages (see Chapter 11 for a discussion of the other epics).

The origins of the *Beowulf* story are obscure, but the poem does contain a few incontrovertible historical facts. General references are made to the Germanic Anglo-Saxons' settlement of England in the sixth century and their encounters with the Danes in the 830s, and a specific incident refers to the death of Beowulf's liege lord, Heygelac of the Geats,* a historical figure who was killed in battle about 521. The only surviving manuscript, an unrhymed poem containing 3,182 lines, with four accented beats per line, is the Christianized version from the late tenth or early eleventh century. It is the longest extant poem written in Old English.

As the poem opens, the reader is introduced to *Evil* in the guise of the monster, Grendel, who each evening terrorizes the court of Hrothgar, the

---

* The poet presents the Geats as a tribe situated in the southeastern part of Sweden.

Danish king, by devouring a number of his warriors. *Good* is presented in the form of Beowulf, a prince of the Geats, who seeks to gain a name for himself by slaying Grendel. During his first encounter with Grendel at Hrothgar's court, Beowulf tears the monster's arm off at the shoulder. Later that night, Beowulf confronts Grendel's mother who seeks vengeance on Hrothgar's court by carrying off his chief adviser. Beowulf becomes a hero in the eyes of the Danes when he follows Grendel's mother to a haunted lake and slays her with a magical sword under the water. The Danes give Beowulf treasure and lands as a reward for helping them rid their territory of the race of evil monsters.

Boasting about his accomplishment, Beowulf is upbraided for his pride by King Hrothgar, who also warns him about the finiteness of life:

> Turn not to pride, O brave champion!
> Your fame lives now, in one strong time.
> Soon in their turn sickness or war
> will break your strength, or the grip of fire,
> overwhelming wave, or sword's swing,
> a thrown spear, or hateful old age;
> the lights will darken that were your eyes.
>
> Death overcomes you all at once, warrior.[8]

Beowulf then returns to the Geats, tells his uncle, King Hygelac, of his deeds, and honors his liege lord by giving him his reward. This brings to a close the long first part of the poem, which scholars regard as the period covering Beowulf's youth.

The second section of the poem opens with Beowulf ascending the throne of the Geats after his uncle and his cousin are killed on the battlefield. He rules the kingdom peacefully for fifty years, "until a certain one, a dragon, began to rule in the dark nights."[9] Knowing that if he is successful in slaying the dragon he will gain the dragon's treasure, Beowulf, even though he is an old man, challenges the dragon to single combat. During the dragon's first attack, Beowulf is engulfed in flames and his terrified men betray him by fleeing. When the dragon attacks a second time, Beowulf stabs it in the neck and breaks his magical sword. It is Beowulf, however, who is severely wounded in the third attack, when the dragon bites him in the neck. Finally, Beowulf's loyal retainer Wiglaf, his only defender, attempts to avenge his lord's mortal wound by driving his sword into the dragon's stomach, but it is Beowulf who wields the fatal blow.

Just as the poem opened with a funeral for the founder of the Danes, King Scyld, so too does it end with a funeral—for Beowulf. In his funeral oration, Wiglaf chastises Beowulf's troops for violating the code of honor. The poet then summarizes the virtues of the age—bravery, honor, and loyalty to one's lord.

> . . . Too few defenders
> pressed round the king when his worst time
>   came.
> Now all treasure, giving and receiving,
> all home-joys, ownership, comfort,
> shall cease for your kin; deprived of their rights
> each man of your families will have to be exiled,
> once nobles afar hear of your flight,
> a deed of no glory. Death is better
> for any warrior than a shameful life.[10]

Christian Themes

Christian concerns did not predominate in early medieval literature, but neither were they absent. A number of Irish poems extolled the virtues of monastic life, whereas others dealt with penance, pilgrimage, and purgatory. Women also wrote religious lyrics such as *The Vision of Ita*—in which Jesus, as an infant, is entrusted to Ita's care. *The Heavenly Banquet,* written by a nun named Brigid, treats Christian themes with a uniquely Irish perspective, especially with her references to vats of beer.

> I would like to have the men of Heaven
> in my own house,
>
> with vats of good cheer
> laid out for them. . . .
>
> I would like a great lake of beer
> for the King of Kings [Christ]
> I would like to be watching Heaven's family
> drinking it for all eternity.[11]

Religious themes pervaded the six poems of the German nun, Hroswitha (see p. 214). Her first poem is an account of the life of the Virgin Mary; the second concerns the ascension of Christ; the third is about a virtuous knight, Gongolf, who resists the devil's attempts to tempt him, but whose adulterous wife instigates a plot to murder Gongolf; the fourth poem details an eyewitness account of the martyrdom of the ninth-century Spanish saint, Pelagius; the fifth and sixth poems are the first literary accounts of the Faustian[†] theme—of selling one's soul to the devil—in Germany; the final poem details the martyrdom of Dionysius, bishop of Paris.

The best known of Hroswitha's works are her six dramas—the first since Roman times—for which she acknowledged her indebtedness to the

---

[†] The historical Faust was a German magician who died in Germany about 1540. However, in 1587, an anonymous Lutheran collected medieval tales of the occult and attributed them to Faust. The most famous story is the one in which Faust, in exchange for power and knowledge, agrees to sell his soul to the devil.

Roman poet Terence, especially on the theme of sensual love. Hroswitha intended to instruct her sister nuns in the ways of morality in these rhymed, rhythmic, prose dramas. In *Gallicanus,* her first drama, Hroswitha describes the desire of Emperor Constantine's pagan general, Gallicanus, to marry Constantia, Constantine's daughter, who had taken a vow of chastity. Hroswitha demonstrates the power of God by having Saints John and Paul convert Gallicanus to Christianity; subsequently, Gallicanus rejects marriage and dies as a Christian martyr.

Hroswitha's second drama, *Dulcitius,* which takes place at the time of Diocletian's persecution of Christians, blends humor and dramatic action. Dulcitius, an executioner for Emperor Diocletian, is intent on compelling three Christian maiden sisters into marrying three court officials. They, however, refuse to renounce their faith or their vow of chastity, and Dulcitius imprisons them in a kitchen where they spend their time in prayer. As Dulcitius prepares to have his way with the young women, God confuses him and Dulcitius ends up embracing the pots and pans instead. He emerges from the kitchen covered with so much soot that the soldiers think he is possessed by the devil and drive him out of the palace.

The violence of passion is the hallmark of Hroswitha's third drama, *Callimachus.* Callimachus, a young pagan man, is in love with Drusiana, a Christian woman who has taken the vow of chastity. When Drusiana learns of Callimachus' passionate love for her, she prays to be delivered from temptation and dies. Callimachus then bribes the guard at her tomb, intending to have sex with her corpse. However, both men die before Callimachus can defile her corpse, and both are resurrected by Saint John and are converted to Christianity. The fourth and fifth dramas, *Abraham* and *Paphnutius,* concern the conversion to Christianity of two harlots. Hroswitha intends the women to represent the vice of *luxuria carnis* (pleasures of the flesh). Hroswitha's final drama relates the martyrdom of Faith, Hope, and Charity—the daughters of Wisdom.

In all of her dramas, Hroswitha skillfully casts the Virgin Mary as the ideal for all subsequent heroines, so that her heroines acquire their boldness from their adherence to their vow of chastity. She thus further augments the elevation of Mary as the replacement for Eve. Whereas Eve's happiness issued from marriage, Hroswitha's heroines obtain their joy from maidenhood. Therefore, Hroswitha's heroines defy the stereotypical image of women, drawn primarily from Paul and Augustine (see Chapter 7), that women are purveyors of sin. With her emphasis on the moral ideal of chastity, she is a precursor of the morality plays that came into existence more than one and a half centuries after her death (see Chapter 11).

EARLY MEDIEVAL ART

Early medieval art spans the period of the Carolingian and Ottonian rulers, who revived the idea of empire. Under the emperors Otto I, the Great (936–973), Otto II (973–983), Otto III (983–1002), and Henry II (1002–1024), Germany became the artistic leader of Europe in architecture, in painting, and in the resurgence of monumental sculpture. The art of the Ottonian dynasty integrated Carolingian, Roman, and Byzantine antecedents, producing the distinctive new Romanesque style; this development marked the liberation of the Germanic peoples of the north from their artistic dependence on the Greco-Roman past and was a point of departure for later development of art in the medieval West.

During the Early Middle Ages, *manuscript illumination*—detailed and vividly colored miniature paintings on the pages of manuscripts—developed into a unique form of art. The most popular type of illumination was done for manuscripts of the Gospels, and although the illuminators were Christians, their work was inspired by the ornamental metalwork of their Germanic and Celtic ancestors, who were pagan. One of the finest examples of this art form is the *Lindisfarne Gospels,* executed about 700 at the Monastery of Lindisfarne on Holy Island, just off the west coast of England. A note inserted into the manuscript sometime around 950 states: "Eadfrith, Bishop of the Lindisfarne Church, originally wrote this book, for God and for Saint Cuthbert [a bishop who died in 670] and . . . for all the saints whose relics are in the Island."[12] The interlacing of geometric forms with bird and animal motifs on the Cross Page (Figure 9.1) demonstrates the precision with which Eadfrith blended mirror images, repetitive shapes, and vivid colors into a work of jewel-like splendor. It is called a cross page because the design included a repetition of the Cross, the most abstract Christian symbol.

Another copy of the Gospels, the *Books of the Kells,* was illuminated between 760 and 820 in southeastern Ireland, at Iona. One of the most famous pages of the manuscript (see chapter opening) contains the first three Greek letters of the name *Christ*—Chi (X), Rho (P), and Iota (I). The longer tendril of the X bears three winged angels on its outside edge, while the P, as the I slices through it, terminates in the face of a unknown man. Although the whirling spirals and circles-within-circles create a dizzying effect, naturalistic mice and a cat are visible on the inside edge at the foot of the X, just above the whorl.

Carolingian literature details the mosaics, wall paintings, and relief sculptures that adorned churches, but unfortunately, none of these artistic creations has survived intact. However, a number of illuminated manuscripts, including the *Gospel Book of Charlemagne,* did survive—reputedly it was found laying on Charlemagne's knees when his tomb was opened in 1000. Following the custom of manuscripts of the Palace School, they contain full-page portraits of the Gospel writers as well as biblical references to the Gospels. The portrait of *Matthew* (Figure 9.2) shows him adorned in classical garb and seated on a stool. If it were not for the golden halo around his head he could

be easily mistaken for a Greco-Roman philosopher. In his left hand he holds an inkhorn as he writes his Gospel with his right hand. The landscape—with its soft brushwork and gentle colors—hearkens back to the illusionistic tradition of the Romans (see Chapter 6).

In architecture, the Germanic emperors revived the ancient tradition of the Roman emperors and built opulent palaces and homes for their families and members of their court. Charlemagne built palaces at Nijmegen and Ingelheim, but only the palace at Aachen (French, Aix-la-Chapelle) has survived relatively intact. The ground plan (Figure 9.3) at Aachen was a rectangle of 590 feet in length, which covered over 50 acres. The northern end of the grounds was marked by an *aula* (court or hall), and a chapel bounded the southern end; a courtyard extended between the two structures. The religious buildings at

Figure 9.1 Cross Page, *Lindisfarne Gospels,* **c. 700, 13 1/2" x 9 1/4" (34.3 x 23.5 cm), British Library, London** The most popular type of manuscript illumination was done for the Gospels, and this cross page was executed at the Monastery of Lindisfarne on Holy Island, just off the west coast of England. The artistry of the Christian illuminators was inspired by the ornamental metalwork of their Germanic and Celtic ancestors. *(British Library, Cott. Nero.D.IV, f. 26V)*

Figure 9.2 *Saint Matthew, Gospel Book of Charlemagne, c. 800–810, 13" x 10" (33 x 25.4 cm), Kunsthistorisches Museum, Vienna* Adorned in classical garb and seated on a stool, Matthew holds an inkhorn in his left hand as he writes his Gospel with his right hand. *(Kunsthistoriches Museum, Vienna)*

Figure 9.3 **Aachen, Ground Plan, begun 790, Germany** Covering more than 50 acres, the plan of Aachen was a rectangle, 590 feet in length. A courtyard extended between the aula, on the northern end, and the chapel, on the southern end. *(From the* World Atlas of Architecture, *New York: Crescent Books, an imprint of Random House, Inc. 1994, p. 188)*

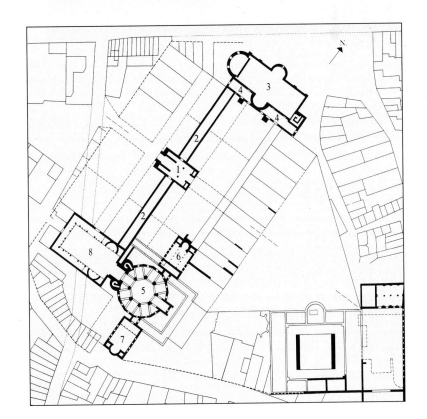

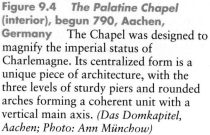

Figure 9.4 *The Palatine Chapel* (interior), begun 790, Aachen, Germany The Chapel was designed to magnify the imperial status of Charlemagne. Its centralized form is a unique piece of architecture, with the three levels of sturdy piers and rounded arches forming a coherent unit with a vertical main axis. *(Das Domkapitel, Aachen; Photo: Ann Münchow)*

the southern end were organized in the form of the Latin cross, and at the center was *The Palatine Chapel* (Figure 9.4).

The Chapel, begun in 790 and dedicated to the Virgin Mary in 800, was designed to magnify the imperial status of Charlemagne. Its centralized form is reminiscent of San Vitale at Ravenna and the Dome of the Rock in Jerusalem (see Chapter 8). Nonetheless, the Chapel is a unique piece of architecture, the dimensions of which were based on an interpretation of Revelation 21. As part of his seventh vision, John is shown the twelve city gates of the "New Jerusalem" by the seventh angel. The angel measured the city with a golden reed, and the length, the height, and the breadth of the city were equal—144 cubits—(a cubit being roughly 18 to 22 inches). Measured by the *"Carolingian foot"* of 13 inches, the Chapel's height, length, and width are relatively equal—constructed according to the proportions of 7, 12, and 144 Carolingian feet. The three levels of sturdy piers

and rounded arches form a coherent unit with a vertical main axis. The exterior wall has sixteen sides and is defined by its westwork with its twin towers. In 800, Charlemagne ordered colored marble and granite columns with white capitals to be sent from Rome and Ravenna to complete the Chapel.

The octagonal interior has eight massive arches on the lowest level that support the upper level galleries. The middle level allowed Charlemagne to attend Mass in seclusion from the other parishioners. Through an opening into the courtyard, however, he could also address as many as 7,000 of his subjects. From Otto I in 962 to Charles V in 1520, the German emperors were customarily crowned in the Palatine Chapel at Aachen. The Palatine Chapel determined the style of Carolingian architecture in the pre-Romanesque period. The massive columns, the rounded arches, and the twin towers of the westwork became standard features of the later style.

However, most religious architecture during the period was basilica style (see p. 175), characterized by exteriors that were dominated by the monumental main entrance with its twin towers—the westwork (from the German *Westwerk*). The interiors had smooth wall surfaces and flat, wooden ceilings that were supported by massive piers and columns. Archbishop Bruno, the brother of Otto I, was instrumental in the building or rebuilding of many of the churches of Cologne that were done in this style. One such church was the Benedictine abbey church of *Saint Pantaleon* (Figure 9.5); consecrated in 980, it was named after a martyr who lived in the late third century. Although the church was largely modified in the later Middle Ages, the original nave and the massive westwork with its two bell towers have survived. It has two transepts with a lantern tower over the crossing of the west transept. Both Archbishop Bruno and the wife of Otto II are buried in the church.

Figure 9.5 *Saint Pantaleon* (exterior), **consecrated 980, Cologne, Germany** This Benedictine abbey was named after the martyr who lived during the late third century. Although much of the initial structure has not survived, the original nave and the massive westwork, with its two bell towers, are still intact. *(Foto Marburg/Art Resource, NY)*

Figure 9.6 *Saint Michael* (exterior), **completed by 1033, Hildesheim, Germany** Designed by Bernward of Hildesheim, Saint Michael features identical square towers over the two crossings and four bell towers attached to the transept walls at the four corners, making it a typical Ottonian westwork. *(Gian Berto Vanni/Art Resource, NY)*

Figure 9.7 *Saint Michael* **(interior), completed by 1033, Hildesheim, Germany** The nave is divided into a series of square bays formed by two piers with two columns inserted between them. Unlike later Romanesque churches, which would be vaulted, Saint Michael's nave has a flat ceiling. *(Gian Berto Vanni/Art Resource, NY)*

The most famous of the Ottonian churches, begun shortly after 1000 and completed in 1033, is the basilica-style abbey church of *Saint Michael* (Figure 9.6) at Hildesheim in lower Saxony. It was designed by Bernward of Hildesheim (c. 960–1022), son of a prominent Saxon family; Bernward was tutor to Otto III who, in 993, appointed him Bishop of Hildesheim. A devoted patron of the arts, Bernward also worked for the social and spiritual advancement of Hildesheim. In contrast to later Romanesque churches, which would be vaulted, Bernward's design for Saint Michael features a flat nave ceiling (Figure 9.7). The nave terminates in a choir at both the east and west ends; each choir is bounded by a transept that leads into an apse. The exterior—with identical square towers over the two crossings and four bell towers attached to the transept walls at the four corners—is a typical Ottonian westwork. Break-

ing with tradition, however, Bernward placed the entrance to the church on the south side aisle, rather than through the façade.

Bernward's design for Saint Michael was also innovative, and several features from his design became commonplace in later Romanesque churches—the nave is divided into a series of square bays formed by two piers with two columns inserted between them; the floor of the western choir is raised above the level of the rest of the church to accommodate the crypt (or basement chapel), which could be entered from the western ambulatory or from the transept. Although the ambulatory and crypt were designed on a grand scale, Bernward was able to integrate them harmoniously with the rest of the structure.

From ancient times through the Carolingian period, plain and unadorned bronze doors had traditionally marked the entrance of churches. The

Figure 9.8 *Bernward's Doors,*
1015, height 16′ (4.87 m),
Hildesheim, Germany These
immense doors were ingeniously
cast in one piece. Each door contains
eight scenes, with the left door
illustrating events from the book of
Genesis, up to the time of Cain and
Abel, and the right door depicting
the gospel story of Christ redeeming
the fallen world. *(Hirmer Verlag
München)*

sculpture contained on the sixteen metal panels of
Bernward's bronze doors (Figure 9.8) for the crypt
of Saint Michael's church constitute a major innovation that was emulated throughout the Middle
Ages and the Renaissance in Europe. The doors
were completed the year the church was consecrated (1015), but they probably were not

installed until 1035. Instead of casting each plate
individually and then joining them together, it
appears that each of the nearly 16-foot-tall doors
was ingeniously cast as one piece. Bernward, an
amateur artist, probably supervised the design and
execution of the doors. Each door has eight
scenes—the left door (from top to bottom)

Figure 9.9 *Bernward's Doors, Adam and Eve Reproached by the Lord,* **1015, c. 23" x 43" (58.4 x 109.2 cm), Hildesheim, Germany** Following their commission of the original sin, God confronts Adam and Eve and reproaches them, as they cower before him, trying to cover their naked bodies. Adam blames Eve, who in turn points to the dragonlike serpent, which responds with an angry gesture. *(Hirmer Verlag München)*

illustrates events from the book of Genesis beginning with the fall of humanity through the murder of Cain by Abel; the right door (from bottom to top) tells the gospel story of Christ's redemption of humanity.

Even though the bodies are somewhat unnatural (due to their positioning), the high relief with which they are sculpted marks an improvement over earlier Christian sculpture (which flattened figures against the background). This tendency anticipates the more natural and realistic portrayal of the human form executed by later sculptors. The drama of each scene outweighs the barrenness of the background, as is evidenced in *Adam and Eve Reproached by the Lord* (Figure 9.9). The couple is portrayed after having eaten the forbidden fruit. As God confronts them with their sin and reproaches them, they cower before God and try to cover their nude bodies. Adam blames Eve,

who in turn points to the dragonlike serpent, which responds with an angry gesture. At the bottom of this panel is a Latin inscription: "In the year of our Lord 1015, the Bernward of esteemed memory cast these doors."

━━━ ⬥ ━━━

The Birth of Europe

Many historians still find it helpful to use the traditional periodization of Western history: ancient, medieval and modern. The civilization of the Ancient World, which was centered on the Mediterranean Sea and unified by a common Greco-Roman culture, came to an end with the fragmentation of the Roman Empire and the establishment of Germanic kingdoms on once

Roman lands. The Middle Ages mark the birth of Europe; a high civilization gradually evolved in old Roman lands and Germanic lands that, in the Ancient World, were primitive by Roman standards. Medieval Europe inherited Greco-Roman, Germanic, and Christian traditions, but it was Christianity that gave it form and coherence. The church, the major institution of the Middle Ages, instructed people what to believe and how to behave. Medieval people were certain that only by adhering to God's revelation as taught by the church would they gain entrance to heaven, the ultimate aim of life. The church was a great unifying force that made people in different lands feel that they shared a common faith and outlook.

The civilization of Latin Christendom developed its own distinctive style, which made it different from both Byzantine and Islamic civilizations, the other two contemporary civilizations built on former Roman lands. Both of these Eastern civilizations were far more advanced than Europe for much of the Middle Ages, but it was Europe that eventually produced those movements that shaped the modern world.

The Renaissance, which began in Italy in the late fourteenth century, is generally considered to be the starting point of the modern age. Other movements associated with the breaking away from the Middle Ages and the rise of modernity are the Reformation, the Commercial Revolution, the Scientific Revolution, and the Enlightenment. The period from the Renaissance through the Enlightenment of the eighteenth century is referred to as Early Modern. Modern Europe begins with the dual revolutions, French and Industrial, that transformed European politics and society, starting in the late eighteenth century.

Because of the great interaction of the West with Asian and African lands—a trend that started in early modern times—some historians call the contemporary period an Age of Globalism. What defines this age is the spread of Western science, technology, institutions, and ideas throughout the world. Europe, which was born in the Early Middle Ages after the demise of the Roman Empire, has in many ways transformed the world.

Key Terms

feudalism	Carolingian Renaissance
vassalage	Mabinogion
chivalry	Ulster cycle
manorialism	Leinster cycle
Carolingian minuscule script	manuscript illumination "Carolingian foot"

Notes

1. Cited in Frances Gies and Joseph Gies, *Women in the Middle Ages* (New York: Thomas Y. Crowell, 1978), p. 46.
2. Quoted in Jaroslav Pelikan, *Mary Through the Centuries: Her Place in the History of Culture* (New Haven and London: Yale University Press, 1996), p. 199.
3. Sabina Flanagan, *Hildegard of Bingen, 1098–1179: A Visionary Life* (London and New York: Routledge, 1989), p. 4.
4. Boethius, *The Consolation of Philosophy,* trans. W. V. Cooper (New York: Modern Library, 1943), p. 26.
5. Ibid., p. 29.
6. Ibid., p. 34.
7. Ruth P. M. Lehmann, *Early Irish Verse* (Austin: University of Texas Press, 1982), pp. 22–23.
8. *Beowulf: A Dual Language Edition*, trans. Howell D. Chickering, Jr. (New York: Doubleday, 1977), p. 151.
9. Ibid., p. 179.
10. Ibid., p. 223.
11. Quoted in Marcia L. Colish, *Medieval Foundations of the Western Intellectual Tradition 400–1400* (New Haven and London: Yale University Press, 1997), p. 80.
12. Quoted in H. W. Janson, *History of Art* (New York: Harry N. Abrams, Inc., 1995), p. 389.

The High Middle Ages I: The Flowering of Medieval Thought

MANORIALISM AND FEUDALISM PRESUPPOSED a hierarchical, organic, and stable social order: clergy who prayed, lords who fought, and peasants who toiled. People believed that society functioned smoothly when individuals accepted their status and performed their proper role. Consequently, a person's rights, duties, and relationship to law depended on his or her ranking in the social order. To change position was to upset the organic unity of society. And no one, serfs included, should be deprived of the traditional rights associated with his or her rank. This arrangement was justified by the clergy who maintained that "God himself has willed that among men, some must be lords and some serfs."[1]

During the High Middle Ages (1050–1300), however, the revival of an urban economy and the reemergence of central authority undermined feudal and manorial relationships. By the end of the eleventh century, Europe showed many signs of recovery. The invasions of Magyars* and Vikings had ended, and powerful lords and kings imposed greater order in their territories. A period of economic vitality, the High Middle Ages witnessed an agricultural revolution, a commercial revolution, the rebirth of towns, and the rise of an enterprising and dynamic middle class.

Offensives against the Muslims—in Spain, in Sicily, and in the Holy Land—demonstrated Europe's growing might and self-confidence. Reform movements strengthened the bonds between the church and the people and increased the power of the papacy. During the High Middle Ages the pope, as Christ's deputy, sought to direct, if not rule, all Christendom. European economic and religious vitality was paralleled by a cultural flowering in philosophy, literature, and the visual arts. The civilization of Latin Christendom had entered its golden age.

ECONOMIC EXPANSION: AGRICULTURAL IMPROVEMENTS, REVIVAL OF TRADE, AND GROWTH OF TOWNS

During the Middle Ages, important advances were made in agriculture—the heavy plow, the collar harness, the windmill, and the three-field system. The heavy plow, which cut deeply into the soil, enabled farmers to cultivate land that had offered too much resistance to the light plow. The old yoke harness worked well with oxen, but it tended to choke horses—and horses, because

Confirmation of the Rule of Saint Francis

Francis wandered into villages and towns, preaching, healing, and befriending the poor, the helpless, and the sick. The saintly Francis soon attracted disciples, who followed in their leader's footsteps. In 1209, he wrote a short rule, which was accepted by Pope Innocent III three years later.

(Scala/Art Resource, NY)

* The Magyars, originally from western Asia, had established themselves on the plains of the Danube; their horsemen launched lightning raids into northern Italy, western Germany, and parts of France. Defeated in Germany in 933 and again in 955, the Magyars withdrew to what is now Hungary; they ceased their raids and adopted Christianity.

Map 10.1 The Holy Roman Empire, c. 1200 Frederick Barbarossa tried to use the feudal bond to tie the different provinces to the imperial monarchy.

they move faster and have greater stamina than oxen, are more valuable for agricultural work. In the old, widely used two-field system, half the land was planted in autumn with winter wheat, whereas the other half was left fallow to restore its fertility. In the new three-field system, one-third of the land was planted in autumn with winter wheat, a second third was planted the following spring with oats and vegetables, and the last third remained fallow. The advantages of the three-field system were that two-thirds of the land was farmed and only one-third was left unused.

By the end of the thirteenth century, medieval agriculture had reached a technical level far superior to that of the ancient world. Higher agricultural production reduced the number of deaths from starvation and dietary disease and thus contributed to a population increase. Soon the farmlands of a manorial village could not support its

growing population. Consequently, peasants had to look beyond their immediate surroundings and colonize trackless wastelands. Lords vigorously promoted this conversion of uncultivated soil into agricultural land because it increased their incomes. Almost everywhere, peasants were draining swamps, clearing forests, and establishing new villages. Their endeavors during the eleventh and twelfth centuries brought vast areas of Europe under cultivation for the first time. New agricultural land was also acquired through expansion, the most notable example being the organized settlement of lands to the east by German colonists. Surplus food and the increase in population freed people to work at nonfarming occupations, making possible the expansion of trade and the revival of town life.

In the eleventh century, sea forces of Italian trading cities cleared the Mediterranean of Muslim fleets that preyed on Italian shipping. As in Roman times, goods could circulate once again from one end of the sea to the other. The principal arteries of trade flowed between the eastern Mediterranean and the Italian cities; between Scandinavia and the Atlantic coast; between northern France, Flanders, and England; and from the Baltic Sea in the north to the Black Sea and Constantinople via Russian rivers. In the twelfth and thirteenth centuries, local, regional, and long-distance trade gained such momentum that some historians describe the period as a commercial revolution that surpassed the commercial activity of the Roman Empire during the Pax Romana.

In the eleventh century, towns emerged anew throughout Europe, and in the twelfth, they became active centers of commercial and intellectual life. One reason for town growth was the increased food supply stemming from advances in agricultural technology. Surplus farm production meant that the countryside could support an urban population of artisans and professionals. Another reason for the rise of urban centers was the expansion of trade. Towns emerged in locations that were natural for trade: seacoasts, riverbanks, crossroads, and market sites.

Towns were a new and revolutionary force—socially, economically, and culturally. A new class of merchants and craftspeople came into being. This new class—the middle class—was made up of those who, unlike the lords and serfs, were not affiliated with the land. The townsman was a new man with a different value system from that of the lord, the serf, and the clergyman.

Merchants and artisans organized *guilds* to protect their members from outside competition. The merchant guild in a town prevented outsiders from doing much business. A craftsman who was new to a town had to be admitted to the guild of his trade before he could open a shop. Competition between members of the same guild was discouraged. To prevent one guild member from making significantly more money than another, a guild required its members to work the same number of hours, pay employees the same wages, produce goods of equal quality, and charge customers a just price. These rules were strictly enforced.

Women took an active part in the economic life of towns, working with men, usually their husbands, in the various crafts—as cobblers, tailors, hatters, bakers, goldsmiths, and so forth. Women brewed beer; made and sold charcoal; sold vegetables, fish, and poultry; and ran inns. In many towns, the wives and widows of master craftsmen were admitted to guilds. These guildswomen had many of the privileges of a master, including the right to train apprentices.

Townspeople, or *burghers,* refused to be treated as serfs bound to a lord and liable for personal services and customary dues. The burghers wanted to travel, trade, marry, and dispose of their property as they pleased; they wanted to make their own laws and levy their own taxes. Sometimes by fighting, but more often by payments of money, the townspeople obtained charters from the lords giving them the right to set up their own councils. These assemblies passed laws, collected taxes, and formed courts that enforced the laws. Towns became more or less self-governing city–states, the first since Greco-Roman days.

In a number of ways, towns loosened the hold of lords on serfs. Seeking freedom and fortune, serfs fled to the new towns, where, according to custom, lords could no longer reclaim them after a year and a day. Enterprising serfs earned money by selling food to the townspeople. When they acquired a sufficient sum, they bought their freedom from lords, who needed cash to pay for goods bought from merchants. Lords increasingly began to accept fixed cash payments from serfs in place of labor services or foodstuffs. As serfs met their obligations to lords with money, they gradually became rent-paying tenants and, in time, were no longer bound to the lord's land. The manorial system of personal relations and mutual obligations was disintegrating.

The activities of townspeople made them a new breed; they engaged in business and had money and freedom. Their world was the market rather than the church, the castle, or the manor. Townspeople were freeing themselves from the prejudices both of feudal aristocrats, who considered trade and manual work degrading, and of the clergy, who cursed the pursuit of riches as an obstacle to salvation. The townspeople were critical, dynamic, and progressive—a force for change. Medieval towns nurtured the origins of the bourgeoisie (literally, "citizens of the burg," the walled town), the urban middle class, which would play a crucial role in modern European history.

THE RISE OF STATES

The revival of trade and the growth of towns were signs of the vitality of Latin Christendom. Another sign of strength was the greater order and security provided by the emergence of states. Aided by educated and trained officials who enforced royal law, tried people in royal courts, and collected royal taxes, kings expanded their territory and slowly fashioned strong central governments. These developments laid the foundations of European states. Not all areas followed the same pattern. Whereas England and France achieved a large measure of unity during the Middle Ages, Germany and Italy remained divided into numerous independent territories.

England

In 1066, the Normans—those Northmen who had first raided and then later settled in France—conquered Anglo-Saxon England. Determined to establish effective control over his new kingdom, William the Conqueror (1027–1087), duke of Normandy, made certain that no feudal baron had enough land or soldiers to threaten his power. Because he had conquered England in one stroke, his successors did not have to travel the long, painful road to national unity that French monarchs had to take.

A crucial development in shaping national unity was the emergence of *common law.* During the reigns of Henry I (1100–1135) and Henry II (1154–1189), royal judges traveled to different parts of the kingdom. Throughout England, important cases began to be tried in the king's court rather than in local courts, thereby increasing royal power. The decisions of royal judges were recorded and used as guides for future cases. In this way, a law common to the whole land gradually came to prevail over the customary law of a specific locality. Because common law applied to all England, it served as a force for unity. It also provided a fairer system of justice. Common law remains the foundation of the English legal system and the legal systems of lands settled by English people, including the United States.

Henry II made trial by jury a regular procedure for many cases that were heard in the king's court, thus laying the foundations of the modern judicial system. Twelve men familiar with the facts of the case appeared before the king's justices and under oath were asked if the plaintiff's statement was true. The justices based their decisions on the answers.

King John (1199–1216) inadvertently precipitated a situation that led to another step in the political development of England. Fighting a costly and losing war with the king of France, John coerced his vassals into giving him more and more revenue; he had also punished some vassals without a proper trial. In 1215, the angry barons rebelled and compelled John to fix his seal to a document called the *Magna Carta,* or Great Charter. The Magna Carta is celebrated as the root of the unique English respect for basic rights and liberties. Although essentially a feudal document directed against a king who had violated the rights of feudal barons, the Magna Carta stated certain

principles that could be interpreted more widely.

Over the centuries, these principles were expanded to protect the liberties of the English against governmental oppression. The Magna Carta stated that no unusual feudal dues "shall be imposed in our kingdom except by the common consent of our kingdom." In time, this right came to mean that the king could not levy taxes without the consent of Parliament, the governmental body that represents the English people. The Magna Carta also provided that "no freeman shall be taken or imprisoned . . . save by the lawful judgment of his peers or by the law of the land." The barons who drew up the document had intended it to mean that they must be tried by fellow barons. As time passed, these words were regarded as a guarantee of trial by jury for all men, a prohibition against arbitrary arrest, and a command to dispense justice fully, freely, and equally. Implied in the Magna Carta is the idea that the king cannot rule as he pleases but must govern according to the law—that not even the king can violate the law of the nation. Centuries afterward, when Englishmen sought to limit the king's power, they would interpret the Magna Carta in this way.

By the thirteenth century, it became accepted custom that the king should not decide major issues without consulting the leading nobles and bishops, who assembled in the Great Council. Lesser nobility and townspeople also began to be summoned to meet with the king. These two groups were eventually called the House of Lords (bishops and nobles) and the House of Commons (knights and burghers). Thus, the English Parliament evolved; by the mid-fourteenth century, it had become a permanent institution of government. Frequently in need of money but unable to levy new taxes without the approval of Parliament, the king had to turn to that body for help. Over the centuries, Parliament would use this control over money matters to increase its power. The tradition grew that the power to govern rested not with the king alone, but with the king and Parliament together.

During the Middle Ages, England became a centralized and unified state. The king, however, did not have unlimited power; he was not above the law. The rights of the people were protected by certain principles implicit in the common law, the Magna Carta, and the emergence of Parliament.

France

In 987, the great lords of France chose Hugh Capet (987–996), the count of Paris, as king. Because many great lords held territories far larger than those of Hugh, the French king did not seem a threat to noble power. But Hugh strengthened the French monarchy by having the lords also elect his son as his coruler. This practice continued until it became understood that the crown would remain with the Capetian family.

In the twelfth and thirteenth centuries, the king's power steadily increased. A decisive figure in the expansion of royal power was Philip Augustus (1180–1223). Philip struck successfully at King John of England (of Magna Carta fame), who held more territory as feudal lord in France than Philip did. By stripping King John of most of his French territory (Normandy, Anjou, and much of Aquitaine), Philip trebled the size of his kingdom and became stronger than any French lord.

Departing from feudal precedent, kings issued ordinances for the entire realm without seeking the consent of their vassals and added to their lands through warfare and marriage. They also devised new ways of raising money, including taxing the clergy. A particularly effective way of increasing the monarch's power was by extending royal justice; many cases previously tried in lords' courts were transferred to the king's court.

By the end of the Middle Ages, French kings had succeeded in creating a unified state. But regional and local loyalties remained strong and persisted for centuries. Whereas the basis for limited monarchy had been established in England, no comparable checks on the king's power developed in France.

Germany

After the destruction of Charlemagne's empire, its German territories were broken into large duchies. Following an ancient German practice, the ruling dukes elected one of their own as king. The German king, however, had little authority outside his own duchy. Some German kings tried not to antagonize the dukes, but Otto the Great was determined to control them. He entered into an alliance with German bishops and archbishops, who could provide him with fighting men and trained administrators—a policy continued by his successors. In 962, emulating the coronation of Charlemagne, the pope crowned Otto "Emperor of the Romans." (Later the title would be changed to Holy Roman Emperor.)

Otto and his successors wanted to dominate Italy and the pope—an ambition that embroiled the Holy Roman emperor in a life-and-death struggle with the papacy. The papacy allied itself with the German dukes and the Italian cities, enemies of the emperor. The intervention in papal and Italian politics was the principal reason that German territories did not achieve unity in the Middle Ages.

MEDIEVAL RELIGION: DEVOTION, POWER, HERESY

In the High Middle Ages, a growing spiritual vitality accompanied economic recovery and the increased political stability. The church tried with great determination to make society follow divine standards; that is, it tried to shape all institutions and cultural expressions according to a comprehensive Christian outlook.

As the sole interpreters of God's revelation and the sole ministers of his *sacraments*—the sacred rites by which God was said to confer his grace—the clergy imposed and supervised the moral outlook of Christendom. Divine grace was channeled through the sacraments, which could be administered only by the clergy, the indispensable intermediary between the individual and God. The church could impose the penalty of *excommunication* (expulsion from the church and denial of the sacraments, without which there could be no salvation) on those who resisted its authority.

The Sacraments

Through the seven sacraments, the community of the church encompassed the individual from birth to death. The rite of baptism cleansed the individual—usually an infant—of the stain of original sin. Confirmation granted the young adult additional grace to that received at baptism. Matrimony made marriage a holy union. Extreme unction was administered to the dying in an effort to remove the remnants of sin. The sacrament of the Eucharist, derived from the Gospel accounts of Jesus' Last Supper with his disciples, took place within a liturgical service, the Mass. In a solemn ceremony, the bread and wine were miraculously transformed into the substance of the body and blood of Christ, which the priest administered, allowing the faithful to partake of Christ's saving grace. The sacrament of penance required sinners to show sorrow for their sins, to confess them to a priest, and to perform an act of penance: prayer, fasting, almsgiving, or a pilgrimage to a holy shrine. Through the priest, the sinner could receive absolution and be rescued from spending eternity in hell. This sacrament enabled the church to enforce its moral standards throughout Latin Christendom. The final sacrament, ordination, was used in consecrating men to serve as clergy.

The Gregorian Reform

By the tenth century, the church was western Europe's leading landholder, owning perhaps a third of the land in Italy and vast properties in other lands. However, the papacy was in no position to exercise commanding leadership over Latin Christendom. The office of pope had fallen under the domination of aristocratic families; they conspired and on occasion murdered in order to place one of their own on the wealthy and powerful throne of Saint Peter. As the papacy became a prize for Rome's leading families, it was not at all unusual for popes themselves to be involved in conspiracies and assassinations. Also weakening the authority of the papacy were local lords, who dominated churches and monasteries by appointing bishops and abbots and by collecting the income from church taxes. These bishops and abbots, appointed by lords for political reasons, lacked the spiritual devotion to maintain high standards of discipline among the priests and monks.

What raised the power of the papacy to unprecedented heights was the emergence of a reform movement, particularly in French and German monasteries. High-minded monks called for a reawakening of spiritual fervor and the elimination of moral laxity among the clergy. They particularly denounced the concern for worldly goods, the taking of mistresses, and the diminishing commitment to the Benedictine rule. Of the many monasteries that took part in this reform movement, the Benedictine monks of Cluny, in Burgundy, France, were the most influential. Many monks were also engaged in preserving the Bible and the writings of the Church Fathers (Figure 10.1) by copying the works by hand—letter by letter, line by line—and ornamenting them through a process called manuscript illumination (discussed in the next chapter).

In the middle of the eleventh century, popes came under the influence of the monastic reformers. In 1059, a special synod, convened by the reform-minded Pope Nicholas II, moved to end the interference of Roman nobles and German Holy Roman emperors in choosing the pope. Henceforth, a select group of clergymen in Rome, called cardinals, would be responsible for picking a new pontiff.

The reform movement found its most zealous exponent in the person of Hildebrand, who became Pope Gregory VII in 1073. For Gregory, human society was part of a divinely ordered universe, governed by God's universal law. As the supreme spiritual leader of Christendom, the pope was charged with the mission of establishing a Christian society on earth. As successor to Saint Peter, the pope had the final word on matters of faith and doctrine. All bishops came under his authority; so did kings, whose powers should be used for Christian ends. The pope was responsible for instructing rulers in the proper use of their God-given powers, and kings had the solemn duty to obey these instructions. If

the king failed in his Christian duty, the pope could deny him his right to rule. Responsible for implementing God's law, the pope could never take a subordinate position to kings.

Like no other pope before him, Gregory VII made a determined effort to assert the preeminence of the papacy over both the church hierarchy and secular rulers. This determination led to a bitter struggle between the papacy and the German monarch and future Holy Roman emperor Henry IV. The dispute was a dramatic confrontation between two competing versions of the relationship between secular and spiritual authority.

Through his reforms, Gregory VII intended to improve the moral quality of the clergy and to liberate the church from all control by secular authorities. He forbade priests who had wives or concubines to celebrate Mass, deposed clergy who had bought their offices, excommunicated bishops and abbots who received their estates from a lay lord, and expelled from the church lay lords who invested bishops with their office. The appointment of bishops, Pope Gregory insisted, should be controlled by the church.

This last point touched off the conflict, called the *Investiture Controversy,* between Henry IV and Pope Gregory. Bishops served a dual function. On the one hand, they belonged to the spiritual community of the church; on the other, as members of the nobility and holders of estates, they were also integrated into the feudal order.

Seeking allies in the conflict with feudal nobility in earlier times, German kings had made vassals of the upper clergy. In return for a fief, bishops had agreed to provide troops for a monarch in his struggle against the lords. But if kings had no control over the appointment of bishops—in accordance with Pope Gregory's view—they would lose the allegiance, military support, and financial assistance of their most important allies. Henry IV regarded Gregory VII as a fanatic who trampled on custom, meddled in German state affairs, and challenged legitimate rulers established by God, thereby threatening to subordinate kingship to the papacy.

With the approval of the German bishops, Henry called for Pope Gregory to descend from the throne of Saint Peter. Gregory in turn excommunicated Henry and deposed him as king. German lands were soon embroiled in a civil war, as German lords used the quarrel to strike at Henry's power. Finally, Henry's troops crossed the Alps, successfully attacked Rome, and installed a new pope, who crowned Henry emperor of the Romans. Gregory died in exile in 1085.

In 1122, the papacy and Emperor Henry V reached a compromise. Bishops were to be elected exclusively by the church and to be invested with the staff and the ring—symbols of spiritual power—by

Figure 10.1 School of Bologna manuscript illumination After a text had been transcribed, it could then be illuminated. This was accomplished by applying decoration in the spaces left blank by the scribe. One illuminator was charged with the pen decoration, executed with colored inks. Another was the overseer of all the painted ornamentation, including borders, frames, and decorated letters. The amount of time required to illuminate a manuscript was dependent on the size of the undertaking and how many layers of color were used, because each fresh layer required its own drying time. *(Staatliche Museen zu Berlin/Bildarchiv Preussischer Kulturbesitz)*

the archbishop, not the king. This change signified that the bishop owed his role as spiritual leader to the church only. But the king would grant the bishop the scepter, to indicate that the bishop was also the recipient of a fief and the king's vassal, owing feudal obligations to the crown. This compromise, called the *Concordat of Worms,* recognized the dual function of the bishop as a spiritual leader in the church and a feudal landowner. Similar settlements had been reached with the kings of France and England several years earlier.

The conflict between the papacy and the German rulers continued after the Concordat of Worms—a contest for supremacy between the heir of Saint Peter and the heir of Charlemagne. German monarchs wanted to control the papacy and the prosperous northern Italian cities. War in Italy weakened German monarchs, enabling German princes to strengthen themselves at the expense of the monarchy, thereby continuing to preclude German unity.

The Crusades

Like the movement for spiritual renewal associated with the Cluniac reformers, the *Crusades*—

wars to regain the Holy Land from the Muslims—were an outpouring of Christian zeal and an attempt by the papacy to assert its preeminence. Along with the renewal of commerce and the growth of towns, the Crusades signaled the increased vitality and self-confidence of western Europe. The victims of earlier Muslim attacks, Latin Christians now took the offensive.

Seeking to regain lands taken from Byzantium by the Seljuk Turks, the Byzantine emperor Alexius appealed to the West for mercenaries. Pope Urban II, at the Council of Clermont (in France) in 1095, exaggerated the danger confronting Eastern Christianity. He called for a holy crusade against the heathen Turks, whom he accused of defiling and destroying Christian churches. A Christian army, mobilized by the papacy to defend the faith and to regain the Holy Land from nonbelievers, accorded with the papal concept of a just war; it would channel the endemic violence of Europe's warrior class in a Christian direction.

What motivated the knights and others who responded to Urban's appeal? No doubt, the Crusaders regarded themselves as armed pilgrims dedicated to rescuing holy places from the hated

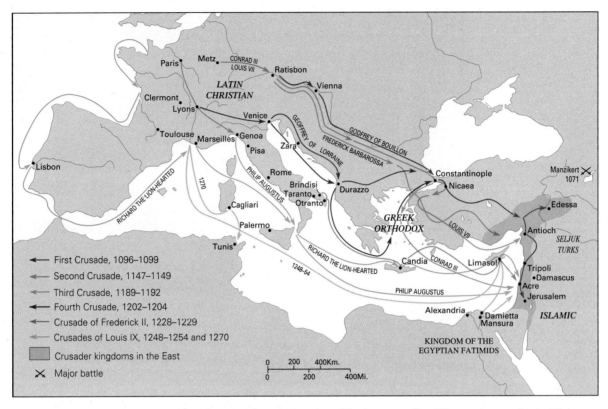

Map 10.2 **The Crusades, 1095–1270** The long-standing Western interest in the Holy Land is vividly illustrated by the Crusades. Note the numerous routes taken, lands traversed, destinations attained, and points of cultural encounter.

Muslims. Moreover, Urban declared that participation in a crusade was itself an act of penance, an acceptable way of demonstrating sorrow for sin. To the warrior nobility, a crusade was a great adventure, promising land, glory, and plunder, but it was also an opportunity to remit sins by engaging in a holy war. The enthusiasm with which knights became Christian warriors revealed to what extent Christian principles had permeated the warrior mentality of the nobles.

Stirred by popular preachers, the common people also became gripped by the crusading spirit. The most remarkable of the evangelists was Peter the Hermit. Swayed by this old man's eloquence, thousands of poor people abandoned their villages and joined Peter's march to Jerusalem. After reaching Constantinople, Peter's recruits crossed into Turkish territory, where they were massacred.

An army of Christian knights also departed for Constantinople. In June 1099, three years after leaving Europe, this army stood outside the walls of Jerusalem. Using siege weapons, it broke into the city and slaughtered the Muslim and Jewish inhabitants. Besides capturing Jerusalem, the Crusaders carved out four principalities in the Near East. Never resigned to the establishment of Christian states in their midst, Muslim leaders called for a jihad, or holy war. Other crusades were called to

quell the resurgent forces of Islam. But in 1291, almost two centuries after Pope Urban's appeal, the last Christian strongholds in the Near East fell.

The Crusades increased the wealth of the Italian cities that furnished transportation for the Crusaders and benefited from the increased trade with the East. They may have contributed to the decline of feudalism and the strengthening of monarchy because many lords were killed in battle or squandered their wealth financing expeditions to the Holy Land. Over the centuries, some have praised the Crusades for inspiring idealism and heroism. Others, however, have castigated the movement for corrupting the Christian spirit and unleashing religious intolerance and fanaticism—including the massacre of Jews in the Rhineland and of Muslims and Jews in Jerusalem—which would lead to strife in future centuries.

Dissenters and Reformers

Freedom of religion is a modern concept; it was totally alien to the medieval outlook. Regarding itself as the possessor and guardian of divine truth, the church felt a profound obligation to purge Christendom of heresy—beliefs that challenged Christian orthodoxy. To the church, heretics had committed treason against God and were carriers of a deadly infection. Heresy was the work of Satan; lured by false ideas, people might abandon the true faith and deny themselves salvation. In the eyes of the church, heretics not only obstructed individual salvation, but also undermined the foundations of society.

To compel obedience, the church used its power of excommunication. An excommunicated person could not receive the sacraments or attend church services—fearful punishments in an age of faith. In dealing with a recalcitrant ruler, the church could declare an interdict on his territory, which in effect denied the ruler's subjects the sacraments (although exceptions could be made). The church hoped that the pressure exerted by an aroused populace would compel the offending ruler to mend his ways.

The church also conducted heresy trials. Before the thirteenth century, local bishops were responsible for finding heretics and putting them on trial. In 1233, the papacy established the *Inquisition,* a court specially designed to fight heresy. The accused were presumed guilty until proven innocent; they were not told the names of their accusers, nor could they have legal defense. To wrest a confession from the accused, torture (which had been sanctioned by Roman law) was permitted. Those who persisted in their beliefs might be turned over to the civil authorities to be burned at the stake.

THE WALDENSIANS Dissent in the Middle Ages was often reformist in character. Inspired by the Gospels, reformers criticized the church for its wealth and involvement in worldly affairs. They called for a return to the simpler, purer life of Jesus and the Apostles.

In their zeal to emulate the moral purity and material poverty of the first followers of Jesus, these reform-minded dissenters attacked ecclesiastical authority. The Waldensians, followers of Peter Waldo, a rich merchant of Lyons, were a case in point. In the 1170s, Peter distributed his property to the poor and attracted both male and female supporters. Like their leader, they committed themselves to poverty and to preaching the Gospel in the vernacular, or native tongue, rather than in the church's Latin, which many Christians did not understand.

The Waldensians, believing that they were the true Christians faithful to the spirit of the Sermon on the Mount and preservers of the apostolic church, considered the contemporary church as the community of Satan. They asserted that all Christians were possessed of the Holy Spirit, not just the clergy, and that they could preach to one another. Repelled by Waldensian attacks against the immorality of the clergy and by the fact that these laypeople were preaching the Gospel without the permission of ecclesiastical authorities, the church condemned the movement as heretical. Despite persecution, however, the Waldensians continued to survive as a group in northern Italy, and during the period of the Reformation, the Waldensians became Protestant.

THE CATHARI The term *Cathari* comes from the Greek word *katharoi* (the pure ones). This belief represented a curious mixture of Eastern religious movements that had competed with Christianity in the days of the Roman Empire. Cathari tenets differed considerably from those of the church. The Cathari believed in an eternal conflict between the forces of the god of good and those of the god of evil. Because the evil god, whom they identified with the God of the Old Testament, had created the world, this earthly home was evil. The soul, spiritual in nature, was good, but it was trapped in wicked flesh.

The Cathari taught that, because the flesh is evil, Christ would not have taken a human form; hence, he could not have suffered on the cross or have been resurrected. Nor could God have issued forth from the evil flesh of the Virgin. According to Catharism, Jesus was not God but an angel. In order to enslave people, the evil god created the church, which demonstrated its wickedness by pursuing power and wealth. Repudiating the church, the Cathari organized their own ecclesiastical hierarchy.

The center for the Catharist heresy was at Albi, in southern France, where a strong tradition of protest existed against the moral laxity and materialism of the clergy. In 1169, the Council of Tours renamed the Cathari Albigensians. When the Albigensians did not submit to peaceful persuasion, Innocent III (1198–1216) called on kings and lords to exterminate Albigensianism with the sword (Figure 10.2). Lasting from 1208 to 1229, the war against the Albigensians was marked by brutality and fanaticism. Under Innocent's successor, Dominican and Franciscan inquisitors completed the task of exterminating them.

THE FRANCISCANS AND THE DOMINICANS Driven by a zeal for reform, devout laypeople condemned the clergy for moral abuses. Sometimes, their piety and resentment exploded into heresy; at other times, it was channeled into movements that served the church. Such was the case with the two great orders of friars, the Franciscans and the Dominicans.

Like Peter Waldo, Saint Francis of Assisi (c. 1181–1226) (Figure 10.3) came from a wealthy merchant family. After undergoing an intense religious experience, Francis abandoned his posses-

Figure 10.2 Expulsion of the Albigensians manuscript Because the Albigensians would not submit to peaceful persuasion, Innocent III (1198–1216) called on kings and lords to exterminate them, using the sword. Characterized by fanaticism and brutality, this task was accomplished between 1208 and 1229. *(British Library)*

sions and devoted his life to imitating Christ. Dressed as a beggar, he wandered into villages and towns, preaching, healing, and befriending the poor, the helpless, the sick, and even lepers, whom everyone feared to approach. In 1209, Francis wrote a short rule, which was accepted by Pope Innocent III in 1212 (see chapter opening). The saintly Francis soon attracted disciples, called *Little Brothers,* who followed in their leader's footsteps.

As the *Franciscans* grew in popularity, the papacy exercised greater control over their activities. In time, the order was transformed from a spontaneous movement of inspired laymen into an organized agent of papal policy. The Franciscans served the church as teachers and missionaries in eastern Europe, North Africa, the Near East, and China. The papacy set aside Francis's prohibition against the Brothers owning churches, houses, and lands corporately. His desire to keep the movement a lay order was abandoned when the papacy granted the Brothers the right to hear confession. Francis's opposition to formal learning as irrelevant to preaching Gospel love was rejected when the movement began to urge university education for its members. Those who protested against these changes as a repudiation of Francis's spirit

were persecuted, and a few were even burned at the stake as heretics.

The Dominican order was founded by Saint Dominic (c. 1170–1221), a Spanish nobleman, who had preached against the Cathari in southern France. Believing that those who were well versed in Christian teaching could best combat heresy, Dominic, unlike Francis, insisted that his followers engage in study. Eventually, *Dominicans* became some of the leading theologians in the universities. Like the Franciscans, they went out into the world to preach the Gospel and to proselytize. Dominican friars became the chief operators of the Inquisition. For their zeal in fighting heresy, they were known as the "hounds of the Lord."

Innocent III: The Apex of Papal Power

During the pontificate of Innocent III (1198–1216), papal theocracy reached its zenith. More than any earlier pope, Innocent made the papacy the center of European political life; in the tradition of Gregory VII, he forcefully asserted the theory of papal monarchy. As head of the church, Vicar of Christ, and successor of Saint Peter, Innocent claimed the authority to intervene in the internal affairs of secular rulers when they threatened the good order of Christendom. According to Innocent, the pope, "lower than God but higher than man . . . judges all and is judged by no one."[2]

Innocent applied these principles of papal supremacy in his dealings with the princes of Europe and called the Fourth Crusade against the Muslims as well as a crusade against the heretical Cathari. The culminating expression of Innocent's supremacy was the Fourth Lateran Council, convened in 1215. Comprising some twelve hundred

Figure 10.3 Saint Francis of Assisi fresco Francis came from a wealthy merchant family, but after undergoing an intense religious experience, he abandoned his possessions and devoted his entire life to imitating Christ. *(Scala/Art Resource, NY)*

clergy and representatives of secular rulers, the council issued several far-reaching decrees. It maintained that the Eastern Orthodox church was subordinate to the Roman Catholic church. It prohibited the state from taxing the clergy and declared laws detrimental to the church null and void. It also made bishops responsible for ferreting out heretics in their dioceses and ordered secular authorities to punish convicted heretics. Furthermore, the council insisted on high standards of behavior for the clergy and required each Catholic to confess his or her sins to a priest at least once a year.

Christians and Jews

In their relations with heretics, pagans, and Muslims, medieval Christians demonstrated a narrow and hostile attitude, which ran counter to the Gospel message that all human beings were children of God and that Christ had suffered for all humanity. Muslims were seen, in the words of Pope Urban II, as a "vile breed," "infidels," and "enemies of God."

Medieval Christians also showed hatred for Jews—a visibly alien group in a society dominated by the Christian worldview. In 1096, bands of Crusaders massacred Jews in French and German towns. In 1290, Jews were expelled from England, and in 1306 from France. Between 1290 and 1293, expulsions, massacres, and forced conversions led to the virtual disappearance of a centuries-old Jewish community life in southern Italy. In Germany, savage riots periodically led to the torture and murder of Jews.

Several factors contributed to anti-Jewish feelings during the Middle Ages. To medieval Christians, the refusal of the Jews to embrace Christianity was an act of wickedness, particularly because the church taught that the Old Testament had prophesied the coming of Christ. Related to this prejudice was the portrayal of the Crucifixion in the Gospels. In the minds of medieval Christians, the crime of deicide—the killing of God—eternally tainted the Jews as a people. The flames of hatred were fanned by the absurd allegation that Jews, made bloodthirsty by the spilling of Christ's blood, tortured and murdered Christians, particularly children, to obtain blood for ritual purposes. This blood libel was widely believed and incited numerous riots, which led to the murder, torture, and expulsion of countless Jews, despite the fact that popes condemned the charge as groundless.

The role of Jews as moneylenders also provoked animosity toward them. Increasingly excluded from international trade and most professions, barred from the guilds, and in some areas from landholding as well, Jews found that virtually the only means of livelihood open to them was moneylending. This activity, which was in theory forbidden to Christians, aroused the hatred of individual peasants, clergy, lords, and kings, who did the borrowing.

The policy of the church toward the Jews was that they should not be harmed, but that they should live in humiliation, a fitting punishment for their act of deicide and continued refusal to embrace Christianity. Thus, the Fourth Lateran Council barred Jews from public office, required them to wear a distinguishing badge on their clothing, and ordered them to remain off the streets during Christian festivals. Christian art, literature, and religious instruction depicted the Jews in a derogatory manner, often identifying them with the Devil, who was very real and very terrifying to medieval Christians. Such people deserved no mercy, reasoned medieval Christians. Indeed, nothing was too bad for them. Deeply etched into the minds and hearts of Christians, the distorted image of the Jew as a contemptible creature persisted in the European mentality into the twentieth century and has not entirely disappeared.

Despite their precarious position, medieval Jews maintained their faith, expanded their tradition of biblical and legal scholarship, and developed a flourishing Hebrew literature. The work of Jewish translators, doctors, and philosophers contributed substantially to the flowering of medieval culture in the High Middle Ages.

The foremost Jewish scholar of the Middle Ages, Moses ben Maimon (1135–1204), also called by the Greek name Maimonides, was born in Córdoba, Spain, then under Muslim rule. Maimonides received an excellent orthodox Jewish education, as well as training in law, medicine, and philosophy. When a fanatical Muslim sect from North Africa invaded Spain and persecuted Jews, his family fled, and Maimonides eventually settled in Egypt, where he became physician to the sultan. During his lifetime, Maimonides achieved fame as a philosopher, theologian, mathematician, and physician. He was recognized as the leading Jewish sage of his day, and Christian and Muslim thinkers respected his writings as well.

In addition to his popular Jewish devotional literature, Maimonides compiled a major philosophical codification of Jewish law, written in Arabic, called *The Guide for the Perplexed.* Like Christian and Muslim philosophers, Maimonides sought to harmonize faith with reason, to reconcile the Hebrew Scriptures and the Talmud (Jewish biblical commentary) with Greek philosophy. Maimonides believed in the rationality of God and that it was a person's duty to connect with God's reason. Nevertheless, he also emphasized the limits of human rea-

son—no one can know what it is like to *be* God and no one can know, with certainty, God's plan for the natural world. Therefore, each individual must be open to revelation and faith. In his writings on ethical themes, Maimonides demonstrated piety, wisdom, and humanity, as is evident in the concluding chapter of *The Guide for the Perplexed,* where he discusses the four perfections to be found in humans—possessions, physical well-being, moral virtues, and rational virtues. He describes the "ultimate perfection":

> It is clear that the perfection of man that may truly be gloried in is the one acquired by him who has achieved, in a measure corresponding to his capacity, apprehension of Him [God]. . . . The way of life of such an individual, after he has achieved this apprehension, will always have in view *loving-kindness, righteousness,* and *judgment,* through assimilation to His action, may He be exalted.[3]

Maimonides also reveals his humanity in his discussion of charity. This system of charity was adopted by Jews in several Palestinian and Babylonian cities.

> There are eight degrees in alms-giving, one higher than the other: Supreme above all is to give assistance to a co-religionist who has fallen on evil times by presenting him with a gift or loan, or entering into partnership with him, or procuring him work, thereby helping him to become self-supporting. Inferior to this is giving charity to the poor in such a way that the giver and recipient are unknown to each other. This is indeed, the performance of a commandment from disinterested motives; and it is exemplified by the Institution of the Chamber of The Silent which existed in the Temple,* where the righteous secretly deposited their alms and the respectable poor were secretly assisted.[4]

REVIVAL OF LEARNING

Europe in the High Middle Ages showed considerable vitality. The population grew, long-distance trade revived, new towns emerged, states started to take shape, and papal power increased. The culminating expression of this recovery and resurgence was the cultural flowering in philosophy, the visual arts, and literature. Creative intellects achieved on a cultural level what the papacy accomplished on an institutional level: the integration of life around a Christian viewpoint. The

---

* The Temple to which Maimonides refers was the Temple in Jerusalem, destroyed by the Romans in A.D. 70.

LU YU: CHINESE BARD

THE ACKNOWLEDGED MASTER OF LYRIC POETRY IN CHINA during the twelfth century was Lu Yu (1125–1210). In nearly ten thousand poems, he covered a wide variety of themes, including romance and commonplace events. Around the age of twenty, Lu married his childhood sweetheart, but because his mother found the wife unacceptable, she forced him to divorce. Many years after the event, Lu composed a poem about his lost love: "In a boat on a summer evening, I heard the cry of a water bird. It was very sad and seemed to be saying, 'Madam is cruel!' Moved, I wrote this poem."

A girl grows up hidden in far-off rooms,
no glimpse of what may lie beyond her wall and hedge.
Then she climbs the carriage, moves to her new lord's home;
father and mother become strangers to her then.
"I was stupid, to be sure, yet I knew
that Madam, my mother-in-law, must be obeyed.
Out of bed with the first cock's crowing,
I combed and bound my hair, put on blouse and skirt.
I did my work, tidied the hall, sprinkling and sweeping,
in the kitchen prepared their plate of food. . . .
When the least displeasure showed in Madam's face,
the sleeves of my robe were soon damp with tear stains.
My wish was that I might bear a son,
to see Madam dandle a grandson in her arms.
But those hopes in the end failed and came to nothing;
ill-fated, they made me the butt of slander.
Driven from the house, I didn't dare grumble,
only grieved that I'd betrayed Madam's kindness."
On the old road that runs along the rim of the swamp,
when fox fire glimmers through drizzling rain,
can you hear the voice crying "Madam is cruel?"
Surely it's the soul of the wife sent home.

In the poem "Written in a Carefree Mood" (1192), Lu described his good feelings on a spring day.

Old man pushing seventy,
in truth he acts like a little boy,
whooping with delight when he spies some mountain fruits,
laughing with joy, tagging after village mummers;[1]
with the others having fun stacking tiles to make a pagoda,
standing alone staring at his image in the jardiniere pool.
Tucked under his arm, a battered book to read,
just like the time he first set off for school.

[1] Villagers dressed up in costume who went from house to house early in the spring to drive out evil spirits.

Source: The Old Man Who Does as He Pleases: Selections from the Poetry and Prose of Lu Yu, trans. Burton Watson (New York: Columbia University Press, 1973), pp. 21, 26–27, 39.

High Middle Ages saw the restoration of some of the learning of the ancient world, the rise of universities, the emergence of an original form of architecture (the Gothic), and the erection of an imposing system of thought, called scholasticism. Medieval theologian–philosophers fashioned Christian teachings into an all-embracing philosophy, which represented the spiritual character of medieval civilization. They perfected what Christian thinkers in the Roman Empire had initiated and what the learned men of the Early Middle Ages were groping for: a synthesis of Greek philosophy and Christian revelation.

In the twelfth and thirteenth centuries, a rich civilization with a distinctive style united the educated elite in the lands from England to Sicily. Gothic cathedrals, an enduring testament to the creativity of the religious impulse, were erected throughout Europe. Universities sprang up in many cities. Roman authors were again read and their style imitated; the quality of written Latin— the language of the church, learning, and education—improved, and secular and religious poetry, both in Latin and in the vernacular, abounded. Roman law emerged anew in Italy, spread to northern Europe, and regained its importance (lost since Roman times) as worthy of study. Some key works of ancient Greece were translated into Latin and studied in universities. Employing the rational tradition of Greece, men of genius harmonized Christian doctrines and Greek philosophy. During this period the status and influence of learned men grew considerably.

Several conditions contributed to this cultural explosion, known as the Twelfth-Century Awakening. As attacks of Vikings, Muslims, and Magyars ended and kings and great lords imposed more order and stability, people found greater opportunities for travel and communication. The revival of trade and the growth of towns created a need for literacy and provided the wealth required to support learning. Increasing contact with Islamic and Byzantine cultures in Spain and Sicily led to the translation into Latin of ancient Greek works preserved by these Eastern civilizations. By preserving Greek philosophy and science—and by commenting creatively on these classical works—Islamic civilization acted as a bridge between antiquity and the cultural revival of the High Middle Ages. The Twelfth-Century Awakening was also kindled by the legacy of the Carolingian Renaissance, whose cultural lights had dimmed but never wholly vanished in the period of disorder after the dissolution of Charlemagne's empire.

In the Early Middle Ages, the principal educational centers were the monastic schools. During the twelfth century, cathedral schools in towns gained importance. Their teachers were paid a stipend by a local church and taught grammar, rhetoric, and logic. But the chief expression of expanding intellectual life was the university, a distinct creation of the Middle Ages.

The origins of the medieval university are obscure and varied. The first universities were not planned but grew spontaneously. They developed as students eager for knowledge and skills needed for high positions in government gathered around prominent teachers. The renewed importance of Roman law for business and politics, for example, drew students to Bologna to study with acknowledged masters.

The university was really a guild or corporation of masters or students who joined together to defend their interests against church or town authorities or the townspeople. A university might emerge when students united because of common needs, such as protection against townspeople who overcharged them for rooms and necessities. Organized into a body, students could also make demands on their instructors. At Bologna, professors faced fines for being absent or for giving lectures that drew fewer than five students; they were required to leave behind a deposit as security to ensure their return if they took a journey. A corporation of students formed the University at Bologna. The University of Paris, which evolved from the Cathedral School of Notre Dame, was the creation of a corporation of masters.

University students attended lectures, prepared for examinations, and earned degrees. They studied grammar, rhetoric, logic, arithmetic, geometry, astronomy, music, medicine, and when ready, Roman and church law and theology, which was considered the queen of the sciences. The curriculum relied heavily on Latin translations of ancient texts, chiefly the works of Aristotle. In mathematics and astronomy, students read Latin translations of Euclid and Ptolemy, whereas students of medicine studied the works of two great medical men of the ancient world, Hippocrates and Galen.

But sometimes students followed other pursuits. Instead of studying, they turned to drinking, gambling, and fighting. At Oxford University, it was reported that students "went through the streets with swords and bows and arrows and assaulted all who passed by."[5] Fathers complained that their sons preferred "play to work and strumming a guitar while the others are at their studies."[6] Students often faced financial problems, and they knew whom to ask for help: "Well-beloved father, to ease my debts . . . at the tavern, at the baker's, with the doctor . . . and to pay . . . the laundress and the barber, I send you word of greetings and of money."[7]

Universities performed a crucial function in the Middle Ages. Students learned the habit of reasoned argument. Universities trained professional secretaries and lawyers, who administered the affairs of church and state and of the growing cities; these institutions of learning also produced theologians and philosophers, who shaped the climate of public opinion. Because the curriculum and the texts studied were essentially the same in all lands, the learning disseminated by universities tightened the cultural bonds that united Christian Europe. Medieval universities established in the West a tradition of learning that has never died; there is direct continuity between the universities of our own day and the medieval ones.

PHILOSOPHY–THEOLOGY

Medieval philosophy, or *scholasticism,* applied reason to revelation. It explained and clarified Christian teachings by means of concepts and principles of logic derived from Greek philosophy. Scholastics tried to show that the teachings of faith, although not derived from reason, were not contrary to reason. They tried to prove through reason what they already held to be true through faith. For example, the existence of God and the immortality of the soul, which every Christian accepted on faith, could also, they thought, be demonstrated by reason. In struggling to harmonize faith with reason, medieval thinkers constructed an extraordinary synthesis of Christian revelation and Greek thought.

The scholastic masters used reason not to challenge but to serve faith: to elucidate, clarify, and buttress it. They did not break with the central concern of Christianity, that of earning God's grace and achieving salvation. Although this goal could be realized solely through faith, scholastic thinkers insisted that a science of nature did not obstruct the pursuit of grace and that philosophy could assist the devout in the contemplation of God. They did not reject Christian beliefs, which were beyond the grasp of human reason and therefore could not be deduced by rational argument. Instead, they held that such truths rested entirely on revelation and were to be accepted on faith. To medieval thinkers, reason did not have an independent existence but ultimately had to acknowledge a suprarational, superhuman standard of truth. They wanted rational thought to be directed by faith for Christian ends and guided by scriptural and ecclesiastical authority. Ultimately, faith had the final word.

Not all Christian thinkers welcomed the use of reason. Regarding Greek philosophy as an enemy of faith (Would not reason lead people to question belief in miracles?), a fabricator of heresies (Would not reason encourage disbelief in essential church teachings?), and an obstacle to achieving communion of the soul with God (Would not a deviation from church teachings, under the influence of pagan philosophy, deprive people of salvation?), conservative theologians opposed the use of reason to elucidate Christian revelation. For if reason could demonstrate the proof of Christian teachings, as its advocates insisted, it could also be used, warned conservatives, to challenge and reject those teachings. In a sense, the conservatives were right. By revitalizing Greek thought, medieval philosophy nurtured a powerful force, which would eventually shatter the medieval concepts of nature and society and weaken Christianity. Modern Western thought was created by thinkers who refused to subordinate reason to religious authority. Reason proved a double-edged sword: It both ennobled and undermined the medieval worldview.

Anselm

An early scholastic, Anselm (1033–1109) was abbot of the Benedictine monastery of Bec in Normandy. He used rational argument to serve the interests of faith. Like Augustine before him and other thinkers who followed him, Anselm said that faith was a precondition for understanding. Without belief there could be no proper knowledge. He developed philosophical proof for the existence of God. Anselm argued as follows: We can conceive of no being greater than God. But if God were to exist only in thought and not in actuality, his greatness would be limited; he would be less than perfect. Hence he exists. Anselm's motive and method reveal something about the essence of medieval philosophy. He does not begin as a modern might: "If it can be proven that God exists, I will adopt the creed of Christianity; if not, I will either deny God's existence (atheism) or reserve judgment (agnosticism)." Rather, Anselm accepts God's existence as an established fact because he believes what Holy Scripture says and what the church teaches. He then proceeds to employ logical argument to demonstrate that God can be known not only through faith but also through reason. He would never use reason to subvert what he knows to be true by faith. In general, this attitude would characterize later medieval thinkers, who also applied reason to faith.

Abelard

As a young teacher of theology at the Cathedral School of Notre Dame, Peter Abelard (1079–1142) acquired a reputation for brilliance and combativeness. He tutored Héloise, who lived with her uncle and guardian, Fulbert, a canon at Notre Dame. In Abelard's *Story of His Misfortunes,* he describes his fascination with Héloise's mind, his lust for her, and his unbounded confidence that he can lure her into his bed.

> In looks she did not rank lowest, while in the extent of her learning she stood supreme. A gift for letters is so rare in women that it added greatly to her charm and had won her renown throughout the realm. I considered all the usual attractions for a lover and decided she was the one to bring to my bed, confident that I should have an easy success; for at that time I had youth and exceptional good looks as well as my great reputation to recommend me, and feared no rebuff from any woman I might choose to honor with my love.[8]

Abelard describes the tutorial:

> Her studies allowed us to withdraw in private, as love desired, and then with our books open before us, more words of love than of our reading passed between us, and more kissing than teaching. My hands strayed oftener to her bosom than to the pages; love drew our eyes to look on each other more than reading kept them on our texts.[9]

Héloise had a child and later entered a nunnery; Abelard was castrated on orders of Fulbert and sought temporary refuge in a monastery. Héloise continued to express her love for Abelard, but ultimately she put the past behind her and learned to love Abelard as a brother in Christ. When Abelard died in 1142, Héloise sought a written absolution of their sins from the church, which she hung over his tomb. When Héloise died twenty-two years later, she was buried at his side. This affair, detailed in the letters the two exchanged, has become one of the great tragic romances in Western literature.

After resuming his career as a teacher in Paris, Abelard again had to seek refuge, this time for writing an essay on the Trinity that church officials found offensive. After further difficulties and flights, he again returned to Paris to teach dialectics. Not long afterward, his most determined opponent, Bernard of Clairvaux, accused Abelard of using the method of dialectical argument to attack faith. To Bernard, a monk and mystic, subjecting revealed truth to critical analysis was fraught with danger:

> [T]he deepest matters become the subject of undignified wrangling. . . . Virtues and vices are discussed with no trace of moral feelings, the sacraments of the Church with no evidence of faith, the mystery of the Holy Trinity with no spirit of humility or sobriety: all is presented in a distorted form, introduced in a way different from the one we learned and are used to.[10]

Hearkening to Bernard's powerful voice, the church condemned Abelard and confined him to a monastery for the rest of his days.

Abelard believed that it was important to apply reason to faith and that careful and constant questioning led to wisdom. Because all knowledge derives from God, said Abelard, it is good to pursue learning. In *Sic et Non* (Yes and No), he took 150 theological issues and, by presenting passages from the Bible and the church fathers, showed that there were conflicting opinions. He suggested that the divergent opinions of authorities could be reconciled through proper use of dialectics. But like Anselm before him, Abelard did not intend to refute traditional church doctrines. Reason would buttress, not weaken, the authority of faith. He wrote after his condemnation in 1141:

> I will never be a philosopher, if this is to speak against St. Paul, I would not be an Aristotle if this were to separate me from Christ. . . . I have set my building on the cornerstone on which Christ has built his Church. . . . I rest upon the rock that cannot be moved.[11]

The Recovery of Aristotle

During the Early Middle Ages, scholars in the Muslim world translated the works of Aristotle into Arabic and wrote commentaries on them. The preservation of ancient Greek thought was a major contribution of Islamic civilization. During the High Middle Ages, learned Europeans translated these works into Latin.

The introduction into Latin Christendom of the major works of Aristotle created a dilemma for religious authorities. Aristotle's comprehensive philosophy of nature and man, a product of human reason alone, conflicted in many instances with essential Christian doctrine. For Aristotle, God was an impersonal principle that accounted for order and motion in the universe, the unmoved mover. For Christianity, not only was God responsible for order in the physical universe, but he was also a personal being—a loving Father concerned about the deeds of his children. Whereas Christianity taught that God created the universe at a specific point in time, Aristotle held that the universe was eternal. Nor did Aristotle believe in the personal immortality of the soul, another cardinal principle of Christianity. For Aristotle, it was impossible for the soul to exist independently of the body.

Some church officials feared that the dissemination of Aristotle's natural philosophy would endanger faith. Would the teachings of Christ and the church fathers have to answer to pagan philosophy? Would Athens prevail over Jerusalem? At

Figure 10.4 Triumph of Saint Thomas Aquinas fresco With his monumental systematic exposition of Christian thought, *Summa Theologica*, Aquinas sought to reconcile Aristotelianism with Christianity. Aquinas never doubted that reason and revelation could be harmonized, and he even used Aristotelian categories in his five proofs of God's existence. *(Scala/Art Resource, NY)*

various times in the first half of the thirteenth century, the teaching of Aristotle's scientific works was forbidden at the University of Paris. However, because the ban did not apply throughout Christendom and was not consistently enforced in Paris, Aristotle's philosophy continued to be studied.

Thomas Aquinas: Synthesis of Christian Belief and Reason

Rejecting the position of conservatives, who insisted that philosophy would contaminate faith, Thomas Aquinas (c. 1225–1274) (Figure 10.4) upheld the value of human reason and natural knowledge. He set about reconciling Aristotelianism with Christianity. Aquinas taught at Paris and at various institutions in Italy. His greatest work, *Summa Theologica,* is a systematic exposition of Christian thought. As a devout Catholic and member of the Dominican order, he of course accepted the truth of revelation. He never used reason to undermine faith.

Aquinas divided revealed truth into two categories: beliefs whose truth can be demonstrated by reason and beliefs that reason cannot prove to be either true or false. For example, he believed that philosophical speculation could prove the exis-

tence of God and the immortality of the human soul, but that it could not prove or disprove the doctrines of the Trinity, the Incarnation, and the Redemption; these articles of faith wholly surpassed the capacity of human reason. This fact, however, did not detract from their certainty. Doctrines of faith did not require rational proof to be valid. They were true because they originated with God, whose authority is unshakable.

Can the teachings of faith conflict with the evidence of reason? For Aquinas, the answer was emphatically no. He said that revelation could not be the enemy of reason because revelation did not contradict reason, and reason did not corrupt the purity of faith. Revelation supplemented and perfected reason. If there appeared to be a conflict between philosophy and faith, it was certain that reason had erred somewhere, for the doctrines of faith were infallible. Because both faith and reason came from God, they were not in competition with each other but, properly understood, supported each other and formed an organic unity. Consequently, reason should not be feared, for it was another avenue to God. Because there was an inherent agreement between true faith and correct reason—they both ultimately stemmed from God—contradictions between the two were only a misleading appearance. Although philosophy had not yet been able to resolve the dilemma, for God no such contradictions existed. In heaven, human beings would attain complete knowledge, as well as complete happiness. While on earth, however, they must allow faith to guide reason; they must not permit reason to oppose or undermine faith.

Because reason was no enemy of faith, applying it to revelation need not be feared. As human reasoning became more proficient, said Aquinas, it also became more Christian, and apparent incompatibilities between faith and reason disappeared. Recognizing that both faith and reason point to the same truth, the wise person accepts the guidance of religion in all questions that relate directly to knowledge needed for salvation. There also existed a wide range of knowledge that God had not revealed and that was not required for salvation. Into this category fell much knowledge about the natural world of things and creatures, which human beings had perfect liberty to explore.

Thus, in exalting God, Aquinas also paid homage to human intelligence, proclaimed the value of rational activity, and asserted the importance of physical reality revealed through human senses. Therefore, he valued the natural philosophy of Aristotle. Correctly used, Aristotelian thought would provide faith with valuable assistance. Aquinas's great effort was to synthesize Aristotelianism with the divine revelation of Christianity. That the two could be harmonized, he had no doubt. He made use of Aristotelian categories in his five proofs of God's existence. In his first proof, for example, Aquinas argued that a thing cannot move itself. Whatever is moved must be moved by something else, and that by something else again. "Therefore, it is necessary to arrive at a first mover, moved by no other; and this everyone understands to be God."[12]

Aquinas also found a place for Aristotle's conception of man. Aristotle, said Aquinas, was correct to regard man as a natural being and to devise for man a natural system of ethics and politics. Aristotle, however, did not go far enough. Aquinas said that, in addition, human beings are also special children of God. Consequently, they must define their lives according to the standards God has set. Aquinas insisted that much of what Aristotle had to say about man is accurate and valuable, for he was a gifted philosopher, but he possessed no knowledge of God. The higher insight provided by revelation did not disqualify what natural reason had to say about human beings but improved on it.

Aquinas upheld the value of reason. To love the intellect was to honor God and not to diminish the truth of faith. He had confidence in the power of the rational mind to comprehend most of the truths of revelation, and he insisted that in nontheological questions about specific things in nature—those questions not affecting salvation—people should trust only to reason and experience.

Aquinas gave new importance to the empirical world and to scientific speculation and human knowledge. The traditional medieval view, based largely on Augustine, drew a sharp distinction between the higher world of grace and the lower world of nature, between the world of spirit and the world of sense experience. Knowledge derived from the natural world was often seen as an obstacle to true knowledge. Aquinas altered this tradition by affirming the importance of knowledge of the social order and the physical world. He gave human reason and worldly knowledge a new dignity. Thus, the City of Man was not merely a sinful place from which people tried to escape in order to enter God's city; it was worthy of investigation and understanding. But Aquinas remained a medieval thinker, for he always maintained that secular knowledge should be supervised and corrected by revealed truth, and he never questioned the truth of the medieval Christian view of the world and the individual. As historian Steven Ozment explains,

> Aquinas brought reason and revelation together, but strictly as unequals. . . . In this union, reason, philosophy, nature, secular man and the state ultimately had value only in subservience to the higher goals of revelation, theology, grace, religious man, and the church. . . . Thomist theology was the most sophisticated statement of the medieval belief in the secondary significance of the lay and secular world, a congenial ideology for a church besieged by independent and aggressive secular political powers.[13]

Strict Aristotelianism: The Challenge to Orthodoxy

Some teachers in the Faculty of Arts at Paris, relying heavily on the commentaries of Averroës, the great Muslim thinker (see Chapter 8), found Aquinas's approach of Christianizing or explaining away Aristotle unacceptable. Unlike Aquinas, they did not seek to reconcile Aristotle's philosophy with Christian dogma. They held that certain Aristotelian propositions contradicting faith were philosophically true, or at least could not be proven false. These teachers maintained that it was impossible to refute these propositions by natural reason alone—that is, without recourse to faith. For example, by reason alone Aristotle had demonstrated that the world was eternal and that the processes of nature were unalterable. The first doctrine conflicted with the Christian belief that God created the universe at a point in time; the second conflicted with the belief that God could work miracles.

But these teachers did not take the next step and argue that Aristotle was correct and faith wrong. They maintained only that Aristotle's arguments could not be refuted by natural reason, and that philosophers—as philosophers, not as Christians—should base their judgments on rational arguments only, not on miracles and revelation. These **strict Aristotelians** did not deny the truths of faith, but they did assert that natural reason could construct conclusive proofs for propositions that the church had explicitly stated to be false.

In 1277, the bishop of Paris condemned 219 propositions, many of them taught by these expositors of Aristotle at the University of Paris. Included in the condemnation were some propositions held by the great Aquinas. This move attempted to prevent Aristotle's philosophical naturalism from undermining Christian beliefs. Consequently, the condemnation was a triumph for conservative theologians, who had grown increasingly worried about the inroads made by Aristotelianism. To them, even the Christian Aristotelianism of Aquinas was suspect.

Condemnations generally hinder the pursuit of knowledge, but, ironically, the condemnation of 1277 may have had the opposite effect. It led some thinkers to examine critically and reject elements of Aristotle's natural philosophy. This development may have served as a prelude to modern science, which, born in the sixteenth and seventeenth centuries, grew out of a rejection of Aristotelian physics.

Joachim of Fiore: A Challenge to the Traditional View of History

Joachim of Fiore (c. 1135–1202) was a monk who developed a theology of history that clashed with the traditional Augustinian view of history. Augustine had taught that the incarnation of Christ was the central event in history: Before Christ, all history was progressing toward the redemptive work of Christ; after Christ, history was advancing toward the second coming of Christ and the Last Judgment. For Augustine, there would be no literal millennium, as alluded to in the book of Revelation, during which Jesus would rule with his saints for a thousand years. Rather, Augustine believed that the City of God—the Christian church—would gradually overcome the earthly city until it was triumphant at the last day. His interpretation was based on a metaphorical rendering of the book of Revelation, instead of a literal one.

Joachim, however, asserted that he had discovered the key to interpreting the book of Revelation by means of a type of mystical knowledge that he called **spiritual intelligence.** He thought that he understood the meaning of history and the path of the future—history was ascending in three stages, culminating in a literal millennium. Dividing the past into two ages paralleling the Old and New Testaments, he predicted the advent of a third age, which would be the climax of history, a period when both the church and society would be renewed. One member of the Trinity governed each of the three ages. The first age—the age of the Father, the Law, and the Old Testament—lasted from creation to the advent of Christ. Joachim counted 42 generations of 30 years each in the Old Testament for a total of 1,260 years. The second age—the age of the Son, the New Testament, and the Gospel—would also last 1,260 years, from Christ to the advent of the third age. Consequently, Joachim believed that the year 1260 would usher in the beginning of the third age, the millennium of Revelation—the age of the Spirit and the "Everlasting Gospel," when God would speak directly to perfected humans.

After his death, Joachim's mystical theology of history gave rise to radical ideas of reform of both church and society, especially among the Franciscan Spirituals. Following the example of Francis, the Spirituals insisted that all friars should live in absolute poverty, and they severely criticized the Order when it modified its position on poverty and allowed the Order to become wealthy. In the middle of the thirteenth century, the Spirituals began to teach that Joachim had been the prophet of the third age and Francis had been the person chosen by God to begin the reform of the church and Christian society. Their passion for poverty was closely connected with their expectations that the third age was about to dawn.

In *The Pursuit of the Millennium,* British historian Norman Cohn links Joachim's three ages to "latter day 'philosophies of history' which are most emphatically anti-Christian," particularly Marxism and Nazism: "Horrified though the unworldly mystic would have been to see it happen, it is unmistakably the Joachite phantasy of the three ages that reappeared in . . . the Marxian dialectic of the three stages of primitive communism, class society and a final communism which is to be the realm of freedom and in which the state will have withered away," as well as the Nazi "phrase 'the Third Reich', as a name for that 'new order' which was to last a thousand years."[14]

SCIENCE

During the Early Middle Ages, few scientific works from the ancient world were available to western Europeans. Scientific thought was at its lowest ebb since its origination more than a thousand years earlier in Greece. By contrast, both Islamic and Byzantine civilizations preserved and, in some instances, added to the legacy of Greek science. In the High Middle Ages, however, many ancient texts were translated from Greek and Arabic into Latin and entered Latin Christendom for the first time. The principal centers of translation were Spain, where Christian and Muslim civilizations met, and Sicily, which had been controlled by Byzantium up to the last part of the ninth century and then by Islam until Christian Normans completed conquest of the island by 1091. Often learned Jews, who knew both Arabic and Latin, served as translators. These translations of ancient Greek scientific works and of Arabic commentaries stimulated interest in nature.

In the thirteenth and fourteenth centuries, a genuine scientific movement did occur. Impressed with the naturalistic and empirical approach of Aristotle, some medieval schoolmen spent time examining physical nature. Among them was the Dominican Albert the Great (Albertus Magnus). Born in Germany, Albert (c. 1206–1280) studied at Padua and taught at the University of Paris, where Thomas Aquinas was his student. To Albert, philosophy meant more than employing Greek reason to contemplate divine wisdom; it also meant making sense of nature. Albert devoted himself to mastering, editing, and commenting on the vast body of Aristotle's works.

While retaining the Christian stress on God, revelation, the supernatural, and the afterlife, Albert (unlike many earlier Christian thinkers) considered nature a valid field for investigation. In his writings on geology, chemistry, botany, and zoology, Albert, like Aristotle, displayed a respect for the concrete details of nature, using them as empirical evidence:

> I have examined the anatomy of different species of bees. In the rear, i.e. behind the waist, I discovered a transparent, shining bladder. If you test this with your tongue, you find that it has a slight taste of honey. In the body there is only an insignificant spiral-shaped intestine and nerve fibers which are connected with the sting. All this is surrounded with a sticky fluid.[15]

Showing a modern-day approach, Albert approved of inquiry into the material world, stressed the value of knowledge derived from experience with nature, sought rational explanations for natural occur-

rences, and held that theological debates should not stop scientific investigations. He pointed to a new direction in medieval thought.

Robert Grosseteste (c. 1175–1253), chancellor of Oxford University, was also a scholar of the scientific movement. He declared that the roundness of the earth could be demonstrated by reason. In addition, he insisted that mathematics was necessary in order to understand the physical world, and he carried out experiments on the refraction of light.

Another Englishman, the monk and philosopher Roger Bacon (c. 1214–1294) foreshadowed the modern attitude of using science to gain mastery over nature. He recognized the practical advantages that might come and predicted these great changes:

> Machines for navigation can be made without rowers so that the largest ships on rivers or seas will be moved by a single man in charge with greater velocity than if they were full of men. Also oars can be made so that without animals they will move with unbelievable rapidity. . . . Also flying machines can be constructed so that a man sits in the midst of the machine revolving some engine by which artificial wings are made to beat the air like a flying bird. Also a machine small in size can be made for walking in the sea and rivers, even to the bottom without danger.[16]

Bacon valued the study of mathematics and read Arabic works on the reflection and refraction of light. Among his achievements were experiments in optics and the observation that light travels much faster than sound. His description of the anatomy of the vertebrate eye and optic nerves was the finest of that era, and he recommended dissecting the eyes of pigs and cows to obtain greater knowledge of the subject.

The study of the ancient texts of Hippocrates and Galen and their Islamic commentators, particularly Avicenna's *Canon of Medicine,* which synthesized Greek and Arabic medicine, elevated medicine to a formal discipline. Although these texts contained numerous errors and contradictions, they had to be mastered, if only to be challenged, before modern medicine could emerge. In addition, medieval doctors dissected animals and, in the late fourteenth century, human bodies. From practical experience, medieval doctors, monks, and laypersons added to the list of plants and herbs that would ease pain and heal.

Medieval scholars did not make the breakthrough to modern science. They kept the belief that the earth was at the center of the universe and that different sets of laws operated on earth and in the heavens. They did not invent analytic geometry or calculus or arrive at the modern concept of inertia (see Chapter 17). Although some medieval thinkers explicitly urged seeking natural explanations to account for physical occurrences, medieval science was never wholly removed from a theological setting. Modern science self-consciously seeks the advancement of specifically scientific knowledge, but in the Middle Ages, many questions involving nature were raised merely to clarify a religious problem.

Medieval scholars and philosophers did, however, advance knowledge about optics, the tides, and mechanics. They saw the importance of mathematics for interpreting nature, and they performed experiments. By translating and commenting on ancient Greek and Arabic works, medieval scholars provided future ages with ideas to reflect on and to reject and surpass, a necessary precondition for the emergence of modern science.

Medieval thinkers also developed an anti-Aristotelian physics, which some historians of science believe influenced Galileo, the creator of modern mechanics, more than two centuries later. To explain why heavy objects do not always fall downward—why an arrow released by a bow moves in a straight line before it falls—Aristotle said that when the arrow leaves the bow, it separates the air, which then moves behind the arrow and pushes it along.

Aristotle, of course, had no comprehension of the law of inertia, which, as formulated by Isaac Newton in the seventeenth century, states that a body in motion will continue in a straight line unless interfered with. Unable to imagine that a body in motion is as natural a condition as a body at rest, Aristotle maintained that an outside force must maintain continual contact with the moving object. Hence, the flying arrow requires the "air-engine" to keep it in motion.

In the fourteenth century, Jean Buridan, a professor at the University of Paris, rejected Aristotle's theory. Buridan argued that the bowstring transmits to the arrow a force called impetus, which keeps the arrow in motion. Whereas Aristotle attributed the arrow's motion to the air, which was external to the arrow, Buridan found the motive force to be an agent imparted to the arrow by the bowstring. Although still far from the modern theory of inertia, Buridan's impetus theory was an advance over Aristotle's air-engine. In the impetus theory, a moving body requires a cause to keep it in motion. In the theory of inertia, once a body is in motion, no force is required to keep it moving in a straight line. The state of motion is as natural as the state of rest.

Late medieval physics went beyond Aristotle in other ways as well, particularly in the importance given to expressing motion mathematically. The extent to which late medieval thinkers influenced the thinkers of the Scientific Revolution is a matter of debate. Some historians view modern science as the child of the Middle Ages. Other historians believe that the achievements of medieval science were slim and that modern science owes very little to the Middle Ages.

THE RECOVERY OF ROMAN LAW

During the Early Middle Ages, western European law essentially consisted of Germanic customs, some of which had been written down. Although some elements of Roman law endured as custom, the formal study of Roman law had disappeared. The late eleventh and the twelfth centuries saw the revival of Roman law, particularly in Bologna, Italy. Irnerius lectured on the *Corpus Juris Civilis*, the imperial code drawn up in the sixth century by order of the Byzantine Emperor Justinian. He made Bologna the leading center for the study of Roman law. Irnerius and his students applied to the study of law the methods of organization and logical analysis that scholastic theologians used in studying philosophical texts.

Unlike traditional Germanic law, which was essentially tribal law, Roman law assumed the existence of universal principles, which could be grasped by the human intellect and expressed in the law of the state. Roman jurists had systematically and rationally structured the legal experience of the Roman people. The example of Roman law stimulated medieval jurists to organize their own legal tradition. Intellectuals increasingly came to insist on both a rational analysis of evidence and judicial decisions based on rational procedures. Law codes compiled in parts of France and Germany and in the kingdom of Castile were influenced by the recovery of Roman law.

The Roman legal experience contained political principles that differed markedly from feudal practices. According to feudal tradition, lords, by virtue of their large estates, were empowered to exercise political authority. Roman jurists, on the other hand, had attributed governmental powers to the state and had granted wide powers to the emperor. The *Corpus Juris Civilis* stated that the power to make laws had originally resided with the Roman people, but that they had surrendered this power to the emperor. Medieval lawyers in the service of kings used this concept to justify royal absolutism, holding that the monarch possessed the absolute powers that the Roman legal tradition had granted to the Roman emperor. This strong defense of the monarch's power helped kings maintain their independence from the papacy.

Roman law also influenced church law, which was derived from the Bible, the church fathers, church councils, and the decisions of popes. In the last part of the eleventh century, church scholars began to codify church (or canon) law and were helped by the Roman legal tradition.

— ◼ —

The Medieval Worldview

A distinctive worldview, based essentially on Christianity, evolved during the Middle Ages. This outlook differed from both the Greco-Roman and the modern scientific and secular views of the world. In the Christian view, not the individual but the Creator determined what constituted the good life. Thus, reason that was not illuminated by revelation was either wrong or inadequate, for God had revealed the proper rules for the regulation of individual and social life. Ultimately, the good life was not of this world but came from a union with God in a higher world. This Christian belief, as formulated by the church, made life and death purposeful and intelligible; it dominated the thought of the Middle Ages.

The Universe: Higher and Lower Worlds

Medieval thinkers sharply differentiated between spirit and matter, between a realm of grace and an earthly realm, between a higher world of perfection and a lower world of imperfection. Moral values derived from the higher world, which was also the final destination for the faithful. Two sets of laws operated in the medieval universe, one for the heavens and one for the earth. The cosmos was a giant ladder, with God at the summit; earth, composed of base matter, stood at the bottom, just above hell.

From Aristotle and Ptolemy, medieval thinkers inherited the theory of an earth-centered universe—the *geocentric theory*—which they imbued with Christian symbolism. The geocentric theory held that revolving around the motionless earth at uniform speeds were seven transparent spheres, in which were embedded each of the seven "planets"—the moon, Mercury, Venus, the sun, Mars, Jupiter, and Saturn. A sphere of fixed stars enclosed this planetary system. Above the firmament of the stars were the three heavenly spheres. The outermost, the Empyrean Heaven, was the abode of God and the Elect. Through the sphere below, God, the Prime Mover, transmitted motion to the planetary spheres. Underneath this was the lowermost sphere, the Crystalline Heaven.

An earth-centered universe accorded with the Christian idea that God created the universe for men and women and that salvation was the primary aim of life. Because God had created people in his image, they deserved this central position. Though they might be at the bottom of the cosmic ladder, only they, of all living things, had the capacity to ascend to heaven, the realm of perfection.

Also acceptable to the Christian mentality was the sharp distinction drawn by Aristotle between the world above the moon and the one below it. Aristotle held that terrestrial bodies were made of four elements: earth, water, air, and fire. Celestial bodies, which occupied the region encompassing the moon and the area above, were composed of a fifth element, the ether—too clear, too pure, and too perfect to be found on earth. The planets and stars existed in a world apart; they were made of the divine ether and followed celestial laws, which did not apply to earthly objects. Whereas earthly bodies underwent change—ice converting to water, a burning log converting to ashes—heavenly objects were incorruptible and immune to all change. Unlike earthly objects, they were indestructible.

Heavenly bodies also followed different laws of motion than earthly objects. Aristotle said that it was natural for celestial bodies to move eternally in uniform circles, such motion being considered a sign of perfection. According to Aristotle, it was also natural for heavy bodies (stone) to fall downward and for light objects (fire, smoke) to move upward toward the celestial world; the falling stone and the rising smoke were finding their natural place in the universe. This view of the universe would be shattered by the Scientific Revolution of the sixteenth and seventeenth centuries (see Chapter 17).

The Individual: Sinful but Redeemable

At the center of medieval belief was the idea of a perfect God and a wretched and sinful human being. God had given Adam and Eve freedom to choose; rebellious and presumptuous, they had used their freedom to disobey God. In doing so, they made evil an intrinsic part of the human personality. But God, who had not stopped loving human beings, showed them the way out of sin. God became man and died so that human beings might be saved. Men and women were weak, egocentric, and sinful. With God's grace, they could overcome their sinful nature and gain salvation; without grace, they were utterly helpless.

The medieval individual's understanding of self related to a comprehension of the universe as a hierarchy culminating in God. On earth, the basest objects were lifeless stones devoid of souls; higher than stones were plants, endowed with a primitive type of soul, which allowed for reproduction and growth. Still higher were animals, which had the capacity for motion and sensation. The highest of the animals were human beings; unlike other animals, they could grasp some part of universal truth. Far superior to them were the angels, for they apprehended God's truth without difficulty. At the summit of this graduated universe was God, who was pure Being, without limitation, and the source of all existence. God's revelation reached down to humanity through the hierarchical order. From God, revelation passed first to the angels, who were also arranged hierarchically. From the angels, the truth reached men and women, grasped first by prophets and apostles and then later by the multitudes. Thus, all things in the universe, from angels to men and women to the lowest earthly objects, occupied a place peculiar to their nature and were linked by God in a great, unbroken chain.

Medieval individuals derived a sense of security from this hierarchical universe, in which the human position was clearly defined. Although they were sinners who dwelt on a corruptible earth at the bottom of the cosmic hierarchy, they could ascend to the higher world of perfection above the moon. As children of God, they enjoyed the unique distinction that each human soul was precious; all individuals commanded respect, unless they were heretics. (A heretic forfeited dignity and could be justly executed.)

Medieval thinkers also arranged knowledge in a hierarchical order: Knowledge of spiritual things surpassed all worldly knowledge, all the sciences. Therefore, the true Christian understood that the pursuit of worldly knowledge could not proceed properly unless guided by divine revelation. To know what God wanted of the individual was the summit of self-knowledge and permitted entry into heaven. Thus, God was both the source and the end of knowledge. The human capacity to think and to act freely constituted the image of God within each individual; it ennobled man and woman and offered them the promise of associating with God in heaven.

True, human nobility derived from intelligence and free will. But if individuals disobeyed God, they brought misery on themselves. To challenge the divine will with human will constituted the sin of pride, contempt for God, and a violation of the divine order. Such sinful behavior invited self-destruction.

In the medieval view, neither nature nor human beings could be understood apart from God and his revelation. All reality emanated from God and was purposefully arranged in a spiritual hierarchy. Three great expressions of this view of life were scholastic philosophy, *The Divine Comedy* of Dante, and the Gothic cathedral.

Key Terms

guilds	Little Brothers
burghers	Inquisition
common law	Franciscans
Magna Carta	Dominicans
sacraments	scholasticism
excommunication	strict Aristotelians
Investiture Controversy	"spiritual intelligence"
Concordat of Worms	geocentric theory
Crusades	

Notes

1. Quoted in V. H. H. Green, *Medieval Civilization in Western Europe* (New York: St. Martin's Press, 1971), p. 35.
2. Excerpted in Brian Tierney, ed., *The Crisis of Church and State, 1050–1300* (Upper Saddle River, N.J.: Prentice Hall, 1964), p. 132.
3. Moses Maimonides, *The Guide of the Perplexed*, trans. Shlomo Pines (Chicago: University of Chicago Press, 1963), pp. 634–635, 638.
4. Quoted in A. Cohen, *The Teachings of Maimonides* (New York: KTAV Publishing House, Inc., 1968), p. 248.
5. Quoted in G. G. Coulton, *Life in the Middle Ages* (New York: Macmillan, 1928), 1:74.
6. Quoted in Charles Homer Haskins, *The Rise of Universities* (Ithaca, N.Y.: Cornell University Press, 1957), p. 79.
7. Quoted in Coulton, *Life in the Middle Ages*, 3:113.
8. Betty Radice, trans., *The Letters of Abelard and Heloise* (New York: Penguin Books, 1974), p. 66.
9. Ibid., p. 67.
10. Quoted in Anders Piltz, *The World of Medieval Learning* (Oxford: Blackwell, 1981), p. 83.
11. Quoted in David Knowles, *The Evolution of Medieval Thought* (New York: Vintage Books, 1964), p. 123.
12. *Summa Theologica*, excerpted in Anton C. Pegis, ed., *Introduction to Saint Thomas Aquinas* (New York: Modern Library, 1948), p. 25.
13. Steven Ozment, *The Age of Reform* (New Haven: Yale University Press, 1980), p. 20.
14. Norman Cohn, *The Pursuit of the Millennium: Revolutionary Messianism in Medieval and Reformation Europe and Its Bearing on Modern Totalitarian Movements* (New York: Harper Torchbooks, 1961), p. 101.
15. Quoted in Piltz, *The World of Medieval Learning*, p. 176.
16. Quoted in A. C. Crombie, *Medieval and Early Modern Science* (Garden City, N.Y.: Doubleday Anchor Books, 1959), 1:55–56.

The High Middle Ages II: The Flowering of Medieval Literature, Art, and Music

THE SAME VITALITY THAT FOSTERED A REVIVAL of learning during the High Middle Ages also found expression in literature, architecture, painting, and music. Like philosophy, the arts were dominated by Christian otherworldliness; but, at the same time, a rich, chivalric secular literature also emerged.

Not too long ago, some intellectuals viewed the Middle Ages as a period of ignorance and superstition, an era of cultural sterility that stood between the high civilizations of ancient Greece and Rome and the modern West. This view of the Middle Ages as the "Dark Ages" has been abandoned, and quite properly so, for the High Middle Ages saw the crystallization of a prolific and creative civilization. To be sure, its religious orientation sets it apart both from classical civilization and from our own modern secular and scientific civilization. But the *Summa Theologica* of Aquinas, the *Divine Comedy* of Dante, the Gothic cathedral, and the innovations in church music all attest to the creativity and genius of the medieval religious spirit.

MEDIEVAL LITERATURE

Medieval literature was written both in Latin and in the vernacular, the normal spoken language as distinct from the language of learning. Much of medieval literature consisted of religious hymns and dramas. Other forms of literature included epic poems of heroic deeds that had first been told orally. One of the greatest works of medieval literature is Dante's *Divine Comedy*, an allegory of the Christian's struggle to overcome sin and achieve salvation.

Religious Hymns and Drama

Religious hymns glorified the life of saints and expressed great love for Jesus and Mary. The hymn quoted below—*Stabat Mater dolorosa* (Mother of Sorrows), describing Mary standing vigil as her son dies—has been attributed either to Pope Innocent III or to a Franciscan monk named Jacaponi di Benedetti (d. 1306). The text has been translated into many languages and put to music by numerous composers. It became part of the Roman liturgy early in the eighteenth century. Today it is often part of the *Tenebrae*—a "service of darkness" commemorating the crucifixion of Jesus on Good Friday. The *Tenebrae*, dating from the eighth century and celebrated on Wednesday, Thursday, or Friday of Holy Week, incorporated hymns reputedly depicting "the seven last words [sayings] of Christ" spoken from the cross. This hymn is based on the third word, "Woman, behold your son. Behold your mother" (John 19:26–27).

The Unicorn in Captivity,
c. 1500,
height, 12'1" (3.68m)

The series of seven unicorn tapestries is the most famous ever executed. The setting is patterned after a medieval stag hunt, but the search is for a unicorn, which, according to Christian tradition, is such a fierce animal that no hunter can apprehend it without the help of a virgin maiden.

(The Metropolitan Museum of Art, Gift of John D. Rockefeller Jr., 1937 (37.80.6) Photograph © 1998 The Metropolitan Museum of Art)

O how sad and sore distressed
Was that mother highly blest
  Of the sole-begotten One!
Christ above in torment hangs:
She beneath Him holds the pangs
  Of her dying glorious Son.

Is there one who would not weep
Whelmed in miseries so deep
  Christ's dear mother to behold?
Can the human heart refrain
  From partaking in her pain,
  In that mother's pain untold?

O thou mother, fount of love,
Touch my spirit from above,
  Make my heart with thine accord!
Make me feel as thou hast felt;
Make my soul to glow and melt
  With the love of Christ my Lord.[1]

Religious hymns also expressed a disdain for worldly pursuits, such as this thirteenth-century anonymous hymn, entitled *The Vanity of This World*.

Why does the world war for glory that's vain?
All its successes wax only to wane;
Quickly its triumphs are frittered away,
Like vessels the potter casts out of frail clay.
As well trust to letters imprinted in ice
As trust the frail world with its treacherous
    device,
Its prizes a fraud and its values all wrong;
Who would put faith in its promise for long?
. . . .
Whither is Caesar the great Emperor fled,
or [King] Croesus whose show on his table was
    spread?
Cicero's eloquence now is in vain;
Where's Aristotle's magnificent brain?

All those great noblemen, all those past days,
All kings' achievements and all prelates' praise,
All the world's princes in all their array—
In the flash of an eye comes the end of the play.
Short is the season of all earthly fame;
Man's shadow, man's pleasure, they both are the
    same,
And the prizes eternal he gives in exchange
For the pleasure that leads to a land that is strange.
. . . .
Call not your own what one day ye may lose;
The world will take back all it gives you to use.
Let your hearts be in heaven, your thought in the
    skies;
Happy is he who the world can despise.[2]

Medieval drama drew on the classical tradition, traditional folklore, and vulgar pantomime and burlesque for source material. Masked actors, called mummers, performed plays that often contained songs, dances, and bawdy dialogue, and village children took up a collection from the audience. Although the earliest extant texts date from the thirteenth and fourteenth centuries, mummers' plays were performed early in the Middle Ages.

As time went on, mummers' plays incorporated Christian moral teachings, and some of them evolved into liturgical dramas, known as *mystery plays*, the earliest of which appeared in the ninth century. Mystery plays were dramatic allegories about important religious events, especially the activities of Holy Week (between Palm Sunday and Easter). Written in Latin and performed by the clergy, these mystery plays dramatized scriptural passages of the New Testament, for example, Christ's entry into Jerusalem, the Last Supper, the Crucifixion, the Empty Tomb, and the Ascension.

The plays became so popular that they were lengthened and extended to include themes from the Old Testament—Adam and Eve, Abraham and Isaac, and David and Bathsheba. As the staging became more complex, a church could no longer contain the action, and the play was moved outside to the square in front of the church or to the porch surrounding the church.

By the thirteenth century, a fair amount of secular themes entered the mystery plays, and they were translated into the vernacular; the staging was assumed by some of the guilds in the towns, and students, local laypeople, and wandering minstrels played the roles previously performed by the clergy. Mystery plays were dominant throughout the Early and High Middle Ages, but by the Late Middle Ages (1330s), they were broadened to include other types of religious drama—the morality and miracle plays (see Chapter 12).

Goliardic Poetry

Medieval university students, like their modern counterparts, lampooned their elders and social conventions, engaged in drinking bouts, and rebelled against the rigors of study. They put their feelings into poetry written in Latin but also in the vernacular. One of the leaders of these student poets, the Archpoet (c. 1300), was given the nickname "Golias," and the term *goliards* was soon applied to the entire group of poets. On the fringes of university life, the goliards wandered from university to university (and from tavern to tavern) reveling in the pleasure of youth, wine, and song.

We in our wandering,
  Blithesome and squandering;
    Tara, tantara, teino!

Eat to satiety,
Drink with propriety;
  Tara, tantara, teino!
Laugh till our sides we split,
Rags on our hides we fit;
  Tara, tantara, teino!
Jesting eternally,
Quaffing infernally;
  Tara, tantara, teino![3]

For the goliards, youth and study did not mix.

Let's away with study,
  Folly's sweet.
Treasure all the pleasure of our youth:
  Time enough for age
To think of Truth.

So short a day,
And life so quickly hasting
And is study wasting
  Youth that would be gay!. . .[4]

And, of course, their thoughts turned to romance.

Think no evil, have no fear,
  If I play with Phyllis;
I am but the guardian dear
  Of her girlhood's lilies,
Lest too soon her bloom should swoon
  Like spring's daffodillies.

All I care for is to play,
  Gaze upon my treasure,
Now and then to touch her hand,
  Kiss in modest measure;
But the fifth act of love's game,
  Dream not of that pleasure!
. . . .
Sweet above all sweets that are
  Tis to play with Phyllis;
For her thoughts are white as snow,
  In her heart no ill is;
And the kisses that she gives
  Sweeter are than lilies.
. . . .
Whatsoe'er the rest may do,
  Let us then be playing:
Take the pastime that is due
  While we're yet a-Maying;
I am young and young are you;
  'Tis the time for playing.[5]

Epics

THE SONG OF ROLAND The French epic poems, *chansons de geste*, were written in the vernacular of northern France. Many of the poems dealt with Charlemagne's battles against the Mus-

lims, with rebellious nobles, and with medieval warfare. The finest of these epic poems, *The Song of Roland* (*La chanson de Roland*), relates the adventures and death of Charlemagne's nephew, Roland.

In 778, Charlemagne invaded Spain hoping to extend the influence of Frankish Christendom at the expense of the Saracens (Muslims) in Spain. When he reached Zaragoza, south of Pamplona, Charlemagne received word of an uprising in Saxony and began his withdrawal to France. Passing back through Pamplona, he destroyed the city and ascended the Pyrenees Mountains by way of the Roncevaux Pass, where his army was ambushed on August 15 by the Christian Basques, whom he had not spared on his southward march into Spain. In the Battle of Roncevaux, many of Charlemagne's military leaders, including Roland, lost their lives. It was Charlemagne's greatest defeat. More than 300 years later, an anonymous author* told about the disaster in a song—for which the music is no longer extant—written in Old French.

The Song of Roland presents these historical events as a classic confrontation between good and evil, in the guise of the Christian king, Charlemagne, and the Saracen king of Spain, Marsile. The poem begins with Charlemagne as conqueror of all of Spain except for Zaragoza, which is under the control of Marsile. As a peace overture, Marsile offers to convert to Christianity and to become Charlemagne's vassal if he will return with his army to Aachen. Roland counsels Charlemagne to reject the offer, but Roland's stepfather, Ganelon, argues that it would be wrong to continue to fight against a foe who seeks clemency. Roland then nominates Ganelon for the treacherous task of negotiating with Marsile. Resentful of Roland, Ganelon conspires with Marsile to bring about Roland's death in battle, agreeing to manipulate the situation so that Roland will be in command of the rear guard. As Charlemagne's army withdraws from Spain, the rear guard is overwhelmed by the Saracens in the pass at Roncevaux, where Roland loses his life. When Charlemagne finds Roland's body, he vows vengeance. Back in Aachen, Ganelon is put on trial for treason, found guilty, and executed by being pulled apart by four horses. The scene near the end of the poem affirms the theme of the Christian quest to rid Europe of the

* Scholars date the oldest surviving manuscript to between 1130 and 1170. Although the authorship of the poem cannot be known with certainty, its final line, *Ci falt la geste que Turoldus declinet* (*Here ends the story which Turold relates*), offers the intriguing possibility that the author was a man named Turold. Perhaps this is a reference to Turold, the son or nephew of William the Conqueror's half brother Odo, Bishop of Bayeux.

"pagan" Muslims by relating the details of the conversion of Bramimonde, queen of Spain, to Christianity. Charlemagne exclaims:

> "In my house there is a noble captive;
> She has heard so many sermons and parables
> That, wishing to believe in God, she seeks
>   Christianity.
> Baptize her, so that God may have her soul." . . .
> In the baths at Aix there is a vast gathering;
> There they baptize the Queen of Spain.
> They found for her the name of Juliana;
> She is a Christian, convinced of the truth.[6]

That same night, the angel Gabriel appears to the war-weary Charlemagne and instructs him to continue to wage battle against the pagans: "The emperor had no wish to go. 'God,' said the king, 'how wearisome my life is!'" [7]

The clash of Charlemagne's forces with those of Marsile is the contextual framework for the overriding theme of *The Song of Roland*—the struggle between good and evil. Instances of this conflict are Ganelon's betrayal of Roland, presented as a surrender of a Christian's will to the wiles of the devil (symbolized by Marsile), and Bramimonde's affirmation of the truth of the Christian message, culminating with her being christened "Juliana." The theme of justice and vengeance is graphically depicted through scenes of violence. As Roland surveys the carnage of battle, he praises the valor and courage of his comrades and vows "I must not fail you. I shall die of grief, if nothing else kills me. Lord companion, let us get back to the fray." Then, as Roland kills twenty-five enemies in succession, the poet exclaims, "Never will any man be so bent on vengeance."[8]

The execution of the traitor Ganelon connects the theme of vengeance with the ideas of commitment to family, country, and one's lord. All of the tribes of the Frankish kingdom assemble to show their support for the judgment:

> That Ganelon should die in terrible agony.
> They have four war-horses brought forward;
> Then they bind him by his hands and feet.
> The horses are mettlesome and swift;
> Four servants goad them on
> Towards a stream which flows through a field.
> Ganelon was given over to total perdition.
> All his ligaments are stretched taut
> And he is torn limb from limb;
> His clear blood spills out on to the green grass.
> Ganelon died a traitor's death.[9]

Ganelon's treachery was a violation of the sacred trust that bound medieval society together. As Charlemagne's vassal, he was obligated to serve his lord faithfully, with unwavering courage,

enduring all forms of suffering, even unto death. Therefore, treason against the king or lord was the greatest of all crimes, punishable by death. In contrast to Ganelon, Roland is idealized as the brave Christian knight who battles God's enemies; a warrior of heroic proportions with great physical prowess, he is exceedingly loyal to God, the king, his knightly entourage, and to "sweet France."

THE NIBELUNGENLIED The *Nibelungenlied*, which is often called "the *Iliad* of the Germans," is the best expression of the heroic epic in Germany. The *Nibelungenlied* literally means the song of the Nibelungs. According to the Germanic tradition, the Nibelungs are legendary people whose name is thought to mean "Children of the Mist." The Nibelungs, however, are never actually identified by the poet until near the end of the poem, when they are equated with the Burgundians, a German tribe.

Like *The Song of Roland*, the *Nibelungenlied* contains traditional demonstrations of courtly graces as well as scenes typified in chivalric literature—ceremonious arrivals and departures, tournament spectacles, and sumptuous banquets—but in a much darker fashion. The *Nibelungenlied* is filled with gruesome details of death and revenge and with brutality, treachery, and greed, but unlike *The Song of Roland*, it is not framed by Christian morality wherein good triumphs over evil.

The legend of the *Nibelungenlied* dates from the early sixth century and is based on stories from both Scandinavia and Germany. It draws on themes from the Germanic past, especially the migration of the tribes; even Attila, leader of the Huns, appears in the second part of the epic. The poem was probably first performed as a ballad by *Minnesingers* (minstrels or troubadours) along the Rhine River. Scholars assume that the first complete German text was executed sometime between 1195 and 1205. Like other epics, the *Nibelungenlied* is concerned with violence, the quest for honor, and loyalty to one's lord. However, the preeminent theme is unholy vengeance, which is carried out by Kriemhild, the Burgundian princess of Worms. With great skill the poet depicted personal antagonisms and confrontations.

The poet begins the story with Siegfried, the son of the king of the Netherlands, who learns of Kriemhild's beauty and lively spirit and vows to marry her.[10] At Worms he meets King Gunther, Kriemhild's brother, as well as Hagen, one of Gunther's chief vassals, who knows of Siegfried's physical prowess, his grandiose escapades, but most importantly, that Siegfried possesses the treasure of the Nibelungs. Siegfried endears himself to the Burgundian court by demonstrating his courage, strength, and prowess in battle against the Danes and finally meets Princess Kriemhild at the victory celebration.

At this point, the poet interrupts the love story of Kriemhild and Siegfried and shifts the reader's attention to Gunther's fascination with Brunhild, Queen of Iceland. Hearing stories of Brunhild's "vast strength and surpassing beauty" and her intention to marry any man who could defeat her in a series of athletic tests, Gunther solicits the aid of Siegfried who agrees to help Gunther acquire Brunhild, provided he be allowed to marry Kriemhild. Although Gunther wins the contest, it is actually Siegfried, wearing a cloak of invisibility, who does the deeds. This deception will ultimately bring about the downfall of both Gunther and Siegfried. Then Siegfried marries Kriemhild, and Gunther weds Brunhild. Suspicious about the circumstances of her defeat, Brunhild refuses to consummate her marriage. The poet makes it clear that this is a violation of a wife's duty to her husband and describes a violent scene in which Siegfried, again in disguise, forces Brunhild to submit to her husband.

A turning point of the Siegfried/Kriemhild and Gunther/Brunhild saga is the fateful encounter between Queen Kriemhild and Queen Brunhild who quarrel about whose husband is superior. During their argument, Kriemhild reveals Siegfried's deceptions to Brunhild.

Anxious to gain the treasure of the Nibelungs, Hagen convinces King Gunther to aid in the betrayal of his brother-in-law. Feigning a desire to protect Siegfried in battle, Hagen wins Kriemhild's confidence, and she reveals to him her husband's vulnerable spot.* Hagen then convinces her to sew a cross on the spot between Siegfried's shoulder blades, and during a hunt, he kills him by stabbing him in the back as he drinks from a spring. Still intent on acquiring for himself the Nibelungs' treasure, which rightfully belongs to Kriemhild, Hagen convinces Gunther to betray his own sister. The death of Siegfried and the loss of the Nibelungs' treasure, which Hagen has thrown into the Rhine River, closes the first part of the poem. Kriemhild's revenge on Hagen and Gunther dominates the second, and longer, part of this most brutal of all medieval epics and eventually leads to the destruction of the Burgundians.

* The poet has Kriemhild tell Hagen the story of how Siegfried killed a dragon (a story drawn from a much earlier Nordic myth) and bathed in its blood so that he might become invincible. As he bathed, a leaf from a linden tree fell between his shoulder blades, which prevented the blood from touching that area.

TALES OF KING ARTHUR Originating in France between 1130 and 1150, the literary genre of the *roman d'aventure*—better known as the **romance**—combined the legendary oral traditions of Britain, France, and Germany with chivalric ideals and Christian concepts to create tales of love, adventure, war, and the miraculous. Enchanting damsels and demonic conjurers found their way into these venerable stories; charmed knights began to dash around Europe on impetuous errands in behalf of their ladyloves. Among the most famous romances are the tales of King Arthur and his Knights of the Round Table.

The invasion of Britain in the fifth century is the foundation for the legend of King Arthur. The invaders were the Germanic Anglo-Saxons who came to be known as the English, a word derived from *Anglo (Engle* or *Englisc).*

Arthur may have been an actual British king who battled the English invaders. Whether or not Arthur was a historical person is, however, less important than how the legendary king was perceived. The medieval legend was worked and reworked until it could account for Arthur's birth, marriage, ascendancy to the English throne, and death. A compilation of various medieval legends relates that Arthur was born of an adulterous relationship between Uther Pendragon (Dragon's Head), King of England, and Igrena (wife of the Duke of Cornwall). After Uther's death, English nobles seek to determine the true king of England by having several candidates attempt to remove a sword embedded in stone. Arthur successfully extracts the sword, succeeds his father, chooses Camelot for his home, and marries Guinevere, the daughter of the dwarf-king, Leodegrance. As part of her dowry, Guinevere gives Arthur a huge round table, which he uses when his esteemed one hundred and fifty knights meet. After numerous victories over their foes, the "Knights of the Round Table" push the invaders out of Britain.

The theme of adultery is reintroduced when Arthur's retainer, Launcelot, betrays his king by seducing Queen Guinevere. Gawain, Arthur's nephew, suggests he follow Launcelot to France and seek to avenge the knight's adulterous betrayal of his king. While in France, Arthur receives word that his bastard son, Mordred, has usurped the throne. At the moment of his return to England, Arthur is mortally wounded by Mordred. However, before Arthur dies, he is carried away to the island of Avalon by mysterious women. The legend then reports that King Arthur will one day return from Avalon.

Although these romances were sometimes criticized over the centuries for being too stylistically and intellectually inferior to later literary genre, they nonetheless continued to delight millions of readers, who remained impervious to changing literary styles. The romances were pure escapist literature; herein lay their appeal. Today, the legend of Arthur's sword, "Excalibur," his idyllic home of Camelot, the machinations of his wily wizard, Merlin, and Arthur's quest for the Holy Grail have provided source material for full-length, animated feature films, Broadway musicals, and television miniseries.

The Poetry of Chivalric Love

Another form of medieval poetry, which flourished particularly in Provence, in southern France, dealt with the romantic glorification of women. Sung by *troubadours*, many of them nobles and some of whom were women (*trobairitz*), the chivalric (or courtly) love poetry expressed a changing attitude toward women. Although medieval men generally regarded women as inferior and subordinate, chivalric love poetry ascribed superior qualities of virtue to noble ladies. To the nobleman, the lady became a goddess worthy of all devotional loyalty, and worship. He would honor her and serve her as he did his lord; for her love, he would undergo any sacrifice. Troubadours sang love songs that praised ladies for their beauty and charm and expressed both the joys and the pains of love:

> I sing of her, yet her beauty
> is greater than I can tell,
> with her fresh color, lively eyes,
> and white skin, untanned
> and untainted by rouge.
> She is so pure and noble
> that no one can speak ill of her.
> But above all, one must praise,
> it seems to me, her truthfulness,
> her manners and her gracious speech
> for she never would betray a friend. . . .[11]

Troubadours could also be playful. Sometimes they mocked women who labored too hard to preserve a youthful beauty.

> That creature so splendid is but an old jade;
> Of ointment and padding her beauty is made;
> Unpainted if you had the hap to behold her,
> You'd find her all wrinkles from forehead
>   to shoulder
>
> What a shame for a woman who has lost all
>   her grace
> To waste thus her time in bedaubing her face!
> To neglect her poor soul I am sure is not right
>   of her,
> For a body that's going to corruption in spite
>   of her.[12]

Troubadours sometimes even mocked the obsession with romance that was associated with the poetry of chivalric love.

> You say the moon is all aglow,
>   The nightingale a-singing —
> I'd rather watch the red wine flow,
>   And hear the goblets ringing.
>
> You say 'tis sweet to hear the gale
>   Creep sighing through the willows —
> I'd rather hear a merry tale,
>   'Mid a group of jolly fellows!
>
> You say 'tis sweet the stars to view
>   Upon the waters gleaming —
> I'd rather see, 'twixt me and you
>   And the post, my supper steaming.[13]

Noblewomen actively influenced the rituals and literature of chivalric (or courtly) love. They often invited poets to their courts and wrote poetry themselves. Sometimes a lady troubadour expressed disdain for her husband and desire for the knight whom she truly loved.

> I should like to hold my knight
> Naked in my arms at eve,
> That he might be in ecstasy
> As I cushioned his head against my breast,
> For I am happier far with him
> Than Floris with Blancheflor;
> I grant him my heart, my love,
> My mind, my eyes, my life.
>
> Fair friend, charming and good,
> When shall I hold you in my power?
> And lie beside you for an hour
> And amorous kisses give to you;
> Know that I would give almost anything
> To have you in my husband's place,
> But only if you swear
> To do everything I desire.[14]

Ladies demanded that knights treat them with gentleness and consideration and that knights dress neatly, bathe often, play instruments, and compose (or at least recite) poetry. To prove worthy of his lady's love, a knight had to demonstrate patience, charm, bravery, and loyalty. It was believed that a knight would ennoble his character by devoting himself to a lady. The rituals of chivalric love also enhanced the skills and refined the tastes of the noble. The rough warrior acquired wit, manners, charm, and a facility with words. He was becoming a courtier and a gentleman. Chivalric love did not involve a husband–wife relationship but a noble's admiration and yearning for another woman of his class. Among nobles, marriages were arranged for political and eco-

POPOL VUH: MAYAN CREATION MYTH

THE *POPOL VUH* IS THE ANCIENT SACRED BOOK of the Quiché Maya people of Guatemala. For centuries, the Popol Vuh was transmitted orally from one generation to another, but in the middle of the sixteenth century, it was finally written down. One hundred and fifty years later, it was translated into Spanish, but was not published until 1857. The Popol Vuh begins with an account of creation by the gods.

> This is the account of how all was in suspense, all calm, in silence; all motionless, still, and the expanse of the sky was empty. . . .
>
> There was nothing standing. . . . Nothing existed. . . .
>
> [The gods] planned the creation [and they said:] "Thus let it be done! Let the emptiness be filled! Let the water recede and make a void, let the earth appear and become solid; let it be done. Thus they spoke. Let there be light, let there be dawn in the sky and on the earth!"

Creation, however, was not complete: "There shall be neither glory nor grandeur in our creation . . . until the human being is made." After three failed attempts at making human beings, the gods finally created four men.

> They were endowed with intelligence; they saw and instantly they could see far, they succeeded in seeing, they succeeded in knowing all that there is in the world. . . .
>
> Then they gave thanks to the Creator and the Maker: "We really give you thanks, two and three times! We have been created, we have been given a mouth and a face, we speak, we hear, we think, and walk; we feel perfectly, and we know what is far and what is near. We also see the large and the small in the sky and on earth." . . .
>
> But the Creator and the Maker did not hear this with pleasure. . . . "Let us check a little their desires, because it is not well what we see. Must they perchance be the equals of ourselves, . . . who can see afar, who know all and see all?" . . .
>
> Then the Heart of Heaven blew mist into their eyes, which clouded their sight as when a mirror is breathed upon. Their eyes were covered and they could see only what was close, only that was clear to them.
>
> In this way the wisdom and all the knowledge of the four men . . . were destroyed. In this way were created and formed our grandfathers, our fathers, by the Heart of Heaven, the Heart of Earth.

The story continues with the creation of four women, who became the wives of the first four men, from whom the Quiché people descended. The remainder of Popol Vuh concerns the history of the Quiché and the chronology of their rulers up to 1550.

Delia Goetz and Sylvanus G. Morley, Popol Vuh: The Sacred Book of the ancient Quiché Maya, *from the translation of Adrián Recinos (Norman: University of Oklahoma Press, 1950), pp. 81–83, 89, 167–169.*

nomic reasons. The passion of adulterous love became so idealized in chivalric love poetry that it became an accepted part of the medieval chivalric code. Even though the church condemned adultery, many people of the High Middle Ages hoped that because the passionate, gallant knight was introduced to an exalted domain of heightened awareness through the instruction of his ladylove, not even the church would consider their love impious.

A prominent woman troubadour poet of the twelfth century was Marie de France. She composed literary works, particularly the Lais (songs), which vicariously enabled women to fulfill both their emotional and intellectual needs. Although little is known about her life, Marie de France is the first woman known to have written narrative poetry in the West. Her extant works—twelve *Lais*, 102 *Fables*, and *Saint Patrick's Purgatory*—were written in French some time between 1160 and 1214.

Both the morals of her fables and the themes of her lais demonstrate that she wrote for prestigious, intellectually capable people. Concerned with their emotional needs, Marie writes about the internal dynamics of family life, as well as relationships between lovers, husbands and wives, and lords and vassals. Common themes in her literature suggest that marriage restrains people and makes them sad, that the chivalric ideal necessitates sacrifice of self in behalf of one's lord, and that people inevitably suffer because of their own covetousness and conceit. However, the main message of Marie's poetry is that people have the power in their innermost selves to be emotionally free of life's cruelty and oppression.

In her lai *Yonec*, Marie describes a beautiful, young woman from a "good family" who marries an aged, jealous husband who "[b]ecause she was beautiful and noble . . . made very effort to guard her. He locked her inside his tower in a great paved chamber, . . . [for] more than seven years."[15] Bemoaning her fate, the young woman weeps bitterly and wishes she had never been born:

> I should never have been born!
> My fate is very harsh.
> I'm imprisoned in this tower
> and I'll never leave it unless I die.
> What is this jealous old man afraid of
> that he keeps me so imprisoned?[16]

She then curses her family for forcing her to marry this man, whom she suspects was baptized in "the river of hell."[17] Aware of chivalry and courtly romance, she dreams about having a "handsome, courtly, brave, and valiant"[18] lover. Within moments, a hawk flies into her chamber and becomes a handsome knight. The young wife

agrees to take him as her lover, but only if he believes in God, which he demonstrates by receiving the Eucharist.

Eventually their love is revealed to the young woman's husband by the old woman who guards the tower. The husband fashions "great spikes of iron forged, their tips sharpened—no razor on earth could cut better,"[19] which mortally wound the hawk when he next comes to visit his ladylove. Now pregnant with the knight's child, the young woman leaps from her window and follows his trail of blood to a palace in another town. Before he dies, her lover gives her a magical ring that will cause her husband to forget the past and free her from her prison. He also gives her a sword to bestow on their son, Yonec, when he becomes "a brave and valiant knight."[20] Soon after Yonec's investiture as a knight, the townspeople bring him and his mother to the tomb of "the best knight, the strongest, the most fierce, and the most handsome and the best loved, that had ever lived . . . [who was] killed for the love of a lady."[21] Realizing it is the tomb of her beloved, the woman gives Yonec his father's sword, declares her love for her lover and their son, and dies. Marie concludes her lai with Yonec avenging his mother's betrayal and death by beheading his stepfather and becoming lord of the land.

Dante Alighieri: *The Divine Comedy*

As a young man in Florence, Dante (1265–1321) began to read the ancient classical authors, as well as the church fathers, but because their Latin was so different from medieval Latin, he found them almost impossible to understand. Nonetheless, he persevered in his quest and eventually mastered their learning and their language. When Dante began to write, however, he wrote in the vernacular—his native Italian—rather than in Latin, the traditional language of intellectual discourse.

Dante was also familiar with the chivalric literature of southern France, and while still a teenager, he began to write poems in Italian, many of which are contained in his first work, *The New Life* (*La Vita Nuova*), written about 1292. In *The New Life*, Dante explains his fascination and love for a woman named Beatrice, who became the most important person in Dante's life, as well as in his literary career. He describes how he first saw Beatrice when he was nine years old:

> From then on indeed Love ruled over my soul, which was thus wedded to him [Love] early in life, and he began to acquire such assurance and mastery over me, owing to the power which my imagination gave him, that I was obliged to fulfil all his wishes perfectly.[22]

When Dante was eighteen, he and Beatrice exchanged a brief greeting:

> It was exactly the ninth hour of day when she gave me her sweet greeting. As this was the first time she had ever spoken to me, I was filled with such joy that, my senses reeling, I had to withdraw from the sight of others. So I returned to the loneliness of my room and began to think about this gracious person.[23]

Beatrice died suddenly when Dante was twenty-five.

In the final chapter of *The New Life,* Dante relates "a marvelous vision in which I saw things which made me decide to write no more of this blessed one [Beatrice] until I could do so more worthily." He then tells of his hope to write something concerning Beatrice "what has never been written in rhyme of any woman."[24] At the age of twenty-seven, Dante received another vision, this time of Beatrice, which inspired him to write his most famous work, *Divine Comedy,* in which he was able to fulfill his pledge to write "more worthily" about Beatrice.

The structure of the *Comedy* represents the significance of the three encounters he had with Beatrice as well as the importance of the Trinity. Written while Dante was in exile,* the *Comedy* is divided into three parts—the *Inferno,* the *Purgatorio,* and the *Paradiso*—which describe the poet's journey through hell, purgatory, and paradise. In the *Comedy,* Dante synthesized the various elements of the medieval outlook and summed up, with immense feeling, the medieval understanding of the purpose of life.

Written as an allegory, the *Inferno* relates the power of God, the Father; the *Purgatorio* depicts the wisdom of Jesus as God's son; and the *Paradiso* portrays the love of the Holy Spirit. Furthermore, to illustrate the importance of the Trinity, Dante designed the *Comedy* with a strict numerological plan—each part contains thirty-three cantos, plus one canto for the introduction, for a total of one hundred cantos. (A canto is a major division of a lengthy poem.) Dante wrote thirty-three cantos for each part to correspond with the traditional belief that Jesus lived thirty-three years. One hundred is the square of ten, and for Dante, ten was a perfect number because it consisted of the square of the Trinity (three) plus one to symbolize the triune God—God the "Three-In-One." Because the *Comedy* symbolizes the spiritual journey of every Christian who yearns for salvation but fears it will be denied because of human sinfulness, the *Comedy* later came to be better known as the "Divine Comedy." Like Aquinas's *Summa Theologica* and the Gothic cathedral, the *Divine Comedy* exemplified the medieval Christian spirit.

The first canto of the *Divine Comedy* opens on Good Friday (the Friday before Easter, the day Christians traditionally associate with the crucifixion of Jesus) as Dante—the symbol for every Christian—wanders from "the True Way" and finds himself "alone in a dark wood" of error and despair.[25] He then meets the Latin poet, Virgil—Dante's symbol for human reason—who becomes Dante's guide through hell to the base of Mount Purgatory. In the second canto, Dante describes his descent into hell, and in the third canto, he describes the entrance to hell and reads an inscription that states, "Abandon all hope ye who enter here."[26] Dante arranges hell into nine concentric circles; in each region, sinners are punished in proportion to their earthly sins.

In Limbo, which Dante describes in the fourth canto as the first circle of hell, Dante and Virgil meet the virtuous pagans and unbaptized children who because "they lacked Baptism's grace, which is the door of the true faith"[27] are neither permitted to enter heaven nor to suffer in hell proper. Here they also encounter the poets of antiquity—Homer, Horace, Ovid, and Lucan—and they pass into "a great Citadel" of reason where they meet celebrated heroes—including Hector, Aeneas, and Caesar. Finally, they are greeted by Aristotle, "the master of those who know," who is surrounded by "the great souls of philosophy," such as Thales, Heraclitus, Anaxagoras, Socrates, Hippocrates, Democritus, Plato, Diogenes, Zeno, Ptolemy, and Galen.[28]

In the lower circles of hell, Dante and Virgil experience all of hell's torments—burning sand, violent storms, darkness, and fearful monsters that whip, claw, bite, and tear sinners apart. The ninth circle, the lowest, is reserved for Lucifer and traitors. Lucifer has three faces, each a different color, and two batlike wings. In each mouth he gnaws on the greatest traitors in history: Judas Iscariot, who betrayed Jesus, and Brutus and Cassius, who assassinated Caesar. Dante and Virgil climb over the body of Lucifer, and Dante describes how they emerge from hell after three days—symbolic of Christ's "harrowing of hell"†—on Easter morning.

---

* Dante belonged to the moderate faction of the Guelphs (the Whites) and was one of six priors (magistrates) in Florence in 1301. The extreme papal faction (the Blacks) convicted him on trumped-up charges of graft and corruption and ordered him to pay an extraordinary fine. Unable to pay the fine, Dante was sentenced to death by fire; rather than die, he fled Florence in 1302 and remained in exile until his death.

† After his crucifixion, Christians believe that Jesus descended into hell for three days where he released the souls of all the saintly ones who had been held captive there since the beginning of the world. Furthermore, they believe that Jesus was then resurrected from the dead on Easter.

My Guide and I crossed over and began
to mount that little known and lightless road
  [the path of salvation]
to ascend into the shining world again.
He first, I second, without thought of rest
  we climbed the dark until we reached the point
  where a round opening brought in sight
    the blest and beauteous shining of the
    Heavenly cars.
And we walked out once more beneath
    the Stars.[29]

In Purgatory, Dante and Virgil meet sinners who, although they undergo punishment, will eventually enter paradise. As they are about to reach the summit of Mount Purgatory, Beatrice replaces Virgil as Dante's guide. Dante and Beatrice then ascend to the highest heaven, the Empyrean, which is located beyond Saturn, the last of the seven planets, beyond the circle of stars that encloses the planets and above the Primum Mobile—the outermost sphere revolving around the earth. Here at the summit of the universe is a realm of pure light that radiates truth, goodness, and gentleness. In paradise, the poet meets the great saints and the Virgin Mary. He glimpses the Vision of God. In this mystical experience, the aim of life is realized.

MEDIEVAL ART

The art and architecture of the Middle Ages served a religious function: Its purpose was to lift the mind to God. Depicting a spiritual universe in which the supernatural was the supreme reality, it gave expression to the vitality of the religious faith among medieval Christians and emphasized the central role the church played in their daily lives.

To remind people of the majesty and power of God, medieval architects designed huge cathedrals that soared toward the heavens. Fundamental spiritual truths were also articulated by pictorial arts—stained-glass windows in the cathedrals told biblical stories to remind worshipers of their religious obligations; illustrations in devotional manuscripts were meant to educate Christians; even tapestries, at times, articulated religious concerns. Painting conveyed many of the same spiritual values that are found in the other pictorial arts. Dark colors and contorted figures generally expressed evil beings, whereas the saved were often light, airy creatures painted with lighter colors. Medieval art was, therefore, the perfect forum to express the Christian view of the proper relationship between the individual and the universe.

Architecture

Building on the architectural style of the Carolingian and Ottonian period, the architects of the Middle Ages further developed Roman principles of vaulting, which allowed them to enclose vast areas without internal walls to support the vaulting. Beginning in the Romanesque period, during the eleventh and twelfth centuries, architects introduced the use of stone barrel vaults for churches to replace timbered ceilings, which were susceptible to fire. Commencing with the Gothic period, in the middle of the twelfth century, architects used the pointed arch to design cathedrals, which daringly surpassed anything previously built in the history of architecture. These medieval principles of vaulting were used until the nineteenth century when it became possible to enclose large areas of uninterrupted space using structural steel.

ROMANESQUE During the *Romanesque* period, from approximately 1050 to 1200, there was a conscious attempt—using the basilica form, arches, arcades, barrel vaults, and domes—to revive the architecture of ancient Rome. The most important innovation of the Romanesque period was the vaulting of nave ceilings. Although Carolingian and Ottonian architects had incorporated some vaulting for ground floor areas, they constructed flat, timbered ceilings for the naves. Moreover, in contrast to the cold, plain exteriors of the earlier period, which did little to encourage the attendance of worshipers, the exteriors of Romanesque churches seemed to welcome worshipers. The twin towers, with their accompanying spires and tolling bells, beckoned the faithful to come inside the church walls. Upon their arrival, as they entered the church through the expansive doors of the west façade, Christians were educated by the sculpture that now adorned the exterior.

Once inside the church, they could view relics of the saints. Devotion to relics had its origins in the early church. During the Crusades many relics were brought from the Holy Land—some real, others concocted. The Cult of Relics—veneration of the preserved bodies, or parts of bodies, of saints of the church as well as articles or clothing they used during their lives—was officially approved by the Council of Nicaea II (787) and the Council of Constantinople (1084) and became exceedingly popular during the Middle Ages. Many Christians believed the grace of God could be acquired through these relics. Therefore, magnificent reliquaries—receptacles containing relics—were fashioned, and shrines exhibiting acclaimed relics became centers for pilgrimages.

Romanesque architecture was fundamentally ecclesiastical architecture. During the period, sev-

Figure 11.1 *Baptistery of San Giovanni,* consecrated 1059, Florence, Italy
This octagonal structure, with its classical and restrained styling, is indicative of Italian Romanesque. The exterior makes use of both white and green marble, which was quarried in the mountains of Carrara, to the west of Florence. *(Scala/Art Resource, NY)*

eral types of church buildings were constructed: the cathedral, the principle church of a diocese and the seat of a bishop; the monastic/abbey church, serving the monks; the pilgrimage church, a stopover for pilgrims on their way to a sacred site or shrine; and the small parish church, ministering to the needs of the laity in a town or village. Numerous regional styles of Romanesque developed, but all of them generally made use of some common elements—thick walls, massive piers, rounded arches, small windows, and barrel vaults. Today there are more than ten thousand extant Romanesque structures, although some of them have been modified significantly.

Italian Romanesque is characterized by a classical and restrained style that developed particularly in the region of Tuscany—most notably at Florence and Pisa. To the north of Pisa, the mountains of Carrara were the source of white marble for church buildings, and green marble was quarried just to the west of Florence. The famous *Baptistery of San Giovanni* (Figure 11.1), consecrated in 1059, included both of these components. The design of this octagonal structure—incorporating rounded arcades and pilasters topped with Corinthian capitals—is highly classical. The stark

interior, which utilizes white marble, is a further illustration of classical simplicity and restraint. This classicism was deliberate—the architects intended both the interior and the exterior to contrast with the Byzantine structures at Ravenna and Saint Mark's Basilica in Venice.

The most ambitious undertaking of Romanesque architectural style in Italy was the complex at Pisa, known as *Campo dei Miracoli* (Figure 11.2), or "Field of Miracles"—the cathedral (1063), the baptistery (1153), the famous "Leaning Tower" or campanile (1174–1350), and the *camposanto,* the cemetery (1278). Busketos, the original Greek architect of the cathedral, utilized the design of an Early Christian basilica, but each of the large transept arms terminates in its own apse, giving the appearance of not one, but three basilicas. The extension of the nave and the apse and its intersection with the large transept resulted in the configuration known as the *cruciform,* resembling the Latin cross. The intersection is covered by a dome rather than the customary tower of the earlier period. The original timbered ceiling of the nave was covered with a coffered ceiling during the Renaissance. The pointed Gothic arch at the crossing of the nave and transept was also

Figure 11.2 *Campo dei Miracoli*, **Pisa, Italy** The "field of miracles" includes the cathedral (1063), the baptistery (1153), the famous "Leaning Tower," called a campanile (1174–1350), and the camposanto, or cemetery (1278). *(Guido Alberto Rossi/ Altitude)*

added later and is distinct from the other, rounded Romanesque arches. Measuring 325 feet in length x 115 feet in width x 111 feet in height, the cathedral is the largest of all Tuscan Romanesque structures. Like most Romanesque churches and in contrast to the simple exteriors of Early Christian basilica-form churches, the exterior of the cathedral is ornamented. Upward movement is suggested by the series of four arcades on the west façade.

The baptistery, begun in 1153 and designed by Diotisalvi, is 114 feet in diameter and 180 feet high. Only the lower arcade is Romanesque, for the upper levels and the dome are later Gothic additions. Although the campanile (bell tower) was begun more than a century after the cathedral, in 1174, its eight stories of stone arches and marble columns mirror the arcades of the cathedral. The 183-foot tower is faced with white marble banded in gray and black and is 63½ feet in diameter. The tower, finished in 1372, began to sink even before the third story was complete. By 1990, it was nearly five degrees out of plumb (approximately 17 feet) and was closed to the public so that reconstruction efforts could begin. On

December 15, 2001, the tower was reopened to the public so that people could once again climb the 293 steps to ascend to the top of the tower and look out across "The Field of Miracles." The *camposanto,* the enclosed cemetery behind the baptistery, was constructed from 1278 to 1283. The elongated classical arcades enclose a green field, under which are the tombs of famous Pisans. The structure was badly damaged in World War II but has been largely rebuilt except for the frescoes, which were beyond repair.

French Romanesque was more experimental than its conservative Italian counterpart. *Saint Sernin Basilica* at Toulouse (Figure 11.3) is the largest barrel-vaulted church in France. Begun in 1077, it was constructed to be a stopover church for pilgrims on their journey to Santiago de Compostela in northwestern Spain. Built of brick, Saint Sernin's cruciform design clearly was adapted to accommodate large crowds of pilgrims. Its nave was elongated, the side aisles were doubled, galleries above the side aisles opening into the nave were constructed, and the eastern end of the nave was extended into an ambulatory—a passageway with radiating chapels around the apse. The ambulatory and radiating chapels allowed pilgrims to pause before relics to offer their prayers and devotions.

More importantly, the side aisles served to transfer the lateral loads from the barrel vaults of the nave ceiling to the thick outer walls of the aisles. The nave ceiling is divided into *bays*—the subdivisions created by two sets of piers and their arches. The lower level of the nave includes arcades leading into the side aisles, above which are the galleries. Like many Romanesque churches, the interior of Saint Sernin was very dark because, except for the apse, it had no clerestory windows. The only lighting for the interior was drawn from the outer side aisles and the gallery, although the bell tower at the intersection of the nave and transept, completed during the Gothic period, did provide additional lighting.

From Toulouse, pilgrims traveled to Roncevalle in the Pyrenees Mountains, and then embarked on a fourteen-day journey through northern Spain, stopping at numerous pilgrimage churches along the way before they reached the climax of their pilgrimage experience, the cathedral *Santiago de Compostela* (Figure 11.4) in the northwest corner of Spain. The original cathedral was built at the supposed site of the tomb of Santiago, Saint James the Greater. According to the Spanish tradition Santiago preached the gospel in Spain, but was killed on his return to Jerusalem. Later, disciples reputedly returned his body to Spain; however, the location of the burial place was forgotten. In the early ninth century, relics of Saint James were found, and Alfonso II proclaimed him patron saint of Spain and ordered a sanctuary to be erected in his honor. Saint James also is viewed as the saint of Spanish Christian efforts to purge the area of Muslim influence.

Built in 899, the cathedral was destroyed by Muslims in 997 and replaced by a second cathedral in 1003. Then, in 1075, Alfonso VI, King of Castile, commissioned the French architect, Bernard le Vieux, to rebuild the cathedral in the French Romanesque style. Built by 50 stonemasons, the new cathedral was substantially complete by 1122. The barrel-vaulted nave is 143 feet long x 48 feet wide x 68 feet high and has 20 piers that divide it into eleven bays. At each end of the large transept is a chapel; five additional chapels radiate around the apse. Other churches in Spain were influenced by the architecture of Santiago de Compostela but, due to the exorbitant cost, none was so magnificent or monumental.

The Benedictine abbey church of *Saint Étienne* at Caen, which was consecrated in 1077, features a three-story nave, with an arcade into the side aisles, a gallery, and a clerestory. It also contains

Figure 11.3 *Saint Sernin Basilica* **(interior), begun 1077, Toulouse, France** This basilica is the largest barrel-vaulted church in France, and it was designed to be a stopover church for pilgrims on their journey to Santiago de Compostela in northwestern Spain. *(Editions Gaud)*

innovative six-part stone *ribbed* groin vaulting (Figure 11.5), which was a significant innovation in replacing *simple* groin vaulting. With the introduction of a second transverse rib or arch, crossing the vault from side to side, the two diagonal ribs divide the bay into six parts. Not only did the stone ribs add strength to the vaulting, but they also further reinforced the vaulting and articulated the parts of each bay.

GOTHIC The *Gothic* style, which began to develop around 1150 in Paris, replaced the Romanesque as the dominant form of architecture until it was supplanted by a new classicism during the Renaissance. Reaching toward God, the Gothic cathedral, like medieval scholasticism, subordinated this world to a higher world and earthly concerns to the divine. The Gothic cathedral, with its flying buttresses, soared toward heaven, rising in ascending tiers; it gave visual expression to the medieval conception of a hierarchical universe, with God at its apex. Although Gothic architects

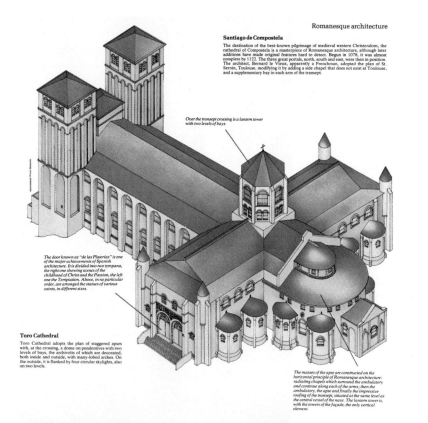

Romanesque architecture

Santiago de Compostela
The destination of the best-known pilgrimage of medieval western Christendom, the cathedral of Compostela is a masterpiece of Romanesque architecture, although later additions have made original features hard to detect. Begun in 1078, it was almost complete by 1122. The three great portals, north, south and east, were then in position. The architect, Bernard le Vieux, apparently a Frenchman, adopted the plan of St. Sernin, Toulouse, modifying it by adding a side chapel that does not exist at Toulouse, and a supplementary bay in each arm of the transept.

Over the transept crossing is a lantern tower with two levels of bays.

The door known as "de las Platerías" is one of the major achievements of Spanish architecture. It is divided into two tympana, the right one showing scenes of the childhood of Christ and the Passion, the left one the Temptation. Above, in no particular order, are arranged the statues of various saints, in different sizes.

Toro Cathedral
Toro Cathedral adopts the plan of staggered apses with, at the crossing, a dome on pendentives with two levels of bays, the archivolts of which are decorated, both inside and outside, with many-lobed arches. On the outside, it is flanked by four circular skylights, also on two levels.

The masses of the apse are constructed on the horizontal principle of Romanesque architecture: radiating chapels which surround the ambulatory and continue along each of the arms; then the ambulatory, the apse and finally the impressive roofing of the transept, situated at the same level as the central vessel of the nave. The lantern tower is, with the towers of the façade, the only vertical element.

Figure 11.4 *Santiago de Compostela*, completed by 1122, Spain   The original cathedral was reputedly built at the site of the tomb of Santiago, Saint James the Greater. According to the Spanish tradition, Santiago preached the gospel in Spain but was killed on his return to Jerusalem. Later, his disciples reputedly returned his body to Spain. (*From* The World Atlas of Architecture, *New York: Crescent Books, imprint of Random House, Inc., 1994, p. 207*)

Figure 11.5 *Saint Étienne* (interior), consecrated in 1077, Caen, France   By introducing a second transverse rib, or arch, to cross the vault from side to side, the two diagonal ribs divide the bay into six parts. The stone ribs add strength to the vaulting, reinforce the vaulting, and give definition to the parts of each bay. (*Editions Gaud*)

appropriated most of the features of Romanesque architecture—ambulatory and radiating chapels, ribbed groin vaulting, and pointed arches—they transformed these features and added new elements, especially flying buttresses, which made it possible to infuse the Gothic cathedral with light.

The Gothic period of architecture began with the transformation of the Carolingian abbey church of *Saint Denis,* between 1137 and 1144, under the leadership of Adam Suger (1081–1151). Saint Denis, who came to France as a missionary in 250, was beheaded by the Romans in 258 and, according to the legend, walked two miles carrying his head to the spot where he wished to be buried—the future site of the church. Pilgrims thus venerated the location of the church, and Saint Denis became the patron saint of France. The original church had long been associated with royal authority, for both Pepin and Charlemagne were consecrated as kings there, and it served as the burial place for Charles Martel, Pepin, and the Capetian kings of France. Because Suger was not only the abbot of the monastery but also chief minister to kings Louis VI and Louis VII, he aspired to make the new church of Saint Denis both a symbol of royal power and the spiritual center of France.

In his writings, Suger provides a florid description of the beauties of the church and its decorations, but in his account of the construction of the west façade and the new choir—the area between the apse and the nave, or transept—he neglects to mention the master architect's structural creativity or even name him. Suger first directed the addition of a new west façade for the old church:

> Thus we began with the former main entrance, dismantling a certain addition said to have been built by Charlemagne on very worthy occasion, because his father, the Emperor Pepin, had ordered that he be buried outside that entrance, face down, for the sins of his father Charles Martel. As is obvious, we exerted ourselves, vehemently enlarging the body of the church, tripling the entrance and doors, and erecting tall, worthy towers.[30]

The west façade, with its three portals with columnlike figures on the jambs, became the standard arrangement for the Gothic style.

Suger then addressed the rebuilding of the choir and the ambulatory, which still bears the imprint of his original design and embodies his fascination with light. In his little book, *On the Consecration of the Church of Saint Denis,* Suger describes the stained-glass windows of the "circular string of chapels" in the ambulatory "by virtue of which the whole [church] would shine with the wonderful and uninterrupted light of most sacred windows, pervading the interior beauty."[31] Unlike earlier chapels (see previous discussion of Saint Sernin) the radiating chapels of Saint Denis were fully integrated into a much larger ambulatory and were more like bay windows. The function of the ambulatory was to receive the multitudes of pilgrims who came to venerate the relics of saints, especially those of Saint Denis.

The most innovative feature of the ambulatory (Figure 11.6) is the use of ribbed groin vaulting. The pointed arches of the vaults facilitated the replacement of the huge piers of the Romanesque style with slender columns, which in turn made possible the piercing of the walls with many large

Figure 11.6 *Saint Denis* (interior), c. **1137–1144, Paris, France** The pointed arches of the vaults facilitated the replacement of the huge piers of the Romanesque style with slender columns, making it possible to pierce the walls with many large stained-glass windows, flooding the interior with light. *(Anthony Scibilia/Art Resource, NY)*

Figure 11.7 *Notre-Dame de Paris* (exterior), c. 1163–1220, Paris, France
The west façade encompasses most of the elements of the fully developed French Gothic style: three recessed portals lead into the nave and side aisles, above the portals is the Gallery of Kings, the third level consists of a rose window and two long, narrow lancet windows. *(Scala/Art Resource, NY)*

stained-glass windows to flood the interior with light. The outward thrust of the vaulting was supported by exterior buttresses (stone supports that counteract the force of the outward thrust exerted by an arch or a vault), which jutted out between the chapels. The principles of vaulting employed by Suger were further developed by later Gothic architects, who constructed naves of great height that were infused with light.

The cathedral *Notre-Dame de Paris* ("Our Lady of Paris") (Figure 11.7) echoes the new features that were first developed at Saint Étienne and then

at Saint Denis. Construction began in 1163 during the reign of Louis VII, and Pope Alexander III laid the first stone. The west façade, constructed between 1190 and 1220, encompasses most of the elements of the fully developed French Gothic style. Three recessed portals (doors) lead into the nave and side aisles; above the portals is the *Gallery of Kings*, which contains sculpture representing the kings of Israel; the third level embraces a circular window (*rose window*), which is situated between two long, narrow lancet windows. Although the twin towers of most Gothic cathedrals were topped with spires, Notre-Dame de Paris is a notable exception.

The choir is the oldest section of the interior (Figure 11.8) of the cathedral. The choir is located in front of the apse and is separated from the ambulatory by a carved screen (*choir screen*) to permit the clergy to pray without interruption. The 427-foot-long nave terminates in a short transept. The 107-foot-high six-part vaulting, the highest vaulting in Europe at the time, is reminiscent of the vaulting at Saint Étienne in Caen. The distinctive pointed arches of the interior are arranged according to the customary Gothic pattern—nave arcade, triforium gallery, and clerestory.

Some time after 1250, the most significant structural advancement of the Gothic period was added to reinforce the exterior walls of the Notre-Dame de Paris—*flying buttresses.* As the interior walls of churches became higher and higher, they tended to push outward, necessitating extra support to restrain this outward thrust. Flying buttresses accomplished this task by connecting the high, upper vaults to strong piers anchored to the ground (Figure 11.9). These buttresses enabled architects to design and construct naves of increasingly greater height; the result was a competition among towns to build the highest cathedral.

The advent of the High Gothic architectural style is marked by the rebuilding of the Romanesque styled *Notre-Dame de Chartres* (Figure 11.10). On July 10, 1194, a tremendous fire destroyed most of the town of Chartres and most of the cathedral. Under the direction of an unknown architect, the cathedral was rebuilt in

Figure 11.8 *Notre-Dame de Paris* (interior), c. 1163–1220, Paris, France   The 107-foot-high six-part vaulting is reminiscent of the vaulting at Saint Étienne in Caen. The distinctive pointed arches of the interior are arranged according to the customary Gothic pattern: nave arcade, triforium gallery, and clerestory. *(Ancient Art & Architecture Collection Ltd.)*

Figure 11.9 *Notre-Dame de Paris* (buttresses), after 1250, Paris, France   As the interior walls of churches became higher and higher, they tended to push outward, necessitating extra support to restrain the outward thrust. Flying buttresses accomplished this task by connecting the high, upper vaults to strong piers anchored to the ground. *(Anthony Scibilia/Art Resource, NY)*

Figure 11.10 *Notre-Dame de Chartres* (exterior), begun c. 1194, Chartres, France
Because the two spires topping the west façade towers were constructed nearly four centuries apart, they provide an interesting contrast between early and late Gothic architecture. The simple north spire was built between 1160 and 1170; the south spire, constructed in the early sixteenth century, is a good example of the flamboyant Gothic style. *(Guido Alberto Rossi/Altitude)*

three stages covering a period of less than thirty years. The 446-foot-long interior (Figure 11.11) consists of a nave culminating in an apse that houses the crypt bearing the relic of Mary, "The Veil of the Virgin," a piece of the garment supposedly worn by Mary when she gave birth to Jesus. The nave is divided into three levels—arcade, triforium gallery, and clerestory. The wide side aisles of the nave, which also run around the transept, were designed to hold the many pilgrims without bothering worshipers. The nave aisles then join other aisles at the choir to form an ambulatory, which is connected to the chapels surrounding the

Figure 11.11 *Notre-Dame de Chartres* (interior), begun c. 1194, Chartres, France   The wide side aisles of the nave, which also run around the transept, were designed to hold many pilgrims without disturbing the worshipers. At the center of the nave is the prayer labyrinth—a meandering stone path designed to symbolize Jesus carrying his cross to the crucifixion—which penitents circled on their knees as they recite their prayers. *(Notre Dame Chartres int, Editions Gaud)*

apse. At the center of the nave is the prayer labyrinth—a meandering stone path designed to symbolize Jesus carrying his cross to the crucifixion—which penitents circled on their knees.

As compared with the Romanesque style, the triforium at Chartres was modified from a wide gallery into a mere passageway, and the clerestory was enlarged until it was nearly as high as the nave arcade. The clerestory windows, consisting of a sequence of paired lancet windows beneath a small rose window, admitted more light than had the clerestory windows in Romanesque churches. In contrast to the double bays of Romanesque churches, the basic element for the design of the nave vaulting was a single rectangular bay. The narrow shafts of the nave piers appear to rise unimpeded to the 120-foot-high four-part ribbed vaults, making the cathedral three times higher than it is wide.

Because the two spires topping the west façade towers were constructed nearly four centuries apart, they provide an interesting contrast between early and late Gothic architecture. The simple north spire was built between 1160 and 1170; the south spire, constructed in the early sixteenth century, is a good example of the *flamboyant* Gothic style of the Late Middle Ages (see Chapter 12). The remaining features of the west façade reflect the usual elements of a French Gothic façade but, unlike Notre-Dame de Paris, the thirteenth-century gallery of kings is located above the rose window, instead of below it.

The Gothic style of architecture was introduced to England in 1175, when the French architect Guillaume of Sens began to rebuild the choir of Canterbury Cathedral, which had been destroyed by a devastating fire. A uniquely English style of Gothic architecture developed within fifty years after the reconstruction efforts at Canterbury. The most striking difference between the French and English styles was the English emphasis on the horizontal instead of the vertical.

Salisbury Cathedral was begun in 1220, and completed by 1258, except for the spire. However, in contrast to the French Gothic cathedrals, the four-part vaults of Salisbury are only 80 feet high and terminate at the triforium. The west façade (Figure 11.12), with its short, squat towers, is

Figure 11.12 *Salisbury Cathedral* (exterior), begun 1220, Salisbury, England The west façade, with its short, squat towers, is wider than the church itself. The 400-foot spire of the tower, marking the crossing of the nave and one of the two transepts, was the highest medieval stone spire. (© *Clive Hicks*)

wider than the church itself. Double transepts were characteristic of many English Gothic cathedrals; the second transept essentially converted the choir area into a second cruciform-type church. The 400-foot spire of the tower, which marks the crossing of the nave and one of the transepts, the highest medieval stone spire, was constructed in the fourteenth century.

Even though the interior of Salisbury (Figure 11.13) employs the same elements as those of the French Gothic style, it emulates the horizontal emphasis of the exterior. The triforium gallery is large and the clerestory is small, inserted between the ribs of the nave vaulting, which curve steeply upward from the triforium. This tends to compartmentalize the clerestory and hide it beneath the vaults. English Gothic architecture in general, and Salisbury Cathedral in particular, embraced such conservative, solid construction as a matter of choice, rather than out of necessity.

Because Italian Gothic architects tended to look backward to the older traditions of the Romanesque style and even to the early Christian basilica, the Gothic style in Italy was the most conservative in Europe. Even more than the English Gothic style, Italian Gothic emphasized width at the expense of height. Due to the sunny Mediterranean weather, Italian architects attempted to keep the interiors of the cathedrals cool by designing thicker interior walls that contained fewer and smaller windows.

The cathedral for the city of Florence was, from the beginning, a civic endeavor. In the late thirteenth century, the citizens, because their city was flourishing, decided that their present cathedral, Santa Reparata, was inadequate and not distinguished enough for them. The building history for *Santa Maria del Fiore* (Figure 11.14) is one of the longest and most fascinating of all cathedrals. In 1296, the committee of citizens accepted the design of Arnolfo di Cambio for the façade—to include a triple portal, pilasters, mosaics, and sculptures in niches. The facing of the side walls of the exterior imitated the colors and types

Figure 11.13 *Salisbury Cathedral (interior), begun 1220, Salisbury, England*   Although the cathedral employs the same elements as those of the French Gothic style, it emulates the horizontal emphasis of the exterior. The triforium gallery is large, and the clerestory is small—inserted between the ribs of the nave vaulting, which curve steeply upward from the triforium and tend to compartmentalize the clerestory and hide it beneath the vaults. *(Ancient Art & Architecture Collection Ltd.)*

Figure 11.14 *Santa Maria del Fiore* (exterior), c. 1296–1360, Florence, Italy The design of the façade includes a triple portal, pilasters, mosaics, and sculptures in niches. The facing of the exterior side walls copies the colors—rose, white, and green—and types of stone used for the nearby baptistery. *(Alinari/Art Resource, NY)*

of stone used for the nearby Romanesque baptistery of San Giovanni (see earlier description)—Maremma rose, Carrara white, and Prato green. After Arnolfo died in 1302, work on the cathedral proceeded slowly until 1334, when the painter Giotto (see Chapter 12) took over and designed the campanile. When Giotto died in 1337, a trio of architects (Andrea Pisano, Francesco Talenti, and Giovanni di Lapo Ghini) succeeded him and essentially completed the Gothic-style cathedral by 1360. Eight years later, the committee of architects decided to design new, higher vaulting. Although the actual height of the vaulting for the Florentine cathedral is nearly equal to that of the French Gothic cathedrals, the interior consists of only four bays and is three times as wide as the French cathedrals, which makes it appear to be not nearly as high as they are. The overall effect is of an interior composed of a single broad level, which significantly diminishes the clerestory. Because no flying buttresses were used to support the outward

thrust of the vaults, tie-rods had to be installed at the upper levels to contain the thrust.

There was, however, one huge problem that the architects could not solve in the fourteenth century—how to cover the immense octagonal space of the interior. This feat was not accomplished until the early Renaissance when Filippo Brunelleschi not only supervised the construction of the choir for the cathedral, but also designed its most outstanding feature—the dome—which towers over the surrounding streets. In 1587, the original façade of Arnolfo was demolished and a new design was commissioned. The present façade of the cathedral was not completed until 1887.

Germany was the last of the European countries to embrace the Gothic style, primarily because of its roots in the Holy Roman Empire and its accompanying affinity for the Romanesque architectural style. Beginning in 1230, the style was adopted at Strasbourg, Trier, and Marburg, and then at Cologne. In 1248, when the Carolingian church burned, the archbishop, Konrad of Hochstaden, decided to rebuild *Cologne Cathedral* (Figure 11.15) in the Gothic style. The most striking feature of the west façade is its twin towers of four stories, which, beginning at the clerestory level, culminate in two ornamented spires topping out at 515 feet.

The interior, designed by Master Gerhard in 1322, was to imitate the French Gothic style—five aisles, basilica style, ambulatory and radiating chapels, and extraordinarily high vaults. The columns of the nave were to rise unencumbered to vaults, and the walls were to be permeated with long, narrow, pointed windows. Unfortunately, only the choir and south tower were completed before construction was stopped in 1560. The plans were subsequently lost and were not redis-covered until the nineteenth century. Today, the nave (Figure 11.16) is 472 feet long x 147 feet wide x 143 feet high.

Following the completion of Cologne Cathedral in the nineteenth century, Gothic architectural style was also adopted in the United States—most notably in Saint Patrick's Cathedral and the Church of Saint John the Divine (the world's largest cathedral) in New York City and in the National Cathedral in Washington D.C.

Sculpture

Large-scale stone sculpture went into a steady decline after the fifth century and was nearly nonexistent in western Europe in the eighth and

Figure 11.15 *Cologne Cathedral* (exterior), begun **1248, Cologne, Germany** In 1248, when the Carolingian church burned, the archbishop decided to replace it with a Gothic-style cathedral. The west façade, with its twin towers of four stories, is the most striking feature. Starting at the clerestory level, they culminate in two ornamented spires reaching a height of 515 feet. *(Gian Berto Vanni/Art Resource, NY)*

Figure 11.16 *Cologne Cathedral* **(interior), begun 1248, Cologne, Germany** Imitating the French Gothic style, the columns of the nave were designed to rise unencumbered to extraordinarily high vaults, and the walls were to be penetrated by long, narrow, pointed windows. The nave alone measures 472 feet long x 147 feet wide x 143 feet high. *(Ancient Art & Architecture Collection Ltd.)*

ninth centuries. Although some statues were rendered in metal or ivory, the preponderance of the ornamental relief that has endured was fashioned of wood and was executed only on a small scale. Therefore, the revival of monumental stone sculpture during the Romanesque period was a profound artistic accomplishment. Sculpted figures were constricted and distorted because they were subordinate to the architecture. In the early Gothic period, however, the human form was partially freed from the constraints of architecture. Sculpture remained essentially religious in its subject matter and intent throughout the Middle Ages, but in the late Gothic, the sculpted human form became free standing and independent of the architecture and acquired a growing naturalism

and individualized realism—a trend that reached its heights in the Renaissance.

ROMANESQUE Initially, with the Romanesque revival of stone sculpture, statues were randomly placed throughout the church—places chosen for convenience rather than religious purposes—in the ambulatory, near the altar, in window moldings, and on the capitals of columns. Later, however, to facilitate better viewing with the intent of religious instruction, architectural sculpture was arranged on and around the portals of churches. As was the case in architecture, so, too, were there a variety of influences on the development of sculpture—Classical, Islamic, Byzantine, Near Eastern, and Carolingian or Ottonian.

Generally, sculpture during the Romanesque period was integrated into the architectural scheme of the structure, even if it meant distorting the figures to do so. *The Prophet* (Figure 11.17) at the abbey church of Saint Pierre at Moissac, northwest of Toulouse, is an excellent example of such distortion of the human body. This unnatural figure, either the prophet Jeremiah or Isaiah, is sculpted on the *trumeau,* or central pier, of the south portal. Holding the scroll of prophecy, the stylized, elongated body is contorted to fit into the space, with legs crossed and head turned. His pensive face is turned to one side, as his long hair flows over his shoulders and his beard streams across his chest. On the front of the trumeau are three pairs of lions, their bodies crisscrossed like Jeremiah's legs.

The Jeremiah *trumeau* is the central support for the tympanum of the south portal at Moissac. The figures of *Christ in Glory* (Figure 11.18) are sculpted to conform with the arched space of the tympanum. The entire scene depicts the second coming of Christ as recorded in the book of Revelation. The central figure represents Christ as king and judge: "[L]o a throne stood in heaven, with one seated on the throne" (Revelation 4:2). Christ is surrounded by the traditional symbols for the evangelists—the angel (Matthew); the winged lion (Mark); the eagle (John); and the winged ox (Luke)—flanked by two additional angels holding scrolls that contain the deeds by which Christ will judge humans. The smaller figures, twenty-four musicians turned toward Christ, represent the twenty-four elders who, in Revelation 4:11, worship Christ as king of all creation: "Worthy art thou, our Lord and God, to receive glory and honor and power, for thou didst create all things, and by thy will they existed and were created." The Romanesque appreciation of pattern is evidenced in the decoration around the tympanum and the portal. The rosette motif of the lintel and the arabesque designs of the archivolts (the arched bands enclosing the tympanum) demonstrate Islamic influence, and the scalloped decoration of the doorjambs reflects the influence of Spain.

The monastic church of Saint Madeleine, Vézelay, in Burgundy, was an important stop for pilgrims, who were drawn there because of its legendary origins, on their journey to Santiago de Compostela. According to tradition, Mary Magdalene traveled to southern France following Jesus' ascension to heaven and lived there for thirty years; after her death, her remains were taken to Vézelay for burial; then the church at Vézelay was named Saint Madeleine in her honor. The present Romanesque church, built early in the

eleventh century, contains a wealth of sculpture that played an important role in inspiring and instructing the Christian Crusaders of both the Second and Third Crusades. For the French, the Second Crusade began in the spring of 1146 at the monastery in Vézelay when Saint Bernard of Clairvaux preached a sermon, in the presence of King Louis VII, promoting the sacred cause. Nearly fifty years later, in 1190, the English joined the French Crusaders at Vézelay to launch the Third Crusade.

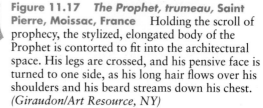

Figure 11.17 *The Prophet, trumeau,* **Saint Pierre, Moissac, France** Holding the scroll of prophecy, the stylized, elongated body of the Prophet is contorted to fit into the architectural space. His legs are crossed, and his pensive face is turned to one side, as his long hair flows over his shoulders and his beard streams down his chest. *(Giraudon/Art Resource, NY)*

Figure 11.18 *Christ in Glory,* **tympanum, Moissac, France** The entire scene depicts the Second Coming of Christ as recorded in the Book of Revelation. The central figure represents Christ as king and judge, flanked by two angels holding scrolls. The twenty-four musicians turned toward him represent the twenty-four elders who worship Christ as king of all creation. *(Gian Berto Vanni/Art Resource, NY)*

Figure 11.19 *Notre-Dame de Chartres* **(tympanum above the central portal, west façade), c. 1145–1155, Chartres, France** Reflecting a vision derived from the Book of Revelation, each figure at Chartres is defined and singular. Surrounding Christ are the twenty-four elders in the outer archivolts, the twelve angels in the inner archivolts, the twelve apostles on the lintel, and symbols for the four evangelists. *(Giraudon/Art Resource, NY)*

GOTHIC Like the sculpted figures of the Romanesque period, the figures of early Gothic sculpture were, for the most part, unnatural and columnlike. Unlike the figures of the Romanesque period, the Gothic figures can theoretically be construed as freestanding sculpture distinct from their architectural setting. This was achieved by treating each figure as a natural entity rather than distorting figures to fit the architectural scheme—as in the tympanum *Christ in Glory* and the *trumeau* of *The Prophet* at Moissac.

This new trend was already in evidence in the sculpture on the Royal Portal of the west façade at Chartres. Sculpted from about 1145 to 1155, the entire design details the life of Christ from his Nativity to his Second Coming. Like the tympanum of the south portal at Moissac, the tympanum above the central portal at Chartres (Figure 11.19) is a depiction of the vision of John recorded in the Book of Revelation. Unlike the confused scene at Moissac, however, each figure at Chartres is defined and singular—the twenty-four elders in the outer archivolts; the twelve angels in the inner archivolts; the twelve apostles, along with Enoch and Elijah, on the lintel; and the symbols for the four evangelists, which surround the imposing, central figure of Christ.

PICTORIAL ART

During the Middle Ages, the influence of the Christian church extended beyond architecture and sculpture to include the pictorial arts—metalwork, stained glass, manuscript illuminations, tapestries, and paintings. In all of these endeavors, the artists were both imaginative and creative, seeking to convey Christian teachings visually. They portrayed God as a mysterious being characterized by both justice and love. Whereas images of the imminence of the Last Judgment and Hell were designed to frighten the faithful into obeying God's commandments, images of the Virgin Mary and Jesus enthroned in heaven were rendered to offer Christians hope of salvation and a heavenly afterlife. In contrast to the three dimensions of architecture and sculpture, these medieval artists visually represented their subject matter on a two-dimensional surface using line and color.

Executed in metal, reliquaries, altar crosses, candlesticks, incense censers, crucifixes, chalices, and medallions to adorn sacred vessels are the most exquisite examples of ecclesiastical art. Most of the decoration was done using enamel, a technique that scholars assume came from Byzantium in the early part of the eleventh century, when it was embraced by German craftsmen. Toward the middle of the twelfth century artisans at Limoges, in east central France, became famous for the art of enameling, which remained centered at Limoges throughout the medieval period. The most outstanding and significant type of pictorial art was, however, the creation of stained-glass windows for the magnificent Gothic cathedrals.

Artisans were familiar with the process of making stained-glass windows during the Romanesque period, but it was not until Gothic times, when window surfaces became significantly larger, that it became a crucial art form. Abbot Suger, in his commentary about the beautiful stained-glass windows for the choir at Saint Denis, makes it clear that stained-glass windows were an integral element of Gothic architecture from the beginning. According to the twelfth-century German monk Theophilus, the glass was made from one part river sand and two parts dried beechwood potash. The exquisite colors were achieved by adding various metal oxides—blue (cobalt oxide), red (copper oxide), purple (manganese oxide), green (iron oxide), and yellow (sulphur or soot). Resembling a giant jigsaw puzzle, the many panels of a stained-glass window were mounted on a metal armature and set in lead on cross sections shaped like the letter *H*. The master glazier began his work by drawing the design on a wooden table smeared with chalk; the glass was then cut to correspond with the chalk shapes outlined on the table. Details were added by brushing the inner surfaces of the glass with various glass fillings, including copper oxide, vinegar, iron oxide, and urine, which were then fused onto the glass in a kiln. The completed pieces were then leaded into panels and attached to the metal armature.

The most numerous, and best-preserved, stained-glass windows are those that were created for the cathedral at Chartres. The four central panels for the famous *Notre-Dame de la Belle Verrière* (Our Lady of the Beautiful Window) were fashioned for the south ambulatory in the twelfth century. Because of the beauty of its blue glass, this window is often referred to as "The Blue Virgin Window" (Figure 11.20). It depicts the Virgin Mary with a crown on her head, seated on a throne supported by angels, holding her young son, Jesus, in her lap. In the early thirteenth century, angels holding incense burners were added on either side of Mary, and six panels depicting Jesus' first miracle at Cana (John 2:11) are positioned beneath her. Illustrations of the three temptations of Jesus by Satan are at the very bottom of the window.*

---

* Satan asked Jesus to turn a stone into bread, told him he would make Jesus king of the world if he would only worship

Figure 11.20 *Notre-Dame de la Belle Verrière,* c. 1170, Notre-Dame de Chartres, France "The Blue Virgin Window" depicts the Virgin Mary with a crown on her head, seated on a throne supported by angels, holding her young son, Jesus, in her lap. *(© Clive Hicks)*

The high point for making stained glass came between 1200 and 1250 and is typified by the three rose windows at Chartres—one for the Royal Portal (c. 1215), one for the south transept (c. 1224), and one for the north transept (c. 1231). The central figure in each of the three windows is Christ—in the north window, he is a child with his mother; in the south window, he is Christ in glory after his ascension; and in the rose window of the Royal Portal, he is judge of the world (Figure 11.21). In this west rose window, the figure

Satan, and took him to the summit of the temple and asked him to throw himself from it to prove that he was truly God's son (Luke 4:1-12).

of Jesus has visible, bleeding wounds. Jesus, flanked by the traditional symbols for the four evangelists, is surrounded by the elliptical and circular patterns containing scenes of angels and his twelve apostles assisting him during the Last Judgment.

As cathedral building declined, so too did the demand for stained glass. As a result, manuscript illumination came to the forefront of the pictorial arts. One of the best surviving examples is the elaborately illuminated Bible, executed by a man simply known as Hugo, for the Abbey of Bury Saint Edmunds in England. Hugo also carved the crucifix for the abbey, cast a bell, and carved the

Figure 11.21 *West Rose Window*, c. *1215, Notre-Dame de Chartres, Chartres, France* In this Royal Portal window, Jesus has visible, bleeding wounds, and he is flanked by the traditional symbols for the four evangelists. Scenes of the angels and his twelve apostles, who assist him during the Last Judgment, are evident in the surrounding elliptical and circular patterns. *(© Clive Hicks)*

bronze doors for the main entrance of the abbey (the only known bronze doors in medieval England). Between 1135 and 1140, he illuminated the "Bury Bible" with vivid colors that are almost enamel-like. *Moses Expounding the Law* (Figure 11.22) is the frontispiece for the Book of Deuteronomy. The upper panel depicts Moses and Aaron explaining the law to the Jews after the Exodus, and the lower panel shows Moses pointing out the clean and unclean animals (the happy, red pigs are the unclean ones). Moses is portrayed with horns because Jerome mistranslated the Hebrew word *karan* (Exodus 34:29) as Moses' "face was *horned*" instead of "his face *shone*." This mistranslation led to the traditional artistic rendition of Moses with horns in the Middle Ages and Renaissance. The entire page is bordered by a symmetrical leaf motif, which also separates the two panels. The human figures, stylized and formal, are structured by the patterns of their drapery and are typical of the period.

Medieval tapestries were impressive types of pictorial design reminiscent of the continuous-relief carvings of the friezes of the ancient Greeks and the carvings on victory columns such as the one for the Roman Emperor Trajan. The *Bayeux Tapestry* (c. 1073–1083), commissioned by the brother of William the Conqueror, is without precedent during the Romanesque period. This detailed design of needlework is a wool embroidery executed on eight bolts of natural linen cloth, employing only two types of stitches. In a *tapestry* the colored yarns form a design, which completely penetrates the resulting fabric. This is accomplished by interlacing colored weft yarns with those of the warp. It narrates the story of the Norman invasion of England in 1066 from the perspective of the Normans, depicting both the triumphs and brutality of war. The tapestry also contains scenes of daily life, and considering the preponderance of ecclesiastical art during the period, this was a rarity. Designed to run clockwise around the nave of the Cathedral of Bayeux in Normandy, the tapestry is 230 feet long but only twenty inches high. Scholars assume that it was fashioned by the women of Queen Matilda's court, all of whom would have been skilled embroideresses, for they probably worked on ecclesiastical vestments and other liturgical accoutrements used in the Mass. Some scholars suggest, however, that men must have worked on the tapestry because only they would have had such a detailed knowledge of military expeditions.

Latin titles were included for those who could read, but the formation of some of the letters suggests that an Anglo-Saxon embroiderer also worked on the tapestry. The scene shown here (Figure 11.23) depicts the death of the Anglo-Saxon king, Edward, and the coronation of Harold, the king whom William defeated. The people on the left rejoice at the news of this event, whereas the people on the right view it with trepidation because they interpret the comet (in the upper right-hand corner) as a portent of disaster, which is further suggested by the ghostlike Norman ships detailed in the lower border.

The series of seven *Unicorn Tapestries*—*The Start of the Hunt, The Unicorn at the Fountain, The Unicorn Leaps the Stream, The Unicorn Defends Himself, The Unicorn Is Captured by a Maiden, The Unicorn is Killed and Brought to the Castle,* and *The Unicorn in Captivity*—were woven by an unknown artist about 1500, and they

are the most famous tapestries ever executed. The setting is patterned after a medieval stag hunt, but the search is for a unicorn, which, according to Christian tradition, is such a fierce animal that no hunter can apprehend it without the help of a virgin maiden. The virgin charms the unicorn, who jumps into her lap and embraces her; he is then trapped and killed by the hunters and brought to the palace of the king. Each tapestry (except the badly damaged fifth one) is twelve feet, one inch high and has a background called *millefleurs*—a fanciful stylized scene imitating a flowery meadow—illustrating more than a hundred varieties of flora and fauna.

The entire series is both a secular cycle—similar to the poetry of chivalric love, in which a dauntless lover undergoes numerous trials to win the

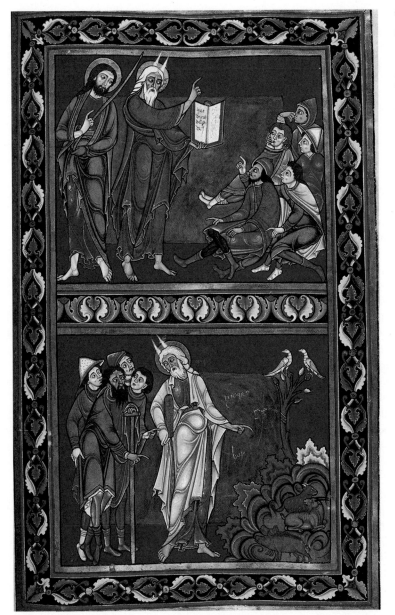

Figure 11.22 *Moses Expounding the Law: Bible of Bury Saint Edmunds,* c. 1135–1140, Bury Saint Edmunds, England, Corpus Christi College, Cambridge, England This illumination is the frontispiece for the Book of Deuteronomy. The upper panel depicts Moses and Aaron explaining the law to the Jews after the Exodus, and the lower panel shows Moses pointing out the clean and unclean animals. The entire page is bordered by a symmetrical leaf motif, which also separates the two panels. *(Courtesy, The Masters and Fellows of Corpus Christi College, Cambridge)*

Figure 11.23   *Bayeux Tapestry*, c. 1073–1083   This scene portrays the death of the Anglo-Saxon king, Edward, and the coronation of Harold. The people on the left rejoice at the news of this event, whereas the people on the right view it as a portent of disaster. *(Tapisserie de Bayeux and with special authorization from the town of Bayeux)*

acceptance of his ladylove; and a religious allegory—illustrating God's divine plan for the redemption of the human race. In the second tapestry, for example, the secular tradition of the medieval legend concerns the magical power of a unicorn's horn to extract a snake's venom from water to protect the birds and the beasts of the forest; whereas the sacred tradition asserts that the serpent represents evil, and that the unicorn is a symbol for Christ the redeemer of the world, with the animals signifying the redeemed of this world. Once the unicorn is killed in the sixth tapestry, the religious symbolism is advanced even further—the dead unicorn is adorned with a wreath of hawthorn, holly, and oak branches to symbolize the "crown of thorns" Jesus reputedly wore at his crucifixion. In the final tapestry, *The Unicorn in Captivity* (see chapter opening), the unicorn miraculously comes back to life and rests in a meadow surrounded by a circular fence. The theme is not related to a medieval stag hunt, but rather it is the culmination of both the sacred and secular purposes for which the series of tapestries was created: the unicorn, Christ, has fulfilled God's plan for redemption; the unicorn, wearing a *chaîne d'amour* (love chain) and tied to a tree, represents the suitor-bridegroom who has been captured by his bride in the hunt for love. This refers to the medieval poetry of chivalric love, in which the chaîne d'amour was often used to portray the courtier's devotion to his ladylove and his complete submission to her will.

Although painting mirrored the other Romanesque arts—in that numerous regional styles developed—no great advances were made to distinguish it from Carolingian or Ottonian painting. The most common type of church decoration was the wall mural, which generally depicted biblical scenes, particularly those illustrating the life of Jesus. Originally, the walls of Romanesque churches were covered with murals. For a variety of reasons—disapproval of the subject matter, lack of appreciation, and damp climatic conditions—few have survived. Nonetheless, painting continued to develop in Italy because Italian Gothic churches contained fewer and smaller windows and emphasized width rather than height. Subsequently, a new naturalism emerged in Italian painting during the late thirteenth century—on church and chapel walls as well as on painted wood panels (see Chapter 12).

MEDIEVAL MUSIC

Although the practice of music in the medieval West was founded in the Jewish tradition of sacred songs and chants, the development of music theory was rooted in the Greeks' concept of music as *musica*—a mathematical science and a pattern of thought that connected all things. The music of all earlier cultures, Mesopotamian, Hebrew, Greek, Roman, Byzantine, was essentially monophonic; that is, it consisted of a single melodic line. In the medieval West, however, there was a gradual transition from monophony to **polyphony** (two or more independent melodies performed at the same time). This had fundamental implications for the further development of music; it led to the discovery of harmony, to a greater emphasis on instrumental music, and to a heightened awareness of the intrinsic beauty of music itself.

Several early medieval thinkers theorized about music. Cassiodorus, in his *Institutiones,* divided instrumental music into "strings, winds, and percussion,"[32] and stated: "The discipline of music permeates all the acts of our life."[33] His words were echoed by Isidore of Seville, who declared, "No discipline can be complete without music."[34] Like the Greeks before him, Boethius associated the mathematics of music with the soul of the universe:

> [O]f the four mathematical disciplines,* the others are concerned with the pursuit of truth, but music is related not only to speculation but to morality as well. Nothing is more characteristic of human nature than to be soothed by sweet modes and stirred up by their opposites. . . . From this may be discerned the truth of what Plato not idly said, that the soul of the universe is united by musical concord. For when, by means of what in ourselves is well and fitly ordered, we apprehend what in sounds is well and fitly combined, and take pleasure in it, we recognize that we ourselves are united by this likeness.[35]

In the early sixth century, Boethius wrote *The Fundamentals of Music,* wherein he transmitted the Pythagoreans' idea of ratios (see Chapter 4) and developed a theory of music that held sway throughout the Middle Ages. Applying to music his penchant for philosophy, Boethius conceived of three types of music—music of the cosmos (*musica mundana*), human music (*musica humana*), and music of instruments (*musica instrumentalis*). Boethius determined that the music of the cosmos, because of its rational structure, was the supreme type of music.

> The first kind, the cosmic, is discernible especially in those things which are observed in heaven itself or in the combination of elements or the diversity of seasons. . . . But all this diversity gives birth to variety of both seasons and fruits in such a way that it nevertheless imparts one structure to the year. . . . [O]n the one hand, adjustment of pitch in lower strings is such that lowness does not descend into silence, while, on the other hand, adjustment of sharpness in higher strings is carefully monitored lest the excessively stretched strings break because of the tenuity of pitch, but the whole corpus of pitches is coherent and harmonious with itself, in the same way we discern in cosmic music that nothing can be so excessive that it destroys something else by its own intemperance. Everything is such that it either bears its own fruit or aids others in bearing theirs.[36]

Human music, however, sought to balance the rational with the irrational—the soul with the body.

Whoever penetrates into his own self perceives human music. For what unites the incorporeal nature of reason with the body if not a certain harmony and, as it were, a careful tuning of low and high pitches as though producing one consonance? What other than this unites the parts of the soul . . . of the rational and the irrational? What is it that intermingles the elements of the body or holds together the parts of the body in an established order?[37]

Because music with instruments had no text, it bore little relationship to human music and appealed specifically to the senses.

> The third kind of music is that which is said to rest in various instruments. This music is governed either by tension, as in strings, or by breath, as in the aulos or those instruments activated by water or by a certain percussion, as in those which are cast in concave brass.[38]

Boethius' *Fundamentals of Music* became the authoritative work about Greek musical theories for medieval musicians, but knowledge about most of the musical systems of classical antiquity was extinguished when the Western empire came under the control of the Germanic rulers. The art of making musical instruments was virtually lost so that only their names remained. It was chiefly from the Byzantines and Muslims that new prototypes for musical instruments were found, including the shawm, buisine, bagpipe, naker, tabor, rebec, lute, and guitar.

The Carolingian Renaissance brought a renewed interest in the manufacture and use of musical instruments for the festivities of the court: ceremonial processions, banquets, dances, tournaments, and hunts. By the tenth century, guilds of musicians were organized along the same lines as artisans. Particularly notable were the *meistersinger* (mastersingers) of Germany, for whom music was a craft with rules to be followed. Examinations were administered and contests were held to assess a musician's skills.

Church officials during the High Middle Ages objected to the sensual nature of the troubadours' music, particularly its use of instruments. Instead, following their Pythagorean predecessors, they viewed music as a philosophical discipline of the mind. Nonetheless, the music scholars of the medieval church attempted to appropriate the Pythagorean system to provide music for the celebration of the Mass. However, they

---

* The medieval quadrivium includes four mathematical sciences—arithmetic, geometry, astronomy, and music—which, along with the verbal arts of the trivium—grammar, rhetoric, and logic—constitute the seven liberal arts.

misunderstood its theoretical basis and subsequently transformed the seven modes of Pythagoras' "music of the spheres" (see Chapter 4) into eight *church* modes. The term Mass (Latin, *missa*) is derived from the chant sung at the end of the service—*Ite, missa est congregatio*—"Depart, the congregation is dismissed." For centuries to come, the medieval musicians' understanding of modes dominated the discussions about music theory in the West.

According to the medieval tradition, Pope Gregory I (the Great), pope from 590 until 604, inscribed the chants of a heavenly dove for use in the sacred music of the church—hence the use of the term **"Gregorian chant."** Also called *plainchant*, Gregorian chant was the first truly Western music. It began monophonically and flourished throughout the Middle Ages and the Renaissance. Consisting of thousands of melodies in the service of the liturgical functions of the church, Gregorian chant also served as the supporting structure for the further development of polyphony. In addition, the standardization of Gregorian chant paved the way for further advancements in Western music. For example, the advent of staff notation to indicate the relative pitch of the notes of a melody enabled singers to "read" music, instead of rote memorization of chants through constant practice. Schools of music also came into existence, including the so-called Notre Dame School of Music near Paris, which taught music as the *ars antiqua* (ancient arts). The *ars antiqua* served as the foundation for music theory for composers throughout Europe during the Middle Ages, and today Gregorian chants continue to be an integral part of worship services in many Christian churches.

To focus on the human voice and the spirituality of the Christian message, the chants were sung *a capella*, and throughout the Middle Ages, they provided an emotionally compelling vehicle for celebration of the Mass. Medieval Christians shunned the use of musical instruments in worship not only because they had been used by pagans, but also because they were generally associated only with secular activities, such as dancing. The first part of the medieval Mass was the *Ordinary—Kyrie, Gloria, Credo, Sanctus,* and *Agnus Dei*—which had chant texts that did not change, even though the music varied according to the occasions of the liturgical year. For example, the music would change for the Sundays of Advent leading to Christmas, the Sundays of Lent preceding Good Friday and Easter, and feast days for the Virgin Mary or the saints of the church. The second part of the Mass was the *Proper—Introit, Gradual, Alleluia, Offertory,* and *Communion*—in which

both the texts and the music were changed. Additional chant settings were required for the eight *Canonical Hours* (called *Offices*), which were done each day in a precise order, at specific times. The chants of *Matins* (before dawn), *Lauds* (at dawn), *Prime* (at 6:00 A.M.), *Terce* (at 9:00 A.M.), *Sext* (noon), *Nones* (at 3:00 P.M.), *Vespers* (at sunset), and *Compline* (after Vespers) were recited publicly only in monasteries or cathedral churches.

The person credited with inventing *staff notation* was Odo (c. 878–942), a Benedictine monk from the monastery at Cluny in France. Due to his success at fostering an interest in music at monasteries besides his own, Odo found it necessary to write down the music for the chants in an orderly fashion. To facilitate the "reading" of music, he assigned a letter of the alphabet to each tone of the scale—from A to G.

Later, Guido of Arezzo (c. 995–c. 1050), another Cluniac monk, refined Odo's system by designating a particular syllable for each tone—*ut, re, mi, fa, sol, la*—and arranged them on Odo's standardized four-line staff. Guido's advancement in teaching Western harmonic tones is called **solmization.** His Latin syllables were later modified to the familiar *do, re, mi, fa, so, la, ti, do,* which is the standard octave for music today. Guido's system was based on the *hexachord*; a hexachord could begin on one of three possible notes—C, F, or G—and regardless of which beginning note was chosen, *ut* was always the first tone of that scale. To assist musicians in memorizing the various scales, Guido is credited with creating a scheme whereby tones of the scale were assigned to specific parts of the hand. The "Guidonian hand" (Figure 11.24) subsequently became the standard for all treatises on music throughout the Renaissance.

During the Romanesque period, chants became more expressive, because intervals besides the octave, fourth, and fifth were added to the melodic line. During this period, most significant developments in Gregorian chant occurred in regions to the north of the Alps Mountains. In fact, the interval of the third became the hallmark of northern chants. This expressiveness is particularly evident in the chants associated with the Virgin Mary and further demonstrates the increasing popularity of the Cult of Mary (see p. 214). Whereas the earliest chants had depicted Mary in a generic manner (comparable to her portrayal in Byzantine mosaics), the later chants characterized her as a unique individual—*Ave Maris Stella* (Hail, Star of the Sea), *Mater dolorosa* (Mother of Sorrows), and *Salve regina* (Hail Holy Queen) and *Ave Maria* (Hail Mary as the mother of God).

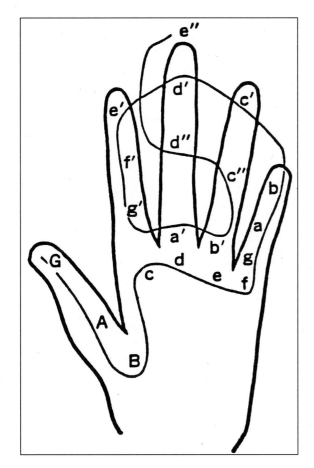

Figure 11.24 *"Guidonian hand"* To assist musicians in memorizing the various scales, Guido assigned tones of the scale to specific parts of the hand. The "Guidonian hand" subsequently became the standard for all treatises on music throughout the Renaissance. (*From the* Harvard Brief Dictionary of Music, *compiled by Don Michael Randel, Cambridge, MA: Belknap Press of Harvard University Press, 1978, p. 202).*

From the twelfth century forward, the chants of the Mass were composed *polyphonically.* The use of polyphony was often ceremonial, for it was designed to heighten the importance of various parts of the Mass—Kyrie, Gloria, Sanctus, Agnus Dei— or to accord prominence to important religious holidays, including Christmas and Easter. Sung by several soloists, the earliest type of polyphony was identified as *parallel organum*—the voices followed the same musical line (the plainsong, or melody) but were separated by a consistent interval (a fourth above or a fifth below the plainsong). Eventually, the musical lines deviated slightly (known as *free organum*) and finally developed into a more complex style of composition (known as *melismatic organum*). The first known composers of polyphony were associated with the Notre Dame School of Music: Leonin (c. 1135–c. 1201), who compiled a large volume of chants (*magnus liber*), and Perotin (c. 1160–c. 1205/25), who revised them.

Other forms of chant, although still religious, were not associated with the Mass. This can be seen in the compositions of Hildegard of Bingen (see p. 214), who created numerous innovative approaches to chant. She set to music a cycle of seventy lyrical poems, entitled *Symphony of the Harmony of Celestial Revelations (Symphonia harmoniae caelestium revelationum)*. Her morality play, *The Order of the Virtues (Ordo virtutum),* portraying the soul's struggle between sixteen virtues and the devil, contains eighty-two melodies and is viewed as a prototype of opera. Finally, her personal spirituality is apparent in the numerous *antiphons** that she composed concerning the Virgin Mary. The lyrics for *Antiphon #11*, for example, show Hildegard's understanding of the incarnation as she recalls that God chose women—Eve and Mary—to bring both sin and redemption into the world.

> O great wonder
> that in a hidden female body
> a king entered.
> God did this
> as humility rises above all.
> And O great the happiness
> in that woman,
> because the evil that came from woman,
> this one then swept away.
> She [Mary] built up sweet-smelling virtues
> and adorned Heaven yet more than
> she [Eve] had first marred earth.[39]

In the thirteenth century a new genre of music came into being—the *motet*—from the French *mot,* which means *word.* Originally a sacred work, a *motet* took a *cantus firmus,* fixed song, that is the fundamental melody of a sacred Latin text and superimposed additional melodies, with their own texts, on top of it. Quite often the texts of these additional melodies were secular love songs sung in the vernacular. Because the church generally shunned the use of musical instruments, except for the organ, musical instruments were rarely used and only for ceremonial occasions. But as the genre of motet further developed, the sacred Latin text of the cantus firmus was dropped, and its melody was played by instruments while the upper voices sang secular songs.

Mystery plays depended on musicians playing instruments to heighten the religious meaning of the dramatic story. The

---

* The term *antiphon* comes from the Greek word *antiphonia,* which means "countersound." In medieval music, it referred to free melodies sung in the same mode and alternating between a chorus of men and a chorus of women.

MUSICAL TERM	DEFINITION	EXAMPLE
Cantus firmus	Literally, "fixed song"; the fundamental melody; also called the *tenor*, derived from the Latin *tenere* meaning "to hold"	The melody a congregation sings, regardless of the type of accompaniment offered by the choir or the organ
A capella	Music sung without instrumental accompaniment	Singing in the shower, without the radio
Monophony	A single melodic line, sung or played	"London Bridges Falling Down" sung or played in unison
Polyphony	Two or more parts, each with its own melody, sung or played simultaneously	One person sings "London Bridges Falling Down," while another sings "Mary Had a Little Lamb," and a third person joins in singing "Twinkle, Twinkle, Little Star"
Harmony	The simultaneous occurrence of two or more musical tones; in contrast to a single line of melody	Barbershop quartets are a popular form of singing songs in harmony. The singers sing different parts, but the combination of notes produces chords which are pleasant to the ear.
Hexachord	A group of six consecutive tones of the scale, with a half tone (the smallest interval in music notation) between *mi* and *fa*	*(notation example: halftone; do re mi fa so la)*
Staff Notation	In medieval music, each musical note written on one of four parallel lines to indicate the pitch of each note; today the staff contains five lines	*(notation example: C D E F G A B C)*
Longa	A long note* in medieval musical notation; twice as long as a breve	⌐ longa
Brevis	A breve, used in medieval musical notation; if it were still used today it would equal a double whole note	▢ brevis
Semibrevis	The longest note in modern musical notation; the smaller values are each half as long as the preceding one; thus— half, quarter, eighth, sixteenth notes, etc.	◆ semibrevis = ○ (◼) whole note
Dissonance	A subjective term used to characterize intervals that sound unpleasant to one's ears; in the 12th and 13th centuries, the church considered the third and the sixth to be unpleasant and pushed the continuation of the prime, fourth, fifth, and octave as appropriate intervals	*(notation example: 3rd, 6th)*

* The term "note" properly connotes a written symbol, but the term is often used to represent the sound of the note, i.e., tone. In English, the terms are used interchangeably performances, often lasting several days, were sponsored by secular sources (such as municipal guilds) but were supervised by the clergy. The musicians performed at specific times of each play to heighten dramatic moments—the Annunciation, Christ's entry into Jerusalem on Palm Sunday, the Crucifixion, the Resurrection. Each instrument also had a symbolic meaning—the organ, playing three parts, represented the triune God; stringed instruments symbolized Christ; trumpets were employed to suggest solemn or regal occasions; hell was depicted through the use of metal pipes, barrels filled with stones, or genuine gunshots. Inevitably, each play would end with the singing of the *Te Deum* ("Thee, O Lord [we praise]"), which was occasionally accompanied by the organ or bells. The *Te Deum* is a hymn of thanksgiving and praise, which is sung as part of matins.

By the thirteenth century a system of rhythmic modes (based loosely on the meters of the poetry of antiquity) developed. This resulted in a precise way to connote the duration of each note on a musical staff. The church modes stabilized around three values—*longa* (the single), *brevis* (the double), and *semibrevis* (the third). Accompanying this was the movement away from the sacred texts of Gregorian chant, the use of secular love songs sung in the vernacular, and the increased use of musical instruments, which paved the way for the development of the *ars nova* (new art) of the fourteenth century (see Chapter 12). The *ars nova* was characterized by the addition of new intervals—principally, the third and the sixth—dissonance, and disjointed rhythms. Altogether, these innovations ultimately removed music from the realm of metaphysics— music as an avenue to truth and spiritual insight. In time, the function of music was transformed. Instead of concentrating on its reputed association with higher truth, moral behavior, and healing, music came to be composed, sung, and played for its aesthetic qualities, and appeal. Rather than viewing music as a science based on mathematical ratios deciphered by the analytic mind, music came to be seen as an art whose structures and sounds are discerned by our sense of hearing.

Christianity and the Arts

Christian themes were central to the arts of the Middle Ages. Christian writers extolled the virtues of monastic life and wrote about the power of the seven sacraments. In addition, they acknowledged the significance of the ideal of the Virgin Mary, who served as a model for all subsequent heroines, and encouraged young women to become morally virtuous.

Religious hymns and dramas, as well as epic poems such as Dante's *Divine Comedy,* detailed the battle each Christian waged against sin. This literature also expressed a disdain of worldly, sensual pleasures of the flesh; allegorized religious events such as Jesus' Crucifixion, Resurrection, and Ascension; and emphasized loving one's neighbor, pursuing a life of virtue, and obeying God's commandments. Such themes also provided inspiration for innumerable artists, writers, and musicians.

Even nonliterate people were able to comprehend biblical truths and stories because of manuscript illuminations, frescoes, sculptures, tapestries, mosaics, and stained-glass windows. In some way, each kind of pictorial art portrayed a spiritual universe in which God was the supreme reality. In addition, monumental Romanesque towers and soaring Gothic vaulting in Christian cathedrals reminded people of the power and majesty of God. Most importantly, like the Gothic cathedral that appeared to touch heaven itself, so too could the human mind ascend to the mind of God wherein the human will and God's will became fused. Even when Gothic architecture was modified to fit the cultural tastes of various countries, the Christian message was not diminished.

Christian motifs would continue to pervade the arts after the Middle Ages came to a close. Renaissance artists achieved their greatest triumphs by depicting biblical stories, as with Michelangelo's rendering of Old Testament stories on his ceiling frescoes in the Sistine Chapel, his depiction of the Last Judgment for its apse wall, and his portrayal of Moses and David in monumental statues. Renaissance artists were also concerned with the Christian themes of God's justice, love, mercy, wrath, vengeance, and compassion. Even after the Protestant Reformation shattered the unity of Christendom, both Catholic and Protestant writers, artists, and composers continued to depict biblical epics, the miracles of Jesus, the Day of Judgment, and the Apocalypse. From the Renaissance on, countless *Madonna and Child* paintings show the enduring imprint of Christian symbols on the European mind.

During the seventeenth century a number of Christian writers wrote works that are regarded as literary monuments. Edmund Spenser's *The Faerie Queen* sought to fuse Christian revelation with Greek and Roman sources, and it has remained enormously popular, because readers continue to view the adventures of the Red Cross Knight as a type of Christian "everyman" who wanders in error but emerges as a Christlike figure. John Milton's *Paradise Lost* and John Bunyan's *The Pilgrim's Progress* helped to define further the Christian conception of Satan, sin, and salvation and became "classical" sources for works such as William Makepeace Thackeray's *Vanity Fair* in the nineteenth century and T. S. Eliot's *The Wasteland* in the twentieth century.

In addition to developing a system of musical notation that made it possible to preserve and transmit music from one generation to another, medieval musicians also produced sacred music that would inspire both listeners and composers for centuries. During the eighteenth and nineteenth centuries, composers were drawn to the power and mystery of the Mass and arranged music for it. Many of them also composed *Requiem Masses,* including Johann Sebastian Bach, Wolfgang Amadeus Mozart, Giuseppe Verdi, and Johannes Brahms. The eighteenth-century oratorio *The Creation,* by Franz Joseph Haydn, combined the six days of creation in the Genesis story with the Enlightenment's skeptical view of Adam and Eve and the fall of the human race. Some compositions have even come to epitomize Christian holidays, such as George Frederick Handel's *Messiah* and Bach's *Magnificat,* pertaining to Christmas, and Bach's *St. Matthew Passion* and numerous musical renderings of *The Seven Last Words of Christ,* associated with Christian Holy Week and Easter. For centuries, the revered Virgin Mary also was the subject of important musical compositions; perhaps the most famous and beloved is *Ave Maria* by the nineteenth-century composer Franz Peter Schubert.

But today, in an increasingly secular world, few artists, writers, and composers try to produce specifically "Christian art"; unlike past ages, they are not directly inspired by Christian doctrines and feelings. Notable exceptions are gospel music and Christian rock, whose creative renditions continue to attract talented composers and appreciative audiences. Yet, a close analysis of some important works in the arts demonstrates that beneath the secular layer lies a Christian influence that is still recognizable, even if the artist did not intentionally intend it. For instance, the connection between black gospel music and jazz and rock 'n' roll is well known. Moreover, Christian symbols and motifs still find their way into numerous surrealist paintings of the Crucifixion and The Last Supper; and in literature, Christian-related concepts of guilt, repression, sin, and salvation often compete with modern-day psychological interpretations of repression, neuroses, and psychoses. Finally, many works of Christian art, literature, and music of past centuries are still admired for their aesthetic qualities, and for some, they remain a constant source of spiritual insight and inspiration.

Key Terms

mystery plays	flying buttresses
goliards	tapestry
romance	polyphony
troubadours	Gregorian chant
Romanesque	solmization
Gothic	antiphons

Notes

1. Excerpted in Charles W. Jones, ed., *Medieval Literature in Translation* (New York: Longmans, Green, 1950), pp. 904–905.
2. Ibid., trans. Edward James Martin, pp. 919–920.
3. Quoted in Charles Homer Haskins, *The Rise of Universities* (Ithaca, N.Y.: Cornell University Press, 1957), pp. 86–87.
4. Quoted in Marcia L. Colish, *Medieval Foundations of the Western Intellectual Tradition 400–1400* (New Haven, Conn.: Yale University Press, 1997), p. 202.
5. Excerpted in David C. Riede and J. Wayne Baker, eds., *The Western Intellectual Tradition,* vol. 1 (Dubuque, Ia.: Kendall/Hunt Publishing Company, 1980), p. 162.
6. Glyn Burgess, trans., *The Song of Roland* (London: Penguin Books, 1990), p. 156.
7. Ibid.
8. Ibid., pp. 88–89.
9. Ibid., pp. 155–156.
10. A. T. Hatto, trans., *The Nibelungenlied* (London: Penguin Books, 1969), p. 23.
11. Excerpted in Anthony Bonner, ed., *Songs of the Troubadours* (New York: Schocken Books, 1972), pp. 42–43.
12. John Rutherford, *The Troubadours: Their Lives and Their Lyrics* (London: Smith, Elder & Co., 1873), p. 142.
13. Ibid., p. 41.
14. Quoted in Frances Gies and Joseph Gies, *Women in the Middle Ages* (New York: Crowell, 1978), p. 45.
15. Marie de France, *Yonec,* in *Medieval Women Writers,* ed. Katharina M. Wilson (Athens: The University of Georgia Press, 1984), p. 71.
16. Ibid., p. 72.
17. Ibid.
18. Ibid., p. 73.
19. Ibid., p. 77.
20. Ibid., p. 80.
21. Ibid., p. 82.
22. Dante Alighieri, *La Vita Nuova (Poems of Youth),* trans. Barbara Reynolds (Baltimore: Penguin Books, 1969), p. 30.
23. Ibid., p. 31.
24. Ibid., p. 99.
25. Dante Alighieri, *The Inferno,* ed. and trans. John Ciardi (New York: New American Library, 1954), p. 28.

26. Ibid., p. 42.

27. Ibid., p. 50.

28. Ibid., pp. 53–54.

29. Ibid., p. 287.

30. David Burr, *Abbot Suger, What Was Done During His Administration* [Online] Available http://history.hanover.edu/courses/excerpts/344sug.htm, February 27, 1998.

31. Quoted in Byrce D. Lyon, *The High Middle Ages: 1000-1300,* (New York: The Free Press, 1964), p. 213.

32. Anicius Manlius Severinus Boethius, *Fundamentals of Music,* trans. Calvin M. Bower, ed. Claude V. Palisca (New Haven: Yale University Press, 1989), p. 10.

33. Quoted in Joseph R. Strayer, *Dictionary of the Middle Ages,* vol. 8 (New York: Charles Scribner's Sons, 1987), p. 579.

34. Ibid., trans. J. Wayne Baker.

35. Quoted in David L. Wagner, ed., *The Seven Liberal Arts in the Middle Ages* (Bloomington: Indiana University Press, 1983), p. 171.

36. Boethius, *Fundamentals of Music,* pp. 9–10.

37. Ibid., p. 10.

38. Ibid.

39. Sabina Flanagan, *Hildegard of Bingen, 1098–1179: A Visionary Life* (London and New York: Routledge, 1989), p. 110.

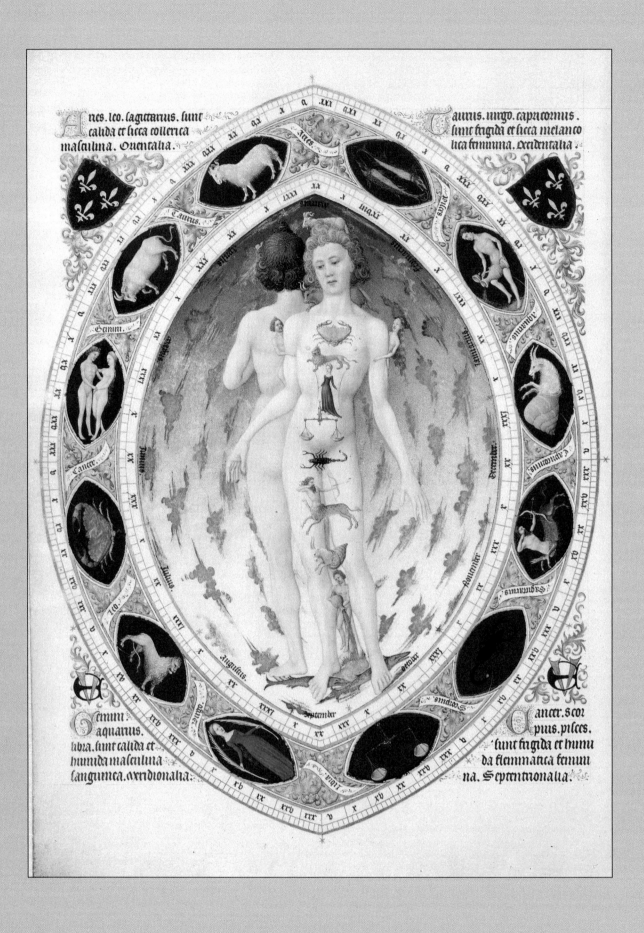

The Late Middle Ages: Crisis, Continuity, and Change

B Y THE START OF THE FOURTEENTH CENTURY, Latin Christendom had experienced more than 250 years of growth. On an economic level, agricultural production had expanded, commerce and town life had revived, and the population had increased. On a political level, kings had become more powerful, bringing greater order and security to large areas. On a religious level, the papacy had demonstrated its strength as the spiritual leader of Christendom, and the clergy had been reformed. On a cultural level, a unified worldview, blending faith and reason, had been forged.

During the Late Middle Ages, roughly the fourteenth and early fifteenth centuries, medieval civilization was in decline. The fourteenth century, an age of adversity, was marked by crop failures, famine, population decline, plagues, stagnating production, unemployment, inflation, devastating warfare, and abandoned villages. Violent rebellions by the poor of the towns and countryside were ruthlessly suppressed by the upper classes. The century witnessed flights into mysticism, outbreaks of mass hysteria, and massacres of Jews; it was an age of pessimism and general insecurity. The papacy declined in power, heresy proliferated, and the synthesis of faith and reason, erected by Christian thinkers during the High Middle Ages, began to disintegrate. These developments were signs that the stable and coherent civilization of the thirteenth century was drawing to a close.

But all was not decline and gloom. On the positive side, representative institutions developed, and thinkers showed a greater interest in the world of nature. And in Italy, the dynamic forces of urbanism and secularism were producing a period of cultural and humanistic flowering known as the Renaissance.

THE FOURTEENTH CENTURY: AN AGE OF ADVERSITY

In the fourteenth century, Latin Christendom was afflicted with an agricultural crisis. Limited use of fertilizers and limited knowledge of conservation exhausted the topsoil. From 1301 to 1314, there was a general shortage of food, and from 1315 to 1317, famine struck Europe. Throughout the century, starvation and malnutrition were widespread.

Adding to the economic crisis was the *Black Death,* or bubonic plague. This disease was carried by fleas on black rats and probably first struck Mongolia in 1331–1332. From there, it crossed into Russia. Carried back from Black Sea ports, the plague reached Sicily in 1347. Spreading swiftly throughout much of Europe, it attacked an already declining and undernourished population. The

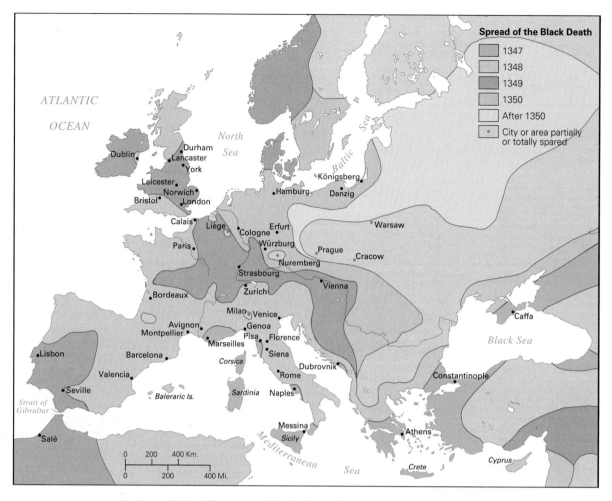

Map 12.1   The Course of the Black Death in Fourteenth-Century Europe   Note the routes that the bubonic plaque took across Europe.

first onslaught lasted until 1351, and other serious outbreaks occurred in later decades. The crowded cities and towns had the highest mortalities. Perhaps twenty million people—about one-quarter to one-third of the European population—perished in the worst natural disaster in recorded history.

Panic-stricken people drifted into debauchery, lawlessness, and frenzied forms of religious life. Organized bands of flagellants marched from region to region, beating themselves and each other with sticks and whips in a desperate effort to appease God, who, they believed, had cursed them with the plague. Art concentrated on morbid scenes of decaying flesh, open graves laden with worm-eaten corpses, dances of death, and the torments of hell. Sometimes, this hysteria was directed against Jews, who were accused of causing the plague by poisoning wells. Terrible massacres of Jews, often by mass burnings, occurred despite the pleas of the papacy.

Compounding the adversity were the conflicts known as the Hundred Years' War (1337–1453).

Because English kings had ruled parts of France, conflicts between the two monarchies were common. The war continued on and off throughout the fourteenth century. In a portentous development, the later stages of the Hundred Years' War saw the use of gunpowder and heavy artillery.

After the battle of Agincourt (1415), won by the English under Henry V, the English controlled most of northern France. It appeared that England would shortly conquer France and join the two lands under one crown. At this crucial moment in French history, a young and illiterate peasant girl, Joan of Arc (1412–1431), helped rescue France. Believing that God commanded her to drive the English out of France, Joan rallied the demoralized French troops, leading them in battle. In 1429, she liberated the besieged city of Orléans. Imprisoned by the English, Joan was condemned as a heretic and a witch in 1431 by a handpicked church court. She was burned at the stake. Inspired by Joan's heroism, the French drove the English from all French territory except the port of Calais.

THE DECLINE OF THE PAPACY

The principal sign of the decline of medieval civilization in the Late Middle Ages was the waning authority and prestige of the papacy. In the High Middle Ages, the papacy had been the dominant institution in Christendom, but in the Late Middle Ages its power declined. The medieval ideal of a unified Christian commonwealth guided by the papacy was shattered. Papal authority weakened in the face of the growing power of kings, who championed the parochial interests of states. As the pope became more embroiled in European politics, papal prestige and the pope's capacity to command diminished. Many pious Christians felt that the pope behaved more like a secular ruler than like an apostle of Christ. Political theorists and church reformers further undermined papal authority.

Conflict with France

Philip IV of France (1285–1314) taxed the church in his country to raise revenue for war. In doing so, he disregarded the church prohibition against taxing its property without papal permission. In 1296, Pope Boniface VIII (1294–1303) decreed that kings and lords who imposed taxes on the clergy and the clergy who paid them would be excommunicated. Far from bowing to the pope's threat, Philip acted forcefully to assert his authority over the church in his kingdom. Boniface backed down from his position, declaring that the French king could tax the clergy in times of national emergency. Thus, the matter was resolved to the advantage of the state.

A second dispute had more disastrous consequences for Boniface. Philip tried and imprisoned a French bishop despite Boniface's warning that this was an illegal act and a violation of church law and tradition, which held that the church, not the state, must judge the clergy. Philip summoned the first meeting of the Estates General to gain the backing of the nation. Consequently, in 1303, Boniface issued the bull *Unam sanctam*, which claimed that the pope had the power to establish and depose temporal rulers and threatened to excommunicate Philip. The outraged monarch raided the papal summer palace at Anagni in September and captured the pope. Although Boniface was released, this shocking event proved too much for him, and a month later he died.

Boniface's two successors, Benedict XI (1303–1304) and Clement V (1305–1314), tried to conciliate Philip. In particular, Clement decided to remain at Avignon, a town on the southeastern French frontier, where he had set up a temporary residence. From 1309 to 1377, a period known as the *Babylonian Captivity,* all of the popes were French and resided in Avignon, not Rome, and were often forced to pursue policies favorable to France. Moreover, the luxurious style of living at Avignon repulsed the laity, and they resented the appointment of high churchmen to lands where they did not know the language and showed little concern for the local population.

The Great Schism and the Conciliar Movement

Pope Gregory XI returned the papacy to Rome in 1377, ending the Babylonian Captivity. But the papacy was to endure an even greater humiliation: the *Great Schism.* Elected pope in 1378, Urban VI abused and imprisoned a number of cardinals. Fleeing from Rome, the cardinals declared that the election of Urban had been invalid and elected Clement VII as the new pope. Urban refused to step down and excommunicated Clement, who responded in kind. To the utter confusion and anguish of Christians throughout Europe, there were now two popes: Urban ruling from Rome and Clement from Avignon.

Prominent churchmen urged the convening of a general council—the Council of Pisa (1409)—to end the disgraceful schism, which obstructed the papacy from performing its sacred duties. Attended by hundreds of churchmen, the Council of Pisa deposed both Urban and Clement and elected a new pope. Neither deposed pope recognized the council's decision, so Christendom then had three popes. A new council was called at Constance (1414–1418). In the struggle that ensued, each of the three popes either abdicated or was deposed in favor of an appointment by the council. In 1417, the Great Schism ended.

The underlying premise of the *Conciliar Movement*—the theory that the authority of a general council of the church is superior to that of the pope—reached its peak at the councils of Pisa and Constance but had depleted itself by the end of the Council of Basel (1431–1449). Thus, the Conciliar Movement attempted to transform the papal monarchy into a constitutional system. Supporters of the movement held that the papacy could not reform the church as effectively as a general council representing the clergy. However, as the papacy regained its authority over the higher clergy and the Conciliar Movement lost its political support, Pope Pius II (1458–1464) was able to condemn it as heretical in 1460.

Deeply embroiled in European power politics, the papacy often neglected its spiritual and moral responsibilities. Many devout Christians longed for a religious renewal, a return to simple piety.

The papacy barely heard this cry for reform. Its failure to provide creative leadership for reform made possible the Protestant Reformation of the sixteenth century. By splitting Christendom into Catholic and Protestant, the Reformation destroyed forever the vision of a Christian world commonwealth guided by Christ's vicar, the pope.

LATE MEDIEVAL THOUGHT

Critics of Papal Power

The conflict between Boniface and Philip provoked a battle of words between proponents of papal supremacy and defenders of royal rights. In his treatise *On Ecclesiastical Power*, Giles of Rome (c. 1245–1316) vigorously supported the doctrine of papal power. Because the spiritual is inherently superior to the temporal, he argued, the pope has the authority to judge temporal rulers. All temporal lords ought to be governed by spiritual and ecclesiastical authority, and especially by the pope, who heads the church.

Defenders of royal prerogatives challenged the pope's claim to primacy over both secular rulers and the clergy. In taking this position, they weakened the medieval church. *On Kingly and Papal Power* (1302) by John of Paris (c. 1241–1306) attacked the theory of papal monarchy championed by Giles of Rome and asserted the independence of the French monarchy. For John, the church was primarily a spiritual body charged with administering the sacraments; as such, its authority did not extend to temporal affairs. Indeed, clerical interference in secular affairs threatened the state's stability. While granting that "the priest is superior to the ruler in dignity," John maintained that "it is not necessary to be superior to him in all things." Because both rulers and priests derive their power from God, said John, they are each superior in their own sphere. "The priest is, therefore, superior in spiritual matters and conversely, the ruler is superior in temporal matters."[1]

The most extreme denial of papal and clerical authority in the Middle Ages came from Marsilius of Padua (c. 1290–c. 1343). In his *The Defender of the Peace* (1324), Marsilius held that the state ran according to its own principles, which had nothing to do with religious commands originating in a higher realm. Religion dealt with a supranatural world and with principles of faith that could not be proved by reason, wrote Marsilius. Politics, on the other hand, dealt with the natural world and the affairs of the human community. Political thinkers should not try to make the earthly realm conform to articles of faith. For Marsilius, the state was self-sufficient; it needed no instruction from a higher authority. Thus, Marsilius denied the essential premises of medieval papal political theory: that the pope, as God's vicar, was empowered to guide kings; that the state, as part of a divinely ordered world, must conform to and fulfill supranatural ends; and that the clergy were above the laws of the state.

Marsilius viewed the church as a spiritual institution with no temporal power. The state, with the consent of the people, exercises coercive authority over both the political community and the church. Consequently, the clergy are subject to the state in all temporal affairs and even in the spiritual realm. Thus, by transferring power from the church to the state, Marsilius essentially made the church a state institution.

Pope John XXII excommunicated Marsilius for his ideas in 1327, and his work was again condemned as heretical at the beginning of the Great Schism in 1378. Marsilius's view on church–state relations influenced the reformers John Wycliffe and Jan Hus (see following section), but no one was willing to go as far as Marsilius in subjecting the church to state authority until the Reformation.

Fourteenth-Century Heresies

In the Late Middle Ages, another threat to papal power and the medieval ideal of a universal Christian community guided by the church came from the radical reformers who questioned the function and authority of the entire church hierarchy. The theories of these heretics foreshadowed the Reformation.

The two principal dissenters—the Englishman John Wycliffe (c. 1320–1384) and the Bohemian (Czech) Jan Hus (c. 1369–1415)—made important contributions to the debate over the power of the papacy and the relationship between the church and the state. By stressing a personal relationship between the individual and God and by claiming the Bible itself, rather than church teachings, to be the ultimate Christian authority, Wycliffe challenged the fundamental position of the medieval church: that the avenue to salvation passed through the church alone. He denounced the wealth of the higher clergy and sought a return to the spiritual purity and material poverty of the early church. Until 1379, Wycliffe accepted the jurisdiction of the pope, but during the Great Schism, his thought underwent a radical change—he denied the legitimacy of the papacy, arguing that it was not a divine institution created by God, but a human institution that had been created by the emperor Constantine.

To Wycliffe, the wealthy, elaborately organized hierarchy of the church was unnecessary and wrong. The splendidly dressed and propertied bishops bore no resemblance to the simple people who first followed Christ. Indeed, these worldly bishops, headed by a princely and tyrannical pope, were really anti-Christians, the "fiends of Hell." Although Wycliffe did not agree with Marsilius that the state should rule the church, he did want the state to confiscate church property and the clergy to embrace poverty.

By denying that priests changed the bread and wine of communion into the substance of the body and blood of Christ, Wycliffe rejected the sacramental power of the clergy. The church, in response, deprived the *Lollards*—an order of poor priests that spread Wycliffe's teachings—of their priestly functions. In the early fifteenth century, some of Wycliffe's followers were burned at the stake.

Wycliffe's ideas were enthusiastically received by Czech reformers in Bohemia led by Jan Hus. Like Wycliffe, Hus advocated vernacular translations of the Bible, which would be accessible to common people, and upbraided the upper clergy for their luxury and immorality. Although he also closely followed Wycliffe's thought on civil and ecclesiastical authority, Hus did not deny the legitimacy of the papal office. He affirmed that the pope received his spiritual authority from Christ. However, if the pope were to abuse his authority, as Hus thought some popes had, he was not to be obeyed.

Although both movements were declared heretical and Hus was burned at the stake by the Council of Constance (even though he had been promised safe conduct to and from the Council), the church could not crush the dissenters' followers or eradicate their teachings. To some extent, the doctrines of the Reformation would parallel the teachings of Wycliffe and Hus.

Breakup of the Thomistic Synthesis

In the Late Middle Ages, the papacy lost power as kings, political theorists, and religious dissenters challenged papal claims to supreme leadership. The great theological synthesis constructed by the scholastic theologians of the twelfth and thirteenth centuries was breaking down. The process of fragmentation seen in the history of the church took place in philosophy as well.

Thomas Aquinas's system had culminated the scholastic attempt to show the basic agreement of philosophy and religion. In the fourteenth century, a number of thinkers cast doubt on the possibility of synthesizing Aristotelianism and Christianity, that is, reason and faith. Denying that reason could demonstrate the truth of Christian doctrines with certainty, philosophers tried to separate reason from faith. Whereas Aquinas had said that reason proved or clarified much of revelation, fourteenth-century thinkers asserted that the basic propositions of Christianity were not open to rational proof. Whereas Aquinas had held that faith supplemented and perfected reason, some philosophers were now proclaiming that reason often contradicted faith.

To be sure, this new outlook did not urge abandoning faith in favor of reason. Faith had to prevail in any conflict with reason because faith rested on God, the highest authority in the universe. But the relationship between reason and revelation was altered.

Articles of faith, it was now held, had nothing to do with reason; they were to be believed, not proved. Reason was not an aid to theology but rather a separate sphere of activity. This new attitude snapped the link between reason and faith that Aquinas had so skillfully forged. The scholastic synthesis was disintegrating.

The chief proponent of this new outlook was William of Ockham (c. 1285–1349). In contrast to Aquinas, Ockham insisted that natural reason could not prove God's existence, the soul's immortality, or any other essential Christian doctrine. Reason could only say that God probably exists and that he probably endowed human beings with an immortal soul. But it could not prove these propositions with certainty. The tenets of faith were beyond the reach of reason, said Ockham; there was no rational foundation to Christianity. For Ockham, reason and faith did not necessarily complement each other as they did for Aquinas; it was neither possible nor helpful to join reason to faith. He did not, however, seek to undermine faith—only to disengage it from reason.

In the process of proclaiming the authority of faith, Ockham also furthered the use of reason to comprehend nature. Ockham's approach, separating natural knowledge from religious dogma, made it easier to explore the natural world empirically, without fitting it into a religious framework. Ockham, thus, is a forerunner of the modern mentality, which is characterized by the separation of reason from religion and by an interest in the empirical investigation of nature.

LATE MEDIEVAL LITERATURE: CONTINUITY WITH TRADITIONAL THEMES

Much of the literature of the fourteenth century continued to focus on traditional Christian themes: God, who ordained the natural order for both this world and the next, and the love of God as the means to the perfection of self and this world. Whatever the medium—letters, poems, romances, allegories, or morality plays—the literature spotlights devotion to Christ and the Virgin Mary, the authority of the pope, and the value of the clergy as administrators of the sacraments. A traditional morality is evident in all genres of literature—in the face of death, individuals struggle to find assurance of their salvation from sin. Sometimes, however, the chivalric knight is held to such lofty goals and becomes so idealized that only Christ himself could achieve such perfection.

The Letters of Catherine of Siena

Catherine of Siena (1347–1380) was the twenty-third child born to her family, and very early in her life she evidenced a deep devotion to Christ. Declaring that Christ alone would be her bridegroom, Catherine vowed never to marry. In 1365, she entered the Dominican order of nuns to consecrate herself to self-discipline and prayer. While in the convent she had a series of mystical experiences, including a marriage to Christ and the imposition of **stigmata**. (Stigmata are marks resembling the wounds on the hands and feet of the crucified Christ.) Francis of Assisi is also said to have had stigmata, but unlike Catherine's, his were said to be visible. Mystical experiences such as these continued for the rest of her life.

Catherine's ecstatic spiritual experiences drew widespread attention, and her piety became well known. Beginning in the 1370s, Catherine, who was illiterate, dictated more than 350 letters, including some to popes. Her *Dialogue on Divine Providence* and her letters reveal a commitment to the belief that "perfect love"—love of God—can transform the world and keep people in harmony with God. Echoing Augustine, she also believed that love of self upsets the natural order of things. Self-love, Catherine asserted, was the evil power responsible for the Great Schism. Thus, she reproved Urban VI, whose abuse of the clergy precipitated the crisis.

> Most holy and most dear Father in sweet Jesus Christ. I, Catherine, the servant and the slave of the servants of Jesus Christ, write to you in His precious blood. . . . And truly, most holy Father, he alone is established in charity who is ready to die for the love of God and the salvation of souls, since he is stripped of all self-love, of all love of himself. The man taken up with self-love is not ready to give his life. It is not simply a matter of his life; he doesn't seem willing to endure the slightest trouble. He fears for himself, for the life

of his body, and for his comforts. So what he does is both imperfect and corrupt because his principal desire for which he strives is corrupt. And in every station of life he achieves little good, whether he be shepherd or subject.[2]

Catherine died in Rome in 1380 and, in 1461 was canonized (declared a saint) by Pope Pius II. Her veneration extends well into the modern world. In 1939, Pope Pius XII bestowed on her the title "Patron of Italy," thus combining her patronage with that of Francis of Assisi. And in 1970, Pope Paul VI proclaimed Catherine a "Doctor of the Church"—to date, she is the only woman ever to have received such a distinction.

The Vision of Piers Plowman

Written by William Langland (c. 1330–c. 1400) in the late fourteenth century, *The Vision of Piers Plowman* is a moral allegory that holds to a mystical ideal similar to that of Catherine of Siena—human beings are saved by a deep-seated faith that remains unaffected by external circumstances. At the same time, it is a satire that mocks the immorality and hypocrisy of both polite English society and the clergy. The text of *Piers Plowman* exists in three versions, which scholars simply call A, B, and C. The A version is 2,000 lines long; the B version is a revision of A with 4,000 new lines, and the C version is a revision of B. Because nothing is known about the author, it is unclear if Langland wrote all three versions.

The poem begins with a prologue describing the dream of a poet in May (a common opening for medieval poets) in which he sees a variety of people in a field engaged in simple tasks; the field is bordered on the west by the Dale of Death, and on the east, by the Tower of Truth. The Dreamer first meets Lady Holy Church, who instructs him in the fundamental tenets of Christianity.

The Plowman finally appears, more than a thousand lines into the poem. Although he is portrayed as an ordinary, principled farmer, the Plowman comes to represent biblical figures—Adam, Moses, Jesus, the Apostle Peter—as well as the "good" popes. Therefore, the Plowman symbolizes both the fallen humanity Christ was sent to redeem and the human nature Jesus assumed to redeem humans. The Plowman promises to lead the people to Holy Truth, but as more and more pilgrims fall by the wayside, the road to Holy Truth comes to symbolize each individual's personal spiritual journey. The Dreamer searches for the Plowman, believing he can assist him in his pilgrimage to truth. This account of the Dreamer's quest for truth also includes a portrayal of Christ's

Passion and his "Harrowing of Hell" (I Peter 3:18–19), pertaining to the three days Jesus spent in hell overcoming evil prior to his resurrection.

> A voice loud in that light cried to Lucifer,
> "Princes of this place, unpin and unlock,
> For he comes here with crown who is King
>   of Glory."
> Then Satan sighed and said to hell, . . .
> "If this King comes in he will carry off
>   mankind. . . .
> And now I see where a soul comes
>   descending hitherward
> With glory and with great light; God it is,
>   I'm sure.
> My advice is we all flee.". . .
> Again the light bade them unlock, and
>   Lucifer answered,
>   "*Who is that?*
> What lord are you?" said Lucifer. The light at
>   once replied,
>   "*The King of Glory.*
> The Lord of might and of main and all manner
>   of powers:
> *The Lord of Powers. . . .*
> And with that breath hell broke." . . .
> And those that the Lord loved his light
>   caught away,
> And he said to Satan, "Lo, here's my soul
>   in payment
> For all sinful souls, to save those that
>   are worthy."[3]

The Vision of Piers Plowman became a staple of English literature for the next three centuries. During the sixteenth and seventeenth centuries, however, English reformers consistently borrowed Langland's reproof of the corrupt Roman church as they sought the separation of the English church from the Roman papacy—a notion that would have exasperated the medieval poet who thought he was defending the true church.

Sir Gawain and the Green Knight

The beautiful verses of *Sir Gawain and the Green Knight* were composed by the Pearl Poet around 1375. A lone English manuscript from the fourteenth century contains four poems—*The Pearl, Purity, Patience,* and *Sir Gawain and the Green Knight*—which are stylistically so much alike that scholars have designated a single author for all of them, calling him the Pearl Poet. Because Gawain's exploits had been known previously through the Welsh *Mabinogion* and Celtic legends, the poem can be viewed as a continuation of Arthurian legend, but it is not a *typical* chivalric romance.

Rather, it is a didactic *moral* romance, for the hero, Gawain, is held to highly idealized moral standards. The fact that the poem focuses on only two adventures, instead of numerous ones, also makes it an atypical romance. Both of Gawain's adventures—the challenge to his faithfulness to his word when his life is at risk and the test of his moral integrity by the lady of the castle—are found in earlier sources, but the themes are uniquely united in this poem.

Gawain is first introduced to the reader during the New Year's festivities at Camelot, when the Green Knight unexpectedly enters to challenge anyone to strike him with his own ax, with the expectation that he will reciprocate the act a year and a day later. Because no one accepts the Green Knight's invitation, the embarrassed King Arthur assumes the challenge himself. But as Arthur raises the ax, Gawain breaks in and offers to be Arthur's substitute.

> Would you grant me the grace, . . .
> To be gone from this bench and stand by
>   you there. . . .
> Though you be tempted thereto, to take it
>   on yourself
> While so bold men about upon benches sit. . . .
> I am the weakest, well I know, and of
>   wit feeblest;
> And the loss of my life would be least of any;
> That I have you for uncle is my only praise;
> My body, but for your blood is barren of worth;
> And for that this folly befits not a king.[4]

Gawain then cuts off the head of the Green Knight with one blow. Through his courteous words and brave actions, Gawain diffuses a volatile situation and restores the credibility of the Knights of the Round Table.

A year later, as part of the initial challenge, the much-heralded Gawain must submit to the promised reciprocal blow by the Green Knight (who is remarkably intact, although the author never tells us how he came to be restored). Anticipation of the event causes great sorrow in Camelot.

> All this courtly company comes to the king
> To counsel their comrade, with care in
>   their hearts;
> There was much secret sorrow suffered that day
> That one so good as Gawain must go in
>   such wise
> To bear a bitter blow, and his bright sword
>   lay by.[5]

As Gawain arrays himself in his armor, the poet describes the manifold symbolism of the gold pentangle on Gawain's shield (reputedly patterned after the sign of King Solomon) as a means of further developing his image of Gawain as the perfect knight. The pentangle represents not only the five senses, but also the five wounds of Christ on the cross, the five joys of Mary,* and five virtues—beneficent love, boundless love, brotherly love, pure mind and manners, and compassion.

On his way to meet the Green Knight, Gawain endures many perils—serpents, wolves, wild men in the woods, bulls, bears, boars, giants, and a dreadful winter. On Christmas Day, as he is praying, Gawain becomes aware of a magnificent castle that proves to be the dwelling of Bercilak de Hautdesert. On numerous occasions, Bercilak's wife attempts to seduce Gawain, but he deftly rebuffs her advances and remains chaste and faithful to his host. She then tries to entice him with an expensive ring, but again, he refuses her gift. Finally, she offers him her girdle with its power to bestow strength. At first, he rejects the gift, but then the lady tells him of its supposed powers.

> For the man that possesses this piece of silk,
> If he bore it on his body, belted about,
> There is no hand under heaven that could hew
>   him down,
> For he could not be killed by any craft on earth.[6]

Knowing that he must meet the Green Knight in two days' time, Gawain accepts the gift. That evening, however, Gawain neglects to tell Bercilak of the gift his wife has given him. Therefore, Gawain is guilty not only of lying to his host but also of betraying him.

Having compromised his standards, Gawain sets out for the Green Chapel. Along the way, his guide entreats him to flee, but Gawain remains true to his word—he will meet the Green Knight. Once Gawain reaches the Green Chapel, he discovers that the Green Knight is actually Bercilak. Mortified that his betrayal of his host is known, Gawain listens as Bercilak tells him that it was he and his wife who forced Gawain to submit to a series of tests, and that Bercilak admires Gawain for choosing life over death when he accepted the girdle.

> . . . I know well the tale,
> And the count of your kisses and your
>   conduct too,
> And the wooing of my wife—it was all
>   my scheme!
> She made trial of a man most faultless by far
> Of all that ever walked over the wide earth. . . .
> Yet you lacked, sir, a little in loyalty there,
> But the cause was not cunning, nor
>   courtship either,
> But that you loved your own life; the less, then,
>   to blame.[7]

Despite what Bercilak says, Gawain, who holds himself to unrealistically high moral standards, cannot forgive himself. Therefore, Gawain keeps the girdle, wears it around his neck as a symbol of his disgrace, and confesses his shame:

> This is the blazon of the blemish that I bear on
>   my neck;
> This is the sign of sore loss that I have
>   suffered there
> For the cowardice and coveting that I came
>   to there;
> This is the badge of false faith that I was found
>   in there,
> And I must bear it on my body till I breathe
>   my last.
> For one may keep a deed dark, but undo it
>   no whit,
> For where a fault is made fast, it is
>   fixed evermore.[8]

The poem then quickly concludes with the epithet *Hony Soyt Qui Mal Pense*, (shame be to the man who has evil in his mind), which stands for Gawain's credo. Because the phrase that concludes the poem was the motto of the Order of the Garter, which was founded by King Edward III, some scholars believe that the Pearl Poet was a courtier of the king.

Until the elevation in stature of other Knights of the Round Table (Lancelot, by the French writer Chrétien de Troyes, and Parcival, by the German author Wolfram von Eschenbach), Gawain remained the ideal of a knight—courteous, faithful, noble, and trustworthy.

Roman de la Rose

The *Roman de la Rose* (The Romance of the Rose) is arguably the most famous French allegory. Guillaume de Lorris, about whom virtually nothing is known, wrote the original 4,000-line poem in the latter half of the thirteenth century. The reader comes to understand the psychology of love through the poet's (the Lover of the poem) quest for the Rose (the symbol for his beloved) and his encounters with characters representing the emotions of love.

In the style of Dante's *Divine Comedy*, the poem is a dream sequence in which the poet dreams about a garden encircled by a sculpted wall. The figures on the wall—Greed, Sorrow, Envy, Hate, Hypocrisy, Villainy, Greed, Felony, Covetousness,

---

* According to the medieval Christian tradition, the five joys of Mary were the Annunciation—when the angel of God told Mary she would bear Jesus; the Nativity—when Jesus was born; the Resurrection—when Jesus was raised from the dead; the Ascension—when Jesus ascended to heaven to sit at the right hand of God; and the Assumption—when Mary herself was taken to heaven by God.

IBN BATTUTA: WORLD TRAVELER

IBN BATTUTA (1304–1369), A DEVOUT MUSLIM, was a native of Morocco who traveled throughout the Near East, India, China, and Spain, journeying approximately 75,000 miles. In 1352, toward the end of his journeys, he traveled south from his home in Tangier through the Sahara Desert to the Kingdom of Mali. In the following passage, Battuta makes observations about his accommodations and about the sultan. He praises the black Muslims' sense of justice and cleanliness and admires their respect for the Koran, but he also notes their "bad qualities."

I reached the city of Malli [Mali], the capital of the king of the blacks. I . . . went to the quarter occupied by the whites, where I asked for Muhammad ibn al-Faqih. I found that he had hired a house for me and went there. . . . I met the qadi [judge] of Malli, . . . who . . . is a negro, a pilgrim, and a man of fine character. . . .

The sultan of Malli . . . is a miserly king, not a man from whom one might hope for a rich present. . . . On certain days the sultan holds audiences in the palace yard. . . . The sultan comes out of a door in a corner of the palace, carrying a bow in his hand and a quiver on his back. On his head he has a golden skull-cap, bound with a gold band. . . . His usual dress is a velvety red tunic. . . . The sultan is preceded by his musicians, who carry gold and silver guimbris [two-stringed guitars], and behind him come three hundred armed slaves. He walks in a leisurely fashion, affecting a very slow movement, and even stops from time to time. . . . As he takes his seat the drums, trumpets, and bugles are sounded. Three slaves go out at a run to summon the sovereign's deputy and the military commanders, who enter and sit down. . . . The negroes are of all people the most submissive to their king and the most abject in their behaviour before him. . . . If he summons any of them while he is holding an audience in his pavilion, the person summoned takes off his clothes and puts on worn garments, removes his turban and dons a dirty skullcap, and enters with his garments and trousers raised knee-high. . . .

The negroes possess some admirable qualities. They are seldom unjust, and have a greater abhorrence of injustice than any other people. Their sultan shows no mercy to anyone who is guilty of the least act of it. There is complete security in their country. Neither traveller nor inhabitant in it has anything to fear from robbers or men of violence. . . . They are careful to observe the hours of prayer, and assiduous in attending them in congregations, and in bringing up their children to them. On Fridays, if a man does not go early to the mosque, he cannot find a corner to pray in, on account of the crowd. . . .

Another of their good qualities is their habit of wearing clean white garments on Fridays. . . . Yet another is their zeal for learning the Koran by heart. They put their children in chains if they show any backwardness in memorizing it, and they are not set free until they have it by heart. . . . Among their bad qualities are the following. The women servants, slave-girls, and young girls go about in front of everyone naked, without a stitch of clothing on them. Women go into the sultan's presence naked and without coverings, and his daughters also go about naked. Then there is their custom of putting dust and ashes on their heads, as a mark of respect. . . . Another reprehensible practice among many of them is the eating of carrion, dogs, and asses.

Source: *Ibn Battuta*, Travels in Asia and Africa, 1325–1354, *trans. H. A. R. Gibb, The Broadway Travellers, ser. ed. E. Denison Ross and Eileen Power (New York: Augustus M. Kelley, 1969), pp. 323–324, 326–327, 329–331.*

Old Age, and Sorrow—represent the vices that can prevent the poet from obtaining the Rose from the garden. The poet then meets Love, attended by Youth, Riches, Sweet-looks, Franchise, Courtesy, and Jollity, who lead the poet to a bed of roses, where he finds his special Rose. Cupid shoots the poet with the arrows of Beauty, Companionship, Courtesy, Simplicity, and Fair Seeming, which further incite him with love of the Rose. (Although Cupid does not shoot his other arrows—Infidelity, Shame, Pride, Villainy, and Despair—they do suggest the intrinsic incongruities of love.) Cupid then tells the poet how he can be worthy of the Rose, and the poet agrees to serve Cupid as his lord. However, his path to the Rose is hindered by Fear, Danger, Slander, and Shame, who also drive out Fair Welcome. Subsequently, Reason encourages the poet to suspend his quest for the Rose, because it is motivated by lust and nonprocreative love; she also points out the transitory nature of love and the capriciousness of fortune. The Lover's Friend then arrives to attack Reason's arguments. Finally, with the assistance of Pity, Franchise, and Venus, the poet obtains the Rose and is allowed to caress it with his lips, but before he can go further, Jealousy, Fear, and Shame burst in, build an impregnable castle, and imprison Fair Welcome and the Rose.

In the early part of the fourteenth century, Jean de Meun continued the story—adding 18,000 lines, nearly four and a half times as many as the original. His portion of the poem opens with the Rose being guarded in the castle by the Old Woman and the poet in despair. Reason returns and again admonishes him about the transience of love and the fickleness of women; she encourages him to find happiness in eternal things. In contrast, the Lover's Friend advocates a plan of action—storm the castle with Deceit, Bribery, and Hypocrisy. The poet, however, is repulsed by the Friend's advice; undaunted, the Friend produces the Jealous Husband, who lodges a long list of complaints against women—that they are silly, giddy, liars, spendthrifts, unfaithful, and wicked. They also are licentious and entice men with their contrived beauty.

> Therefore I swear . . . that a woman who wants to be beautiful, . . . examines herself and takes great trouble to deck herself out and look attractive, because she wants to wage war on Chastity, who certainly has many enemies. In cloisters and abbeys all the women are sworn against her. They will never be so walled in that they do not hate Chastity. . . . They all do homage to Venus, with no consideration for worth or harm; they primp and paint in order to fool those who look at them,

and they go searching along through the streets in order . . . to arouse desire in people, so that they will want to lie with them.[9]

The Friend then advances his own arguments, both pro and con, about the value of women, but decides to champion the poet's quest for the Rose. Apologizing to Cupid for listening to Reason, the poet asks for his help. Cupid offers him False Seeming, Forced Abstinence, Courtesy, and Largesse, and together they free Fair Welcome from the castle.

The poem digresses to long speeches by the Old Woman, Nature, and Genius about the nature of love. The Old Woman, for whom love is nothing more than the satisfying of a natural drive, unencumbered by moral restraints, recites her rules of love—manipulation, infidelity, and mirth. Nature, however, rebuffs the Old Woman's argument and points out that the human will is naturally free to reject her doctrines and other doctrines, especially those limiting sex to a procreative act. Genius, interceding with Cupid on behalf of Nature, then tells the poet that he must banish False Seeming and Forced Abstinence and take the love that he bears for the Rose and surrender it to procreation. Genius's point is that by sublimating his natural sexual desire to the virtue of the procreative act, the poet will bring heaven down to earth. As Jean de Meun's portion of the poem concludes, the poet agrees with Genius, storms the castle, reunites with the Rose, and awakens from his dream.

Everyman

Everyman, written in Middle English about 1485, is the best extant example of the genre of drama known as the **morality play**. (There are also late medieval Dutch and German versions of this morality play.) Whereas mystery plays (see Chapter 11) attempted to make the Christian message more understandable for the illiterate masses by dramatizing biblical events, morality plays used allegory to dramatize the moral struggle against evil in which every Christian is engaged. The moral themes—trust in God, do good, love mercy, and do justice—are often presented in an unduly didactic way, especially in comparison to the mystery plays. Both genres, however, employ a sort of bawdy humor, even though humor is not particularly evident in *Everyman*.

The plot focuses on Everyman being stripped of all that he possesses, including family, friends, and wealth. Each character in the drama—including Fellowship, Good Deeds, Knowledge, Beauty, Strength, and Discretion—epitomizes his or her name. The overarching theme is how every individual—Everyman—struggles, in the face of Death, to be worthy of salvation and everlasting life; but in the end, all anyone possesses is Good Deeds—the harsh moral of the play.

In the manner of the chorus of a Greek tragedy, the play opens with a prologue, spoken by the Messenger, who explains the plot to the audience:

> *The Summoning of Everyman* called it is,
> That of our lives and ending shows
> How transitory we be all day. . . .
> Here shall you see how Fellowship and Jollity,
> Both Strength, Pleasure, and Beauty,
> Will fade from thee as flower in May;
> For ye shall hear how our Heaven King
> Calleth every man to a general reckoning.[10]

The audience immediately becomes aware that Everyman is nearing the end of his life and is about to be held accountable for having been enamored of the "seven deadly sins." God speaks:

> To get them life I suffered to be dead. . .
> I could do no more than I did, truly.
> And now I see the people do clean forsake me.
> They use the seven deadly sins damnable,
> As pride, covetise, wrath, and lechery
> Now in the world be made commendable.[11]

Subsequently, Everyman is approached by Death and is amazed to discover the meaning of such phrases as "Death gives no warning" and the "Tide abides no man." Death's greater function, however, is to educate Everyman into the larger issues of life and death, and at times, Death is almost sympathetic to Everyman's struggle against sin. Characters representing his friends and family—Fellowship, Goods, Kindred, and Cousin—then relate incidents of Everyman's earlier lifestyle in a universal way, carefully avoiding any indication that such behavior is unique to Everyman. Recognizing that none of these brings hope of salvation, Everyman, in despair, asks: "My Good Deeds, where are you?" and implores her to help him. In her reply, Good Deeds offers the assistance of her sister, Knowledge, because she is too weak to help him alone, due to Everyman's neglect of her.

For the remainder of the play, Knowledge (recognition of one's sins) is Everyman's guide. With her help, Everyman acquires new "friends"—Beauty, Strength, Discretion, and Five Wits. Knowledge then counsels him to go to a priest and receive the sacraments. Content to stand before God on his own diminutive merits, Everyman questions Knowledge's advice, but Five Wits admonishes him and reminds him that salvation from sin only comes from the administration of the sacraments by the priesthood of the church.

> Everyman, that is the best that ye can do.
> God will you to salvation bring,
> For priesthood exceedeth all other things.
> To us holy scripture they do teach,
> And converteth man from sin heaven to reach.
> God hath to them more power given
> Than to any angel that is in heaven. . . .
> No remedy we find under God
> But all only priesthood.[12]

As his strength wanes, Everyman asks his new friends to accompany him to the grave, but for their own reasons, they refuse. Good Deeds, however, offers to go with him and speaks to him about the vanity of human existence.

> All earthly things is but vanity—
> Beauty, Strength, and Discretion do man forsake,
> Foolish friends, and kinsmen, that fair spake—
> All fleeth save Good Deeds, and that am I.[13]

Everyman and Good Deeds then descend into the grave, the Angel speaks, and the drama concludes with an epilogue spoken by the Doctor, who relates the moral of the play:

> This moral men may have in mind.
> Ye hearers, take it of worth, old and young.
> And forsake Pride, for he deceiveth you in
>   the end;
> And remember Beauty, Five Wits, Strength,
>   and Discretion—
> They all at the last do every man forsake,
> Save his Good Deeds there doth he take.[14]

LATE MEDIEVAL LITERATURE: NEW DIRECTIONS

Late medieval literature evidenced both traditional Christian concerns and new literary forms and themes that pointed away from the Middle Ages. These innovations presage the Renaissance and the birth of modernity. In this respect, Dante is a pivotal figure. On the one hand, his *Divine Comedy* is profoundly medieval in its overriding concern with salvation and its creative integration of Aristotelian–Ptolemaic cosmology with the Christian viewpoint. On the other hand Dante was also a precursor of change; he colored the traditional view of salvation with his own creative interpretation and gave a new value to vernacular literature, regarding it as a worthy companion to both classical and biblical literature. He held distinct opinions, which he wove into the fabric of the *Divine Comedy.* Based only on his own judgment, and with no influence from the church, Dante placed popes, kings, his contemporaries, and literary figures (both past and present) in Hell, Purgatory, or

Paradise. The value he placed on vernacular poetry is typified by his treatment of it in the *Paradiso*—as Dante approaches God, the angels cease to sing in Latin and begin to sing in Italian. His final mention of the vernacular occurs when Adam tells Dante that even if he and Eve had not disobeyed God and had remained in the Garden of Eden, eventually the language of the Garden would have been altered. Consequently, no absolute language governs creation, and Latin is not superior to Italian. Other writers—Francesco Petrarch, Giovanni Boccaccio, Geoffrey Chaucer, and Christine de Pizan—were influenced by Dante and also displayed a fresh spirit.

The writers of the fourteenth century whose works evidence change hardly abandoned the familiar forms of poem, romance, allegory, and dream vision, but they did transform them to fit their own purposes. Within these forms, themes appear that had not been seen since antiquity—appreciation of human talents, the value of worldly activities, and the significance of the natural love that exists between men and women. The authors often display an inner conflict: They are constrained by traditional Christian piety but also feel compelled to break the bonds of artistic convention. Thus, the literature fluctuates between the writer's desire to withdraw from the world, discipline the passions, and contemplate salvation, and the aspiration to become involved in the world and to assist in its transformation. As the literature progresses, the writers become less inhibited, the themes become less Christian and idealized, and the tone becomes more secular. Nowhere is this more evident than in the literature about women—concerning their dignity, merit, and worth. The image of women is altered in numerous literary works, in which single men and women communicate about the status and ability of women within society. The success of Christine de Pizan further illustrates the affinity for a more natural literature unaffected by piety and convention.

Francesco Petrarch

Francesco Petrarch (1304–1374), like Dante, for whom he expressed great admiration, wrote poetry in the vernacular Tuscan dialect and was influenced by the chivalric literature of southern France. For nearly a century after his death, Petrarch's reputation as an author was based on his *Italian sonnets,* which were inspired by a woman named Laura with whom he was infatuated for twenty-one years, much as Dante was with Beatrice. (A sonnet is a poem of fourteen lines expressing a single thought; an Italian sonnet, also

know as a Petrarchan sonnet, consists of an octave of eight lines followed by a sextet of six lines.) In a sonnet written in about 1338, Petrarch describes how he was snared by the love of Laura:

> The radiance of her eyes outdid the sun,
> transfiguring the earth in a holy blaze.
> Then with her ivory hand she twitched the rope!
> And so I fell in the net, and was undone
> by her angelic words, her darling ways;
> also by pleasure; by desire; by hope.[15]

On the twenty-first anniversary of their first meeting, April 6, 1348, Petrarch had a presentiment of Laura's death; six weeks later, he received a letter from a friend confirming that Laura had indeed died of the plague on that very date.

Despite the popularity of his sonnets, however, Petrarch's real passion was for the authors of antiquity whose wisdom, he thought, could instruct his own day. Therefore, he sought not only to revive their works but also to recapture the essence of the Roman virtues and integrate them with Christian values. When Petrarch was a child, his father read aloud to him the orations and letters of Cicero, and as an adult, Petrarch held Cicero in the highest esteem. In 1345, Petrarch discovered a previously unknown collection of Cicero's letters written about everyday concerns, which inspired him to make a collection of his own Latin letters—*Epistolae familiares* (*Letters on Familiar Matters*). Included in the collection were epistles to his heroes of antiquity, such as Livy, Virgil, and Horace, but especially Cicero. In a letter to Cicero, written at Avignon and dated December 19, 1345, Petrarch criticizes him for his political machinations, lauds his mind and his eloquence, and informs Cicero of the fate of his works.

> . . . O great father of Roman eloquence, I thank you, as do all who bedeck themselves with the flowers of the Latin language. It is from your fount that we draw the waters that bathe our field. We are sustained by your leadership, by your words of encouragement, by the light that illumines our simplicity. It is by your presence in spirit that we have gained whatever art and principles in writing we may possess.
>
> . . .You have heard what I think of your life and genius. Are you interested in hearing about your books, how fate has treated them, how they are regarded by the general public and by scholars? Some brilliant volumes are still in existence. We are barely able to list them, much less absorb them utterly. The reputation of your works is immense; your name is on everyone's lips; but your serious students are few, whether because the times are unpropitious or because men's wits are dull and

sluggish, or, as I think more likely, because greed diverts our minds to other ends.[16]

One of Petrarch's most important Latin writings, his *Secretum* (The Secret Book), written in 1342 and 1343, reveals the inner conflict between his Christian piety and his preoccupation with the literature and culture of antiquity. Its theme is similar to Dante's in the *Divine Comedy*—a soul, though wandering from the path of truth and wisdom into sin and error, finds salvation. The *Secretum* is Petrarch's personal confession, patterned after Augustine's *Confessions* (see Chapter 7), with whom he has a conversation.

Petrarch engages Augustine in a dialogue about whether an individual should live the contemplative life of a philosopher or the active life of a citizen of the world. Petrarch informs Augustine that he wants to do something useful with his life; in response, Augustine chastises Petrarch for his vanity and lusting for fame as an author. The dialogue concludes with Augustine advising Petrarch to abandon his writing and to contemplate death philosophically.

> And, to return to the point from which we started, begin to think deeply about death, which little by little and all unconscious you are approaching. You are part of the great procession; exulting in the prime of your life, you are treading on the heels of others; but others are treading on yours. Remember Cicero: "All the life of a philosopher is meditation on death." You can find the right path by listening to your own spirit, which tells you: "This is the way home."[17]

There are distinctly new and modern elements in Petrarch's work: his love for classical literature, his criticism of medieval Latin as barbaric in contrast to the style of Cicero, Seneca, and other Romans, and his literary works based on classical models. Also new is the subjective and individualistic character of his writing. In talking about himself and probing his own feelings, Petrarch demonstrates a self-consciousness characteristic of the modern outlook.

Giovanni Boccaccio

Due to his father's success as a banker, Giovanni Boccaccio (1313–1375) received a good education. In the early 1330s, Boccaccio was sent to Naples and came under the influence of Cino da Pistoia, a poet and professor of jurisprudence. It was Cino who fostered Boccaccio's interest in the "new" poetry of Petrarch and Dante, whose prominence was already well established in Florence. Because of his familial connection to Dante—his stepmother was related to Dante's Beatrice—and his interest in the new poetry, Boccaccio developed a lifelong adulation for Dante and his work. He also became great friends with Petrarch, with whom he exchanged many letters on a variety of topics.

The earliest works of Boccaccio, begun in Naples between 1334 and 1341, illustrate both continuity and change. Disciplining the passions was a standard theme of medieval literature, and allegory was often the method used to explore the psychology of love and the problems, and emotions, associated with it. Boccaccio's first three works—*Il Filocolo (Matters of Love), Il Filostrato (The Story of Troilus),* and *Il Teseida dell nozze d' Emilia (The Book of Teseo)*—written in the traditional form of the medieval romance, feature his deep interest in antiquity and a growing interest in the worldly life, but also confirm his commitment to Christian principles. The overwhelming theme of these early works is that only the Christian faith, with its offer of salvation from sin, provides hope that individuals can control self-destructive passions.

The 7,000 stanzas of *Filostrato*, set against the backdrop of the Trojan War, describe the tragic love affair of Troilus, the son of the king of Troy, and Criseida, the daughter of the prophet Calchas. Troilus, the embodiment of an innocent lover, is betrayed by Criseida, who abandons him for the Greek hero Diomedes. Through the death of Troilus and the destruction of Troy, the message of *Filostrato* is that love that is disobedient to the divine will leads to both personal and civic disaster.*

Boccaccio's *II Teseida dell nozze d'Emilia* is divided into two sections: The first part recounts the wars fought by Teseo, king of Athens, against Thebes; the second deals with the love two Theban prisoners bear for Emilia. Using Thebes to symbolize carnal love and Athens to represent virtuous love, Boccaccio concludes that without Christian faith, all love is merely lust.

Boccaccio also wrote four anthologies in Latin that revived classical, historical, and geographical knowledge and became immensely popular with his contemporaries. Begun in 1351, Boccaccio's first anthology, *Genealogy of the Pagan Gods*, is a compendium of classical mythology, which he continued to revise until his death in 1375. Designed to facilitate the reading of classical literature, the work affirms the value of poetry in teaching and encouraging moral reform, themes that had an immense influence on Renaissance writers.

---

* In Homer's *Iliad*, Troilus is portrayed as having been killed before the Trojan War began. Boccaccio's story is further developed by both Geoffrey Chaucer and William Shakespeare.

Despite the popularity of Latin works among his contemporaries, Boccaccio's long-lasting fame rests with his vernacular works, most notably his *Decameron* (1350). The work evidences the changes in literary taste that came to fruition during the Renaissance. In the *Decameron*, Boccaccio abandons Latin for the vernacular, shuns the didactic tone of Dante, which he had so often employed, and develops a naturalistic theme, one that has nothing to do with salvation from sin. Through the work, Boccaccio reveals himself to be a master of prose dialogue.

The *Decameron* opens in Florence just after the bubonic plague ravaged Europe in 1348–1349. In striking detail, Boccaccio describes the effects of the disease and the fanatical fear people had of being infected.

In the year 1348, . . . in the beginning of the spring . . . its horrible results began to appear . . . both in men and women with certain swellings in the groin or under the armpit. They grew to the size of a small apple or an egg . . . and were vulgarly called tumours. In a short space of time these tumours . . . spread . . . all over the body. Soon after this the symptoms changed and black or purple spots appeared on the arms or thighs or any other part of the body. . . . These spots were a certain sign of death. . . . The violence of this disease was such that the sick communicated it to the healthy who came near them. . . . To speak to or go near the sick brought infection and a common death to the living; and moreover, to touch the clothes or anything else the sick had touched or worn gave the disease to the person touching. . . . No doctor's advice, no medicine could overcome or alleviate this disease. . . . One citizen avoided another, hardly any neighbour troubled about others, relatives never or hardly ever visited each other. Moreover, such terror was struck into the hearts of men and women by this calamity, that brother abandoned brother, and the uncle his nephew, and the sister her brother, and very often the wife her husband. What is even worse and nearly incredible is that fathers and mothers refused to see and tend their children, as if they had not been theirs.[18]

The plot commences as seven ladies and three young men meet at church on a Sunday morning, and fearful of the plague, they decide to flee into the country. They gather their servants and provisions and elect a leader for each day they are to travel. The leaders determine the appropriate times for such activities as bathing, eating, fasting, celebrating, and going to church. But the central activity is telling stories—each person is to tell ten tales over a ten-day period with the leaders designating the theme for each day.

With the exception of the days during which they may consider any topic, the theme for the stories of one day is countered with a conflicting theme on the succeeding day. For example, one day the theme is how love is a ruinous force and the next day how love is beneficial; another day, they describe the degree to which fortune controls human destiny, and the next day how fortune can be turned to one's own advantage. In contrast to the poetry of courtly love and chivalric romances, the love discussed in the *Decameron* is neither idealized nor Christianized; it is the natural love that exists between women and men. No matter who is speaking, the tone of the speakers is decidedly secular. Often the theme of love is coupled with criticism of licentious clergymen, as is evident in *The Eighth Day, Second Tale.*

Fair ladies, I mean to tell you a little tale about those who are constantly injuring us without our being able to injure them in the same way—I mean the priests, who have declared a Crusade against our wives, and seem to think that when they can get on one of them they have obtained forgiveness of their sins.[19]

The tale then relates how a priest of Varlungo arranges to have sex with Monna Belcolore on a day when her husband, a laborer named Bentivegna del Mazzo, decides to go into town for business. As the priest enters her home, Boccaccio describes the scene in such a way as to make clear that this is not the first time the priest has attempted to be intimate with Belcolore.

Belcolore came down and took a seat and began to sift some cabbage seed which her husband had gathered.

"Ah, Belcolore," said the priest, "must you always make me die in this way?"

Belcolore giggled, and said:

"Why, what do I do?"

"You don't do anything," said the priest, "but you won't let me do to you what I want to do and what God commands."

"Get away with you!" said Belcolore, "Priests don't do such things."

"Yes we do," said the priest, "and better than other men. Why not? And we are better workers than other men. Do you know why? Because we only grind at harvest time. But you'll find it out for yourself if you'll only lie still and let me go."[20]

However, before Belcolore agrees to have sex with the priest, she asks for a token of his pledge to her, and he offers his cloak. Boccaccio then describes their tryst in the hayloft:

"Father, come along to the hayloft. Nobody ever goes there."

There the priest gave her the sweetest flopping kisses and enjoyed her for a long space of time, making her a relative of the Lord God. He then departed in his cassock, as if he had been to a wedding; and returned to his church.[21]

The next day, the priest, realizing he has made a mistake, plots to get Belcolore to return his cloak. He sends a young boy who asks to borrow a stone mortar from Belcolore. That evening, while Belcolore and Bentivegna are eating dinner at their home, the priest summons the parish clerk and asks him to return the mortar to them saying: "The parson thanks you and will you send him back the cloak which the little boy left as a pledge?"[22] When the clerk asks for the cloak, Belcolore angrily tries to speak but is interrupted by her husband. The confrontation between Belcolore and Bentivegna about the return of the priest's cloak further illustrates the bawdy humor and the secular tone of the *Decameron*.

"So you take pledges from the parson, do you? By Christ, I'd like to give you a good wipe in the nose, . . . henceforth if he wants anything of ours, even the ass, don't you say 'No' to him!"

Belcolore got up grumbling and went to the chest under the bed, took out the cloak, and as she gave it to the clerk, she said:

"Say to the priest: 'Belcolore says that she prays God you may never again grind sauce in her mortar, not having done her any honour in this.'"

The clerk went off with the cloak and delivered the message to the priest, who said, laughing:

"When you see her, tell her that if she won't lend the mortar, I won't lend the pestle."[23]

Boccaccio had a lifelong obsession with Dante, and beginning in 1355, he wrote his *Life of Dante*. In 1373, the government of Florence appointed him to be the first public lecturer on Dante's *Divine Comedy*. Boccaccio gave his first lecture on October 23, 1373, and his last on September 4, 1374. These lectures succeeded in immortalizing Dante and elevating his status among both scholars and the educated citizenry of Florence.

Geoffrey Chaucer

Many of the tales related in the *Decameron* were subsequently transformed by Geoffrey Chaucer for his *Canterbury Tales*. As the son of a successful wine merchant, Chaucer (c. 1340–1400) received a good education and had an intimate understanding of the merchant class. However, he spent most of his life serving members of the royal family.

Sometime after 1386, Chaucer began his masterpiece, *Canterbury Tales,* the first major work written in vernacular English. For source material, Chaucer drew on his reading of ancient authors, including Virgil and Ovid; contemporary works, including the *Roman de la Rose*; and the writings of Dante, Petrarch, and Boccaccio. But most importantly, Chaucer employed his understanding of all classes of society, about whom he had been curious all his life. Consequently, in many cases, Chaucer's characters are *caricatures*—personifying virtues and vices to which all human beings are subject—which makes the *Canterbury Tales* reminiscent of medieval morality plays. Using the framing device of Boccaccio's *Decameron*—tales within a tale—Chaucer presents thirty people assembled at the Tabard Inn who are about to embark on a pilgrimage to the shrine of Saint Thomas à Becket, who became the Archbishop of Canterbury in 1162 and was murdered by agents of King Henry II eight years later, as he said his evening prayers at his own altar in Canterbury Cathedral. To pass the time, each pilgrim is to tell two stories going to the shrine and two on the way back, for a total of 120 tales. (Chaucer, however, only completed twenty-four of them.)

The *Canterbury Tales* opens with a "General Prologue," whereby Chaucer creates vignettes of his pilgrims, including a "KNIGHT, a worthy man . . a valiant warrior for his lord"; a "youthful SQUIRE, a lover and knight bachelor to admire"; a "nun, a PRIORESS, [who] excelled at singing when church services were held, intoning through her nose melodiously"; a "MONK, . . . a manly man . . . [who] let old things pass away so that the modern world might have its day"; an "Oxford STUDENT . . . of highest moral virtue was his speech, and gladly he would learn and gladly teach"; and "from near the town of BATH a good WIFE . . . of remedies of love she had good notions, for of that art's old dance she knew the motions"; a "SUMMONER. . . who like a cherub had a fire-red face . . . eyes puffed and narrow. He was hot and lecherous as a sparrow"; a "gentle PARDONER [Church official] . . . who'd come straight from the court of Rome. And he would loudly sing 'Come hither, love, to me!'"; and finally, "Our HOST made welcome each and every one, . . . [h]e served us with the finest in good food; the wine was strong to fit our festive mood."[24]

Once the pilgrims begin their tales, a discerning reader can see the parallels between the tales of Chaucer's pilgrims and a number of tales detailed in Boccaccio's *Decameron*. For example, in *The Seventh Day, Ninth Tale*, Boccaccio relates the story of a wife and her lover who lust for a sexual encounter. They tell her husband to climb a tree but caution him to disregard what he sees with his eyes (even if it happens to be his wife having sex with another man) for it will merely be an illusion. The man does climb the tree—thus leaving his wife and her lover to copulate with impunity. This is the background for Chaucer's *Merchant's Tale*, but instead of having the husband climb the tree, it is the lovers who copulate in the tree, and the husband goes blind, only to regain his sight later. A similar correspondence can be found between the *Decameron: The Eighth Day, First Tale* and Chaucer's *Shipman's Tale*. Boccaccio conveys the story of a merchant who lends a man money, without knowing that the man intends to use it to seduce the merchant's wife. Once he has had sex with the merchant's wife, the man tells the merchant that he has repaid the loan to his wife. The merchant then goes to his wife and gets the money. Although the wife is deservedly punished for being unfaithful to her husband, the man is rewarded for his cunning. However, in Chaucer's tale the lover is a monk, not a merchant, and the wife has time to spend the money on new clothes for herself before her husband discovers that the loan was repaid to her.

Another example of Chaucer's indebtedness to Boccaccio is *The Ninth Day, Sixth Tale* from the *Decameron*, which Chaucer uses as a framework for his *Reeve's Tale*. In Boccaccio's story, two young men, desirous of having sex with a certain man's daughter, visit his home on the pretense of seeking shelter for the night. He cheerfully offers to help them, but tells them that because his house is so small, they will all have to sleep in the same room. Undaunted, the young men rearrange the furniture in the room, particularly the baby's cradle, and create such confusion for everyone that the host's wife unwittingly sleeps with one young man and his daughter with the other. The lesson of Boccaccio's story is that cunning is rewarded by the gratification of lust. In contrast, Chaucer transforms the lusty youths into Oxford scholars and has them play the same trick on the local miller, who regularly cheats his customers. Therefore, Chaucer's moral is: "He who cheats gets his comeuppance in the end."

Boccaccio, as we have already seen, was not the only inspiration for Chaucer's *Canterbury Tales*. In fact, one of the most notorious figures in all of the tales is the Wife of Bath, whose character reminds us of the Old Woman in Jean de Meun's version of the *Roman de la Rose*. In the "Prologue" to her tale, the Wife of Bath explains that she has been married five times, but her fifth husband, Jenkin, she found difficult to subdue, because he kept reading to her from a book about wicked wives.

> One night this Jenkin, who was my fifth sire,
> Was reading in his book beside the fire.

He read of Eve, who by her wickedness
Had brought all of mankind to wretchedness,
The reason Jesus Christ himself was slain
To bring us back with his heart's blood again,
"Of women here expressly you may find
That woman was the ruin of all mankind."[25]

She then explains how they fought and that she pushed him into the fire. Once free from the flames, Jenkin came to her, and sought her forgiveness, which she granted with several conditions:

> We finally reached accord between us two,
> The bridle he put wholly in my hand
> To have complete control of house and land,
> And of his tongue and hands as well—and when
> He did, I made him burn his book right then.[26]

Having given the pilgrims background for her story, the Wife of Bath then relates her tale, set at the time of King Arthur, about a forlorn young maiden who is raped by one of Arthur's knights as she walks by the river. Demands to the king for justice are counterbalanced by pleas of mercy from the queen and her ladies. Arthur allows the queen to mete out the judgment to the guilty knight—she will spare his life if, within a year and a day, he can tell her "what it is that women most desire."[27] The knight searches far and wide for an answer to the queen's question; he seeks the advice of friends and family and reads the books of antiquity, but feels hopeless that he will ever find the answer. Then one day he happens on an old wife, whom Chaucer describes as "an uglier creature no mind could devise."[28] She explains that she will tell him the answer to the queen's question if he will do the next thing that she requests of him. On the day of his hearing before the queen and her court, the knight reports:

> What women most desire is sovereignty
> Over their husbands or the ones they love,
> To have mastery, to be above. . . .
> This is what you most desire, though you
>   may kill
> Me if you wish. I'm here, do as you will.[29]

All those in attendance agree with him, and his life is spared. However, the old wife then makes her request—"take me as your wife." Horrified, the knight states that he would rather be dead. However, for reasons unknown, he ultimately marries her but is loathe to consummate their marriage.

The wife then decides to amend their deal with the provision that he treat her more kindly. Rather than make a choice, he defers to his wife's judgment, and she responds:

> Unless I am to you as good and true
> As any wife since this old world was new.

> Come dawn, if I'm not as fair to be seen . . .
>   Who ever lived. . . .
> Then take my life or do whatever's best.
> Lift up the curtains now, see how it is.[30]

When he raises the curtains he discovers that she is young and fair. The Wife of Bath then concludes her tale with a moral about the virtue of men submitting to their wives.

> And may Christ Jesus send
> Us husbands meek and young and fresh abed,
> And then the grace to outlive those we wed;
> I also pray that Jesus shorten lives
> Of those who won't be governed by their wives.[31]

In December of 1399, Chaucer rented a house in the garden of Westminster Abbey where, after a life of service to the English court and a prodigious literary output, he died on October 25, 1400, and was buried in the Abbey.

Christine de Pizan

Christine de Pizan (c. 1364–c. 1430) was an exceptional woman in an age when most females were under the authority of men and received, at best, only an elementary education. Christine was born in Venice, and when she was five years old, her father, Tomasso de Pizzano, an astrologer, natural philosopher, and mathematician, accepted a position at the court of Charles V in France. Interested in learning and education, Charles founded the royal library, commissioned translations of classical, philosophical, and scientific works, and redecorated the Louvre to house an eminent library.

In 1380, when Christine was fifteen years old, she was married to Etienne de Castel, the husband her father had chosen for her. Through Etienne's position as a court secretary, Christine came into contact with educated men who introduced her to Latin prose and the works of Petrarch and Boccaccio. Charles V's untimely death in 1380 was followed by the death of her father in 1387 and, three years later, of her beloved husband. Suddenly, at the age of twenty-five, Christine found herself a widow with a daughter, two sons, a niece, and her mother to support. Seeking consolation for her grief, she began to write poetry. Learning that her poetry was well received, Christine proceeded to write courtly love poetry, as well as poems about the French court, and mythology. Later, however, like Dante, Petrarch, and Boccaccio, she turned her interest toward the writers of antiquity. The success of her works accorded her the patronage of such distinguished people as Philip the Bold, Duke of Burgundy, Queen Isabella of Bavaria, the English Earl of Salisbury, and Jean, Duke of Berry (see following discussion).

Christine is best remembered for her two extended works on the role of women in society, in which she addresses such weighty issues as the ability of women to govern, their aptitude for learning, and the criminality of rape. In 1405, she authored *The Book of the City of Ladies*. The structure of the book is patterned after Augustine's *City of God*; the thematic material depends heavily on the works of Boccaccio—particularly his *Concerning Famous Women* and the *Decameron*—which she completely reorganizes. The book, divided into three parts, describes Christine's vision of a city—founded by the goddesses Reason, Discretion, and Justice—reserved for women who have made significant contributions to society. In Parts one and two, using examples from classical antiquity, biblical history, and French history, Christine and the three virtues argue that women possess the same moral and intellectual qualities as men; Part three is devoted to the Virgin Mary and female Christian saints. The first chapter of Part three tells how Justice leads the women to entreat the Virgin Mary to live in the city. Justice states,

> Let all women now accompany me, and let us say to her: "We greet you, Queen of Heaven. . . . May all the devout sex of women humbly beseech you that it please you well to reside among them with grace and mercy, as their defender, protector, and guard against all assaults of enemies and of the world, that they may drink from the fountain of virtues which flows from you and be so satisfied that every sin and vice be abominable to them. Now come to us, Heavenly Queen. . . . My Lady, what man is so brazen to dare think or say that the feminine sex is vile in beholding your dignity? For if all other women were bad, the light of your goodness so surpasses and transcends them that any remaining evil would vanish. Since God chose His spouse from among women, most excellent Lady, because of your honor, not only should men refrain from reproaching women but should also hold them in great reverence."[32]

Subsequently, in 1406, Christine wrote *The Book of Three Virtues*, also known as *The Treasury of the City of Ladies*, dedicated to Marguerite of Burgundy, to establish the criteria for women who desired to live in the city.

In her final work, dated July 31, 1429, a joyous poem about Joan of Arc's victory at Orléans and the coronation of Charles VII (1422–1461) at Reims, Christine lauds Joan of Arc's triumph, which she sees as a victory for womanhood:

> I, Christine, who have wept for eleven years in a walled abbey . . . now, for the first time begin to laugh. . . . Oh! What honour for the female sex! It

is perfectly obvious that God has special regard for it when all these wretched people who destroyed the whole Kingdom—now recovered and made safe by a woman, something that 5000 *men* could not have done—and the traitors [have been] exterminated. Before the event they would scarcely have believed this possible. A little girl of sixteen . . . who . . . drives her enemies out of France, recapturing castles and towns. Never did anyone see greater strength, even in hundreds or thousands of men! And she is the supreme captain of our brave and able men. Neither Hector nor Achilles had such strength![33]

LATE MEDIEVAL ART

Late medieval architects, sculptors, painters, and musicians continued to employ traditional artistic forms and look to the past for thematic material, which they persisted in rendering in religious terms. Some of them, however, were precursors not only of a momentous change in attitude about human beings and their place in the great scheme of things but also in the closer attention they paid to the portrayal of the human form. In addition, they successfully created a more realistic representation of tangible space, which began to include a degree of spatial depth and perspective. In all their endeavors, the artists' works evidence an increasing naturalism, realism, and individualism, which would reach full fruition in the Italian Renaissance.

Sculpture

Although late medieval sculptors continued to employ traditional artistic forms and Christian themes, some displayed changes in attitudes and styles that made them precursors of the Italian Renaissance. They began to pay closer attention to the portrayal of the individual human form and, by including a degree of spatial depth and perspective, represented tangible space more realistically. The naturalism and individualism tentatively demonstrated by late medieval artists would reach full fruition in the Renaissance.

Sculptors of the fourteenth century sought to maintain continuity with the past in their rendering of the human form. Thus, many late medieval sculptures resembled the detailed figures for the doorjambs on the Cathedral of Chartres. Nevertheless, their work also foreshadowed change, for they paid attention to portraying the human figure with greater naturalism and realism. This tendency is particularly evident in the Pisan and Burgundian schools of sculpture.

From approximately 1250 until 1350, Italian sculpture was dominated by the so-called Pisani sculptors, which included Nicola Pisano (c. 1220/5–c. 1280), who founded the Pisan school; his son, Giovanni, (c. 1245/50–c. 1314); the unrelated Andrea Pisano (c. 1290–1348), who worked on the sculpture for the campanile for the Florentine Cathedral with Giotto (see the following discussion); and his son, Nino (fl. 1349–c. 1368).

Like Petrarch, Boccaccio, and Chaucer, Nicola was fascinated by antiquity and made a study of classical sculpture. For this reason, some scholars regard him as the first Renaissance sculptor, but Nicola applied what he learned about classical sculpture to Gothic structures. Consequently, Nicola's work evidences both change and continuity, for he developed a naturalistic relief style that was inspired by antiquity but integrated it into the northern Gothic style. His prominence rests on his ability to create large-scale sculptural arrangements. In this effort, he and his son are most famous for the sculpting of a series of pulpits, including the *Pulpit for the Baptistery of Pisa* (Figure 12.1), which Nicola signed in 1260, and the one Giovanni did for the cathedral itself. Nicola's pulpit evidences his classical interest—instead of a line of figures set on a flat background, he arranges them in groups and creates each figure as a unique individual against a background marked by spatial depth and perspective. However, the sculpted capitals, the design of the arches, and the corner figures all are reminiscent of the styling of the French Gothic. The panels of the pulpit include portrayals of the Annunciation, the Nativity, and the shepherds in the field receiving the news of Jesus' birth. Nicola's last documented work was the sculpture for the fountain in the marketplace of Perugia, which he completed in 1278.

The preeminent sculptor of the short-lived Burgundian school was Claus Sluter (c. 1350–1406). His symbolic *Well of Moses* (Figure 12.2) for the cloister of Chartreuse de Champmol, in Dijon, was executed between 1395 and 1406. The monumental masterpiece was originally designed to be a giant crucifix in the center of the fountain, symbolizing Christ as the fountain of life. Most of the crucifix was destroyed by Protestant extremists in the sixteenth century, but the pedestal with its five prophets, including Moses and Isaiah, is still intact. Although at first glance the figures remind us of the portal jambs on Gothic cathedrals, the importance of architecture has been diminished, for the figures lean forward and distinguish themselves from the architecture. The realistic detailing of the figures, their life-sized volume, and the naturalistic rendering of their forms all point forward to the Renaissance. Looking to the right is Moses, with his customary horns (see Chapter 11), whose form appears to protrude outward into the adjoin-

Figure 12.1 Nicola Pisano, *Pulpit for the Baptistery of Pisa,* signed 1260, marble, height 15' (4.6m), Pisa, Italy Nicola's arrangement of his figures in groups and his creation of each one as a unique individual against a background with spatial depth and perspective evidences his interest in classical styling. The sculpted panels of the pulpit include portrayals of the Annunciation, the Nativity, the Crucifixion, and the shepherds in the field receiving the news of Jesus' birth. *(Scala/Art Resource, NY)*

ing space, as does the scroll in his left hand. The gentle folds of his garment, however, fall naturally over his broad body. The figure of Isaiah, in contrast to Moses, is rendered less prominently but more individually, as can be seen in his wrinkled skin, the texturing of his garment, and the detailing of his face. Sluter's Isaiah, arguably the first portrait sculpture since antiquity, evidences traits that were soon to become hallmarks of the Renaissance—the tangible rendering of space, the attention to detail, and the realistic portrayal of the human figure and personality.

Painting

By the second half of the thirteenth century, the tradition of painting in northern Europe had nearly disappeared, mostly because the available wall space had been allocated for windows by the Gothic architects. During the same period, however, a revolution in painting was taking place in Italy. Although the Byzantine style remained dominant in most of Italy, a new style began to develop through the works of Cimabue, Duccio, and Giotto, characterized by a new naturalism. This outburst of painting in northern Italy combined architectural space with pictorial design to produce an overall sense of unity. Human figures were rendered more softly in both posture and gesture and revealed real emotions, in contrast to earlier works where the faces tended to be unexpressive. A more convincing perspective accompanied these changes. All of these elements of the new style were enlarged and expanded on by the painters of the Renaissance.

MANUSCRIPT ILLUMINATION: THE LIMBOURG BROTHERS Manuscript illumination continued to be the basis of painting in northern Europe. The late Gothic style of manuscript illumination was defined by the Limbourg Brothers—Jean, Paul, and Herman—although some scholars claim there may have been a fourth brother, Arnold. Their father was a sculptor in Nijmegen, in the Netherlands, and their mother was the sister of the famous painter Jean Malouel, official painter for the court of Burgundy. We know that the brothers flourished as artists during the late fourteenth century and the early fifteenth century, first for Philip the Bold and, when he died in 1404, for Jean, Duke of Berry, brother of King Charles V. The first documented work of the Limbourg brothers, begun between 1402 and 1404, was a *Bible moralisée* (moralized Bible) for Philip the Bold. Following a previous model, the miniature paintings are framed and the text appears in Latin with a French translation in the margins.

The brothers were then commissioned by the Duke of Berry to complete two **books of hours**, a personal book of devotions for laypeople for the calendar year. Because the brothers were not constrained by an existing model, they emerged as innovators in the *Belles Heures* (Good Hours). Completed by 1408, the *Belles Heures* consists of the customary calendar, designating signs of the zodiac and the tasks associated with each month, but also contains portraits of the duke and his wife. After the calendar, however, the brothers included people and events that were atypical. For example, they detailed eleven episodes

in the life of Catherine of Siena (see previous discussion), who was the patron saint of the duke's wife, Jeanne of Boulogne. Although they did not include some of the better-known events of Catherine's life (such as her mystical death), they did include scenes of Catherine in prison.

The last commission the brothers undertook for the duke was *Les Très Riches Heures du Duc de Berry (The Very Rich Hours of the Duke of Berry)*. Begun in 1413, it is, perhaps, the finest example of manuscript illumination ever. The brothers were able to complete illustrations for eleven of the months; another artist completed *November*. The background—landscape, sky, architectural setting—was executed first, then the figures, and finally the faces of the figures. At the top of each calendar page is a two-tiered arch—the outer arch consists of the zodiac sign, in gold, along with information about the phases of the moon and the days of the week; the inner arch shows the blue dome of heaven and Apollo, in his chariot pulled by winged horses, holding the blazing sun. Below the arch, filling the remainder of the page, is a landscape depicting the labor associated with each month.

Figure 12.2 Claus Sluter, *Well of Moses*, 1395–1406, stone, height of figures 6' (1.8 m), Dijon, France
The realistic detailing of the five figures and their naturalistic forms point forward to the Renaissance. For example, Moses, with his customary horns, appears to protrude outward into the adjoining space, as does the scroll in his left hand. Although the figure of Isaiah is less prominent, he is rendered more individualistically. Particularly noteworthy is his wrinkled skin, the texturing of his garment, and the detailing of his face. *(Erich Lessing/Art Resource, NY)*

Figure 12.3   Limbourg Brothers, *Les Très Riches Heures du Duc de Berry*, February 1413–1416, Musée Condé, Chantilly   At the top of each calendar page is a two-tiered arch. The outer arch consists of the zodiac sign, the inner arch shows the blue dome of heaven and Apollo, and below the arch is the labor associated with each month, as is evident in this snowy February scene. *(Victoria & Albert Museum, London/The Bridgeman Art Library International Ltd)*

One unique feature is that the zodiac signs and the occupations take up the entire page. For the first time in the history of Western art, peasant activities are included in six of the months. *February* (Figure 12.3) convincingly illustrates a snowy landscape; *March*, plowing the fields; *June*, haymaking; *July*, sheepshearing; *October*, tilling and sowing winter grain; and *September*, harvesting grapes. The other five months depict courtly affairs—*January*, a banquet with the duke, including the giving of gifts; *April*, the engagement of a courtly couple; *May*, aristocrats enjoying horseback riding; *August*, opulently dressed aristocrats riding off to engage in falconry; and *December*, boar hunting in the forest of Vincennes, a popular hunting place for the kings of France.

Immediately following the calendar is a painting that does not exist in any other illuminated manuscript—a full-page rendering of *Anatomical Man*

(see chapter opening). Scholars assume that the Limbourgs' inclusion of it reflects Charles V's passionate interest in astrology (his astrologer was the father of Christine de Pizan), which was also shared by his brothers. Because the miniature purports to illustrate the effect of the stars of the zodiac on the human body, "astrological" man would be a more appropriate title for this painting. The inscriptions in the corners indicate that human temperaments—sanguine, phlegmatic, choleric, and melancholic—are affected by the mixture of the traditional four humors—blood, phlegm, black bile, and yellow bile—as well as by the conditions of heat and moisture, particularly as they are associated with being male or female. The combination of these qualities results in four main groups of signs.* The qualities are symbolized by the two figures standing back-to-back—the front figure represents the feminine, and the figure in the back the masculine. An ellipse bearing the signs of the zodiac surrounds the figures. Immediately above the inscriptions in the upper corners, the Duc de Berry's coat of arms is evident, whereas in the lower corners, his enigmatic initials "VE" can be seen.

Events illustrating the lives of various saints, including the four Evangelists and Augustine, are also depicted; so too are biblical events that the duke and the Limbourgs deemed important, including *The Garden of Eden, The Annunciation, David Foresees the Coming of Christ*, and *The Last Judgment*. Interspersed with texts taken from various Psalms and the Offices (see Chapter 11) are the customary lives of the Virgin Mary and Christ. They are, however, rendered with more precision and detail than the brothers' predecessors and often with a vision that is uniquely their own.

Their miniature that depicts *Hell* (Figure 12.4) is a good example of their creative vision. Although the Limbourgs' portrayal of Satan is reminiscent of the character of Satan in Dante's *Inferno* and anticipates the image of Satan envisioned by John Milton in his monumental work, *Paradise Lost* (1667), the Limbourgs' vision of Satan was inspired by the description of the leviathan described in the Book of Job:

> Out of his mouth go flaming torches;
>   sparks of fire leap forth.
> Out of his nostrils comes forth smoke,
>   as from a boiling pot and burning rushes.

* The groupings are as follows: (1) Pisces, Cancer, Scorpio are phlegmatic, cold, wet, and feminine; (2) Taurus, Virgo, and Capricorn are melancholic, cold, dry, and feminine; (3) Gemini, Aquarius, and Libra are sanguineous, hot, wet, and masculine; and (4) Aries, Leo, and Sagittarius are choleric, hot, dry, and masculine.

His breath kindles coals,
  and a flame comes forth from his mouth.
(Job 41:19–21)

Satan, reclining on a fiery grill, strangles representatives of the damned in each hand, while the flames of his grill incinerate all others who are nearby. The demons on either side of him fuel his fire with huge bellows, and additional batlike demons mete out punishments on hapless sinners. (They include a number of clergymen but very few women.) The coloring is primarily gray, black, and red. The mountains in the background act as gigantic furnaces, and between them is the fountain of fire and smoke spewed forth by Satan's nostrils as he disgorges the bodies of additional sinners.

The Limbourg brothers' attention to detail, unique vision, precision, and vibrant coloring was emulated in the fifteenth century by other artists in the Netherlands—including Hubert and Jan Van Eyck and Hieronymus Bosch—who appropriated the Limbourgs' style for painting on panels. Moreover, when the famous Netherlandish school of painting came into being, it rivaled the early Renaissance school in Italy.

PAINTING IN ITALY: CIMABUE, DUCCIO, AND GIOTTO Although northern Europe manuscript illumination showed continuity with the past, innovation was the hallmark of Italian painters, particularly those from the region of Tuscany. Italian painters began to confront the problems of creating believable space and depicting divine themes in human form. Cenni di Pepo, better known as Cimabue (c. 1240–c. 1301), was the first Florentine painter to do so.

Cimabue traveled to Rome in 1272, and in 1302, at Pisa, he executed the Saint John apse mosaic for the cathedral. In the last quarter of the thirteenth century, he rendered frescoes for the church of Saint Francis in Assisi. Although now badly damaged, the frescoes originally depicted Matthew, Mark, Luke, and John in the vaults of the transept crossing; the crucifixion and apocalypse in the left transept arm; the lives of Saint Peter and Saint Paul in the right transept arm; and the life of the Virgin Mary in the apse. One of Cimabue's most magnificent works, still extant, is the altarpiece he constructed for the church of Saint Trinitá in Florence, sometime about 1285. Measuring more than twelve feet by seven feet,

Figure 12.4 Limbourg Brothers, *Les Très Riches Heures du Duc de Berry, Hell*, 1413–1416, Musée Condé, Chantilly
Satan, reclining on a fiery grill, strangles representatives of the damned in each hand, while the fountain of fire and smoke spewing forth from his nostrils disgorges the bodies of additional sinners. The flames of his grill, fueled by batlike demons who mete out punishments on hapless sinners, incinerate all others who are nearby. *(Musée Condé, Chantilly/The Bridgeman Art Library International Ltd)*

reinforced with linen cloth. Subsequently, a design was executed for the panel, and the actual work was begun by first sizing the background in red and then filling it in, frequently with gold leaf, and finally, an underpainting of *terra verde* (green earth) pigment was applied. Once the background was complete, the picture was painted in multiple layers, using tempera on delicate brushes. Such a process left little room for human error.

A quarter of a century later, Duccio di Buoninsegna (c. 1255–1319) executed another altarpiece, the *Maestà,* for the cathedral in his hometown of Siena. The central panel of the altarpiece portrays *The Virgin as Queen of Heaven* (Figure 12.6). Duccio's rendering of the scene is, however, more natural than Cimabue's—the angular draperies have been replaced by gentle folds and the gold leaf has been greatly reduced. More importantly, the figures display a fragile, three-dimensional quality that makes them appear softer and rounder, and the throne has been moved back into space. This hearkens back to the earlier Hellenistic and Roman illusionism (see Chapters 5 and 6), but also evidences the influence of the Pisani school of sculpture. (Giovanni Pisano is known to have been in Siena between 1285 and 1295.) The compartments on the reverse side of Duccio's altarpiece depict scenes from the life of Mary and Jesus, but this time the elements demonstrate the blending of Byzantine and Gothic styling, as well as the effectiveness of Duccio's narrative technique. During the sixteenth century, the altarpiece was dismantled, and some of the panels can now be viewed individually in museums throughout the world.

The definitive break with the Byzantine tradition in painting—flat, expressionless figures set against a stylized background—was effected by Giotto di Bondone (1266–1337), whom Dante described in his *Purgatorio* as the preeminent painter of the fourteenth century.

> In painting Cimabue thought to hold
> The field, and now his fame is quite obscured
> While everywhere men cry up Giotto's name.[34]

Today, art historians credit Giotto with having revolutionized the course of painting in Europe. He was born in Colle di Vespignano, but few details of his life are known. Some scholars believe that Giotto may have been a student of Cimabue, but most agree that he traveled to Rome and probably also worked in Padua, Milan, and Naples. All scholars are in agreement that in 1305 to 1306 Giotto executed his masterpiece—the design for the *Arena Chapel* in Padua (Figure 12.7)—which was commissioned by Enrico Scrovegni, a wealthy merchant, reputedly as reparation for his father's

Figure 12.5   Cimabue, *Madonna Enthroned,* c. 1285, tempera on wood, 12′7 1/2′ x 7′4″ (3.9 x 2.2 m), Church of Saint Trinitá, Florence, Italy   The gable-shaped panel encases the softly shrouded, round-faced figure of Mary, holding the Christ child and surrounded by a layering of angels. At the base of the panel are four Old Testament prophets. *(Uffizi/Scala/Art Resource, NY)*

Madonna Enthroned (Figure 12.5), depicts the softly shrouded figure of Mary holding the Christ child, surrounded by angels; at the base of the panel are four Old Testament prophets. The gold-streaked draperies, Mary's round face, and the formal, dignified pose all indicate the influence of Byzantine mosaics. However, the gable shape of the panel, the layering of the angels bordering Mary, and the three-dimensional perspective of Mary's throne, as well as its decorative architecture, are all unique to Tuscany.

Paintings such as Cimabue's altarpiece were painstakingly done on wooden panels using tempera—an egg-based substance that dried swiftly, forming a hard surface. First the panel needed to be smoothed and covered with *gesso,* a combination of glue and plaster, which was occasionally

Figure 12.6 Duccio, *Majestà, The Virgin as Queen of Heaven,* c. 1310, tempera on panel, 6'10 1/2" (2.1 m), Siena, Italy Mary's throne has been moved back into space, and the figures display a fragile, three-dimensional quality that makes them appear softer and rounder than Cimabue's. The angular draperies also have been replaced by gentle folds, and the gold leaf has been greatly reduced. *(Scala/Art Resource, NY)*

Figure 12.7 Giotto, *Arena (Scrovegni) Chapel,* c. 1305–1306, Padua, Italy Giotto believed that placing his figures and the viewer in the same space would cause the viewer to become more emotionally involved in each scene. The scenes of the top row tell the early life of the Virgin Mary and the story of Joachim and Anna, reputedly Mary's parents. The middle and bottom rows relate stories about the life and passion of Jesus. *(Scrovegni Chapel, Padua/Scala/Art Resource, NY)*

Figure 12.8   Giotto, *Arena (Scrovegni) Chapel, Lamentation,* c. 1305–1306, Padua, Italy   Mary serenely holds Jesus' head, while anonymous mourners cradle his pierced hands and feet. Angels weep from the clouds, and John, standing above Mary, cries conspicuously. *(Alinari/Art Resource, NY)*

usurious undertakings. The thirty-nine frescoes, which cover the walls and the ceiling of the chapel in three tiers, were designed by Giotto as a series of three narratives to be read from the center, then down and clockwise.

The top row illustrates both the story of *Joachim and Anna* and the *Early Life of the Virgin.* According to the medieval tradition, Joachim and Anna were the Virgin Mary's parents. The middle and bottom rows tell the story of the *Life and Passion of Christ.* Giotto's simple, yet dramatic style causes the viewer to become a participant in each scene, rather than just a casual bystander. He accomplishes this feat by making all of the action of each scene occur in the foreground. In addition, he crafts the design of the fresco to place the action at eye level—in the lower half of the fresco. Thus the viewer stands on the same plane as the participants of each scene. Establishing this relationship between the viewer and the painting was nothing short of revolutionary in the history of painting. Undoubtedly, Giotto was aware that by placing his figures and the viewer in the same space the viewer would become

more emotionally involved in each scene. Giotto's renown as a painter led to his appointment, in 1334, as head of the Florentine Cathedral workshop (a position that, until that time, only sculptors and architects had occupied). While its director, he was able to realize his dream of making painting superior to sculpture. He did so by redefining pictorial space—the figures, not the architectural setting, are the focus of the painted surface. For the first time in the history of painting, three-dimensional forms are adequately depicted on a flat, two-dimensional surface.

The somber tragedy of Giotto's *Lamentation* (Figure 12.8), from the third row of frescoes, illustrates his compositional precision and his authority in the production of the human drama played out at Christ's crucifixion. The figures grieve in a manner consistent with each personality—Mary serenely holds Jesus' head, while anonymous mourners cradle his pierced hands and feet; angels weep from the clouds (a symbol for the supernatural); John, Jesus' beloved disciple, stands above Mary and cries most conspicuously. The overall unity of the scene is achieved by the diagonal slope of the hill, which moves from the upper right of the fresco to focus on Mary and her son. The leafless tree in the upper right typifies the sorrow of the setting, but also symbolizes the biblical reference to Adam and Eve having caused the Tree of Knowledge to wither, but that Christ's atonement made the tree fruitful again. The serenity of the brushwork further enhances the image of the necessity of Christ's sacrifice.

Giotto's affinity for the human form and the feeling he allowed it to convey set his work apart from that of Cimabue and Duccio. Although Giotto's disciples further cultivated his perspective and developed his setting, they were unable to duplicate his psychological depiction of the human form. Furthermore, the bubonic plague caused artists to return to traditional medieval themes, concentrating on death and the torments of hell. Giotto's facility to create believable space and convincing objects within a two-dimensional surface anticipated Renaissance techniques, and Renaissance artists in Florence in the early fifteenth century did make the next advancements in painting.

THE *ARS NOVA* (NEW ART) IN MUSIC

Modern scholars have appropriated the title of a musical treatise written by Phillipe de Vitry (1291–1361), *ars nova*, to designate the music of the fourteenth century and to differentiate it from the *ars antiqua* of the thirteenth century, which consisted largely of late-medieval motet compositions. The music of this century, like its literature and visual arts, was characterized by great innovation, but also continuity with the past. Most innovations in music came from the French composers, who emphasized flexibility of rhythm and a wide range of vocalists, instead of just the tenor singing the cantus firmus. But in the latter half of the century, Italian composers developed a more natural melodic line, which was charming, smooth, and utilized the immense range of the human voice. New forms of music also came into being—most notably, polyphonic secular music in France and the *madrigal* and *caccia* in Italy. Throughout the fourteenth century, far more secular music than sacred music was composed and performed. Moreover, there were some innovations in the liturgical music of the church that incurred the disdain of the papal hierarchy.

The early fourteenth-century illuminated manuscript of the satiric play *Roman de Fauvel* (The Story of Fauvel) (Figure 12.9) tells us a great deal about the character of late medieval music. Written by members of the French court, including de

Vitry, the allegorical play contains 150 musical compositions ranging from monophonic Gregorian chants to secular motets. The main character is Fauvel, a donkey, whose name is an acronym for six vices—*F*lattery, *A*varice, *U*ntruthfulness, *V*ariability, *E*nvy, and *L*aziness. Fauvel has turned the world inside out as people revel in wickedness, including chivalric knights, who engage in sinful acts, and clergymen, who are equally licentious. As the pope and the king cater to Fauvel, Fortune raises him to great power. He marries Pride amidst a scene of great pomp and ceremony and their children come to reign over the world. The music essentially veiled the actual meaning of a text such as this one, which is critical of the papal hierarchy.

> The pope sits on his holy chair, which stood
> For rock of Peter once, but now is wood.
> He looks at Fauvel there in his presence,
> To whom the assembled make great reverence,
> And groom him constantly from morn
>   till night. . .
> And now, while softly rubbing Fauvel's head,
> He says, "A lovely beast, he must be fed."
> The cardinals, who wish to please anew,
> Reply, "O holy Father, thou speak'st true."[35]

The musical innovation of the *Roman de Fauvel* was the structural device known as the *isorhythm* (same rhythm)—taking the tenor melody and repeating it in a complex pattern of pitch and rhythm—the musical principle that became the basis for the *ars nova*.

Around 1320, three important musical treatises were published—the *Ars novae musicae (Art of the New Music)* by Jean de Muris, the *Speculum musicae (Mirror of Music)* by Jacob of Liège, and most importantly, Philippe de Vitry's *Ars nova*, which gave the movement its name. These three treatises advocated a new style of music characterized by "imperfection," including new rhythms and new intervals as a complement to the customary ones. Moreover, staff notation was expanded to designate the duration of the various pitches, and five new note shapes appeared. The new music was, however, soon officially condemned by the church, not only for these innovations but also for using secular texts along with the sacred chants. Pope John XXII (1316–1334), writing from Avignon in 1325, declared the *ars nova* to be nothing short of blasphemous.

> Certain disciples of the new school . . . display their prolation in notes which are new to us, preferring to devise methods of their own rather than to continue singing in the old way. . . .Their voices are incessantly . . . intoxicating the ear, not soothing it. . . . We now hasten therefore to banish those

Figure 12.9 *Roman de Fauvel,* **early 14th century.** Written by members of the French court, the allegory contains 150 musical compositions ranging from monophonic Gregorian chants to secular motets. The main character is Fauvel, a donkey, whose name is an acronym for six vices—*Flattery, Avarice, Untruthfulness, Variability, Envy,* and *Laziness. (Bibliothèque Nationale, Paris/Flammarion/ The Bridgeman Art Library International Ltd)*

methods . . . far from the house of God. . . . [W]e straitly command that no one henceforward shall think himself at liberty to attempt those methods, or methods like them.[36]

After Philippe de Vitry, the foremost composer of the *ars nova* in France was Guillaume de Machaut (c. 1304–1377). Much of his work is still extant and has been published in modern critical editions. Machaut was also esteemed as a poet and often likened to his contemporary, Petrarch. He was educated in theology and became a priest in northern France. When he was twenty years old, Machaut served as secretary to King John of Bohemia (brother of John XXII) and accompanied him on numerous military expeditions throughout Europe. In 1346, with King John's death at the Battle of Crécy, Machaut entered the service of the Dauphin of France (soon to be Charles V) and his brother, Jean, Duke of Berry.

The vast majority of Machaut's pieces are secular songs written in the spirit of the troubadours and reflective of his nostalgic longing for the chivalric age, which was waning. He composed most of his secular works polyphonically, but some of his songs hearken back to earlier monophonic music. Machaut's sacred music is generally more conservative than his secular pieces, except for his arrangement of the Mass—*Messe de Notre Dame (Mass of Our Lady)*—the first known unified setting of the Ordinary. Reputedly composed for the coronation of Charles V in 1364, it is Machaut's most acclaimed sacred composition. Machaut organized the Ordinary, both stylistically and thematically, according to the same mode, resulting in a single, complete piece of music, instead of the customary five independent compositions. He also employed a motet styling for the mass, including isorhythms, fascinating rhythmic patterns between the cantus firmus and the upper voices, and instrumental accompaniment. Machaut's Mass set the standard for composition into the sixteenth century, and for some composers, even beyond.

During the second half of the fourteenth century, northern Italian composers endorsed new forms of music, including the *madrigal* and the *caccia*. Although the genre of madrigal changed over time, fourteenth-century *madrigals* were musical poems of two or three stanzas of three lines each, using the same music, which concluded with a stanza of different music called the *ritornello*. A *caccia*—a term that is actually a play on words meaning both *canon* and *hunt*—has three parts. The two upper voices are highly elaborate, whereas the music for the lower voice is written with longer note values. Because caccia were very lively pieces, they became popular at courtly gatherings. One of the most notable composers of madrigals and caccia was Giovanni da Firenze (c. 1320–1362), a Florentine clergyman who composed both liturgical music and secular songs. An exquisite fifteenth-century manuscript, called the *Squarcialupi Codex,* not only contains a miniature painting of Giovanni but also a copy of one of his caccia.

Additionally, the *Squarcialupi Codex* includes a portrait of Italy's most celebrated composer of the fourteenth century, Francesco Landini (1325–1397). Landini's father was a painter and a close associate of Giotto. Due to a smallpox infection, which he incurred as a small child, Landini became blind. Since he knew he could never be a painter, Landini gravitated toward music and became an accomplished singer, instrumentalist, music director, and organist. The hallmark of Landini's music is its lyrical quality: *dolcezza,* an Italian word meaning sweetness and the term most often used to describe Landini's musical compositions, as well as his playing. Landini was also called on to fashion the design for the organ of the Florentine Cathedral (see Chapter 11). Landini's contemporaries acknowledged him as the most significant composer of the period, and nearly half of the *Squarcialupi Codex* is filled with the compositions of "Master Francesco the Blind."

Even after the Middle Ages came to an end, its music continued to permeate the thinking of the next generation of composers. Plainchant continued to be a popular mode of expression, and after the Great Schism ended in 1417, musicians once again began to compose rich music for the liturgy in the church. Similarly, the literary themes concerning the dignity and worth of the individual and the value of this world were fully probed in secular songs and instrumental music. In the final analysis, the Middle Ages presided over the connection of music with text, the further evolution of musical instruments, the practical analysis of melody, the advancement of polyphony, the extension of musical notation and rhythm, and the development of musical drama, which were to inspire and to benefit all future musicians.

The Middle Ages and The Modern World: Continuity and Discontinuity

Medieval civilization began to decline in the fourteenth century, but no dark age comparable to the three centuries following Rome's fall descended on Europe; its economic and political institutions and technological skills had grown too strong. Instead, the waning of the Middle Ages opened up possibilities for another stage in Western civilization: the modern age.

The modern world is linked to the Middle Ages in innumerable ways. European cities, the middle class, the state system, English common law, universities—all had their origins in the Middle Ages. During medieval times, important advances were made in business practices, including partnerships, systematic bookkeeping, and the bill of exchange. By translating and commenting on the writings of Greek and Arabic thinkers, medieval scholars preserved a priceless intellectual heritage, without which the modern mind could never have evolved. In addition, numerous strands connect the thought of the scholastics and that of early modern philosophers. Romanesque and Gothic styles served as models for western architecture for centuries after the Middle Ages. Medieval love lyrics still endure, and religious hymns continue to be sung. Moreover, without the medieval discovery of polyphony, harmony, and staff notation, modern music could not have evolved in the manner it did.

Feudal traditions lasted long after the Middle Ages. Up to the French Revolution, for instance, French aristocrats enjoyed special privileges and exercised power over local government. In England, the aristocracy controlled local government until the Industrial Revolution transformed English society in the nineteenth century. Retaining the medieval ideal of the noble warrior, aristocrats continued to dominate the officer corps of European armies through the nineteenth century and even into the twentieth. Aristocratic notions of duty, honor, loyalty, and courtly love have endured into our own day.

During the Middle Ages, Europeans began to take the lead over the Muslims, the Byzantines, the Chinese, and all the other peoples in the use of technology. Medieval technology and inventiveness stemmed in part from Christianity, which taught that God had created the world specifically for human beings to subdue and exploit. Consequently, medieval people tried to employ animal power and laborsaving machinery to relieve human drudgery. Moreover, Christianity taught that God was above nature, not within it, so the

Christian had no spiritual obstacle to exploiting nature—unlike, for instance, the Hindu. In contrast to classical humanism, the Christian outlook did not consider manual work degrading; even monks combined it with study.

The Christian stress on the sacred worth of the individual and on the higher law of God has never ceased to influence Western civilization. Even though in modern times the various Christian churches have not often taken the lead in political and social reform, the ideals identified with the Judeo-Christian tradition have become part of the Western heritage. As such, they have inspired social reformers, who may no longer identify with their ancestral religion.

Believing that God's law was superior to state or national decrees, medieval philosophers provided a theoretical basis for opposing tyrannical kings who violated Christian principles. The idea that both the ruler and the ruled are bound by a higher law would, in a secularized form, become a principal element of modern liberal thought.

Feudalism also contributed to the history of liberty. According to feudal custom, the king, as a member of the feudal community, was duty-bound to honor agreements made with his vassals. Lords possessed personal rights, which the king was obliged to respect. Resentful of a king who ran roughshod over customary feudal rights, lords also negotiated contracts with the crown, such as the famous Magna Carta, to define and guard their customary liberties. To protect themselves from the arbitrary behavior of a king, feudal lords initiated what came to be called government by consent and the rule of law.

During the Middle Ages, then, there gradually emerged the idea that law was not imposed on inferiors by an absolute monarch but required the collaboration of the king and his subjects; that the king, too, was bound by the law; and that lords had the right to resist a monarch who violated agreements. A related phenomenon was the rise of representative institutions, with which the king was expected to consult on the realm's affairs. The most notable such institution was the British Parliament; although subordinate to the king, it became a permanent part of the state. Later, in the seventeenth century, Parliament would successfully challenge royal authority. Thus, continuity exists between the feudal tradition of a king bound by law and the modern practice of limiting the authority of the head of state.

Although the elements of continuity are clear, the characteristic outlook of the Middle Ages is as different from that of the modern age as it was from the outlook of the ancient world. Religion was the integrating feature of the Middle Ages, whereas science and secularism—a preoccupation with worldly life—determine the modern outlook. The period from the Italian Renaissance of the fifteenth century through the eighteenth-century Age of Enlightenment constituted a gradual breaking away from the medieval worldview—a rejection of the medieval conception of nature, the individual, and the purpose of life. The transition from medieval to modern was neither sudden nor complete, for there are no sharp demarcation lines separating historical periods. Although many distinctively medieval ways endured in the sixteenth, seventeenth, and even eighteenth centuries, these centuries saw as well the rise of new intellectual, political, and economic forms, which marked the emergence of modernity.

Medieval thought began with the existence of God and the truth of his revelation as interpreted by the church. In medieval thought, says historian–philosopher Ernst Cassirer,

> neither science nor morality, neither law nor state, can be erected on its own foundation. Supernatural assistance is always needed to bring them to true perfection. . . . Reason is and remains the servant of revelation; within the sphere of natural intellectual and psychological forces, reason leads toward, and prepares the ground for, revelation.[37]

The medieval mind rejected the fundamental principle of Greek philosophy—the autonomy of reason. Without the guidance of revealed truth, reason was seen as feeble.

Scholastics engaged in genuine philosophical speculation, but they did not allow philosophy to challenge the basic premises of their faith. Unlike either ancient or modern thinkers, medieval schoolmen ultimately believed that reason alone could not provide a unified view of nature or society. A rational soul had to be guided by a divine light. For all medieval philosophers, the natural order depended on a supernatural order for its origin and purpose. To understand the natural world properly, it was necessary to know its relationship to the higher world. The discoveries of reason had to accord with Scripture as interpreted by the church.

In the modern view, both nature and the human intellect are self-sufficient. Nature is a mathematical system that operates without miracles or any other form of divine intervention. To comprehend nature and society, the mind needs no divine assistance; it accepts no authority above reason. The modern mentality finds it unacceptable to reject the conclusions of science on the basis of clerical authority and revelation or to ground politics, law, or economics on religious dogma. It refuses to settle public issues by appeals to religious belief.

The medieval philosopher understood both nature and society to be a hierarchical order. God was the source of moral values, and the church was responsible for teaching and upholding these ethical norms. Kings acquired their right to rule from God. The entire social structure constituted a hierarchy: The clergy guided society according to Christian standards; lords defended Christian society from its enemies; and serfs, lowest in the social order, toiled for the good of all. In the hierarchy of knowledge, a lower form of knowledge derived from the senses, and the highest type of knowledge, theology, dealt with God's revelation. To the medieval mind, this hierarchical ordering of nature, society, and knowledge had divine sanction.

Rejecting the medieval division of the universe into higher and lower realms and superior and inferior substances, the modern view postulated the uniformity of nature and of nature's laws: The cosmos knows no privilege of rank; heavenly bodies follow the same laws of nature as earthly objects. Space is geometric and homogeneous, not hierarchical, heterogeneous, and qualitative. The universe was no longer conceived as finite and closed but as infinite, and the operations of nature were explained mathematically. The modern thinker studies mathematical law and chemical composition, not grades of perfection. Spiritual meaning is not sought in an examination of the material world. Roger Bacon, for example, described seven coverings of the eye and then concluded that God had fashioned the eye in this manner in order to express the seven gifts of the Spirit. This way of thinking is alien to the modern outlook. So, too, is the medieval belief that natural disasters, such as plagues and famines, are God's punishments for people's sins.

The outlook of the modern West also broke with the rigid division of medieval society into three orders: clergy, nobles, and commoners. The intellectual justification for this arrangement, as expressed by the English prelate John of Salisbury (c. 1115–1180), has been rejected by modern westerners: "For inferiors owe it to their superiors to provide them with service, just as the superiors in their turn owe it to their inferiors to provide them with all things needful for their protection and succor."[38] Opposing the feudal principle that an individual's obligations and rights are a function of his or her rank in society, the modern view stressed equality of opportunity and equal treatment under the law. It rejected the idea that society should be guided by clergy, who were deemed to possess a special wisdom; by nobles, who were entitled to special privileges; and by monarchs, who were thought to receive their power from God.

The modern West also rejected the personal and customary character of feudal law. As the modern state developed, law assumed an impersonal and objective character. For example, if the lord demanded more than the customary forty days of military service, the vassal might refuse to comply because he would see the lord's request as an unpardonable violation of custom and agreement, as well as an infringement on his liberties. In the modern state, with a constitution and a representative assembly, if a new law increasing the length of military service is passed, it merely replaces the old law. People do not refuse to obey it because the government has broken faith or violated custom.

In the modern world, the individual's relationship to the universe has been radically transformed. Medieval people lived in a geocentric universe, which was finite in space and time. The universe was small, enclosed by a sphere of stars, beyond which were the heavens. The universe, it was believed, was some four thousand years old, and in the not-too-distant future, Christ would return and human history would end. People in the Middle Ages knew why they were on earth and what was expected of them; they never doubted that heaven would be their reward for living a Christian life. Preparation for heaven was the ultimate aim of life. J. H. Randall, Jr., a historian of ideas, eloquently sums up the medieval view of a purposeful universe, in which the human being's position was clearly defined:

> The world was governed throughout by the omnipotent will and omniscient mind of God, whose sole interests were centered in man, his trial, his fall, his suffering and his glory. Worm of the dust as he was, man was yet the central object in the whole universe. . . . And when his destiny was completed, the heavens would be rolled up as a scroll and he would dwell with the Lord forever. Only those who rejected God's freely offered grace and with hardened hearts refused repentance would be cut off from this eternal life.[39]

This comforting medieval vision is alien to the modern outlook. Today, in a universe some twelve billion years old, in which the earth is a tiny speck floating in an endless cosmic ocean, where life evolved over tens of millions of years, many westerners no longer believe that human beings are special children of God; that heaven is their ultimate goal; that under their feet is hell, where grotesque demons torment sinners; and that God is an active agent in human history. To many intellectuals, the universe seems unresponsive to the religious supplications of people, and life's purpose is sought within the limits of earthly existence. Science and secularism have driven Christianity and faith from their central position to the periphery of human concerns.

In the nineteenth, twentieth, and twenty-first centuries, Christian thinkers lamented the waning of faith. Distressed by an all-consuming secularism, a crude materialism, and vicious class and national antagonisms, these thinkers attributed the ills of the modern West to a diminishing commitment to Christianity and called for spiritual renewal. Some of them, looking back nostalgically to the Middle Ages when life had an overriding religious purpose and few doubted the truth of Christian teachings, contended that the modern West would benefit from a reaffirmation of those Christian concerns and values that had energized medieval society.

The modern outlook developed gradually in the period from the Renaissance to the eighteenth-century Age of Enlightenment. Mathematics rendered the universe comprehensible. Economic and political thought broke free of the religious frame of reference. Science became the great hope of the future. The thinkers of the Enlightenment wanted to liberate humanity from superstition, ignorance, and traditions that could not pass the test of reason. They saw themselves as emancipating culture from theological dogma and clerical authority. Rejecting the Christian idea of a person's inherent sinfulness, they held that the individual was basically good and that evil resulted from faulty institutions, poor education, and bad leadership. Thus, the concept of a rational and free society in which individuals could realize their potential slowly emerged.

Key Terms

Black Death	morality play
Babylonian Captivity	Italian sonnets
Great Schism	caricatures
Conciliar Movement	books of hours
Lollards	*ars nova*
stigmata	madrigals

Notes

1. Excerpted in Ralph Lerner and Muhsin Mahdi, eds., *Medieval Political Philosophy* (New York: The Free Press, 1963), pp. 413–414.
2. Quoted in Katharina M. Wilson, *Medieval Women Writers*, trans. Joseph Berrigan (Athens: University of Georgia Press), pp. 255–256.
3. William Langland, *Will's Vision of Piers Plowman*, trans. E. Talbot Donaldson, ed. Elizabeth D. Kirk and Judith H. Anderson (New York: W. W. Norton, 1990), pp. 209–211.
4. Excerpted in M. H. Abrams, ed., *The Norton Anthology of English Literature*, vol. 1 (New York: W. W. Norton, Revised edition, 1968), p. 258, ftn. 6.
5. Ibid., p. 232.
6. Ibid., p. 269.
7. Ibid., p. 269.
8. Ibid., p. 272.
9. Guillaume de Lorris and Jean de Meun, *The Romance of the Rose,* trans. Charles Dahlberg (Princeton, N.J.: Princeton University Press, 1971), pp. 163–164.
10. G. A. Lester, *Three Late Medieval Morality Plays: Mankind, Everyman, Mundus et infans* (New York: W. W. Norton, 1981), pp. 63–64.
11. Ibid., pp. 64–65.
12. Ibid., pp. 94–95.
13. Ibid., p. 100.
14. Ibid., p. 102.
15. Quoted in Morris Bishop, *Petrarch and His World* (Bloomington: Indiana University Press, 1966), pp. 153–154.
16. Morris Bishop, ed., trans., *Letters from Petrarch* (Bloomington: Indiana University Press, 1966), pp. 153–154.
17. Ibid., p. 213.
18. Giovanni Boccaccio, *The Decameron,* trans. Richard Aldington (New York: Dell Publishing Co., 1966), pp. 31, 33.
19. Ibid., p. 455.
20. Ibid., p. 457.
21. Ibid., p. 458.
22. Ibid.
23. Ibid., p. 459.
24. Geoffrey Chaucer, *The Canterbury Tales,* trans. Ronald L. Ecker and Eugene J. Crook (Palatka, Fla.: Hodge & Braddock Publishers, 1993), pp. 3, 4, 5, 6, 8, 12, 17, 20.
25. Ibid., p. 172.
26. Ibid., p. 175.
27. Ibid., p. 177.
28. Ibid., p. 180.
29. Ibid., p. 181.
30. Ibid., p. 186.
31. Ibid.
32. Christine de Pizan, *The Book of the City of Ladies,* trans. Earl Jeffrey Richards (New York: Persea Books, 1982), p. 218.
33. Christine de Pizan, *Ditié de Jehanne D'Arc,* trans. Angus J. Kennedy and Kenneth Varty (Oxford: Society for the Study of Mediaeval Languages and Literature, 1977), pp. 41, 46.
34. Dante Alighieri, *The Divine Comedy,* trans. Thomas G. Bergin (New York: Appleton-Century-Crofts, 1955), p. 36.
35. Quoted in Alec Harman, *Mediaeval and Early Renaissance Music up to c. 1525* (Fair Lawn, N.J., 1958), p. 121.
36. H. E. Wooldridge, *The Oxford History of Music, Vol. I. The Polyphonic Period, Part I: Method of Musical Art, 330-1400* (London: Oxford University Press, 192 9), pp. 296–298.
37. Ernst Cassirer, *The Philosophy of the Enlightenment* (Boston: Beacon, 1955), p. 40.
38. John of Salisbury, *Policraticus,* trans. John Dickinson (New York: Russell & Russell, 1963), pp. 243–244.
39. J. H. Randall, Jr., *The Making of the Modern Mind* (Boston: Houghton Mifflin, 1940), p. 34.

antiphons – The term comes from the Greek word *antiphonia*, which means "countersound." In medieval music, it referred to free melodies sung in the same mode and alternating between a chorus of men and a chorus of women.

Apocalyptic – The prophetic literature after the Exile, specifically the prophecies of Obadiah, Zechariah, Malachi, and Daniel, that dealt with catastrophic upheavals and the emergence of a radically different world. Such literature included metaphors of the Messiah, denunciations of evil, and expectations of the "last day," by which was meant the cataclysmic end of the world as people knew it and the emergence of a new kingdom of peace.

Aramaic – A Semitic language related to Hebrew, which became the common tongue of the Jews after the Exile in Babylon.

arch and vault – Acquired from the Etruscans, the arch and vault were used by Roman engineers and architects to design structures that spanned wide distances and supported heavy loads. The arch and vault was a crucial advancement over the "post-and-lintel" design of the Greeks.

"Archimedes Principle" – Developed by the Greek Archimedes (b. c. 287 B.C.), it states that a body immersed in a fluid displaces its own weight. This principle established the general principles of hydrostatics, a branch of physics that treats the pressure and equilibrium of liquids at rest.

ars nova – The title of a musical treatise written by Phillipe de Vitry (1291–1361), the term is used to designate the music of the fourteenth century.

Atomism – A view of physics, originally proposed by Democritus (c. 460–370 B.C.), stating that all things consist of atoms in motion. Epicurus used this theory of nature to postulate that in a universe of colliding atoms, there could be no higher intelligence ordering things and thus, no room for divine activity. This belief calmed Epicurus, whose principal cause of anxiety was the superstitious fear that the gods

intervened in human life and could inflict suffering after death.

Babylonian Captivity (Period of the Exile) – The term for the period in Jewish history after 586 B.C. when the Chaldeans conquered Judah, destroyed Solomon's temple, devastated the land, and deported several thousand Hebrews to Babylon. This period was the darkest moment in the history of the Hebrews up to that time.

Babylonian Captivity of the Church – The period from 1309 to 1377, during which all of the popes were French and resided in Avignon, not Rome, and were often forced to pursue policies favorable to France.

basilica form – A form of architecture (the long rectangular church with a horizontal focus), dictated by the emperor Constantine as the style for Christian churches throughout the Empire. The six main parts of a basilica-form church are the atrium, narthex, nave, side aisles, apse, and transept.

bishop – First used as a synonym for priest, gradually the term was reserved for the one clergyman in the community with the authority to resolve disputes over doctrines and practices. Regarded as the successors to Christ's twelve disciples, bishops supervised religious activities within their regions.

Black Death – Also known as the bubonic plague, this disease was carried by fleas on black rats. Spreading rapidly in the mid-fourteenth century, it killed perhaps twenty million people—about one-quarter to one-third of the European population.

books of hours – Personal books of devotions for laypeople for the calendar year, a famous example of which was commissioned by the Duke of Berry.

burghers – Another name for medieval townspeople, they refused to be treated as serfs bound to a lord and liable for personal services and customary dues. Many burghers obtained charters from the lords giving them the right to set up their own councils, which passed laws, collected taxes, and formed courts that enforced the laws.

calligraphy – A decorative form of writing, used in Islamic religious architecture to carry the sacred message of the Quran. For Muslims, calligraphy was valued above all other art forms and was also utilized as decoration for ceramics, metalwork, and textiles, such as pillows and carpets.

cantillation – The style, represented by a formulaic series of melodies, in which the Hebrew Scriptures were chanted in both the Temple and the synagogue.

caricatures – Characters that personify virtues and vices to which all human beings are subject, an example of which occurs in Chaucer's *Canterbury Tales*.

"Carolingian foot" – A measurement of 13 inches; the Palatine Chapel was constructed according to the proportions of 7 x 12 = 144 Carolingian feet.

Carolingian minuscule script – A style of writing, created by Alcuin. It standardized the written hand in the empire. Later, it became the model for early typefaces during the Renaissance and for the modern printed Latin type.

Carolingian Renaissance – A time of intellectual flowering under Charlemagne, it was designed to improve the educational level of the clergy so that they understood and could properly teach the faith. This process raised the level of literacy and improved the Latin style.

catharsis – An emotional release, often seen in the rituals of mystery cult members. In imitation of Dionysos' ordeal, members of his cult savagely tore apart sacrificial animals to release pent-up, primitive emotions.

cella – One of the two main parts of a Greek temple, which applies to both orders of architecture, it is the area where the figure of the deity was placed.

centralized form – A popular style of early Christian architecture, centralized-form churches were either round or polygonal structures with a vertical focus, which was finished with a dome. Because the number eight was the Christian symbol of the resurrection, the most common geometric design was the octagon, which was used for both baptisteries and funeral chapels.

chivalry – A code of behavior for the feudal nobility. A true knight was expected to fight bravely, demonstrate loyalty to his lord, and treat other knights with respect and courtesy.

chorus – Coming from the Greek word meaning "dance," the chorus was a group of singers in early Greek tragedy who performed hymns. The emotional impact of these hymns was intensified by the music, which was played on either a lyre or an aulos.

Christ Pantocrator – This image of Christ, also referred to as Christ the All-Sovereign, was traditionally used to fill the dome of Byzantine churches. In one hand the stern-faced Christ holds the Law and with the other gestures as if pronouncing a commandment.

Christian – From the name given Jesus, *Christ* (the Lord's Anointed, the Messiah), these followers believed that they were the true Israel, the real people of God, who had recognized the Messiah when he came. Early Christians preached to their fellow Jews that Jesus was the true Messiah and that those who accepted him and repented of their sins would be baptized in his name and would share in the immortality promised in Jesus' resurrection.

code of Hammurabi – The principal collection of laws in ancient Mesopotamia under Hammurabi (c. 1792–c. 1750 B.C.), the Babylonian ruler. The laws included strict punishments for crimes – "an eye for an eye and a tooth for a tooth," yet punishments varied depending on class distinctions.

common law – A unified system of law that developed in England during the reigns of Henry I (1100–1135) and Henry II (1154–1189). During this period important cases began to be tried in the king's court rather than in local courts, thereby increasing royal power and making the system of law more unified and just.

Conciliar Movement – A fifteenth-century movement that stated the authority of a general council of the church is superior to the pope. It attempted to transform the papal monarchy into a constitutional system, until Pope Pius II condemned it as heretical in 1460.

Concordat of Worms – A compromise decision, reached in 1122, to the Investiture Controversy over whether the church or the king had power to elect bishops. The Concordat gave the church sole power to elect bishops, but gave the king power to grant the bishop the scepter, to indicate that the bishop was also the recipient of a fief and the king's vassal, owing feudal obligations to the crown.

contrapposto – A technique in sculpture that shows a pose suspended between resting and walking in which one side of the body is relaxed and the other side tense with the weight carried by one leg. This technique was originated by Polykleitos sometime around 450–440 B.C.

Corpus Juris Civilis – The official body of law of the Byzantine Empire, it was a collection of Rome's ancient laws and the commentaries of learned jurists.

cosmogony – An account of the origins of the universe. An example of this is Hesiod's poem, *Theogony (Generation of the Gods),* which links the creation of the natural world (Heaven, Earth, Sea, Night, and Day), and human life to the existence of immortal gods and goddesses.

Council of Nicaea – The name of the council called in A.D. 325 by the emperor Constantine to settle the dispute over whether Jesus and God were of the same nature and substance. The council ruled that they were coequal and coeternal; this position became the basis of the Nicene Creed, which still remains the official doctrine of the church.

covenant – A belief, central to Hebrew religious thought and decisive in Hebrew history, that God had made a special agreement with the Hebrew people: If they obeyed his commands, they would "be unto Me a kingdom of priests, and a holy nation" (Exodus 19:6). By this act, the Israelites as a nation accepted God's lordship.

Crusades – A series of medieval wars fought by Christians attempting to regain the Holy Land from the Muslims.

cult of Mithras – A mystery religion that had certain parallels with early Christianity and was its principal competitor. The devotion to Mithras began in the Near East over 2,000 years before the Pax Romana and later spread into the Empire from Persia. The god Mithras, whose birth date was celebrated on December 25, had as his mission the rescue of humanity from evil.

Cynics – A group of supreme individualists who regarded laws and public opinion, private property and employ-

ment, and wives and children as hindrances to the free life. The Cynics had no loyalty to family, city, or kingdom and ridiculed religion, philosophy, and literature.

Dark Age – The term given to the period of Greek civilization from 1100 to 800 B.C., during which time the Greeks experienced insecurity, warfare, poverty, and isolation.

Delian League – A confederation of more than 150 Greek city-states, formed immediately after the Persian Wars. The league, named after its treasury on the island of Delos, was created for Greeks to protect themselves against a renewed confrontation with Persia. Dominated by Athens, it aroused resentment and fear among other city-states.

deus ex machina – A Latin phrase meaning "the god from the machine," it refers to a convention in Greek theater in which a crane, attached to a cable with a harness, allowed an actor portraying a god or goddess to appear on the scene from the sky. Today, this phrase is used to refer to any improbable event or character employed in literature to resolve a confounding dilemma.

dialectics – A method of inquiry developed by Socrates, it is also known as logical discussion. As Socrates used it, a dialectical exchange between individuals (or with oneself), a *dialogue,* was the essential source of knowledge.

Dominicans – A Catholic order founded by Saint Dominic (c. 1170–1221), a Spanish nobleman, who had preached against the Cathari in southern France. Believing that those who were well versed in Christian teaching could best combat heresy, Dominic, unlike Francis, insisted that his followers engage in study.

Doric order – One of the two main orders of Greek architecture, it refers to the standard features of the exterior, which are clearly distinguishable. The three main divisions of Doric architecture are the stepped platform, the columns, and the entablature, which consists of everything situated on top of the columns.

Epic of Gilgamesh – Written in about 2000 B.C., this epic is viewed as the greatest work of Mesopotamian literature. It is based on legends about Gilgamesh, probably a historical figure who ruled the city of Uruk in about 2600 B.C., and it reveals the

Mesopotamians' struggle to come to terms with the reality of death.

Epicureanism – A Greek philosophy developed by Epicurus in which people could achieve happiness when their bodies were "free from pain" and their minds were "released from worry and fear." Although Epicurus wanted to increase pleasure for the individual, he rejected unbridled hedonism, believing that happiness must be pursued rationally.

eschatology – A vision of an "end of time"; used in the Zoroastrianism religion as the time when Ahura Mazda's purpose for creating the world is fulfilled, evil is defeated, and good finally triumphs. The two major events leading up to the end of time are: the bodily resurrection of the dead, in both paradise and hell; and the final judgment—during which all of humanity is to be immersed in molten metal.

Essenes – A Jewish sect that established a semimonastic community near the Dead Sea. The Essenes believed in the physical resurrection of the body, like the Pharisees, but gave this doctrine a more compelling meaning by tying it to the immediate coming of God's kingdom.

excommunication – The harshest penalty imposed by the church on those who resisted its authority. It consisted of expulsion from the church and denial of the sacraments, without which there could be no salvation.

Feast of Weeks – A Jewish holy day venerating the receiving of the Ten Commandments on Mount Sinai.

feudalism – A loose medieval system in which the essential unit of government was not a kingdom, but a county or castellany, and political power was the private possession of local lords.

Five Pillars – The basic tenets of the Islamic faith that all Muslims are required to follow. The first pillar is called "The Witness"—a Muslim must accept and repeat the statement of faith: "There is no God but Allah, and Muhammad is his Prophet." The four other pillars—Prayer, Alms, Fasting, and Pilgrimage—are acts of worship.

flying buttresses – Designed to help support the walls of Gothic cathedrals, these buttresses connected the high, upper vaults to strong piers anchored to the ground. They enabled architects to design and construct naves of increasingly greater height; the result was a competition among towns to build the highest cathedral.

Forms – In Plato's philosophy, it meant unchanging, eternal, absolute, and universal standards of beauty, goodness, justice, and truth. Plato postulated the existence of a higher world of reality, the realm of Ideas, or Forms, independent of the world of things that we experience every day.

Franciscans – A Catholic order (also called Little Brothers) whose members followed the teachings of Saint Francis of Assisi, it was transformed from a spontaneous movement of inspired laymen into an organized agent of papal policy. The papacy set aside many of Francis's prohibitions including the owning of property, the right to hear confession, and formal learning.

genre sculpture – A style of sculpture from the Hellenistic age, it was radically different from Classical Hellenic sculpture and further defined individualized realism. Hellenistic genre sculpture depicted people in everyday situations, as individuals, rather than as types.

Gentiles – From the Latin *gens,* or "nation," this word designates non-Jews.

geocentric theory – A medieval view, advocated by Aristotle and Ptolemy and based on Christian beliefs, that we live in an earth-centered universe. The geocentric theory held that revolving around the motionless earth at uniform speeds were seven transparent spheres, in which were embedded each of the seven planets.

Geometric Style – The oldest style of Greek vase painting, beginning after 800 B.C. It is characterized by a wide variety of solid, fixed shapes—concentric circles, triangles, dots, and diamonds—that decorated the vases.

gladiators – Roman men, usually slaves and condemned criminals, who were trained to fight against wild beasts, sometimes until death. Public displays of these spectacles took place in the Colosseum.

Golden Age – The term used by cultural historians to describe Latin literature during the Ciceronian and Augustan periods. Whereas Latin prose reached its apex with Cicero in the late Republic, the reign of Augustus was distinguished by the greatest poetry ever composed in Latin.

goliards – A group of medieval student poets who wandered from university to university, reveling in the pleasure of youth, wine, and song. Their name derives from one of the leaders, the

Archpoet (c. 1300), who had the nickname "Golias."

Gothic – A style of architecture, developed around 1150 in Paris, that gave visual expression to the medieval conception of a hierarchical universe, with God at its apex. Although Gothic architects appropriated most of the features of Romanesque architecture—ambulatory and radiating chapels, ribbed groin vaulting, and pointed arches—they transformed these features and added new elements, especially flying buttresses, which made it possible to infuse the Gothic cathedral with light.

Great Schism – The period from 1378 to 1417 during which there were two popes, Urban VI ruling from Rome and Clement VII from Avignon.

Gregorian chant – Also called plainchant, this form of music is attributed to Pope Gregory I (The Great) who reputedly inscribed the chants of a heavenly dove for use in the sacred music of the church. It was the first truly Western music and served as the supporting structure for the further development of polyphony.

guilds – A medieval group of merchants and artisans organized to protect their members from outside competition. To prevent one guild member from making significantly more money than another, a guild required its members to work the same number of hours, pay employees the same wages, produce goods of equal quality, and charge customers a just price.

Hegira – The name given to Muhammad's flight in 622 from Mecca to Medina. It is one of the most important events in Muslim history and is commemorated by yearly pilgrimages. The date of the Hegira became year one of the Muslim calendar.

Hellenistic Age – The second stage in Greek history, it began with the death of Alexander the Great in 323 B.C. and ended in 30 B.C., when Egypt, the last major Hellenistic state, fell to Rome.

Hellenistic romance – Introduced in the first century B.C. and reaching its height in the second and third centuries A.D., it was the precursor of the modern romance novel. It involves a praiseworthy heroine who is separated from her gallant lover, either because of natural disasters or human maliciousness; she eventually reunites with him.

hieroglyphics – A form of picture writing in ancient Egypt in which figures, such as crocodiles, sails, eyes, and so forth, represented words or sounds that would be combined to form words. Hieroglyphics were often used to write "pyramid texts," which contained fragments from myths, historical annals, and magical lore and provided spells to assist the king in ascending to heaven.

hubris – A term denoting excessive pride or arrogance that leads to suffering; this was typically the fatal flaw of the hero of Greek tragedy.

ichthys – A Greek word meaning "fish", it was often embedded within a fish symbol by early Christians. The word was an acronym formed by using the first letter of the Greek words *Iesous Christos Theou Yios Soter* (Jesus Christ God's Son Savior) to describe the character of Jesus.

iconoclastic controversy – This controversy, which centered on the depiction of Christ in human form, commenced in 726 with an imperial edict against making images and curtailed artistic production for more than a century.

Inquisition – A papal court, established in 1233, designed to fight heresy. Those accused of heresy were presumed guilty, were not told the names of their accusers, and were often tortured to obtain a confession.

Investiture Controversy – A debate between King Henry IV and Pope Gregory VII over whether kings or the church should control the appointment of bishops. A compromise was reached in 1122, the Concordat of Worms, which gave the church sole power to elect bishops, but gave the king power to grant the bishop the scepter, to indicate that the bishop was also the recipient of a fief and the king's vassal, owing feudal obligations to the crown.

Ionic order – One of two styles of Greek architecture, the other being Doric, its distinguishing feature is its column which has an elaborate contoured base, a shaft that is leaner and significantly less tapered than a Doric order, and a capital, which simulates a large double scroll.

Islam – A monotheistic faith, whose name means "surrender to Allah," it emerged in the seventh century among the Arabs of Arabia. Its founder was Muhammad (c. 570–632), a prosperous merchant in Mecca, a trading city near the Red Sea.

Italian sonnets – Sonnets are poems of fourteen lines expressing a single thought; an Italian sonnet, also known as a Petrarchan sonnet, consists of an octave of eight lines followed by a sextet of six lines.

jihad – An Islamic word meaning "to strive for moral and religious perfection." Because Muslims view their religion as universal, jihad is employed to spread Islam or to defend it against its enemies and is often translated "holy war."

jus gentium – A second branch of Roman law developed during the period of the Republic's expansion outside Italy. This branch of law combined Roman civil law with principles selectively drawn from the legal tradition of Greeks and other peoples.

komos – A Greek word meaning "ritual revel," it is the origin of the word comedy. From the earliest of Greek times, revelers would travel to local communities often telling obscene jokes and wearing huge artificial phalluses. The *komos* would always end with a sexual union—an orgy or marriage—as a symbol of increased fertility.

Kontakion – A Byzantine style of hymn, containing as few as eighteen and sometimes more than thirty stanzas, all of which are structured identically.

legends – Stories often about famous people—usually warriors, kings, or religious figures—who may actually have lived or were believed to have lived. Passed on by oral tradition, these stories are often embellished with details that are unhistorical.

Leinster cycle – An Irish epic that depicts the adventures of Finn (Irish for "fair" or "white")—an actual warlord of the Irish army, who lived during the third century A.D. Although some of the texts can be dated as early as the eighth century, the stories of Finn did not become popular until the early thirteenth century.

lex caritatis – The law of love that spurs service to the world community. Roman thinkers wanted the elite to be motivated by this love and embraced the Stoic doctrine that all people, because of their capacity to reason, belong to a common humanity.

linear perspective – An artistic trait, first seen in Roman art, in which the participants in the foreground are larger and project from the image or sculpture whereas those closest to the background appear to be fused with the image or stone.

Lollards – An order of priests who followed the teachings of John Wycliffe (c. 1320–1384). They rejected the sacramental power of the clergy and sought a return to the spiritual purity and poverty of the early church.

lyric poetry – Greek poetry that was intended to be sung to the musical accompaniment of a lyre, a stringed instrument. During the seventh century B.C., lyric poetry began to supplant epic poetry.

Ma'at – An Egyptian word meaning "justice, law, right, and truth." Pharaohs were seen as ruling in accordance with Ma'at.

mabinogi – A Welsh noun meaning "a story for children," it is the basis for the title of the *Mabinogion,* the oldest example of Welsh literature. This collection of pre-Christian stories summarizes the mythology of the Welsh people in narrative form.

madrigals – Developed in the fourteenth century, these musical poems consisted of two or three stanzas of three lines each, using the same music, which concluded with a stanza of different music called the *ritornello.*

Magna Carta – This document, also known as the Great Charter, was created in 1215, in response to King John's violation of the rights of feudal barons. It is celebrated as the root of the unique English respect for basic rights and liberties.

manorialism – An economic practice in which a lord rules over a village community (manor) and its serfs, who remain bound to the land. It became the essential agricultural arrangement for much of the Middle Ages.

manuscript illumination – Detailed and vividly colored miniature paintings on the pages of manuscripts, it developed into a unique form of art during the Early Middle Ages. The most popular type of illumination was done for manuscripts of the Gospels.

meditation poetry – A type of lyric poetry that reflects on a theme, unlike songs, which celebrate a theme. A good example of meditation poetry is Psalm 23, perhaps the most quoted of the Psalms.

Messiah – A term meaning "the anointed one." Jews believed the Messiah would come and return them to their homeland and introduce an era of peace and prosperity. The concept of a Messiah, originating with the Book of Isaiah, would also become a central concept of the Christian religion.

Metaphysics – The branch of philosophy that deals with ultimate reality or Being.

morality play – A genre of drama that used allegory to dramatize the moral struggle against evil in which every Christian is engaged. The moral themes—trust in God, do good, love mercy, and do justice—are often presented in an unduly didactic way, especially in comparison to the mystery plays.

mosaic – A technique for Roman pictorial design, adapted from the tesserae of the Hellenistic Greeks, in which small tiles were placed together to affect the appearance of painting. Although initially little color was used in the tiles of the mosaics in public structures, once the Romans discovered that they could fuse color into glass tiles they began to cover the interior walls of their villas with mosaics.

mosque – A Muslim place of worship. Architects began to construct mosques in the early eighth century. The basic plan—a square structure, broad arches, and a courtyard—was influenced by Muhammad's own house.

mystery plays – First appearing in the ninth century, these plays were dramatic allegories about important religious events, especially the activities of Holy Week (between Palm Sunday and Easter). Written in Latin and performed by the clergy, they dramatized scriptural passages of the New Testament.

mystery religions – Alternate forms of Greek religion in which initiates engaged in secret forms of worship. The Eleusinian and the Orphic-Dionysian mysteries were the two most important cults.

myths – Depicted the deeds of gods, who in some remote past had brought forth the world and human beings. Holding that the gods determined human destiny, the mythmaking mind interpreted human experience through these myths. Mythmaking was humanity's first way of thinking; it was the earliest attempt to make nature's mysteries and life's uncertainties comprehensible.

Neolithic Age – Also known as the New Stone Age, this period began in the Near East about ten thousand years ago. During this time, human beings discovered farming, domesticated animals, established villages, polished stone tools, made pottery, and wove cloth.

Neo-Platonism – Led by the influential spokesman Plotinus (c. A.D. 205–c. A.D. 270), Neo-Platonism strove to achieve union with the One, or the Good, sometimes called God—the source of all existence. Plotinus felt that the intellect could neither describe nor understand the One, which transcended all knowing, and that joining with the One required a mystical leap, a purification of the soul so that it could return to its true eternal home.

New Comedy – The term used to describe Athenian comedy from the death of Alexander the Great in 323 B.C. to the death of Philemon (c. 361–263 B.C.), an important New Comedy dramatist. A distinguishing feature of New Comedy was the shift away from Athenian politics to a depiction of private life, particularly of prosperous families.

oikoumene – For Paul, the new Christian community was not a nation, but an *oikoumene*, a world community. To this extent, Christianity shared in the universalism of the Hellenistic Age.

Oriental Style – A style of Greek vase painting, from 725 and 650 B.C., which exhibited powerful Egyptian and other Near Eastern influences. Rather than emphasizing design, these vases demonstrate a narrative technique, which deals with the larger questions of human existence—the origin of the universe, life after death, and the relationship of immortal deities to finite humans.

Paleolithic Age – This period, also called the Old Stone Age, began some three million years ago. During this time, human beings lived as hunters and food gatherers.

Passover – A Jewish holy day commemorating their Exodus from Egypt.

Pax Romana – A period of peace, order, efficient administration, and prosperity also know as the Roman peace or the "Time of Happiness." It was inaugurated by Augustus and lasted for two hundred years.

pharaoh – An Egyptian ruler who was viewed as both a man and a god. All Egyptians were subservient to the pharaoh, whose word was regarded as a divine ordinance.

Pharisees – One of the four Jewish sects, they adopted a more liberal attitude toward Mosaic Law (Torah) than the Sadducees. The Pharisees allowed discussion on varying interpretations of the Law and granted authority to oral tradition as well as to written Scripture. Unlike the Sadducees, the Pharisees believed in life after death.

polis – A Greek city-state. The mature polis was a self-governing community that expressed the will of free citizens, not the desires of gods, hereditary kings, or priests.

principate – The name given to the rule of Augustus and his successors. In keeping with his policy of maintaining the appearance of traditional republican government, Octavian refused to be called king and took the inoffensive title of *princeps* (first citizen). The Senate also conferred on him the semireligious and revered name of Augustus.

pronaos – The two main parts of the temples, which apply to both orders of architecture, are the *cella* (the area where the figure of the deity was placed) and the *pronaos* (porch).

prophets – Spiritually inspired persons in the Jewish religion who felt compelled to act as God's messengers. For the Hebrews, Moses was the first and the greatest of the prophets. The teachings and deeds of others who followed him—Samuel, Elijah, and Elisha—were recorded in the historical books of Samuel and Kings.

Ptolemaic system – A system synthesized by Ptolemy (A.D. 90–168), in which a motionless, spherical earth stood in the center of the universe; the moon, sun, and planets moved about the earth in circles or in combinations of circles. The Ptolemaic system endured until the sixteenth century when Nicholas Copernicus proposed the modern view that planets revolve around the sun.

Quran – Translated as "recitation" in Arabic, this Muslim holy book contains standards of morality and is the source of the rules that govern Islamic daily life. Muslims believe it contains the words of God as revealed to Muhammad; it is also the first example of Arabic prose.

romance – A literary genre that originated in France between 1130 and 1150, it combines the legendary oral traditions of Britain, France, and Germany with chivalric ideals and Christian concepts to create tales of love, adventure, war, and the miraculous. Among the most famous romances are the tales of King Arthur and his Knights of the Round Table.

Romanesque – The period from approximately 1050 to 1200, during which there was a conscious attempt—using the basilica form, arches, arcades, barrel vaults, and domes—to revive the architecture of ancient Rome. The most important innovation of the Romanesque period was the vaulting of nave ceilings.

sacraments – The sacred rites by which God was said to confer his grace: baptism, confirmation, matrimony, extreme unction, Eucharist, penance, and ordination. Divine grace was channeled through the sacraments, which could be administered only by the clergy, the indispensable intermediary between the individual and God.

Sadducees – One of the four Jewish sects at the time of Jesus, they were religiously conservative and insisted on a strict interpretation of Mosaic Law and the perpetuation of temple ceremonies. Rejecting ideas of the resurrection of the dead and an afterlife, they held that God meted out rewards and punishments on earth.

scholasticism – Medieval philosophy that explained and clarified Christian teachings by means of concepts and principles of logic derived from Greek philosophy. Scholastics tried to show that the teachings of faith, although not derived from reason, were not contrary to reason.

Severe Style – The early Classical period of Hellenic sculpture (480–450 B.C.) during which figures were executed with simplicity and fidelity to texture and form. The greatest contribution of the artists of the Severe Style was their concept of monumental, freestanding statues that appear to be in motion.

Shi'ites – The smaller of the two Islamic sects, their followers maintained that not the existing caliphs, but the descendants of Muhammad, starting with Ali, were the rightful rulers of the Islamic community.

shofar – A horn (made from a he-goat's or a ram's horn) used to herald the beginning of the Jewish New Year and to mark the start of the Day of Atonement. The shofar is the only musical instrument to retain its prominence in Jewish worship services up to the present.

Silver Age – The name given to the period from the death of Augustus in A.D. 14 to about A.D. 150 during which the quality of Latin prose and poetry declined. In comparison to the preceding period, the literature of the Silver Age was characterized by a new type of rhetoric intended more to impress than to persuade and enlighten.

Skepticism – A Greek school of philosophy that attacked the Epicurean and Stoic beliefs that there is a definite avenue to happiness. Skeptics held that one could achieve spiritual comfort by recognizing that none of the beliefs by which people lived was true or could bring happiness.

solmization – A system for organizing harmonic tones, developed by Guido of Arezzo (c. 995–c. 1050), it designated a particular syllable for each tone—*ut, re, mi, fa, sol, la*—and arranged them on a standardized four-line staff. The Latin syllables were later modified to the familiar *do, re, mi, fa, so, la, ti, do,* which is the standard octave for music today.

Sophists – Greek thinkers who insisted that it was futile to speculate about the first principles of the universe, for such knowledge was beyond the grasp of the human mind. Instead, they urged individuals to improve themselves and their cities by applying reason to the tasks of citizenship and statesmanship.

spiritual intelligence – A type of mystical knowledge, advocated by the monk Joachim of Fiore (c. 1135–1202), which was used to interpret the book of Revelation. Joachim believed that history was ascending in three stages, of which the final stage (the year 1260) would be the climax of history, a period when both the church and society would be renewed.

stigmata – Marks that resemble the wounds on the hands and feet of the crucified Christ. Some religious figures, including Catherine of Siena and Francis of Assisi, were said to have had stigmata.

Stoicism – A Greek philosophy, created by Zeno (335–263 B.C.) that taught that the world constituted a single society. At the core of Stoicism was the belief that the universe contained a principle of order, variously called the Divine Fire, God—more the fundamental force of the universe than a living person—and Divine Reason (Logos). The Stoics reasoned since the Logos was in every soul, human beings were essentially brothers and sisters and fundamentally equal.

strict Aristotelians – Medieval thinkers who maintained that Aristotle's arguments could not be refuted by natural reason, and that philosophers should base their judgments on rational arguments only, not on miracles and revelation.

Struggle of the Orders – A conflict during the early Roman Republic between the patricians and the commoners, or plebeians. Resenting their inferior status and eager for economic relief, the plebeians organized and waged a struggle for political, legal, and social equality.

Sufism – An Islamic mystical movement, the name is derived from the Arabic word *suf*—the undyed, woolen robe these mystics wore—as a sign for their asceticism. The Sufis were opposed to the rational speculation of Muslim philosophers, choosing instead to seek union with God through direct, fervid experience.

Sunnites – The major Islamic sect, they followed traditional teachings and established practices as defined by the consensus of the Muslim community.

sympathetic magic – A belief that something done to an image of an animal or a person would produce the same effect on the being itself. This belief can be seen in prehistoric cave drawings of injured animals.

Synoptic Gospels – The Gospels of Mark, Matthew, and Luke are called *synoptic* because their approach to Jesus is very similar. The remaining Gospel of John is quite different from these three.

tapestry – A detailed form of needlework in which colored yarns form a design, which completely penetrates the resulting fabric. This is accomplished by interlacing colored weft yarns with those of the warp.

The Book of Job – A story in the Hebrew Scriptures in which Job's faith in God is repeatedly challenged by personal hardships.

The Book of Psalms – Composed primarily of songs, this book in the Hebrew Scriptures represents the best-known examples of lyric poetry. The Psalms consist of 150 hymns extolling God in exquisite poetic language.

The Song of Solomon – One of the Psalms in the Hebrew Scriptures, it is uncharacteristically provocative and erotic in nature. The figurative language of *simile* (a comparison using *like* or *as*) is the primary vehicle for descriptive phraseology, as the bridegroom praises his bride.

Torah – The Hebrew name given to the first five books—Genesis, Exodus, Leviticus, Numbers, and Deuteronomy—of the Hebrew Scriptures. These books represent Jewish written and oral tradition dating from about 1250 to 150 B.C.

troubadours – Medieval poets, often nobles, who would sing chivalric love songs about the superior qualities of virtue to noble ladies. To these noblemen, the lady became a goddess worthy of all devotional loyalty and worship.

Twelve Tables – Drawn up in the early days of the patrician–plebeian struggle, these Tables established written rules of criminal and civil law for the Roman state that applied to all citizens.

Ulster cycle – Named for the people of northeastern Ireland, the Ulaid, this epic dates from the first century B.C. and focuses on the fictional hero Cuchulainn.

universalism – A central concept of Jewish thought dealing with concern for all humanity, which found expression in those prophets who envisioned the unity of all people under God. This belief was balanced by the Jewish concept of parochialism, stressing the special nature, destiny, and needs of a chosen people.

vassalage – A feudalistic practice in which a knight, in a solemn ceremony, pledged loyalty to a lord in exchange for military support.

volute – The name for the capital on a Greek column; in the Ionic order it simulates a large double scroll.

Zealots – The fourth of the Jewish sects, they demanded that the Jews neither pay taxes to Rome nor acknowledge the authority of the Roman emperor. The Zealots were devoted patriots and engaged in acts of resistance to Rome, which culminated in the great revolt of A.D. 66–70, which was crushed by superior Roman might.

ziggurat – A temple tower located in the heart of the city, it was the most prominent architectural structure in Mesopotamia. The ziggurat was essentially a terraced pyramid with each level smaller than the one below it, with the temple itself resting on the summit.

BIBLIOGRAPHY

Chapter 1

Cook, J. M., *The Persian Empire* (1983). History of ancient Persia.

David, Rosalie A., *The Ancient Egyptians* (1982). Focuses on religious beliefs and practices.

Frankfort, Henri, *Ancient Egyptian Religion* (1961). An interpretation of the origins and nature of Egyptian religion.

Frankfort, Henri, *The Intellectual Adventure of Ancient Man* (1946); paperback edition is entitled, *Before Philosophy*. Discussions of role of myth in ancient Near East by distinguished scholars.

Jacobsen, Thorkild, *The Treasures of Darkness* (1976). Study of Mesopotamian religion.

Oates, Joan, *Babylon* (1979). A survey of the history of Babylon to Hellenistic times.

Roux, Georges, *Ancient Iraq* (1964). A survey of Mesopotamian history and society.

Saggs, H. W. F., *Civilization Before Greece and Rome* (1989). Focuses on culture and society.

Sanders, N. K., *Prehistoric Art in Europe* (1968). Thorough survey of prehistoric art.

Smith, W. Stevenson, *The Art and Architecture of Ancient Egypt,* rev. ed. (1998). An excellent introduction to Egyptian art from 4000 to 332 B.C.

Strouhal, Eugen, *Life of the Ancient Egyptians* (1992). Daily life of Egyptians; lavishly illustrated.

Wilson, John A., *The Culture of Ancient Egypt* (1951). An interpretation by a noted Egyptologist.

Chapter 2

Albright, W. F., *The Biblical Period from Abraham to Ezra* (1963). Analyzes the culture and history of ancient Israel and explains the growing spiritual nature of the Hebrew conception of God.

Alter, Robert and Frank Kermode, eds., *The Literary Guide to the Bible* (1978). Specialists discuss the literary qualities and significance of both the Old and New Testament.

Anderson, Bernhard, *Understanding the Old Testament,* 2nd ed. (1966). A survey of the Old Testament in its historical setting.

Boadt, Lawrence, *Reading the Old Testament* (1984). Written by a Catholic scholar for Catholic students, it is an excellent introduction to ancient Israel's religious experience.

Bright, John, *A History of Israel* (1972). A thoughtful, clearly written survey.

Ehrlich, E. L., *A Concise History of Israel* (1965). An interpretive essay.

Grant, Michael, *The History of Ancient Israel* (1984). A lucid account.

Heschel, Abraham, *The Prophets,* 2 vols. (1962). A penetrating analysis of the nature of prophetic inspiration.

Idelsohn, A. Z., *Jewish Music in Its Historical Development* (1929). The standard work on the historical development of Jewish music.

Kaufmann, Yehezkel, *The Religion of Israel* (1960). An abridgment and translation of Kaufman's classic multivolume work.

Kuntz, Kenneth J., *The People of Ancient Israel* (1974). An introduction to Old Testament literature, history, and thought.

Snaith, N. H., *The Distinctive Ideas of the Old Testament* (1964). A discussion of the central ideas that distinguish Hebrew religion from other religions of the Near East.

von Rad, Gerhard, *The Message of the Prophet* (1965). An examination of the message of each prophet against the background of his time.

Zeitlin, Irving M., *Ancient Judaism* (1984). A sociologist examines the history and thought of ancient Israel.

Chapter 3

Brunschwig, Jacques and Geoffrey E. R. Lloyd, eds., *Greek Thought: A Guide to Classical Knowledge* (2002). Comprehensive essays on many aspects of Greek intellectual life.

Copelston, Frederick, *A History of Philosophy,* Vol. 1 (1962). An excellent analysis of Greek philosophy.

Cornford, J. M., *Before and After Socrates* (1968). The essential meaning of Greek philosophy clearly presented.

Grant, Michael, *The Rise of the Greeks* (1987). An eminently readable survey of the history of the Greeks from about 1000 to 490 B.C.

Guthrie, W. K. C., *The Greek Philosophers from Thales to Aristotle* (1960). A short, reliable survey of Greek philosophy.

Hammond, N. G. L., *The Classical Age of Greece* (1975). An interpretation of major developments in Greek history.

Jaeger, Werner, *Paideia: The Ideals of Greek Culture* (1939–1944). A three-volume work on Greek culture by a distinguished classicist. The treatment of Homer, the early Greek philosophers, and the Sophists in volume 1 is masterful.

Kitto, H. D. F. *The Greeks* (1957). A stimulating survey of Greek life and thought.

Lloyd, G. E. R., *Early Greek Science* (1970). A survey of Greek science from Thales to Aristotle.

Nilsson, M. P., *A History of Greek Religion* (1964). A highly regarded work on Greek religion.

Schein, Seth L., *The Mortal Hero* (1984). An introduction to Homer's *Iliad*.

Stockton, David, *The Classical Athenian Democracy* (1990). The evolution and nature of Greek democracy.

Chapter 4

See also entries in Chapter 3

Arnott, Peter D., *An Introduction to the Greek Theater* (1967). A helpful guide to the theatrical context of Greek plays.

Finley, M. I., ed., *The Legacy of Greece* (1981). Essays on all phases of Greek culture.

Hadas, Moses, *A History of Greek Literature* (1962). Survey of Greek literature from Homer to the Early Christian period.

Kitto, H. D. F., *Greek Tragedy* (1954). A valuable introduction to Greek drama.

Laisné, Claude, *Art of Ancient Greece: Sculpture, Painting, Architecture* (1995). An excellent introduction to Greek art.

Lawrence, A. W., *Greek and Roman Sculpture* (1972). Reprint of 1929 classic.

Levi, Peter, *The Pelican History of Greek Literature* (1985). Sound insights into Greek writers.

Robertson, Martin, *A Shorter History of Greek Art* (1981). An excellent introduction based on his exhaustive two-volume study.

Woodford, Susan, *The Art of Greece and Rome* (1982). Brief introduction to Greek and Roman art.

Chapter 5

Bury, J. B., et al., *The Hellenistic Age* (1970). First published in 1923; contains valuable essays by leading classicists.

Ferguson, John, *The Heritage of Hellenism* (1973). A good introduction to Hellenistic culture.

Fox, Robin Lane, *Alexander the Great* (1974). A competent biography.

Grant, Michael, *From Alexander to Cleopatra* (1982). A fine survey of all phases of Hellenistic society and culture.

Hadas, Moses, *Hellenistic Culture* (1972). Focuses on the cultural exchanges between East and West.

Havelock, Christine Mitchell, *Hellenistic Art*, 2nd ed. (1981). Thorough survey of Hellenistic art from 323 to 31 B.C.

Pollitt, J. J., *Art in the Hellenistic Age* (1986). Study of Hellenistic art in its cultural setting; organized around themes and styles.

Tarn, W. W., *Alexander the Great* (1956). A controversial interpretation.

Wallbank, F. W., *The Hellenistic World* (1982). A survey of the Hellenistic world that makes judicious use of quotations from original sources.

Welles, C. Bradford, *Alexander and the Hellenistic World* (1970). A useful sketch of the political and cultural history of the age.

Chapter 6

Boren, H. C., *Roman Society* (1977). A social, economic, and cultural history, written with the student in mind.

Clarke, M. L., *The Roman Mind* (1968). Studies in the history of thought from Cicero to Marcus Aurelius.

Dupont, Florence, *Daily Life in Ancient Rome* (1989). Social structure, religion, and notions of time and space.

Grant, Michael, *The Fall of the Roman Empire* (1990). A clearly written synthesis.

_____, *History of Rome* (1978). A synthesis of Roman history by a leading classical scholar.

_____, *Julius Caesar* (1969). A clear explanation of the intricacies of Roman history and politics.

Henig, Martin, ed., *A Handbook of Roman Art: A Comprehensive Survey of All the Arts of the Roman World* (1983). Excellent, comprehensive survey of Roman art.

Jenkyns, Richard, ed., *The Legacy of Rome* (1992). Essays on Rome's impact on Western civilization.

MacMullen, Ramsay, *Constantine* (1969). An account of the man and his times.

Ogilvie, R. M., *Roman Literature and Society* (1980). An introduction to Roman literature.

Sear, Frank, *Roman Architecture* (1983). Excellent coverage.

Starr, C. G., *Civilization and the Caesars* (1965). A fine interpretive essay on the collapse of classical humanism and the spread of religion in the four centuries from Cicero to Augustine.

Wheeler, Mortimer, *Roman Art and Architecture* (1964). An interpretive study, filled with insight.

Wood, Neal, *Cicero's Social and Political Thought* (1988). Cicero's ideas and their impact on Western political philosophy.

Chapter 7

Armstrong, A. G., and R. A. Markus, *Christian Faith and Greek Philosophy* (1960). A presentation of the dialogue between Christianity and Greek philosophy.

Benko, Stephen, *Pagan Rome and the Early Christians* (1984). How Romans and Greeks viewed early Christianity.

Cochrane, C. N., *Christianity and Classical Culture* (1957). A study of thought from Augustus to Augustine; difficult but worth the effort.

Ferguson, Everett, ed., *Background of Early Christianity* (1993). A clear and thorough examination of the milieu in which Christianity was born.

Ferguson, John, *The Religions of the Roman Empire* (1970). A study of the religious milieu of early Christianity.

Jaeger, Werner, *Early Christianity and Greek Paideia* (1961). How the church fathers perpetuated and transformed Greek ideas.

Krautheimer, Richard, *Early Christian and Byzantine Architecture* (1965). Thorough survey of Early Christian and Byzantine architecture; 190 pages of photographs.

Latourette, K. S., *A History of Christianity* (1953). Clearly written and eminently readable.

Nicholls, William, *Christian Antisemitism* (1993). A Christian scholar analyzes the Christian roots of anti-Judaism.

Nock, A. D., *Early Christianity and Its Hellenistic Background* (1964). A superb scholarly treatment of the relationship of Christianity to the wider cultural setting.

Pelikan, Jaroslav, *The Christian Tradition* (1971), Vol. 1, *The Emergence of the Catholic Tradition*. The first of a five-volume series on the history of Christian doctrine.

Perkins, Pheme, *Reading the New Testament* (1978). Introduces the beginning student to the New Testament.

Perry, Marvin, and Frederick M. Schweitzer, eds., *Jewish-Christian Encounters over the Centuries* (1994). Useful essays on Jesus, Paul, the Dead Sea Scrolls, and early Christian anti-Judaism.

Segal, Allan F., *Rebecca's Children* (1986). Judaism and Christianity in the Roman world.

Chapter 8

Arberry, A. J., *Sufism: An Account of the Mystics of Islam* (1990). The standard introduction to Sufism.

Fakhry, Majid, *A History of Islamic Philosophy,* 2nd ed. (1983). An introduction to the philosophy of Islam.

Grant, Michael, *From Rome to Byzantium: The Fifth Century AD* (1998). An insightful view into the nature of the Roman and Byzantine Empire during the fifth century.

Hodgson, Marshall G. S., *The Venture of Islam,* 2 vols. (1974). A magisterial survey of Islamic culture.

Hourani, Albert, *A History of the Arab Peoples* (1991). A panoramic view of Arab history and culture.

Irwin, Robert, *Islamic Art in Context* (1997). Excellent, thorough survey of Islamic art within its religious, social, political, and literary context.

Kritzeck, James, ed., *Anthology of Islamic Literature.* A rich sampling.

Lemerle, Paul, *Byzantine Humanism: The First Phase* (1986). Covers learning and literature to the end of the tenth century.

Lewis, Bernard, *The Arabs in History* (1966). A valuable survey.

Nasr, Seyyed Hossein, *Science and Civilization in Islam* (1968). An analysis of Islamic science with many illuminating extracts from medieval works.

Nicholson, Reynolds A., *A Literary History of the Arabs* (1992). The standard survey of the subject.

Norwich, John Julius, *A Short History of Byzantium* (1997). A sweeping view of the Byzantine Empire from

Constantine to 1453; based on his earlier three-volume study.

Rice, D. Talbot, *Byzantine Art,* rev. ed. (1968). Comprehensive survey of Byzantine art; revised from the original 1935 edition.

Rodley, Lyn, *Byzantine Art and Architecture* (1994). Excellent introduction to the subject.

Schimmel, Annemarie, *Calligraphy and Islamic Culture* (1984). The standard study.

Wellesz, Egon, *A History of Byzantine Music and Hymnography,* 2nd ed. (1962). A thorough survey of the topic.

Chapter 9

Bark, W. C., *Origins of the Medieval World* (1960). The Early Middle Ages as a fresh beginning.

Beckwith, John, *Early Medieval Art* (1964). Covers early European art from Charlemagne to the early twelfth century.

Colish, Marcia L., *Medieval Foundations of the Western Intellectual Tradition, 400–1400* (1997). A magisterial analysis of the course of Western intellectual history between 400 and 1400 A.D.

Conant, Kenneth J., *Carolingian and Romanesque Architecture, 800 to 1200* (1959). A standard study of European architecture during the period.

Dawson, Christopher, *The Making of Europe* (1957). Stresses the role of Christianity in shaping European civilization.

Fletcher, Richard, *The Barbarian Conversion: From Paganism to Christianity* (1997). A masterly survey of Europe's conversion to Christianity between the fourth and the four teenth centuries.

Focillon, Henri, *The Year 1000* (1971). Conditions of life toward the end of the Early Middle Ages.

Herrin, Judith, *The Formation of Christendom* (1987). The transition from antiquity to the Middle Ages.

Kitzinger, Ernst, *Early Medieval Art* (1983). Originally published in 1940, it provides valuable insights into the transition of art from classical naturalism to Christian religious fervor.

Laistner, M. L. W., *Thought and Letters in Western Europe* A.D. *500 to 900* (1957). A comprehensive survey of European thought in the Early Middle Ages.

Zacour, Norman, *An Introduction to Medieval Institutions* (1969). Comprehensive essays on all phases of medieval society.

Chapter 10

Apel, Willi, *Gregorian Chant* (1958). The standard scholarly treatment.

Brooke, Christopher, *The Twelfth-Century Renaissance* (1969). Surveys schools, learning, theology, literature, and leading figures.

Brooke, Christopher, and Rosalind Brooke, *Popular Religion in the Middle Ages* (1984). How the common people viewed the clergy, the Bible, the saints, judgment, heaven, and hell.

Carroll, James, *Constantine's Sword: The Church and the Jews* (2001). Carroll, a novelist, columnist, and former priest, bares his own soul as he explores centuries of Catholic demeaning of Jews and Judaism.

Cohn, Norman, *The Pursuit of the Millennium: Revolutionary Millenarians and Mystical Anarchists of the Middle Ages* (1970). First published in 1957, this treatment quickly became a classic.

Copleston, F. C., *A History of Medieval Philosophy* (1974). A lucid, comprehensive survey of medieval philosophy.

Gilson, Etienne, *Reason and Revelation in the Middle Ages* (1966). A superb brief exposition of the medieval philosophical tradition.

Grant, Edward, *The Foundations of Modern Science in the Middle Ages: Their Religious, Institutional, and Intellectual Contexts* (1996). An excellent synthesis that sees the foundations of modern science in the Middle Ages.

Grout, Donald Jay, *A History of Western Music* (1960). The standard, authoritative treatment of the history of music in the West.

Haskins, C. H., *The Renaissance of the Twelfth Century* (1957). Reprint of a still useful work.

_____, *The Rise of the Universities* (1957). A readable introduction to student life and the working conditions of professors in the Middle Ages, first published in 1923.

Mayer, H. E., *The Crusades* (1972). A short, scholarly treatment.

Mundy, J. H., *Europe in the High Middle Ages, 1150–1309* (1973). All phases of society in the High Middle Ages.

Perry, Marvin, and Frederick M. Schweitzer, eds., *Jewish-Christian Encounters over the Centuries* (1994). Excellent essay by Schweitzer on the medieval view of Jews and Judaism.

Pieper, Josef, *Scholasticism* (1964). Written with intelligence and grace.

Sirat, Colette, *A History of Jewish Philosophy in the Middle Ages* (1985). A comprehensive treatment of medieval Jewish philosophy.

Synan, Edward A., *The Popes and the Jews in the Middle Ages* (1965). An exploration of Jewish-Christian relations in the Middle Ages.

Chapter 11

See also entries in Chapter 10

Conant, Kenneth J., *Carolingian and Romanesque Architecture, 800 to 1200* (1959). Standard study of European architecture during the period.

Duby, Georges, *The Age of the Cathedrals: Art and Society, 980–1420* (1981). A far-reaching survey of the ideas and institutions that are reflected in medieval art and architecture.

Gimpel, Jean, *The Cathedral Builders* (1984). The financial, political, and spiritual forces behind the building of cathedrals.

Grout, Donald Jay, *A History of Western Music* (1960). The standard, authoritative treatment of the history of music in the West.

Lewis, C. S., *The Discarded Image: An Introduction to Medieval and Renaissance Literature* (1994). A masterful overview of the philosophical and intellectual background of medieval literature.

Martindale, Andrew, *Gothic Art from the Twelfth to Fifteenth Centuries* (1967). Excellent introduction to the topic.

Panofsky, Erwin, *Gothic Architecture and Scholasticism* (1976). A classic in the field.

Stokstad, Marilyn, *Medieval Art* (1986). The best one-volume introduction to medieval art.

Wilson, Christopher, *The Gothic Cathedral: The Architecture of the Great Church, 1130–1530* (1990).

Yudkin, Jeremy, *Music in Medieval Europe* (1989). An excellent survey that covers ecclesiastical and secular music as well as musical instruments and patronage.

Zink, Michel, *Medieval French Literature* (1994). An excellent introduction.

Chapter 12

See also entries in Chapters 10 and 11

Black, Antony, *Political Thought in Europe, 1250–1450* (1992). Covers both secular and ecclesiastical theories and compares European political theory with that of Byzantium and Islam.

Bloom, Harold, ed., *Petrarch* (1989). Essays on aspects of Petrarch's life and writings.

Brewer, D. S., *Chaucer and His Time* (1963). Chaucer seen in the background of fourteenth-century England.

Fremantle, Richard, *Florentine Gothic Painters from Giotto to Masaccio: A Guide to Painting in and near Florence* (1975). Covers painting in Florence during the fourteenth and early fifteenth centuries.

Holmes, George, *Europe: Hierarchy and Revolt, 1320–1450* (1975). A good survey of the period.

Hughes, Dom Anselm, and Gerald Abraham, eds., *Ars Nova and the Renaissance, 1300–1540* (1960). Standard scholarly work on the subject.

Huizinga, Johan, *The Autumn of the Middle Ages* (1996). A new translation of an old classic (1924); a still valuable discussion of late medieval culture.

McFarlane, K. B., *John Wycliffe and the Beginnings of English Nonconformity* (1952). The man and his influence.

Mollat, Guillaume, *The Popes at Avignon, 1305–1378* (1963). The papacy in the fourteenth century.

Ozment, Steven E., *The Age of Reform, 1250–1450* (1980). An intellectual and religious history of late medieval and Reformation Europe.

Pächt, Otto, *Book Illumination in the Middle Ages: An Introduction* (1986). Outstanding study of the topic.

Perroy, Edouard, *The Hundred Years' War* (1965). The best treatment of the conflict.

Spinka, Matthew, *John Hus: A Biography* (1968). An excellent treatment of Hus and his influence.

Vasta, Edward, ed., *Middle English Survey: Critical Essays* (1965). Insightful essays.

Ziegler, Philip, *The Black Death* (1969). The spread and impact of the great plague.

CHAPTER 1

Page 11 (c) 1938 by J.M. Dent & Sons Ltd. Reprinted by permission of Everyman Publishers Plc. **Pages 12–13** Pritchard, James, ed, *Ancient Eastern Texts to the Old Testament,* 3/e with supplement. Copyright (c) 1969 by Princeton University Press. Reprinted with permission of Princeton University Press. **Pages 14–15** *The Epic of Gilgamesh* translated by N.K. Sandars (Penguin Classics 1960, Third Edition, 1972), copyright (c) N.K. Sandars, 1960, 1964, 1972. Reproduced by permission of Penguin Books Ltd. **Page 19** From *Life of the Ancient Egyptians,* by Eugene Strohal, translated by Derryck Viney. Copyright (c) 1989, 1992 Eugene Strohal. Published by the University of Oklahoma Press. **Page 21** Lichtheim, Miriam, *Ancient Egyptian Literature: A Book of Readings, Three Volumes,* Vol. 2. Copyright (c) 1973–1980 Regents of the University of California Press. Reprinted with permission. **Page 32** Lichtheim, Miriam, *Ancient Egyptian Literature: A Book of Readings, Three Volumes,* Vol. 1. Copyright (c) 1973–1980 Regents of the University of California Press. Reprinted with permission.

CHAPTER 3

Page 59 From *The Iliad* by Homer, translated by E.V. Rieu (Penguin Classics, 1950) copyright (c) the Estate of E.V. Rieu, 1946. Reproduced with permission of Penguin Books Ltd. **Page 72** From *The Iliad* by Homer, translated by E.V. Rieu (Penguin Classics, 1950) copyright (c) the Estate of E.V. Rieu, 1946. Reproduced with permission of Penguin Books Ltd. **Pages 73–74** From Plato's *Republic,* trans. F.M. Cornford. Copyright (c) 1945 by Oxford University Press. Reprinted by permission of Oxford University Press.

CHAPTER 4

Page 78 Highham, T.F., and C.M. Bowra, eds., *The Oxford Book of Greek Verse in Translation.* Copyright (c) 1938 by Clarendon Press. Reprinted with permission of Oxford University Press. **Page 78** Excerpt from *Sappho A Garland: The Poems and Fragments of Sappho* translated by Jim Powell. Copyright (c) 1993 by Jim Powell. Reprinted by permission of Farrar, Strauss and Giroux, LLC. **Page 78** From *The Greeks* by H D F Kitto (Penguin Books 1951, Revised edition 1957)

copyright (c) H D F Kitto 1951, 1957. Reproduced by permission of Penguin Books Ltd. **Page 81** Reprinted with permission of Pocket Books, an imprint of Simon & Schuster Adult Publishing Group, from Sophocles: *Oedipus The King,* translated by Bernard M.W. Knox. Copyright (c) 1959, and renewed (c) 1967, by Bernard M.W. Knox. **Page 82** Podlecki, Anthony J., trans., *Aeschylus, The Persians.* Copyright (c) 1991. Reprinted with permission of the author. **Page 83** McLeish, Kenneth, trans., *Sophocles: Electra, Antigone, Philocetes.* Copyright (c) 1979 by Cambridge University Press. Reprinted with the permission of Cambridge University Press. **Pages 84–85** Excerpts from "Oedipus Rex" in *Sophocles, The Oedipus Cycle: An English Version* by Dudley Fitts and Robert Fitzgerald, copyright 1949 by Harcourt, Inc. and renewed 1977 by Cornelia Fitts and Robert Fitzgerald, reprinted by permission of the publisher. CAUTION: All rights, including professional, amateur, motion picture, recitation, lecturing, public reading, radio broadcasting, and television are strictly reserved. Inquiries on all rights should be addressed to Harcourt, Inc. Permissions Department, Orlando, Fl 32887-6777. **Page 85** Extract from *The Medea* translated by Rex Warner published by The Bodley Head. Used by permission of The Random House Group Limited. **Page 85** Warner, Rex, trans., *Euripides, Medea.* Copyright © 1993 by Dover Publications, Inc. Reprinted with permission. **Page 86** Murray, Gilbert, trans., *Euripides, Five Plays of Euripides: Alcestis, Medea, The Trojan Women, Iphigenia in Tauris, Electra.* Copyright © 1934 by George Allen & Unwin Ltd. Reprinted with permission of Taylor & Francis, Ltd. **Pages 86, 88** Rogers, Benjamin B., trans., *Five Comedies by Aristophanes* (London: G. Bell & Sons, 1955), pp. 156–157, 169–70. **Page 87** Waley, Arthur, trans., *The Analects of Confucius.* Copyright © 1938 by Allen & Unwin Ltd.

CHAPTER 5

Page 111 From *The Voyage of Argo* (The Argonautica) by Apollonius of Rhodes, translated by E.V. Rieu (Penguin Classics, 1950) copyright (c) the Estate of E.V. Rieu, 1959. Reproduced with permission of Penguin Books Ltd. **Page 113** From *Basic Writings of Mo Tzu, Hsun Tzu, and Han Fei Tzu* by Watson, Burton, trans., (c) 1967

Columbia University Press. Reprinted with permission of the publisher.

CHAPTER 6

Page 133 Plautus quote "Not the throes..." quoted in Duff, J. Wright, *A Literary History of Rome,* 1960, pp. 136–37. **Page 134** Havelock, E.A., *The Lyric Genius of Catullus.* Copyright (c) 1929 by E.A. Havelock. Reprinted with permission. **Pages 134–135** From *The Aeneid* by Virgil, translated by Robert Fitzgerald, copyright (c) 1980, 1982, 1984 by Robert Fitzgerald. Used by permission of Random House, Inc. **Page 135** Clancy, Joseph P., *The Odes, and Epodes of Horace.* Copyright (c) 1960 by University of Chicago Press. Reprinted with permission. **Page 136** Ovid, *The Art of Love and Other Love Books of Ovid* (New York: Grosset and Dunlap, 1959), pp. 117–118, 130–32, 135. **Page 136** Carrington, A.G., *Aspects of Martial's Epigrams.* Copyright (c) 1960 Blackwell Science Publishers Ltd. Reprinted with permission. **Page 136** Creekmore, Hubert, trans., *The Satire of Juvenal.* Copyright © 1963 by the Schaffner Agency. Reprinted with permission. **Page 137** Juvenal, *The Satires,* translated by Rudd, Niall, intro William Barr. Copyright (c) 1991 by Clarendon Press. Reprinted with permission of Oxford University Press. **Page 138** Marcus Aurelius, "Hour by hour resolve..." Marcus Aurelius, *Meditations,* trans. Stanforth, Maxwell, Penguin Classics, 1964, bk. 2. **Page 139** *Bhagavad Gita: The Song of God,* translated by Swami Prabhavananda and Christopher Isherwood, pages 65, 66. Reprinted with permission of Vedenta Press.

CHAPTER 8

Page 186 Wellesz, Egon, *A History of Byzantine Music and Hymnography.* Copyright (c) 1961 by Clarendon Press. Reprinted with permission of Oxford University Press. **Pages 200–201** Kritzeck, James, *Anthology of Islamic Literary from the Rise of Islam to Modern Times.* Copyright © 1975 by Wayland Publications Ltd.

CHAPTER 9

Page 217 Waley, Arthur, trans., *The Pillow Book of Sei Shonagon.* Copyright © 1938 by Allen & Unwin Ltd. **Page 218** Lehmann, Ruth P.M., *Early*

Irish Verse. Copyright (c) 1982 by the Estate of Ruth P.M. Lehmann. Reprinted with permission. **Page 220** Colish, Marcia L., *Medieval Foundations of the Western Intellectual Tradition, 400–1400.* Copyright (c) 1997 by Yale University Press. Reprinted with permission. **Page 220** From *Beowulf* by Howell D. Chickering, Jr., translated by Howell D. Chickering, Jr., copyright (c) 1977 by Howell D. Chickering, Jr. Used by permission of Crown Publishers, a division of Random House, Inc.

CHAPTER 10

Page 243 From *The Old Man Who Does As He Pleases: Selections from the Poetry and Prose of Lu Yu,* Watson, Burton, trans., (c) 1973 Columbia University Press. Reprinted with the permission of the publisher.

CHAPTER 11

Page 256 Jones, Charles W., ed., *Medieval Literature in Translation.* Copyright © 1950 by Dover Publications, Inc. Reprinted with permission. **Page 256** Reprinted from *Charles Homer Haskins: The Rise of Universities.* Copyright (c) 1957 Cornell University. Used by permission of the publisher, Cornell University Press. **Page 257** Waddell, Helen, *Medieval Latin Lyrics.* Reprinted with permission of Mary Martin. **Page 257** David C. Riede and J. Wayne Baker, *The Western Intellectual Tradition, Vol. 1.* Copyright (c) 1980. Reprinted with permission. **Page 258** From *The Song of Roland*

translated by Glyn Burgess (Penguin Classics, 1990) copyright (c) Glyn Burgess, 1990. Reproduced with permission of Penguin Books Ltd. **Page 260** Bonner, Anthony, ed., *Songs of the Troubadours.* Copyright (c) 1972. Reprinted with permission. **Page 260** *Women in the Middle Ages* by Frances Gies and Joseph Gies. Copyright (c) 1978 by Frances and Joseph Gies. Reprinted by permission of Harper-Collins Publishers, Inc. **Page 261** *Popol Vuh: The Sacred Book of the Ancient Quiche Maya,* English version by Delia Goetz and Sylvanus G. Morely, from the translation of Adrian Recinos. Copyright (c) 1950, 1977 by the University of Oklahoma Press. Reprinted by Permission. **Page 262** Yonec by Marie de France from *Lais Of Marie De France,* translated by Hanning, Robert W. and Ferrante, Joan M. Copyright (c) 1995 by Baker Book House. **Page 263** From *The Divine Comedy* by Dante Alighieri, translated by John Ciardi. Copyright 1954, 1957, 1959, 1960, 1961, 1965, 1967, 1970 by the Ciardi Family Publishing Trust. Used by permission of W.W. Norton & Company, Inc. **Page 287** Flanagan, Sabina, *Hildegard of Bingen, 1098–1179: A Visionary Life.* Copyright (c) 1989 by International Thomson Publishing Services Ltd. Reprinted with permission.

CHAPTER 12

Page 299 From *Piers Plowman: An Alliterative Verse Translation* by William Langland, translated by E. Tal-

bot Donaldson. Copyright (c) 1990 by W.W. Norton & Company, Inc. Used by permission of W.W. Norton & Company, Inc. **Pages 299–300** From *Sir Gawain and the Green Knight: A New Verse Translation,* translated by Marie Boroff. Copyright (c) 1967 by W.W. Norton & Company, Inc. Used by permission of W.W. Norton & Company, Inc. **Page 301** Gibb, H.A.R., translator, *Ibn Battuta: Travels in Asia and Africa,* The Haukluyt Society. Reprinted with permission. **Page 302** *The Romance of the Rose* by Guillaume de Lorris and Jean de Meun, trans. Dahlberg, Charles. Copyright (c) 1971 by Princeton University Press. Reprinted by permission of Princeton University Press. **Page 303** From *Three Late Medieval Morality Plays: Mankind, Everyman & Mundus Et Infax-New Mermaids Series,* edited by G.A. Lester. Copyright (c) 1981 by Ernest Benn Limited. Used by permission of W.W. Norton & Company, Inc. **Page 304** Bishop, Morris, *Petrarch and His World.* Copyright (c) 1963 by the Indiana University Press. Reprinted with permission. **Pages 306–307** (c) The Estate of Richard Aldington. Reprinted with permission. **Page 307** From *The Canterbury Tales,* trans. Ronald L. Ecker and Eugene J. Crook, Hodge & Braddock, Publishers, 1993. Reprinted with permission. **Pages 316** Bergin, Thomas, *The Divine Comedy,* Harlan Davidson, Inc., pp. 36. **Page 318** Harman, Alec, *Medieval and Early Renaissance Music up to c. 1525.* Copyright © 1958 by Hutchinson Ltd.

Page numbers in **boldface** indicate pages on which key terms are defined. Page numbers in *italics* indicate figures or maps.

A capella, 288
Aachen, Germany, palace at, 222, *223, 224, 224*
Aaron, Messiah of, 160, 161
Abbasid caliphs of Baghdad, 195, 198, 204–205
Abel, 42, 49
Abelard, Peter, 245–246
Abraham (Hebrew patriarch), *30,* 31, 33, 43, 173–174, 202
Abraham (Hroswitha), 221
Abraham and Isaac (fresco), *30*
Absalom, 48
Achaemenian empire (Iran), 26
Achilles, 59, 60, 79
Acropolis, 99–101, *99, 100*
Acropolis of Pergamum, The, 118, *118*
Adam and Eve, 36, 42, 214, 221, 228, *228*
Adam and Eve Reproached by the Lord (relief sculpture), 228, *228*
Aegean civilizations, early, 53–54
Aegean Sea, 32
Aeneid (Virgil), 134–135
Aeschylus, 81, 82, 83
Afterlife
   in Egyptian religion, 19, 21
   in Persian religion, 26
Agamemnon (Aeschylus), 82
Agincourt, Battle of (1415), 294
Agrarian society, 214–215
Agriculture (farming)
   in early civilizations, 9, 10
   in Egypt, 17
   famine and, 293
   irrigation and, 9, 10
   medieval, 214–215, 231–232, 293
   in Mesopotamia, 10
   in Near East, 5
   in Neolithic Age, 7–8
   in Paleolithic Age, 5
   in Rome, 128
   in Sparta, 55
Ahab, king of Israel, 39
Akhetaten, Egypt, 19
Akhenaton, pharaoh of Egypt, 19–20, 22
Akkadians, 9
Albert the Great, 250
Albi, France, 239
Albigensians (Cathari), 239, *240,* 241

Alcuin of York (medieval scholar), 216, 218
Alexander the Great, 26, 54, 72, 74, 107, 108, 117, *117, 118*
Alexandria, Egypt, 109–110, *109,* 112
Alexiad (Comnena), 185
Alexius I Comnenus, Byzantine emperor, 185, 237
Alfonso VI, king of Castile, 267
Alhambra (Granada, Spain), 205–206, *206*
Allegory of the Cave (Plato), 70, *71*
Almagest (Ptolemy), 138
Altamira Cave (Santander, Spain), 6–7
Altar to Zeus (Pergamum), 118–119, *119*
Amarna religion, 19–20
Amarna style of art, 22, 24
Ambrose (Latin writer), 169–170
Amenhotep IV (Akhenaton), pharaoh of Egypt, 19–20, 22
Amores (Ovid), 136
Amos (prophet), 39
Analects of Confucius, The, 87
Anatomical Man (manuscript illumination), 292, 312
Anaximander, 65
Anglo-Saxons, 211, 234, 283, *284*
Animals
   in agriculture, 231–232
   in art, 6–7, *6, 8, 22, 22, 23, 23,* 27, *30, 191*
   hunting of, 5, 6, 7
   religion and, 15–16, *16*
Anjou, 235
Annals (Tacitus), 137
Anselm, 198, 245
Anthemius of Tralles (master-builder), 191–192
Antigone (Sophocles), 83–84
Antiochus IV (Seleucid king), 110
Antiphons, **287**
Aphrodite of Cyrene (Hellenistic art), 117
Aphrodite of Knidos (Greek sculpture), 76, 96
Aphrodite of Melos (Hellenistic sculpture), 122, *122*
Apocalyptic literature, **40**
Apollo Belvedere (Hellenistic sculpture), 117, 121–122, *121*
Apollodorus of Athens, 92
Apollonius of Rhodes, 111
Apostles, 162–163, 166
Apse, 175, *176*
Aqueduct, 144, *144,* 147

Aquinas, St. Thomas, 247–248, *247,* 249, 250, 255, 297
Aquitaine, 235
Ara Pacis Augustae (Roman relief sculpture), 150–151, *151*
Arab(s)
   art and architecture of, 202–206, *203, 204, 205, 206*
   decline of empire, 195
   invading Constantinople, 184, 195
   religion and, 193–195. *See also* Islam
Arabic language, 195, 207
Aramaic, **110**
Arch, 151–152, *152,* 154
Arch and vault, **143–144,** *143*
Arch of Septimus Severus (relief sculpture), 152
Arch of Titus (relief sculpture), 151, *152*
Archaic age (Greece), 81
Archaic period of Greek art, 90, 91, *91, 92–94, 93, 94*
Archimedes (theoretician), 114
Archimedes Principle, **114**
Architecture
   arch and vault, **143–144,** *143*
   basilica form of, 147, **175–176,** *176, 225, 225*
   Byzantine, 188–193, *188, 189, 191, 192, 193*
   Carolingian foot in, 224
   centralized form of, **177–178,** *177, 178*
   Christian, 175–178, *176, 177, 178. See also* Churches, Christian
   Corinthian order of, 98, 102–103, *103*
   domestic (Roman), 147–148, *148*
   Doric order of, **98–101,** *98, 99, 100*
   English, 273–274, *273, 274*
   flying buttresses in, 267, 268, 271, *271*
   French, 266–273, *267, 269, 270, 271, 272, 279, 280–281, 281, 282, 310*
   German, 222–228, *223, 224, 225, 226, 227, 228,* 275–276, *276, 277*
   Gothic style of, **267–276,** *269, 270, 271, 272, 273, 274, 275, 276, 277*
   Greek, 53, 90, 97–103, *98, 99, 100, 101, 102, 103,* 177
   Hellenistic, 118–119, *118, 119*
   Ionic order of, 98, **101–102,** *101, 102*
   Islamic, 202–206, *203, 204, 205, 206*
   Italian, 187–191, *188, 189, 190, 191,* 265–266, *265, 266,* 274–275, *275*

medieval, 222–228, *223, 224, 225, 226,* 264–276, *265, 266, 267, 268, 269, 270, 271, 272, 273, 274, 275, 276, 277, 279*
Mesopotamian, 15, *15*
public, 144–147, *144, 145, 146, 147*
Roman, 143–148, *143, 144, 145, 146, 147, 148*
Romanesque style of, 264–267, *265, 266, 267, 268*
Spanish, 205–206, *206, 267, 268*
Arena (Scrovegni) Chapel (frescoes), 316–317, *316, 317*
Argonautica (Apollonius of Rhodes), 111
Arianism, **168**
Aristarchus (astronomer), 114
Aristocracy, Greek, 56, 78
Aristophanes, 85, 86, 88, 111
Aristotelians, strict, **249**
Aristotle, 57, 64, 72–74, 83, 84, 112, 138
   on ethical thought, 73–74
   influence on Islamic thought, 198, 199
   influence on medieval thought, 216, 244, 246–247, 248–249, 250, 251
   on music, 79
   on Plato's theory of ideas, 73
   on political thought, 74
Arius (Greek priest), 168
Arnolfo di Cambio, 274, 275
Ars Amatoria (Ovid), 136
Ars nova, 289, **318–320,** *319*
Ars novae musicae (Muris), 318
Art
   Amarna style of, 22, 24
   animals in, 6–7, *6, 8,* 22, *22, 23, 23, 27, 30, 191*
   Archaic period of, 90, 91, *91,* 92–94, *93, 94*
   Black Death and, 294, *294*
   of Byzantine civilization, 186–193
   Christian, 171–178, 289–290
   Classical period of Greek art, 90, 94–97, *94, 95, 96, 97*
   Egyptian, *4,* 22–24, *22, 23, 24*
   frescoes, *30,* 172–173, *172, 241, 247,* 314, 316–318, *316, 317*
   Greek, 89–103, *90, 91, 92, 93, 94, 95, 96, 97*
   Hebrew, 49
   Hellenic, 89–103, *90, 91, 92, 93, 94, 95, 96, 97*
   Hellenistic, 116–123, *117, 118, 119, 120, 121, 122*
   iconoclastic controversy and, 187
   Islamic, 202–206, *203, 204, 205, 206*
   limestone relief, 22, *22*
   linear perspective in, 150–151
   manuscript illumination, 221, *222, 223, 237,* 281–282, *283, 292,* 312–314, *313, 314*
   medieval, 221–228, 264–284, *292,* 310–318
   Mesopotamian, 15–17, *15, 16, 17*

Minoan, *54*
mosaics, 117, *117,* 155–156, 177–178, *177, 178,* 187–190, *187, 189, 190*
Neoclassical style of, 103
painting. *See* Painting
   in Paleolithic Age, 6–7, *6, 7, 8*
Persian, 26–27
relief carvings, 7
Roman, *124, 132,* 142–156
Russian, 193
sculpture. *See* Sculpture
stained-glass windows, 280–281, *281, 282*
symbolism in, *171,* 172–175, *172, 173, 174, 175*
tapestries, *254,* 282–284, *284*
Artaxerxes (Persia), 26
Arthurian legend, 259–260, 299–300
Asia, 8, 108, 109
Asia Minor, 32, 56, 62, 64, 76, 78, 108, 112, 125
Assyrians, 26, 27, 28, 32, 38
Astronomy
   in Egypt, 18, 28, 138
   in Hellenistic Age, 110, 114
   in Islamic world, 198
   in Mesopotamia, 12
   in Roman Empire, 138
Atatürk, Kemal, 193
Athanasius, 168
Athens
   architecture of, 99–102, *99, 100, 101, 102*
   as city-state, 54, 56–57, 67
   democracy in, 56–57, 78, 88, 89, 104
   literature in, 78
   in Peloponnesian War, 56, 57, 58, 86, 89
   philosophy in, 67, 68–69
Atomic theory of Democritus, 66
Atonism (Egyptian religion), 19–20
Atrium, *175, 176*
Attalus I, king of Pergamum, 117–118, 119, *119*
Attis (Catallus), 134
Auden, W. H., 104
Augustine (Christian theologian), 166, 170–171, 248, 249, 305, 309
Augustus as Pontifex Maximus (Roman sculpture), 148–149, *149, 150*
Augustus Caesar, *124,* 128–129, 134, 149–150, *149,* 218
Augustus of Prima Porta (Roman sculpture), *124,* 150
Austria, Paleolithic sculpture in, 7, *7*
Autonomy, moral, 36–37
Ave Maria (Schubert), 290
Averroës (Muslim thinker), 199, 248
Avicenna (Ibn-Sina), 198, 250

Babel, Tower of, 15, 28, 42
Babylon, 9, 12, 15
   conquest of Judah, 32
   Hebrews in, 32, 33
   mathematics in, 66

myths of, 27
   Persian conquest of, 17, 33
Babylonian Captivity
   of Christians, **295**
   of Jews, **32**
Bach, Johann Sebastian, 168, 290
Bacon, Roger, 250, 322
Baghdad, Abbasid caliphs of, 195, 198, 204–205
Bakr, Abu, 194–195
Baptism, 162, 167, 172
Baptistery of San Giovanni (Florence, Italy), *265, 265,* 275
Barbarians, 67
Barbarossa, Frederick, *232*
Basel, Council of (1431–1449), 295
Basilica(s), 147, 176, 184, 266–267
Basilica form architecture, 147, **175–176,** *176, 225, 225*
Basket weaving, 7
Bassus, Junius (Roman prefect), *174*
Baths, public, 146–147, 177
Bathsheba, 48
Battle of Issus (Roman mosaic), *117, 177*
Bayeux Tapestry (Normandy, France), 282, *284*
Becket, Saint Thomas à, 307
Bede, Venerable (historian), 211
Bedouin tribes, 194
ben Asher, Aaron, 49
Benedict, Rule of, 165, 236
Benedict XI, Pope, 295
Benedictine monasticism, 165, 211, 236, 286
Beowulf (Old English epic), 219–220
Bernard le Vieux, 267
Bernard of Clairvaux, Saint, 246, 278
Bernward of Hildesheim (German architect), 225, 226–228, *226, 227, 228*
Bhagavad-Gita, 139
Bible
   Adam and Eve story in, 36, 42
   Book of Proverbs in, 45–46
   Book of Psalms in, 44–45
   creation story in, 42
   epic stories in, 41–44
   Hebrew, *30,* 31, 36, 37, 38, 41–49
   influence on Western literature, 48–49
   as literature, 41–49
   Mesopotamian sources of, 31
   New Testament of, 167–168
   prophets in, 39–41
   Sodom and Gomorrah story in, 43
   wisdom writings in, 43, 45–48
Bible moralisée, 312
Bishop, **165**
Black Death (bubonic plague), **293–294,** *294*
Black-figure vase painting, 91, *91*
Blake, William, 49
Boaz, 38
Boccaccio, Giovanni, 305–307, 308
Boethius (medieval scholar), 79, 215–216, 285
Bohemia, 297, 319

Boniface VIII, Pope, 295, 296
Book of Job, 46, **47–48**
Book of Proverbs, 45–46
Book of Psalms, **44–45**
"Book of the Dead, The" (Egypt), 20
Books of hours, 292, 312–314, *313,*
   314
Books of Instruction (Egypt), 18–19
Books of the Kells, 208, 221–222
Botany, 112
Bowra, C. M., 60
Brahms, Johannes, 290
Brevis, 288, 289
Bright, John, 34
Bronze, 8, 226–228, *227, 228*
Brunelleschi, Filippo, 275
Bruno, Archbishop, 225
Bubonic plague (Black Death),
   293–294, *294*
Buildings, The (Procopius), 185,
   191–192
Bunyan, John, 168, 289
Burghers, **233**
Burgundian school of sculpture, 310
Buridan, Jean, 251
Burton, Sir Richard, 202
"Bury" Bible, 281–282, *283*
Buttresses, flying, 267, 268, **271,** *271*
Byzantine civilization, 183–193
   architecture of, 188–193, *188, 189,*
      191, 192, 193
   art of, 186–193
   attacks by invaders, 184
   government of, 184
   Greek influence in, 185
   history of, 183–184, 185
   iconoclastic controversy in, 187
   invasions of, 184, 195
   language of, 184
   law in, 184–185
   learning in, 183, 184–185
   legacy of, 206
   music in, 185–186
   philosophy in, 184, 185
   religion in, 183–184
Byzantium, 183. *See also* Constantinople; Istanbul, Turkey

Caccia, 318, 320
Caen, France, 267, *268*
Caesar, Julius, 128, 133
Caesar, Octavian (Augustus), *124,*
   128–129, 134, 149–150, *149,* 218
Cain, 42, 48
Calendars
   Islamic, 200
   in Near East, 28
Calf-Bearer, The (Greek sculpture),
   92–93, *93,* 175
Caliph, 194–195, 198, 204–205
Calligraphy, **203**
Callimachus (Alexandrian scholar-poet),
   111
Callimachus (Hroswitha), 221
Calvinism, 171
Camel, Battle of the, 197

Camera obscura, 198
Campo del Miracoli (Pisa, Italy),
   265–266, *266*
Canaan, 31, 32, 38, 43
Canon of Medicine (Avicenna), 250
Canterbury Cathedral, 273
Canterbury Tales (Chaucer), 307–309
Cantillation, **49**
Cantus firmus, 287, 288
Capet, Hugh, 234–235
Caracalla, Baths of, 146–147
Cardinals, 236
Caricatures, **307**
Carneades of Cyrene, 116
Carolingian foot, **224**
Carolingian literature, 222, *223*
Carolingian minuscule script, **218**
Carolingian Renaissance, 216, **218,**
   244, 285
Carthage, 127
Cassiodorus (medieval scholar), 216,
   285
Cassirer, Ernst, 321
Caste, 139
*Catacomb of Saints Peter and Marcelli-
   nus* (fresco), *172, 173*
Catallus, Gaius Valerius (Roman poet),
   133–134
Cathari (Albigensians), 239, *240,* 241
Catharsis, **64**
Catherine of Siena, 298
Catholicism
   Babylonian Captivity and, 32, 295
   Crusades and, 184, 237–238, *238,*
      241, 278
   dissenters and, 239
   division between Roman Catholic and
      Greek Orthodox Churches,
      183–184, 241
   excommunication in, 235, 239, 295,
      296
   Great Schism and, 295–296, 297, 298
   Gregorian reform and, 235–237
   heresy and, 238–239, 296–297
   during High Middle Ages, 235–242,
      245–249
   Inquisition and, **239**
   during Late Middle Ages, 293, 295
   monasticism and, 165, 211, 214, 216,
      236, 239–240, 246
   papacy and, 165, 211, 236–237,
      240–241, 293, 295–296
   reformers and, 239–240, *240*
   sacraments of, *173,* 235
Cave paintings, 6–7, *6, 8*
Cella, **98,** 100, 101
Centralized form architecture, **177–178,**
   177, 178
Chaldeans, 32, 33
Chapel, 224, *224,* 316–317, *316, 317*
Chariot races (Rome), 145
Charioteer of Delphi (Greek sculpture),
   95, *95*
Charlemagne, *210,* 211–212, 216, 218,
   222, 224, 257–258
Charles V, German emperor, 224

Charles V, king of France, 309,
   319
Charles VII, king of France, 309
Chartres, France, cathedral in, 168,
   271–273, *272, 279,* 280–281, *281,*
   282, 310
Chaucer, Geoffrey, 307–309
Chauvet Cave (France), 7, *8*
Cheops, pharaoh of Egypt, 23, *23*
Chephren, pharaoh of Egypt, 23,
   23
China
   legalism in, 113
   lyric poetry in, 243
Chivalric love, poetry of, 260, 262
Chivalry, **213**
Choir screen, 271
Chorus, 80, 81, 82
Chrétien de Troyes, 300
*Christ Gives the Law to Saints Peter
   and Paul* (mosaic), *177, 177*
Christ in Glory (Moissac, France), 278,
   279
Christ Pantocrator, **191**
Christian(s), **161**
   in Crusades, 184, 237–238, *238,* 241,
      278
   in Muslim society, 197–198
Christianity, *158,* 159–179, 320–321
   appeal of, 163–164
   architecture of, 175–178, *176, 177,*
      178. See also Churches, Christian
   art of, 171–178, 289–290
   classical humanism and, 178–179
   Crusades and, 184, 237–238, *238,*
      241, 278
   division between Roman Catholic and
      Greek Orthodox Churches,
      183–184, 241
   Greek philosophy and, 168–169
   Hellenistic Age and, 114
   Hellenization of, 169
   Jews and, 162–163, 166–167, 238,
      241–242
   Latin, 209–215. *See also* Latin
      Christendom
   literature of, 167–171, 220–221
   monasticism in, 165, 211, 214, 216,
      236, 239–240, 246
   origins of, 159–163
   rise of, 209–215
   Rome and, 164–165
   society and, 165–166
   spread of, 163–165, *163*
   symbolism in, *171,* 172–175, *172,*
      173, 174, 175
   theology of, 167–171, 245–249
   women and, 166
Christine de Pizan, 304, 309–310
Chronographia (Psellus), 185
Chrysostom, John, 167
Chthonic deities, 62
Churches, Christian, *158,* 175–178, *176,*
   177, 178, 184, 185, 187, 188–193,
   188, 189, 190, 191, 225–228,
   264–280. *See also* Architecture

Cicero, Marcus Tullius (Roman statesman), 132–133, 134, 140, 216, 304
Cimabue (Cenni di Pepo), 314–315,
315, 316
Cino da Pistoia, 305
Circumcision, 43, 110
Circus Maximus (Rome), 145–146
Citadel, Persian, 26–27
Cité de dames (Christine de Pizan), 309
Cities
deterioration of, 132
early civilizations in, 8–9
in Egypt, 19, 109–110, *109*
fortified walls around, 17
in Hellenistic Age, 109–110, *109*
during High Middle Ages, 233
in Mesopotamia, 9
in Persia, 26
in Roman Empire, 129
See also names of specific cities
City of God, The (Augustine), 170
City-states, 107
Athens, 54, 56–57, 67
conflict between, 56, 57, *58*, 86, 89
decline of, 57–58
in Greece, 54–58, *55*
in Mesopotamia, 9, 16
parochialism in, 107–108
Sparta, *55*, 55, 56
Civil wars, in Rome, 128, 129, 131, 136
Civilization, 5
environmental factors and, 9
rise to, 8–9
*See also names of specific
civilizations*
Classical age (Greece), 81
Classical period of Greek art, 90,
94–97, *94, 95, 96, 97*
Cleisthenes, 56
Clement of Alexandria, 169
Clement V, Pope, 295
Clement VII, Pope, 295
Clouds, The (Aristophanes), 86, 88
Clovis (Merovingian ruler), 211
Code of Hammurabi, **12**
Cohn, Norman, 249
Cologne, Germany, 225, *225*, 228, *228*,
275–276, *276, 277*
Cologne Cathedral (Cologne, Germany),
275–276, *276, 277*
Colosseum (Rome), 145–146, *147*
Comedy
Greek, 86, 88
New, **112**, 133
Commodus, Roman emperor, 140
Common law, **234**
Comnena, Anna (Byzantine historian),
185
Conciliar Movement, **295**
Concordat of Worms, **237**
Confessions (Augustine), 170
*Confirmation of the Rule of Saint
Francis*, 230
Conflict
between Byzantine and Roman
Churches, 183–184

between Catholic Church and France,
295
between city-states, 56, 57, *58*, 86,
89
during Late Middle Ages, 293, 294
in Rome, 125, 127, 128, 129, 131
Struggle of the Orders, 125, 127
See also War(s)
Confucianism, 87
Confucius, 87
Consolation of Philosophy, The
(Boethius), 216
Conspiracy of Catiline (Sallust), 133
Constance, Council of (1414–1418),
295, 297
Constantine, Roman emperor, 131, 132,
152, 165, 175–176, *175*
Constantine IX, Byzantine emperor, 185
Constantinople, 131, 183, 184, 186,
193, 195, 238
Council of, 264
See also Byzantium; Istanbul, Turkey
Contrapposto, **96**, 97
Copper, 8
Córdoba, Great Mosque of, *182*, 205
Corinthian order of architecture, 98,
102–103, *103*
Cornelia (mother of Tiberius and Gaius
Gracchus), 131
Corpus Juris Civilis, **184**–185, 251
Cosmogony, **61**
Cosmologists, 65–67, 68
Cosmopolitanism
in Hellenistic Age, 108–110, 123
in Roman Empire, 131
Council of Basel (1431–1449), 295
Council of Constance (1414–1418),
295, 297
Council of Constantinople, 264
Council of Nicaea (325), **168**
Council of Nicaea II (787), 264
Council of Pisa (1409), 295
Council of Tours (1169), 239
Covenant, **37**–38, 41, 43, 110
Craftspeople, 233
Creation, The (Haydn), 290
Creation stories, 42, 261
Crécy, Battle of, 319
Crete, 54
Crusades, 184, **237**–238, *238*, 241, 278
Cult of Mithras, **141**, 164
Cult of Relics, 264
Cultural diffusion, 107–123
Culture
Hellenistic, 110–116
Jewish contributions to, 242
Mesopotamian, 9, 16–17, *17*
rational investigation of (Greek
philosophy), 67, 140
Roman, 132–142
Sumerian, 9, 16–17, *17*
See also Architecture; Art; Music;
Painting; Sculpture
Cycle of the Patriarchs (Hebrew
Scriptures), 43
Cynics, **116**

Cyrus the Great, king of Persia, 17, 26,
33, 88

Damascus, Great Mosque of, 204
Daniel (prophet), 40
Dante Alighieri, 49, 168, 255, 262–264,
300, 303–304, 305, 307
Daphnis and Chloë (Hellenistic
romance), 112
Darius I, king of Persia, 26, 56
Darius III, king of Persia, 117, *117*
Dark Age (Greece), **54**, 62
"Dark Ages," 255. *See also* Middle
Ages
Dating, radiocarbon, 6
David, Hebrew king, 32, 48, 49, 160,
173
De Clementia (Seneca), 137
De genealogia deorum genilium
(Boccaccio), 305
Dead Sea, 32
"Dead Sea Scrolls, The," 160
Death of Sarpedon, The (vase painting),
91–92, *92*
Deborah (prophetess), 38
Decameron (Boccaccio), 305–307
Defender of the Peace, The (Marsilius
of Padua), 296
Delian League, 57
Delilah, 48
Demagogues, 89
Democracy
danger in, 89
in Greece, 56–57, 78, 88, 89, 104
Plato on, 72
Democritus, 66, **115**
Denis, Saint, 268, 269
Deus ex machina, **81**
Dialectics, **69**, 81
Dialogue
in drama, 81
in philosophy, 69, 81
Dialogue on Divine Providence
(Catherine of Siena), 298
Diaspora, 162, 171
Diocletian, Roman emperor, 131, 132,
141
Diogenes (philosopher), 116
Dionysos, 64, 80, 81, 91, *91*, 96–97, 97
Dionysos in Boat (vase painting), 91,
91
Dipylon Vase (vase painting), 90, *91*
Disciples, of Jesus, 161, 165
Disease, in Late Middle Ages, 293–294,
294
Disibodenberg, monastery of, 214
Dissonance, 288
Divine Comedy (Dante), 49, 168, 255,
262–264, 300, 303–304, 307
Diwan (Rumi), 200–201
Dome of the Rock, 202–203, *203*,
204
Dominic, Saint, 240
Dominicans, 239, **240**
Domitian, Roman emperor, 151
Domus Aurea (Golden House), 147

Doric order of architecture, **98**–101, *98, 99, 100*

Doryphoros, or Spear Bearer (Greek sculpture), 96, *97*

Drama
    chorus in, 80, 81, 82
    comedies, 86, 88
    Greek, 80–88
    Hellenistic, 111
    medieval, 256, 302–303
    morality plays, 302–303
    mystery plays, 256, 287, 289
    Roman, 133
    tragedies, 81–86

Duccio di Buoninsegna, 315–316, *315*

Dulcitius (Hroswitha), 221

Dying Trumpeter (Hellenistic sculpture), 117, 119–120, *119*

Dyskolos (The Grouch), 111

East of Eden (Steinbeck), 49

Ecclesiastical History of the English People (Bede), 211

Economy, during Middle Ages, 231–233, 293

Edict of Milan, 165, 175

Education
    of Greek women, 57
    in Middle Ages, 215–216, 218, 244–246
    Socrates on, 68

Edward (Anglo-Saxon king), 283, *284*

Edward III, king of England, 300

Egypt, 17–24, *18*
    achievements of, 28
    agriculture in, 17
    art of, *4,* 22–24, *22, 23, 24*
    cities in, 19, 109–110, *109*
    early civilizations in, 8, 9
    government of, *4,* 17, 18, 19–20, 22–23, *23,* 24, *24, 25,* 114
    Greek influence in, 109–110
    historical records in, 88
    influence on Greek art, 92, *93*
    influence on Hebrews, 31
    literature in, 18, 20–21
    mathematics in, 20, 28, 138
    medicine in, 18, 20, 28
    Middle Kingdom of, 18
    music in, 19, 24
    New Kingdom of, 18
    Old Kingdom of, 17–18, 23
    pharaohs of, 17, 18, 19–20, 22–23, *23,* 24, *24, 25,* 114
    pyramids of, 17, 18, 19, 20, 23, *23*
    religion in, 18–20, 21, 27–28, 109
    Rome and, 127
    science in, 18, 20, 28, 138
    trade in, 18
    women in, *4,* 20–21, 23–24, *24*

Einhard (medieval writer), 218

Elamites, 9

Elements (Euclid), 114

Eleusinian mystery, 63

Elijah (prophet), 39

Eliot, T. S., 290

Elisha (prophet), 39

Emperor Constantine, The (sculpture), *175*

England
    architecture in, 273–274, *273, 274*
    in Hundred Years' War, 294
    literature of, 219–220, 259–260, 307–309
    medieval, 234, 294

Enuma Elish (epic poem), 12, 41

Epic cycles, 43–44, 219

Epic literature, 12, 13–15, 41–44, 91, 111, 219–220, 257–260

Epic of Gilgamesh, The (Mesopotamian epic poem), **13**–15, 41

Epic poetry, **12,** 13–15, 41–44, 91, 111, 219, 257–260

Epicureanism, 115, 132, 134

Epicurus (Greek philosopher), 115, 132, 134

Epigonos of Pergamum, 119–120

Epigrams (Martial), 136

Epistles (Seneca), 138

Epodes (Horace), 135

Equestrian Statue of Marcus Aurelius, 150, *150*

Eratosthenes of Cyrene (astronomer), 114

Erechtheion (Athens, Greece), 102, *102*

Esau, 42, 43

Eschatology, **26**

Eschenbach, Wolfram von, 300

Essenes, **160**

Esther, 38

Ethics
    Aristotle on, 73–74
    in Egypt, 18–19

Etienne de Castel, 309

Etruscans, 125, 143

Etymologiae, 216

Eucharist, *173,* 235

Euclid, 114, 216, 244

Eumenes II, king of Pergamum, 118, 119, *119*

Eumenides (Aeschylus), 82

Euphrates River, 9, 18

Euripides, 85–86

European civilization, origins of, 212, 228–229

Evans, Arthur, 54

Everett, Reverend Robert A., 167

Everyman (morality play), 302–303

Excommunication, 235, 239, 295, 296

Exekias (Greek vase painter), 91, *91*

Exodus (Jews), 38, 41

Ezekiel (prophet), 32

Faerie Queen, The (Spenser), 289

Famine, 293

Al-Farabi (Islamic philosopher), 198

Farming. *See* Agriculture (farming)

Farrington, Benjamin, 112

Faust, 220

Feast of Weeks, **38**

Fertility cult, 7

Fertility images, 6, 7, *7*

Feudal lords, 213, 215, 231, 233

Feudalism, **212**–214, 231, 321

Fief, 212

Filostrato (Boccaccio), 305

Fire, 5

Firenze, Giovanni da, 320

FitzGerald, Edward, 200

Five Pillars of the faith, **196**

Florence, Italy, 265, *265,* 274–275, *275*

Flying buttresses, 267, 268, **271,** *271*

Food shortage, 293

Food storage, 9, 10

Form(s), **70,** 72, 169

Formative period of Greek art, 90

France
    architecture in, 266–273, *267, 269, 270, 271, 272, 279,* 280–281, *281, 282,* 310
    cave paintings in, 6–7, *6, 8*
    conflict with Catholic Church in, 295
    in Hundred Years' War, 294
    medieval, 234–235
    relief carving in, 7

Francis of Assisi, Saint, 230, 239–240, *241,* 298

Franciscans, 239–**240**

Franks, 195, *210,* 211–212. *See also* France

Free organum (music), 287

Freedom
    in Greece, 104
    lack of, in Persia, 88

Frescoes, *30,* 172–173, *172, 241, 247,* 314, 316–318, *316, 317. See also* Wall paintings

Freud, Sigmund, 84

Friars, 239–240

Fundamentals of Music, The (Boethius), 285

Gaius Gracchus, 128

Galen (Roman physician), 112, 138, 140, 244, 250

Galileo, 251

Galla Placidia, Byzantine empress, 187–188, *187*

Gallicanus (Hroswitha), 221

Garden of Eden, 36, 42

Genesis, 42, 43

Gaul and His Wife (Hellenistic sculpture), 117, 120, *120*

Gelon, king of Syracuse, 114

Genre sculpture, **122,** *122*

Gentiles, **162**

Geocentric theory, **252**

Geography, in Hellenistic Age, 114

Geometric Style of Greek vase painting, 90–91, *90*

Geometry, 20, 28

Gerhard, Master, 276

Germania (Tacitus), 137

Germanic tribes, 129, 131, 132, 183, 184, 209, 211, 212, 222

Germany
    architecture in, 222–228, *223, 224, 225, 226, 227, 228,* 275–276, *276, 277*

independent territories in, 234, 235
medieval, 209, 211, 212, 222, 234, 235
Giles of Rome, 296
Giotto di Bondone, 275, 316–318, *316, 317*
Giza (Egypt), 23, *23,* 24
Gladiators, 127, 138, **146**
Globalism, Age of, 229
Gods and goddesses. *See* Religion
Golden Age of Roman literature, **134–136**
Golden Calf, 42
Golden Rule, 161
Goliards, **256–257**
Good Shepherd, The (mosaic), 187–188, *187*
Good Shepherd, The (sculpture), 174–175, *175*
Gospel(s)
    Lindisfarne Gospels, 221, 222
    Synoptic, **167–168**
Gospel Book of Charlemagne, 222, *223*
Gothic style
    of architecture, **267–276,** *269, 270, 271, 272, 273, 274, 275, 276, 277*
    of sculpture, *279, 280*
Government
    in Athens, 56–57
    in Byzantine civilization, 184
    in early civilizations, 8
    in Egypt, *4,* 17, 18, 19–20, 22–23, *23,* 24, *24,* 25, 114
    in Hellenistic Age, 109
    during High Middle Ages, 234–235
    legalism and, 113
    in Ottoman Empire, 195
    papal power vs., 295–297
    religion and, 8, 9, 18, 28
    Roman, 125, 127, 128–129, 131
Granada, Spain, 205–206, *206*
Great Mosque of Córdoba, *182,* 205
Great Mosque of Damascus, 204
Great Mosque of Samarra, 204–*205*
Great Schism, **295–296,** 297, 298
Greco-Roman Age, 107
Greece, 53–123
    architecture in, 53, 90, 97–103, *98, 99, 100, 101, 102, 103,* 177
    art of, 89–103, *90, 91, 92, 93, 94, 95, 96, 97*
    city-states in, 54–58, *55*
    Dark Age in, 54, 62
    democracy in, 56–57, 78, 88, 89, 104
    drama in, 80–88
    early Aegean civilizations in, 53–54
    freedom in, 104
    humanism in, 77–104
    influence on Byzantine civilization, 185
    influence on Egyptian civilization, 109–110
    influence on Hellenistic Age, 109–110
    influence on Islamic thought, 198, 199, 246

influence on Rome, 102, 127, 132, 142
    literature in, 41, 58–62, 77–88
    Macedonia and, 57–58
    mathematics in, 53, 65, 66, 79
    medicine in, 66–67
    Mesopotamian influence on, 28
    moral values in, 68, 88
    music of, 49, 79–80
    Mycenean, 54, 98
    philosophy in, 53, 64–75, 114–116, 140, 168–169, 321
    politics in city-states, 53–54, 55, 56
    rational thought in, 36, 53, 55, 64–75, 77, 89, 103, 115–116, 140, 142
    religion in, 55, 61, 62–64
    sculpture of, *52, 53, 55,* 68, *76,* 90, 92–97, *93, 94, 95, 96, 97, 99,* 175
    vase painting in, *54,* 79, 90–92, *90, 91, 92*
    view of history in, 88–89, 172
    See also Hellenic civilization
Gregorian chant, **286–287**
Gregory I, Pope, 211, 286
Gregory VII, Pope, 236, 240
Grosseteste, Robert, 250
Guatemala, Mayan creation myth of, 261
Gudea, king of Sumeria, 16–17, *17*
Guelphs, 263
Guest, Lady Charlotte, 218
Guide for the Perplexed, The (Maimonides), 242
Guido of Arezzo, 286
"Guidonian hand," 286, *287*
Guilds, **233**
Guillaume de Lorris, 300, 302
Guillaume de Machaut, 319
Guillaume of Sens, 273
Gymnasia, 109

Hadassah, 38
Hadith, 196, 197
Hadrian, Roman emperor, 147, 152
Hagia Sophia (Istanbul, Turkey), 185, 191–193, *192, 193*
Al-Hallaj, Al-Husayn ibn Mansur, 197
Ham (son of Noah), 42
Hamilton, Edith, 62
Hammurabi, code of, **12**
Han Fei Tzu, 113
Handel, George Friedrich, 168, 290
Hanging Gardens (Babylon), 17
Hannibal, 128
Hanukkah, Festival of Lights, 110
Harmony, 288
Harp, 15–16, *16*
Hawthorne, Nathaniel, 49
Haydn, Franz Josef, 290
Heavenly Banquet, The (Brigid), 220
Hebrew(s), 31–50
    art of, 49
    history and, 31–34, 38–39, 88
    kings of, 32, *35,* 45–46, 48, 49, 160, 173

Law of, 33, 34, 37–38, 41, 110, 160, 161, 162, 163, 282, *283*
    legacy of, 50
    literature of, 242
    Mesopotamian influence on, 28, 31
    moral autonomy of, 36–37
    music of, 49, *50*
    patriarchs of, *30,* 31, 33, 42, 43–44, 48, 173–174, 202
    prophets of, 32, 34, 38, 39–41
    religion of, *30,* 31–49, *33,* 110. *See also* Judaism
    in Sinai wilderness, 31–32
    temples of, 32, 33, *33, 35,* 38, 110, 151, 242
    See also Jews
Hebrew Scriptures, 33, 34, 37–38, 41–49
    Bible, *30,* 31, 36, 37, 38, 41–49
    Christians and, 166, 167–168
    epic stories and poetry in, 41–44
    in first century B.C., 160
    in Hellenistic Age, 110
    lyric poetry in, 44–45
    Western authors and language in, 48–49
    wisdom writings in, 43, 45–48
Hector, 59
Hegira, **194**
Hellenic civilization, 62–123
    architecture of, 53, 90, 97–103, *98, 99, 100, 101, 102, 103*
    art of, 89–103, *90, 91, 92, 93, 94, 95, 96, 97*
    city-states in, 54–58, *55*
    drama in, 80–88
    humanism in, 77–104
    literature in, 58–62, 77–88
    parochialism in, 107–108
    philosophy in, 64–75
    religion in, 55, 61, 62–64
    view of history in, 88–89
    See also Greece
Hellenistic Civilization, **107–123**
    architecture in, 118–119, *118, 119*
    art in, 116–123, *117, 118, 119, 120, 121, 122*
    changes in, 107–108
    cities in, 109–110, *109*
    cosmopolitanism in, 108–110, 123
    culture of, 110–116
    Greek influence in, 109–110
    legacy of, 123
    literature of, 110–112
    mathematics in, 114
    medicine in, 112, 114
    philosophy in, 110, 114–116
    science in, 110, 112, 114, 115
    sculpture in, *106,* 110, 117–122, *118, 119, 120, 121, 122*
    universalism in, 108–110, 123
Hellenistic Romance, **111–112**
Hellenization, 109–110, 169
Héloise, 245–246
Henry I, king of England, 234
Henry II, emperor of Germany, 221

Henry II, king of England, 234
Henry IV, Holy Roman Emperor, 236
Henry V, Holy Roman Emperor, 236
Henry V, king of England, 294
Herculaneum, 147–148
Heresy, 238–239, 296–297
Hermes with the Infant Dionysos
    (Greek sculpture), 96–97, *97*
Herodotus, 88–89, 185
Heroides (Ovid), 136
Herophilus (Hellenistic physician), 112
Hesiod, 60–62
Hexachord, 288
Hieroglyphics, **19**
Hieron II, king of Syracuse, 114
High Middle Ages, 231–291
    architecture of, 264–276, *265, 266,
        267, 268, 269, 270, 271, 272, 273,
        274, 275, 276, 277, 279*
    changes during, 231
    economic expansion in, 231–233
    law in, 251–252
    literature in, 255–264
    music of, 284–289
    philosophy in, 245–249
    poetry in, 256–264
    religion in, 235–242, 245–249
    revival of learning in, 218, 242–249
    rise of states in, 233–235
    science in, 250–251
    sculpture in, 276–280, *278, 279*
    Twelfth-Century Awakening in, 218,
        244
    worldview in, 252–253
Hildebrand, 236
Hildegard of Bingen (medieval writer),
    214, 287
Hildesheim, Germany, 225, 226–228,
    226, 227, 228
Hillel (Jewish sage), 166
Hinduism, 11, 139
Hipparchus of Nicaea (astronomer),
    114
Hippo, bishop of, 170
Hippocrates, 66, 112, 114, 244, 250
Hippocratic school of medicine, 66–67
Histories (Herodotus), 88
Histories (Tacitus), 137
History
    Byzantine, 183–184, 185
    Greek view of, 88–89, 112
    Hebrews and, 31–34, 38–39, 88
    Hellenistic, 112
    Islamic view of, 199
    Roman view of, 135–136, 137
    theology of, 249
History of Rome (Livy), 135
History of the Franks (Gregory I), 211
History of the Goths (Cassiodorus),
    216
Holidays
    Islamic, 196
    Jewish, 38, 110
Holofernes (Assyrian leader), 38
Holy Roman Emperor, 235, 236
Holy Roman Empire, 232

Homer, 41, 53–54, *54,* 58–60, 62, 79,
    134, 219, 305
Horace (Quintus Horatius Flaccus), 135
Hosea (prophet), 39
Houses, Roman, 147–148, *148,* 153,
    154
Hroswitha (medieval poet), 214,
    220–221
Hubris, **59,** 62, 82, 84, 88
Hugh, king of France, 234–235
Hugo (illuminated Bible), 281–282
Humanism
    Christianity and, 178–179
    in Greece, 77–104
    in literature, 77–79
    in Rome, 132
Hun(s), 132, 183
Hundred Years' War, 294
Hungary, 195, 231
Hunting, 5, 6, 7
Hus, Jan, 296, 297
Hyksos, 18
Hymn(s), religious, 255–256, 289
Hymn of Pentecost (Romanus), 186
Hyperbole, 201

Ibn Battuta, 301
Ibn Hazm (Islamic poet and scholar),
    199–200
Ibn Khaldûn (Islamic philosopher), 199
Ibn-Rushd (Averroës), 199, 248
Ibn-Sina (Avicenna), 198, 250
Ichthys (fish), **172**–173, *173*
Iconoclastic controversy, **187**
Ideas, theory of, 70, 72, 73
Idolatry, 36, 42, 49
Iktinos (Greek architect), *99,* 100
Iliad (Homer), 58–60, 79, 134, 305
Immaculate Conception, 214
Incest, 20
India, religion in, 11, 139
Individualism, 41
Innocent III, Pope, 240–241
Inquisition, **239**
Insula at Ostia, 148, *148*
Intelligence, spiritual, **249**
Investiture Controversy, **236**
Ionian Greeks, 56
Ionian philosophers, 64–65, 66
Ionic order of architecture, *98,*
    101–102, *101, 102*
Iran, 26. *See also* Persia
Iraq, 16. *See also* Sumeria
Ireland, *208,* 211, 218–219, 221–222
Irenaeus, 251
Irrigation, in early civilizations, 9, 10
Isaac (Hebrew patriarch), *30,* 31, 43
Isaiah (prophet), 32, 39, 40
Isidore of Seville, 216, 285
Isidorus of Miletus (master-builder),
    192
Islam, **193**–207
    art and architecture of, 202–206,
        203, 204, 205, 206
    Five Pillars of, **196**
    Greek influence on, 198, 199, 246

inner divisions of, 196–197
    legacy of, 206–207
    literature of, 199–202
    origins and expansion of, 193–195,
        194
    theology of, 195–196
    thought and learning of, 198–199
    women of, 197
Isolt, 219
Isorhythm, 318
Israel, 32, *32*
    Twelve Tribes of, 43–44
    See also Hebrew(s); Jews; Judaism
Issus, Battle of, 117, *117,* 177
Istanbul, Turkey, 185, 191–193, *192,
    193,* 195. *See also* Byzantium;
    Constantinople
Italian sonnets, **304**–305
Italy
    architecture in, 187–191, *188, 189,
        190, 191,* 265–266, *265, 266,*
        274–275, *275*
    art in, *187, 190,* 314–318, *315, 316,
        317*
    Doric temple in, 98–99, *99*
    independent territories in, 234
    trade and, 232–233

Jacob (Hebrew patriarch), 31, 42, 43
Jacob of Liège, 318
Jaeger, Werner, 60
James the Greater, Saint, 267
Japan, medieval, 217
Japheth (son of Noah), 42
Jean, Duke of Berry, 319
Jean de Meun, 302
Jeremiah (prophet), 32, 39, 41
Jericho, Battle of, 48
Jerome (Latin writer), 169
Jerusalem, 32, 33, *35*
    as holy city, 202–203, *203*
    Temple of, 110, 151, 242
Jesus, 159–162, 167, 168, 172, 191,
    195, 214, *282, 317*
Jews
    in Babylon, 32, 33
    Christians and, 162–163, 166–167,
        238, 241–242
    contributions to medieval culture, 242
    Crusades and, 238, 241–242
    Exodus from Egypt, 38, 41
    in Hellenistic Age, 110
    in High Middle Ages, 241–242
    holidays of, 38, 110
    hostility toward, 166–167, 238,
        241–242, 293, 294
    Jesus and, 159, 160–161, 167, 168,
        172, 191, 195, 214, *282, 317*
    in Late Middle Ages, 293, 294
    literature of, 242
    Muhammad and, 194
    in Muslim society, 197–198
    religion of. *See* Judaism
    under Rome, 33
    sects of, 160
    See also Hebrew(s)

Jihad (holy war), **195**, 238
Joachim of Fiore, 249
Joan of Arc, 294, 309–310
Job, 43, *46*
   Book of, 46, **47–48**
John, king of Bohemia, 319
John, king of England, 234, 235
John of Paris, 296
John of Salisbury, 322
John the Baptist, 161
John XXII, Pope, 296, 318–319
Jonah, 48, 173
Jordan River, *32*
Joseph (Hebrew patriarch), 43–44, 48
Joshua, 48
Judah, 32, 33, 41
Judah the Maccabeus, 110
Judaism, 32–49, *33*
   covenant in, 37–38, 41, 43, 110
   early Christians and, 162–163,
      166–167
   in first century B.C., 160, 161
   in Hellenistic Age, 110
   moral autonomy in, 36–37
   Satan in, 47
   sects of, 160
   Universalism and, 40–41
   wisdom writings of, 43, 45–48
   women in, 38
Judea, 110
Julius II, Pope, 176
jus gentium, **140**
Just state, 71–72
Justice, social, 39–40
Justinian, Byzantine emperor, 184, 185,
   186, 191–192
Juvenal (Decimus Junius Juvanlis),
   136–137

Kaaba, shrine of (Mecca), 196
Kallikrates (Greek architect), 99, 100,
   101–102, *101*
Kepler, Johannes, 198
Ketubim (writings of Jews), 34
Khan, Chingis, 195
Khayyam, Omar, 200
King, Martin Luther, Jr., 40
King Arthur, tales of, 259–260
King Gudea (Sumerian statue), 16–17
"King Tut," 24, *25*
Kitto, H. D. F., 59
Kitzinger, Ernst, 171
Knidos, 76
Komos, *86*
Konrad of Hochstaden, 276
Kontakion, **186**
Korai (Greek sculpture), 92, 93–94, *93,
   94*
Koran (*See* Quran)
Kritios Boy (Greek sculpture), *94, 95*
Küng, Hans, 159

La Magdelaine Cave (France), 7
Lagash (Sumerian city-state), 16
Lais (Marie de France), 262
Lamentation (fresco), 317–318, *317*

Lamentations (Pierluigi da Palestrina),
   168
Landini, Francesco, 320
Langland, William, 298–299
Language(s)
   Arabic, 195, 207
   Aramaic, 110
   in Byzantine civilization, 184
   in Hebrew Scriptures, 48–49
   Latin, 132, 184, 215, 244, 304
   in Paleolithic Age, *5*
   in Roman Empire, 131, 132
Laocoön Group, The (Hellenistic sculpture), *106,* 117, 121
Lascaux (France) cave painting, 6–7, *6*
Last Supper (da Vinci), 168
Late Middle Ages, *292,* 293–323
   adversity in, 293–296
   art in, *292,* 310–318
   Black Death (bubonic plague) in,
      293–294, *294*
   decline of civilization in, 293–295
   learning and thought in, 296–297
   literature in, 297–310
   music in, 318–320, *319*
   papal power in, 295–297
   poetry in, 298–302, 303–307
   religion in, 295–297
Lateran Council, Fourth (1215), 241,
   242
Latin Christendom
   adversity in, 293–296
   Crusades and, 184, 237–238, *238,*
      241, 278
   Great Schism in, 295–296, 297, 298
   Gregorian reform and, 235–237
   heresy in, 238–239, 296–297
   during High Middle Ages, 235–242,
      245–249
   Inquisition in, 239
   during Late Middle Ages, 293, 295
   medieval civilization and, 209–211
   monasticism in, 165, 211, 214, 216,
      236, 239–240, 246
   papacy and, 165, 176, 211, 212, 214,
      236–238, 240–241, 286, 293,
      295–296, 318–319
   rise of, 209–215
   See also Catholicism
Latin language, 132, 184, 215, 244,
   304
Law(s)
   Aristotle on, 74
   Byzantine, 184–185
   code of Hammurabi, 12
   common, **234**
   Corpus Juris Civilis, 184–185, 251
   in early civilizations, 8–9
   Greek philosophy on, 67
   Hebrew, 33, 34, 37–38, 41, 110, 160,
      161, 162, 163, 282, *283*
   in Hellenistic Age, 109, 110
   during High Middle Ages, 251–252
   jus gentium, 140
   of love (*lex caritatis*), **137**
   Mesopotamian, 12

   natural, 133, 142
   Roman, 125, 127, 140, 251–252
   Twelve Tables, 140
Learning
   in Byzantine civilization, 183,
      184–185
   Islamic, 198–199
   during Middle Ages, 215–218,
      242–249, 296–297
   revival of, 242–245
Legalism, 113
Legends, *54,* 259–260, 299–300
Leinster cycle, **219**
Leo III, Pope, 212
Leonin (composer), 287
Lex caritatis (law of love), **137**
Libation Bearers, The (Aeschylus),
   82
Libraries
   in Hellenistic Age, 112
   in Middle Ages, 216
   in Roman Empire, 132
Liège, Jacob of, 318
Life of Augustus (Suetonius), 218
Limbourg Brothers, *292,* 311–314, *313,
   314*
Limestone relief, 22, *22*
Lindisfarne Gospels, 221, *222*
Linear perspective, **150–151**
Literature
   apocalyptic, **40**
   Bible as, 41–49
   Carolingian, 222, *223*
   Christianity and, 167–171, 220–221
   Egyptian, 18, 20–21
   English, 219–220, 259–260,
      307–309
   epic, 12, 13–15, 41–44, 91, 111,
      219–220, 257–260
   Golden Age of (Roman), **134–136**
   Greek, 41, 58–62, 77–88
   Hellenistic, 110–112
   humanism in, 77–79
   Irish, 218–219, 221–222
   Islamic, 199–202
   Jewish, 242
   Leinster cycle in, 219
   manuscript illumination and, 221,
      222, 223, 237, 281–282, 283, 292,
      312–314, *313, 314*
   medieval, 218–221, 255–264,
      297–310
   Mesopotamian, 12–15, 28, 41
   religious, 220–221, 255–256
   Roman, 132–137
   romance, 111–112, 259–260,
      299–300
   Silver Age of (Roman), **134,** 136–137
   tragedy, 81–86
   Ulster cycle in, 219
   Welsh mythology, 218
   women in, 214, 220–221, 262, 304,
      309–310
   See also Drama; Poetry
Little Brothers, **240**
Livia (wife of Augustus Caesar), 131

Livre des trois vertus (Christine de Pizan), 309
Livy, 135
Logic, formal, 66
Logos (Divine Reason), 115, 167, 169
Lollards, **297**
Longa, 288, 289
Lords, feudal, 213, 215, 231, 233
Lorris, Guillaume de, 300, 302
Love
   chivalric, 260, 262
   law of *(lex caritatis)*, 137
Lu Yu, 243
Lucian (Greek writer), 116
Lucretius (Roman philosopher), 132
Lun Yu (Confucius), 87
Lustration, 83
Luther, Martin, 171
Lyceum, 72, 112
Lyric poetry, **77**
   Chinese, 243
   Greek, 77–79
   in Hebrew Scriptures, 44–45
   Irish, 218
Lysistrata (Aristophanes), 86

Ma'at, **18**
Mabinogi, **218**
Mabinogion, 218
Macedonia, 57–58, 108, 109, 127
Machaut, Guillaume de, 319
Madonna Enthroned (painting), 314–315, *315*
Madrigals, 318, **320**
Magic
   in Egypt, 18
   in Rome, 140–141
   sympathetic, **6**
Magna Carta, **234**, 321
Magnificat (Bach), 290
Magyars, 231
Mahdi, 197
Maimonides (Moses ben Maimon), 242
Main Hall of Lascaux (cave painting), 6–7, *6*
Maison Carrée (Nîmes, France), 144, *145*
Majestà, The Virgin as Queen of Heaven (painting), 315–316, *315*
Malachi (prophet), 40
al-Malik, Abd, 202
Malouel, Jean, 311
Manichaeism, 170
Manorialism, **214**–215, 231, 233
Manual of Discipline, The, 160
Manual of Harmonics, The (Nicomachus of Gerasa), 79
Manufacturing, in early civilizations, 8
Manuscript illumination, **221**, 222, *223*, 237, 281–282, *283*, 292, 312–314, *313*, *314*
Marathon, 56, 82, 88
Marcus Agrippa, 144
Marcus Aurelius, Roman emperor, 138, 142, 150, *150*, 152
Marie de France, 262

Marriage of Peleus and Thetis (Catallus), 134
Marsile, king of Spain, 257, 258
Marsilius of Padua, 296
Martial (Marcus Valerius Martialis), 136
Martyrs, 165, 189
Mary, mother of Jesus, 168, 214, 221, *281, 315, 316, 317*
Masaccio, 168
Masks, in Greek drama, 81
Mathematical Composition (Ptolemy), 138
Mathematics
   in Babylon, 66
   in Egypt, 20, 28, 138
   in Greece, 53, 65, 66, 79
   in Hellenistic Age, 114
   in High Middle Ages, 250, 251
   in Islamic world, 198, 200
   in Mesopotamia, 12, 28
   music and, 79, 80, 285
   in Near East, 28
Mathnawi (Rumi), 200
Mattathias (Jewish priest), 110
Matthew (Carolingian literature), 222, 223
Mausoleum of Galla Placidia (Ravenna, Italy), 187–188, *187*
Maximian, Bishop, 188–189, 190
Mayan creation myth, 261
Mecca, 193, 194, 196
Medea (Euripides), 85
Medicine
   in Egypt, 18, 20, 28
   in Greece, 66–67
   healing power of music and, 79
   in Hellenistic Age, 112, 114
   in High Middle Ages, 250
   Hippocratic school of, 66–67
   in Islamic world, 198
   Jewish contributions to, 242
   in Mesopotamia, 12
   in Rome, 138, 140
Medieval civilization. *See* Middle Ages
Medina, 194
Meditation poetry, 44–45
Meditations (Marcus Aurelius), 138
Megiddo, 38
Mehmed II (Ottoman Turk ruler), 195
Meistersinger, 285
Melismatic organum (music), 287
Melville, Herman, 49
Menander (dramatist), 111, 133
Merchants, 233
Merovingian rulers, 211
Mesopotamia, 9–17
   achievements of, 28
   agriculture in, 10
   art in, 15–17, *15, 16, 17*
   cities in, 9
   city-states in, 9, 16
   conquests and invasions in, 9, 10, 12
   culture of, 9, 16–17, *17*
   early civilizations in, 8
   flooding in, 10

   historical records in, 88
   influence on Greeks, 28
   influence on Hebrews, 28, 31
   law in, 12
   literature in, 12–15, 28, 41
   mathematics in, 12, 28
   medicine in, 12
   music in, 15–16, *16*, 17
   religion in, 9–12, 15, 16–17, *17*
   science in, 12, 28
   social classes in, 12
   temples in, 9–10, 15, *15*
   trade in, 12
Messe de Notre Dame (sacred music), 319
Messenians, *55*
Messiah, **40**
Messiah (Handel), 168, 290
Messiah of Aaron, 160, 161
Metal, use of, 8, 226–228, *227, 228*
Metamorphoses (Ovid), 136
Meun, Jean de, 302
Michael V, Byzantine emperor, 185
Middle Ages, 209–229
   agrarian society in, 214–215
   architecture of, 222–228, *223, 224, 225, 226*, 264–276, *265, 266, 267, 268, 269, 270, 271, 272, 273, 274, 275, 276, 277, 279*
   art in, 221–228, 264–284, 310–318
   birth of Europe in, 212, 228–229
   Carolingian empire in, *210*, 211–212
   deterioration of Roman civilization in, 209, 212
   education in, 215–216, 218, 244–246
   feudalism in, 212–214, 231, 321
   High. *See* High Middle Ages
   invasions during, 212, *213*
   Late. *See* Late Middle Ages
   learning and thought in, 215–218, 242–249, 296–297
   literature in, 218–221, 255–264, 297–310
   modern world and, 320–323
   monasticism in, 211, 214, 216, 236, 239–240, 246
   music of, 284–289, 318–320, *319*
   philosophy in, 216, 245–249, 296–297, 321–322
   poetry in, 214, 218–221, 256–264, 298–302, 303–307
   rise of Latin Christendom in, 209–215
   sculpture in, 228, *228*, 276–280, *278, 279*, 310–311, *311, 312*
Middle class
   Aristotle on, 74
   during High Middle Ages, 233
   in Rome, 131
Middle Kingdom of Egypt, 18
Milan, Edict of, 165, 175
Millefleurs, 283
Milton, John, 49, 168, 289
Minaret, 205, *205*
Minoan civilization, 54
Miriam (prophetess), 38

Misogyny, in Egypt, 21
Mithraism, 141, 164
Mnseicles (Greek architect), *100,* 101, 102, *102*
Moby Dick (Melville), 49
Moissac, France, 278, *279*
Monasticism, 165, 211, 214, 216, 236, 239–240, 246, 280, 286
Mongols, 132, 195
Monks. *See* Monasticism
Monophony, 284, 288
Monotheism, 19–20, 25, 34
Moral autonomy, 36–37
Moral Dialogues (Seneca), 137
Moral transformation, 160–161, 177–178
Moral values
    in Greece, 68, 88
    in Rome, 133
Morality play, **302**–303
Mosaics, 117, *117,* **155**–156, 177–178, *177, 178,* 187–190, *187, 189, 190*
Moses, 20, 31, 33, 34, 39, 42–43, 160, 173, 282, *283, 312*
Moses Expounding the Law (manuscript illumination), 282, *283*
Mosques, *182,* **203**–205, *205*
Motet, 287
Mount Sinai, 33, 38, 43
Mount Vesuvius, 147–148
Mozart, Wolfgang Amadeus, 290
Muhammad (prophet), 193–195, 196, 197, 202
Muhammad III, 205
Muhammad V, 206
Mummers, *256*
Mummification, 21
Muqaddimah (Ibn Khaldûn), 199
Murals. *See* Frescoes; Wall paintings
Muris, Jean de, 318
Muses, 61
Museum, in Hellenistic Age, 112
Music
    antiphons, 287
    ars nova, 289, 318–320, *319*
    Byzantine, 185–186
    caccia, 318, 320
    cantillation, 49
    dissonance in, 288
    Egyptian, 19, 24
    Greek, 49, 79–80
    Gregorian chant, 286–287
    healing power of, 79
    Hebrew, 49, *50*
    isorhythm, 318
    Kontakion, 186
    madrigals, 318, 320
    mathematics and, 79, 80, 285
    medieval, 284–289, 318–320, *319*
    Mesopotamian, 15–16, *16,* 17
    modes of, 79
    monophony, 284, 288
    motet, 287
    in Paleolithic Age, 7
    polyphony, 284, 287, 288

religion and, 79, 80–81, 168, 285–289, 290, 319, 320
    schools of, 286, 287
    solmization, 286
    songs, 19
    staff notation, 286, 288, 289
Musical instruments, 49, *50, 79,* 285
Muslims
    Crusades and, 237–238, *238,* 241
    invading Byzantine civilization, 184, 195
    invading Carolingian civilization, 212, *213*
    learning of, 198–199
    Shi'ites, **196**–197
    society of, 197–198
    Sunnites, **196**–197
    women, 197
    See also Islam
Mycenean civilization, 54, 98
Mycerinus, pharaoh of Egypt, 23, *23, 24, 24*
Mycerinus and His Queen (Egyptian statue), 24, *24*
Mystery plays, *256,* 287, 289
Mystery religions, 63–64, 141–142, 155, *155*
Myth(s), 54
    creation, 261
    Mayan, 261
    in Near East, 27–28
    in Rome, 140–141
    Sumerian, 9
    Welsh, 218
Mythmaking, 27–28

Naomi, 38
Narthex, 175, *176*
Natural History (Pliny the Elder), 92
Natural law, 133, 142
Natural Questions (Seneca), 137
Nature
    in Egyptian religion, 19, 22, *22,* 27–28
    in Greek philosophy, 64, 65–67
    in Judaism, 35
    in Near Eastern religions, 27–28
Nave, 175, *176*
Near East
    achievements in, 28
    farming in, 5
    Hebrews in, 31–34
    in Neolithic Age, 7–8
    in Paleolithic Age, 5
    religions in, 25–26, 27–28, 35, 36
    technology of, 28
    See also Egypt; Mesopotamia
Nebi'im (Hebrew Scriptures), 34
Nebuchadnezzar, king of Babylon, 17
Nefertiti, queen of Egypt, *4,* 24
Neoclassical style of art, 103
Neolithic Age (New Stone Age), 7–8
Neolithic Revolution, 7
Neo-Platonism, **142,** 170, 184, 185, 198, 199, 216
Nero, Roman emperor, 137, 147

New Comedy, **112,** 133
New Kingdom of Egypt, 18
New Life, The (Dante Alighieri), 263
New Testament, 167–168
Newton, Isaac, 251
Nibelungenlied, The (German epic poem), 258–259
Nicaea, Council of, **168**
Nicaea II, Council of, 264
Nicholas II, Pope, 236
Nicomachean Ethics (Aristotle), 73
Nicomachus of Gerasa, 79
Nike of Samothrace (Hellenistic sculpture), 117, 120–121, *121*
Nile River, 17, 19
Nile Valley, *18*
Nîmes, France, 144, *144, 145*
Noah, 42
Noblewomen, 213–214
Normandy, France, 234, 235, 282, *284*
Notre-Dame de Chartres (Chartres, France), 168, 271–273, *272, 279,* 280–281, *281, 282,* 310
Notre-Dame de la Belle Verrière (stained-glass window), 280, *281*
Notre-Dame de Paris (Paris, France), 270–271, *270, 271*
Notre Dame School of Music, 286, 287
Nuns, 211, 214, 220–221, 246

Obadiah (prophet), 40
Obed, 38
Odes (Horace), 135
Odo (Benedictine monk), 286
Odoacer, Roman emperor, 132, 188
Odyssey (Homer), *54, 58, 59, 60,* 134
Oedipus complex, 84
Oedipus the King (Sophocles), 84–85
Oikoumene, 163
Old Kingdom of Egypt, 17–18, 23
Old Market Woman (Hellenistic sculpture), 117, 122, *122*
Old Saint Peter's Church (Rome), 176–177, *176*
Oligarchy, in Roman Republic, 127
Olympian religion, 62–63
On Ecclesiastical Power (Giles of Rome), 296
On Kingly and Papal Power (John of Paris), 296
On the Consecration of the Church of Saint Denis (Suger), 269
On the Nature of Things (Lucretius), 132
One Thousand and One Arabian Nights, 201–202
Optics, 198, 250, 251
Orchestra, 81
Orestia trilogy (Aeschylus), 82
Oriental Style of Greek vase painting, 91
Origen, 167
Orpheus, 174
Orphism, 63–64
Ostrogoth rulers, 188, 216

Otto I, the Great, German emperor, 221, 224, 225, 235
Otto II, German emperor, 221
Otto III, German emperor, 221, 226
Ottoman Empire, 184, 193, 195
Ottonian dynasty, 221
Ovid (Publius Ovidius Naso), 136
Oxford University, 244
Ozment, Steven, 248

Padua, Italy, 316–318, *316, 317*
Paestum, Italy, 98–99, *99*
Painting
   in caves, 6–7, *6, 8*
   Hellenistic, 117
   Italian, 314–318, *315, 316, 317*
   in Late Middle Ages, *292,* 311–318, *313, 314, 315, 316, 317*
   portrait, 155, *156*
   tempera, 315, *315*
   vase painting, *54,* 79, 90–92, *90, 91, 92*
   wall paintings, 24, 90, 92, 152–156, *154, 155. See also* Frescoes
Palace(s), 205–206, *206,* 222, 223, 224, *224*
Palace of the Lions (Granada, Spain), 205–206, *206*
Palatine Chapel, The (Aachen, Germany), 224, *224*
Paleolithic Age (Old Stone Age), 5–7, *6, 7, 8*
Palestine, 31, 38
Palestrina, Giovanni Pierluigi da, 168
Pandora, 61–62
Pantheon (Rome), 144–145, *145, 146,* 177
Papacy, 165, 176, 211, 212, 214, 236–238, 240–241, 286, 293, 295–296, 318–319
Paphnutius (Hroswitha), 221
Paradise Lost (Milton), 49, 168, 289
Parallel organum (music), 287
Paris, France, 268–271, *269, 270, 271*
Parliament, English, 234
Parmenides, 65–66
Parochialism, in Hellenic civilization, 107–108
Parthenon (Athens, Greece), 99–100, *99*
Passover (Jewish holiday), **38**
Patriarchs
   Cycle of the, 43
   of Hebrews, *30,* 31, 33, 42, 43–44, 48, 173–174, 202
Patricians, 125, 127
Patrick, Saint, 211
Paul, Saint, 162–163, 166, 177, *177*
Paul VI, Pope, 298
Paulinus (Roman judge), 189
Pax Romana, **129,** 131, 134–140
Pearl Poet, 299–300
Peasants
   in Egypt, 18
   in Greece, 55
   in Middle Ages, 212, 214, 215, 231, 233

in Rome, 128
Pelikan, Jaroslav (theologian), 191
Peloponnesian League, 57
Peloponnesian peninsula, *55*
Peloponnesian War, 56, 57, *58,* 86, 89
Penelope, *54,* 60
Pentateuch (Torah), 33, 34, 160
"People of the book," 197–198
Pepin II (Carolingian ruler), 211
Peplos Maiden, The (Greek sculpture), 93–94, *94*
Pergamum, 108, 117–120, *118, 119,* 127, 138
Pericles, 56, 82, 99, 100
Perotin (composer), 287
Persepolis, Iran, 26
Persia, 25–27
   art of, 26–27
   Athens and, 56
   attack on Roman Empire, 131
   conquest of Babylon by, 17, 33
   lack of freedom in, 88
   religion in, 25–26, *26*
   rulers of, 26, *26, 27*
   tomb in, *26, 27*
Persian Wars, 57
Persians, The (Aeschylus), 82
Pesach (Passover), 38
Peter, Saint, 165, *172,* 173, 176, 177, *177*
Peter the Hermit, 238
Petrarch, Francesco, 304–305
Pharaohs, 17, **18,** 19–20, 22–23, *23, 24, 24, 25,* 114
Pharisees, **160**
Phidias (Greek sculptor), *99,* 100
Philemon (dramatist), 111
Philip Augustus, king of France, 235
Philip II, king of Macedonia, 57–58, 108
Philip IV, king of France, 295, 296
Philistines, 32, 48
Philosophy
   of Aristotle. *See* Aristotle
   Byzantine, 184, 185
   Christianity and, 168–169
   cosmologists, 65–67, 68
   Cynicism, 116
   dialectics, 69, 81
   Epicureanism, 115, 132, 134
   Greek, 53, 64–75, 114–116, 140, 168–169, *321*
   Hellenistic, 110, 114–116
   Islamic, 198–199
   medieval, 216, 245–249, 296–297, 321–322
   Neo-Platonism, 142, 170, 184, 185, 198, 199, 216
   of Plato, 64, 66, 69–72, 73
   Roman, 132–134, 137–138, 141, 142
   Skepticism, 116
   of Socrates, 68–69
   Sophists, 67, 68, 85, 86, 88, 89
   spiritualization of, 142
   Stoicism, 115–116, 133, 137–138, 169

Philoxenos of Eretria (Hellenistic painter), 117
Physics
   in Hellenistic Age, 112, 114, 115
   in Islamic world, 198
Phythokritos (Hellenistic sculptor), 120
Pilate, Pontius, 161
Pilgrim's Progress (Bunyan), 168, 289
Pillow-Book, The (Sei Shonagon), 217
Pinakotheke (gallery for paintings), 101
Pindar, 78–79
Pisa, Italy, 265–266, *266*
   Council of (1409), 295
Pisan school of sculpture, 310, 316
Pisano, Andrea, 275, 310
Pisano, Giovanni, 310, 316
Pisano, Nicola, 310, *311*
Pius II, Pope, 295, 298
Pius IX, Pope, 214
Pius XII, Pope, 298
Pizzano, Tomasso de, 309
Plainchant, 286
Plato, *52,* 64, 66, 69–72, 74, 142
   on Forms, 70, 72, 169
   on just state, 71–72
   on music, 79
   theory of ideas, 70, 72, 73
Plautus (Roman playwright), 111, 133
Plays
   morality, **302**–303
   mystery, **256,** 287, 289
   satyr, 81
   See also Drama
Plebians, in Rome, 127
Pliny the Elder, 92
Plotinus (Roman philosopher), 142
Poetics (Aristotle), 84
Poetry
   Chinese, 243
   of chivalric love, 260, 262
   Egyptian, 21
   epic, **12,** 13–15, 41–44, 91, 111, 219, 257–260
   goliardic, 256–257
   Greek, 58–62, 77–79
   Hellenistic, 111
   Islamic, 199–201
   Italian sonnets, 304–305
   lyric, 44–45, **77**–79, 218, 243
   medieval, 214, 218–221, 256–264, 298–302, 303–307
   meditation, **44**–45
   Mesopotamian, 12–15, 41
   Roman, 133–137
   similes in, 45
Polis, **54**–55, 107. *See also* City-states
Political areté, 67
Politics (Aristotle), 74
Politics, in Greek city-states, 53–54, *55,* 56
Polybius (Hellenistic historian), 112
Polygamy, 197
Polykleitos (Greek sculptor), 96, *97*
Polyphony, **284,** 287, 288
Pompeii, 147–148

Pont du Gard (Nîmes, France), 144, *144*
Pope, 165, 176, 211, 212, 214, 236–238, 240–241, 286, 293, 295–296, 318–319
Popol Vuh (Mayan creation myth), 261
Porphyry (Neo-Platonic scholar), 216
Portrait of a Boy (portrait painting), 155, *156*
Portrait paintings, 155, *156*
Portrait sculpture, 148–150, *149, 150*
Pottery
  Greek, *54*
  in Neolithic Age, 8
Praxiteles (Greek sculptor), *76*, 96–97, *97, 175*
Prehistory, 5–8
  Neolithic Age (New Stone Age), 7–8
  Paleolithic Age (Old Stone Age), 5–7, *6, 7, 8*
Prince, The (Machiavelli), 113
Principate, **129**
Procopius of Caesarea (Byzantine historian), 185, 191–192
Pronaos (Greek porch), 98, 100
Prophet(s), **39**
  Hebrew, 32, 34, 38, 39–41
  Islamic, 193–195, 196, 197, 202
  Persian, 25–26
  social justice and, 39–40
  See also names of specific prophets
Prophet, The (Romanesque sculpture), 278, *278*
Propylaea (Athens, Greece), 100–101, *100*
Protagoras, 67
Protestant Reformation, 171, 296, 297
Proverbs, Book of, 45–46
Psalms, Book of, **44–45**
Psellus, Michael (Byzantine historian), 185
Ptolemaic system, **138**
Ptolemy (Egyptian astronomer), 79, 138, 198, 244
Ptolemy I, pharaoh of Egypt, 114
Public architecture (Roman), 144–147, *144, 145, 146, 147*
Pulpit for the Baptistery of Pisa (sculpture), 310, *311*
Pursuit of the Millennium, The (Cohn), 249
Putti Harvesting Grapes (mosaic), 177–178, *178*
Pyramid(s)
  Egyptian, 17, 18, 19, 20, 23, *23*
  Mesopotamian, 15, *15*
  ziggurat, 15, *15*
Pyramid Age (Egypt), 17, 23
Pyramids of Giza, 23, *23*
Pythagoras, 65, 79, 80

Queen Nefertiti (Egyptian sculpture), *4*, 24
Qumran, 160
Quran, **195**–196, 197, 198, 199, 203

Ramadan, 196
Randall, J. H., Jr., 322
ar-Rashid, Harun, 201
Rational thought
  in Greece, 36, 53, 55, 64–75, 77, 89, 103, 115–116, 140, 142
  in Hellenistic Age, 107–108, 114, 115–116
Ravenna, Italy, 187–191, *187, 188, 189, 190, 191*
Red-figure vase painting, 91–92, *92*
Reincarnation, 139
Relativism, 68
Relief, limestone, 22, *22*
Relief carvings, 7
Relief sculpture, 22, *22*, 150–152, *151, 152, 153, 154*, 173, *173*, 174, *174*, 228, *228*
Religion
  Amarna, 19–20
  animals and, 15–16, *16*
  arts and, 171–178, 289–290
  in Byzantine civilization, 183–184
  Confucianism, 87
  Crusades and, 184, 237–238, *238*, 241, 278
  in early civilizations, 8–9
  in Egypt, 18–20, 21, 27–28, 109
  government and, 8, 9, 18, 28
  in Greece, 55, 61, 62–64
  of Hebrews, *30*, 31–49, *33*, 110. *See also* Judaism
  in Hellenistic Age, 110
  heresy and, 238–239, 296–297
  during High Middle Ages, 235–242, 245–249
  Hinduism, 11, 139
  iconoclastic controversy and, 187
  idolatry and, 36, 42, 49
  Inquisition and, 239
  during Late Middle Ages, 295–297
  literature and, 220–221, 255–256
  in Macedonia, 109
  in Mesopotamia, 9–12, 15, 16–17, *17*
  Mithraism, 141, 164
  monotheism, 19–20, 25, 34
  moral autonomy and, 36–37
  music and, 79, 80–81, 168, 285–289, 290, 319, 320
  mystery, **63–64**, 141–142, 155, *155*
  in Near East, 25–26, 27–28, 35, 36
  Olympian, 62–63
  in Paleolithic Age, 5–6
  in Persia, 25–26, *26*
  polytheism, 19
  in Rome, 141–142, 164–165
  social justice and, 39–40
  wars and, 9, 184, 195, 237–238, *238*, 241, 278
  Zoroastrianism, 25–26, *26*, 170
  See also Christianity; Islam
Religious hymns, 255–256, 289
Renaissance
  Carolingian, 216, **218**, 244, 285
  Italian, 229, 310
Republic, The (Plato), 71–72, 74

Rhazes (al-Razi), 198
Rhetoric, 132, 215
Rhythmos, 96, 97, 100, 103
Roads, Roman, 143
Roland (French military leader), 257–258
Roman d'aventure, 259–260
Roman de Fauvel (play with music), 318, *319*
Roman de la Rose (Guillaume de Lorris), 300, 302
Roman Empire, 125, 128–132, *130*
  cities in, 129
  decline of, 131–132, 211, 215
  expansion of, *126*, 127
  foundations of, 128–131
  languages in, 131, 132
  legacy of, 156
Roman Patrician with Portrait Heads (Roman sculpture), 148–149, *149*
Roman Republic, 125–128
  beginning of, 125, 127
  collapse of, 127–128
Romance, **259**
  Hellenistic, **111**–112
  medieval, 259–260, 299–300
Romanesque style
  of architecture, **264**–267, *265, 266, 267, 268*
  of sculpture, 277–278, *278, 279*
Romanus (Byzantine clergyman), 186
Rome, 124–156, *126*
  agriculture in, 128
  architecture of, 143–148, *143, 144, 145, 146, 147, 148*
  art of, *124*, 132, 142–156
  Christianity and, 164–165
  conflict in, 125, 127, 128, 129, 131
  creation of world-state by, 125, 129, 131
  culture of, 132–142
  Etruscans in, 125, 143
  government of, 125, 127, 128–129, 131
  Greek influence on, 102, 127, 132, 142
  Jews under, 33
  land reform in, 128
  law of, 125, 127, 140, 251–252
  literature of, 132–137
  Pax Romana in, 129, 131, 134–140
  philosophy of, 132–134, 137–138, 141, 142
  religion in, 141–142, 164–165
  science in, 138, 140
  sculpture of, *106, 124*, 148–152, *149, 150, 151, 152, 153, 154*
  sense of community in, 108
  slavery in, 127, 128, 129, 145, 166
  social classes in, 125, 127, 128, 131
  Struggle of the Orders in, 125, 127
  women in, 129, 131
Romulus, Roman emperor, 132
Roncevaux, Battle of, 257
Rubaiyat (Khayyam), 200
Rule of Benedict, 165, 236

Rumi, Jalal al-Din, 200–201
Russia, art of, 193
Ruth, 38

Sacraments, *173*, **235**
Sadducees, **160**
Saint Apollinare in Classe Church
(Ravenna, Italy), 190–191, *191*
Saint Apollinare Nuovo Church
(Ravenna, Italy), 188, *188*
Saint Denis (Paris, France), 268–270,
269
Saint Étienne (Caen, France), 267, *268*
Saint Madeleine Church (Vézelay,
France), 278
Saint Mark's Basilica, 184
Saint Matthew (Carolingian literature),
222, *223*
St. Matthew Passion (Bach), 168,
290
Saint Michael (Hildesheim, Germany),
225, 226–228, *226*, *227*, *228*
Saint Pantaleon (Cologne, Germany),
225, *225*
Saint Patrick's Purgatory (Marie de
France), 262
Saint Peter's Basilica, 176
Saint Sernin Basilica (Toulouse, France),
266–267, *267*
Saint Sophia Cathedral (Kiev), 193
Sakok (Jewish priest), 160
Salisbury, England, 273–274, *273*, *274*
Salisbury Cathedral (Salisbury, England),
273–274, *273*, *274*
Sallust (Gaius Sallustius Crispus), 133
Samarra, Great Mosque of, 204–205,
205
Samuel (prophet), 39
San Vitale (mosaics), 189, *189*, *190*
San Vitale Church (Ravenna, Italy),
189–190, *189*, *190*
Santa Costanza Church (Rome, Italy),
158, 177–178, *177*, *178*
Santa Croce Church (Ravenna, Italy),
187
Santa Maria del Fiore (Florence, Italy),
274–275, *275*
Santiago de Compostela (Spain), 267,
268
Sappho, 78
Sarcophagus, 24, *25*
Sarcophagus of Baebia Hertofila (relief
sculpture), 173, *173*
Sarcophagus of Junius Bassus (relief
sculpture), 174, *174*
Satan, 166
in art, 313–314, *314*
in Judaism, 47
Satires I–VI (Juvenal), 136–137
Satyr play, 81
Saul, Hebrew king, 32, 49
Scarlet Letter, The (Hawthorne), 49
Scenes of a Dionysiac Mystery Cult
(Roman painting), 155, *155*
Scheherazade, 201–202
Schliemann, Heinrich, 54

Scholasticism, **245–249**. *See also* Learning; Philosophy
Schubert, Franz Peter, 290
Science
in Egypt, 18, 20, 28, 138
in Greece, 66
in Hellenistic Age, 110, 112, 114,
115
during High Middle Ages, 250–251
in Islamic world, 198
in Mesopotamia, 12, 28
in Near East, 28
in Rome, 138, 140
See also specific disciplines
Scientific Revolution, 251
Scivias (Hildegard of Bingen), 214
Scrovegni, Enrico, 316
Sculpture
in Archaic period, 92–94, *93*, *94*
Burgundian school of, 310
Christian, 173, *173*, 174–175
contrapposto technique in, 96, 97
Egyptian, *4*, 24, *24*
genre, **122**, *122*
Gothic style of, 279, 280
Greek, *52*, *53*, *55*, *68*, *76*, 90, 92–97,
93, *94*, *95*, *96*, *97*, *99*, 175
Hellenistic, *106*, 110, 117–122, *118*,
119, *120*, *121*, *122*
medieval, 228, *228*, 276–280, *278*,
279, 310–311, *311*, *312*
Mesopotamian, 15, 16–17, *16*, *17*
Paleolithic, 7, *7*
Pisan school of, 310, 316
portrait, 148–150, *149*, *150*
relief, 22, *22*, 150–152, *151*, *152*,
153, *154*, 173, *173*, 174, *174*, 228,
228
Roman, *106*, *124*, 148–152, *149*,
150, *151*, *152*, *153*, *154*
Romanesque style of, 277–278, *278*,
279
Severe Style of Greek sculpture, *94*,
95–96, *95*, *96*
Secret History, The (Procopius), 185
Secretum (Petrarch), 305
Secularism, 293
Sei Shonagon, 217
Seleucia, 108, 109, 110, 127
Seljuk Turks, 184, 195, 237
Semibrevis, 288, 289
Seneca, Lucius Annaeus, 137–138
Sens, Guillaume of, 273
Serfs, 215, 231, 233
Severe Style of Greek sculpture, *94*,
95–96, *95*, *96*
Shaft of the Dead Man, The (cave paint-
ing), 6–7
Shem (son of Noah), 42
Shiel, James, 53
Shi'ites, **196**–197
Shofar, 49, *50*
Sic et Non (Abelard), 246
Side aisles of Christian church, 175, *176*
Silver Age (Roman) of literature, **134**,
136–137

Simile, 45
Sinai
Jews in wilderness of, 31–32
Mount, 33, 38, 43
Sir Gawain and the Green Knight (Pearl
Poet), 299–300
Skepticism, **116**
Slavery
in Athens, 56–57
Christians and, 166
in Rome, 127, 128, 129, 145, 166
in Sparta, 55
Sluter, Claus, 310–311, *312*
Social classes
in Christianity, 164, 165–166
in Egypt, 18, 19
under feudalism, 212–214, 231
in Greece, 55, 56, 78
in Hinduism, 139
law and, 12
in Mesopotamia, 12
in Rome, 125, 127, 128, 131
See also Middle class; Peasants
Social justice, 39–40
Society
agrarian, 214–215
Christianity and, 165–166
feudal, 212–214, 231
Socrates, 68–69, *68*, 88, 104, 115, 137
Sodom and Gomorrah, 43
Solmization, **286**
Solomon, Hebrew king, 32, 35, 160
sayings of, 45–46
Song of, **45**
Solon, 56, 82
Song of Roland, The (French epic
poem), 257–258
Song of Solomon, The, 45
Sonnets, Italian, **304**–305
Sophists, *67*, 68, 85, 86, 88, 89
Sophocles, 81, 82–85
Sophrosyne, 67
Spain
architecture in, 205–206, *206*, 267,
268
cave paintings in, 6–7
Sparta, 55, *55*, 56
in Peloponnesian War, 56, 57, 58, 86,
89
Spartacus, 127
Spear(s), 6
Spear Bearer, or Doryphoros (Greek
sculpture), 96, *97*
Speculum musicae (Liège), 318
Spenser, Edmund, 289
Sphinx, 23, *23*
"Spiritual intelligence," **249**
Spoils from the Temple of Jerusalem
(relief sculpture), 151
Spring (Irish lyric poem), 218
Squarcialupi Codex (fifteenth-century
manuscript), 320
Stabat Mater dolorosa (religious hymn),
186, 255–256
Stace, W. T., 142
Staff notation, 286, 288, 289

Stained-glass windows, 280–281, *281, 282*

State(s)
  just, 71–72
  rise during High Middle Ages, 233–235
  See also City-states

Statue(s). *See* Sculpture

Statues from the Abu Temple, 15, *16*

Staurotheotokion, 186

Steinbeck, John, 49

Stigmata, **298**

Stoicism, **115**–116, 133, 137–138, 169

Stone Age
  New Stone Age (Neolithic), 7–8
  Old Stone Age (Paleolithic), **5**–7, *6, 7, 8*

Story of His Misfortunes (Abelard), 245–246

Strato (Greek scientist), 112

Strict Aristotelians, **249**

Struggle of the Orders, **125**, 127

Suetonius (Roman biographer), 218

Sufism, **197**

Suger, Adam, 268–269

Sumeria
  culture of, 9, 16–17, *17*
  early civilizations in, 9
  influence on other civilizations, 9
  invention of writing in, 28
  See also Mesopotamia

Sumerian Harp, 15–16, *16*

Summa Theologica (Aquinas), 247–248, 255

Sunnites, **196**–197

Sylvester I, Pope, 176

Symbolism, in early Christian art, *171, 172, 173, 174, 175*

Symmetria, 96, 97, 100, 103

Sympathetic magic, **6**

Symposium (Plato), 72

Synoptic Gospels, **167**–168

Syracuse, 114

Syria, 109, 132

Tacitus, 137

Talenti, Francesco, 275

Tamerlane (Mongolian conqueror), 195

Tanak. See Hebrew Scriptures

Tapestries, **254**, 282–284, *284*

Taxation, of Catholic Church, 295

Te Deum, 289

Tempera, 315, *315*

Temple(s)
  Greek, 90, 98–100, *99,* 101–102, *101,* 177
  Hebrew, 32, 33, *33, 35,* 38, 110, 151, 242
  Mesopotamian, 9–10, 15, *15*
  Roman, 144–145, *145, 146*
  ziggurat, 15, *15*

Temple of Athene Nike (Athens, Greece), 101–102, *101*

Temple of Hera I (Paestum, Italy), 98–99, *99*

Ten Commandments, The, 33, 37, 38, 43

Tenebrae (Good Friday service), 255–256

Terence (Roman playwright), 111, 133

Tertullian (Latin church father), 168–169

Teseida dell nozze d' Emilia (Boccaccio), 305

Tesserae (mosaic tiles), 177

Tetralogy, 81

Thackeray, William Makepeace, 290

Thales, 65

Theater at Epidauros, 103, *103*

Theocritus (Hellenistic poet), 111

Theodora, Byzantine empress, 184, 185

Theodorakopoulos, John N., 64–65

Theodoric (Ostrogothic ruler), 188, 216

Theodosius I, Roman emperor, 165

Theogony (Hesiod), 60–61, 62

Theology
  of Christianity, 167–171, 245–249
  of Islam, 195–196

Theophilus (German monk), 280

Theophrastus (Greek scientist), 112

Thomistic synthesis, 297

Thucydides, 56, 89, 133, 185

Ti Watching a Hippopotamus Hunt (limestone relief), 22, *22*

Tiberius, Roman emperor, 147, 159

Tiberius Gracchus, 128

Tigris River, 9

Timaeus (Plato), 72

Timelines, 2–3, 180–181

Titus' Triumph (relief sculpture), 151

Tombs
  Egyptian, 22, *22,* 24, *25. See also* Pyramid(s)
  Persian, 26, *27*
  of Xerxes, 26, *27*

Tools
  in Neolithic Age, 7, 8
  in Paleolithic Age, 5

Torah, 33, 34, 160

Toulouse, France, 266–267, *267*

Tours, France
  Battle of, 195
  bishop of, 211
  Council of (1169), 239

Tower of Babel, 15, 28, 42

Towns, medieval, 233

Trade
  in early civilizations, 8
  in Egypt, 18
  during High Middle Ages, 232–233
  in Italy, 232–233
  in Mesopotamia, 12
  in Neolithic Age, 7
  in Sparta, 55

Tragedy, Greek, 81–86

Trajan, Roman emperor, 146, 151–152, *153,* 282

Trajan's Column (relief sculpture), 151–152, *153*

Transept, 175, *176*

Treaty of Verdun, *210*

Très Riches Heures du Duc de Berry, Les, 292, 312–314, *313, 314*

Tribute Money, The (Masaccio), 168

Trilogy, 81, 82

Tristan and Isolt, 219

Trojan War, 59

Trojan Women, The (Euripides), 85–86

Troubadours, **260,** 262

Troy, 59

Truth, 70

Turkey, 184, 185, 191–193, *192, 193,* 195, 237

Turold, 257

Tutankhamen (Egypt), 24, *25*

Twelfth-Century Awakening, 218, 244

Twelve Tables, **140**

Twelve Tribes of Israel, 43–44

Ulster cycle, **219**

Umayyad dynasty, *194, 195,* 204, *205*

Unam sanctam (papal bull), 295

Unicorn Tapestries, **254,** 283–284

Universal History (Ibn Khaldûn), 199

Universalism, **41**
  in Carolingian empire, 212
  in Hellenistic Age, 108–110, 123
  Judaism and, 40–41
  in Roman Empire, 131

Universities, medieval, 244–245

Ur, 43

Urban II, Pope, 237–238, 241

Urban VI, Pope, 295, 298

Urbanism, 293

Vandals, 132

Vanity Fair (Thackeray), 290

Vanity of This World, The (religious hymn), 256

Vase painting
  in Archaic period, 91, *91*
  black-figure, 91, *91*
  Geometric Style of, 90–91, *90*
  Greek, *54, 79,* 90–92, *90, 91, 92*
  Oriental Style of, 91
  red-figure, 91–92, *92*

Vassalage, **212**

Vault, in Roman architecture, **143**–144, *143*

Veda (Hindu Books of Knowledge), 11

"Venus" of Willendorf (sculpture), 7, *7*

Verdi, Giuseppe, 290

Verdun, Treaty of, *210*

Vermeer, Jan, 198

Vesuvius, Mount, 147–148

Vézelay, France, 278

Vienna, 195

Vikings, 212, *213,* 231

Villa of Livia (Roman painting), 153, *154*

Villages, in Neolithic Age, 7–8

Vinci, Leonardo da, 168, 198

Virgil (Publius Vergillius Maro), 134–135, 219

Visigoths, 132, 170, 184

Vision of Ita, The, 220

Vision of Piers Plowman, The (Langland), 298–299
Vita Caroli Magni (Einhard), 218
Vitalis, Saint, 189
Vitry, Phillipe de, 318, 319
Volcano, 147–148
Volute, **101**, 102
Vryonis, Speros, 206

Wady Qumran Manuscripts, 160
Waldensians, 239
Waldo, Peter, 239
Wall paintings
    in Egypt, 24
    in Greece, 90, 92
    in Rome, 152–156, *154, 155*
    See also Frescoes
War(s)
    between Athens and Persia, 56
    Christianity and, 166, 184, 237–238, *238,* 241, 278
    civil, 128, 129, 131, 136
    Crusades, 184, 237–238, *238,* 241, 278
    Hundred Years', 294
    jihad, 195, 238
    Mycenean civilization and, 54
    Peloponnesian, 56, 57, *58,* 86, 89
    Persian, 57
    religion and, 9, 184, 195, 237–238, *238,* 241, 278
    in Roman Empire, 127–128, 131, 136
    Sparta and, 55
    Trojan, 59

War of the Sons of Light with the Sons of Darkness, The, 160
Wars, The (Procopius), 185
Wasteland, The (Eliot), 290
Watt, W. Montgomery, 207
Well of Moses (sculpture), 310–311, *312*
Welsh mythology, 218
West Rose window (stained glass), 281, *282*
William of Ockham, 297
William the Conqueror, 234
Wilson, John A., 31
Wilson, Lyn Hatherly, 78
Windows, stained-glass, 280–281, *281, 282*
Wisdom writings, 43, 45–48
Women
    in art, *4, 7, 16, 24, 54, 55,* 76, *92, 93–94, 94, 120, 121, 122, 122, 190, 228, 281, 292, 315, 316, 317*
    in Athens, 57, 74
    in Byzantine civilization, 185
    Christianity and, 166
    education of, 57
    in Egypt, *4,* 20–21, 23–24, *24*
    in Greek plays, 83–84, 85–86
    guildswomen, 233
    during High Middle Ages, 233
    Islamic, 197
    Jewish, 38
    in Late Middle Ages, 304, 309–310
    in literature, 214, 220–221, 262, 304, 309–310

    in medieval Japan, 217
    in Mesopotamia, 12
    in Middle Ages, 213–214, 220–221
    poetry by, 78
    in Rome, 129, 131
    in Sparta, *55, 55*
    wife beating, 213–214
Works and Days (Hesiod), 60–62
World-state, Roman, 125, 129, 131
Writing
    calligraphy, 203
    Carolingian minuscule script, 218
    Egyptian (hieroglyphics), 19
    invention of, 8, 9, 28
    "Written in a Carefree Mood" (Lu), 243
Wycliffe, John, 296–297

Xenophanes, 63
Xerxes, king of Persia, *26, 26,* 27, 56, 82, 88
Ximénez, Francisco, 261

Yoga, 139
Yonec (Marie de France), 262

Zaragoza, 257
Zarathustra (prophet), 25–26
Zealots, **160**
Zechariah (prophet), 40
Zeno (Greek philosopher), 115–116
Zeus (Greek sculpture), 95–96, *96*
Ziggurat, **15**, *15*
Zoroastrianism, 25–26, *26,* 170